Almanac
of the
50 States

Comparative Data Profiles &
Guide to Government Data

2008 Edition

Almanac of the 50 States

Comparative Data Profiles &
Guide to Government Data

2008 Edition

State & Municipal Profiles Series

[ip] information
publications

Woodside, California

Books from Information Publications

State & Municipal Profiles Series

Almanac of the 50 States

California Cities, Towns & Counties   *Connecticut Municipal Profiles*

Florida Cities, Towns & Counties   *Massachusetts Municipal Profiles*

The New Jersey Municipal Data Book   *North Carolina Cities, Towns & Counties*

American Profiles Series

Asian Americans: A Statistical Sourcebook and Guide to Government Data

Black Americans: A Statistical Sourcebook and Guide to Government Data

Hispanic Americans: A Statistical Sourcebook and Guide to Government Data

Essential Topics Series

Energy, Transportation & the Environment:
A Statistical Sourcebook and Guide to Government Data

Almanac of the 50 States, 2008
ISBN 978-0-929960-47-0 Paper
ISBN 978-0-929960-46-3 Cloth

Information Publications, Inc.
2995 Woodside Rd., Suite 400-182
Woodside, CA 94062-2446

www.informationpublications.com
info@informationpublications.com

Toll Free Phone 877.544.INFO (4636)
Toll Free Fax 877.544.4635

Direct Dial Phone 650.568.6170
Direct Dial Fax 650.568.6150

REF
HA 203
.A55
2008

Table of Contents

1139307

Table of Contents

Comparative Tables

Table of Contents

Comparative Tables *(continued)*

Education *(con't)*

Social Insurance and Welfare

Housing and Construction

Government Finance

Crime and Law Enforcement

Table of Contents

Comparative Tables *(continued)*

Introduction

The *Almanac of the Fifty States* is a comprehensive, easy to use statistical reference book, providing a general overview of every state and the District of Columbia, along with tables of comparative rankings.

The book is divided into two parts. The first, **State Profiles**, is comprised of 52 profile sections: one for each of the 50 states, one for the District of Columbia, and one for the US in summary. Each profile is eight pages long, utilizes the same format of 13 subject categories, and has been compiled from the same sources of information. The result is a set of basic data profiles that are readable, understandable, and provide a strong basis for comparative analysis.

The individual profiles are the heart of the book. They have been designed to include information that has the greatest appeal to the broadest cross-section of users. The information comes from the latest reports of federal government agencies, augmented with data from business and trade organizations. No original material or new surveys are included, as our objective is to provide the most vital and significant information about each state, from the most reliable and respected collectors of data. A discussion outlining the data sources for the profiles is provided below.

The second part of the book, **Comparative Tables**, is composed of 100 tables. Each ranks the 50 states, the District of Columbia, and the US as a whole, according to a selected characteristic from the profiles. The purpose here is to provide straightforward tabular data, grouped by subject, on how states compare with regard to a given characteristic.

Scope of this Book

The overall goal of the *Almanac of the 50 States* is to bring together into a single volume a wide variety of diverse information and present it, state by state, in a clear, comprehensible format. It is not intended as a detailed research tool, but rather as a ready reference source, the first place to turn to answer basic questions about the states. For readers requiring more depth of coverage or a different focus, the full range of federal government resources should be examined. The Bureau of the Census, beyond the Decennial Census for which it is best known, collects many other samples of data on a biennial, annual, or even monthly basis, depending on the subject matter. Most Census data has been published online and can be found by visiting www.census.gov and clicking on the appropriate topic. The Census website is relatively easy to navigate and contains a wealth of information.

One particularly useful publication is the Census Bureau's *Statistical Abstract*. This publication, updated annually, contains a summary of all the Bureau's programs (as well as other federal agencies'), and collectively presents a thorough profile of the United States and its population, economy, and government. The abstract is available online at

Introduction

http://www.census.gov/prod/www/statistical-abstract.html. All information from the *Abstract* that appears in this book was taken from the 2008 edition. Besides *Statistical Abstract* (and its supplements *City and County Data Book* and *State and Metropolitan Area Data Book*), the annual reports and serial publications of individual departments and agencies merit some attention. The federal government is the largest publishing enterprise in the United States, and once the initial hurdle of access is overcome, the researcher is well rewarded: the available materials cover a wide range of topics in great depth and detail.

Additionally, the publications of various trade and professional associations provide an excellent source of state information. Most of these organizations produce monographs and annual reports which provide statistical information that is not available elsewhere. Such publications have been useful in compiling this book, and the most pertinent of proprietary information has been reprinted here with permission.

Finally, state governments are themselves publishers of note. Frequently they bring together and make available valuable information on a state and regional level. Most of their material is collected and made available by the respective state libraries.

The Profiles

All information in the profiles has been selected from federal government reports and publications, or from materials published by business and trade organizations. The use of such sources ensures an internal consistency and reliability of data, and enables the users of this book to go back to the more detailed original source materials for further information.

To enhance this consistency, all headings and terms used in the profiles have been carried over as they appear in the original sources. Those unfamiliar with government terminology may at times be puzzled by either the meaning of a specific term, or why the data was gathered in a certain way. We define a few unclear terms (as the data collection agency uses them) and present the original source for each item of information; readers seeking more detailed definitions and fuller explanations of data-collection procedures are referred there.

Each profile has been designed to be clear and stand on its own. The headings are clear, abbreviations have been avoided whenever possible, and indents have been used to indicate subgroups of the main heading. However, users are cautioned to pay attention to the wording of a heading, and to note whether a dollar amount, median (midway point), mean (average), rate, or percent is being provided. Additionally, not all subgroups add to the total shown. This may be due to rounding, or to only selected subgroups being displayed. Finally, while we strive to include the most complete set of information available, not all agencies are uniform in their data-tracking; in several cases, data is not available for all 50 states. In these cases, or when something does not apply (such as state government employees and payroll for Washington, DC, which is not a state), or when a sample size too small to produce a reliable estimate, "NA" appears in the place of the data item.

Note on Data Sources

Since the majority of the data presented here comes from the Census Bureau, one change in their data-collection methods warrants mentioning. The American Community Survey (ACS), a monthly sample of the population, is beginning to track much of the information previously only measured by the Decennial Census. Currently the ACS provides data on a nationwide and statewide level, as well as for individual communities with populations over 65,000. In 2008, the ACS coverage will expand to all communities with populations greater than 20,000. By 2010, the Bureau of the Census hopes to use the ACS to track all the information collected in the long form of the Decennial Census. One caution in using American Community Survey data is that, owing to the margin of error inherent in any sampling process, the ACS provides different figures for the total population from the Census Bureau's Population Division statistics. In order to avoid confusion, information obtained from the two sources should never be presented together; here, such data is kept under separate headings. You can find out more information about the ACS at http://www.census.gov/acs/www.

Categories, Headings & Terms

A review of the 13 categories that make up each of the profiles appears below. In addition to citing the source of origin, the paragraphs contain a brief identification of terms and some background methodology on the data collection.

State Summary

All information in this section is taken from the other 12 categories, and individual sources are identified in these sections' discussions.

Geography & Environment

General coastline data represents the length of the outline of the coast. Tidal shoreline data represents the shoreline of the outer coast, off-shore islands, sounds, bays, rivers, and creeks to the head of the tidewater. The original source of this information is *The Coastline of the United States, 1975*.

Introduction

Federally-owned land data comes from the *Federal Real Property Profile*, published on September 30, 2004 by the US General Services Administration, Office of Governmentwide Policy, located online at www.gsa.gov.

Information on highest and lowest elevations, land and water area, and state parks comes from *Statistical Abstract*.

Cropland and forest land data comes from the *2003 National Resources Inventory (NRI) Land Use report*, from the National Resources Conservation Service (NRCS).

Number of cities with population over 100,000, and population data for the largest and capital cities come from the 1990 and 2000 Decennial Censuses, and the US Census Bureau Population Division's *Annual Population Estimates*.

National Forest System data comes from the US Department of Agriculture Forestry Service's 2007 *Land Area Reports*.

Demographics & Population Characteristics

All 1980, 1990, and 2000 items are from the 1980, 1990, and 2000 Decennial Censuses of Population, respectively, conducted by the Bureau of the Census. Figures for the 2006 and 2007 population, changes in population, and information on age, sex, and race & Hispanic origin, as well as projections and breakdowns for future years, come from ongoing reports published by the Bureau of the Census. Note that population projections were made in 2005 and do not reflect events that have happened since then. For example, population projections for Louisiana are now very different from the current figures due to the loss of population in the aftermath of hurricane Katrina.

Persons per square mile is calculated based on land size estimates and the 2007 population estimates.

Core-Based Statistical Area (CBSA) population information comes from the Bureau of Census' Annual Population Estimates, reprinted in *Statistical Abstract*. Core-Based Statistical Area populations encompass the all the people living in categories of Metropolitan and Micropolitan areas in the state. CBSAs, Metropolitan, and Micropolitan Areas are defined by the US Office of Management and Budget (OMB). The most recent definitions, effective June, 2003, are fairly complicated, but generally, each category consists of a large population nucleus, together with adjacent communities which have a high degree of economic and social integration with that nucleus. A Metropolitan Area must include at least one place with 50,000 or more inhabitants. A Micropolitan Area must include at least one place with a population of greater than 10,000, but less than 50,000. (In addition, states in New England use slightly different criteria due to their population distributions.) Non-CBSA area population is everyone not included in the Core-Based Statistical Area population of the state. The data presented here represents a change from previous editions of *Almanac of the 50 States*, which presented only metropolitan and non-metropolitan populations. Although the census no longer publishes data organized into metropolitan and non-metropolitan areas, this information can be found in the 2006 edition of *Almanac of the 50 States*, or in previous (2003 and earlier) editions of *Statistical Abstract.*

Racial statistics are provided, although they are a highly sensitive subject. The breakdown represents the self-identification of respondents in regard to pre-set Census categories, and does not in any way denote any scientific of biological notion of race. The terms used in this book, such as "Black," "Asian," and "Hispanic," are presented because they are the terms used by the Federal government for data collection purposes. Hispanic origin is not racial group as defined by the Bureau, and persons may be of any race and be of Hispanic origin as well. Readers should note that racial category information comes from the US Census Bureau's Population Division, while more specific breakdowns about the Asian and Hispanic populations comes from the American Community Survey. Because the Population Survey and American Community Survey are different estimates, they present different figures for the total population.

A household is defined as the person or persons occupying a housing unit. A housing unit is defined below, under "Housing & Construction." Briefly, a housing unit is a separate set of living quarters such as a house, apartment, mobile home, etc. A family is a type of household and consists of a householder and one or more other persons living in the same household who are related to the householder by birth, marriage, or adoption. Married couples, and female heads of household with dependent children and no husband present, are subgroups, or types of families. Data on households, languages spoken at home, marital status, and nativity within state of residence are all obtained from the 2006 American Community Survey. Under marital status, "married" includes all people who are currently separated. Data on the group quarters population (including people living in college dormitories, residential treatment centers, group homes, military barracks, correctional facilities, and workers' dormitories) are also taken from the ACS, and marks the first time this population has been included in the survey.

Immigration and naturalization data is from the *Yearbook of Immigration Statistics*, an annual publication of the US Department of Homeland Security (www.dhs.gov).

Vital Statistics & Health

Birth, death, infant death, marriage, and divorce data comes from *National Vital Statistics Reports*, publications from the National Center for Health Statistics, a division of the Department of Health & Human Services' Centers for Disease Control (www.cdc. gov/nchs). All death rates are age-adjusted.

Introduction

Statistics on abortion come from *Morbidity and Mortality Weekly Report (MMWR)*, a publication of the Centers for Disease Control. Note that several states do not provide information on abortion, and the statistics provided cover only legal, reported abortions.

Percentages of adults who smoke, and those who are overweight and obese are from the CDC's Behavioral Risk Factor Surveillance Service (BRFSS). "Overweight" is defined as having a Body Mass Index (defined as kg/m^2) greater than 25, and "obese" is defined by a Body Mass Index over 30. Data on exercise also comes from the BRFSS, published in MMWR's "Surveillance of Certain Health Behaviors Among States and Selected Local Areas" report for 2005. "Moderate" physical activity is defined as causing a small increase in heart rate and breathing for 30 minutes per day, at least 5 times per week. "Vigorous" activity is defined as causing a large increase in heart rate and breathing for 20 minutes per day, at least 3 times per week. For all BRFSS data, the US Summary figure is the median of the state values.

Data for physicians are counts of active, non-federally employed practitioners. Physicians exclude doctors of osteopathy. This information comes from the American Medical Association, reprinted in *Statistical Abstract*, and is reprinted here with permission.

Hospital data comes from the American Hospital Association, is reprinted in *Statistical Abstract*, and appears here with permission. Data reflects American Hospital Association member hospitals only. The average daily census refers to the average total number of inpatients receiving treatment each day, excluding newborns.

Information on disability status of the population comes from the 2006 American Community Survey.

Education

Educational attainment data comes from the 2006 American Community Survey.

Higher education enrollment, minority enrollment, institutions, and degrees conferred come from *Digest of Education Statistics 2005*, compiled by the National Center for Educational Statistics, US Department of Education (www.nces.ed.gov). Public elementary and secondary school enrollment, as well as high school graduates, also come from the NCES. Testing proficiency data for grades 4 and 8 comes from the NCES' *National Assessment of Educational Progress* (NAEP) report. Public library data is taken from the NCES' report *Public Libraries in the US* for Fiscal Year 2005.

Public school finance and teacher data is from the National Education Association's *Rankings & Estimates* report for 2006-07, and is reproduced here with permission. Per capita spending data was calculated using the NEA's estimate for total current expenditures (which do not count capital outlay or interest on school debt) and the Census' population estimate for July 1, 2006.

Information on state and local financial support for higher education comes from the State Higher Education Executive Officers' (SHEEO) report for the 2006 Fiscal Year.

SAT test scores and the percentage of high school graduates who take the test are from www.collegeboard.com.

Social Insurance & Welfare Programs

All Social Security information has been obtained from the Social Security Administration's *Annual Statistical Supplement, 2006*. Detail is provided for three major Social Security programs: those for the retired; for the survivors of enrollees; and for the disabled covered under the program. The current Statistical Supplement, as well as several older editions, can be found online at www.socialsecurity.gov, in the Office of Policy Data. Supplemental Security Income data also comes from the *Annual Statistical Supplement*.

Medicare and health care expenditure data are produced by the US Centers for Medicare and Medicaid Services, accessible online at www.cms.hhs.gov.

State Children's Health Insurance Program and Medicaid information is from the US Centers for Medicare and Medicaid Services, reprinted in *Statistical Abstract*.

Information on persons without health insurance is gathered by the Census Bureau's *Current Population Reports*.

State unemployment insurance data comes from the US Department of Labor, Employment and Training Administration's *Unemployment Insurance Financial Data Handbook*, reprinted in *Statistical Abstract*.

Information on Temporary Assistance for Needy Families comes from the Administration for Children & Families, a division of the US Department of Health & Human Services, and refers to the total recipients for the year.

Food Stamp program data is obtained from the US Department of Agriculture's Food and Nutrition Service.

Housing & Construction

The Bureau defines some key terms as follows: a housing unit is a house, apartment, mobile home or trailer, group of rooms, or single room occupied as separate living

Introduction

quarter or, if vacant, intended as a separate living quarter. Separate living quarters are those in which occupants live and eat separately from any other persons in the building and which have direct access from the outside of the building or from a common hall.

Home ownership and vacancy rate data comes from the Census Bureau's Housing and Vacancy Survey.

Data for total housing units can be found at the Census' Population Division.

Owner- and renter-occupied, seasonally-occupied housing units, and median rent and home values, are obtained from the American Community Survey.

Figures for existing home sales come from the National Association of Realtors, and are reprinted here with permission.

New authorizations for housing unit construction are obtained from the Manufacuring, Mining, and Construction Statistics division of the US Census Bureau.

Information on new home construction comes from the National Association of Home Builders, reprinted in *Statistical Abstract.*

Government and Elections

Names of state officials have been obtained from websites for the National Governors Association, the National Lieutenant Governors Association, the National Association of Secretaries of State, the National Association of Attorneys General, and the Conference of Chief Justices. Party in majority information comes from the National Conference of State Legislatures (www.ncsl.org), and is reprinted with permission.

Information about the governorship and legislative structure of each state was obtained from respective legislative manuals and annual election reports, as well as the 2007 edition of *The Book of the States*, published by the Council of State Governments.

State and local employee data is from *State Government Employment and Payroll, 2006*, and *Local Government Employment and Payroll, 2006,* respectively, published by the Federal, State, and Local Government division of the Bureau of the Census. Figures represent March 2006, full-time equivalent employees, along with March payroll data. Federal government employment and payroll is taken from the US Office of Personnel Management's *Federal Employment Statistics: Employment and Trends* report for September 2006, and pertains to the fiscal year ending September 30, 2006.

Information on local governments comes from the 2002 *Census of Governments* (conducted every 5 years by the Bureau of the Census). Data provided concerns governmental units, as opposed to geographic entities. For example, in Connecticut there are eight counties, but no county governments, hence Connecticut's profile lists zero under "county."

Voting estimates for the 2006 election come from the November 2006 *Voting and Registration Survey* from Current Population Reports, a monthly sample of about 56,000 households published by the US Census Bureau of the Census. Note that the figures are estimates calculated from a survey performed the week after the election, in which respondents were asked whether they had voted in the election, and will differ from official vote tallies.

Women holding public office data comes from press releases provided by the Center for American Women and Politics at the Eagleton Institute of Rutgers University, and is reprinted with permission. More data can be found online at www.cawp.rutgers.edu.

Data concerning Black elected officials are from the Joint Center for Political & Economic Studies, printed in *Statistical Abstract*, and is reproduced here with permission.

Hispanic public officials information is from the National Association of Latino Elected and Appointed Officials, reprinted in *Statistical Abstract*.

Names, parties and terms of office for Senators come from the federal website, www.senate.gov. The number of Representatives by party, congressional election results, and vote totals come from the Clerk of the House of Representatives, clerkweb.house.gov. At press time, there were three vacancies in the House due to the deaths or resignations of representatives in Illinois, Indiana, and Mississippi. Special elections to fill these seats until the 2008 general election were to be held after this book went to press, so this edition reflects those vacant seats. Vote for president in 2004 is from the Federal Election Commission.

Governmental Finance

Revenue, expenditure and debt information comes from the *2006 State Government Finance Data* report. Federal government grants information comes from the *2005 Consolidated Federal Funds Report*. Finance data for the District of Columbia comes from the *State and Local Government Finance: 2004-05* report. All are publications from the Federal, State and Local Governments section of the US Census Bureau and are available on their website, www.census.gov/govs/www/index.html.

Federal budget data comes from the US Office of Management and Budget's annual report *Historical Tables, Budget of the United States Government, Fiscal Year 2008*. Per capita national debt was calculated using the Census' population estimate for 2007.

Introduction

Crime & Law Enforcement

Information on crime, crime rates, police agencies, and arrests comes from *Crime in the United States, 2006*, published by the Uniform Crime Reports division of the Federal Bureau of Investigation (FBI). The information is located online at www.fbi.gov/ucr/ucr.htm. Readers are cautioned that crime information is based on crimes known to police, and may not include all crimes that have been committed. Hate crime data comes from the FBI's report *Hate Crime Statistics, 2006*.

Fraud and identity theft data come from the US Federal Trade Commission's report *Consumer Fraud and Identity Theft Complaint Data, January–December 2006*.

Information on the number of persons under sentence of death is as of January 1, 2008, and comes from *Sourcebook of Criminal Justice Statistics, 2003* with ongoing updates online.

Information on prisoners comes from *Prisoners in 2006* and *Prisoners at Mid-year 2005*. Data for adults on probation and parole comes from *Probation and Parole Statistics in the United States, 2006*. State court information comes from *State Court Organization 2004*. These sources are publications of the Bureau of Justice Statistics, US Department of Justice.

Labor & Income

Most of the civilian labor force and unemployment data comes from *Geographic Profile of Employment and Unemployment, 2003*, and the *Profile*'s *Annual Averages 2006*, published by the Department of Labor, Bureau of Labor Statistics. The Bureau of Labor Statistics can be found online at www.bls.gov. Civilian labor force includes all civilians who are either employed or unemployed.

Generally, employed persons are those who: 1) did any work as a paid employee; 2) worked 15 hours or more as an unpaid employee in a family enterprise; or 3) had jobs but were not working due to illness, vacation, etc. A full-time employee is one who works at least 35 hours per week. Unemployed persons are those who: 1) had no paid employment and were both available for and looking for work; or 2) were waiting to be recalled to a job; or 3) were waiting to report to a new job.

Labor union membership comes from *Union Members*, published in the Current Population Summary from the Bureau of Labor Statistics.

Experienced civilian labor force by occupation is from the *Occupational Employment Statistics Survey*, published by Bureau of Labor Statistics.

Hours and earnings data comes from *Current Employment Statistics*, a division of the Bureau of Labor Statistics.

Average annual pay and experienced civilian labor force by private industry come from the Census of Employment and Wages' *Annual Averages 2006*, published by the Bureau of Labor Statistics. It includes the workers who are covered by state unemployment insurance laws, and federal civilian workers covered by federal unemployment. This represents approximately 98% of total civilian employment. It excludes members of the armed forces, elected officials in most states, railroad employees, most self-employed persons, and some others. Pay includes bonuses, the cash value of meals and lodging, and tips and other gratuities.

Household income and poverty information comes from *Income, Earnings, and Poverty Data from the 2006 American Community Survey*, published by the US Bureau of the Census.

Personal (per capita) income information was obtained from the Bureau of Economic Analysis, reprinted in *Statistical Abstract*.

Federal individual income tax data is from the Internal Revenue Service's latest *Statistics of Income Bulletin*. Further information can be found at www.irs.gov/taxstats/ Charitable contribution data also comes from the *Statistics of Income Bulletin*, reprinted in *Statistical Abstract*.

Economy, Business, Industry & Agriculture

Fortune 500 companies come from a count of listed corporations found in the annual directory issue of *Fortune*, reprinted here with permission.

Information on patents and trademarks issued is from the US Trademark Office's annual report.

Bankruptcy information is from statistical tables for the Federal Judiciary's bankruptcy courts (www.uscourts.gov).

Business firm ownership is from the *2002 Survey of Business Owners (SBO)*, published by Bureau of the Census as part of the 2002 Economic Census. The 2002 SBO can be found online at www.census.gov/csd/sbo.

Gross Domestic Product (formerly Gross State Product) is taken from the Department of Commerce's Bureau of Economic Analysis, available at www.bea.gov. The industries represented are major categories under the North American Industry Classification System (NAICS). The NAICS has replaced the US SIC (Standard Industrial Classification)

Introduction

system, and was developed jointly by the US, Canada, and Mexico to provide new comparability in statistics about business activity across North America. For more information on NAICS and to understand the correspondence between NAICS and SIC, please visit the US Bureau of the Census website, www.census.gov, and search for NAICS.

Agricultural data comes from the US Department of Agriculture's Economic Research Service, www.ers.usda.gov.

Federal economic activity data is from the *Consolidated Federal Funds Report, 2005*.

Department of Defense expenditure information comes from *Atlas/Data Abstract for the United States and Selected Areas*, published annually by the department.

Homeland security information comes from the Department of Homeland Security, State and Local Government Coordination and Preparedness, Office for Domestic Preparedness, and is accessible at www.dhs.gov.

FDIC-insured institution data comes from US Federal Deposit Insurance Corporation, and was obtained directly from the agency.

Fishing data is from *Fisheries of the United States, 2006*, a publication of the National Oceanic and Atmospheric Administration (NOAA).

Mining statistics are from the US Geological Survey, obtained from the current *Mineral Commodity Summaries* report. It can be found at http://minerals.usgs.gov.

Establishment, annual payroll and paid employee data come from the 2005 *County Business Patterns*, a 52-volume report issued annually by the Bureau of the Census. Receipts data comes from the 2002 Economic Census. Both the Economic Census and *County Business Patterns* follow NAICS classifications; however, the two reports are separate (and measure different time periods), and their data should be treated separately. *In particular, the 2002 receipts data should not be combined with the 2005 establishment, employee, or payroll data in any calculations.*

Trade statistics and export information come from the *US International Trade in Goods and Services* report for December 2006, from the Census Bureau's Foreign Trade Statistics division.

Foreign investment in US affiliates refers to US business enterprises (excluding banks) with at least one foreign owner with a direct or indirect voting interest of at least 10%. Data shown here comes from the US Bureau of Economic Analysis' *Survey of Current Business* for August 2006 and *Foreign Direct Investment in the United States, Operations of US Affiliates of Foreign Companies* report, reprinted in *Statistical Abstract*.

Communication, Energy & Transportation

The percent of households with computers and internet access are from the US Department of Commerce's National Telecommunications and Information Division, reprinted in *Statistical Abstract*.

The number of FCC-licensed TV and radio stations comes from the FCC's database, which is updated daily. Data presented here is as of January 1, 2008. Wireless customer information comes from the FCC Industry Analysis and Technology Division's *Local Telephone Competition* report, which is based on reports from individual carriers. Data on high-speed internet providers comes from the FCC's report *High-Speed Services for Internet Access: Status as of December 31, 2006*.

All energy information except gas utility data has been obtained from the US Energy Information Administration, www.eia.doe.gov. Energy consumption data comes from the *State Energy Data Report*, electricity information from the *Electric Power Annual*, and renewable energy data from *Renewable Energy Consumption and Electricity Preliminary 2006 Statistics*, and nuclear power plant from the EIA's annual power plant report.

Natural gas utility information comes from the American Gas Association's *Gas Facts*, and is reprinted with permission.

All transportation information comes from *Highway Statistics, 2006*, an annual publication of the Department of Transportation. It can be accessed online at www.fhwa.dot.gov. For the purpose of registration figures, the definition of motor vehicles includes automobiles, buses, and trucks, but not motorcycles. Gasoline figures include gasohol, a mixture of gasoline and alcohol (usually ethanol). Road system statistics refer to public roads.

Commuting statistics are from the 2006 American Community Survey.

Introduction

Disclaimer

The *Almanac of the 50 States* contains thousands of pieces of information. Every reasonable precaution, along with a good deal of care, was taken in its preparation. Despite all efforts, it is possible that some of the information contained in this book may not be accurate. Some errors may be due to errors in the original source materials, others may have been made by the compilers of this volume. An incorrect spelling may occur, a figure may be inverted and similar mistakes may exist. The compilers, editors, typist, printers, and others are all human, and in a work of this magnitude the possibility of error can never be fully eliminated. If any piece of information is believed to be inaccurate, please contact the publisher. We are eager to eliminate any errors from coming editions and we will be pleased to check a piece of information.

The publisher is also aware that some users may apply the data in this book in various remunerative projects. Although we have taken reasonable, responsible measures to insure total accuracy, we cannot take responsibility for liability or losses suffered by users of the data. The information provided here is believed to be correct at the time of publication. No other guarantees are made or implied.

The publisher assumes no liability for losses incurred by users, and warrants only that diligence and due care were used in the production of this volume.

A Final Word

In order to continue to meet its goals, *Almanac of the 50 States* is revised and updated on an annual basis. The best suggestions for improvement in a ready-reference source such as this come from the regular users of the work. Therefore, we actively solicit your comments and ideas. If you know how this book could become more useful to you, please contact us.

The Editors
Almanac of the 50 States
Information Publications, Inc.
2995 Woodside Road, Suite 400-182
Woodside, CA 94062

www.informationpublications.com
info@informationpublications.com

Toll Free Phone: 877-544-4636
Toll Free Fax: 877-544-4635

State Summary

Capital city . . . . Montgomery
Governor . . . . Bob Riley
State Capitol
600 Dexter Ave
Montgomery, AL 36130
334-242-7100
Admitted as a state 1819
Area (square miles) 52,419
Population, 2007 (estimate). 4,627,851
Largest city . . . . .Birmingham
Population, 2006 229,424
Personal income per capita, 2006
(in current dollars) $31,295
Gross domestic product, 2006 ($ mil) . . . $160,569

Leading industries by payroll, 2005

Manufacturing, Health care/Social assistance,
Professional/Scientific/Technical

**Leading agricultural commodities
by receipts, 2005**

Broilers, Cattle and calves, Greenhouse/nursery,
Chicken eggs, Cotton

Geography & Environment

Total area (square miles). 52,419
land 50,744
water 1,675
Federally-owned land, 2004 (acres) 513,913
percent. 1.6%
Highest point . . . . Cheaha Mountain
elevation (feet) 2,405
Lowest point . . . . Gulf of Mexico
elevation (feet) . . . . sea level
General coastline (miles) 53
Tidal shoreline (miles) 607
Cropland, 2003 (x 1,000 acres) 2,509
Forest land, 2003 (x 1,000 acres). 21,530
Capital city . . . . .Montgomery
Population 2000 201,568
Population 2006 201,998
Largest city . . . . .Birmingham
Population 2000 242,820
Population 2006 229,424

Number of cities with over 100,000 population
1990 4
2000 4
2006 4

State park and recreation areas, 2005
Area (x 1,000 acres) 48
Number of visitors (x 1,000) 2,961
Revenues ($1,000) $22,363
percent of operating expenditures 66.6%

National forest system land, 2007
Acres 668,947

Demographics & Population Characteristics

Population
1980 3,893,800
1990 4,040,587
2000 4,447,351
2006 4,599,030
Male 2,229,469
Female 2,369,561
Living in group quarters, 2006 115,155
percent of total. 2.5%
2007 (estimate) .4,627,851
persons per square mile of land 91.2
2008 (projected) .4,568,983
2010 (projected) .4,596,330
2020 (projected) .4,728,915
2030 (projected) .4,874,243

**Population of Core-Based Statistical Areas
(formerly Metropolitan Areas), x 1,000**

	CBSA	Non-CBSA
1990	3,559	482
2000	3,945	503
2006	4,109	490

Change in population, 2000-2007
Number 180,500
percent 4.1%
Natural increase (births minus deaths) 102,880
Net internal migration 59,843
Net international migration 30,650

Persons by age, 2006
Under 5 years 299,377
5 to 17 years 814,924
18 years and over 3,484,729
65 years and over 615,597
85 years and over 79,530
Median age 37.1

Persons by age, 2010 (projected)
Under 5 years 298,302
18 and over 3,504,146
65 and over 648,889
Median age 38.5

Race, 2006
One Race
White. 3,276,561
Black or African American 1,211,583
Asian 41,881
American Indian/Alaska Native. 23,799
Hawaiian Native/Pacific Islander. 1,749
Two or more races. 43,457

Persons of Hispanic origin, 2006
Total Hispanic or Latino 111,432
Mexican. 71,146
Puerto Rican 8,629
Cuban 5,312

Persons of Asian origin, 2006

Total Asian	45,882
Asian Indian	10,184
Chinese	8,876
Filipino	2,682
Japanese	3,835
Korean	6,402
Vietnamese	8,761

Marital status, 2006

Population 15 years & over	3,682,816
Never married	988,715
Married	1,978,644
Separated	95,558
Widowed	272,160
Divorced	443,297

Language spoken at home, 2006

Population 5 years and older	4,305,303
English only	4,124,326
Spanish	107,806
French	8,932
German	9,180
Chinese	7,221

Households & families, 2006

Households	1,796,058
with persons under 18 years	612,801
with persons over 65 years	435,989
persons per household	2.50
Families	1,222,858
persons per family	3.06
Married couples	888,609
Female householder, no husband present	259,482
One-person households	496,850

Nativity, 2006

Number of residents born in state	3,261,356
percent of population	70.9%

Immigration & naturalization, 2006

Legal permanent residents admitted	4,278
Persons naturalized	1,946
Non-immigrant admissions	71,983

Vital Statistics and Health

Marriages

2004	42,536
2005	41,962
2006	39,627

Divorces

2004	22,405
2005	22,430
2006	22,054

Health risks, 2006

Percent of adults who are:

Smokers	23.2%
Overweight (BMI > 25)	65.0%
Obese (BMI > 30)	30.5%

Births

2005	60,453
Birthrate (per 1,000)	13.3
White	41,252
Black	18,136
Hispanic	4,020
Asian/Pacific Islander	875
Amer. Indian/Alaska Native	190
Low birth weight (2,500g or less)	10.7%
Cesarian births	31.8%
Preterm births	16.7%
To unmarried mothers	35.7%
Twin births (per 1,000)	32.2
Triplets or higher order (per 100,000)	198.3
2006 (preliminary)	63,235
rate per 1,000	13.7

Deaths

2004

All causes	46,121
rate per 100,000	992.5
Heart disease	12,774
rate per 100,000	276.3
Malignant neoplasms	9,756
rate per 100,000	203.7
Cerebrovascular disease	2,986
rate per 100,000	65.0
Chronic lower respiratory disease	2,361
rate per 100,000	50.0
Diabetes	1,449
rate per 100,000	30.7
2005 (preliminary)	47,088
rate per 100,000	997.9
2006 (provisional)	47,032

Infant deaths

2004	516
rate per 1,000	8.7
2005 (provisional)	546
rate per 1,000	9.1

Exercise routines, 2005

None	29.7%
Moderate or greater	42.8%
Vigorous	20.3%

Abortions, 2004

Total performed in state	11,370
rate per 1,000 women age 15-44	12
% obtained by out-of-state residents	15.2%

Physicians, 2005

Total	9,786
rate per 100,000 persons	215

Community hospitals, 2005

Number of hospitals	109
Beds (x 1,000)	15.5
Patients admitted (x 1,000)	706
Average daily census (x 1,000)	9.9
Average cost per day	$1,198
Outpatient visits (x 1 mil)	7.5

Disability status of population, 2006
5 to 15 years 7.5%
16 to 64 years 17.5%
65 years and over 48.4%

Education

Educational attainment, 2006
Population over 25 years 3,022,878
    Less than 9th grade...................... 6.6%
    High school graduate or more 80.1%
    College graduate or more.............. 21.1%
    Graduate or professional degree......... 7.7%

Public school enrollment, 2005-06
Total............................... 741,758
    Pre-kindergarten through grade 8.....527,479
    Grades 9 through 12.................212,414

Graduating public high school seniors, 2004-05
Diplomas (incl. GED and others) 39,990

SAT scores, 2007
Average critical reading score.............. 563
Average writing score...................... 554
Average math score....................... 556
Percent of graduates taking test 9%

Public school teachers, 2006-07 (estimate)
Total (x 1,000) 50.0
    Elementary...........................28.5
    Secondary............................21.5
Average salary $43,389
    Elementary........................ $43,055
    Secondary......................... $43,800

State receipts & expenditures for public schools, 2006-07 (estimate)
Revenue receipts ($ mil) $6,139
Expenditures
Total ($ mil) $6,444
    Per capita $1,234
    Per pupil $7,908

NAEP proficiency scores, 2007

	Reading		Math	
	Basic	Proficient	Basic	Proficient
Grade 4	61.6%	28.9%	70.2%	25.8%
Grade 8	62.3%	21.2%	55.3%	18.2%

Higher education enrollment, fall 2005
Total................................. 28,236
    Full-time men 10,151
    Full-time women.................... 13,496
    Part-time men 1,783
    Part-time women.................... 2,806

Minority enrollment in institutions of higher education, 2005
Black, non-Hispanic 74,968
Hispanic 3,717
Asian/Pacific Islander 3,577
American Indian/Alaska Native..........1,895

Institutions of higher education, 2005-06
Total.................................... 66
    Public................................ 39
    Private 27

Earned degrees conferred, 2004-05
Associate's.............................9,274
Bachelor's.............................21,616
Master's...............................9,993
First-professional......................1,100
Doctor's 571

Public Libraries, 2006
Number of libraries...................... 207
Number of outlets 302
Annual visits per capita 3.2
Circulation per capita....................4.1

State & local financial support for higher education, FY 2006
Full-time equivalent enrollment (x 1,000)....181.0
Appropriations per FTE.................$5,617

Social Insurance & Welfare Programs

Social Security benefits & beneficiaries, 2005
Beneficiaries (x 1,000) 904
    Retired & dependents................... 546
    Survivors............................ 140
    Disabled & dependents................. 218
Annual benefit payments ($ mil) $9,259
    Retired & dependents................. $5,370
    Survivors...........................$1,741
    Disabled & dependents...............$2,149
Average monthly benefit
    Retired & dependents.................. $960
    Disabled & dependents................ $907
    Widowed............................ $897

Medicare, July 2005
Enrollment (x 1,000)..................... 755
Payments ($ mil) $4,897

Medicaid, 2004
Beneficiaries (x 1,000)................... 118
Payments ($ mil) $905

State Children's Health Insurance Program, 2006
Enrollment (x 1,000)................... 84.3
Expenditures ($ mil)...................$111.1

Persons without health insurance, 2006
Number (x 1,000)........................ 689
    percent............................. 15.2%
Number of children (x 1,000) 82
    percent of children 7.4%

Health care expenditures, 2004
Total expenditures..................... $23,199
    per capita $5,135

Federal and state public aid

State unemployment insurance, 2006
Recipients, first payments (x 1,000) 105
Total payments ($ mil) $206
Average weekly benefit $184
Temporary Assistance for Needy Families, 2006
Recipients (x 1,000) 533.8
Families (x 1,000) 228.5
Supplemental Security Income, 2005
Recipients (x 1,000) .163.7
Payments ($ mil) $776.4
Food Stamp Program, 2006
Avg monthly participants (x 1,000) 546.7
Total benefits ($ mil) $593.7

Housing & Construction

Housing units
Total 2005 (estimate) 2,081,960
Total 2006 (estimate) 2,110,154
Seasonal or recreational use, 2006 65,853
Owner-occupied, 2006 1,289,272
   Median home value $107,000
   Homeowner vacancy rate 2.8%
Renter-occupied, 2006 506,786
   Median rent $573
   Rental vacancy rate 13.4%
Home ownership rate, 2005 . . . . 76.6%
Home ownership rate, 2006 . . . . 74.2%

New privately-owned housing units
Number authorized, 2006 (x 1,000) 32.0
   Value ($ mil) $4,402.0
Started 2005 (x 1,000, estimate) 20.9
Started 2006 (x 1,000, estimate) 21.1

Existing home sales
2005 (x 1,000) 128.0
2006 (x 1,000) 125.8

Government & Elections

State officials 2008
Governor . . . . .Bob Riley
   Republican, term expires 1/11
Lieutenant Governor . . . . Jim Folsom Jr
Secretary of State . . . . Beth Chapman
Attorney General . . . . Troy King
Chief Justice . . . . Sue Bell Cobb

Governorship
Minimum age 30
Length of term . . . . 4 years
Consecutive terms permitted 2
Who succeeds . . . . Lieutenant Governor

Local governments by type, 2002
Total 1,171
   County 67
   Municipal 451
   Township 0
   School District 128
   Special District 525

State legislature
Name . . . . Legislature
Upper chamber . . . . .Senate
   Number of members 35
   Length of term . . . . 4 years
   Party in majority, 2008 . . . . Democratic
Lower chamber . . . . House of Representatives
   Number of members 105
   Length of term . . . . 4 years
   Party in majority, 2008 . . . . .Democratic

Federal representation, 2008 (110th Congress)
Senator . . . . Jeff Sessions
   Party . . . . Republican
   Year term expires 2009
Senator . . . . .Richard Shelby
   Party . . . . Republican
   Year term expires 2011
Representatives, total 7
   Democrats 2
   Republicans 5

Voters in November 2006 election (estimate)
Total 1,667,457
   Male 792,343
   Female 875,113
   White 1,241,244
   Black 400,946
   Hispanic 8,488
   Asian . . . . NA

Presidential election, 2004
Total Popular Vote 1,883,449
   Kerry 693,933
   Bush 1,176,394
Total Electoral Votes 9

Votes cast for US Senators
2004
Total vote (x 1,000) 1,839
Leading party . . . . Republican
Percent for leading party 67.5%
2006
Total vote (x 1,000) . . . . NA
Leading party . . . . NA
Percent for leading party . . . . NA

Votes cast for US Representatives
2004
Total vote (x 1,000) 1,793
   Democratic 708
   Republican 1,080
Leading party . . . . Republican
Percent for leading party 60.2%
2006
Total vote (x 1,000) 1,140
   Democratic 502
   Republican 628
Leading party . . . . Republican
Percent for leading party 55.0%

State government employment, 2006
Full-time equivalent employees 85,223
Payroll ($ mil) $304.2

Local government employment, 2006
Full-time equivalent employees 187,312
Payroll ($ mil) $534.9

Women holding public office, 2008
US Congress............................... 0
Statewide elected office...................... 5
State legislature 18

Black public officials, 2002
Total.................................... 757
   US and state legislatures 36
   City/county/regional offices 569
   Judicial/law enforcement................. 56
   Education/school boards................. 96

Hispanic public officials, 2006
Total...................................... 0
   State executives & legislators 0
   City/county/regional offices 0
   Judicial/law enforcement................... 0
   Education/school boards................... 0

Governmental Finance

State government revenues, 2006
Total revenue (x $1,000)............$23,670,922
   per capita $5,156.79
General revenue (x $1,000) $20,306,022
   Intergovernmental 7,587,663
   Taxes 8,529,676
     general sales.................... 2,221,506
     individual income tax 2,766,239
     corporate income tax 558,768
   Current charges................... 2,831,624
   Miscellaneous 1,357,059

State government expenditure, 2006
Total expenditure (x $1,000) $22,260,824
   per capita $4,849.60
General expenditure (x $1,000) $20,010,410
   per capita, total................... $4,359.34
     Education..................... 1,880.57
     Public welfare 1,116.88
     Health....................... 208.62
     Hospitals...................... 242.78
     Highways 291.14
     Police protection................ 35.26
     Corrections 98.44
     Natural resources 61.81
     Parks & recreation 8.22
     Governmental administration 106.93
     Interest on general debt............. 54.10

State debt & cash, 2006 ($ per capita)
Debt $1,388.38
Cash/security holdings............... $8,425.34

Federal government grants to state & local government, 2005 (x $1,000)
Total............................$7,346,245
by Federal agency
   Defense 62,908
   Education 613,336
   Energy........................... 32,674
   Environmental Protection Agency 53,366
   Health & Human Services. 3,934,254
   Homeland Security................. 510,384
   Housing & Urban Development...... 403,224
   Justice 65,806
   Labor 108,019
   Transportation 891,539
   Veterans Affairs.................... 10,156

Crime & Law Enforcement

Crime, 2006 (rates per 100,000 residents)
Property crimes 181,021
   Burglary 44,571
   Larceny 121,610
   Motor vehicle theft 14,840
   Property crime rate.................. 3,936.1
Violent crimes....................... 19,557
   Murder 382
   Forcible rape....................... 1,649
   Robbery.......................... 7,059
   Aggravated assault 10,467
   Violent crime rate 425.2
Hate crimes............................ 1

Fraud and identity theft, 2006
Fraud complaints...................... 4,708
   rate per 100,000 residents 102.4
Identity theft complaints 2,774
   rate per 100,000 residents 60.3

Law enforcement agencies, 2006
Total agencies.......................... 358
Total employees 15,697
   Officers 10,347
   Civilians 5,350

Prisoners, probation, and parole, 2006
Total prisoners....................... 28,241
   percent change, 12/31/05 to 12/31/06 .... 1.3%
   in private facilities 0%
   in local jails 4.1%
Sentenced to more than one year 27,526
   rate per 100,000 residents 595
Adults on probation 55,766
Adults on parole....................... 8,658

Prisoner demographics, June 30, 2005 (rate per 100,000 residents)
Male.................................. 1,665
Female 161
White................................. 542
Black................................. 1,916
Hispanic .... NA

6   Alabama

Arrests, 2006
Total 189,558
   Persons under 18 years of age 11,577

Persons under sentence of death, 1/1/07
Total 195
   White 100
   Black 93
   Hispanic 2

State's highest court
Name . . . . .Supreme Court
Number of members 9
Length of term . . . . 6 years
Intermediate appeals court? . . . . .yes

Labor & Income

Civilian labor force, 2006 (x 1,000)
Total 2,210
   Men 1,179
   Women 1,031
   Persons 16-19 years 84
   White 1,640
   Black 516
   Hispanic 53

Civilian labor force as a percent of civilian
  non-institutional population, 2006
Total 62.1%
   Men 69.8
   Women 55.2
   Persons 16-19 years 37.2
   White 63.1
   Black 59.0
   Hispanic 74.5

Employment, 2006 (x 1,000)
Total 2,119
   Men 1,133
   Women 986
   Persons 16-19 years 72
   White 1,590
   Black 478
   Hispanic 53

Unemployment rate, 2006
Total 4.1%
   Men 3.9
   Women 4.4
   Persons 16-19 years 14.4
   White 3.0
   Black 7.5
   Hispanic 1.1

Full-time/part-time labor force, 2003 (x 1,000)
Full-time labor force, employed 1,723
Part-time labor force, employed 299
Unemployed, looking for
   Full-time work 108
   Part-time work 16
Mean duration of unemployment (weeks) 20.0
   Median 10.6

Labor unions, 2006
Membership (x 1,000) 170
   percent of employed 8.8%

Experienced civilian labor force
  by private industry, 2006
Total 1,574,558
   Natural resources & mining 21,888
   Construction 110,025
   Manufacturing. 302,792
   Trade, transportation & utilities 383,473
   Information 30,305
   Finance 96,572
   Professional & business 213,949
   Education & health 197,774
   Leisure & hospitality. 169,709
   Other 48,070

Experienced civilian labor force
  by occupation, May 2006
Management. 77,880
Business & financial 61,520
Legal. 10,160
Sales 205,000
Office & admin. support. 303,160
Computers & math 33,590
Architecture & engineering. 40,360
Arts & entertainment 17,840
Education 106,540
Social services 18,150
Health care practitioner & technical 108,640
Health care support 47,670
Maintenance & repair. 92,800
Construction 102,010
Transportation & moving 160,950
Production 227,380
Farming, fishing & forestry 7,130

Hours and earnings of production workers
  on manufacturing payrolls, 2006
Average weekly hours 40.9
Average hourly earnings $15.56
Average weekly earnings $636.40

Income and poverty, 2006
Median household income. $38,783
Personal income, per capita (current $) . . . $31,295
   in constant (2000) dollars $27,319
Persons below poverty level 16.6%

Average annual pay
2006 . . . . $36,204
   increase from 2005 . . . . 4.6%

Federal individual income tax returns, 2005
Returns filed. 1,955,914
Adjusted gross income ($1,000) $88,628,735
Total tax liability ($1,000) $10,434,751

Charitable contributions, 2004
Number of contributions 516.2
Total amount ($ mil) $2,492.7

Economy, Business, Industry & Agriculture

Fortune 500 companies, 2007 1
Bankruptcy cases filed, FY 2007 23,176

Patents and trademarks issued, 2007
Patents 386
Trademarks 382

Business firm ownership, 2002
Women-owned 81,821
   Sales ($ mil) $11,435
Black-owned 28,666
   Sales ($ mil) $1,651
Hispanic-owned 2,524
   Sales ($ mil) $748
Asian-owned 4,270
   Sales ($ mil) $1,491
Amer. Indian/Alaska Native-owned 2,908
   Sales ($ mil) $470
Hawaiian/Pacific Islander-owned 96
   Sales ($ mil) $5

Gross domestic product, 2006 ($ mil)
Total gross domestic product $160,569
   Agriculture, forestry, fishing and
      hunting 2,466
   Mining 2,574
   Utilities 4,349
   Construction 8,085
   Manufacturing, durable goods 18,284
   Manufacturing, non-durable goods 11,687
   Wholesale trade 9,180
   Retail trade 12,673
   Transportation & warehousing 4,476
   Information 4,609
   Finance & insurance 8,342
   Real estate, rental & leasing 15,388
   Professional and technical services 9,234
   Educational services 751
   Health care and social assistance 11,248
   Accommodation/food services 3,629
   Other services, except government 3,881
   Government 24,185

Establishments, payroll, employees & receipts, by major industry group, 2005

Total 101,976
   Annual payroll ($1,000) $53,365,320
   Paid employees 1,667,526

Forestry, fishing & agriculture 980
   Annual payroll ($1,000) $188,609
   Paid employees 6,955

Mining 268
   Annual payroll ($1,000) $405,665
   Paid employees 7,427
   Receipts, 2002 ($1,000) $2,615,060

Utilities 413
   Annual payroll ($1,000) $1,329,504
   Paid employees 20,254
   Receipts, 2002 ($1,000) . . . . .NA

Construction 9,952
   Annual payroll ($1,000) $3,597,814
   Paid employees 105,850
   Receipts, 2002 ($1,000) $15,582,292

Manufacturing 4,953
   Annual payroll ($1,000) $10,526,271
   Paid employees 282,136
   Receipts, 2002 ($1,000) $66,686,220

Wholesale trade 5,533
   Annual payroll ($1,000) $3,259,343
   Paid employees 78,099
   Receipts, 2002 ($1,000) $43,641,369

Retail trade 19,451
   Annual payroll ($1,000) $4,846,484
   Paid employees .237,503
   Receipts, 2002 ($1,000) $43,784,342

Transportation & warehousing 3,144
   Annual payroll ($1,000) $1,974,948
   Paid employees 58,881
   Receipts, 2002 ($1,000) $4,794,369

Information 1,702
   Annual payroll ($1,000) $1,717,058
   Paid employees .37,341
   Receipts, 2002 ($1,000) . . . . .NA

Finance & insurance .6,743
   Annual payroll ($1,000) $4,040,625
   Paid employees .77,144
   Receipts, 2002 ($1,000) . . . . .NA

Professional, scientific & technical 9,180
   Annual payroll ($1,000) $4,919,444
   Paid employees 95,543
   Receipts, 2002 ($1,000) $8,757,629

Education 785
   Annual payroll ($1,000) $607,875
   Paid employees 25,390
   Receipts, 2002 ($1,000) $185,253

Health care & social assistance 9,820
   Annual payroll ($1,000) $7,920,889
   Paid employees 228,797
   Receipts, 2002 ($1,000) $16,594,961

Arts and entertainment 1,130
   Annual payroll ($1,000) $251,848
   Paid employees 16,286
   Receipts, 2002 ($1,000) $706,653

Real estate 4,055
   Annual payroll ($1,000) $671,937
   Paid employees 23,860
   Receipts, 2002 ($1,000) $2,636,384

Accommodation & food service 7,529
   Annual payroll ($1,000) $1,591,435
   Paid employees 145,447
   Receipts, 2002 ($1,000) $4,692,297

Exports, 2006

Value of exported goods ($ mil) $13,878
   Manufactured $12,142
   Non-manufactured...................$1,436

Foreign direct investment in US affiliates, 2004

Property, plants & equipment ($ mil) ... $16,857
Employment (x 1,000).....................70.6

Agriculture, 2006

Number of farms 43,000
Farm acreage (x 1,000) 8,600
   Acres per farm....................... 200
Farm marketings and income ($ mil)
Total................................ $3,739.1
   Crops............................. $695.9
   Livestock..........................$3,043.1
Net farm income $1,579.8

Principal commodities, in order by marketing receipts, 2005

Broilers, Cattle and calves, Greenhouse/nursery,
Chicken eggs, Cotton

Federal economic activity in state

Expenditures, 2005 ($ mil)
   Total............................. $42,061
      Per capita $9,247.55
   Defense $9,781
   Non-defense..................... $32,280
Defense department, 2006 ($ mil)
   Payroll........................... $3,503
   Contract awards $6,954
   Grants $64
Homeland security grants ($1,000)
   2006..............................$15,578
   2007..............................$11,574

FDIC-insured financial institutions, 2005

Number 159
Assets ($ billion) $233.3
Deposits ($ billion) $171.3

Fishing, 2006

Catch (x 1,000 lbs)..................... 34,052
Value ($1,000)......................... $48,566

Mining, 2006 ($ mil)

Total non-fuel mineral production $1,200
Percent of U.S. 1.86%

Communication, Energy & Transportation

Communication

Households with computers, 2003........ 53.9%
Households with internet access, 2003 .... 45.7%
High-speed internet providers 63
Total high-speed internet lines........ 898,850
   Residential 616,392
   Business......................... 282,458
Wireless phone customers, 12/2006 3,374,701

FCC-licensed stations (as of January 1, 2008)

TV stations 43
FM radio stations....................... 193
AM radio stations 153

Energy

Energy consumption, 2004
   Total (trillion Btu).................2,160
   Per capita (million Btu) 478.1
By source of production (trillion Btu)
   Coal............................ 854
   Natural gas...................... 404
   Petroleum....................... 639
   Nuclear electric power 330
   Hydroelectric power 107
By end-use sector (trillion Btu)
   Residential 394
   Commercial 270
   Industrial 1,001
   Transportation 495
Electric energy, 2005
   Primary source of electricity......... Coal
   Net generation (billion kWh) 137.9
      percent from renewable sources...... 10.1%
   Net summer capability (million kW) 30.7
   CO_2 emitted from generation 83.8
Natural gas utilities, 2005
   Customers (x 1,000) 867
   Sales (trillion Btu)..................... 226
   Revenues ($ mil) $1,294
Nuclear plants, 2007 5
Total CO_2 emitted (million metric tons).....136.0
Energy spending, 2004 ($ mil) $15,180
   per capita $3,360
   Price per million Btu $11.29

Transportation, 2006

Public road & street mileage 96,521
   Urban............................. 21,846
   Rural.............................74,675
   Interstate......................... 908
Vehicle miles of travel (millions) 60,414
   per capita 13,161.4
Total motor vehicle registrations.......4,630,314
   Automobiles......................1,795,596
   Trucks 2,825,636
   Motorcycles 104,074
Licensed drivers........................3,665,180
   19 years & under 216,227
Deaths from motor vehicle accidents 1,208
Gasoline consumed (x 1,000 gallons) 2,627,049
   per capita 572.3

Commuting Statistics, 2006

Average commute time (min) 23.6
   Drove to work alone 83.6%
   Carpooled.......................... 11.3%
   Public transit 0.5%
   Walk to work 1.1%
   Work from home..................... 2.5%

State Summary

Capital city . . . . Juneau
Governor . . . . Sarah Palin
PO Box 110001
Juneau, AK 99811
907-465-3500
Admitted as a state 1959
Area (square miles) 663,267
Population, 2007 (estimate). 683,478
Largest city . . . . Anchorage
Population, 2006 278,700
Personal income per capita, 2006
(in current dollars) $37,271
Gross domestic product, 2006 ($ mil) $41,105

Leading industries by payroll, 2005

Health care/Social assistance, Construction,
Transportation & Warehousing

Leading agricultural commodities by receipts, 2005

Greenhouse/nursery, Hay, Cattle and calves,
Potatoes, Dairy products

Geography & Environment

Total area (square miles) 663,267
land 571,951
water 91,316
Federally-owned land, 2004 (acres) . . 252,495,811
percent 69.1%
Highest point . . . . Mt. McKinley
elevation (feet) 20,320
Lowest point . . . . Pacific Ocean
elevation (feet) . . . . sea level
General coastline (miles) 6,568
Tidal shoreline (miles) 33,904
Cropland, 2003 (x 1,000 acres) . . . . NA
Forest land, 2003 (x 1,000 acres). . . . . NA
Capital city . . . . Juneau
Population 2000 30,711
Population 2006 30,737
Largest city . . . . Anchorage
Population 2000 260,283
Population 2006 278,700

Number of cities with over 100,000 population

1990 1
2000 1
2006 1

State park and recreation areas, 2005

Area (x 1,000 acres) 3,353
Number of visitors (x 1,000) 4,678
Revenues ($1,000) $2,511
percent of operating expenditures 38.9%

National forest system land, 2007

Acres 21,972,605

Demographics & Population Characteristics

Population

1980 401,851
1990 550,043
2000 626,931
2006 670,053
Male 346,411
Female 323,642
Living in group quarters, 2006 23,100
percent of total 3.4%
2007 (estimate). 683,478
persons per square mile of land 1.2
2008 (projected) 680,082
2010 (projected) 694,109
2020 (projected) 774,421
2030 (projected) 867,674

Population of Core-Based Statistical Areas (formerly Metropolitan Areas), x 1,000

	CBSA	Non-CBSA
1990	398	152
2000	461	166
2006	503	167

Change in population, 2000-2007

Number 56,547
percent. 9.0%
Natural increase (births minus deaths) 53,166
Net internal migration . . . . -5,125
Net international migration 4,236

Persons by age, 2006

Under 5 years 49,771
5 to 17 years 131,663
18 years and over 488,619
65 years and over 45,630
85 years and over 4,148
Median age 33.4

Persons by age, 2010 (projected)

Under 5 years 58,380
18 and over 510,126
65 and over 56,548
Median age 32.5

Race, 2006

One Race
White 473,645
Black or African American 25,108
Asian 31,113
American Indian/Alaska Native 103,497
Hawaiian Native/Pacific Islander 4,138
Two or more races 32,552

Persons of Hispanic origin, 2006

Total Hispanic or Latino 37,498
Mexican 21,987
Puerto Rican 2,495
Cuban 510

Persons of Asian origin, 2006

Total Asian	30,151
Asian Indian	689
Chinese	2,447
Filipino	16,885
Japanese	1,267
Korean	3,211
Vietnamese	1,537

Marital status, 2006

Population 15 years & over	524,378
Never married	171,898
Married	274,300
Separated	8,277
Widowed	20,329
Divorced	57,851

Language spoken at home, 2006

Population 5 years and older	622,572
English only	526,829
Spanish	22,649
French	2,470
German	4,716
Chinese	875

Households & families, 2006

Households	229,878
with persons under 18 years	90,661
with persons over 65 years	30,161
persons per household	2.81
Families	157,939
persons per family	3.36
Married couples	117,329
Female householder, no husband present	28,062
One-person households	57,133

Nativity, 2006

Number of residents born in state	260,324
percent of population	38.9%

Immigration & naturalization, 2006

Legal permanent residents admitted	1,554
Persons naturalized	831
Non-immigrant admissions	100,647

Vital Statistics and Health

Marriages

2004	5,594
2005	5,446
2006	5,309

Divorces

2004	2,829
2005	2,865
2006	2,968

Health risks, 2006

Percent of adults who are:

Smokers	24.0%
Overweight (BMI > 25)	64.2%
Obese (BMI > 30)	26.2%

Births

2005	10,459
Birthrate (per 1,000)	15.8
White	6,536
Black	422
Hispanic	779
Asian/Pacific Islander	778
Amer. Indian/Alaska Native	2,723
Low birth weight (2,500g or less)	6.1%
Cesarian births	21.9%
Preterm births	10.6%
To unmarried mothers	36.0%
Twin births (per 1,000)	26.9
Triplets or higher order (per 100,000)	68.0
2006 (preliminary)	10,991
rate per 1,000	16.4

Deaths

2004

All causes	3,051
rate per 100,000	750.5
Heart disease	589
rate per 100,000	158.3
Malignant neoplasms	728
rate per 100,000	183.8
Cerebrovascular disease	172
rate per 100,000	52.1
Chronic lower respiratory disease	139
rate per 100,000	39.4
Diabetes	93
rate per 100,000	22.5
2005 (preliminary)	3,170
rate per 100,000	750.8
2006 (provisional)	3,318

Infant deaths

2004	69
rate per 1,000	6.7
2005 (provisional)	54
rate per 1,000	5.2

Exercise routines, 2005

None	21.4%
Moderate or greater	59.2%
Vigorous	35.9%

Abortions, 2004

Total performed in state	1,937
rate per 1,000 women age 15-44	14
% obtained by out-of-state residents	0.2%

Physicians, 2005

Total	1,515
rate per 100,000 persons	228

Community hospitals, 2005

Number of hospitals	22
Beds (x 1,000)	1.4
Patients admitted (x 1,000)	51
Average daily census (x 1,000)	0.8
Average cost per day	$2,246
Outpatient visits (x 1 mil)	1.7

Disability status of population, 2006
5 to 15 years 5.9%
16 to 64 years 14.1%
65 years and over 47.9%

Education

Educational attainment, 2006
Population over 25 years 415,630
    Less than 9th grade. 3.8%
    High school graduate or more 89.7%
    College graduate or more. 26.9%
    Graduate or professional degree. 9.5%

Public school enrollment, 2005-06
Total. 133,288
    Pre-kindergarten through grade 8. 91,225
    Grades 9 through 12 42,063

Graduating public high school seniors, 2004-05
Diplomas (incl. GED and others) 7,236

SAT scores, 2007
Average critical reading score 519
Average writing score 491
Average math score 517
Percent of graduates taking test 48%

Public school teachers, 2006-07 (estimate)
Total (x 1,000) 8.0
    Elementary. 5.3
    Secondary. 2.7
Average salary $54,658
    Elementary. $54,658
    Secondary. $54,658

State receipts & expenditures for
  public schools, 2006-07 (estimate)
Revenue receipts ($ mil) $1,346
Expenditures
Total ($ mil) $1,486
    Per capita $2,060
    Per pupil $11,900

NAEP proficiency scores, 2007

	Reading		Math	
	Basic	Proficient	Basic	Proficient
Grade 4	61.7%	28.7%	78.8%	37.9%
Grade 8	70.8%	27.1%	73.0%	32.2%

Higher education enrollment, fall 2005
Total. 1,365
    Full-time men 252
    Full-time women. 432
    Part-time men 222
    Part-time women. 459

Minority enrollment in institutions
  of higher education, 2005
Black, non-Hispanic .1,016
Hispanic 1,071
Asian/Pacific Islander 1,476
American Indian/Alaska Native. 4,078

Institutions of higher education, 2005-06
Total. 8
    Public. 5
    Private 3

Earned degrees conferred, 2004-05
Associate's. 879
Bachelor's 1,427
Master's 655
First-professional. 0
Doctor's 25

Public Libraries, 2006
Number of libraries. 89
Number of outlets 107
Annual visits per capita 5.2
Circulation per capita. 6.1

State & local financial support for
  higher education, FY 2006
Full-time equivalent enrollment (x 1,000) 18.8
Appropriations per FTE. $12,097

Social Insurance & Welfare Programs

Social Security benefits & beneficiaries, 2005
Beneficiaries (x 1,000) 65
    Retired & dependents. 42
    Survivors. 10
    Disabled & dependents. 13
Annual benefit payments ($ mil) $659
    Retired & dependents. $415
    Survivors. $120
    Disabled & dependents. $124
Average monthly benefit
    Retired & dependents. $962
    Disabled & dependents. $912
    Widowed. $913

Medicare, July 2005
Enrollment (x 1,000) 52
Payments ($ mil) $343

Medicaid, 2004
Beneficiaries (x 1,000). 808
Payments ($ mil) $3,857

State Children's Health Insurance Program, 2006
Enrollment (x 1,000). 22.2
Expenditures ($ mil) $27.8

Persons without health insurance, 2006
Number (x 1,000). 109
    percent. 16.5%
Number of children (x 1,000) 19
    percent of children 10.5%

Health care expenditures, 2004
Total expenditures. $4,237
    per capita $6,450

Federal and state public aid

State unemployment insurance, 2006
Recipients, first payments (x 1,000) 41
Total payments ($ mil) $110
Average weekly benefit $198
Temporary Assistance for Needy Families, 2006
Recipients (x 1,000) 114.8
Families (x 1,000) 42.5
Supplemental Security Income, 2005
Recipients (x 1,000) 11.0
Payments ($ mil) $53.2
Food Stamp Program, 2006
Avg monthly participants (x 1,000) 57.2
Total benefits ($ mil) $86.0

Housing & Construction

Housing units
Total 2005 (estimate) 274,182
Total 2006 (estimate) 276,571
Seasonal or recreational use, 2006 23,131
Owner-occupied, 2006 148,249
    Median home value $213,200
    Homeowner vacancy rate 1.7%
Renter-occupied, 2006 81,629
    Median rent $883
    Rental vacancy rate 8.5%
Home ownership rate, 2005 . . . . 66.0%
Home ownership rate, 2006 . . . . 67.2%

New privately-owned housing units
Number authorized, 2006 (x 1,000) 2.7
    Value ($ mil) $511.5
Started 2005 (x 1,000, estimate) 2.3
Started 2006 (x 1,000, estimate) 2.3

Existing home sales
2005 (x 1,000) 24.6
2006 (x 1,000) 30.7

Government & Elections

State officials 2008
Governor . . . . .Sarah Palin
        Republican, term expires 12/10
Lieutenant Governor . . . . Sean Parnell
Secretary of State . . . . (no secretary of state)
Attorney General . . . . Talis Colberg
Chief Justice . . . . .Dana Fabe

Governorship
Minimum age 30
Length of term . . . . 4 years
Consecutive terms permitted 2
Who succeeds . . . . Lieutenant Governor

Local governments by type, 2002
Total 175
    County 12
    Municipal 149
    Township 0
    School District 0
    Special District 14

State legislature
Name . . . . Legislature
Upper chamber . . . . .Senate
    Number of members 20
    Length of term . . . . 4 years
    Party in majority, 2008 . . . . Republican
Lower chamber . . . . . . .House of Representatives
    Number of members 40
    Length of term . . . . 2 years
    Party in majority, 2008 . . . . Republican

Federal representation, 2008 (110th Congress)
Senator . . . . Ted Stevens
    Party . . . . Republican
    Year term expires 2009
Senator . . . . Lisa Murkowski
    Party . . . . Republican
    Year term expires 2011
Representatives, total 1
    Democrats 0
    Republicans 1

Voters in November 2006 election (estimate)
Total 247,901
    Male 118,516
    Female 129,384
    White 202,045
    Black 5,753
    Hispanic 1,905
    Asian 3,908

Presidential election, 2004
Total Popular Vote 312,598
    Kerry 111,025
    Bush 190,889
Total Electoral Votes 3

Votes cast for US Senators
2004
Total vote (x 1,000) 308
Leading party . . . . Republican
Percent for leading party 48.6%
2006
Total vote (x 1,000) . . . . NA
Leading party . . . . NA
Percent for leading party . . . . NA

Votes cast for US Representatives
2004
Total vote (x 1,000) 300
    Democratic 67
    Republican 213
Leading party . . . . Republican
Percent for leading party 71.1%
2006
Total vote (x 1,000) 235
    Democratic 94
    Republican 133
Leading party . . . . Republican
Percent for leading party 56.6%

State government employment, 2006
Full-time equivalent employees 25,151
Payroll ($ mil) $107.5

Local government employment, 2006
Full-time equivalent employees 27,480
Payroll ($ mil) $111.9

Women holding public office, 2008
US Congress 1
Statewide elected office 1
State legislature 13

Black public officials, 2002
Total 2
    US and state legislatures 1
    City/county/regional offices 1
    Judicial/law enforcement 0
    Education/school boards 0

Hispanic public officials, 2006
Total 1
    State executives & legislators 0
    City/county/regional offices 1
    Judicial/law enforcement 0
    Education/school boards 0

Governmental Finance

State government revenues, 2006
Total revenue (x $1,000) $10,844,814
    per capita $16,008.29
General revenue (x $1,000) $8,920,140
    Intergovernmental 2,155,908
    Taxes 2,484,422
        general sales 0
        individual income tax 0
        corporate income tax 821,664
    Current charges .519,470
    Miscellaneous .3,760,340

State government expenditure, 2006
Total expenditure (x $1,000) $8,599,090
    per capita $12,693.32
General expenditure (x $1,000) $7,528,220
    per capita, total $11,112.58
        Education 2,672.91
        Public welfare 2,147.40
        Health 303.76
        Hospitals 45.70
        Highways 1,673.24
        Police protection 105.75
        Corrections 310.29
        Natural resources 404.43
        Parks & recreation 15.93
        Governmental administration 729.13
        Interest on general debt 445.84

State debt & cash, 2006 ($ per capita)
Debt $9,240.46
Cash/security holdings $76,637.60

Federal government grants to state & local government, 2005 (x $1,000)
Total $3,131,207
by Federal agency
    Defense 42,948
    Education 306,817
    Energy 8,488
    Environmental Protection Agency 101,021
    Health & Human Services 1,321,234
    Homeland Security 16,181
    Housing & Urban Development 187,412
    Justice 56,303
    Labor 47,501
    Transportation 537,548
    Veterans Affairs 2,406

Crime & Law Enforcement

Crime, 2006 (rates per 100,000 residents)
Property crimes 24,155
    Burglary 4,136
    Larceny 17,490
    Motor vehicle theft 2,529
    Property crime rate 688.0
Violent crimes 4,610
    Murder 36
    Forcible rape 509
    Robbery 605
    Aggravated assault 3,460
    Violent crime rate 688.0
Hate crimes 11

Fraud and identity theft, 2006
Fraud complaints 1,079
    rate per 100,000 residents 161.0
Identity theft complaints 384
    rate per 100,000 residents 57.3

Law enforcement agencies, 2006
Total agencies 42
Total employees 1,937
    Officers 1,220
    Civilians 717

Prisoners, probation, and parole, 2006
Total prisoners 5,069
    percent change, 12/31/05 to 12/31/06 . . . . 5.3%
    in private facilities 33.2%
    in local jails . . . . NA
Sentenced to more than one year 3,116
    rate per 100,000 residents 462
Adults on probation 6,095
Adults on parole 1,044

Prisoner demographics, June 30, 2005 (rate per 100,000 residents)
Male 1,232
Female 141
White 500
Black 2,163
Hispanic 380

6 Alaska

Arrests, 2006
Total 36,994
   Persons under 18 years of age 4,136

Persons under sentence of death, 1/1/07
Total 0
   White 0
   Black 0
   Hispanic 0

State's highest court
Name . . . . .Supreme Court
Number of members 5
Length of term . . . . 10 years
Intermediate appeals court? . . . . .yes

Labor & Income

Civilian labor force, 2006 (x 1,000)
Total 349
   Men 187
   Women 162
   Persons 16-19 years 20
   White 273
   Black 11
   Hispanic 13

Civilian labor force as a percent of civilian non-institutional population, 2006
Total 72.0%
   Men 77.1
   Women 66.8
   Persons 16-19 years 50.0
   White 73.7
   Black 75.8
   Hispanic 77.9

Employment, 2006 (x 1,000)
Total 325
   Men 172
   Women 153
   Persons 16-19 years 17
   White 258
   Black 10
   Hispanic 12

Unemployment rate, 2006
Total 6.9%
   Men 8.0
   Women 5.7
   Persons 16-19 years 14.7
   White 5.3
   Black 10.7
   Hispanic 10.3

Full-time/part-time labor force, 2003 (x 1,000)
Full-time labor force, employed 250
Part-time labor force, employed 55
Unemployed, looking for
   Full-time work 22
   Part-time work 5
Mean duration of unemployment (weeks) 15.6
   Median 7.6

Labor unions, 2006
Membership (x 1,000) 62
   percent of employed 22.2%

Experienced civilian labor force by private industry, 2006
Total 231,542
   Natural resources & mining 13,196
   Construction 17,994
   Manufacturing 13,208
   Trade, transportation & utilities 63,780
   Information 6,947
   Finance 13,700
   Professional & business 24,342
   Education & health 37,054
   Leisure & hospitality 31,371
   Other 9,487

Experienced civilian labor force by occupation, May 2006
Management 23,980
Business & financial 9,660
Legal 2,090
Sales 25,760
Office & admin. support 50,970
Computers & math 3,930
Architecture & engineering 6,330
Arts & entertainment 3,010
Education 21,720
Social services 5,630
Health care practitioner & technical 13,150
Health care support 6,220
Maintenance & repair 16,260
Construction 20,810
Transportation & moving 23,200
Production 11,520
Farming, fishing & forestry 700

Hours and earnings of production workers on manufacturing payrolls, 2006
Average weekly hours .40.5
Average hourly earnings $14.30
Average weekly earnings $579.15

Income and poverty, 2006
Median household income $59,393
Personal income, per capita (current $) . . . $37,271
   in constant (2000) dollars $32,535
Persons below poverty level 10.9%

Average annual pay
2006 . . . . $41,750
   increase from 2005 . . . . 3.8%

Federal individual income tax returns, 2005
Returns filed 346,927
Adjusted gross income ($1,000) $16,725,880
Total tax liability ($1,000) $2,215,386

Charitable contributions, 2004
Number of contributions 69.7
Total amount ($ mil) $260.4

Economy, Business, Industry & Agriculture

Fortune 500 companies, 2007 0
Bankruptcy cases filed, FY 2007 696

Patents and trademarks issued, 2007
Patents 27
Trademarks 74

Business firm ownership, 2002
Women-owned 16,308
 Sales ($ mil) $2,348
Black-owned 926
 Sales ($ mil) $81
Hispanic-owned 1,241
 Sales ($ mil) $171
Asian-owned 1,908
 Sales ($ mil) $421
Amer. Indian/Alaska Native-owned 5,019
 Sales ($ mil) $648
Hawaiian/Pacific Islander-owned 152
 Sales ($ mil) $10

Gross domestic product, 2006 ($ mil)
Total gross domestic product $41,105
 Agriculture, forestry, fishing and
  hunting 306
 Mining 12,133
 Utilities 416
 Construction 1,882
 Manufacturing, durable goods 153
 Manufacturing, non-durable goods 779
 Wholesale trade 805
 Retail trade 1,881
 Transportation & warehousing 3,561
 Information 910
 Finance & insurance 1,205
 Real estate, rental & leasing 3,301
 Professional and technical services 1,399
 Educational services 129
 Health care and social assistance 2,262
 Accommodation/food services 997
 Other services, except government 615
 Government 7,272

Establishments, payroll, employees & receipts, by major industry group, 2005

Total 19,808
 Annual payroll ($1,000) $9,774,285
 Paid employees 231,088

Forestry, fishing & agriculture 332
 Annual payroll ($1,000) . . . . NA
 Paid employees . . . . NA

Mining 123
 Annual payroll ($1,000) $620,607
 Paid employees .6,780
 Receipts, 2002 ($1,000) $8,254,126

Utilities 85
 Annual payroll ($1,000) $120,284
 Paid employees .1,721
 Receipts, 2002 ($1,000) . . . . .NA
Construction 2,773
 Annual payroll ($1,000) $1,272,040
 Paid employees .19,353
 Receipts, 2002 ($1,000) $4,417,369
Manufacturing 514
 Annual payroll ($1,000) $402,806
 Paid employees 9,860
 Receipts, 2002 ($1,000) $3,832,024
Wholesale trade 736
 Annual payroll ($1,000) $386,296
 Paid employees 8,239
 Receipts, 2002 ($1,000) $3,616,674
Retail trade 2,675
 Annual payroll ($1,000) $911,704
 Paid employees 34,897
 Receipts, 2002 ($1,000) $7,437,071
Transportation & warehousing 1,149
 Annual payroll ($1,000) $961,489
 Paid employees 18,549
 Receipts, 2002 ($1,000) $3,205,233
Information 380
 Annual payroll ($1,000) $366,003
 Paid employees .7,824
 Receipts, 2002 ($1,000) . . . . .NA
Finance & insurance 744
 Annual payroll ($1,000) $393,778
 Paid employees .7,836
 Receipts, 2002 ($1,000) . . . . .NA
Professional, scientific & technical 1,832
 Annual payroll ($1,000) $676,383
 Paid employees .12,014
 Receipts, 2002 ($1,000) $1,362,539
Education 224
 Annual payroll ($1,000) $58,716
 Paid employees .2,709
 Receipts, 2002 ($1,000) $56,481
Health care & social assistance 1,959
 Annual payroll ($1,000) $1,627,019
 Paid employees .37,476
 Receipts, 2002 ($1,000) $3,393,974
Arts and entertainment 522
 Annual payroll ($1,000) $68,344
 Paid employees .4,215
 Receipts, 2002 ($1,000) $282,921
Real estate 876
 Annual payroll ($1,000) $145,988
 Paid employees 4,443
 Receipts, 2002 ($1,000) $675,209
Accommodation & food service 1,966
 Annual payroll ($1,000) $483,353
 Paid employees .23,939
 Receipts, 2002 ($1,000) $1,393,225

Exports, 2006

Value of exported goods ($ mil) $4,044
    Manufactured $577
    Non-manufactured $3,400

Foreign direct investment in US affiliates, 2004

Property, plants & equipment ($ mil) $31,121
Employment (x 1,000) 11.3

Agriculture, 2006

Number of farms 640
Farm acreage (x 1,000) 900
    Acres per farm 1,406
Farm marketings and income ($ mil)
Total $64.2
    Crops $24.9
    Livestock $39.4
Net farm income $20.0

Principal commodities, in order by marketing receipts, 2005

    Greenhouse/nursery, Hay, Cattle and calves, Potatoes, Dairy products

Federal economic activity in state

Expenditures, 2005 ($ mil)
    Total $9,230
        Per capita $13,915.75
    Defense $3,217
    Non-defense $6,012
Defense department, 2006 ($ mil)
    Payroll $1,640
    Contract awards $1,656
    Grants $43
Homeland security grants ($1,000)
    2006 . . . . $8,294
    2007 . . . . $7,195

FDIC-insured financial institutions, 2005

Number 7
Assets ($ billion) $4.3
Deposits ($ billion) $3.1

Fishing, 2006

Catch (x 1,000 lbs) 5,421,263
Value ($1,000) $1,342,294

Mining, 2006 ($ mil)

Total non-fuel mineral production $2,850
Percent of U.S. 4.43%

Communication, Energy & Transportation

Communication

Households with computers, 2003 . . . . 72.7%
Households with internet access, 2003 . . . . 67.6%
High-speed internet providers 18
Total high-speed internet lines 145,008
    Residential 123,538
    Business 21,470
Wireless phone customers, 12/2006 412,112

FCC-licensed stations (as of January 1, 2008)

TV stations 17
FM radio stations 80
AM radio stations 39

Energy

Energy consumption, 2004
    Total (trillion Btu) 779
    Per capita (million Btu) 1,186.1
By source of production (trillion Btu)
    Coal 14
    Natural gas 412
    Petroleum 335
    Nuclear electric power 0
    Hydroelectric power 15
By end-use sector (trillion Btu)
    Residential 56
    Commercial 63
    Industrial 393
    Transportation 266
Electric energy, 2005
    Primary source of electricity . . . . Gas
    Net generation (billion kWh) 6.6
        percent from renewable sources 22.3%
    Net summer capability (million kW) 1.9
    CO_2 emitted from generation 4.3
Natural gas utilities, 2005
    Customers (x 1,000) 123
    Sales (trillion Btu) 90
    Revenues ($ mil) $348
Nuclear plants, 2007 0
Total CO_2 emitted (million metric tons) 44.8
Energy spending, 2004 ($ mil) $4,164
    per capita $6,339
    Price per million Btu $11.09

Transportation, 2006

Public road & street mileage 14,787
    Urban 2,370
    Rural 12,417
    Interstate 1,081
Vehicle miles of travel (millions) 4,967
    per capita 7,331.9
Total motor vehicle registrations 675,094
    Automobiles 242,487
    Trucks 429,901
    Motorcycles 24,114
Licensed drivers 489,024
    19 years & under 23,645
Deaths from motor vehicle accidents 74
Gasoline consumed (x 1,000 gallons) 293,351
    per capita 433.0

Commuting Statistics, 2006

Average commute time (min) 17.7
    Drove to work alone 67.7%
    Carpooled 12.7%
    Public transit 1.1%
    Walk to work 9.1%
    Work from home 5.1%

State Summary

Capital city . . . . Phoenix
Governor . . . . Janet Napolitano
State Capitol
1700 W Washington
Phoenix, AZ 85007
602-542-4331
Admitted as a state 1912
Area (square miles) 113,998
Population, 2007 (estimate) 6,338,755
Largest city . . . . Phoenix
Population, 2006 1,512,986
Personal income per capita, 2006
(in current dollars) $31,458
Gross domestic product, 2006 ($ mil) . . . $232,463

Leading industries by payroll, 2005

Health care/Social assistance, Construction,
Manufacturing

**Leading agricultural commodities
by receipts, 2005**

Cattle and calves, Dairy products, Lettuce, Cotton, Hay

Geography & Environment

Total area (square miles) 113,998
land 113,635
water 364
Federally-owned land, 2004 (acres) . . .34,933,236
percent 48.1%
Highest point . . . . Humphreys Peak
elevation (feet) 12,633
Lowest point . . . . .Colorado River
elevation (feet) 70
General coastline (miles) 0
Tidal shoreline (miles) 0
Cropland, 2003 (x 1,000 acres) 934
Forest land, 2003 (x 1,000 acres) 4,141
Capital city . . . . Phoenix
Population 2000 1,321,045
Population 2006 1,512,986
Largest city . . . . Phoenix
Population 2000 1,321,045
Population 2006 1,512,986

Number of cities with over 100,000 population

1990 6
2000 9
2006 9

State park and recreation areas, 2005

Area (x 1,000 acres) 64
Number of visitors (x 1,000) 2,224
Revenues ($1,000) $9,188
percent of operating expenditures 43.3%

National forest system land, 2007

Acres 11,264,377

Demographics & Population Characteristics

Population

1980 2,718,215
1990 3,665,228
2000 5,130,632
2006 6,166,318
Male 3,085,755
Female 3,080,563
Living in group quarters, 2006 109,501
percent of total 1.8%
2007 (estimate) 6,338,755
persons per square mile of land 55.8
2008 (projected) .6,320,874
2010 (projected) 6,637,381
2020 (projected) .8,456,448
2030 (projected) 10,712,397

**Population of Core-Based Statistical Areas
(formerly Metropolitan Areas), x 1,000**

	CBSA	Non-CBSA
1990	3,512	153
2000	4,944	187
2006	5,964	203

Change in population, 2000-2007

Number 1,208,140
percent 23.5%
Natural increase (births minus deaths) 353,002
Net internal migration 655,354
Net international migration 214,014

Persons by age, 2006

Under 5 years 480,491
5 to 17 years 1,147,707
18 years and over 4,538,120
65 years and over 790,286
85 years and over .105,104
Median age 34.6

Persons by age, 2010 (projected)

Under 5 years 515,408
18 and over 4,948,917
65 and over 922,010
Median age 36.4

Race, 2006

One Race

White 5,380,815
Black or African American 231,677
Asian 146,725
American Indian/Alaska Native 294,118
Hawaiian Native/Pacific Islander 12,132
Two or more races 100,851

Persons of Hispanic origin, 2006

Total Hispanic or Latino 1,803,377
Mexican 1,601,082
Puerto Rican 31,273
Cuban 9,119

Persons of Asian origin, 2006

Total Asian 144,858
  Asian Indian........................ 28,015
  Chinese 32,461
  Filipino 23,653
  Japanese 10,707
  Korean..............................10,792
  Vietnamese......................... 26,308

Marital status, 2006

Population 15 years & over 4,806,252
  Never married 1,441,518
  Married......................... 2,518,326
  Separated 96,570
  Widowed.......................... 277,749
  Divorced 568,659

Language spoken at home, 2006

Population 5 years and older......... 5,687,173
  English only 4,094,302
  Spanish 1,244,012
  French 14,946
  German........................... 23,855
  Chinese 21,515

Households & families, 2006

Households.........................2,224,992
  with persons under 18 years 760,124
  with persons over 65 years.......... 543,788
  persons per household 2.72
Families...........................1,476,269
  persons per family.....................3.33
Married couples.....................1,104,808
Female householder,
  no husband present................ 256,384
One-person households 596,850

Nativity, 2006

Number of residents born in state 2,200,209
  percent of population................. 35.7%

Immigration & naturalization, 2006

Legal permanent residents admitted......21,530
Persons naturalized 9,707
Non-immigrant admissions 769,491

Vital Statistics and Health

Marriages

2004...............................37,882
2005............................... 38,308
2006............................... 38,983

Divorces

2004............................... 24,403
2005............................... 24,535
2006............................... 24,274

Health risks, 2006

Percent of adults who are:
  Smokers.......................... 18.2%
  Overweight (BMI > 25)............... 59.6%
  Obese (BMI > 30)..................... 22.9%

Births

2005................................ 96,199
  Birthrate (per 1,000)....................16.2
  White...............................83,147
  Black 3,645
  Hispanic 42,852
  Asian/Pacific Islander 2,953
  Amer. Indian/Alaska Native 6,454
  Low birth weight (2,500g or less)........ 6.9%
  Cesarian births 24.7%
  Preterm births 13.2%
  To unmarried mothers............... 43.1%
  Twin births (per 1,000) 26.5
  Triplets or higher order (per 100,000)....164.9
2006 (preliminary)................... 102,475
  rate per 1,000 ....16.6

Deaths

2004

All causes 43,198
  rate per 100,000.....................758.1
Heart disease 10,539
  rate per 100,000.....................185.7
Malignant neoplasms.....................9,618
  rate per 100,000.....................167.2
Cerebrovascular disease.............. 2,446
  rate per 100,000.....................43.3
Chronic lower respiratory disease 2,416
  rate per 100,000.....................42.4
Diabetes............................1,196
  rate per 100,000.....................20.9
2005 (preliminary) 45,837
  rate per 100,000.....................771.8
2006 (provisional) 46,073

Infant deaths

2004................................. 630
  rate per 1,000 ....6.7
2005 (provisional) 667
  rate per 1,000 ....6.9

Exercise routines, 2005

None................................ 22.6%
Moderate or greater.................. 53.4%
Vigorous 28.9%

Abortions, 2004

Total performed in state............... 12,690
  rate per 1,000 women age 15-44.......... 11
  % obtained by out-of-state residents 3.0%

Physicians, 2005

Total............................... 12,503
  rate per 100,000 persons 210

Community hospitals, 2005

Number of hospitals 67
Beds (x 1,000)............................11.8
Patients admitted (x 1,000) 665
Average daily census (x 1,000) 8.0
Average cost per day $1,769
Outpatient visits (x 1 mil) 6.8

Disability status of population, 2006
5 to 15 years 5.9%
16 to 64 years 11.3%
65 years and over 38.9%

Education

Educational attainment, 2006
Population over 25 years 3,953,375
  Less than 9th grade. 7.1%
  High school graduate or more 83.8%
  College graduate or more. 25.5%
  Graduate or professional degree. 9.2%

Public school enrollment, 2005-06
Total. 1,094,454
  Pre-kindergarten through grade 8. . . . 739,359
  Grades 9 through 12 354,901

Graduating public high school seniors, 2004-05
Diplomas (incl. GED and others) 59,498

SAT scores, 2007
Average critical reading score 519
Average writing score 502
Average math score 525
Percent of graduates taking test 32%

Public school teachers, 2006-07 (estimate)
Total (x 1,000) 47.1
  Elementary 29.3
  Secondary 17.8
Average salary $45,941
  Elementary $45,941
  Secondary $45,941

State receipts & expenditures for public schools, 2006-07 (estimate)
Revenue receipts ($ mil) $8,431
Expenditures
Total ($ mil) $7,173
  Per capita $955
  Per pupil $5,896

NAEP proficiency scores, 2007

	Reading		Math	
	Basic	Proficient	Basic	Proficient
Grade 4	55.9%	24.2%	73.7%	30.6%
Grade 8	64.9%	24.3%	66.5%	26.3%

Higher education enrollment, fall 2005
Total. 224,732
  Full-time men 81,214
  Full-time women. 130,752
  Part-time men 4,392
  Part-time women. 8,374

Minority enrollment in institutions of higher education, 2005
Black, non-Hispanic 48,521
Hispanic 85,654
Asian/Pacific Islander 19,763
American Indian/Alaska Native. 17,880

Institutions of higher education, 2005-06
Total. 76
  Public. 25
  Private 51

Earned degrees conferred, 2004-05
Associate's. 15,918
Bachelor's 29,133
Master's 19,882
First-professional. 788
Doctor's. 906

Public Libraries, 2006
Number of libraries. 86
Number of outlets 200
Annual visits per capita 4.0
Circulation per capita. 7.3

State & local financial support for higher education, FY 2006
Full-time equivalent enrollment (x 1,000). . . . 219.5
Appropriations per FTE. $6,316

Social Insurance & Welfare Programs

Social Security benefits & beneficiaries, 2005
Beneficiaries (x 1,000) 919
  Retired & dependents. 654
  Survivors. 110
  Disabled & dependents. 155
Annual benefit payments ($ mil) $10,030
  Retired & dependents. $6,887
  Survivors. $1,505
  Disabled & dependents. $1,638
Average monthly benefit
  Retired & dependents. $1,023
  Disabled & dependents. $970
  Widowed. $1,002

Medicare, July 2005
Enrollment (x 1,000). 794
Payments ($ mil) $3,906

Medicaid, 2004
Beneficiaries (x 1,000). 708
Payments ($ mil) $2,358

State Children's Health Insurance Program, 2006
Enrollment (x 1,000). 96.7
Expenditures ($ mil). $95.8

Persons without health insurance, 2006
Number (x 1,000). 1,311
  percent. 20.9%
Number of children (x 1,000) 283
  percent of children 17.0%

Health care expenditures, 2004
Total expenditures. $23,576
  per capita $4,103

Federal and state public aid

State unemployment insurance, 2006
Recipients, first payments (x 1,000) 68
Total payments ($ mil) $209
Average weekly benefit $198
Temporary Assistance for Needy Families, 2006
Recipients (x 1,000) .1,009.2
Families (x 1,000) 460.5
Supplemental Security Income, 2005
Recipients (x 1,000) 97.7
Payments ($ mil) $481.7
Food Stamp Program, 2006
Avg monthly participants (x 1,000) 540.8
Total benefits ($ mil) $626.3

Housing & Construction

Housing units
Total 2005 (estimate) 2,516,563
Total 2006 (estimate) 2,605,283
Seasonal or recreational use, 2006 160,512
Owner-occupied, 2006 1,523,041
   Median home value. $236,500
   Homeowner vacancy rate. 3.0%
Renter-occupied, 2006 701,951
   Median rent $762
   Rental vacancy rate. 9.3%
Home ownership rate, 2005. . . . . 71.1%
Home ownership rate, 2006. . . . . 71.6%

New privately-owned housing units
Number authorized, 2006 (x 1,000) 65.4
   Value ($ mil) $11,203.1
Started 2005 (x 1,000, estimate) 61.9
Started 2006 (x 1,000, estimate) 60.1

Existing home sales
2005 (x 1,000) 199.2
2006 (x 1,000) 142.9

Government & Elections

State officials 2008
Governor . . . . Janet Napolitano
        Democratic, term expires 1/11
Lieutenant Governor. . (no Lieutenant Governor)
Secretary of State . . . . .Jan Brewer
Attorney General . . . . Terry Goddard
Chief Justice . . . . Ruth McGregor

Governorship
Minimum age 25
Length of term . . . . 4 years
Consecutive terms permitted 2
Who succeeds . . . . Secretary of State

Local governments by type, 2002
Total 638
   County 15
   Municipal 87
   Township 0
   School District 231
   Special District 305

State legislature
Name . . . . Legislature
Upper chamber . . . . .Senate
   Number of members 30
   Length of term . . . . 2 years
   Party in majority, 2008 . . . . Republican
Lower chamber. . . . . . . .House of Representatives
   Number of members 60
   Length of term . . . . 2 years
   Party in majority, 2008 . . . . Republican

Federal representation, 2008 (110th Congress)
Senator . . . . John McCain
   Party . . . . Republican
   Year term expires 2011
Senator . . . . .Jon Kyl
   Party . . . . Republican
   Year term expires 2013
Representatives, total 8
   Democrats. 4
   Republicans 4

Voters in November 2006 election (estimate)
Total 1,777,409
   Male 797,135
   Female 980,274
   White 1,669,501
   Black 35,422
   Hispanic 166,397
   Asian 11,775

Presidential election, 2004
Total Popular Vote 2,012,585
   Kerry 893,524
   Bush 1,104,294
Total Electoral Votes 10

Votes cast for US Senators
2004
Total vote (x 1,000) .1,962
Leading party . . . . Republican
Percent for leading party 76.7%
2006
Total vote (x 1,000) .1,527
Leading party . . . . Republican
Percent for leading party 53.3%

Votes cast for US Representatives
2004
Total vote (x 1,000) .1,871
   Democratic 598
   Republican 1,128
Leading party . . . . Republican
Percent for leading party 60.3%
2006
Total vote (x 1,000) .1,493
   Democratic 627
   Republican 771
Leading party . . . . Republican
Percent for leading party 51.7%

State government employment, 2006
Full-time equivalent employees 66,858
Payroll ($ mil) $240.7

Local government employment, 2006
Full-time equivalent employees 218,226
Payroll ($ mil) $807.7

Women holding public office, 2008
US Congress 1
Statewide elected office..................... 3
State legislature 30

Black public officials, 2002
Total...................................... 13
  US and state legislatures 1
  City/county/regional offices 1
  Judicial/law enforcement.................. 6
  Education/school boards 5

Hispanic public officials, 2006
Total..................................... 357
  State executives & legislators 17
  City/county/regional offices 141
  Judicial/law enforcement................. 47
  Education/school boards 152

Governmental Finance

State government revenues, 2006
Total revenue (x $1,000)............$27,834,655
  per capita $4,514.44
General revenue (x $1,000) $22,978,622
  Intergovernmental 8,093,916
  Taxes 11,713,167
    general sales................... 5,189,786
    individual income tax 3,253,279
    corporate income tax 890,004
  Current charges................... 1,419,649
  Miscellaneous 1,751,890

State government expenditure, 2006
Total expenditure (x $1,000) $25,731,467
  per capita $4,173.33
General expenditure (x $1,000) $23,284,278
  per capita, total.................. $3,776.43
  Education 1,311.99
  Public welfare 1,091.53
  Health 219.04
  Hospitals........................ 10.03
  Highways 325.03
  Police protection................. 36.12
  Corrections 142.72
  Natural resources 45.56
  Parks & recreation 36.18
  Governmental administration........ 99.68
  Interest on general debt............. 65.68

State debt & cash, 2006 ($ per capita)
Debt $1,364.01
Cash/security holdings............... $7,119.00

Federal government grants to state & local government, 2005 (x $1,000)
Total.............................$8,603,017
by Federal agency
  Defense 68,647
  Education 855,247
  Energy............................ 14,239
  Environmental Protection Agency 61,308
  Health & Human Services. 5,457,773
  Homeland Security.................. 33,270
  Housing & Urban Development...... 417,228
  Justice 107,311
  Labor 112,346
  Transportation 712,630
  Veterans Affairs..................... 5,531

Crime & Law Enforcement

Crime, 2006 (rates per 100,000 residents)
Property crimes 285,370
  Burglary 57,055
  Larceny 173,466
  Motor vehicle theft 54,849
  Property crime rate............... 4,627.9
Violent crimes...................... 30,916
  Murder 465
  Forcible rape...................... 1,941
  Robbery.......................... 9,226
  Aggravated assault 19,284
  Violent crime rate 501.4
Hate crimes........................ 215

Fraud and identity theft, 2006
Fraud complaints.................... 9,222
  rate per 100,000 residents 149.6
Identity theft complaints 9,113
  rate per 100,000 residents 147.8

Law enforcement agencies, 2006
Total agencies........................ 98
Total employees 21,434
  Officers 11,932
  Civilians 9,502

Prisoners, probation, and parole, 2006
Total prisoners..................... 35,892
  percent change, 12/31/05 to 12/31/06 .... 6.9%
  in private facilities 14.5%
  in local jails 0.1%
Sentenced to more than one year 31,830
  rate per 100,000 residents 509
Adults on probation 73,265
Adults on parole...................... 6,463

Prisoner demographics, June 30, 2005 (rate per 100,000 residents)
Male................................. 1,443
Female 171
White................................ 590
Black................................ 3,294
Hispanic 1,075

Arrests, 2006

Total 307,695
  Persons under 18 years of age 50,744

Persons under sentence of death, 1/1/07

Total 124
  White 88
  Black 13
  Hispanic 20

State's highest court

Name . . . . .Supreme Court
Number of members 5
Length of term . . . . 6 years
Intermediate appeals court? . . . . .yes

Labor & Income

Civilian labor force, 2006 (x 1,000)

Total 2,969
  Men 1,659
  Women 1,310
  Persons 16-19 years 170
  White 2,670
  Black 113
  Hispanic 848

Civilian labor force as a percent of civilian non-institutional population, 2006

Total 64.7%
  Men 73.4
  Women 56.3
  Persons 16-19 years 47.5
  White 64.9
  Black 70.6
  Hispanic 65.6

Employment, 2006 (x 1,000)

Total 2,844
  Men 1,597
  Women 1,247
  Persons 16-19 years 148
  White 2,563
  Black 106
  Hispanic 806

Unemployment rate, 2006

Total 4.2%
  Men 3.7
  Women 4.8
  Persons 16-19 years 13.2
  White 4.0
  Black 6.1
  Hispanic 4.9

Full-time/part-time labor force, 2003 (x 1,000)

Full-time labor force, employed 2,090
Part-time labor force, employed 450
Unemployed, looking for
  Full-time work 117
  Part-time work 34
Mean duration of unemployment (weeks) 17.8
  Median 8.4

Labor unions, 2006

Membership (x 1,000) 197
  percent of employed 7.6%

Experienced civilian labor force by private industry, 2006

Total 2,225,734
  Natural resources & mining 37,927
  Construction 239,650
  Manufacturing .187,057
  Trade, transportation & utilities 510,489
  Information 44,885
  Finance 181,637
  Professional & business 394,485
  Education & health 284,407
  Leisure & hospitality 266,285
  Other 70,024

Experienced civilian labor force by occupation, May 2006

Management 122,110
Business & financial 111,310
Legal 16,000
Sales 273,050
Office & admin. support 500,150
Computers & math 51,500
Architecture & engineering 57,910
Arts & entertainment 26,940
Education 133,870
Social services 25,960
Health care practitioner & technical 107,110
Health care support 58,410
Maintenance & repair 98,840
Construction 203,180
Transportation & moving 162,450
Production 128,430
Farming, fishing & forestry 13,760

Hours and earnings of production workers on manufacturing payrolls, 2006

Average weekly hours 40.6
Average hourly earnings $14.88
Average weekly earnings $604.13

Income and poverty, 2006

Median household income $47,265
Personal income, per capita (current $) . . . $31,458
  in constant (2000) dollars $27,461
Persons below poverty level 14.2%

Average annual pay

2006 . . . . $40,019
  increase from 2005 . . . . 4.9%

Federal individual income tax returns, 2005

Returns filed 2,474,093
Adjusted gross income ($1,000) $135,510,440
Total tax liability ($1,000) $17,288,262

Charitable contributions, 2004

Number of contributions 789.3
Total amount ($ mil) $2,726.7

Economy, Business, Industry & Agriculture

Fortune 500 companies, 2007 4
Bankruptcy cases filed, FY 2007 9,749

Patents and trademarks issued, 2007
Patents 1,814
Trademarks 1,597

Business firm ownership, 2002
Women-owned 109,748
  Sales ($ mil) $15,761
Black-owned 6,330
  Sales ($ mil) $530
Hispanic-owned 35,104
  Sales ($ mil) $4,295
Asian-owned 10,215
  Sales ($ mil) $2,396
Amer. Indian/Alaska Native-owned 6,614
  Sales ($ mil) $960
Hawaiian/Pacific Islander-owned 348
  Sales ($ mil) $38

Gross domestic product, 2006 ($ mil)
Total gross domestic product $232,463
  Agriculture, forestry, fishing and
    hunting 2,121
  Mining 3,343
  Utilities 4,214
  Construction 18,096
  Manufacturing, durable goods 15,834
  Manufacturing, non-durable goods 2,993
  Wholesale trade 13,575
  Retail trade 19,908
  Transportation & warehousing 6,021
  Information 6,519
  Finance & insurance 19,603
  Real estate, rental & leasing 33,555
  Professional and technical services 13,471
  Educational services 1,681
  Health care and social assistance 16,321
  Accommodation/food services 7,666
  Other services, except government 4,423
  Government 28,108

Establishments, payroll, employees & receipts, by major industry group, 2005

Total 131,651
  Annual payroll ($1,000) $76,340,525
  Paid employees 2,159,823

Forestry, fishing & agriculture 204
  Annual payroll ($1,000) $38,512
  Paid employees 1,531

Mining 229
  Annual payroll ($1,000) $443,346
  Paid employees 8,882
  Receipts, 2002 ($1,000) $2,180,922

Utilities 244
  Annual payroll ($1,000) $752,361
  Paid employees 10,415
  Receipts, 2002 ($1,000) . . . . NA

Construction 15,082
  Annual payroll ($1,000) $7,954,878
  Paid employees 211,584
  Receipts, 2002 ($1,000) $28,926,214

Manufacturing 4,858
  Annual payroll ($1,000) $7,827,619
  Paid employees 167,886
  Receipts, 2002 ($1,000) $41,910,739

Wholesale trade 6,646
  Annual payroll ($1,000) $4,437,410
  Paid employees 95,027
  Receipts, 2002 ($1,000) $60,976,999

Retail trade 18,228
  Annual payroll ($1,000) $7,311,713
  Paid employees 306,113
  Receipts, 2002 ($1,000) $56,457,863

Transportation & warehousing 3,092
  Annual payroll ($1,000) $2,748,306
  Paid employees 72,724
  Receipts, 2002 ($1,000) $6,602,709

Information 2,224
  Annual payroll ($1,000) $2,478,510
  Paid employees 51,772
  Receipts, 2002 ($1,000) . . . . NA

Finance & insurance 9,187
  Annual payroll ($1,000) $7,004,350
  Paid employees 131,283
  Receipts, 2002 ($1,000) . . . . NA

Professional, scientific & technical 15,426
  Annual payroll ($1,000) $6,193,259
  Paid employees 118,943
  Receipts, 2002 ($1,000) $11,751,755

Education 1,625
  Annual payroll ($1,000) $1,152,769
  Paid employees 38,802
  Receipts, 2002 ($1,000) $616,930

Health care & social assistance 13,843
  Annual payroll ($1,000) $9,831,310
  Paid employees 252,401
  Receipts, 2002 ($1,000) $18,821,645

Arts and entertainment 1,782
  Annual payroll ($1,000) $1,222,715
  Paid employees 43,895
  Receipts, 2002 ($1,000) $3,416,701

Real estate 8,866
  Annual payroll ($1,000) $1,945,948
  Paid employees 48,118
  Receipts, 2002 ($1,000) . . . . NA

Accommodation & food service 10,688
  Annual payroll ($1,000) $3,238,141
  Paid employees 238,838
  Receipts, 2002 ($1,000) $8,612,730

Exports, 2006
Value of exported goods ($ mil) $18,287
   Manufactured $12,960
   Non-manufactured $1,622

Foreign direct investment in US affiliates, 2004
Property, plants & equipment ($ mil) $9,333
Employment (x 1,000). 62.9

Agriculture, 2006
Number of farms 10,000
Farm acreage (x 1,000) 26,100
   Acres per farm 2,610
Farm marketings and income ($ mil)
Total. $2,879.2
   Crops. $1,558.5
   Livestock. $1,320.7
Net farm income $773.7

Principal commodities, in order by marketing receipts, 2005
  Cattle and calves, Dairy products, Lettuce, Cotton, Hay

Federal economic activity in state
Expenditures, 2005 ($ mil)
  Total. $44,639
    Per capita $7,498.49
  Defense $12,001
  Non-defense. $32,638
Defense department, 2006 ($ mil)
  Payroll. $2,656
  Contract awards $9,696
  Grants $79
Homeland security grants ($1,000)
  2006. . . . .$20,171
  2007 . . . .$33,774

FDIC-insured financial institutions, 2005
Number 55
Assets ($ billion) $18.9
Deposits ($ billion) $14.2

Fishing, 2006
Catch (x 1,000 lbs) . . . . NA
Value ($1,000). . . . . NA

Mining, 2006 ($ mil)
Total non-fuel mineral production $6,710
Percent of U.S. 10.42%

Communication, Energy & Transportation

Communication
Households with computers, 2003 . . . . .64.3%
Households with internet access, 2003 . . . . 55.2%
High-speed internet providers 52
Total high-speed internet lines. 1,832,564
  Residential 1,220,053
  Business. 612,511
Wireless phone customers, 12/2006 4,405,032

FCC-licensed stations (as of January 1, 2008)
TV stations 31
FM radio stations. 143
AM radio stations 74

Energy
Energy consumption, 2004
  Total (trillion Btu). 1,437
  Per capita (million Btu) 250.0
By source of production (trillion Btu)
  Coal 425
  Natural gas 355
  Petroleum 563
  Nuclear electric power 293
  Hydroelectric power 70
By end-use sector (trillion Btu)
  Residential 369
  Commercial 326
  Industrial 231
  Transportation 511
Electric energy, 2005
  Primary source of electricity. . . . . Coal
  Net generation (billion kWh) 101.5
    percent from renewable sources. 6.4%
  Net summer capability (million kW) 24.9
  CO_2 emitted from generation 51.4
Natural gas utilities, 2005
  Customers (x 1,000) 1,100
  Sales (trillion Btu). 87
  Revenues ($ mil) $915
Nuclear plants, 2007 4
Total CO_2 emitted (million metric tons). . . .88.8
Energy spending, 2004 ($ mil) $13,779
  per capita $2,398
  Price per million Btu $15.24

Transportation, 2006
Public road & street mileage 60,376
  Urban. 22,560
  Rural 37,816
  Interstate. 1,169
Vehicle miles of travel (millions) 62,468
  per capita 10,131.6
Total motor vehicle registrations. 4,182,332
  Automobiles. .2,189,979
  Trucks 1,987,392
  Motorcycles 114,435
Licensed drivers .4,032,643
  19 years & under 165,665
Deaths from motor vehicle accidents 1,288
Gasoline consumed (x 1,000 gallons) 2,870,781
  per capita 465.6

Commuting Statistics, 2006
Average commute time (min) 25.0
  Drove to work alone 74.6%
  Carpooled. 13.9%
  Public transit 2.1%
  Walk to work 2.3%
  Work from home 4.5%

State Summary

Capital city . . . . Little Rock
Governor . . . . Mike Beebe

State Capitol
Room 250
Little Rock, AR 72201
501-682-2345

Admitted as a state 1836
Area (square miles) 53,179
Population, 2007 (estimate) 2,834,797
Largest city . . . . Little Rock
    Population, 2006 184,422
Personal income per capita, 2006
    (in current dollars) $27,935
Gross domestic product, 2006 ($ mil) $91,837

Leading industries by payroll, 2005

Manufacturing, Health care/Social assistance,
Retail trade

**Leading agricultural commodities
by receipts, 2005**

Broilers, Rice, Cotton, Soybeans, Cattle and
calves

Geography & Environment

Total area (square miles) 53,179
    land 52,068
    water 1,110
Federally-owned land, 2004 (acres) 2,407,948
    percent 7.2%
Highest point . . . . Magazine Mountain
    elevation (feet) .2,753
Lowest point . . . . Ouachita River
    elevation (feet) 55
General coastline (miles) 0
Tidal shoreline (miles) 0
Cropland, 2003 (x 1,000 acres) 7,522
Forest land, 2003 (x 1,000 acres) 15,008
Capital city . . . . Little Rock
    Population 2000 .183,133
    Population 2006 184,422
Largest city . . . . Little Rock
    Population 2000 .183,133
    Population 2006 184,422

Number of cities with over 100,000 population

1990 1
2000 1
2006 1

State park and recreation areas, 2005

Area (x 1,000 acres) 53
Number of visitors (x 1,000) 9,751
Revenues ($1,000) $16,174
    percent of operating expenditures 41.6%

National forest system land, 2007

Acres 3,598,417

Demographics & Population Characteristics

Population

1980 2,286,435
1990 2,350,725
2000 2,673,398
2006 2,810,872
    Male 1,377,711
    Female 1,433,161
Living in group quarters, 2006 78,322
    percent of total 2.8%
2007 (estimate) .2,834,797
    persons per square mile of land 54.4
2008 (projected) 2,836,580
2010 (projected) .2,875,039
2020 (projected) .3,060,219
2030 (projected) 3,240,208

**Population of Core-Based Statistical Areas
(formerly Metropolitan Areas), x 1,000**

	CBSA	Non-CBSA
1990	1,802	549
2000	2,082	591
2006	2,224	587

Change in population, 2000-2007

Number 161,399
    percent 6.0%
Natural increase (births minus deaths) 78,302
Net internal migration 62,982
Net international migration 27,119

Persons by age, 2006

Under 5 years 192,891
5 to 17 years 498,295
18 years and over 2,119,686
65 years and over 390,421
85 years and over 54,889
    Median age 36.8

Persons by age, 2010 (projected)

Under 5 years 194,806
18 and over 2,172,383
65 and over 412,152
    Median age 37.9

Race, 2006

One Race

White 2,279,839
Black or African American 442,155
Asian 29,312
American Indian/Alaska Native 21,635
Hawaiian Native/Pacific Islander 2,649
Two or more races 35,282

Persons of Hispanic origin, 2006

Total Hispanic or Latino 138,283
Mexican 104,920
Puerto Rican 2,615
Cuban 650

Persons of Asian origin, 2006

Total Asian 28,168
  Asian Indian. 5,279
  Chinese 4,672
  Filipino 3,839
  Japanese 793
  Korean. 3,431
  Vietnamese. 2,488

Marital status, 2006

Population 15 years & over 2,237,108
  Never married 538,460
  Married. 1,253,688
  Separated 53,052
  Widowed. 167,095
  Divorced 277,865

Language spoken at home, 2006

Population 5 years and older. 2,616,131
  English only 2,456,301
  Spanish 116,396
  French 4,352
  German. 5,050
  Chinese 3,611

Households & families, 2006

Households. 1,103,428
  with persons under 18 years 379,411
  with persons over 65 years. 274,524
  persons per household 2.48
Families. 758,195
  persons per family. 2.99
Married couples. .567,229
Female householder,
  no husband present. 142,145
One-person households 296,225

Nativity, 2006

Number of residents born in state 1,723,478
  percent of population 61.3%

Immigration & naturalization, 2006

Legal permanent residents admitted 2,926
Persons naturalized .1,133
Non-immigrant admissions 39,848

Vital Statistics and Health

Marriages

2004 36,806
2005 35,882
2006 34,261

Divorces

2004 16,874
2005 16,728
2006 16,150

Health risks, 2006

Percent of adults who are:
  Smokers. 23.7%
  Overweight (BMI > 25). 63.8%
  Obese (BMI > 30). 26.9%

Births

2005 39,208
  Birthrate (per 1,000). 14.1
  White. 30,807
  Black 7,473
  Hispanic 4,038
  Asian/Pacific Islander 687
  Amer. Indian/Alaska Native 241
  Low birth weight (2,500g or less). 8.9%
  Cesarian births 31.5%
  Preterm births. 13.4%
  To unmarried mothers. 40.2%
  Twin births (per 1,000) 29.4
  Triplets or higher order (per 100,000). . . .100.4
2006 (preliminary). 40,973
  rate per 1,000 . . . . .14.6

Deaths

2004
All causes 27,528
  rate per 100,000 . . . . 924.7
Heart disease 7,534
  rate per 100,000 .250.9
Malignant neoplasms 6,304
  rate per 100,000 . . . . 208.9
Cerebrovascular disease. 1,948
  rate per 100,000 .65.0
Chronic lower respiratory disease 1,428
  rate per 100,000 .47.4
Diabetes. 838
  rate per 100,000 .28.0
2005 (preliminary). 28,055
  rate per 100,000. . . . . 930.2
2006 (provisional) 28,032

Infant deaths

2004 319
  rate per 1,000 . . . . .8.3
2005 (provisional) 294
  rate per 1,000 . . . . .7.5

Exercise routines, 2005

None. 30.6%
Moderate or greater. 46.4%
Vigorous 24.8%

Abortions, 2004

Total performed in state. 4,644
  rate per 1,000 women age 15-44. 8
  % obtained by out-of-state residents 17.4%

Physicians, 2005

Total. 5,619
  rate per 100,000 persons 202

Community hospitals, 2005

Number of hospitals 85
Beds (x 1,000). 9.4
Patients admitted (x 1,000) 380
Average daily census (x 1,000) 5.5
Average cost per day $1,238
Outpatient visits (x 1 mil) 5.0

Disability status of population, 2006
5 to 15 years 9.4%
16 to 64 years 18.7%
65 years and over 50.5%

Education

Educational attainment, 2006
Population over 25 years 1,847,325
Less than 9th grade..................... 7.4%
High school graduate or more 80.5%
College graduate or more.............. 18.2%
Graduate or professional degree........ 6.2%

Public school enrollment, 2005-06
Total............................... 474,206
Pre-kindergarten through grade 8.... 335,223
Grades 9 through 12 138,237

Graduating public high school seniors, 2004-05
Diplomas (incl. GED and others) 26,698

SAT scores, 2007
Average critical reading score.............. 578
Average writing score 565
Average math score 566
Percent of graduates taking test 5%

Public school teachers, 2006-07 (estimate)
Total (x 1,000) 34.1
Elementary 16.6
Secondary.............................17.5
Average salary $44,245
Elementary........................ $44,245
Secondary......................... $44,245

State receipts & expenditures for public schools, 2006-07 (estimate)
Revenue receipts ($ mil) $4,308
Expenditures
Total ($ mil) $4,515
Per capita $1,441
Per pupil $10,398

NAEP proficiency scores, 2007

	Reading		Math	
	Basic	Proficient	Basic	Proficient
Grade 4	63.5%	28.6%	80.7%	36.7%
Grade 8	69.6%	25.4%	64.7%	24.4%

Higher education enrollment, fall 2005
Total....................................15,155
Full-time men 5,652
Full-time women.....................6,833
Part-time men 837
Part-time women.....................1,833

Minority enrollment in institutions of higher education, 2005
Black, non-Hispanic 26,242
Hispanic 2,913
Asian/Pacific Islander 2,059
American Indian/Alaska Native...........1,576

Institutions of higher education, 2005-06
Total..................................... 48
Public................................. 33
Private 15

Earned degrees conferred, 2004-05
Associate's.............................5,166
Bachelor's 11,191
Master's 2,851
First-professional...................... 505
Doctor's 249

Public Libraries, 2006
Number of libraries...................... 48
Number of outlets 216
Annual visits per capita 3.2
Circulation per capita....................4.4

State & local financial support for higher education, FY 2006
Full-time equivalent enrollment (x 1,000)....101.3
Appropriations per FTE................ $5,899

Social Insurance & Welfare Programs

Social Security benefits & beneficiaries, 2005
Beneficiaries (x 1,000) 558
Retired & dependents................... 346
Survivors.............................. 80
Disabled & dependents................. 132
Annual benefit payments ($ mil) $5,564
Retired & dependents................$3,332
Survivors........................... $961
Disabled & dependents................$1,271
Average monthly benefit
Retired & dependents.................. $935
Disabled & dependents................ $887
Widowed..............................$868

Medicare, July 2005
Enrollment (x 1,000)..................... 472
Payments ($ mil) $3,132

Medicaid, 2004
Beneficiaries (x 1,000)...................1,070
Payments ($ mil) $3,888

State Children's Health Insurance Program, 2006
Enrollment (x 1,000)......................3.4
Expenditures ($ mil).................... $60.4

Persons without health insurance, 2006
Number (x 1,000)........................ 521
percent........................... 18.9%
Number of children (x 1,000) 65
percent of children 9.3%

Health care expenditures, 2004
Total expenditures.....................$13,357
per capita $4,863

Federal and state public aid

State unemployment insurance, 2006
Recipients, first payments (x 1,000) 80
Total payments ($ mil) $243
Average weekly benefit $244
Temporary Assistance for Needy Families, 2006
Recipients (x 1,000) 219.8
Families (x 1,000) 99.8
Supplemental Security Income, 2005
Recipients (x 1,000) 91.0
Payments ($ mil) $406.6
Food Stamp Program, 2006
Avg monthly participants (x 1,000) 384.9
Total benefits ($ mil) $414.4

Housing & Construction

Housing units

Total 2005 (estimate) 1,248,831
Total 2006 (estimate) 1,273,615
Seasonal or recreational use, 2006 39,144
Owner-occupied, 2006 753,412
   Median home value $93,900
   Homeowner vacancy rate 1.9%
Renter-occupied, 2006 350,016
   Median rent $566
   Rental vacancy rate 13.5%
Home ownership rate, 2005 . . . . 69.2%
Home ownership rate, 2006 . . . . 70.8%

New privately-owned housing units

Number authorized, 2006 (x 1,000) 13.9
   Value ($ mil) $1,793.8
Started 2005 (x 1,000, estimate) 13.6
Started 2006 (x 1,000, estimate) 13.6

Existing home sales

2005 (x 1,000) 75.3
2006 (x 1,000) 82.6

Government & Elections

State officials 2008

Governor . . . . Mike Beebe
    Democratic, term expires 1/11
Lieutenant Governor . . . . Bill Halter
Secretary of State . . . . Charlie Daniels
Attorney General . . . . Dustin McDaniel
Chief Justice . . . . Jim Hannah

Governorship

Minimum age 30
Length of term . . . . 4 years
Consecutive terms permitted 2
Who succeeds . . . . Lieutenant Governor

Local governments by type, 2002

Total 1,588
   County 75
   Municipal 499
   Township 0
   School District 310
   Special District 704

State legislature

Name . . . . General Assembly
Upper chamber . . . . Senate
   Number of members 35
   Length of term . . . . 4 years
   Party in majority, 2008 . . . . Democratic
Lower chamber . . . . House of Representatives
   Number of members 100
   Length of term . . . . 2 years
   Party in majority, 2008 . . . . Democratic

Federal representation, 2008 (110th Congress)

Senator . . . . Mark Pryor
   Party . . . . Democratic
   Year term expires 2009
Senator . . . . Blanche Lincoln
   Party . . . . Democratic
   Year term expires 2011
Representatives, total 4
   Democrats 3
   Republicans 1

Voters in November 2006 election (estimate)

Total 910,565
   Male 430,602
   Female 479,963
   White 792,177
   Black 101,004
   Hispanic 7,811
   Asian . . . . NA

Presidential election, 2004

Total Popular Vote 1,054,945
   Kerry 469,953
   Bush 572,898
Total Electoral Votes 6

Votes cast for US Senators

2004
Total vote (x 1,000) 1,039
Leading party . . . . Democratic
Percent for leading party 55.9%
2006
Total vote (x 1,000) . . . . NA
Leading party . . . . NA
Percent for leading party . . . . NA

Votes cast for US Representatives

2004
Total vote (x 1,000) 791
   Democratic 426
   Republican 358
Leading party . . . . Democratic
Percent for leading party 53.9%
2006
Total vote (x 1,000) 763
   Democratic 457
   Republican 306
Leading party . . . . Democratic
Percent for leading party 59.8%

State government employment, 2006
Full-time equivalent employees 58,147
Payroll ($ mil) $177.8

Local government employment, 2006
Full-time equivalent employees 103,776
Payroll ($ mil) $277.4

Women holding public office, 2008
US Congress 1
Statewide elected office. 1
State legislature 28

Black public officials, 2002
Total. 535
  US and state legislatures 15
  City/county/regional offices 374
  Judicial/law enforcement. 17
  Education/school boards 129

Hispanic public officials, 2006
Total. 0
  State executives & legislators 0
  City/county/regional offices 0
  Judicial/law enforcement. 0
  Education/school boards 0

Governmental Finance

State government revenues, 2006
Total revenue (x $1,000) $16,424,851
  per capita $5,846.99
General revenue (x $1,000) $13,644,838
  Intergovernmental 4,288,097
  Taxes 6,959,438
    general sales. 2,772,131
    individual income tax 2,012,835
    corporate income tax 368,523
  Current charges. 1,696,823
  Miscellaneous 700,480

State government expenditure, 2006
Total expenditure (x $1,000) $14,370,337
  per capita $5,115.62
General expenditure (x $1,000) $13,302,770
  per capita, total. $4,735.58
    Education 2,017.23
    Public welfare 1,224.39
    Health 124.95
    Hospitals. 237.19
    Highways 339.82
    Police protection. 36.57
    Corrections .140.61
    Natural resources 81.42
    Parks & recreation 33.75
    Governmental administration 193.25
    Interest on general debt 55.96

State debt & cash, 2006 ($ per capita)
Debt $1,614.11
Cash/security holdings. $8,496.33

Federal government grants to state & local government, 2005 (x $1,000)
Total. $4,681,690
by Federal agency
  Defense 45,249
  Education 386,623
  Energy 5,503
  Environmental Protection Agency 31,133
  Health & Human Services. 2,933,378
  Homeland Security. 29,581
  Housing & Urban Development. 249,928
  Justice 42,706
  Labor 69,227
  Transportation 435,771
  Veterans Affairs. 6,457

Crime & Law Enforcement

Crime, 2006 (rates per 100,000 residents)
Property crimes 111,521
  Burglary 32,042
  Larceny 72,016
  Motor vehicle theft 7,463
  Property crime rate. 3,967.5
Violent crimes. 15,506
  Murder 205
  Forcible rape. 1,308
  Robbery. 2,766
  Aggravated assault 11,227
  Violent crime rate 551.6
Hate crimes. 133

Fraud and identity theft, 2006
Fraud complaints. 2,428
  rate per 100,000 residents 86.4
Identity theft complaints 1,537
  rate per 100,000 residents 54.7

Law enforcement agencies, 2006
Total agencies. 264
Total employees 8,266
  Officers 5,405
  Civilians 2,861

Prisoners, probation, and parole, 2006
Total prisoners. 13,729
  percent change, 12/31/05 to 12/31/06 . . . . 1.4%
  in private facilities 0%
  in local jails 6.1%
Sentenced to more than one year 13,713
  rate per 100,000 residents 485
Adults on probation 31,508
Adults on parole. 18,405

Prisoner demographics, June 30, 2005 (rate per 100,000 residents)
Male. 1,231
Female 136
White. 478
Black. 1,846
Hispanic 288

6 Arkansas

Arrests, 2006
Total 113,791
  Persons under 18 years of age 11,389

Persons under sentence of death, 1/1/07
Total 37
  White 14
  Black 23
  Hispanic 0

State's highest court
Name . . . . .Supreme Court
Number of members 7
Length of term . . . . 8 years
Intermediate appeals court? . . . . .yes

Labor & Income

Civilian labor force, 2006 (x 1,000)
Total 1,374
  Men 724
  Women 650
  Persons 16-19 years 69
  White 1,137
  Black 194
  Hispanic 76

Civilian labor force as a percent of civilian non-institutional population, 2006
Total 63.5%
  Men 69.3
  Women 58.0
  Persons 16-19 years 45.3
  White 63.6
  Black 62.6
  Hispanic 74.9

Employment, 2006 (x 1,000)
Total 1,302
  Men 684
  Women 617
  Persons 16-19 years 57
  White 1,087
  Black 174
  Hispanic 72

Unemployment rate, 2006
Total 5.3%
  Men 5.4
  Women 5.1
  Persons 16-19 years 17.2
  White 4.4
  Black 10.3
  Hispanic 4.7

Full-time/part-time labor force, 2003 (x 1,000)
Full-time labor force, employed 996
Part-time labor force, employed 191
Unemployed, looking for
  Full-time work 67
  Part-time work 11
Mean duration of unemployment (weeks) 16.7
  Median 9.2

Labor unions, 2006
Membership (x 1,000) 58
  percent of employed 5.1%

Experienced civilian labor force by private industry, 2006
Total 973,615
  Natural resources & mining 18,550
  Construction 56,956
  Manufacturing 198,822
  Trade, transportation & utilities 244,917
  Information 19,911
  Finance 51,171
  Professional & business 114,216
  Education & health 145,778
  Leisure & hospitality 97,450
  Other 25,845

Experienced civilian labor force by occupation, May 2006
Management 44,020
Business & financial 34,560
Legal 5,620
Sales 117,740
Office & admin. support 184,070
Computers & math 14,430
Architecture & engineering 13,910
Arts & entertainment 8,670
Education 69,800
Social services 14,470
Health care practitioner & technical 64,750
Health care support 31,320
Maintenance & repair 52,420
Construction 49,700
Transportation & moving 126,680
Production 152,190
Farming, fishing & forestry 6,600

Hours and earnings of production workers on manufacturing payrolls, 2006
Average weekly hours .41.0
Average hourly earnings $13.35
Average weekly earnings $547.35

Income and poverty, 2006
Median household income $36,599
Personal income, per capita (current $) . . . $27,935
  in constant (2000) dollars $24,385
Persons below poverty level 17.3%

Average annual pay
2006 . . . . $32,389
  increase from 2005 . . . . 3.6%

Federal individual income tax returns, 2005
Returns filed 1,153,654
Adjusted gross income ($1,000) $47,857,444
Total tax liability ($1,000) $5,382,410

Charitable contributions, 2004
Number of contributions 235.0
Total amount ($ mil) $1,224.1

Economy, Business, Industry & Agriculture

Fortune 500 companies, 2007 5
Bankruptcy cases filed, FY 2007 11,494

Patents and trademarks issued, 2007
Patents 151
Trademarks 246

Business firm ownership, 2002
Women-owned 49,618
  Sales ($ mil) $6,339
Black-owned 8,942
  Sales ($ mil) $442
Hispanic-owned 2,094
  Sales ($ mil) $374
Asian-owned 2,013
  Sales ($ mil) $614
Amer. Indian/Alaska Native-owned 2,283
  Sales ($ mil) $317
Hawaiian/Pacific Islander-owned 61
  Sales ($ mil) $4

Gross domestic product, 2006 ($ mil)
Total gross domestic product $91,837
  Agriculture, forestry, fishing and
    hunting 2,306
  Mining 1,293
  Utilities 1,924
  Construction 4,079
  Manufacturing, durable goods 9,679
  Manufacturing, non-durable goods 8,350
  Wholesale trade 6,260
  Retail trade 6,847
  Transportation & warehousing 4,408
  Information 3,527
  Finance & insurance 3,585
  Real estate, rental & leasing 7,953
  Professional and technical services 3,423
  Educational services 395
  Health care and social assistance 6,866
  Accommodation/food services 2,099
  Other services, except government 2,074
  Government 12,492

Establishments, payroll, employees & receipts, by major industry group, 2005
Total 66,039
  Annual payroll ($1,000) $30,185,779
  Paid employees 1,017,424
Forestry, fishing & agriculture 829
  Annual payroll ($1,000) $157,170
  Paid employees 5,413
Mining 305
  Annual payroll ($1,000) $191,156
  Paid employees 3,999
  Receipts, 2002 ($1,000) $917,469

Utilities 370
  Annual payroll ($1,000) $420,862
  Paid employees 7,059
  Receipts, 2002 ($1,000) . . . . NA
Construction 6,348
  Annual payroll ($1,000) $1,634,994
  Paid employees 49,959
  Receipts, 2002 ($1,000) $6,623,949
Manufacturing 3,105
  Annual payroll ($1,000) $6,577,058
  Paid employees 198,288
  Receipts, 2002 ($1,000) $46,721,413
Wholesale trade 3,473
  Annual payroll ($1,000) $1,904,796
  Paid employees 49,206
  Receipts, 2002 ($1,000) $34,470,795
Retail trade 11,880
  Annual payroll ($1,000) $2,724,653
  Paid employees 140,465
  Receipts, 2002 ($1,000) $25,611,630
Transportation & warehousing 2,596
  Annual payroll ($1,000) $2,037,033
  Paid employees 61,474
  Receipts, 2002 ($1,000) $5,222,960
Information 1,034
  Annual payroll ($1,000) $1,077,266
  Paid employees 24,579
  Receipts, 2002 ($1,000) . . . . NA
Finance & insurance 4,304
  Annual payroll ($1,000) $1,496,807
  Paid employees 37,092
  Receipts, 2002 ($1,000) . . . . NA
Professional, scientific & technical 5,474
  Annual payroll ($1,000) $1,455,707
  Paid employees 36,141
  Receipts, 2002 ($1,000) $2,599,015
Education 507
  Annual payroll ($1,000) $216,266
  Paid employees 12,572
  Receipts, 2002 ($1,000) $71,850
Health care & social assistance 6,828
  Annual payroll ($1,000) $5,001,545
  Paid employees 154,792
  Receipts, 2002 ($1,000) $9,675,926
Arts and entertainment 856
  Annual payroll ($1,000) . . . . NA
  Paid employees . . . . NA
  Receipts, 2002 ($1,000) $391,164
Real estate 2,983
  Annual payroll ($1,000) $321,152
  Paid employees 12,612
  Receipts, 2002 ($1,000) $1,397,076
Accommodation & food service 4,878
  Annual payroll ($1,000) $890,819
  Paid employees 86,916
  Receipts, 2002 ($1,000) $2,766,905

Exports, 2006

Value of exported goods ($ mil) $4,265
   Manufactured $3,906
   Non-manufactured.................... $203

Foreign direct investment in US affiliates, 2004

Property, plants & equipment ($ mil) $4,913
Employment (x 1,000)....................32.0

Agriculture, 2006

Number of farms 46,500
Farm acreage (x 1,000) 14,300
   Acres per farm......................... 308
Farm marketings and income ($ mil)
Total................................$6,164.1
   Crops............................$2,396.7
   Livestock........................ $3,767.4
Net farm income $1,950.9

Principal commodities, in order by marketing receipts, 2005

Broilers, Rice, Cotton, Soybeans, Cattle and calves

Federal economic activity in state

Expenditures, 2005 ($ mil)
   Total............................. $20,387
      Per capita $7,344.76
   Defense $1,862
   Non-defense $18,525
Defense department, 2006 ($ mil)
   Payroll............................$1,080
   Contract awards $881
   Grants $64
Homeland security grants ($1,000)
   2006............................... $8,343
   2007...............................$7,238

FDIC-insured financial institutions, 2005

Number............................... 156
Assets ($ billion) $48.5
Deposits ($ billion) $39.3

Fishing, 2006

Catch (x 1,000 lbs)..................... NA
Value ($1,000)......................... NA

Mining, 2006 ($ mil)

Total non-fuel mineral production $617
Percent of U.S. 0.96%

Communication, Energy & Transportation

Communication

Households with computers, 2003........ 50.0%
Households with internet access, 2003 .... 42.4%
High-speed internet providers 45
Total high-speed internet lines......... 424,685
   Residential 385,669
   Business...........................39,016
Wireless phone customers, 12/2006 2,044,217

FCC-licensed stations (as of January 1, 2008)

TV stations 27
FM radio stations......................... 207
AM radio stations 84

Energy

Energy consumption, 2004
   Total (trillion Btu)....................1,136
   Per capita (million Btu) 413.5
By source of production (trillion Btu)
   Coal 270
   Natural gas 229
   Petroleum............................ 388
   Nuclear electric power 161
   Hydroelectric power................... 37
By end-use sector (trillion Btu)
   Residential 218
   Commercial 155
   Industrial 474
   Transportation 289
Electric energy, 2005
   Primary source of electricity............ Coal
   Net generation (billion kWh) 47.8
      percent from renewable sources...... 10.1%
   Net summer capability (million kW) 14.1
   CO_2 emitted from generation 26.4
Natural gas utilities, 2005
   Customers (x 1,000) 627
   Sales (trillion Btu)..................... 159
   Revenues ($ mil) $741
Nuclear plants, 2007 2
Total CO_2 emitted (million metric tons)......62.4
Energy spending, 2004 ($ mil) $8,718
   per capita $3,174
   Price per million Btu $11.89

Transportation, 2006

Public road & street mileage 99,005
   Urban...............................11,272
   Rural 87,733
   Interstate 655
Vehicle miles of travel (millions) 33,007
   per capita 11,750.0
Total motor vehicle registrations.......1,994,255
   Automobiles....................... 958,640
   Trucks 1,027,414
   Motorcycles 58,686
Licensed drivers 2,034,975
   19 years & under 105,116
Deaths from motor vehicle accidents 665
Gasoline consumed (x 1,000 gallons) 1,447,192
   per capita 515.2

Commuting Statistics, 2006

Average commute time (min) 20.7
   Drove to work alone 80.2%
   Carpooled...........................12.9%
   Public transit 0.4%
   Walk to work 1.8%
   Work from home..................... 3.3%

State Summary

Capital city . . . . .Sacramento
Governor . . . . .Arnold Schwarzenegger
Office of the Governor
State Capitol
Sacramento, CA 95814
916-445-2841
Admitted as a state 1850
Area (square miles) 163,696
Population, 2007 (estimate) 36,553,215
Largest city . . . . .Los Angeles
　Population, 2006 3,849,378
Personal income per capita, 2006
　(in current dollars) $38,956
Gross domestic product, 2006 ($ mil) . .$1,727,355

Leading industries by payroll, 2005

Professional/Scientific/Technical, Manufacturing, Health care/Social assistance

Leading agricultural commodities by receipts, 2005

Dairy products, Greenhouse/nursery, Grapes, Almonds, Cattle and calves

Geography & Environment

Total area (square miles) 163,696
　land 155,959
　water 7,736
Federally-owned land, 2004 (acres) . . .45,393,238
　percent 45.3%
Highest point . . . . .Mt. Whitney
　elevation (feet) 14,494
Lowest point . . . . .Death Valley
　elevation (feet) . . . . -282
General coastline (miles) 840
Tidal shoreline (miles) 3,427
Cropland, 2003 (x 1,000 acres) 9,468
Forest land, 2003 (x 1,000 acres). 13,903
Capital city . . . . .Sacramento
　Population 2000 407,018
　Population 2006 453,781
Largest city .Los Angeles
　Population 2000 3,694,820
　Population 2006 3,849,378

Number of cities with over 100,000 population

1990 43
2000 56
2006 62

State park and recreation areas, 2005

Area (x 1,000 acres) .1,554
Number of visitors (x 1,000) 77,119
Revenues ($1,000) $82,819
　percent of operating expenditures 17.8%

National forest system land, 2007

Acres 20,802,641

Demographics & Population Characteristics

Population

1980 23,667,902
1990 29,760,021
2000 33,871,653
2006 36,457,549
　Male 18,224,444
　Female 18,233,105
Living in group quarters, 2006 863,207
　percent of total 2.4%
2007 (estimate) 36,553,215
　persons per square mile of land 234.4
2008 (projected) 37,262,310
2010 (projected) 38,067,134
2020 (projected) 42,206,743
2030 (projected) 46,444,861

Population of Core-Based Statistical Areas (formerly Metropolitan Areas), x 1,000

	CBSA	Non-CBSA
1990	29,540	218
2000	33,628	243
2006	36,195	262

Change in population, 2000-2007

Number 2,681,560
　percent 7.9%
Natural increase (births minus deaths) . . 2,232,397
Net internal migration . . . . -1,223,992
Net international migration 1,807,426

Persons by age, 2006

Under 5 years 2,678,019
5 to 17 years 6,854,595
18 years and over 26,924,935
65 years and over 3,931,514
85 years and over 555,473
　Median age 34.4

Persons by age, 2010 (projected)

Under 5 years 2,853,032
18 and over 28,570,156
65 and over 4,392,708
　Median age 34.9

Race, 2006

One Race
　White 28,043,733
　Black or African American 2,445,228
　Asian 4,510,534
　American Indian/Alaska Native. 421,346
　Hawaiian Native/Pacific Islander. 153,193
Two or more races. 883,515

Persons of Hispanic origin, 2006

Total Hispanic or Latino 13,074,155
　Mexican. 10,841,524
　Puerto Rican 160,130
　Cuban 85,992

Persons of Asian origin, 2006

Total Asian 4,483,252
  Asian Indian. 475,118
  Chinese 1,165,605
  Filipino 1,100,767
  Japanese 300,355
  Korean. 430,913
  Vietnamese. 533,893

Marital status, 2006

Population 15 years & over 28,569,779
  Never married 9,732,918
  Married. 14,552,553
  Separated 709,120
  Widowed. 1,550,349
  Divorced 2,733,959

Language spoken at home, 2006

Population 5 years and older. 33,784,883
  English only 19,414,977
  Spanish 9,588,622
  French 136,449
  German 150,299
  Chinese 936,113

Households & families, 2006

Households. .12,151,227
  with persons under 18 years 4,696,427
  with persons over 65 years. 2,710,892
  persons per household 2.93
Families. 8,303,793
  persons per family. 3.54
Married couples. 6,051,701
Female householder,
  no husband present. 1,553,660
One-person households 2,994,372

Nativity, 2006

Number of residents born in state . . . 19,089,635
  percent of population 52.4%

Immigration & naturalization, 2006

Legal permanent residents admitted. . . . 264,677
Persons naturalized 152,836
Non-immigrant admissions 5,573,588

Vital Statistics and Health

Marriages

2004 227,486
2005 228,762
2006 215,985

Divorces

2004 . . . . NA
2005 . . . . NA
2006 . . . . NA

Health risks, 2006

Percent of adults who are:
  Smokers. 14.9%
  Overweight (BMI > 25). 58.8%
  Obese (BMI > 30). 23.3%

Births

2005 548,882
  Birthrate (per 1,000). 15.2
  White. 445,277
  Black 32,252
  Hispanic 282,842
  Asian/Pacific Islander 68,232
  Amer. Indian/Alaska Native 3,121
  Low birth weight (2,500g or less) 6.9%
  Cesarian births 30.7%
  Preterm births 10.7%
  To unmarried mothers. 35.7%
  Twin births (per 1,000) 29.0
  Triplets or higher order (per 100,000). . . .149.6
2006 (preliminary). 562,431
  rate per 1,000 . . . . .15.4

Deaths

2004
All causes 232,525
  rate per 100,000. . . . . .715.6
Heart disease 64,999
  rate per 100,000. . . . . .202.1
Malignant neoplasms 53,700
  rate per 100,000. . . . . .166.8
Cerebrovascular disease. 16,882
  rate per 100,000. . . . . .52.7
Chronic lower respiratory disease 12,522
  rate per 100,000. . . . . .39.7
Diabetes. 7,117
  rate per 100,000. . . . . .22.2
2005 (preliminary). 237,079
  rate per 100,000. . . . . .713.1
2006 (provisional) 238,011

Infant deaths

2004 2,811
  rate per 1,000 . . . . .5.2
2005 (provisional) 2,800
  rate per 1,000 . . . . .5.1

Exercise routines, 2005

None. 23.9%
Moderate or greater. 53.4%
Vigorous 36.2%

Abortions, 2004

Total performed in state. . . . . NA
  rate per 1,000 women age 15-44 . . . . NA
  % obtained by out-of-state residents . . . . . . NA

Physicians, 2005

Total. 94,341
  rate per 100,000 persons 261

Community hospitals, 2005

Number of hospitals 357
Beds (x 1,000). 70.2
Patients admitted (x 1,000) 3,434
Average daily census (x 1,000) 50.0
Average cost per day $1,994
Outpatient visits (x 1 mil) 49.0

Disability status of population, 2006
5 to 15 years 4.8%
16 to 64 years 10.3%
65 years and over 41.1%

Education

Educational attainment, 2006
Population over 25 years 23,133,174
   Less than 9th grade.................... 10.6%
   High school graduate or more 80.1%
   College graduate or more............. 29.0%
   Graduate or professional degree....... 10.4%

Public school enrollment, 2005-06
Total................................6,437,202
   Pre-kindergarten through grade 8...4,431,994
   Grades 9 through 12...............1,953,077

Graduating public high school seniors, 2004-05
Diplomas (incl. GED and others) 355,217

SAT scores, 2007
Average critical reading score.............. 499
Average writing score...................... 498
Average math score 516
Percent of graduates taking test 49%

Public school teachers, 2006-07 (estimate)
Total (x 1,000) 304.2
   Elementary...........................222.9
   Secondary.............................81.3
Average salary $63,640
   Elementary.......................... $63,640
   Secondary........................... $63,640

State receipts & expenditures for public schools, 2006-07 (estimate)
Revenue receipts ($ mil) $67,460
Expenditures
Total ($ mil) $71,622
   Per capita $1,523
   Per pupil $9,156

NAEP proficiency scores, 2007

	Reading		Math	
	Basic	Proficient	Basic	Proficient
Grade 4	53.2%	22.9%	69.6%	29.7%
Grade 8	62.3%	21.5%	59.1%	23.9%

Higher education enrollment, fall 2005
Total................................391,678
   Full-time men 130,335
   Full-time women.....................169,171
   Part-time men 39,913
   Part-time women..................... 52,259

Minority enrollment in institutions of higher education, 2005
Black, non-Hispanic 185,659
Hispanic 632,358
Asian/Pacific Islander 451,454
American Indian/Alaska Native......... 22,007

Institutions of higher education, 2005-06
Total..................................... 408
   Public..................................... 146
   Private..................................... 262

Earned degrees conferred, 2004-05
Associate's........................... 92,687
Bachelor's 146,959
Master's.............................. 54,254
First-professional.....................9,188
Doctor's.............................. 6,203

Public Libraries, 2006
Number of libraries...................... 179
Number of outlets.....................1,153
Annual visits per capita 4.1
Circulation per capita.....................5.4

State & local financial support for higher education, FY 2006
Full-time equivalent enrollment (x 1,000) .. 1,662.1
Appropriations per FTE............... $6,586

Social Insurance & Welfare Programs

Social Security benefits & beneficiaries, 2005
Beneficiaries (x 1,000) 4,460
   Retired & dependents...................3,193
   Survivors............................. 571
   Disabled & dependents.................. 697
Annual benefit payments ($ mil) $48,106
   Retired & dependents...............$32,751
   Survivors...........................$7,946
   Disabled & dependents...............$7,409
Average monthly benefit
   Retired & dependents.................$1,003
   Disabled & dependents............... $955
   Widowed............................ $995

Medicare, July 2005
Enrollment (x 1,000).................... 4,201
Payments ($ mil) $22,477

Medicaid, 2004
Beneficiaries (x 1,000).................10,015
Payments ($ mil) $27,444

State Children's Health Insurance Program, 2006
Enrollment (x 1,000).................. 1,391.4
Expenditures ($ mil)................. $1,801.1

Persons without health insurance, 2006
Number (x 1,000).......................6,791
   percent............................. 18.8%
Number of children (x 1,000) 1,225
   percent of children 12.8%

Health care expenditures, 2004
Total expenditures................... $166,236
   per capita $4,638

Federal and state public aid

State unemployment insurance, 2006
Recipients, first payments (x 1,000) 948
Total payments ($ mil) $4,485
Average weekly benefit $289
Temporary Assistance for Needy Families, 2006
Recipients (x 1,000) 12,874.3
Families (x 1,000) 5,451.5
Supplemental Security Income, 2005
Recipients (x 1,000) 1,212.1
Payments ($ mil) $8,146.4
Food Stamp Program, 2006
Avg monthly participants (x 1,000) 1,999.7
Total benefits ($ mil) $2,376.7

Housing & Construction

Housing units
Total 2005 (estimate) 12,993,870
Total 2006 (estimate) 13,174,378
Seasonal or recreational use, 2006 275,870
Owner-occupied, 2006 7,102,197
   Median home value $535,700
   Homeowner vacancy rate 1.9%
Renter-occupied, 2006 5,049,030
   Median rent $1,029
   Rental vacancy rate 5.8%
Home ownership rate, 2005 . . . . 59.7%
Home ownership rate, 2006 . . . . 60.2%

New privately-owned housing units
Number authorized, 2006 (x 1,000) 160.5
   Value ($ mil) $29,614.4
Started 2005 (x 1,000, estimate) 165.0
Started 2006 (x 1,000, estimate) 154.2

Existing home sales
2005 (x 1,000) 601.1
2006 (x 1,000) 459.9

Government & Elections

State officials 2008
Governor . . . . Arnold Schwarzenegger
           Republican, term expires 1/11
Lieutenant Governor . . . . John Garamendi
Secretary of State . . . . Debra Bowen
Attorney General . . . . Jerry Brown
Chief Justice . . . . Ronald George

Governorship
Minimum age 18
Length of term . . . . 4 years
Consecutive terms permitted 2
Who succeeds . . . . Lieutenant Governor

Local governments by type, 2002
Total 4,409
   County 57
   Municipal 475
   Township 0
   School District 1,047
   Special District 2,830

State legislature
Name . . . . Legislature
Upper chamber . . . . Senate
   Number of members 40
   Length of term . . . . 4 years
   Party in majority, 2008 . . . . Democratic
Lower chamber . . . . Assembly
   Number of members 80
   Length of term . . . . 2 years
   Party in majority, 2008 . . . . Democratic

Federal representation, 2008 (110th Congress)
Senator . . . . Barbara Boxer
   Party . . . . Democratic
   Year term expires 2011
Senator . . . . Dianne Feinstein
   Party . . . . Democratic
   Year term expires 2013
Representatives, total 53
   Democrats 34
   Republicans 19

Voters in November 2006 election (estimate)
Total 10,103,659
   Male 4,806,091
   Female 5,297,568
   White 8,335,875
   Black 608,009
   Hispanic 868,190
   Asian 882,153

Presidential election, 2004
Total Popular Vote 12,421,852
   Kerry 6,745,485
   Bush 5,509,826
Total Electoral Votes 55

Votes cast for US Senators
2004
Total vote (x 1,000) 12,053
Leading party . . . . Democratic
Percent for leading party 57.7%
2006
Total vote (x 1,000) 8,541
Leading party . . . . Democratic
Percent for leading party 59.4%

Votes cast for US Representatives
2004
Total vote (x 1,000) 11,624
   Democratic 6,224
   Republican 5,031
Leading party . . . . Democratic
Percent for leading party 53.5%
2006
Total vote (x 1,000) 8,296
   Democratic 4,720
   Republican 3,314
Leading party . . . . Democratic
Percent for leading party 56.9%

State government employment, 2006
Full-time equivalent employees 393,609
Payroll ($ mil) $2,051.1

Local government employment, 2006
Full-time equivalent employees 1,425,123
Payroll ($ mil) $6,931.5

Women holding public office, 2008
US Congress 21
Statewide elected office..................... 1
State legislature 34

Black public officials, 2002
Total.................................. 234
  US and state legislatures 10
  City/county/regional offices 78
  Judicial/law enforcement................. 76
  Education/school boards 70

Hispanic public officials, 2006
Total.................................. 1,059
  State executives & legislators 30
  City/county/regional offices 388
  Judicial/law enforcement................. 41
  Education/school boards 600

Governmental Finance

State government revenues, 2006
Total revenue (x $1,000) $263,764,713
  per capita $7,276.29
General revenue (x $1,000) $188,443,700
  Intergovernmental 53,685,005
  Taxes 111,346,857
    general sales................... 32,199,800
    individual income tax 51,219,823
    corporate income tax 10,316,467
  Current charges................ 13,328,957
  Miscellaneous 10,082,881

State government expenditure, 2006
Total expenditure (x $1,000) $225,317,442
  per capita $6,215.68
General expenditure (x $1,000) $191,607,263
  per capita, total................... *$5,285.74*
  Education 1,910.55
  Public welfare 1,464.38
  Health 270.05
  Hospitals....................... 153.50
  Highways 344.88
  Police protection................... 36.49
  Corrections 187.48
  Natural resources 117.91
  Parks & recreation 14.15
  Governmental administration 218.90
  Interest on general debt 145.79

State debt & cash, 2006 ($ per capita)
Debt $3,018.40
Cash/security holdings.............. $13,837.40

Federal government grants to state & local government, 2005 (x $1,000)
Total.......................... $55,334,202
by Federal agency
  Defense 375,279
  Education 4,613,968
  Energy.......................... 267,414
  Environmental Protection Agency 312,186
  Health & Human Services. 34,997,223
  Homeland Security................. 367,844
  Housing & Urban Development.... 4,344,298
  Justice 640,662
  Labor 533,832
  Transportation 4,000,705
  Veterans Affairs................... 35,877

Crime & Law Enforcement

Crime, 2006 (rates per 100,000 residents)
Property crimes 1,156,017
  Burglary 246,464
  Larceny 666,860
  Motor vehicle theft 242,693
  Property crime rate............... 3,170.9
Violent crimes....................... 194,120
  Murder 2,485
  Forcible rape..................... 9,212
  Robbery......................... 70,968
  Aggravated assault 111,455
  Violent crime rate 532.5
Hate crimes.......................... 1,604

Fraud and identity theft, 2006
Fraud complaints..................... 49,070
  rate per 100,000 residents 134.6
Identity theft complaints 41,396
  rate per 100,000 residents 113.5

Law enforcement agencies, 2006
Total agencies.......................... 460
Total employees 115,912
  Officers 75,483
  Civilians 40,429

Prisoners, probation, and parole, 2006
Total prisoners....................... 175,512
  percent change, 12/31/05 to 12/31/06 .... 2.8%
  in private facilities 1.8%
  in local jails 1.4%
Sentenced to more than one year 173,942
  rate per 100,000 residents 475
Adults on probation 401,707
Adults on parole..................... 118,592

Prisoner demographics, June 30, 2005 (rate per 100,000 residents)
Male................................. 1,246
Female 119
White 460
Black................................ 2,992
Hispanic 782

Arrests, 2006

Total 1,543,797
   Persons under 18 years of age 231,735

Persons under sentence of death, 1/1/07

Total 660
   White 254
   Black 235
   Hispanic 136

State's highest court

Name . . . . .Supreme Court
Number of members 7
Length of term . . . . 12 years
Intermediate appeals court? . . . . .yes

Labor & Income

Civilian labor force, 2006 (x 1,000)

Total 17,751
   Men 9,876
   Women 7,875
   Persons 16-19 years 740
   White 13,833
   Black 1,058
   Hispanic 5,822

Civilian labor force as a percent of civilian non-institutional population, 2006

Total 65.1%
   Men 73.9
   Women 56.7
   Persons 16-19 years 36.1
   White 65.6
   Black 61.1
   Hispanic 68.4

Employment, 2006 (x 1,000)

Total 16,892
   Men 9,410
   Women 7,482
   Persons 16-19 years 611
   White 13,188
   Black 959
   Hispanic 5,493

Unemployment rate, 2006

Total 4.8%
   Men 4.7
   Women 5.0
   Persons 16-19 years 17.5
   White 4.7
   Black 9.4
   Hispanic 5.6

Full-time/part-time labor force, 2003 (x 1,000)

Full-time labor force, employed 13,408
Part-time labor force, employed 2,875
Unemployed, looking for
   Full-time work 1,004
   Part-time work 173
*Mean duration of unemployment (weeks) *19.8
   Median 10.0

Labor unions, 2006

Membership (x 1,000) 2,273
   percent of employed 15.7%

Experienced civilian labor force by private industry, 2006

Total 13,125,809
   Natural resources & mining 402,871
   Construction 929,950
   Manufacturing 1,495,034
   Trade, transportation & utilities 2,854,723
   Information 470,144
   Finance 934,448
   Professional & business 2,222,644
   Education & health 1,576,182
   Leisure & hospitality 1,514,160
   Other 700,575

Experienced civilian labor force by occupation, May 2006

Management 790,790
Business & financial 740,470
Legal 109,180
Sales 1,568,140
Office & admin. support 2,713,590
Computers & math 391,960
Architecture & engineering 324,780
Arts & entertainment 308,110
Education 968,230
Social services 186,650
Health care practitioner & technical 615,630
Health care support 318,080
Maintenance & repair 511,120
Construction 823,290
Transportation & moving 1,034,210
Production 974,890
Farming, fishing & forestry 182,520

Hours and earnings of production workers on manufacturing payrolls, 2006

Average weekly hours .40.4
Average hourly earnings $15.95
Average weekly earnings $644.38

Income and poverty, 2006

Median household income $56,645
Personal income, per capita (current $) . . . $38,956
   in constant (2000) dollars $34,006
Persons below poverty level 13.1%

Average annual pay

2006 . . . . $48,345
   increase from 2005 .4.6%

Federal individual income tax returns, 2005

Returns filed 15,572,877
Adjusted gross income ($1,000) $970,448,917
Total tax liability ($1,000) $136,858,733

Charitable contributions, 2004

Number of contributions 5,287.9
Total amount ($ mil) $21,867.9

Economy, Business, Industry & Agriculture

Fortune 500 companies, 2007 52
Bankruptcy cases filed, FY 2007 62,951

Patents and trademarks issued, 2007
Patents 22,888
Trademarks 13,965

Business firm ownership, 2002
Women-owned 870,496
  Sales ($ mil) $137,692
Black-owned 112,815
  Sales ($ mil) $9,741
Hispanic-owned 427,678
  Sales ($ mil) $57,186
Asian-owned 371,530
  Sales ($ mil) $125,757
Amer. Indian/Alaska Native-owned 40,541
  Sales ($ mil) $4,387
Hawaiian/Pacific Islander-owned 7,074
  Sales ($ mil) $1,230

Gross domestic product, 2006 ($ mil)
Total gross domestic product $1,727,355
  Agriculture, forestry, fishing and
    hunting 24,222
  Mining 12,954
  Utilities 28,123
  Construction 82,664
  Manufacturing, durable goods 100,665
  Manufacturing, non-durable goods . . . 68,312
  Wholesale trade .101,757
  Retail trade 119,716
  Transportation & warehousing 38,813
  Information 103,269
  Finance & insurance 115,104
  Real estate, rental & leasing 292,786
  Professional and technical services 147,869
  Educational services 13,909
  Health care and social assistance 103,704
  Accommodation/food services 46,020
  Other services, except government 38,871
  Government 189,935

Establishments, payroll, employees & receipts, by major industry group, 2005
Total 860,866
  Annual payroll ($1,000) $588,450,315
  Paid employees 13,382,470
Forestry, fishing & agriculture 2,034
  Annual payroll ($1,000) $705,641
  Paid employees 23,719
Mining 819
  Annual payroll ($1,000) $1,420,222
  Paid employees 19,651
  Receipts, 2002 ($1,000) $7,293,240

Utilities 1,140
  Annual payroll ($1,000) $5,026,299
  Paid employees 59,422
  Receipts, 2002 ($1,000) . . . . .NA
Construction 75,151
  Annual payroll ($1,000) $39,863,707
  Paid employees 865,810
  Receipts, 2002 ($1,000) $150,527,556
Manufacturing 44,825
  Annual payroll ($1,000) $71,776,365
  Paid employees 1,450,372
  Receipts, 2002 ($1,000) $378,661,414
Wholesale trade 59,252
  Annual payroll ($1,000) $47,831,555
  Paid employees 816,186
  Receipts, 2002 ($1,000) $655,954,708
Retail trade 112,382
  Annual payroll ($1,000) $43,416,017
  Paid employees 1,651,973
  Receipts, 2002 ($1,000) $359,120,365
Transportation & warehousing 20,086
  Annual payroll ($1,000) $17,941,928
  Paid employees 448,607
  Receipts, 2002 ($1,000) $45,507,276
Information 20,837
  Annual payroll ($1,000) $40,284,426
  Paid employees 509,258
  Receipts, 2002 ($1,000) . . . . .NA
Finance & insurance 51,819
  Annual payroll ($1,000) $54,895,842
  Paid employees 703,282
  Receipts, 2002 ($1,000) . . . . .NA
Professional, scientific & technical 108,411
  Annual payroll ($1,000) $74,611,098
  Paid employees 1,192,324
  Receipts, 2002 ($1,000) $145,236,098
Education 10,492
  Annual payroll ($1,000) $9,169,034
  Paid employees 301,561
  Receipts, 2002 ($1,000) $4,270,794
Health care & social assistance 93,546
  Annual payroll ($1,000) $63,344,431
  Paid employees 1,507,717
  Receipts, 2002 ($1,000) $136,397,384
Arts and entertainment 18,817
  Annual payroll ($1,000) $11,677,810
  Paid employees 298,786
  Receipts, 2002 ($1,000) $26,292,138
Real estate 50,007
  Annual payroll ($1,000) $13,602,382
  Paid employees 317,240
  Receipts, 2002 ($1,000) $54,377,915
Accommodation & food service 71,625
  Annual payroll ($1,000) $19,887,731
  Paid employees 1,285,138
  Receipts, 2002 ($1,000) $55,559,669

Exports, 2006
Value of exported goods ($ mil) $127,746
   Manufactured $93,348
   Non-manufactured $12,109

Foreign direct investment in US affiliates, 2004
Property, plants & equipment ($ mil) . . . $90,622
Employment (x 1,000) 547.0

Agriculture, 2006
Number of farms 76,000
Farm acreage (x 1,000) 26,300
   Acres per farm 346
Farm marketings and income ($ mil)
Total $31,402.7
   Crops $23,787.7
   Livestock $7,615.0
Net farm income $5,905.7

Principal commodities, in order by marketing receipts, 2005
   Dairy products, Greenhouse/nursery, Grapes, Almonds, Cattle and calves

Federal economic activity in state
Expenditures, 2005 ($ mil)
   Total $242,023
      Per capita $6,694.20
   Defense $45,124
   Non-defense $196,900
Defense department, 2006 ($ mil)
   Payroll $15,270
   Contract awards $32,126
   Grants $350
Homeland security grants ($1,000)
   2006 . . . .$231,951
   2007 . . . . $242,245

FDIC-insured financial institutions, 2005
Number 304
Assets ($ billion) $573.6
Deposits ($ billion) $371.3

Fishing, 2006
Catch (x 1,000 lbs) 341,573
Value ($1,000) $129,929

Mining, 2006 ($ mil)
Total non-fuel mineral production $4,500
Percent of U.S. 6.99%

Communication, Energy & Transportation

Communication
Households with computers, 2003 . . . . .66.3%
Households with internet access, 2003 . . . . 59.6%
High-speed internet providers 77
Total high-speed internet lines 11,753,765
   Residential 7,707,939
   Business. 4,045,826
Wireless phone customers, 12/2006 . . . 29,717,334

FCC-licensed stations (as of January 1, 2008)
TV stations 108
FM radio stations. 600
AM radio stations 251

Energy
Energy consumption, 2004
   Total (trillion Btu). 8,365
   Per capita (million Btu) 233.4
By source of production (trillion Btu)
   Coal 69
   Natural gas 2,474
   Petroleum 3,788
   Nuclear electric power 316
   Hydroelectric power 342
By end-use sector (trillion Btu)
   Residential 1,556
   Commercial 1,556
   Industrial 2,053
   Transportation 3,200
Electric energy, 2005
   Primary source of electricity. . . . . Gas
   Net generation (billion kWh) 200.3
      percent from renewable sources. 31.6%
   Net summer capability (million kW) 61.7
   CO_2 emitted from generation 54.7
Natural gas utilities, 2005
   Customers (x 1,000) 10,600
   Sales (trillion Btu). 1,542
   Revenues ($ mil) $7,922
Nuclear plants, 2007 4
Total CO_2 emitted (million metric tons). . . .388.9
Energy spending, 2004 ($ mil) $90,260
   per capita $2,518
   Price per million Btu $15.12

Transportation, 2006
Public road & street mileage 170,290
   Urban. 86,565
   Rural 83,725
   Interstate. 2,460
Vehicle miles of travel (millions) 327,478
   per capita 9,033.9
Total motor vehicle registrations 33,182,058
   Automobiles 19,835,554
   Trucks 13,289,690
   Motorcycles 726,096
Licensed drivers 23,021,279
   19 years & under 938,414
Deaths from motor vehicle accidents 4,236
Gasoline consumed (x 1,000 gallons) . . .15,844,687
   per capita 437.1

Commuting Statistics, 2006
Average commute time (min) 26.8
   Drove to work alone 73.0%
   Carpooled. 12.4%
   Public transit 5.0%
   Walk to work 2.7%
   Work from home 4.8%

Colorado 1

State Summary

Capital city . . . . Denver
Governor . . . . Bill Ritter

136 State Capitol
Denver, CO 80203
303-866-2471

Admitted as a state 1876
Area (square miles) 104,094
Population, 2007 (estimate). 4,861,515
Largest city . . . . Denver
  Population, 2006 566,974
Personal income per capita, 2006
  (in current dollars) $39,186
Gross domestic product, 2006 ($ mil) . . . $230,478

Leading industries by payroll, 2005

Professional/Scientific/Technical, Health care/
  Social assistance, Construction

**Leading agricultural commodities
by receipts, 2005**

Cattle and calves, Dairy products, Greenhouse/
  nursery, Corn, Hay

Geography & Environment

Total area (square miles). 104,094
  land 103,718
  water 376
Federally-owned land, 2004 (acres) . . . 24,354,713
  percent. 36.6%
Highest point . . . . Mt. Elbert
  elevation (feet) 14,433
Lowest point . . . . Arikaree River
  elevation (feet) 3,315
General coastline (miles) 0
Tidal shoreline (miles) 0
Cropland, 2003 (x 1,000 acres) 8,348
Forest land, 2003 (x 1,000 acres). 3,289
Capital city . . . . Denver
  Population 2000 554,636
  Population 2006 566,974
Largest city . . . . Denver
  Population 2000 554,636
  Population 2006 566,974

Number of cities with over 100,000 population
1990 4
2000 8
2006 9

State park and recreation areas, 2005
Area (x 1,000 acres) 410
Number of visitors (x 1,000) 11,377
Revenues ($1,000) $19,500
  percent of operating expenditures 67.1%

National forest system land, 2007
Acres 14,519,030

Demographics & Population Characteristics

Population
1980 2,889,964
1990 3,294,394
2000 4,302,015
2006 4,753,377
  Male 2,393,004
  Female 2,360,373
Living in group quarters, 2006 102,994
  percent of total 2.2%
2007 (estimate) 4,861,515
  persons per square mile of land 46.9
2008 (projected). 4,746,528
2010 (projected) 4,831,554
2020 (projected). 5,278,867
2030 (projected). 5,792,357

**Population of Core-Based Statistical Areas
(formerly Metropolitan Areas), x 1,000**

	CBSA	Non-CBSA
1990	2,989	306
2000	23,922	380
2006	4,356	397

Change in population, 2000-2007
Number 559,496
  percent 13.0%
Natural increase (births minus deaths) 291,317
Net internal migration 132,566
Net international migration 141,730

Persons by age, 2006
Under 5 years 341,069
5 to 17 years 828,232
18 years and over 3,584,076
65 years and over 477,186
85 years and over 61,232
  Median age 35.4

Persons by age, 2010 (projected)
Under 5 years 353,009
18 and over 3,642,971
65 and over 517,419
  Median age 35.7

Race, 2006
One Race
  White 4,282,804
  Black or African American 195,978
  Asian 125,724
  American Indian/Alaska Native. 54,626
  Hawaiian Native/Pacific Islander. 6,755
Two or more races. 87,490

Persons of Hispanic origin, 2006
Total Hispanic or Latino 934,410
  Mexican. 671,341
  Puerto Rican 18,148
  Cuban 4,917

Persons of Asian origin, 2006

Total Asian	133,079
Asian Indian	15,144
Chinese	28,753
Filipino	12,537
Japanese	13,166
Korean	25,722
Vietnamese	19,646

Marital status, 2006

Population 15 years & over	3,778,016
Never married	1,096,726
Married	2,065,116
Separated	67,812
Widowed	181,840
Divorced	434,334

Language spoken at home, 2006

Population 5 years and older	4,414,382
English only	3,653,462
Spanish	545,112
French	19,827
German	33,463
Chinese	20,839

Households & families, 2006

Households	1,846,988
with persons under 18 years	629,349
with persons over 65 years	335,325
persons per household	2.52
Families	1,196,223
persons per family	3.11
Married couples	934,148
Female householder, no husband present	181,646
One-person households	521,377

Nativity, 2006

Number of residents born in state	2,000,357
percent of population	42.1%

Immigration & naturalization, 2006

Legal permanent residents admitted	12,714
Persons naturalized	5,526
Non-immigrant admissions	355,991

Vital Statistics and Health

Marriages

2004	33,826
2005	35,132
2006	36,121

Divorces

2004	20,230
2005	20,504
2006	21,138

Health risks, 2006

Percent of adults who are:

Smokers	17.9%
Overweight (BMI > 25)	54.9%
Obese (BMI > 30)	18.2%

Births

2005	68,944
Birthrate (per 1,000)	14.8
White	62,856
Black	3,123
Hispanic	21,785
Asian/Pacific Islander	2,390
Amer. Indian/Alaska Native	575
Low birth weight (2,500g or less)	9.2%
Cesarian births	24.6%
Preterm births	12.3%
To unmarried mothers	27.1%
Twin births (per 1,000)	31.7
Triplets or higher order (per 100,000)	153.8
2006 (preliminary)	70,750
rate per 1,000	14.9

Deaths

2004

All causes	28,309
rate per 100,000	736.4
Heart disease	6,079
rate per 100,000	162.7
Malignant neoplasms	6,196
rate per 100,000	160.1
Cerebrovascular disease	1,638
rate per 100,000	44.6
Chronic lower respiratory disease	1,899
rate per 100,000	51.7
Diabetes	696
rate per 100,000	18.2
2005 (preliminary)	29,628
rate per 100,000	742.8
2006 (provisional)	29,502

Infant deaths

2004	434
rate per 1,000	6.3
2005 (provisional)	451
rate per 1,000	6.5

Exercise routines, 2005

None	17.3%
Moderate or greater	54.4%
Vigorous	32.6%

Abortions, 2004

Total performed in state	11,415
rate per 1,000 women age 15-44	11
% obtained by out-of-state residents	9.2%

Physicians, 2005

Total	12,101
rate per 100,000 persons	259

Community hospitals, 2005

Number of hospitals	71
Beds (x 1,000)	9.6
Patients admitted (x 1,000)	417
Average daily census (x 1,000)	5.8
Average cost per day	$1,751
Outpatient visits (x 1 mil)	7.4

Disability status of population, 2006
5 to 15 years 5.2%
16 to 64 years 10.5%
65 years and over 38.3%

Education

Educational attainment, 2006
Population over 25 years 3,118,500
   Less than 9th grade. 4.6%
   High school graduate or more 88.0%
   College graduate or more. 34.3%
   Graduate or professional degree. 12.4%

Public school enrollment, 2005-06
Total. 779,826
   Pre-kindergarten through grade 8. . . . 549,875
   Grades 9 through 12 229,951

Graduating public high school seniors, 2004-05
Diplomas (incl. GED and others) 45,058

SAT scores, 2007
Average critical reading score 560
Average writing score 549
Average math score 565
Percent of graduates taking test 24%

Public school teachers, 2006-07 (estimate)
Total (x 1,000) 47.0
   Elementary 24.0
   Secondary 23.0
Average salary $45,833
   Elementary $45,520
   Secondary $46,110

State receipts & expenditures for public schools, 2006-07 (estimate)
Revenue receipts ($ mil) $7,428
Expenditures
Total ($ mil) $8,516
   Per capita $1,486
   Per pupil $9,592

NAEP proficiency scores, 2007

	Reading		Math	
	Basic	Proficient	Basic	Proficient
Grade 4	70.0%	36.2%	81.8%	41.2%
Grade 8	78.7%	34.6%	75.1%	37.4%

Higher education enrollment, fall 2005
Total. 68,163
   Full-time men 21,914
   Full-time women .27,752
   Part-time men 8,508
   Part-time women. .9,989

Minority enrollment in institutions of higher education, 2005
Black, non-Hispanic 15,528
Hispanic 33,856
Asian/Pacific Islander 11,710
American Indian/Alaska Native. 4,370

Institutions of higher education, 2005-06
Total. 78
   Public. 27
   Private 51

Earned degrees conferred, 2004-05
Associate's. 9,788
Bachelor's 25,230
Master's 10,921
First-professional. 1,054
Doctor's 1,062

Public Libraries, 2006
Number of libraries. 115
Number of outlets 253
Annual visits per capita 6.2
Circulation per capita. 11.0

State & local financial support for higher education, FY 2006
Full-time equivalent enrollment (x 1,000) 158.9
Appropriations per FTE. $3,364

Social Insurance & Welfare Programs

Social Security benefits & beneficiaries, 2005
Beneficiaries (x 1,000) 588
   Retired & dependents. 419
   Survivors. 77
   Disabled & dependents. 92
Annual benefit payments ($ mil) $6,227
   Retired & dependents. $4,206
   Survivors. $1,065
   Disabled & dependents. $955
Average monthly benefit
   Retired & dependents. $982
   Disabled & dependents. $934
   Widowed. $977

Medicare, July 2005
Enrollment (x 1,000) 522
Payments ($ mil) $2,647

Medicaid, 2004
Beneficiaries (x 1,000). 503
Payments ($ mil) $2,399

State Children's Health Insurance Program, 2006
Enrollment (x 1,000). 70.0
Expenditures ($ mil) $77.1

Persons without health insurance, 2006
Number (x 1,000). 826
   percent. 17.2%
Number of children (x 1,000) 176
   percent of children 14.6%

Health care expenditures, 2004
Total expenditures. $21,691
   per capita $4,717

Federal and state public aid

State unemployment insurance, 2006
Recipients, first payments (x 1,000) 69
Total payments ($ mil) $288
Average weekly benefit $312
Temporary Assistance for Needy Families, 2006
Recipients (x 1,000) 426.0
Families (x 1,000) 165.5
Supplemental Security Income, 2005
Recipients (x 1,000) 55.4
Payments ($ mil) $263.8
Food Stamp Program, 2006
Avg monthly participants (x 1,000) 251.4
Total benefits ($ mil) $321.0

Housing & Construction

Housing units
Total 2005 (estimate) 2,053,794
Total 2006 (estimate) 2,094,898
Seasonal or recreational use, 2006 95,893
Owner-occupied, 2006 1,269,421
   Median home value $232,900
   Homeowner vacancy rate 3.0%
Renter-occupied, 2006 577,567
   Median rent $780
   Rental vacancy rate 10.5%
Home ownership rate, 2005 . . . . 71.0%
Home ownership rate, 2006 . . . . 70.1%

New privately-owned housing units
Number authorized, 2006 (x 1,000) 38.3
   Value ($ mil) $7,769.5
Started 2005 (x 1,000, estimate) 36.8
Started 2006 (x 1,000, estimate) 37.7

Existing home sales
2005 (x 1,000) 130.4
2006 (x 1,000) 123.7

Government & Elections

State officials 2008
Governor . . . . Bill Ritter
      Democratic, term expires 1/11
Lieutenant Governor . . . . Barbara O'Brien
Secretary of State . . . . Mike Coffman
Attorney General . . . . .John Suthers
Chief Justice . . . . .Mary Mullarkey

Governorship
Minimum age 30
Length of term . . . . 4 years
Consecutive terms permitted 2
Who succeeds . . . . Lieutenant Governor

Local governments by type, 2002
Total 1,928
   County 62
   Municipal 270
   Township 0
   School District 182
   Special District 1,414

State legislature
Name . . . . General Assembly
Upper chamber . . . . .Senate
   Number of members 35
   Length of term . . . . 4 years
   Party in majority, 2008 . . . . .Democratic
Lower chamber . . . . . . .House of Representatives
   Number of members 65
   Length of term . . . . 2 years
   Party in majority, 2008 . . . . .Democratic

Federal representation, 2008 (110th Congress)
Senator . . . . .Wayne Allard
   Party . . . . Republican
   Year term expires 2009
Senator . . . . .Ken Salazar
   Party . . . . .Democratic
   Year term expires 2011
Representatives, total 7
   Democrats 4
   Republicans 3

Voters in November 2006 election (estimate)
Total 1,729,916
   Male 805,406
   Female 924,510
   White 1,659,514
   Black 24,618
   Hispanic 85,614
   Asian 19,579

Presidential election, 2004
Total Popular Vote 2,130,330
   Kerry 1,001,732
   Bush 1,101,255
Total Electoral Votes 9

Votes cast for US Senators
2004
Total vote (x 1,000) 2,107
Leading party .Democratic
Percent for leading party 51.3%
2006
Total vote (x 1,000) . . . . NA
Leading party . . . . NA
Percent for leading party . . . . NA

Votes cast for US Representatives
2004
Total vote (x 1,000) 2,039
   Democratic 995
   Republican 992
Leading party .Democratic
Percent for leading party 48.8%
2006
Total vote (x 1,000) 1,539
   Democratic 833
   Republican 624
Leading party .Democratic
Percent for leading party 54.1%

State government employment, 2006
Full-time equivalent employees 67,451
Payroll ($ mil) $290.9

Local government employment, 2006
Full-time equivalent employees 187,551
Payroll ($ mil) $691.2

Women holding public office, 2008
US Congress................................ 2
Statewide elected office.................... 2
State legislature 35

Black public officials, 2002
Total...................................... 17
   US and state legislatures 4
   City/county/regional offices 5
   Judicial/law enforcement................... 8
   Education/school boards.................. 0

Hispanic public officials, 2006
Total.................................... 145
   State executives & legislators 7
   City/county/regional offices 101
   Judicial/law enforcement................... 7
   Education/school boards................ 30

Governmental Finance

State government revenues, 2006
Total revenue (x $1,000)............$23,466,755
   per capita $4,923.53
General revenue (x $1,000) $17,493,287
   Intergovernmental 4,725,831
   Taxes 8,522,307
      general sales....................2,105,049
      individual income tax 4,258,944
      corporate income tax 457,673
   Current charges.................. 2,404,244
   Miscellaneous 1,840,905

State government expenditure, 2006
Total expenditure (x $1,000).......$20,150,921
   per capita $4,227.84
General expenditure (x $1,000) $16,965,585
   per capita, total................... *$3,559.53*
   Education 1,465.92
   Public welfare 851.19
   Health 151.25
   Hospitals.........................74.55
   Highways 264.72
   Police protection.................. 23.20
   Corrections 171.56
   Natural resources 59.34
   Parks & recreation................18.30
   Governmental administration...... 146.53
   Interest on general debt............137.88

State debt & cash, 2006 ($ per capita)
Debt....................................$2,783.59
Cash/security holdings.............. $11,778.13

Federal government grants to state & local government, 2005 (x $1,000)
Total.............................$5,433,177
by Federal agency
   Defense 45,419
   Education 475,650
   Energy....................... 64,729
   Environmental Protection Agency 63,271
   Health & Human Services. 2,682,837
   Homeland Security...................20,917
   Housing & Urban Development...... 403,828
   Justice 85,459
   Labor 110,307
   Transportation 595,647
   Veterans Affairs.................. 9,364

Crime & Law Enforcement

Crime, 2006 (rates per 100,000 residents)
Property crimes 164,054
   Burglary 32,422
   Larceny 110,837
   Motor vehicle theft 20,795
   Property crime rate................3,451.3
Violent crimes........................18,616
   Murder 158
   Forcible rape......................2,076
   Robbery..........................3,835
   Aggravated assault 12,547
   Violent crime rate 391.6
Hate crimes. 174

Fraud and identity theft, 2006
Fraud complaints.......................7,657
   rate per 100,000 residents 161.1
Identity theft complaints 4,395
   rate per 100,000 residents 92.5

Law enforcement agencies, 2006
Total agencies........................... 235
Total employees 16,471
   Officers 11,298
   Civilians 5,173

Prisoners, probation, and parole, 2006
Total prisoners....................... 22,481
   percent change, 12/31/05 to 12/31/06 .... 4.8%
   in private facilities 21.6%
   in local jails 1.9%
Sentenced to more than one year 22,481
   rate per 100,000 residents 469
Adults on probation 63,032
Adults on parole.......................9,551

Prisoner demographics, June 30, 2005 (rate per 100,000 residents)
Male....................................1,279
Female 166
White.................................... 525
Black....................................3,491
Hispanic 1,042

Arrests, 2006

Total	247,536
Persons under 18 years of age	44,178

Persons under sentence of death, 1/1/07

Total	2
White	0
Black	1
Hispanic	1

State's highest court

Name	Supreme Court
Number of members	7
Length of term	10 years
Intermediate appeals court?	yes

Labor & Income

Civilian labor force, 2006 (x 1,000)

Total	2,610
Men	1,424
Women	1,186
Persons 16-19 years	114
White	2,389
Black	85
Hispanic	428

Civilian labor force as a percent of civilian non-institutional population, 2006

Total	72.7%
Men	80.0
Women	65.6
Persons 16-19 years	47.8
White	73.0
Black	67.8
Hispanic	71.4

Employment, 2006 (x 1,000)

Total	2,499
Men	1,368
Women	1,131
Persons 16-19 years	96
White	2,294
Black	79
Hispanic	398

Unemployment rate, 2006

Total	4.2%
Men	4.0
Women	4.6
Persons 16-19 years	15.9
White	4.0
Black	6.6
Hispanic	6.9

Full-time/part-time labor force, 2003 (x 1,000)

Full-time labor force, employed	1,899
Part-time labor force, employed	429
Unemployed, looking for	
Full-time work	123
Part-time work	26
Mean duration of unemployment (weeks)	18.8
Median	9.9

Labor unions, 2006

Membership (x 1,000)	165
percent of employed	7.7%

Experienced civilian labor force by private industry, 2006

Total	1,890,640
Natural resources & mining	35,514
Construction	167,647
Manufacturing	149,147
Trade, transportation & utilities	415,032
Information	75,633
Finance	156,739
Professional & business	331,871
Education & health	228,145
Leisure & hospitality	264,980
Other	65,664

Experienced civilian labor force by occupation, May 2006

Management	107,070
Business & financial	114,640
Legal	17,630
Sales	257,450
Office & admin. support	372,340
Computers & math	77,980
Architecture & engineering	54,890
Arts & entertainment	31,630
Education	120,890
Social services	26,380
Health care practitioner & technical	99,920
Health care support	41,610
Maintenance & repair	89,030
Construction	141,740
Transportation & moving	137,740
Production	103,820
Farming, fishing & forestry	3,450

Hours and earnings of production workers on manufacturing payrolls, 2006

Average weekly hours	39.2
Average hourly earnings	$16.58
Average weekly earnings	$649.94

Income and poverty, 2006

Median household income	$52,015
Personal income, per capita (current $)	$39,186
in constant (2000) dollars	$34,207
Persons below poverty level	12.0%

Average annual pay

2006	$43,506
increase from 2005	4.6%

Federal individual income tax returns, 2005

Returns filed	2,160,153
Adjusted gross income ($1,000)	$125,994,344
Total tax liability ($1,000)	$16,946,987

Charitable contributions, 2004

Number of contributions	758.9
Total amount ($ mil)	$2,790.8

Economy, Business, Industry & Agriculture

Fortune 500 companies, 2007.............. 12
Bankruptcy cases filed, FY 2007........ 14,238

Patents and trademarks issued, 2007
Patents............................. 2,071
Trademarks.......................... 1,866

Business firm ownership, 2002
Women-owned..................... 135,220
  Sales ($ mil) $16,359
Black-owned........................7,066
  Sales ($ mil) $758
Hispanic-owned.................... 24,054
  Sales ($ mil)......................$5,114
Asian-owned 10,910
  Sales ($ mil) $2,451
Amer. Indian/Alaska Native-owned 3,950
  Sales ($ mil) $490
Hawaiian/Pacific Islander-owned 391
  Sales ($ mil) $35

Gross domestic product, 2006 ($ mil)
Total gross domestic product $230,478
  Agriculture, forestry, fishing and
    hunting 1,920
  Mining............................ 12,775
  Utilities............................3,635
  Construction 14,278
  Manufacturing, durable goods..........9,221
  Manufacturing, non-durable goods 5,791
  Wholesale trade..................... 12,544
  Retail trade........................13,816
  Transportation & warehousing 5,533
  Information.......................19,534
  Finance & insurance................. 13,669
  Real estate, rental & leasing 30,421
  Professional and technical services 20,589
  Educational services..................1,430
  Health care and social assistance.......13,192
  Accommodation/food services......... 6,640
  Other services, except government 5,262
  Government....................... 26,501

Establishments, payroll, employees & receipts, by major industry group, 2005
Total...............................151,070
  Annual payroll ($1,000)..........$75,525,841
  Paid employees 1,936,264
Forestry, fishing & agriculture.............. 269
  Annual payroll ($1,000)............. $35,709
  Paid employees 1,418
Mining...............................1,011
  Annual payroll ($1,000)........... $1,227,392
  Paid employees 16,191
  Receipts, 2002 ($1,000) $5,342,881

Utilities 370
  Annual payroll ($1,000)........... $548,366
  Paid employees 8,013
  Receipts, 2002 ($1,000) ....NA
Construction.........................19,153
  Annual payroll ($1,000).......... $6,620,283
  Paid employees 152,212
  Receipts, 2002 ($1,000) $32,663,596
Manufacturing.........................5,189
  Annual payroll ($1,000)...........$6,279,451
  Paid employees 135,832
  Receipts, 2002 ($1,000) $34,661,144
Wholesale trade 7,269
  Annual payroll ($1,000)...........$5,635,317
  Paid employees 98,511
  Receipts, 2002 ($1,000) $92,092,155
Retail trade 19,208
  Annual payroll ($1,000).......... $6,046,900
  Paid employees 249,433
  Receipts, 2002 ($1,000) $52,226,983
Transportation & warehousing........... 3,285
  Annual payroll ($1,000)...........$2,216,693
  Paid employees 59,969
  Receipts, 2002 ($1,000) $4,357,611
Information.........................3,222
  Annual payroll ($1,000)...........$4,934,931
  Paid employees 79,149
  Receipts, 2002 ($1,000) ....NA
Finance & insurance 10,485
  Annual payroll ($1,000)...........$6,280,715
  Paid employees 102,599
  Receipts, 2002 ($1,000) ....NA
Professional, scientific & technical 21,670
  Annual payroll ($1,000)...........$9,458,401
  Paid employees 155,267
  Receipts, 2002 ($1,000) $20,547,273
Education 1,917
  Annual payroll ($1,000)........... $901,651
  Paid employees 35,311
  Receipts, 2002 ($1,000) $722,991
Health care & social assistance 12,686
  Annual payroll ($1,000).......... $8,294,247
  Paid employees 221,956
  Receipts, 2002 ($1,000) $17,499,334
Arts and entertainment 2,349
  Annual payroll ($1,000)...........$1,069,914
  Paid employees 44,714
  Receipts, 2002 ($1,000) $3,084,694
Real estate...........................9,702
  Annual payroll ($1,000)...........$1,755,618
  Paid employees 46,058
  Receipts, 2002 ($1,000) $6,686,060
Accommodation & food service...........11,697
  Annual payroll ($1,000)...........$3,136,250
  Paid employees 222,283
  Receipts, 2002 ($1,000) $8,808,846

Exports, 2006
Value of exported goods ($ mil) $7,956
    Manufactured $6,056
    Non-manufactured $310

Foreign direct investment in US affiliates, 2004
Property, plants & equipment ($ mil) $16,115
Employment (x 1,000) .71.4

Agriculture, 2006
Number of farms 30,700
Farm acreage (x 1,000) 30,700
    Acres per farm 1,000
Farm marketings and income ($ mil)
Total $5,614.4
    Crops $1,552.5
    Livestock $4,061.9
Net farm income $734.0

Principal commodities, in order by marketing receipts, 2005
Cattle and calves, Dairy products, Greenhouse/
      nursery, Corn, Hay

Federal economic activity in state
Expenditures, 2005 ($ mil)
    Total $31,173
       Per capita $6,684.69
    Defense $6,691
    Non-defense $24,481
Defense department, 2006 ($ mil)
    Payroll $3,210
    Contract awards $4,127
    Grants $46
Homeland security grants ($1,000)
    2006 . . . . $21,080
    2007 . . . . $19,899

FDIC-insured financial institutions, 2005
Number 164
Assets ($ billion) $47.2
Deposits ($ billion) $39.2

Fishing, 2006
Catch (x 1,000 lbs) . . . . NA
Value ($1,000) . . . . NA

Mining, 2006 ($ mil)
Total non-fuel mineral production $1,670
Percent of U.S. 2.59%

Communication, Energy & Transportation

Communication
Households with computers, 2003 . . . . .70.0%
Households with internet access, 2003 . . . . 63.0%
High-speed internet providers 63
Total high-speed internet lines 1,489,091
    Residential 1,018,006
    Business 471,085
Wireless phone customers, 12/2006 3,608,209

FCC-licensed stations (as of January 1, 2008)
TV stations 31
FM radio stations 179
AM radio stations 82

Energy
Energy consumption, 2004
    Total (trillion Btu) 1,384
    Per capita (million Btu) 300.9
By source of production (trillion Btu)
    Coal 390
    Natural gas 438
    Petroleum 500
    Nuclear electric power 0
    Hydroelectric power 12
By end-use sector (trillion Btu)
    Residential 308
    Commercial 285
    Industrial 373
    Transportation 417
Electric energy, 2005
    Primary source of electricity . . . . Coal
    Net generation (billion kWh) 49.6
       percent from renewable sources 4.5%
    Net summer capability (million kW) 11.1
    CO_2 emitted from generation 40.8
Natural gas utilities, 2005
    Customers (x 1,000) 1,667
    Sales (trillion Btu) 322
    Revenues ($ mil) $1,887
Nuclear plants, 2007 0
Total CO_2 emitted (million metric tons) 89.7
Energy spending, 2004 ($ mil) $11,805
    per capita $2,567
    Price per million Btu $12.54

Transportation, 2006
Public road & street mileage 88,021
    Urban 19,066
    Rural 68,955
    Interstate 954
Vehicle miles of travel (millions) 48,641
    per capita 10,205.3
Total motor vehicle registrations 1,807,823
    Automobiles 858,967
    Trucks 943,027
    Motorcycles 117,159
Licensed drivers .3,341,275
    19 years & under 155,126
Deaths from motor vehicle accidents 535
Gasoline consumed (x 1,000 gallons) 2,164,191
    per capita 454.1

Commuting Statistics, 2006
Average commute time (min) 23.9
    Drove to work alone 75.1%
    Carpooled 10.6%
    Public transit 3.2%
    Walk to work 3.1%
    Work from home 5.7%

State Summary

Capital city . . . . Hartford
Governor . . . . M. Jodi Rell
210 Capitol Ave
Hartford, CT 06106
800-406-1527
Admitted as a state 1788
Area (square miles) 5,543
Population, 2007 (estimate) 3,502,309
Largest city . . . . Bridgeport
  Population, 2006 137,912
Personal income per capita, 2006
  (in current dollars) $49,852
Gross domestic product, 2006 ($ mil) . . . $204,134

Leading industries by payroll, 2005

Finance & Insurance, Manufacturing, Health
care/Social assistance

**Leading agricultural commodities
by receipts, 2005**

Greenhouse/nursery, Dairy products, Chicken
eggs, Aquaculture, Tobacco

Geography & Environment

Total area (square miles) 5,543
  land 4,845
  water 699
Federally-owned land, 2004 (acres) 13,938
  percent 0.4%
Highest point . . . . Mt. Frissell (south slope)
  elevation (feet) 2,380
Lowest point . . . . Long Island Sound
  elevation (feet) . . . . sea level
General coastline (miles) 0
Tidal shoreline (miles) 618
Cropland, 2003 (x 1,000 acres) 172
Forest land, 2003 (x 1,000 acres) 1,706
Capital city . . . . Hartford
  Population 2000 121,578
  Population 2006 124,512
Largest city . . . . Bridgeport
  Population 2000 139,529
  Population 2006 137,912

Number of cities with over 100,000 population

1990 5
2000 5
2006 5

State park and recreation areas, 2005

Area (x 1,000 acres) 204
Number of visitors (x 1,000) 6,235
Revenues ($1,000) $4,611
  percent of operating expenditures 32.0%

National forest system land, 2007

Acres 24

Demographics & Population Characteristics

Population

1980 3,107,576
1990 3,287,116
2000 3,405,602
2006 3,504,809
  Male 1,706,188
  Female 1,798,621
Living in group quarters, 2006 113,079
  percent of total 3.2%
2007 (estimate) .3,502,309
  persons per square mile of land 722.9
2008 (projected) .3,550,416
2010 (projected) .3,577,490
2020 (projected) .3,675,650
2030 (projected) .3,688,630

**Population of Core-Based Statistical Areas
(formerly Metropolitan Areas), x 1,000**

	CBSA	Non-CBSA
1990	3,287	0
2000	3,406	0
2006	3,505	0

Change in population, 2000-2007

Number 96,707
  percent 2.8%
Natural increase (births minus deaths) 92,010
Net internal migration . . . .-78,064
Net international migration 97,695

Persons by age, 2006

Under 5 years 202,831
5 to 17 years 615,455
18 years and over 2,686,523
65 years and over 470,443
85 years and over 76,395
  Median age 39.0

Persons by age, 2010 (projected)

Under 5 years 217,712
18 and over 2,763,482
65 and over 515,621
  Median age 39.6

Race, 2006

One Race
  White 2,966,187
  Black or African American 358,210
  Asian 117,986
  American Indian/Alaska Native 12,497
  Hawaiian Native/Pacific Islander 2,597
Two or more races 47,332

Persons of Hispanic origin, 2006

Total Hispanic or Latino 391,935
  Mexican 37,155
  Puerto Rican 221,658
  Cuban 7,159

Persons of Asian origin, 2006

Total Asian 117,054
  Asian Indian. 40,394
  Chinese 26,493
  Filipino 12,352
  Japanese 3,623
  Korean. 11,310
  Vietnamese. 8,324

Marital status, 2006

Population 15 years & over 2,839,111
  Never married 879,704
  Married. 1,503,801
  Separated 44,462
  Widowed. 181,942
  Divorced 273,664

Language spoken at home, 2006

Population 5 years and older. 3,302,738
  English only 2,639,307
  Spanish 308,863
  French 46,702
  German. 11,837
  Chinese 21,772

Households & families, 2006

Households. 1,325,443
  with persons under 18 years 460,658
  with persons over 65 years. 325,996
  persons per household 2.56
Families. 894,348
  persons per family. 3.13
Married couples. 680,656
Female householder,
  no husband present. 160,504
One-person households 359,319

Nativity, 2006

Number of residents born in state 1,953,665
  percent of population. 55.7%

Immigration & naturalization, 2006

Legal permanent residents admitted. 18,700
Persons naturalized .7,231
Non-immigrant admissions 212,993

Vital Statistics and Health

Marriages

2004 20,240
2005 20,514
2006 17,382

Divorces

2004 10,942
2005 10,623
2006 9,773

Health risks, 2006

Percent of adults who are:
  Smokers. 17.0%
  Overweight (BMI > 25). 58.8%
  Obese (BMI > 30). 20.6%

Births

2005 41,718
  Birthrate (per 1,000). 11.9
  White. 33,988
  Black 5,280
  Hispanic 8,004
  Asian/Pacific Islander 2,237
  Amer. Indian/Alaska Native 213
  Low birth weight (2,500g or less). 8.0%
  Cesarian births .32.4%
  Preterm births 10.4%
  To unmarried mothers. 32.2%
  Twin births (per 1,000) 41.5
  Triplets or higher order (per 100,000). . . 245.5
2006 (preliminary). 41,807
  rate per 1,000 . . . . .11.9

Deaths

2004
All causes 29,314
  rate per 100,000. . . . . 706.2
Heart disease 7,868
  rate per 100,000. . . . . .182.5
Malignant neoplasms 7,175
  rate per 100,000. . . . . .181.5
Cerebrovascular disease. 1,635
  rate per 100,000. .37.6
Chronic lower respiratory disease 1,432
  rate per 100,000. .34.7
Diabetes. 767
  rate per 100,000. .18.7
2005 (preliminary). 29,466
  rate per 100,000. . . . . 696.0
2006 (provisional) 29,790

Infant deaths

2004 233
  rate per 1,000 . . . . .5.5
2005 (provisional) 226
  rate per 1,000 . . . . .5.4

Exercise routines, 2005

None. 21.2%
Moderate or greater. 51.2%
Vigorous 31.0%

Abortions, 2004

Total performed in state. 12,189
  rate per 1,000 women age 15-44. 17
  % obtained by out-of-state residents 3.7%

Physicians, 2005

Total. 12,780
  rate per 100,000 persons 365

Community hospitals, 2005

Number of hospitals 36
Beds (x 1,000). 7.7
Patients admitted (x 1,000) 405
Average daily census (x 1,000) 6.3
Average cost per day $1,714
Outpatient visits (x 1 mil) 7.1

Disability status of population, 2006
5 to 15 years 5.4%
16 to 64 years 10.0%
65 years and over 36.3%

Education

Educational attainment, 2006
Population over 25 years 2,367,511
   Less than 9th grade................... 4.8%
   High school graduate or more 88.0%
   College graduate or more............. 33.7%
   Graduate or professional degree....... 14.4%

Public school enrollment, 2005-06
Total............................... 575,059
   Pre-kindergarten through grade 8.... 399,705
   Grades 9 through 12 175,354

Graduating public high school seniors, 2004-05
Diplomas (incl. GED and others) 35,560

SAT scores, 2007
Average critical reading score 510
Average writing score 511
Average math score 512
Percent of graduates taking test 84%

Public school teachers, 2006-07 (estimate)
Total (x 1,000) 42.5
   Elementary........................... 29.0
   Secondary............................ 13.5
Average salary $60,822
   Elementary....................... $60,822
   Secondary........................ $60,822

State receipts & expenditures for public schools, 2006-07 (estimate)
Revenue receipts ($ mil) $8,331
Expenditures
Total ($ mil) $8,339
   Per capita $2,129
   Per pupil $13,370

NAEP proficiency scores, 2007

	Reading		Math	
	Basic	Proficient	Basic	Proficient
Grade 4	72.6%	41.2%	83.9%	44.7%
Grade 8	76.7%	37.1%	72.8%	34.7%

Higher education enrollment, fall 2005
Total................................... 62,970
   Full-time men 21,391
   Full-time women..................... 27,075
   Part-time men 5,193
   Part-time women..................... 9,311

Minority enrollment in institutions of higher education, 2005
Black, non-Hispanic 18,528
Hispanic 14,285
Asian/Pacific Islander 7,877
American Indian/Alaska Native.......... 672

Institutions of higher education, 2005-06
Total.................................... 44
   Public............................... 22
   Private.............................. 22

Earned degrees conferred, 2004-05
Associate's............................. 5,022
Bachelor's 16,617
Master's............................... 8,851
First-professional....................... 1,014
Doctor's............................... 675

Public Libraries, 2006
Number of libraries...................... 194
Number of outlets 251
Annual visits per capita 6.4
Circulation per capita................... 9.0

State & local financial support for higher education, FY 2006
Full-time equivalent enrollment (x 1,000)..... 73.6
Appropriations per FTE............... $9,503

Social Insurance & Welfare Programs

Social Security benefits & beneficiaries, 2005
Beneficiaries (x 1,000) 585
   Retired & dependents.................. 435
   Survivors............................ 68
   Disabled & dependents................. 82
Annual benefit payments ($ mil) $6,917
   Retired & dependents............... $4,994
   Survivors......................... $1,029
   Disabled & dependents................ $894
Average monthly benefit
   Retired & dependents................ $1,096
   Disabled & dependents............... $981
   Widowed........................... $1,072

Medicare, July 2005
Enrollment (x 1,000)..................... 525
Payments ($ mil) $3,996

Medicaid, 2004
Beneficiaries (x 1,000)................... 501
Payments ($ mil) $3,696

State Children's Health Insurance Program, 2006
Enrollment (x 1,000).................... 23.1
Expenditures ($ mil).................... $31.5

Persons without health insurance, 2006
Number (x 1,000)....................... 325
   percent............................. 9.4%
Number of children (x 1,000) 49
   percent of children 6.0%

Health care expenditures, 2004
Total expenditures..................... $22,167
   per capita $6,344

Federal and state public aid
State unemployment insurance, 2006
Recipients, first payments (x 1,000) 119
Total payments ($ mil) $559
Average weekly benefit $304
Temporary Assistance for Needy Families, 2006
Recipients (x 1,000) 432.6
Families (x 1,000) 217.5
Supplemental Security Income, 2005
Recipients (x 1,000) 52.1
Payments ($ mil) $259.8
Food Stamp Program, 2006
Avg monthly participants (x 1,000) 210.3
Total benefits ($ mil) $239.1

Housing & Construction
Housing units
Total 2005 (estimate) 1,423,343
Total 2006 (estimate) 1,432,241
Seasonal or recreational use, 2006 22,144
Owner-occupied, 2006 921,382
   Median home value $298,900
   Homeowner vacancy rate 2.1%
Renter-occupied, 2006 404,061
   Median rent $886
   Rental vacancy rate 7.9%
Home ownership rate, 2005 . . . . 70.5%
Home ownership rate, 2006 . . . . 71.1%

New privately-owned housing units
Number authorized, 2006 (x 1,000) 9.2
   Value ($ mil) $1,874.2
Started 2005 (x 1,000, estimate) 8.5
Started 2006 (x 1,000, estimate) 8.5

Existing home sales
2005 (x 1,000) 80.4
2006 (x 1,000) 70.8

Government & Elections
State officials 2008
Governor . . . . .M. Jodi Rell
       Republican, term expires 1/11
Lieutenant Governor . . . . Michael Fedele
Secretary of State . . . . .Susan Bysiewicz
Attorney General . . . . Richard Blumenthal
Chief Justice . . . . Chase Rogers

Governorship
Minimum age 30
Length of term . . . . 4 years
Consecutive terms permitted . . . . . . not specified
Who succeeds . . . . Lieutenant Governor

Local governments by type, 2002
Total 580
   County 0
   Municipal 30
   Township 149
   School District 17
   Special District 384

State legislature
Name . . . . General Assembly
Upper chamber . . . . .Senate
   Number of members 36
   Length of term . . . . 2 years
   Party in majority, 2008 . . . . .Democratic
Lower chamber . . . . . . .House of Representatives
   Number of members 151
   Length of term . . . . 2 years
   Party in majority, 2008 . . . . .Democratic

Federal representation, 2008 (110th Congress)
Senator . . . . Christopher J. Dodd
   Party . . . . .Democratic
   Year term expires 2011
Senator . . . . Joseph Lieberman
   Party . . . . Independent Democrat
   Year term expires 2013
Representatives, total 5
   Democrats 4
   Republicans 1

Voters in November 2006 election (estimate)
Total 1,219,997
   Male 571,821
   Female 648,176
   White 1,117,425
   Black 80,758
   Hispanic 29,616
   Asian 15,380

Presidential election, 2004
Total Popular Vote 1,578,769
   Kerry 857,488
   Bush 693,826
Total Electoral Votes 7

Votes cast for US Senators
2004
Total vote (x 1,000) .1,425
Leading party . . . . .Democratic
Percent for leading party 66.4%
2006
Total vote (x 1,000) .1,135
Leading party . . . . Independent Democrat
Percent for leading party 49.8%

Votes cast for US Representatives
2004
Total vote (x 1,000) .1,429
   Democratic 786
   Republican 630
Leading party . . . . .Democratic
Percent for leading party 55.0%
2006
Total vote (x 1,000) .1,075
   Democratic 649
   Republican 420
Leading party . . . . .Democratic
Percent for leading party 48.9%

State government employment, 2006
Full-time equivalent employees 61,971
Payroll ($ mil) $305.5

Local government employment, 2006
Full-time equivalent employees 126,251
Payroll ($ mil) $549.7

Women holding public office, 2008
US Congress 1
Statewide elected office. 4
State legislature 53

Black public officials, 2002
Total. 69
   US and state legislatures 14
   City/county/regional offices 46
   Judicial/law enforcement. 3
   Education/school boards 6

Hispanic public officials, 2006
Total. 29
   State executives & legislators 6
   City/county/regional offices 19
   Judicial/law enforcement. 0
   Education/school boards 4

Governmental Finance

State government revenues, 2006
Total revenue (x $1,000) $22,896,537
   per capita $6,549.82
General revenue (x $1,000) $19,460,063
   Intergovernmental 4,176,892
   Taxes 12,131,894
      general sales 3,040,683
      individual income tax 5,777,636
      corporate income tax 634,990
   Current charges. 1,573,469
   Miscellaneous 1,577,808

State government expenditure, 2006
Total expenditure (x $1,000) $20,674,608
   per capita $5,914.21
General expenditure (x $1,000) $17,771,850
   per capita, total. *$5,083.84*
      Education 1,440.38
      Public welfare 1,407.69
      Health 219.97
      Hospitals. 347.70
      Highways 229.12
      Police protection. 56.57
      Corrections .176.78
      Natural resources 25.37
      Parks & recreation 16.56
      Governmental administration 289.13
      Interest on general debt 307.48

State debt & cash, 2006 ($ per capita)
Debt $6,875.68
Cash/security holdings. $10,722.64

Federal government grants to state & local government, 2005 (x $1,000)
Total. $5,438,708
by Federal agency
   Defense 56,863
   Education 366,474
   Energy 47,693
   Environmental Protection Agency 34,677
   Health & Human Services. 3,377,354
   Homeland Security. 25,469
   Housing & Urban Development 582,537
   Justice 63,904
   Labor 99,750
   Transportation 507,432
   Veterans Affairs. 7,247

Crime & Law Enforcement

Crime, 2006 (rates per 100,000 residents)
Property crimes 87,764
   Burglary 14,694
   Larceny 62,680
   Motor vehicle theft 10,390
   Property crime rate. 2,504.1
Violent crimes. 9,841
   Murder 108
   Forcible rape. 636
   Robbery. 4,241
   Aggravated assault 4,856
   Violent crime rate 280.8
Hate crimes. 180

Fraud and identity theft, 2006
Fraud complaints. 4,695
   rate per 100,000 residents 134.0
Identity theft complaints 2,305
   rate per 100,000 residents 65.8

Law enforcement agencies, 2006
Total agencies. 101
Total employees 9,703
   Officers 7,875
   Civilians 1,828

Prisoners, probation, and parole, 2006
Total prisoners. 20,566
   percent change, 12/31/05 to 12/31/06 . . . . 5.8%
   in private facilities .0%
   in local jails . . . . NA
Sentenced to more than one year 13,746
   rate per 100,000 residents 392
Adults on probation 54,511
Adults on parole. 2,567

Prisoner demographics, June 30, 2005 (rate per 100,000 residents)
Male 1,030
Female 85
White 211
Black. 2,532
Hispanic 1,401

Arrests, 2006

Total 96,616
  Persons under 18 years of age 15,185

Persons under sentence of death, 1/1/07

Total 8
  White 3
  Black 3
  Hispanic 2

State's highest court

Name . . . . Supreme Court
Number of members 7
Length of term . . . . 8 years
Intermediate appeals court? . . . . .yes

Labor & Income

Civilian labor force, 2006 (x 1,000)

Total 1,858
  Men 982
  Women 876
  Persons 16-19 years 93
  White 1,592
  Black 182
  Hispanic 186

Civilian labor force as a percent of civilian non-institutional population, 2006

Total 67.9%
  Men 75.1
  Women 61.4
  Persons 16-19 years 48.3
  White 67.3
  Black 72.2
  Hispanic 70.1

Employment, 2006 (x 1,000)

Total 1,778
  Men 939
  Women 839
  Persons 16-19 years 80
  White 1,531
  Black 167
  Hispanic 170

Unemployment rate, 2006

Total 4.3%
  Men 4.4
  Women 4.2
  Persons 16-19 years 14.5
  White 3.8
  Black 8.1
  Hispanic 8.2

Full-time/part-time labor force, 2003 (x 1,000)

Full-time labor force, employed 1,346
Part-time labor force, employed 358
Unemployed, looking for
  Full-time work 80
  Part-time work 20
Mean duration of unemployment (weeks) 20.3
  Median 12.4

Labor unions, 2006

Membership (x 1,000) 247
  percent of employed 15.6%

Experienced civilian labor force by private industry, 2006

Total 1,425,174
  Natural resources & mining 5,868
  Construction 67,157
  Manufacturing 193,714
  Trade, transportation & utilities 307,295
  Information 37,730
  Finance 144,325
  Professional & business 205,869
  Education & health 272,738
  Leisure & hospitality 132,475
  Other 57,761

Experienced civilian labor force by occupation, May 2006

Management 90,860
Business & financial 84,160
Legal 12,760
Sales 179,080
Office & admin. support 294,610
Computers & math 46,360
Architecture & engineering 35,060
Arts & entertainment 20,600
Education 122,480
Social services 30,590
Health care practitioner & technical 89,820
Health care support 51,510
Maintenance & repair 55,590
Construction 55,190
Transportation & moving 94,760
Production 118,720
Farming, fishing & forestry 1,040

Hours and earnings of production workers on manufacturing payrolls, 2006

Average weekly hours .42.2
Average hourly earnings $19.78
Average weekly earnings $834.72

Income and poverty, 2006

Median household income $63,422
Personal income, per capita (current $) . . . $49,852
  in constant (2000) dollars $43,518
Persons below poverty level 8.3%

Average annual pay

2006 . . . . $54,814
  increase from 2005 . . . . 3.5%

Federal individual income tax returns, 2005

Returns filed 1,681,956
Adjusted gross income ($1,000) . . . $132,285,344
Total tax liability ($1,000) $22,513,429

Charitable contributions, 2004

Number of contributions 666.9
Total amount ($ mil) $2,690.0

Economy, Business, Industry & Agriculture

Fortune 500 companies, 2007.............. 11
Bankruptcy cases filed, FY 2007..........5,572

Patents and trademarks issued, 2007
Patents..............................1,632
Trademarks...........................1,040

Business firm ownership, 2002
Women-owned........................82,118
   Sales ($ mil) $12,216
Black-owned.........................10,309
   Sales ($ mil) $723
Hispanic-owned......................9,408
   Sales ($ mil) $1,277
Asian-owned 7,170
   Sales ($ mil) $1,863
Amer. Indian/Alaska Native-owned 1,216
   Sales ($ mil) $148
Hawaiian/Pacific Islander-owned 167
   Sales ($ mil) $78

Gross domestic product, 2006 ($ mil)
Total gross domestic product $204,134
   Agriculture, forestry, fishing and
      hunting 353
   Mining............................. 96
   Utilities...................... 3,400
   Construction 6,726
   Manufacturing, durable goods....... 15,223
   Manufacturing, non-durable goods 8,324
   Wholesale trade....................11,363
   Retail trade.......................11,725
   Transportation & warehousing 3,185
   Information 7,747
   Finance & insurance................ 33,640
   Real estate, rental & leasing 28,502
   Professional and technical services.... 15,369
   Educational services....................3,102
   Health care and social assistance...... 15,295
   Accommodation/food services.........3,672
   Other services, except government 4,039
   Government 18,347

Establishments, payroll, employees & receipts, by major industry group, 2005

Total.............................. 93,561
   Annual payroll ($1,000)......... $75,605,605
   Paid employees 1,529,827
Forestry, fishing & agriculture.............. 81
   Annual payroll ($1,000)................. NA
   Paid employees .... NA
Mining.............................. 74
   Annual payroll ($1,000)............ $61,986
   Paid employees 911
   Receipts, 2002 ($1,000) $208,448

Utilities 140
   Annual payroll ($1,000)..........$1,000,312
   Paid employees 9,947
   Receipts, 2002 ($1,000) ....NA
Construction...........................9,811
   Annual payroll ($1,000)..........$3,385,312
   Paid employees 62,362
   Receipts, 2002 ($1,000) $13,697,394
Manufacturing........................5,037
   Annual payroll ($1,000)..........$9,766,644
   Paid employees 185,259
   Receipts, 2002 ($1,000) $45,053,345
Wholesale trade.......................4,671
   Annual payroll ($1,000).......... $4,873,666
   Paid employees 80,024
   Receipts, 2002 ($1,000) $86,932,049
Retail trade........................ 13,928
   Annual payroll ($1,000)...........$5,083,890
   Paid employees 198,459
   Receipts, 2002 ($1,000) $41,952,682
Transportation & warehousing............1,694
   Annual payroll ($1,000)..........$1,436,078
   Paid employees 38,157
   Receipts, 2002 ($1,000) $4,014,398
Information..........................1,778
   Annual payroll ($1,000)..........$2,828,910
   Paid employees 41,534
   Receipts, 2002 ($1,000) ....NA
Finance & insurance....................6,145
   Annual payroll ($1,000)..........$15,586,173
   Paid employees 133,285
   Receipts, 2002 ($1,000) ....NA
Professional, scientific & technical 10,224
   Annual payroll ($1,000)..........$6,581,420
   Paid employees 99,651
   Receipts, 2002 ($1,000) $14,610,345
Education 1,182
   Annual payroll ($1,000).......... $2,088,379
   Paid employees 58,583
   Receipts, 2002 ($1,000) $525,061
Health care & social assistance 9,651
   Annual payroll ($1,000)..........$9,326,294
   Paid employees 238,784
   Receipts, 2002 ($1,000) $18,512,454
Arts and entertainment 1,678
   Annual payroll ($1,000).......... $605,839
   Paid employees 23,250
   Receipts, 2002 ($1,000) $1,984,816
Real estate........................... 3,544
   Annual payroll ($1,000)..........$1,081,044
   Paid employees 22,750
   Receipts, 2002 ($1,000) $4,603,410
Accommodation & food service............7,579
   Annual payroll ($1,000)..........$2,374,481
   Paid employees 128,777
   Receipts, 2002 ($1,000) $6,681,803

Exports, 2006

Value of exported goods ($ mil) $12,238
   Manufactured $10,988
   Non-manufactured................... $695

Foreign direct investment in US affiliates, 2004

Property, plants & equipment ($ mil) $12,517
Employment (x 1,000)....................102.7

Agriculture, 2006

Number of farms 4,200
Farm acreage (x 1,000) 360
   Acres per farm......................... 86
Farm marketings and income ($ mil)
Total...............................$523.6
   Crops............................. $372.3
   Livestock...........................$151.3
Net farm income $182.8

Principal commodities, in order by marketing receipts, 2005

   Greenhouse/nursery, Dairy products, Chicken eggs, Aquaculture, Tobacco

Federal economic activity in state

Expenditures, 2005 ($ mil)
   Total............................ $30,774
      Per capita $8,790.67
   Defense $9,523
   Non-defense....................... $21,250
Defense department, 2006 ($ mil)
   Payroll............................ $758
   Contract awards $7,781
   Grants $64
Homeland security grants ($1,000)
   2006............................$13,521
   2007............................$10,479

FDIC-insured financial institutions, 2005

Number 57
Assets ($ billion) $63.3
Deposits ($ billion) $47.0

Fishing, 2006

Catch (x 1,000 lbs).....................11,746
Value ($1,000)....................... $36,892

Mining, 2006 ($ mil)

Total non-fuel mineral production $169
Percent of U.S. 0.26%

Communication, Energy & Transportation

Communication

Households with computers, 2003........ 69.2%
Households with internet access, 2003 .... 62.9%
High-speed internet providers 25
Total high-speed internet lines........1,251,241
   Residential 844,344
   Business.......................... 406,897
Wireless phone customers, 12/2006 2,705,023

FCC-licensed stations (as of January 1, 2008)

TV stations 13
FM radio stations.......................... 61
AM radio stations 40

Energy

Energy consumption, 2004
   Total (trillion Btu)................. 924
   Per capita (million Btu) 264.4
By source of production (trillion Btu)
   Coal 44
   Natural gas....................... 163
   Petroleum........................ 471
   Nuclear electric power 173
   Hydroelectric power 5
By end-use sector (trillion Btu)
   Residential 304
   Commercial 211
   Industrial 123
   Transportation 285
Electric energy, 2005
   Primary source of electricity......... Nuclear
   Net generation (billion kWh) 33.5
      percent from renewable sources....... 3.7%
   Net summer capability (million kW) 8.0
   CO_2 emitted from generation 11.5
Natural gas utilities, 2005
   Customers (x 1,000) 531
   Sales (trillion Btu)................... 104
   Revenues ($ mil) $1,182
Nuclear plants, 2007 2
Total CO_2 emitted (million metric tons).....42.4
Energy spending, 2004 ($ mil) $10,595
   per capita $3,032
   Price per million Btu $15.86

Transportation, 2006

Public road & street mileage 21,249
   Urban.............................15,081
   Rural 6,168
   Interstate........................... 346
Vehicle miles of travel (millions) 31,743
   per capita 9,080.4
Total motor vehicle registrations.......1,052,143
   Automobiles.......................1,999,809
   Trucks 1,041,651
   Motorcycles 64,959
Licensed drivers 2,805,124
   19 years & under 104,155
Deaths from motor vehicle accidents 301
Gasoline consumed (x 1,000 gallons) 1,566,875
   per capita 448.2

Commuting Statistics, 2006

Average commute time (min) 24.1
   Drove to work alone 79.7%
   Carpooled......................... 8.4%
   Public transit 4.1%
   Walk to work 3.0%
   Work from home..................... 3.5%

State Summary

Capital city . . . . Dover
Governor. . . . . Ruth Ann Minner
Legislative Hall
Dover, DE 19902
302-577-3210
Admitted as a state 1787
Area (square miles) 2,489
Population, 2007 (estimate). 864,764
Largest city . . . . Wilmington
Population, 2006. 72,826
Personal income per capita, 2006
(in current dollars) $39,022
Gross domestic product, 2006 ($ mil) $60,361

Leading industries by payroll, 2005

Finance & Insurance, Health care/Social assistance, Professional/Scientific/Technical

**Leading agricultural commodities
by receipts, 2005**

Broilers, Corn, Greenhouse/nursery, Soybeans,
Dairy products

Geography & Environment

Total area (square miles). 2,489
land 1,954
water 536
Federally-owned land, 2004 (acres) 25,874
percent. 2.0%
Highest point . . . . Ebright Road
elevation (feet) 442
Lowest point . . . . Atlantic Ocean
elevation (feet) . . . . sea level
General coastline (miles) 28
Tidal shoreline (miles) 381
Cropland, 2003 (x 1,000 acres) 458
Forest land, 2003 (x 1,000 acres). 341
Capital city . . . . Dover
Population 2000 .32,135
Population 2006 .34,745
Largest city . . . . Wilmington
Population 2000 72,664
Population 2006 72,826

Number of cities with over 100,000 population
1990 0
2000 0
2006 0

State park and recreation areas, 2005
Area (x 1,000 acres). 24
Number of visitors (x 1,000) 4,557
Revenues ($1,000) $11,366
percent of operating expenditures. 39.3%

National forest system land, 2007
Acres 0

Demographics & Population Characteristics

Population
1980 594,338
1990 666,168
2000 783,600
2006 853,476
Male. 414,244
Female. 439,232
Living in group quarters, 2006. 24,915
percent of total. 2.9%
2007 (estimate). 864,764
persons per square mile of land 442.6
2008 (projected). 865,705
2010 (projected) 884,342
2020 (projected) 963,209
2030 (projected). 1,012,658

**Population of Core-Based Statistical Areas
(formerly Metropolitan Areas), x 1,000**

	CBSA	Non-CBSA
1990	666	0
2000	784	0
2006	853	0

Change in population, 2000-2007
Number 81,164
percent. 10.4%
Natural increase (births minus deaths) 31,157
Net internal migration 39,573
Net international migration 13,924

Persons by age, 2006
Under 5 years 56,692
5 to 17 years 146,674
18 years and over .650,110
65 years and over .114,574
85 years and over .14,553
Median age 37.5

Persons by age, 2010 (projected)
Under 5 years 58,179
18 and over 682,134
65 and over 124,972
Median age 39.4

Race, 2006
One Race
White. 636,116
Black or African American 178,201
Asian 23,680
American Indian/Alaska Native. 3,454
Hawaiian Native/Pacific Islander. 498
Two or more races. .11,527

Persons of Hispanic origin, 2006
Total Hispanic or Latino 53,836
Mexican. 24,631
Puerto Rican 14,715
Cuban 890

Persons of Asian origin, 2006

Total Asian 24,413
Asian Indian. 11,424
Chinese 5,067
Filipino 2,878
Japanese 949
Korean. 1,797
Vietnamese. 1,314

Marital status, 2006

Population 15 years & over 685,569
Never married 214,894
Married. 351,482
Separated 16,713
Widowed. 44,350
Divorced 74,843

Language spoken at home, 2006

Population 5 years and older. 796,385
English only 700,255
Spanish 51,762
French 6,214
German 4,391
Chinese 4,490

Households & families, 2006

Households. 320,110
with persons under 18 years 107,624
with persons over 65 years. 78,042
persons per household 2.59
Families. 213,565
persons per family. 3.15
Married couples. 157,209
Female householder,
no husband present. 41,147
One-person households 86,967

Nativity, 2006

Number of residents born in state 400,956
percent of population 47.0%

Immigration & naturalization, 2006

Legal permanent residents admitted. 2,265
Persons naturalized 1,187
Non-immigrant admissions 34,511

Vital Statistics and Health

Marriages

2004 5,095
2005 5,015
2006 5,153

Divorces

2004 3,108
2005 3,251
2006 3,849

Health risks, 2006

Percent of adults who are:
Smokers. 21.7%
Overweight (BMI > 25). 63.8%
Obese (BMI > 30). 26.0%

Births

2005 11,643
Birthrate (per 1,000). 13.8
White. 8,192
Black 2,912
Hispanic 1,652
Asian/Pacific Islander 501
Amer. Indian/Alaska Native. 38
Low birth weight (2,500g or less). 9.5%
Cesarian births 30.0%
Preterm births 14.0%
To unmarried mothers. 44.3%
Twin births (per 1,000) 35.6
Triplets or higher order (per 100,000). . . .180.5
2006 (preliminary). 11,988
rate per 1,000 . . . . .14.0

Deaths

2004
All causes 7,143
rate per 100,000. . . . . .823.3
Heart disease 2,015
rate per 100,000. . . . . 232.3
Malignant neoplasms 1,827
rate per 100,000. . . . . .207.4
Cerebrovascular disease. 350
rate per 100,000. . . . . .40.6
Chronic lower respiratory disease 345
rate per 100,000. . . . . .39.8
Diabetes. 210
rate per 100,000. . . . . .24.1
2005 (preliminary). 7,472
rate per 100,000. . . . . 830.5
2006 (provisional) 7,111

Infant deaths

2004 98
rate per 1,000 . . . . .8.6
2005 (provisional) 88
rate per 1,000 . . . . .7.6

Exercise routines, 2005

None. 23.3%
Moderate or greater. 45.2%
Vigorous 24.9%

Abortions, 2004

Total performed in state. 4,588
rate per 1,000 women age 15-44. 26
% obtained by out-of-state residents 28.9%

Physicians, 2005

Total. 2,090
rate per 100,000 persons 248

Community hospitals, 2005

Number of hospitals 6
Beds (x 1,000). 2.0
Patients admitted (x 1,000) 104
Average daily census (x 1,000) 1.7
Average cost per day $1,715
Outpatient visits (x 1 mil) 1.9

Disability status of population, 2006
5 to 15 years 6.7%
16 to 64 years 12.6%
65 years and over 38.8%

Education

Educational attainment, 2006
Population over 25 years 566,312
    Less than 9th grade. 4.8%
    High school graduate or more 85.5%
    College graduate or more. 27.0%
    Graduate or professional degree. 10.5%

Public school enrollment, 2005-06
Total. 120,937
    Pre-kindergarten through grade 8. 84,639
    Grades 9 through 12 36,298

Graduating public high school seniors, 2004-05
Diplomas (incl. GED and others) 7,102

SAT scores, 2007
Average critical reading score 497
Average writing score 486
Average math score 496
Percent of graduates taking test 72%

Public school teachers, 2006-07 (estimate)
Total (x 1,000) 8.0
    Elementary 4.0
    Secondary 4.1
Average salary $54,680
    Elementary $54,855
    Secondary $54,509

State receipts & expenditures for public schools, 2006-07 (estimate)
Revenue receipts ($ mil) $1,676
Expenditures
Total ($ mil) $1,898
    Per capita $1,800
    Per pupil $13,380

NAEP proficiency scores, 2007

	Reading		Math	
	Basic	Proficient	Basic	Proficient
Grade 4	72.6%	33.8%	86.9%	40.0%
Grade 8	77.2%	30.5%	74.3%	31.3%

Higher education enrollment, fall 2005
Total. 12,930
    Full-time men 2,758
    Full-time women 4,009
    Part-time men 2,118
    Part-time women. 4,045

Minority enrollment in institutions of higher education, 2005
Black, non-Hispanic 10,169
Hispanic 1,818
Asian/Pacific Islander 1,500
American Indian/Alaska Native. 154

Institutions of higher education, 2005-06
Total. 10
    Public. 5
    Private 5

Earned degrees conferred, 2004-05
Associate's. 1,262
Bachelor's 5,247
Master's 2,031
First-professional. 335
Doctor's 234

Public Libraries, 2006
Number of libraries. 21
Number of outlets 35
Annual visits per capita 5.0
Circulation per capita. 6.9

State & local financial support for higher education, FY 2006
Full-time equivalent enrollment (x 1,000) 31.3
Appropriations per FTE. $6,632

Social Insurance & Welfare Programs

Social Security benefits & beneficiaries, 2005
Beneficiaries (x 1,000) 152
    Retired & dependents. 108
    Survivors. 19
    Disabled & dependents. 26
Annual benefit payments ($ mil) $1,725
    Retired & dependents. $1,173
    Survivors. $268
    Disabled & dependents. $284
Average monthly benefit
    Retired & dependents. $1,054
    Disabled & dependents. $984
    Widowed. $1,040

Medicare, July 2005
Enrollment (x 1,000). 128
Payments ($ mil) $1,021

Medicaid, 2004
Beneficiaries (x 1,000). 158
Payments ($ mil) $1,269

State Children's Health Insurance Program, 2006
Enrollment (x 1,000). 10.8
Expenditures ($ mil) $10.8

Persons without health insurance, 2006
Number (x 1,000). 105
    percent. 12.2%
Number of children (x 1,000) 24
    percent of children 11.7%

Health care expenditures, 2004
Total expenditures. $5,226
    per capita $6,306

4   Delaware

Federal and state public aid

State unemployment insurance, 2006
Recipients, first payments (x 1,000) 23
Total payments ($ mil) $97
Average weekly benefit $251
Temporary Assistance for Needy Families, 2006
Recipients (x 1,000) 142.3
Families (x 1,000) 64.4
Supplemental Security Income, 2005
Recipients (x 1,000) 13.7
Payments ($ mil) $65.7
Food Stamp Program, 2006
Avg monthly participants (x 1,000) 65.7
Total benefits ($ mil) $70.2

Housing & Construction

Housing units
Total 2005 (estimate) 374,872
Total 2006 (estimate) 382,828
Seasonal or recreational use, 2006 31,435
Owner-occupied, 2006 238,194
    Median home value $227,100
    Homeowner vacancy rate 2.6%
Renter-occupied, 2006 81,916
    Median rent $830
    Rental vacancy rate 12.2%
Home ownership rate, 2005 . . . . 75.8%
Home ownership rate, 2006 . . . . 76.8%

New privately-owned housing units
Number authorized, 2006 (x 1,000) 6.5
    Value ($ mil) $785.5
Started 2005 (x 1,000, estimate) 5.9
Started 2006 (x 1,000, estimate) 5.7

Existing home sales
2005 (x 1,000) 19.3
2006 (x 1,000) 17.8

Government & Elections

State officials 2008
Governor . . . . Ruth Ann Minner
            Democratic, term expires 1/09
Lieutenant Governor . . . . John Carney
Secretary of State . . . . Harriet Smith Windsor
Attorney General . . . . .Joseph Biden III
Chief Justice .Myron Steele

Governorship
Minimum age 30
Length of term . . . . 4 years
Consecutive terms permitted 2
Who succeeds . . . . Lieutenant Governor

Local governments by type, 2002
Total 339
    County 3
    Municipal 57
    Township 0
    School District 19
    Special District 260

State legislature
Name . . . . General Assembly
Upper chamber . . . . .Senate
    Number of members 21
    Length of term . . . . 4 years
    Party in majority, 2008 . . . . .Democratic
Lower chamber . . . . .House of Representatives
    Number of members 41
    Length of term . . . . 2 years
    Party in majority, 2008 . . . . Republican

Federal representation, 2008 (110th Congress)
Senator . . . . Joseph R. Biden Jr
    Party . . . . .Democratic
    Year term expires 2009
Senator . . . . Thomas Carper
    Party . . . . .Democratic
    Year term expires 2013
Representatives, total 1
    Democrats 0
    Republicans 1

Voters in November 2006 election (estimate)
Total 275,407
    Male 123,761
    Female 151,647
    White 219,948
    Black 47,276
    Hispanic 2,290
    Asian 5,417

Presidential election, 2004
Total Popular Vote 375,190
    Kerry 200,152
    Bush 171,660
Total Electoral Votes 3

Votes cast for US Senators
2004
Total vote (x 1,000) . . . . NA
Leading party . . . . NA
Percent for leading party . . . . NA
2006
Total vote (x 1,000) 243
Leading party . . . . .Democratic
Percent for leading party 70.2%

Votes cast for US Representatives
2004
Total vote (x 1,000) 356
    Democratic 106
    Republican 246
Leading party . . . . Republican
Percent for leading party 69.1%
2006
Total vote (x 1,000) 252
    Democratic 98
    Republican 144
Leading party . . . . Republican
Percent for leading party 57.2%

State government employment, 2006
Full-time equivalent employees 25,614
Payroll ($ mil) $98.8

Local government employment, 2006
Full-time equivalent employees 23,874
Payroll ($ mil) $92.7

Women holding public office, 2008
US Congress............................... 0
Statewide elected office...................... 1
State legislature 19

Black public officials, 2002
Total..................................... 29
    US and state legislatures 4
    City/county/regional offices 18
    Judicial/law enforcement.................. 0
    Education/school boards 7

Hispanic public officials, 2006
Total...................................... 2
    State executives & legislators 1
    City/county/regional offices 1
    Judicial/law enforcement.................. 0
    Education/school boards 0

Governmental Finance

State government revenues, 2006
Total revenue (x $1,000)............$6,839,982
   per capita $8,021.12
General revenue (x $1,000) $5,954,563
   Intergovernmental 1,218,950
   Taxes 2,860,749
     general sales............................ 0
     individual income tax 1,018,633
     corporate income tax 295,577
   Current charges................... 807,693
   Miscellaneous 1,067,171

State government expenditure, 2006
Total expenditure (x $1,000).........$6,519,932
   per capita $7,645.80
General expenditure (x $1,000) $6,019,481
   per capita, total.................. $7,058.93
    Education 2,414.19
    Public welfare 1,472.32
    Health 391.50
    Hospitals..........................71.20
    Highways 590.88
    Police protection...................118.81
    Corrections 287.00
    Natural resources 98.75
    Parks & recreation 75.13
    Governmental administration.......569.02
    Interest on general debt............ 202.84

State debt & cash, 2006 ($ per capita)
Debt $4,930.38
Cash/security holdings..............$13,563.53

Federal government grants to state & local government, 2005 (x $1,000)
Total............................$1,265,225
by Federal agency
   Defense 22,524
   Education 119,362
   Energy............................11,104
   Environmental Protection Agency 27,974
   Health & Human Services........... 661,022
   Homeland Security....................3,478
   Housing & Urban Development....... 95,821
   Justice 26,491
   Labor 23,423
   Transportation 140,992
   Veterans Affairs....................19,478

Crime & Law Enforcement

Crime, 2006 (rates per 100,000 residents)
Property crimes 29,171
   Burglary 6,189
   Larceny 20,166
   Motor vehicle theft 2,816
   Property crime rate................. 3,417.9
Violent crimes..........................5,817
   Murder 42
   Forcible rape........................ 400
   Robbery...........................1,735
   Aggravated assault 3,640
   Violent crime rate 681.6
Hate crimes.............................. 72

Fraud and identity theft, 2006
Fraud complaints......................1,119
   rate per 100,000 residents 131.1
Identity theft complaints 569
   rate per 100,000 residents 66.7

Law enforcement agencies, 2006
Total agencies........................... 53
Total employees 3,085
   Officers 2,247
   Civilians 838

Prisoners, probation, and parole, 2006
Total prisoners........................7,206
   percent change, 12/31/05 to 12/31/06 .... 3.4%
   in private facilities 0%
   in local jails .... NA
Sentenced to more than one year 4,195
   rate per 100,000 residents 488
Adults on probation 16,958
Adults on parole......................... 544

Prisoner demographics, June 30, 2005 (rate per 100,000 residents)
Male.................................1,547
Female 128
White................................ 396
Black................................2,517
Hispanic 683

Arrests, 2006

Total 39,832
  Persons under 18 years of age 7,448

Persons under sentence of death, 1/1/07

Total 18
  White 8
  Black 7
  Hispanic 3

State's highest court

Name . . . . .Supreme Court
Number of members 5
Length of term . . . . 12 years
Intermediate appeals court? . . . . no

Labor & Income

Civilian labor force, 2006 (x 1,000)

Total 448
  Men 233
  Women 215
  Persons 16-19 years 23
  White 337
  Black 91
  Hispanic 29

Civilian labor force as a percent of civilian non-institutional population, 2006

Total 67.1%
  Men 73.3
  Women 61.5
  Persons 16-19 years .48.3
  White 66.0
  Black 71.4
  Hispanic 74.4

Employment, 2006 (x 1,000)

Total 432
  Men 224
  Women 208
  Persons 16-19 years 21
  White 327
  Black 86
  Hispanic 28

Unemployment rate, 2006

Total 3.5%
  Men 3.8
  Women 3.2
  Persons 16-19 years .8.9
  White 3.0
  Black 5.5
  Hispanic 4.0

Full-time/part-time labor force, 2003 (x 1,000)

Full-time labor force, employed 338
Part-time labor force, employed 61
Unemployed, looking for
  Full-time work 16
  Part-time work 2
Mean duration of unemployment (weeks) 16.3
  Median 10.3

Labor unions, 2006

Membership (x 1,000) 43
  percent of employed 10.8%

Experienced civilian labor force by private industry, 2006

Total 364,323
  Natural resources & mining 1,406
  Construction 29,247
  Manufacturing 33,245
  Trade, transportation & utilities 81,169
  Information 6,710
  Finance 44,031
  Professional & business 62,212
  Education & health 52,085
  Leisure & hospitality 40,927
  Other 13,291

Experienced civilian labor force by occupation, May 2006

Management 18,600
Business & financial 22,750
Legal 4,580
Sales 47,700
Office & admin. support 78,670
Computers & math 12,560
Architecture & engineering . . . . NA
Arts & entertainment 4,660
Education 21,980
Social services 6,490
Health care practitioner & technical 22,030
Health care support 9,770
Maintenance & repair 16,350
Construction 23,570
Transportation & moving 25,390
Production 26,730
Farming, fishing & forestry 930

Hours and earnings of production workers on manufacturing payrolls, 2006

Average weekly hours .39.9
Average hourly earnings $18.13
Average weekly earnings $723.39

Income and poverty, 2006

Median household income $52,833
Personal income, per capita (current $) . . . $39,022
  in constant (2000) dollars $34,064
Persons below poverty level 11.1%

Average annual pay

2006 . . . . $46,285
  increase from 2005 . . . . 3.7%

Federal individual income tax returns, 2005

Returns filed 402,938
Adjusted gross income ($1,000) $23,183,670
Total tax liability ($1,000) $3,086,150

Charitable contributions, 2004

Number of contributions 129.0
Total amount ($ mil) $483.3

Economy, Business, Industry & Agriculture

Fortune 500 companies, 2007 1
Bankruptcy cases filed, FY 2007 1,897

Patents and trademarks issued, 2007
Patents 353
Trademarks 23,801

Business firm ownership, 2002
Women-owned 15,344
   Sales ($ mil) $2,021
Black-owned 4,258
   Sales ($ mil) $215
Hispanic-owned 879
   Sales ($ mil) $137
Asian-owned 1,895
   Sales ($ mil) $618
Amer. Indian/Alaska Native-owned 333
   Sales ($ mil) . . . . NA
Hawaiian/Pacific Islander-owned 17
   Sales ($ mil) . . . . NA

Gross domestic product, 2006 ($ mil)
Total gross domestic product $60,361
   Agriculture, forestry, fishing and
      hunting 398
   Mining . . . . NA
   Utilities 1,070
   Construction . . . . NA
   Manufacturing, durable goods 1,262
   Manufacturing, non-durable goods 3,292
   Wholesale trade 2,264
   Retail trade 2,504
   Transportation & warehousing 717
   Information 1,075
   Finance & insurance 19,818
   Real estate, rental & leasing 7,124
   Professional and technical services 3,545
   Educational services 328
   Health care and social assistance 3,083
   Accommodation/food services 919
   Other services, except government 1,034
   Government 5,168

Establishments, payroll, employees & receipts, by major industry group, 2005
Total 25,319
   Annual payroll ($1,000) $16,875,311
   Paid employees 392,840
Forestry, fishing & agriculture 44
   Annual payroll ($1,000) . . . . NA
   Paid employees . . . . NA
Mining 28
   Annual payroll ($1,000) . . . . NA
   Paid employees . . . . NA
   Receipts, 2002 ($1,000) $13,860

Utilities 47
   Annual payroll ($1,000) $205,557
   Paid employees 2,593
   Receipts, 2002 ($1,000) . . . . .NA
Construction 2,709
   Annual payroll ($1,000) $1,003,802
   Paid employees 23,925
   Receipts, 2002 ($1,000) $3,882,206
Manufacturing 652
   Annual payroll ($1,000) $1,661,304
   Paid employees 35,624
   Receipts, 2002 ($1,000) $16,417,927
Wholesale trade 999
   Annual payroll ($1,000) $1,399,099
   Paid employees 20,040
   Receipts, 2002 ($1,000) $17,292,794
Retail trade 3,842
   Annual payroll ($1,000) $1,298,046
   Paid employees 54,524
   Receipts, 2002 ($1,000) $10,912,971
Transportation & warehousing 740
   Annual payroll ($1,000) $475,939
   Paid employees 15,054
   Receipts, 2002 ($1,000) $749,566
Information 407
   Annual payroll ($1,000) $499,397
   Paid employees .9,510
   Receipts, 2002 ($1,000) . . . . .NA
Finance & insurance 2,082
   Annual payroll ($1,000) $2,896,158
   Paid employees 40,894
   Receipts, 2002 ($1,000) . . . . .NA
Professional, scientific & technical 2,460
   Annual payroll ($1,000) $1,895,569
   Paid employees 27,202
   Receipts, 2002 ($1,000) $3,135,436
Education 263
   Annual payroll ($1,000) $198,567
   Paid employees 6,426
   Receipts, 2002 ($1,000) $106,335
Health care & social assistance 2,242
   Annual payroll ($1,000) $2,085,645
   Paid employees 51,444
   Receipts, 2002 ($1,000) $3,792,091
Arts and entertainment 376
   Annual payroll ($1,000) $166,810
   Paid employees .6,702
   Receipts, 2002 ($1,000) $675,763
Real estate 1,215
   Annual payroll ($1,000) $243,068
   Paid employees 6,680
   Receipts, 2002 ($1,000) $6,948,051
Accommodation & food service 1,722
   Annual payroll ($1,000) $483,637
   Paid employees 31,094
   Receipts, 2002 ($1,000) $1,231,595

Exports, 2006
Value of exported goods ($ mil) $3,890
   Manufactured $3,593
   Non-manufactured.................... $39

Foreign direct investment in US affiliates, 2004
Property, plants & equipment ($ mil) $4,508
Employment (x 1,000)....................26.1

Agriculture, 2006
Number of farms 2,300
Farm acreage (x 1,000) 515
   Acres per farm 224
Farm marketings and income ($ mil)
Total.................................$969.1
   Crops.............................$182.7
   Livestock........................... $786.4
Net farm income $388.2

Principal commodities, in order by
   marketing receipts, 2005
  Broilers, Corn, Greenhouse/nursery, Soybeans,
           Dairy products

Federal economic activity in state
Expenditures, 2005 ($ mil)
   Total............................ $5,495
     Per capita $6,527.79
   Defense $588
   Non-defense........................ $4,907
Defense department, 2006 ($ mil)
   Payroll.............................$420
   Contract awards $125
   Grants $21
Homeland security grants ($1,000)
   2006............................. $10,296
   2007 .... $6,684

FDIC-insured financial institutions, 2005
Number 34
Assets ($ billion) $559.6
Deposits ($ billion) $255.1

Fishing, 2006
Catch (x 1,000 lbs) 4,380
Value ($1,000)........................ $5,692

Mining, 2006 ($ mil)
Total non-fuel mineral production $22
Percent of U.S. 0.03%

Communication, Energy & Transportation

Communication
Households with computers, 2003........ 59.5%
Households with internet access, 2003 .... 53.2%
High-speed internet providers 22
Total high-speed internet lines......... 273,734
   Residential 169,563
   Business.......................... 104,171
Wireless phone customers, 12/2006 682,636

FCC-licensed stations (as of January 1, 2008)
TV stations 3
FM radio stations.......................... 21
AM radio stations 10

Energy
Energy consumption, 2004
   Total (trillion Btu)..................... 305
   Per capita (million Btu) 367.8
By source of production (trillion Btu)
   Coal 54
   Natural gas............................ 50
   Petroleum............................ 141
   Nuclear electric power 0
   Hydroelectric power...................... 0
By end-use sector (trillion Btu)
   Residential 69
   Commercial 57
   Industrial 109
   Transportation 69
Electric energy, 2005
   Primary source of electricity........... Coal
   Net generation (billion kWh) 8.1
     percent from renewable sources........ NA
   Net summer capability (million kW) 3.4
   CO_2 emitted from generation 6.8
Natural gas utilities, 2005
   Customers (x 1,000) 149
   Sales (trillion Btu)...................... 35
   Revenues ($ mil) $262
Nuclear plants, 2007 0
Total CO_2 emitted (million metric tons)......17.2
Energy spending, 2004 ($ mil) $2,541
   per capita $3,066
   Price per million Btu $13.64

Transportation, 2006
Public road & street mileage 6,179
   Urban............................. 2,920
   Rural 3,259
   Interstate............................ 41
Vehicle miles of travel (millions) 9,442
   per capita 11,072.5
Total motor vehicle registrations........813,188
   Automobiles....................... 432,509
   Trucks 378,512
   Motorcycles 22,786
Licensed drivers 619,877
   19 years & under 29,672
Deaths from motor vehicle accidents 148
Gasoline consumed (x 1,000 gallons) 458,885
   per capita 538.1

Commuting Statistics, 2006
Average commute time (min) 23.6
   Drove to work alone 80.8%
   Carpooled............................ 9.4%
   Public transit 2.8%
   Walk to work 2.7%
   Work from home...................... 2.6%

District of Columbia 1

District Summary

City....................... Washington, DC
Mayor......................... Adrian Fenty

John A. Wilson Building
1350 Pennsylvania Ave NW
Washington, DC 20004
202-727-1000

Founded............................... 1790
Area (square miles) 68
Population, 2007 (estimate)............ 588,292
Largest city .... Washington, DC
  Population, 2006................... 581,530
Personal income per capita, 2006
  (in current dollars) $55,755
Gross domestic product, 2006 ($ mil) $87,664

Leading industries by payroll, 2005

Professional/Scientific/Technical, Health care/
Social assistance, Information

**Leading agricultural commodities
by receipts, 2005**

NA

Geography & Environment

Total area (square miles).................... 68
  land 61
  water 7
Federally-owned land, 2004 (acres) 9,631
  percent............................ 24.7%
Highest point .... Tenleytown
  elevation (feet) 410
Lowest point .... Potomac River
  elevation (feet) .... sea level
General coastline (miles) 0
Tidal shoreline (miles) 0
Cropland, 2003 (x 1,000 acres) .... NA
Forest land, 2003 (x 1,000 acres)............ NA
Capital city .... Washington, DC
  Population 2000 572,059
  Population 2006 581,530
Largest city .... Washington, DC
  Population 2000 572,059
  Population 2006 581,530

Number of cities with over 100,000 population
1990 1
2000 1
2006 1

State park and recreation areas, 2005
Area (x 1,000 acres)...................... NA
Number of visitors (x 1,000) .... NA
Revenues ($1,000) .... NA
  percent of operating expenditures........ NA

National forest system land, 2007
Acres 0

Demographics & Population Characteristics

Population
1980 638,333
1990 606,900
2000 572,059
2006 581,530
  Male............................. 272,664
  Female........................... 308,866
Living in group quarters, 2006.......... 35,225
  percent of total...................... 6.1%
2007 (estimate).................... 588,292
  persons per square mile of land 9,644.1
2008 (projected)................... 538,487
2010 (projected)....................529,785
2020 (projected)................... 480,540
2030 (projected)....................433,414

**Population of Core-Based Statistical Areas
(formerly Metropolitan Areas), x 1,000**

	CBSA	Non-CBSA
1990	607	0
2000	572	0
2006	582	0

Change in population, 2000-2007
Number 16,233
  percent............................. 2.8%
Natural increase (births minus deaths) 15,596
Net internal migration ....-43,431
Net international migration 25,783

Persons by age, 2006
Under 5 years 34,948
5 to 17 years 79,933
18 years and over 466,649
65 years and over 71,331
85 years and over 10,770
  Median age 35.0

Persons by age, 2010 (projected)
Under 5 years 41,737
18 and over 415,721
65 and over 61,036
  Median age 33.8

Race, 2006
One Race
  White............................ 223,033
  Black or African American 328,566
  Asian 18,871
  American Indian/Alaska Native.........2,161
  Hawaiian Native/Pacific Islander......... 511
Two or more races...................... 8,388

Persons of Hispanic origin, 2006
Total Hispanic or Latino 47,775
  Mexican............................ 6,127
  Puerto Rican 2,744
  Cuban 2,346

Persons of Asian origin, 2006

Total Asian 19,827
   Asian Indian. 5,430
   Chinese 5,261
   Filipino 2,652
   Japanese 382
   Korean. 1,327
   Vietnamese. 2,083

Marital status, 2006

Population 15 years & over 486,138
   Never married 262,607
   Married. 147,417
   Separated 16,392
   Widowed. 32,502
   Divorced 43,612

Language spoken at home, 2006

Population 5 years and older. 546,550
   English only 462,774
   Spanish 45,023
   French 9,791
   German. 2,325
   Chinese 3,022

Households & families, 2006

Households. 250,456
   with persons under 18 years 53,390
   with persons over 65 years. 54,239
   persons per household 2.18
Families. 108,759
   persons per family. 3.24
Married couples. 55,871
Female householder,
   no husband present. 43,487
One-person households 118,150

Nativity, 2006

Number of residents born in district. ... 232,943
   percent of population 40.1%

Immigration & naturalization, 2006

Legal permanent residents admitted 3,775
Persons naturalized 1,089
Non-immigrant admissions 312,585

Vital Statistics and Health

Marriages

2004 2,925
2005 2,344
2006 2,276

Divorces

2004 1,043
2005 1,145
2006 1,254

Health risks, 2006

Percent of adults who are:
   Smokers. 17.9%
   Overweight (BMI > 25). 54.6%
   Obese (BMI > 30). 22.5%

Births

2005 7,971
   Birthrate (per 1,000). 14.5
   White. 2,401
   Black 5,368
   Hispanic 1,111
   Asian/Pacific Islander 195
   Amer. Indian/Alaska Native 7
   Low birth weight (2,500g or less) 11.2%
   Cesarian births 30.5%
   Preterm births. 15.9%
   To unmarried mothers. 56.0%
   Twin births (per 1,000) 34.5
   Triplets or higher order (per 100,000). .... NA
2006 (preliminary). 8,529
   rate per 1,000 ....14.7

Deaths

2004
All causes 5,454
   rate per 100,000. ....974.0
Heart disease 1,544
   rate per 100,000. ....274.9
Malignant neoplasms 1,152
   rate per 100,000. ....207.0
Cerebrovascular disease. 218
   rate per 100,000. ....38.9
Chronic lower respiratory disease 165
   rate per 100,000. ....29.5
Diabetes. 224
   rate per 100,000. ....40.2
*2005 (preliminary). *5,483
   rate per 100,000. ....971.4
2006 (provisional) 5,177

Infant deaths

2004 95
   rate per 1,000 ....12.0
2005 (provisional) 74
   rate per 1,000 ....10.2

Exercise routines, 2005

None. 22.5%
Moderate or greater. 53.1%
Vigorous 31.5%

Abortions, 2004

Total performed in district 2,401
   rate per 1,000 women age 15-44. 18
   % obtained by non-DC residents 52.6%

Physicians, 2005

Total. 4,483
   rate per 100,000 persons 770

Community hospitals, 2005

Number of hospitals 11
Beds (x 1,000). 3.5
Patients admitted (x 1,000) 141
Average daily census (x 1,000) 2.7
Average cost per day $1,910
Outpatient visits (x 1 mil) 1.6

Disability status of population, 2006

5 to 15 years 7.9%
16 to 64 years 11.1%
65 years and over 37.6%

Education

Educational attainment, 2006

Population over 25 years 395,630
  Less than 9th grade..................... 6.3%
  High school graduate or more 84.3%
  College graduate or more............. 45.9%
  Graduate or professional degree....... 25.4%

Public school enrollment, 2005-06

Total.................................76,876
  Pre-kindergarten through grade 8......52,186
  Grades 9 through 12..................18,769

Graduating public high school seniors, 2004-05

Diplomas (incl. GED and others) 3,098

SAT scores, 2007

Average critical reading score............. 478
Average writing score..................... 471
Average math score...................... 462
Percent of graduates taking test 78%

Public school teachers, 2006-07 (estimate)

Total (x 1,000) 5.5
  Elementary...........................3.6
  Secondary...........................1.9
Average salary $59,000
  Elementary....................... $59,000
  Secondary....................... $59,000

District receipts & expenditures for public schools, 2006-07 (estimate)

Revenue receipts ($ mil) $882
Expenditures
Total ($ mil) $1,228
  Per capita $1,685
  Per pupil $18,260

NAEP proficiency scores, 2007

	Reading		Math	
	Basic	Proficient	Basic	Proficient
Grade 4	38.7%	13.8%	49.3%	13.5%
Grade 8	47.9%	12.1%	34.1%	8.0%

Higher education enrollment, fall 2005

Total................................. 99,302
  Full-time men 24,900
  Full-time women..................... 34,850
  Part-time men 15,586
  Part-time women..................... 23,966

Minority enrollment in institutions of higher education, 2005

Black, non-Hispanic 36,007
Hispanic 4,922
Asian/Pacific Islander 6,643
American Indian/Alaska Native........... 436

Institutions of higher education, 2005-06

Total................................... 15
  Public................................ 2
  Private................................ 13

Earned degrees conferred, 2004-05

Associate's............................. 447
Bachelor's 9,199
Master's 8,536
First-professional...................... 2,950
Doctor's................................ 613

Public Libraries, 2006

Number of libraries......................... 1
Number of outlets 24
Annual visits per capita 3.4
Circulation per capita....................2.1

State & local financial support for higher education, FY 2006

Full-time equivalent enrollment (x 1,000)..... NA
Appropriations per FTE................... NA

Social Insurance & Welfare Programs

Social Security benefits & beneficiaries, 2005

Beneficiaries (x 1,000) 71
  Retired & dependents.................... 49
  Survivors............................ 11
  Disabled & dependents................. 11
Annual benefit payments ($ mil) $674
  Retired & dependents.................$446
  Survivors.........................$116
  Disabled & dependents...............$112
Average monthly benefit
  Retired & dependents.................$862
  Disabled & dependents................$857
  Widowed..........................$806

Medicare, July 2005

Enrollment (x 1,000)..................... 73
Payments ($ mil) $558

Medicaid, 2004

Beneficiaries (x 1,000) 157
Payments ($ mil) $800

State Children's Health Insurance Program, 2006

Enrollment (x 1,000)....................6.3
Expenditures ($ mil)....................$9.9

Persons without health insurance, 2006

Number (x 1,000)........................ 66
  percent.......................... 11.6%
Number of children (x 1,000) 10
  percent of children 8.7%

Health care expenditures, 2004

Total expenditures..................... $4,809
  per capita $8,295

Federal and state public aid

State unemployment insurance, 2006
Recipients, first payments (x 1,000) 16
Total payments ($ mil) $93
Average weekly benefit $283
Temporary Assistance for Needy Families, 2006
Recipients (x 1,000) 380.5
Families (x 1,000) 157.1
Supplemental Security Income, 2005
Recipients (x 1,000) 21.2
Payments ($ mil) $113.4
Food Stamp Program, 2006
Avg monthly participants (x 1,000) 89.2
Total benefits ($ mil) $104.2

Housing & Construction

Housing units
Total 2005 (estimate) 280,044
Total 2006 (estimate) 282,894
Seasonal or recreational use, 2006 860
Owner-occupied, 2006 114,586
   Median home value $437,700
   Homeowner vacancy rate 3.7%
Renter-occupied, 2006 135,870
   Median rent $914
   Rental vacancy rate 7.8%
Home ownership rate, 2005 . . . . 45.8%
Home ownership rate, 2006 . . . . 45.9%

New privately-owned housing units
Number authorized, 2006 (x 1,000) 2.1
   Value ($ mil) $299.5
Started 2005 (x 1,000, estimate) 0.4
Started 2006 (x 1,000, estimate) 0.4

Existing home sales
2005 (x 1,000) 12.1
2006 (x 1,000) 10.1

Government & Elections

District officials 2008
Mayor . . . . Adrian Fenty
     Democratic, term expires 1/11
Secretary of the District . . . . Stephanie Scott
Attorney General . . . . Linda Singer
Chief Justice . . . . Eric Washington

Mayorship
Minimum age . . . . not specified
Length of term . . . . 4 years
Consecutive terms permitted . . . . .yes
Who succeeds . . . . NA

Local governments by type, 2002
Total 2
   County 0
   Municipal 1
   Township 0
   School District 0
   Special District 1

District legislature
Name . . . . .DC Council
   Number of members 13
      (1 each from 8 wards, 5 at-large)
   Length of term . . 2 years for at-large members,
   4 years for ward-elected members
   Party in majority, 2008 . . . . .Democratic

Federal representation, 2008 (110th Congress)
Delegate . . . . Eleanor Holmes Norton
Shadow Representative . . . . Mike Panetta
Shadow Senator . . . . Paul Strauss
   Party . . . . Democratic
   Year term expires 2009
Shadow Senator . . . . .Michael Brown
   Party . . . . Democratic
   Year term expires 2013
Representatives, total 1
   Democrats 1
   Republicans 0

Voters in November 2006 election (estimate)
Total 186,634
   Male 78,911
   Female 107,723
   White 80,727
   Black 98,324
   Hispanic 1,447
   Asian 5,375

Presidential election, 2004
Total Popular Vote 227,586
   Kerry 202,970
   Bush 21,256
Total Electoral Votes 3

Votes cast for US Senators
2004
Total vote (x 1,000) . . . . NA
Leading party . . . . NA
Percent for leading party . . . . NA
2006
Total vote (x 1,000) . . . . NA
Leading party .Democratic
Percent for leading party . . . . NA

Votes cast for US Representatives
2004
Total vote (x 1,000) 195
   Democratic 169
   Republican . . . . NA
Leading party .Democratic
Percent for leading party 86.3%
2006
Total vote (x 1,000) 115
   Democratic 112
   Republican 0
Leading party .Democratic
Percent for leading party 97.3%

District government employment, 2006

Full-time equivalent employees 46,611
Payroll ($ mil) $226.3

State government employment, 2006

Full-time equivalent employees . . . . NA
Payroll ($ mil) . . . . NA

Women holding public office, 2008

US Congress 1
Statewide elected office. . . . . NA
State legislature . . . . NA

Black public officials, 2002

Total. 174
    US and state legislatures 2
    City/county/regional offices 169
    Judicial/law enforcement. 0
    Education/school boards 3

Hispanic public officials, 2006

Total. 1
    State executives & legislators 0
    City/county/regional offices 0
    Judicial/law enforcement. 0
    Education/school boards 1

Governmental Finance

District government revenues, 2004-05

Total revenue (x $1,000) $9,326,744
    Revenue per capita $16,023.98
General Revenue (x $1,000) $13,924.89
    Intergovernmental 2,814,574
    Taxes 4,297,242
        general sales 846,909
        individual income tax 1,147,940
        corporate income tax 199,310
    Current charges. 388,842
    Miscellaneous 604,313

District government expenditures, 2004-05

Total expenditure (x $1,000) $9,099,596
    per capita. *$15,633.73*
Direct General Expend. (x $1,000). . . . $7,244,305
    Expenditures per capita:
    Total. $12,446.21
    Education $2,295.85
    Public welfare. $2,902.42
    Health $782.84
    Hospitals. $449.51
    Highways $122.45
    Police protection $711.96
    Corrections. $282.41
    Natural resources $0.00
    Parks & recreation. $221.35
    Governmental administration $302.01
    Interest on general debt $479.32

District debt & cash, 2004-05 ($ per capita)

Debt $10,324.75
Cash/security holdings. $11,671.78

Federal government grants to district government, 2005 (x $1,000)

Total. $4,325,307
by Federal agency
    Defense 40,359
    Education 408,011
    Energy 29,452
    Environmental Protection Agency 73,527
    Health & Human Services. 1,682,697
    Homeland Security. 12,040
    Housing & Urban Development 309,662
    Justice 201,903
    Labor 162,032
    Transportation 492,762
    Veterans Affairs. 915

Crime & Law Enforcement

Crime, 2006 (rates per 100,000 residents)

Property crimes 27,063
    Burglary 3,835
    Larceny 15,907
    Motor vehicle theft 7,321
    Property crime rate. 4,653.8
Violent crimes. 8,772
    Murder 169
    Forcible rape. 185
    Robbery. 3,829
    Aggravated assault 4,589
    Violent crime rate 1,508.4
Hate crimes. 64

Fraud and identity theft, 2006

Fraud complaints. .1,139
    rate per 100,000 residents 195.9
Identity theft complaints 765
    rate per 100,000 residents 131.5

Law enforcement agencies, 2006

Total agencies. 3
Total employees 4,880
    Officers 4,196
    Civilians 684

Prisoners, probation, and parole, 2006

Total prisoners. . . . . NA
                    (District of Columbia
                    prisoners have been housed
                    in federal jails since 2001)
Sentenced to more than one year . . . . NA
    rate per 100,000 residents . . . . NA
Adults on probation 6,883
Adults on parole. 5,387

Prisoner demographics, June 30, 2005 (rate per 100,000 residents)

Male 1,202
Female 145
White. 56
Black. 1,065
Hispanic 267

Arrests, 2006

Total 5,681
  Persons under 18 years of age 437

Persons under sentence of death, 1/1/07

Total 0
  White 0
  Black 0
  Hispanic 0

District's highest court

Name . . . . Court of Appeals
Number of members 9
Length of term . . . . 15 years
Intermediate appeals court? . . . . no

Labor & Income

Civilian labor force, 2006 (x 1,000)

Total 291
  Men 141
  Women 151
  Persons 16-19 years 6
  White 144
  Black 131
  Hispanic 30

Civilian labor force as a percent of civilian non-institutional population, 2006

Total 67.1%
  Men 70.4
  Women 64.3
  Persons 16-19 years 27.4
  White 78.4
  Black 57.2
  Hispanic 81.1

Employment, 2006 (x 1,000)

Total 274
  Men 133
  Women 141
  Persons 16-19 years 4
  White 140
  Black 118
  Hispanic 28

Unemployment rate, 2006

Total 5.8%
  Men 5.4
  Women 6.2
  Persons 16-19 years 29.8
  White 2.3
  Black 10.0
  Hispanic 4.2

Full-time/part-time labor force, 2003 (x 1,000)

Full-time labor force, employed 254
Part-time labor force, employed 27
Unemployed, looking for
  Full-time work 19
  Part-time work 2
Mean duration of unemployment (weeks) 26.8
  Median 14.1

Labor unions, 2006

Membership (x 1,000) 25
  percent of employed 10.3%

Experienced civilian labor force by private industry, 2006

Total 440,694
  Natural resources & mining . . . . NA
  Construction 12,575
  Manufacturing 1,755
  Trade, transportation & utilities 27,524
  Information 22,219
  Finance 26,950
  Professional & business 144,118
  Education & health 86,729
  Leisure & hospitality 54,126
  Other 56,496

Experienced civilian labor force by occupation, May 2006

Management 64,190
Business & financial 69,820
Legal 37,520
Sales 28,110
Office & admin. support 104,340
Computers & math .33,710
Architecture & engineering 11,820
Arts & entertainment 27,950
Education 32,220
Social services 8,420
Health care practitioner & technical 25,040
Health care support 7,420
Maintenance & repair 8,100
Construction 11,510
Transportation & moving 13,290
Production 6,770
Farming, fishing & forestry . . . . NA

Hours and earnings of production workers on manufacturing payrolls, 2006

Average weekly hours 38.7
Average hourly earnings $17.30
Average weekly earnings $669.51

Income and poverty, 2006

Median household income $51,847
Personal income, per capita (current $) . . . $55,755
  in constant (2000) dollars $48,671
Persons below poverty level 19.6%

Average annual pay

2006 . . . .$70,151
  increase from 2005 . . . . 5.2%

Federal individual income tax returns, 2005

Returns filed 282,474
Adjusted gross income ($1,000) $19,712,600
Total tax liability ($1,000) $3,164,453

Charitable contributions, 2004

Number of contributions 104.3
Total amount ($ mil) $663.5

Economy, Business, Industry & Agriculture

Fortune 500 companies, 2007 2
Bankruptcy cases filed, FY 2007 670

Patents and trademarks issued, 2007

Patents 67
Trademarks 782

Business firm ownership, 2002

Women-owned 15,675
  Sales ($ mil) $2,403
Black-owned 12,198
  Sales ($ mil) $1,568
Hispanic-owned 2,169
  Sales ($ mil) $548
Asian-owned 2,411
  Sales ($ mil) $1,003
Amer. Indian/Alaska Native-owned 217
  Sales ($ mil) $42
Hawaiian/Pacific Islander-owned 48
  Sales ($ mil) . . . . NA

Gross domestic product, 2006 ($ mil)

Total gross domestic product $87,664
  Agriculture, forestry, fishing and
    hunting 1
  Mining . . . . NA
  Utilities 831
  Construction . . . . NA
  Manufacturing, durable goods 70
  Manufacturing, non-durable goods 111
  Wholesale trade 765
  Retail trade 1,152
  Transportation & warehousing 415
  Information 5,130
  Finance & insurance 4,033
  Real estate, rental & leasing 9,616
  Professional and technical services 17,975
  Educational services 2,321
  Health care and social assistance 3,746
  Accommodation/food services 2,503
  Other services, except government 5,315
  Government 28,932

Establishments, payroll, employees & receipts, by major industry group, 2005

Total 20,481
  Annual payroll ($1,000) $25,152,741
  Paid employees .439,610
Forestry, fishing & agriculture 1
  Annual payroll ($1,000) . . . . NA
  Paid employees . . . . NA
Mining 5
  Annual payroll ($1,000) . . . . NA
  Paid employees . . . . NA
  Receipts, 2002 ($1,000) . . . . .NA

Utilities 33
  Annual payroll ($1,000) $97,551
  Paid employees .1,164
  Receipts, 2002 ($1,000) . . . . .NA
Construction 376
  Annual payroll ($1,000) $305,069
  Paid employees .5,798
  Receipts, 2002 ($1,000) $1,380,689
Manufacturing 142
  Annual payroll ($1,000) $75,172
  Paid employees .1,739
  Receipts, 2002 ($1,000) $246,237
Wholesale trade 448
  Annual payroll ($1,000) $358,165
  Paid employees .6,431
  Receipts, 2002 ($1,000) $2,971,507
Retail trade 1,913
  Annual payroll ($1,000) $481,963
  Paid employees 20,049
  Receipts, 2002 ($1,000) $3,061,401
Transportation & warehousing 188
  Annual payroll ($1,000) $124,179
  Paid employees .3,597
  Receipts, 2002 ($1,000) $905,612
Information 723
  Annual payroll ($1,000) $2,037,549
  Paid employees 24,445
  Receipts, 2002 ($1,000) . . . . .NA
Finance & insurance 954
  Annual payroll ($1,000) $1,786,209
  Paid employees 18,548
  Receipts, 2002 ($1,000) . . . . .NA
Professional, scientific & technical 4,579
  Annual payroll ($1,000) $8,206,840
  Paid employees 88,139
  Receipts, 2002 ($1,000) $17,967,225
Education 492
  Annual payroll ($1,000) $1,769,081
  Paid employees 47,816
  Receipts, 2002 ($1,000) $715,092
Health care & social assistance 2,092
  Annual payroll ($1,000) $2,865,767
  Paid employees 60,171
  Receipts, 2002 ($1,000) $5,772,971
Arts and entertainment 285
  Annual payroll ($1,000) $250,532
  Paid employees .6,081
  Receipts, 2002 ($1,000) $620,458
Real estate 985
  Annual payroll ($1,000) $600,351
  Paid employees .9,697
  Receipts, 2002 ($1,000) . . . . .NA
Accommodation & food service 1,956
  Annual payroll ($1,000) $1,161,792
  Paid employees 49,273
  Receipts, 2002 ($1,000) $2,943,078

Exports, 2006
Value of exported goods ($ mil) $1,040
   Manufactured $947
   Non-manufactured.................... $50

Foreign direct investment in US affiliates, 2004
Property, plants & equipment ($ mil) $4,518
Employment (x 1,000)....................15.7

Agriculture, 2006
Number of farms .... NA
Farm acreage (x 1,000) .... NA
   Acres per farm......................... NA
Farm marketings and income ($ mil)
Total.................................... NA
   Crops................................. NA
   Livestock............................. NA
Net farm income .... NA

Principal commodities, in order by marketing receipts, 2005
NA

Federal economic activity in district
Expenditures, 2005 ($ mil)
   Total................................$37,859
      Per capita $65,044.63
   Defense $5,219
   Non-defense...................... $32,640
Defense department, 2006 ($ mil)
   Payroll............................ $2,561
   Contract awards $4,067
   Grants $38
Homeland security grants ($1,000)
   2006............................ $54,015
   2007............................ $71,985

FDIC-insured financial institutions, 2005
Number 7
Assets ($ billion) $1.2
Deposits ($ billion) $1.0

Fishing, 2006
Catch (x 1,000 lbs)....................... NA
Value ($1,000)........................... NA

Mining, 2006 ($ mil)
Total non-fuel mineral production .... NA
Percent of U.S. .... NA

Communication, Energy & Transportation

Communication
Households with computers, 2003........64.3%
Households with internet access, 2003 ....56.8%
High-speed internet providers 28
Total high-speed internet lines......... 268,008
   Residential 144,289
   Business.......................... 123,719
Wireless phone customers, 12/2006 880,077

FCC-licensed stations (as of January 1, 2008)
TV stations 8
FM radio stations......................... 14
AM radio stations 7

Energy
Energy consumption, 2004
   Total (trillion Btu).................... 190
   Per capita (million Btu) 328.3
By source of production (trillion Btu)
   Coal 1
   Natural gas 33
   Petroleum 31
   Nuclear electric power 0
   Hydroelectric power 0
By end-use sector (trillion Btu)
   Residential 38
   Commercial 121
   Industrial 4
   Transportation 27
Electric energy, 2005
   Primary source of electricity....... Petroleum
   Net generation (billion kWh) 0.2
      percent from renewable sources........ NA
   Net summer capability (million kW) 0.8
   CO_2 emitted from generation 0.2
Natural gas utilities, 2005
   Customers (x 1,000) 151
   Sales (trillion Btu)..................... 32
   Revenues ($ mil) $247
Nuclear plants, 2007 0
Total CO_2 emitted (million metric tons).......3.9
Energy spending, 2004 ($ mil) $1,729
   per capita $2,983
   Price per million Btu $16.87

Transportation, 2006
Public road & street mileage 1,500
   Urban............................. 1,500
   Rural 0
   Interstate............................ 13
Vehicle miles of travel (millions) 3,623
   per capita 6,188.3
Total motor vehicle registrations........219,105
   Automobiles.......................168,916
   Trucks 47,300
   Motorcycles 1,372
Licensed drivers.........................357,569
   19 years & under 8,300
Deaths from motor vehicle accidents 37
Gasoline consumed (x 1,000 gallons) 131,963
   per capita 225.4

Commuting Statistics, 2006
Average commute time (min) 29.2
   Drove to work alone 35.4%
   Carpooled........................... 6.3%
   Public transit 39.0%
   Walk to work 11.8%
   Work from home 4.0%

State Summary

Capital city . . . . Tallahassee
Governor . . . . Charlie Crist

PL 05 The Capitol
400 S Monroe St
Tallahassee, FL 32399
850-488-4441

Admitted as a state 1845
Area (square miles) 65,755
Population, 2007 (estimate). 18,251,243
Largest city . . . . Jacksonville
   Population, 2006. 794,555
Personal income per capita, 2006
   (in current dollars) $35,798
Gross domestic product, 2006 ($ mil) . . . $713,505

Leading industries by payroll, 2005

   Health care/Social assistance, Retail trade, Professional/Scientific/Technical

**Leading agricultural commodities
by receipts, 2005**

   Greenhouse/nursery, Oranges, Tomatoes, Cattle and calves, Cane for sugar

Geography & Environment

Total area (square miles). 65,755
   land 53,927
   water 11,828
Federally-owned land, 2004 (acres) 2,858,782
   percent 8.2%
Highest point .Britton Hill
   elevation (feet) 345
Lowest point . . . . .Atlantic Ocean
   elevation (feet) . . . . sea level
General coastline (miles) 1,650
Tidal shoreline (miles) 8,426
Cropland, 2003 (x 1,000 acres) 2,873
Forest land, 2003 (x 1,000 acres). 12,733
Capital city . . . . Tallahassee
   Population 2000 150,624
   Population 2006 .159,012
Largest city . . . . Jacksonville
   Population 2000 735,617
   Population 2006 794,555

Number of cities with over 100,000 population
1990 9
2000 13
2006 17

State park and recreation areas, 2005
Area (x 1,000 acres). 696
Number of visitors (x 1,000) 18,202
Revenues ($1,000) $38,179
   percent of operating expenditures. 49.3%

National forest system land, 2007
Acres 1,160,324

Demographics & Population Characteristics

Population
1980 9,746,324
1990 12,937,926
2000 15,982,824
2006 18,089,888
   Male. 8,884,135
   Female 9,205,753
Living in group quarters, 2006. 412,218
   percent of total. 2.3%
2007 (estimate). 18,251,243
   persons per square mile of land 338.4
2008 (projected). 18,533,980
2010 (projected) 19,251,691
2020 (projected) 23,406,525
2030 (projected) 28,685,769

**Population of Core-Based Statistical Areas
(formerly Metropolitan Areas), x 1,000**

	CBSA	Non-CBSA
1990	12,645	293
2000	15,620	363
2006	17,692	398

Change in population, 2000-2007
Number 2,268,419
   percent. 14.2%
Natural increase (births minus deaths) 360,972
Net internal migration 1,286,175
Net international migration 674,271

Persons by age, 2006
Under 5 years 1,122,849
5 to 17 years 2,898,706
18 years and over 14,068,333
65 years and over 3,037,704
85 years and over 462,545
   Median age 39.6

Persons by age, 2010 (projected)
Under 5 years 1,195,168
18 and over 15,165,568
65 and over 3,418,697
   Median age 41.9

Race, 2006
One Race
   White. 14,503,894
   Black or African American 2,864,423
   Asian 397,143
   American Indian/Alaska Native. 80,369
   Hawaiian Native/Pacific Islander. 15,401
Two or more races. 228,658

Persons of Hispanic origin, 2006
Total Hispanic or Latino 3,642,989
   Mexican. 563,110
   Puerto Rican 682,432
   Cuban 1,054,371

Persons of Asian origin, 2006

Total Asian 393,427
  Asian Indian. 117,195
  Chinese .... .65,743
  Filipino 74,826
  Japanese 13,391
  Korean........................... 24,980
  Vietnamese......................... 54,204

Marital status, 2006

Population 15 years & over 14,789,121
  Never married 4,040,890
  Married........................ .7,859,691
  Separated 355,551
  Widowed........................... 1,110,370
  Divorced 1,778,170

Language spoken at home, 2006

Population 5 years and older........ 16,972,259
  English only 12,610,892
  Spanish 3,171,968
  French 413,484
  German......................... 83,489
  Chinese 47,727

Households & families, 2006

Households......................... .7,106,042
  with persons under 18 years 2,163,568
  with persons over 65 years......... .2,088,025
  persons per household 2.49
Families........................... .4,632,974
  persons per family.................... .3.05
Married couples..................... .3,452,127
Female householder,
  no husband present................. 861,237
One-person households 1,991,903

Nativity, 2006

Number of residents born in state 6,079,334
  percent of population................. 33.6%

Immigration & naturalization, 2006

Legal permanent residents admitted.... 155,996
Persons naturalized 90,846
Non-immigrant admissions 4,942,206

Vital Statistics and Health

Marriages

2004 156,370
2005 157,976
2006 155,505

Divorces

2004 82,662
2005 .... .81,285
2006 .... .87,789

Health risks, 2006

Percent of adults who are:
  Smokers. 21.0%
  Overweight (BMI > 25)................ 59.6%
  Obese (BMI > 30).................... 23.1%

Births

2005 226,240
  Birthrate (per 1,000)................... .12.7
  White........................... .161,478
  Black 56,503
  Hispanic .... .63,756
  Asian/Pacific Islander 7,565
  Amer. Indian/Alaska Native............ 694
  Low birth weight (2,500g or less)....... 8.7%
  Cesarian births 34.9%
  Preterm births 13.8%
  To unmarried mothers............... .42.8%
  Twin births (per 1,000) 29.9
  Triplets or higher order (per 100,000)....142.7
2006 (preliminary).................. 236,882
  rate per 1,000 .... .13.1

Deaths

2004
All causes 169,008
  rate per 100,000 ....763.6
Heart disease 47,160
  rate per 100,000 .... 204.9
Malignant neoplasms 39,840
  rate per 100,000 ....179.9
Cerebrovascular disease.................9,715
  rate per 100,000 .... .42.0
Chronic lower respiratory disease 8,971
  rate per 100,000 .... .38.8
Diabetes............................. 4,809
  rate per 100,000 .... .21.6
2005 (preliminary)...................170,787
  rate per 100,000 ....749.4
2006 (provisional) 170,007

Infant deaths

2004 1,537
  rate per 1,000 .... 7.1
2005 (provisional) 1,633
  rate per 1,000 .... 7.2

Exercise routines, 2005

None................................26.9%
Moderate or greater.....................45.3%
Vigorous 24.6%

Abortions, 2004

Total performed in state.................91,710
  rate per 1,000 women age 15-44.......... 27
  % obtained by out-of-state residents ...... NA

Physicians, 2005

Total................................ .43,314
  rate per 100,000 persons 244

Community hospitals, 2005

Number of hospitals 205
Beds (x 1,000)........................... .51.2
Patients admitted (x 1,000) 2,371
Average daily census (x 1,000) 33.9
Average cost per day $1,497
Outpatient visits (x 1 mil) 22.3

Disability status of population, 2006

5 to 15 years 6.1%
16 to 64 years 12.4%
65 years and over 38.4%

Education

Educational attainment, 2006

Population over 25 years 12,460,438
 Less than 9th grade. 5.7%
 High school graduate or more 84.5%
 College graduate or more. 25.3%
 Graduate or professional degree. 8.9%

Public school enrollment, 2005-06

Total. 2,675,024
 Pre-kindergarten through grade 8. . . 1,873,395
 Grades 9 through 12 801,629

Graduating public high school seniors, 2004-05

Diplomas (incl. GED and others) 141,868

SAT scores, 2007

Average critical reading score 497
Average writing score 479
Average math score 496
Percent of graduates taking test 65%

Public school teachers, 2006-07 (estimate)

Total (x 1,000) 167.8
 Elementary 84.8
 Secondary 83.0
Average salary $45,308
 Elementary $45,308
 Secondary $45,308

State receipts & expenditures for public schools, 2006-07 (estimate)

Revenue receipts ($ mil) $27,556
Expenditures
Total ($ mil) $29,798
 Per capita $1,251
 Per pupil $8,928

NAEP proficiency scores, 2007

	Reading		Math	
	Basic	Proficient	Basic	Proficient
Grade 4	70.4%	34.0%	86.2%	40.3%
Grade 8	71.5%	28.0%	68.1%	27.4%

Higher education enrollment, fall 2005

Total. 223,663
 Full-time men 68,522
 Full-time women 91,021
 Part-time men 28,062
 Part-time women. 36,058

Minority enrollment in institutions of higher education, 2005

Black, non-Hispanic 155,357
Hispanic 159,572
Asian/Pacific Islander 29,827
American Indian/Alaska Native. 3,476

Institutions of higher education, 2005-06

Total. 169
 Public. 40
 Private 129

Earned degrees conferred, 2004-05

Associate's. 60,441
Bachelor's 65,839
Master's 24,014
First-professional. 3,716
Doctor's 3,064

Public Libraries, 2006

Number of libraries. 78
Number of outlets 531
Annual visits per capita 4.1
Circulation per capita. 5.5

State & local financial support for higher education, FY 2006

Full-time equivalent enrollment (x 1,000) 532.7
Appropriations per FTE. $5,641

Social Insurance & Welfare Programs

Social Security benefits & beneficiaries, 2005

Beneficiaries (x 1,000) 3,424
 Retired & dependents. 2,526
 Survivors. 401
 Disabled & dependents. 497
Annual benefit payments ($ mil) $36,891
 Retired & dependents. $26,145
 Survivors. $5,567
 Disabled & dependents. $5,178
Average monthly benefit
 Retired & dependents. $999
 Disabled & dependents. $943
 Widowed. $993

Medicare, July 2005

Enrollment (x 1,000). 3,046
Payments ($ mil) $21,363

Medicaid, 2004

Beneficiaries (x 1,000). 2,952
Payments ($ mil) $12,834

State Children's Health Insurance Program, 2006

Enrollment (x 1,000). 303.6
Expenditures ($ mil) $300.6

Persons without health insurance, 2006

Number (x 1,000). 3,828
 percent. 21.2%
Number of children (x 1,000) 771
 percent of children 18.9%

Health care expenditures, 2004

Total expenditures. $95,223
 per capita $5,483

Federal and state public aid

State unemployment insurance, 2006
Recipients, first payments (x 1,000) 240
Total payments ($ mil) $719
Average weekly benefit $231
Temporary Assistance for Needy Families, 2006
Recipients (x 1,000) 995.8
Families (x 1,000) 610.3
Supplemental Security Income, 2005
Recipients (x 1,000) 422.5
Payments ($ mil) $2,031.4
Food Stamp Program, 2006
Avg monthly participants (x 1,000) 1,417.7
Total benefits ($ mil) $1,684.3

Housing & Construction

Housing units
Total 2005 (estimate) 8,260,451
Total 2006 (estimate) 8,533,419
Seasonal or recreational use, 2006 655,647
Owner-occupied, 2006 4,994,101
    Median home value $230,600
    Homeowner vacancy rate 4.3%
Renter-occupied, 2006 2,111,941
    Median rent $872
    Rental vacancy rate 10.7%
Home ownership rate, 2005 . . . . 72.4%
Home ownership rate, 2006 . . . . 72.4%

New privately-owned housing units
Number authorized, 2006 (x 1,000) 203.2
    Value ($ mil) $35,716.3
Started 2005 (x 1,000, estimate) 173.6
Started 2006 (x 1,000, estimate) 165.4

Existing home sales
2005 (x 1,000) 547.1
2006 (x 1,000) 395.3

Government & Elections

State officials 2008
Governor . . . . .Charlie Crist
           Republican, term expires 1/11
Lieutenant Governor . . . . .Jeff Kottkamp
Secretary of State . . . . .Kurt Browning
Attorney General . . . . Bill McCollum
Chief Justice . . . . R. Fred Lewis

Governorship
Minimum age 30
Length of term . . . . 4 years
Consecutive terms permitted 2
Who succeeds . . . . Lieutenant Governor

Local governments by type, 2002
Total 1,191
    County 66
    Municipal 404
    Township 0
    School District 95
    Special District 626

State legislature
Name . . . . Legislature
Upper chamber . . . . .Senate
    Number of members 40
    Length of term . . . . 4 years
    Party in majority, 2008 . . . . Republican
Lower chamber . . . . .House of Representatives
    Number of members 120
    Length of term . . . . 2 years
    Party in majority, 2008 . . . . Republican

Federal representation, 2008 (110th Congress)
Senator . . . . Mel Martinez
    Party . . . . Republican
    Year term expires 2011
Senator . . . . Bill Nelson
    Party . . . . .Democratic
    Year term expires 2013
Representatives, total 25
    Democrats 9
    Republicans 16

Voters in November 2006 election (estimate)
Total 5,342,902
    Male 2,538,342
    Female 2,804,559
    White 4,592,237
    Black 642,099
    Hispanic 270,298
    Asian 44,294

Presidential election, 2004
Total Popular Vote 7,609,810
    Kerry 3,583,544
    Bush 3,964,522
Total Electoral Votes 27

Votes cast for US Senators
2004
Total vote (x 1,000) 7,430
Leading party . . . . Republican
Percent for leading party 49.4%
2006
Total vote (x 1,000) 4,794
Leading party . . . . Democratic
Percent for leading party 60.3%

Votes cast for US Representatives
2004
Total vote (x 1,000) 5,627
    Democratic 2,212
    Republican 3,319
Leading party . . . . Republican
Percent for leading party 59.0%
2006
Total vote (x 1,000) 3,852
    Democratic 1,600
    Republican 2,183
Leading party . . . . Republican
Percent for leading party 56.7%

State government employment, 2006
Full-time equivalent employees 191,215
Payroll ($ mil) $657.0

Local government employment, 2006
Full-time equivalent employees 676,044
Payroll ($ mil) $2,365.5

Women holding public office, 2008
US Congress............................... 5
Statewide elected office...................... 1
State legislature 37

Black public officials, 2002
Total.................................... 275
   US and state legislatures 25
   City/county/regional offices 180
   Judicial/law enforcement................. 43
   Education/school boards................. 27

Hispanic public officials, 2006
Total.................................... 121
   State executives & legislators 19
   City/county/regional offices 70
   Judicial/law enforcement................. 26
   Education/school boards.................. 6

Governmental Finance

State government revenues, 2006
Total revenue (x $1,000)...........$83,807,587
   per capita $4,641.15
General revenue (x $1,000) $66,623,771
   Intergovernmental 20,003,686
   Taxes 37,201,518
     general sales...................20,788,525
     individual income tax 0
     corporate income tax 2,405,863
   Current charges..................4,734,440
   Miscellaneous 4,684,127

State government expenditure, 2006
Total expenditure (x $1,000).......$76,142,277
   per capita $4,216.65
General expenditure (x $1,000) $67,862,305
   per capita, total.................. *$3,758.12*
     Education...................... 1,145.98
     Public welfare 943.10
     Health 165.85
     Hospitals..........................33.33
     Highways 353.94
     Police protection.................... 26.07
     Corrections 135.17
     Natural resources 101.58
     Parks & recreation 8.74
     Governmental administration.......145.33
     Interest on general debt..............62.83

State debt & cash, 2006 ($ per capita)
Debt $1,429.42
Cash/security holdings..............$9,492.24

Federal government grants to state & local government, 2005 (x $1,000)
Total........................... $22,552,241
by Federal agency
   Defense 94,808
   Education 1,851,893
   Energy........................... 49,222
   Environmental Protection Agency ... 104,705
   Health & Human Services. 11,699,806
   Homeland Security................2,420,195
   Housing & Urban Development.....1,294,327
   Justice 290,884
   Labor 318,890
   Transportation 2,364,264
   Veterans Affairs....................27,931

Crime & Law Enforcement

Crime, 2006 (rates per 100,000 residents)
Property crimes 721,084
   Burglary 170,873
   Larceny 473,774
   Motor vehicle theft 76,437
   Property crime rate..................3,986.1
Violent crimes........................ 128,795
   Murder 1,129
   Forcible rape........................6,475
   Robbery...........................34,147
   Aggravated assault 87,044
   Violent crime rate 712.0
Hate crimes........................... 257

Fraud and identity theft, 2006
Fraud complaints..................... 25,902
   rate per 100,000 residents 143.2
Identity theft complaints 17,780
   rate per 100,000 residents 98.3

Law enforcement agencies, 2006
Total agencies.......................... 450
Total employees.......................74,051
   Officers 45,723
   Civilians 28,328

Prisoners, probation, and parole, 2006
Total prisoners........................ 92,969
   percent change, 12/31/05 to 12/31/06 .... 3.6%
   in private facilities 6.8%
   in local jails 0%
Sentenced to more than one year 92,874
   rate per 100,000 residents 509
Adults on probation 272,977
Adults on parole........................4,790

Prisoner demographics, June 30, 2005 (rate per 100,000 residents)
Male....................................1,541
Female 155
White...................................588
Black....................................2,615
Hispanic 382

Arrests, 2006

Total............................... 1,110,535
   Persons under 18 years of age 121,173

Persons under sentence of death, 1/1/07

Total.................................... 397
   White.................................. 221
   Black 139
   Hispanic 35

State's highest court

Name ....Supreme Court
Number of members......................... 7
Length of term........................ 6 years
Intermediate appeals court? ....yes

Labor & Income

Civilian labor force, 2006 (x 1,000)

Total...................................9,054
   Men 4,800
   Women 4,254
   Persons 16-19 years................... 356
   White................................7,413
   Black 1,310
   Hispanic 1,954

Civilian labor force as a percent of civilian non-institutional population, 2006

Total..................................63.5%
   Men 70.1
   Women 57.5
   Persons 16-19 years...................40.2
   White................................62.9
   Black 65.7
   Hispanic 67.5

Employment, 2006 (x 1,000)

Total..................................8,762
   Men 4,647
   Women 4,115
   Persons 16-19 years................... 314
   White................................7,206
   Black 1,232
   Hispanic 1,887

Unemployment rate, 2006

Total................................... 3.2%
   Men 3.2
   Women 3.3
   Persons 16-19 years...................11.6
   White................................2.8
   Black 5.9
   Hispanic 3.4

Full-time/part-time labor force, 2003 (x 1,000)

Full-time labor force, employed 6,552
Part-time labor force, employed...........1,191
Unemployed, looking for
   Full-time work......................... 355
   Part-time work......................... 65
*Mean duration of unemployment (weeks)......*18.3
   Median 9.5

Labor unions, 2006

Membership (x 1,000).................... 397
   percent of employed 5.2%

Experienced civilian labor force by private industry, 2006

Total............................6,887,084
   Natural resources & mining 97,141
   Construction 634,751
   Manufacturing...................... 402,317
   Trade, transportation & utilities 1,593,327
   Information 167,289
   Finance 544,294
   Professional & business 1,347,000
   Education & health 939,776
   Leisure & hospitality............. 904,030
   Other 248,095

Experienced civilian labor force by occupation, May 2006

Management....................... 231,960
Business & financial 360,270
Legal............................... 69,320
Sales............................. 984,230
Office & admin. support..............1,508,910
Computers & math 149,660
Architecture & engineering...........127,420
Arts & entertainment 94,400
Education 390,160
Social services 80,800
Health care practitioner & technical.....413,180
Health care support 200,440
Maintenance & repair.................322,170
Construction 513,750
Transportation & moving 515,490
Production 353,550
Farming, fishing & forestry...........38,740

Hours and earnings of production workers on manufacturing payrolls, 2006

Average weekly hours 41.5
Average hourly earnings $14.75
Average weekly earnings $612.13

Income and poverty, 2006

Median household income............. $45,495
Personal income, per capita (current $)... $35,798
   in constant (2000) dollars $31,249
Persons below poverty level.............. 12.6%

Average annual pay

2006 .... $38,485
   increase from 2005 .... 4.6%

Federal individual income tax returns, 2005

Returns filed........................ 8,411,496
Adjusted gross income ($1,000) $481,888,152
Total tax liability ($1,000) $69,937,790

Charitable contributions, 2004

Number of contributions 2,182.1
Total amount ($ mil)................. $9,481.9

Economy, Business, Industry & Agriculture

Fortune 500 companies, 2007 12
Bankruptcy cases filed, FY 2007 36,572

Patents and trademarks issued, 2007
Patents 3,049
Trademarks 5,779

Business firm ownership, 2002
Women-owned 437,355
   Sales ($ mil) $61,275
Black-owned 102,053
   Sales ($ mil) $5,721
Hispanic-owned 266,688
   Sales ($ mil) $40,892
Asian-owned 41,258
   Sales ($ mil) $11,222
Amer. Indian/Alaska Native-owned 10,105
   Sales ($ mil) $647
Hawaiian/Pacific Islander-owned 1,480
   Sales ($ mil) $72

Gross domestic product, 2006 ($ mil)
Total gross domestic product $713,505
   Agriculture, forestry, fishing and
      hunting 6,313
   Mining 805
   Utilities 11,685
   Construction 55,839
   Manufacturing, durable goods 24,430
   Manufacturing, non-durable goods 11,430
   Wholesale trade .47,023
   Retail trade 56,573
   Transportation & warehousing 18,194
   Information 28,841
   Finance & insurance 48,397
   Real estate, rental & leasing 122,221
   Professional and technical services 45,405
   Educational services 5,011
   Health care and social assistance 51,299
   Accommodation/food services 26,032
   Other services, except government 17,954
   Government 78,875

Establishments, payroll, employees & receipts, by major industry group, 2005
Total 504,662
   Annual payroll ($1,000) $239,197,889
   Paid employees 7,107,378
Forestry, fishing & agriculture 1,029
   Annual payroll ($1,000) $353,729
   Paid employees .16,165
Mining 275
   Annual payroll ($1,000) $287,568
   Paid employees 5,588
   Receipts, 2002 ($1,000) $1,562,949

Utilities 645
   Annual payroll ($1,000) $2,099,914
   Paid employees 32,240
   Receipts, 2002 ($1,000) . . . . .NA
Construction 57,346
   Annual payroll ($1,000) $18,452,509
   Paid employees 477,670
   Receipts, 2002 ($1,000) $79,384,681
Manufacturing 14,286
   Annual payroll ($1,000) $14,906,536
   Paid employees 371,432
   Receipts, 2002 ($1,000) $78,474,770
Wholesale trade 31,709
   Annual payroll ($1,000) $13,996,062
   Paid employees 311,270
   Receipts, 2002 ($1,000) $219,490,896
Retail trade 72,469
   Annual payroll ($1,000) $23,452,267
   Paid employees 987,307
   Receipts, 2002 ($1,000) $191,805,685
Transportation & warehousing 12,668
   Annual payroll ($1,000) $8,020,002
   Paid employees 216,297
   Receipts, 2002 ($1,000) $25,805,912
Information 8,693
   Annual payroll ($1,000) $8,829,908
   Paid employees 174,999
   Receipts, 2002 ($1,000) . . . . .NA
Finance & insurance 32,974
   Annual payroll ($1,000) $20,227,493
   Paid employees 370,990
   Receipts, 2002 ($1,000) . . . . .NA
Professional, scientific & technical 65,901
   Annual payroll ($1,000) $21,899,141
   Paid employees 422,953
   Receipts, 2002 ($1,000) $42,457,665
Education 4,966
   Annual payroll ($1,000) $3,481,093
   Paid employees 119,169
   Receipts, 2002 ($1,000) $1,883,151
Health care & social assistance 48,207
   Annual payroll ($1,000) $32,749,098
   Paid employees 866,420
   Receipts, 2002 ($1,000) $70,972,374
Arts and entertainment 7,515
   Annual payroll ($1,000) $4,081,454
   Paid employees 166,236
   Receipts, 2002 ($1,000) $11,319,842
Real estate 33,946
   Annual payroll ($1,000) $6,466,526
   Paid employees 168,266
   Receipts, 2002 ($1,000) $22,785,030
Accommodation & food service 33,049
   Annual payroll ($1,000) $10,738,660
   Paid employees 724,791
   Receipts, 2002 ($1,000) $29,366,940

Exports, 2006
Value of exported goods ($ mil) $38,545
   Manufactured $31,638
   Non-manufactured $2,233

Foreign direct investment in US affiliates, 2004
Property, plants & equipment ($ mil) . . . $26,819
Employment (x 1,000) 238.4

Agriculture, 2006
Number of farms 41,000
Farm acreage (x 1,000) 10,000
   Acres per farm 244
Farm marketings and income ($ mil)
Total $6,974.2
   Crops $5,669.3
   Livestock $1,304.9
Net farm income $2,340.4

Principal commodities, in order by
marketing receipts, 2005
   Greenhouse/nursery, Oranges, Tomatoes, Cattle
      and calves, Cane for sugar

Federal economic activity in state
Expenditures, 2005 ($ mil)
   Total $134,544
      Per capita $7,572.16
   Defense $18,590
   Non-defense $115,954
Defense department, 2006 ($ mil)
   Payroll $8,864
   Contract awards $10,707
   Grants $131
Homeland security grants ($1,000)
   2006 . . . . $100,122
   2007 . . . . $84,743

FDIC-insured financial institutions, 2005
Number 306
Assets ($ billion) $165.8
Deposits ($ billion) $120.0

Fishing, 2006
Catch (x 1,000 lbs) 95,255
Value ($1,000) $237,130

Mining, 2006 ($ mil)
Total non-fuel mineral production $2,790
Percent of U.S. 4.33%

Communication, Energy &
Transportation

Communication
Households with computers, 2003 . . . . 61.0%
Households with internet access, 2003 . . . . 55.6%
High-speed internet providers 60
Total high-speed internet lines 5,346,321
   Residential 4,028,919
   Business 1,317,402
Wireless phone customers, 12/2006 . . . 14,761,666

FCC-licensed stations (as of January 1, 2008)
TV stations 92
FM radio stations 343
AM radio stations 226

Energy
Energy consumption, 2004
   Total (trillion Btu) 4,453
   Per capita (million Btu) 256.4
By source of production (trillion Btu)
   Coal 699
   Natural gas 755
   Petroleum 2,120
   Nuclear electric power 326
   Hydroelectric power 3
By end-use sector (trillion Btu)
   Residential 1,307
   Commercial 1,042
   Industrial 554
   Transportation 1,550
Electric energy, 2005
   Primary source of electricity . . . . Gas
   Net generation (billion kWh) 220.3
      percent from renewable sources 2.1%
   Net summer capability (million kW) 53.2
   CO_2 emitted from generation 130.3
Natural gas utilities, 2005
   Customers (x 1,000) 712
   Sales (trillion Btu) 141
   Revenues ($ mil) $665
Nuclear plants, 2007 5
Total CO_2 emitted (million metric tons) 243.9
Energy spending, 2004 ($ mil) $41,112
   per capita $2,367
   Price per million Btu $15.21

Transportation, 2006
Public road & street mileage 121,995
   Urban 81,789
   Rural 40,206
   Interstate 1,471
Vehicle miles of travel (millions) 203,741
   per capita 11,282.9
Total motor vehicle registrations 16,373,565
   Automobiles 7,425,148
   Trucks 8,899,488
   Motorcycles 588,900
Licensed drivers .13,988,630
   19 years & under 770,196
Deaths from motor vehicle accidents 3,374
Gasoline consumed (x 1,000 gallons) . . . 8,692,569
   per capita 481.4

Commuting Statistics, 2006
Average commute time (min) 25.9
   Drove to work alone 79.3%
   Carpooled 10.9%
   Public transit 2.0%
   Walk to work 1.7%
   Work from home 4.0%

State Summary

Capital city . . . . Atlanta
Governor . . . . Sonny Perdue

203 State Capitol
Atlanta, GA 30334
404-656-1776

Admitted as a state 1788
Area (square miles) 59,425
Population, 2007 (estimate). 9,544,750
Largest city . . . . Atlanta
  Population, 2006 486,411
Personal income per capita, 2006
  (in current dollars) $31,891
Gross domestic product, 2006 ($ mil) . . . $379,550

Leading industries by payroll, 2005

Manufacturing, Health care/Social assistance,
Professional/Scientific/Technical

Leading agricultural commodities by receipts, 2005

Broilers, Cotton, Greenhouse/nursery, Chicken
eggs, Cattle and calves

Geography & Environment

Total area (square miles). 59,425
  land 57,906
  water 1,519
Federally-owned land, 2004 (acres) 1,409,406
  percent. 3.8%
Highest point . . . . Brasstown Bald
  elevation (feet) 4,784
Lowest point . . . . Atlantic Ocean
  elevation (feet) . . . . sea level
General coastline (miles) 100
Tidal shoreline (miles) 2,344
Cropland, 2003 (x 1,000 acres) 4,152
Forest land, 2003 (x 1,000 acres). 21,893
Capital city . . . . Atlanta
  Population 2000 416,474
  Population 2006 486,411
Largest city . . . . Atlanta
  Population 2000 416,474
  Population 2006 486,411

Number of cities with over 100,000 population

1990 4
2000 5
2006 5

State park and recreation areas, 2005

Area (x 1,000 acres) 84
Number of visitors (x 1,000) 10,294
Revenues ($1,000) $32,834
  percent of operating expenditures 55.4%

National forest system land, 2007

Acres 866,024

Demographics & Population Characteristics

Population

1980 5,463,105
1990 6,478,216
2000 8,186,816
2006 9,363,941
  Male 4,611,078
  Female 4,752,863
Living in group quarters, 2006 272,931
  percent of total. 2.9%
2007 (estimate) .9,544,750
  persons per square mile of land 164.8
2008 (projected). 9,325,827
2010 (projected) .9,589,080
2020 (projected) 10,843,753
2030 (projected) 12,017,838

Population of Core-Based Statistical Areas (formerly Metropolitan Areas), x 1,000

	CBSA	Non-CBSA
1990	5,822	656
2000	7,411	776
2006	8,534	830

Change in population, 2000-2007

Number 1,357,934
  percent. 16.6%
Natural increase (births minus deaths) 521,982
Net internal migration 484,919
Net international migration 240,814

Persons by age, 2006

Under 5 years 702,134
5 to 17 years 1,752,886
18 years and over 6,908,921
65 years and over .912,874
85 years and over .113,362
  Median age 34.6

Persons by age, 2010 (projected)

Under 5 years 730,521
18 and over 7,086,694
65 and over 980,824
  Median age 34.7

Race, 2006

One Race
  White 6,158,769
  Black or African American 2,799,625
  Asian 261,401
  American Indian/Alaska Native. 30,893
  Hawaiian Native/Pacific Islander. 7,396
Two or more races. 105,857

Persons of Hispanic origin, 2006

Total Hispanic or Latino 696,146
  Mexican. 455,008
  Puerto Rican 51,349
  Cuban 18,448

Persons of Asian origin, 2006
Total Asian 254,899
  Asian Indian. 74,525
  Chinese 37,017
  Filipino 14,562
  Japanese 6,774
  Korean. 45,846
  Vietnamese. 44,830

Marital status, 2006
Population 15 years & over 7,325,075
  Never married 2,308,808
  Married. 3,756,569
  Separated 183,167
  Widowed. 418,204
  Divorced 841,494

Language spoken at home, 2006
Population 5 years and older. 8,665,006
  English only 7,633,572
  Spanish 610,402
  French 51,396
  German. 26,723
  Chinese 32,902

Households & families, 2006
Households. 3,376,763
  with persons under 18 years 1,253,007
  with persons over 65 years. 636,235
  persons per household 2.69
Families. 2,296,694
  persons per family. 3.27
Married couples. 1,639,379
Female householder,
  no husband present. 492,332
One-person households 892,833

Nativity, 2006
Number of residents born in state 5,200,328
  percent of population. 55.5%

Immigration & naturalization, 2006
Legal permanent residents admitted. 32,202
Persons naturalized 19,785
Non-immigrant admissions 436,905

Vital Statistics and Health

Marriages
2004. 68,897
2005. 62,893
2006. 66,456

Divorces
2004. . . . . NA
2005. . . . . NA
2006. . . . . NA

Health risks, 2006
Percent of adults who are:
  Smokers. 19.9%
  Overweight (BMI > 25). 61.7%
  Obese (BMI > 30). 27.1%

Births
2005 142,200
  Birthrate (per 1,000). 15.7
  White. 90,958
  Black 46,027
  Hispanic 21,891
  Asian/Pacific Islander 4,953
  Amer. Indian/Alaska Native 262
  Low birth weight (2,500g or less). 9.5%
  Cesarian births 30.5%
  Preterm births 13.6%
  To unmarried mothers. 40.6%
  Twin births (per 1,000) 31.2
  Triplets or higher order (per 100,000). . . .149.6
2006 (preliminary). 148,619
  rate per 1,000. . . . . .15.9

Deaths
2004
All causes 65,818
  rate per 100,000. . . . . 924.6
Heart disease 16,557
  rate per 100,000. . . . . .239.7
Malignant neoplasms 14,313
  rate per 100,000. . . . . .196.3
Cerebrovascular disease. 4,063
  rate per 100,000. .60.5
Chronic lower respiratory disease 3,125
  rate per 100,000. .45.8
Diabetes. 1,623
  rate per 100,000. .22.5
2005 (preliminary). 66,735
  rate per 100,000. . . . . 905.8
2006 (provisional) 66,335

Infant deaths
2004 1,181
  rate per 1,000 . . . . .8.5
2005 (provisional) 1,108
  rate per 1,000 . . . . .7.8

Exercise routines, 2005
None. 27.2%
Moderate or greater. 42.0%
Vigorous 23.7%

Abortions, 2004
Total performed in state. 32,513
  rate per 1,000 women age 15-44. 16
  % obtained by out-of-state residents 12.5%

Physicians, 2005
Total. 19,997
  rate per 100,000 persons 219

Community hospitals, 2005
Number of hospitals 149
Beds (x 1,000). 25.0
Patients admitted (x 1,000) 961
Average daily census (x 1,000) 17.0
Average cost per day $1,202
Outpatient visits (x 1 mil) 13.8

Disability status of population, 2006

5 to 15 years	5.6%
16 to 64 years	12.3%
65 years and over	45.1%

Education

Educational attainment, 2006

Population over 25 years	5,968,250
Less than 9th grade	6.4%
High school graduate or more	82.2%
College graduate or more	26.6%
Graduate or professional degree	9.2%

Public school enrollment, 2005-06

Total	1,598,461
Pre-kindergarten through grade 8	1,145,446
Grades 9 through 12	453,015

Graduating public high school seniors, 2004-05

Diplomas (incl. GED and others)	79,128

SAT scores, 2007

Average critical reading score	494
Average writing score	483
Average math score	495
Percent of graduates taking test	69%

Public school teachers, 2006-07 (estimate)

Total (x 1,000)	112.9
Elementary	68.4
Secondary	44.5
Average salary	$49,905
Elementary	$49,357
Secondary	$50,748

State receipts & expenditures for public schools, 2006-07 (estimate)

Revenue receipts ($ mil)	$16,777
Expenditures	
Total ($ mil)	$16,333
Per capita	$1,531
Per pupil	$9,502

NAEP proficiency scores, 2007

	Reading		Math	
	Basic	Proficient	Basic	Proficient
Grade 4	65.6%	28.3%	78.6%	31.6%
Grade 8	70.1%	25.6%	64.2%	24.7%

Higher education enrollment, fall 2005

Total	84,638
Full-time men	28,317
Full-time women	42,432
Part-time men	5,186
Part-time women	8,703

Minority enrollment in institutions of higher education, 2005

Black, non-Hispanic	131,040
Hispanic	10,597
Asian/Pacific Islander	15,790
American Indian/Alaska Native	1,187

Institutions of higher education, 2005-06

Total	132
Public	74
Private	58

Earned degrees conferred, 2004-05

Associate's	12,705
Bachelor's	35,515
Master's	13,111
First-professional	2,029
Doctor's	1,225

Public Libraries, 2006

Number of libraries	58
Number of outlets	396
Annual visits per capita	3.7
Circulation per capita	4.8

State & local financial support for higher education, FY 2006

Full-time equivalent enrollment (x 1,000)	292.7
Appropriations per FTE	$7,824

Social Insurance & Welfare Programs

Social Security benefits & beneficiaries, 2005

Beneficiaries (x 1,000)	1,231
Retired & dependents	799
Survivors	182
Disabled & dependents	250
Annual benefit payments ($ mil)	$12,846
Retired & dependents	$8,048
Survivors	$2,261
Disabled & dependents	$2,537
Average monthly benefit	
Retired & dependents	$978
Disabled & dependents	$924
Widowed	$913

Medicare, July 2005

Enrollment (x 1,000)	1,039
Payments ($ mil)	$7,143

Medicaid, 2004

Beneficiaries (x 1,000)	1,929
Payments ($ mil)	$6,944

State Children's Health Insurance Program, 2006

Enrollment (x 1,000)	343.7
Expenditures ($ mil)	$265.2

Persons without health insurance, 2006

Number (x 1,000)	1,659
percent	17.7%
Number of children (x 1,000)	314
percent of children	12.8%

Health care expenditures, 2004

Total expenditures	$41,097
per capita	$4,600

Federal and state public aid

State unemployment insurance, 2006
Recipients, first payments (x 1,000) 198
Total payments ($ mil) $537
Average weekly benefit $256
Temporary Assistance for Needy Families, 2006
Recipients (x 1,000) 672.7
Families (x 1,000) 351.9
Supplemental Security Income, 2005
Recipients (x 1,000) 202.7
Payments ($ mil) $943.6
Food Stamp Program, 2006
Avg monthly participants (x 1,000) 946.8
Total benefits ($ mil) $1,098.3

Housing & Construction

Housing units

Total 2005 (estimate) 3,772,200
Total 2006 (estimate) 3,873,183
Seasonal or recreational use, 2006 75,646
Owner-occupied, 2006 2,285,179
    Median home value $156,800
    Homeowner vacancy rate 3.4%
Renter-occupied, 2006 1,091,584
    Median rent $738
    Rental vacancy rate 13.0%
Home ownership rate, 2005 . . . . 67.9%
Home ownership rate, 2006 . . . . 68.5%

New privately-owned housing units

Number authorized, 2006 (x 1,000) 104.2
    Value ($ mil) $14,454.8
Started 2005 (x 1,000, estimate) 86.1
Started 2006 (x 1,000, estimate) 84.1

Existing home sales

2005 (x 1,000) 242.1
2006 (x 1,000) 248.8

Government & Elections

State officials 2008

Governor . . . . Sonny Perdue
        Republican, term expires 1/11
Lieutenant Governor . . . . Casey Cagle
Secretary of State . . . . .Karen Handel
Attorney General . . . . Thurbert Baker
Chief Justice . . . . Leah Ward Sears

Governorship

Minimum age 30
Length of term . . . . 4 years
Consecutive terms permitted 2
Who succeeds . . . . Lieutenant Governor

Local governments by type, 2002

Total 1,448
    County 156
    Municipal 531
    Township 0
    School District 180
    Special District 581

State legislature

Name . . . . General Assembly
Upper chamber . . . . .Senate
    Number of members 56
    Length of term . . . . 2 years
    Party in majority, 2008 . . . . Republican
Lower chamber . . . . House of Representatives
    Number of members 180
    Length of term . . . . 2 years
    Party in majority, 2008 . . . . Republican

Federal representation, 2008 (110th Congress)

Senator . . . . Saxby Chambliss
    Party . . . . Republican
    Year term expires 2009
Senator . . . . Johnny Isakson
    Party . . . . Republican
    Year term expires 2011
Representatives, total 13
    Democrats 6
    Republicans 7

Voters in November 2006 election (estimate)

Total 2,671,578
    Male 1,197,134
    Female 1,474,444
    White 1,904,631
    Black 721,981
    Hispanic 30,939
    Asian 26,220

Presidential election, 2004

Total Popular Vote 3,301,875
    Kerry 1,366,149
    Bush 1,914,254
Total Electoral Votes 15

Votes cast for US Senators

2004
Total vote (x 1,000) 3,221
Leading party . . . . Republican
Percent for leading party 57.8%
2006
Total vote (x 1,000) . . . . NA
Leading party . . . . NA
Percent for leading party . . . . NA

Votes cast for US Representatives

2004
Total vote (x 1,000) 2,961
    Democratic 1,141
    Republican 1,820
Leading party . . . . Republican
Percent for leading party 61.5%
2006
Total vote (x 1,000) 2,070
    Democratic 932
    Republican 1,138
Leading party . . . . Republican
Percent for leading party 55.0%

State government employment, 2006
Full-time equivalent employees 124,361
Payroll ($ mil) $420.6

Local government employment, 2006
Full-time equivalent employees 381,283
Payroll ($ mil) $1,203.9

Women holding public office, 2008
US Congress 0
Statewide elected office. 3
State legislature 46

Black public officials, 2002
Total. 640
   US and state legislatures 53
   City/county/regional offices 413
   Judicial/law enforcement. 48
   Education/school boards 126

Hispanic public officials, 2006
Total. 7
   State executives & legislators 3
   City/county/regional offices 2
   Judicial/law enforcement. 2
   Education/school boards 0

Governmental Finance

State government revenues, 2006
Total revenue (x $1,000) $37,594,200
   per capita $4,024.18
General revenue (x $1,000) $32,352,787
   Intergovernmental 10,609,465
   Taxes 17,033,651
      general sales 5,802,913
      individual income tax 8,040,366
      corporate income tax 890,732
   Current charges 2,790,463
   Miscellaneous 1,919,208

State government expenditure, 2006
Total expenditure (x $1,000) $34,944,785
   per capita $3,740.58
General expenditure (x $1,000) $31,300,124
   per capita, total. *$3,350.44*
   Education 1,534.01
   Public welfare 946.84
   Health 106.20
   Hospitals. 74.82
   Highways 152.30
   Police protection. 27.53
   Corrections 148.08
   Natural resources 47.46
   Parks & recreation 18.96
   Governmental administration 69.59
   Interest on general debt 47.99

State debt & cash, 2006 ($ per capita)
Debt $1,123.22
Cash/security holdings. $7,443.82

Federal government grants to state & local government, 2005 (x $1,000)
Total. $11,165,966
by Federal agency
   Defense 49,431
   Education 1,075,668
   Energy 40,810
   Environmental Protection Agency 44,181
   Health & Human Services. 6,317,744
   Homeland Security 47,492
   Housing & Urban Development 773,556
   Justice 211,135
   Labor 161,864
   Transportation 1,373,966
   Veterans Affairs. 13,844

Crime & Law Enforcement

Crime, 2006 (rates per 100,000 residents)
Property crimes 364,183
   Burglary 85,117
   Larceny 235,903
   Motor vehicle theft 43,163
   Property crime rate. 3,889.2
Violent crimes. 44,106
   Murder 600
   Forcible rape. 2,173
   Robbery. 15,509
   Aggravated assault 25,824
   Violent crime rate 471.0
Hate crimes. 16

Fraud and identity theft, 2006
Fraud complaints. 11,941
   rate per 100,000 residents 127.5
Identity theft complaints 8,084
   rate per 100,000 residents 86.3

Law enforcement agencies, 2006
Total agencies. 436
Total employees 30,854
   Officers 22,162
   Civilians 8,692

Prisoners, probation, and parole, 2006
Total prisoners 52,792
   percent change, 12/31/05 to 12/31/06 .... 8.3%
   in private facilities 9.6%
   in local jails 9.4%
Sentenced to more than one year 52,781
   rate per 100,000 residents 558
Adults on probation 422,790
Adults on parole. 22,958

Prisoner demographics, June 30, 2005 (rate per 100,000 residents)
Male 1,877
Female 184
White 623
Black. 2,068
Hispanic 576

Arrests, 2006

Total. 234,735
  Persons under 18 years of age 24,368

Persons under sentence of death, 1/1/07

Total. 107
  White. 53
  Black 50
  Hispanic 3

State's highest court

Name . . . . .Supreme Court
Number of members. 7
Length of term . . . . 6 years
Intermediate appeals court? . . . . .yes

Labor & Income

Civilian labor force, 2006 (x 1,000)

Total. 4,694
  Men 2,511
  Women 2,183
  Persons 16-19 years. 184
  White. 3,177
  Black 1,342
  Hispanic 379

Civilian labor force as a percent of civilian non-institutional population, 2006

Total. 67.9%
  Men 75.5
  Women 60.9
  Persons 16-19 years. 35.9
  White. 67.7
  Black 68.1
  Hispanic 76.9

Employment, 2006 (x 1,000)

Total. 4,476
  Men 2,398
  Women 2,078
  Persons 16-19 years. 146
  White. 3,072
  Black 1,236
  Hispanic 361

Unemployment rate, 2006

Total. 4.6%
  Men 4.5
  Women 4.8
  Persons 16-19 years. 20.5
  White. 3.3
  Black 7.9
  Hispanic 4.8

Full-time/part-time labor force, 2003 (x 1,000)

Full-time labor force, employed 3,654
Part-time labor force, employed. 553
Unemployed, looking for
  Full-time work. 187
  Part-time work. 21
Mean duration of unemployment (weeks). 20.9
  Median 13.0

Labor unions, 2006

Membership (x 1,000). 176
  percent of employed 4.4%

Experienced civilian labor force by private industry, 2006

Total. 3,367,178
  Natural resources & mining 33,050
  Construction 218,511
  Manufacturing. 447,903
  Trade, transportation & utilities 862,887
  Information 115,966
  Finance 227,061
  Professional & business 550,357
  Education & health 414,017
  Leisure & hospitality. 383,810
  Other 98,918

Experienced civilian labor force by occupation, May 2006

Management. 228,460
Business & financial 167,100
Legal. 24,370
Sales 422,650
Office & admin. support. 710,350
Computers & math 92,900
Architecture & engineering. 54,170
Arts & entertainment 35,700
Education 251,300
Social services 42,990
Health care practitioner & technical. . . . 184,650
Health care support 79,160
Maintenance & repair. 188,270
Construction 175,830
Transportation & moving 331,340
Production 345,950
Farming, fishing & forestry. 13,470

Hours and earnings of production workers on manufacturing payrolls, 2006

Average weekly hours 39.5
Average hourly earnings $14.74
Average weekly earnings $582.23

Income and poverty, 2006

Median household income. $46,832
Personal income, per capita (current $). . . $31,891
  in constant (2000) dollars $27,839
Persons below poverty level. 14.7%

Average annual pay

2006 . . . . $40,370
  increase from 2005 . . . . 3.3%

Federal individual income tax returns, 2005

Returns filed. 3,917,976
Adjusted gross income ($1,000) $199,214,881
Total tax liability ($1,000) $24,999,408

Charitable contributions, 2004

Number of contributions. 1,318.1
Total amount ($ mil). $5,889.9

Economy, Business, Industry & Agriculture

Fortune 500 companies, 2007 15
Bankruptcy cases filed, FY 2007......... 48,104

Patents and trademarks issued, 2007
Patents.................................1,614
Trademarks........................... 2,050

Business firm ownership, 2002
Women-owned...................... 196,195
  Sales ($ mil) $30,027
Black-owned.......................... 90,461
  Sales ($ mil) $5,665
Hispanic-owned....................18,310
  Sales ($ mil) $4,200
Asian-owned 26,925
  Sales ($ mil) $7,984
Amer. Indian/Alaska Native-owned 4,472
  Sales ($ mil) $662
Hawaiian/Pacific Islander-owned 176
  Sales ($ mil) $25

Gross domestic product, 2006 ($ mil)
Total gross domestic product $379,550
  Agriculture, forestry, fishing and
    hunting 3,255
  Mining..............................1,030
  Utilities 8,055
  Construction 19,793
  Manufacturing, durable goods........19,437
  Manufacturing, non-durable goods ... 29,564
  Wholesale trade.................... 30,236
  Retail trade........................ 25,370
  Transportation & warehousing 12,601
  Information........................ 23,434
  Finance & insurance................ 22,328
  Real estate, rental & leasing 45,616
  Professional and technical services.... 24,674
  Educational services..................3,332
  Health care and social assistance......22,171
  Accommodation/food services..........9,988
  Other services, except government 7,620
  Government...................... 48,859

Establishments, payroll, employees & receipts, by major industry group, 2005

Total.............................. 220,528
  Annual payroll ($1,000)........$128,827,270
  Paid employees 3,489,046

Forestry, fishing & agriculture............1,081
  Annual payroll ($1,000)............ $239,929
  Paid employees 8,178

Mining.................................. 219
  Annual payroll ($1,000)............ $331,858
  Paid employees 6,494
  Receipts, 2002 ($1,000) $1,635,358

Utilities 572
  Annual payroll ($1,000)..........$1,693,241
  Paid employees 27,291
  Receipts, 2002 ($1,000) ....NA

Construction......................... 22,466
  Annual payroll ($1,000).......... $7,901,149
  Paid employees 201,496
  Receipts, 2002 ($1,000) $41,366,986

Manufacturing........................8,623
  Annual payroll ($1,000)........$16,218,823
  Paid employees 428,467
  Receipts, 2002 ($1,000) $126,156,636

Wholesale trade 13,973
  Annual payroll ($1,000).........$10,510,976
  Paid employees 200,693
  Receipts, 2002 ($1,000) $201,091,040

Retail trade......................... 35,023
  Annual payroll ($1,000).........$10,225,754
  Paid employees 474,458
  Receipts, 2002 ($1,000) $90,098,578

Transportation & warehousing 5,986
  Annual payroll ($1,000)..........$6,188,812
  Paid employees 152,508
  Receipts, 2002 ($1,000) $10,586,256

Information...........................4,198
  Annual payroll ($1,000)..........$7,432,375
  Paid employees 121,905
  Receipts, 2002 ($1,000) ....NA

Finance & insurance 14,779
  Annual payroll ($1,000).........$10,044,949
  Paid employees 174,282
  Receipts, 2002 ($1,000) ....NA

Professional, scientific & technical 26,284
  Annual payroll ($1,000).......... $11,815,810
  Paid employees 209,548
  Receipts, 2002 ($1,000) $25,165,914

Education 2,197
  Annual payroll ($1,000)..........$1,996,873
  Paid employees 67,298
  Receipts, 2002 ($1,000) $748,348

Health care & social assistance 19,446
  Annual payroll ($1,000)......... $14,800,306
  Paid employees 398,607
  Receipts, 2002 ($1,000) $31,478,319

Arts and entertainment 2,693
  Annual payroll ($1,000)..........$1,095,981
  Paid employees 40,022
  Receipts, 2002 ($1,000) $2,449,690

Real estate...........................11,540
  Annual payroll ($1,000)..........$2,599,140
  Paid employees 62,813
  Receipts, 2002 ($1,000) $9,574,062

Accommodation & food service...........17,218
  Annual payroll ($1,000)..........$4,341,413
  Paid employees 336,804
  Receipts, 2002 ($1,000) $12,740,423

Exports, 2006

Value of exported goods ($ mil) $20,073
   Manufactured $16,996
   Non-manufactured.................. $1,619

Foreign direct investment in US affiliates, 2004

Property, plants & equipment ($ mil) ... $23,574
Employment (x 1,000)................... 175.9

Agriculture, 2006

Number of farms 49,000
Farm acreage (x 1,000) 10,800
   Acres per farm........................ 220
Farm marketings and income ($ mil)
Total............................... $6,005.1
   Crops............................ $2,240.2
   Livestock......................... $3,764.9
Net farm income $2,387.6

Principal commodities, in order by marketing receipts, 2005

  Broilers, Cotton, Greenhouse/nursery, Chicken
       eggs, Cattle and calves

Federal economic activity in state

Expenditures, 2005 ($ mil)
  Total............................. $59,846
    Per capita $6,553.09
  Defense......................... $11,868
  Non-defense $47,979
Defense department, 2006 ($ mil)
  Payroll........................... $7,409
  Contract awards $5,515
  Grants $54
Homeland security grants ($1,000)
  2006.......................... $44,406
  2007.......................... $39,959

FDIC-insured financial institutions, 2005

Number 352
Assets ($ billion) $284.7
Deposits ($ billion) $205.8

Fishing, 2006

Catch (x 1,000 lbs)..................... 7,747
Value ($1,000)........................ $10,798

Mining, 2006 ($ mil)

Total non-fuel mineral production $1,970
Percent of U.S. 3.06%

Communication, Energy & Transportation

Communication

Households with computers, 2003........ 60.6%
Households with internet access, 2003 .... 53.5%
High-speed internet providers 81
Total high-speed internet lines........ 2,651,349
  Residential 1,869,159
  Business......................... 782,190
Wireless phone customers, 12/2006 7,281,724

FCC-licensed stations (as of January 1, 2008)

TV stations 47
FM radio stations......................... 266
AM radio stations 185

Energy

Energy consumption, 2004
  Total (trillion Btu)................. 3,141
  Per capita (million Btu) 351.5
By source of production (trillion Btu)
  Coal 835
  Natural gas...................... 410
  Petroleum....................... 1,118
  Nuclear electric power 352
  Hydroelectric power 37
By end-use sector (trillion Btu)
  Residential 720
  Commercial 534
  Industrial 960
  Transportation 928
Electric energy, 2005
  Primary source of electricity........... Coal
  Net generation (billion kWh) 136.7
    percent from renewable sources....... 5.3%
  Net summer capability (million kW) 36.5
  CO_2 emitted from generation 89.3
Natural gas utilities, 2005
  Customers (x 1,000) 1,902
  Sales (trillion Btu)................. 341
  Revenues ($ mil) $656
Nuclear plants, 2007 4
Total CO_2 emitted (million metric tons).... 168.0
Energy spending, 2004 ($ mil) $25,659
  per capita $2,872
  Price per million Btu $12.42

Transportation, 2006

Public road & street mileage 118,199
  Urban............................ 37,325
  Rural 80,874
  Interstate........................ 1,244
Vehicle miles of travel (millions) 113,532
  per capita 12,152.8
Total motor vehicle registrations...... 8,286,454
  Automobiles...................... 4,141,179
  Trucks 4,123,932
  Motorcycles 142,239
Licensed drivers 5,906,834
  19 years & under 286,654
Deaths from motor vehicle accidents 1,693
Gasoline consumed (x 1,000 gallons) 4,982,331
  per capita 533.3

Commuting Statistics, 2006

Average commute time (min) 27.3
  Drove to work alone 78.2%
  Carpooled......................... 11.5%
  Public transit 2.4%
  Walk to work 1.7%
  Work from home.................... 4.2%

State Summary

Capital city . . . . Honolulu
Governor . . . . Linda Lingle

Executive Chambers
State Capitol
Honolulu, HI 96813
808-586-0034

Admitted as a state 1959
Area (square miles) .10,931
Population, 2007 (estimate). 1,283,388
Largest city . . . . Honolulu
　　Population, 2006 377,357
Personal income per capita, 2006
　　(in current dollars) $36,299
Gross domestic product, 2006 ($ mil) $58,307

Leading industries by payroll, 2005

Health care/Social assistance, Accommodation &
Food services, Retail trade

Leading agricultural commodities by receipts, 2005

Greenhouse/nursery, Pineapples, Cane for sugar,
Macadamia nuts, Coffee

Geography & Environment

Total area (square miles). 10,931
　　land 6,423
　　water 4,508
Federally-owned land, 2004 (acres) 796,726
　　percent. 19.4%
Highest point . . . . Mauna Kea
　　elevation (feet) 13,796
Lowest point . . . . Pacific Ocean
　　elevation (feet) . . . . sea level
General coastline (miles) 750
Tidal shoreline (miles) 1,052
Cropland, 2003 (x 1,000 acres) . . . . NA
Forest land, 2003 (x 1,000 acres). . . . . NA
Capital city . . . . Honolulu
　　Population 2000 371,657
　　Population 2006 377,357
Largest city . . . . Honolulu
　　Population 2000 371,657
　　Population 2006 377,357

Number of cities with over 100,000 population

1990 1
2000 1
2006 1

State park and recreation areas, 2005

Area (x 1,000 acres) 27
Number of visitors (x 1,000) . . . . NA
Revenues ($1,000) $2,111
　　percent of operating expenditures 28.2%

National forest system land, 2007

Acres 1

Demographics & Population Characteristics

Population

1980 964,691
1990 1,108,229
2000 1,211,537
2006 1,285,498
　　Male 643,328
　　Female 642,170
Living in group quarters, 2006 37,547
　　percent of total. 2.9%
2007 (estimate). .1,283,388
　　persons per square mile of land 199.8
2008 (projected). 1,317,607
2010 (projected). .1,340,674
2020 (projected). .1,412,373
2030 (projected). .1,466,046

Population of Core-Based Statistical Areas (formerly Metropolitan Areas), x 1,000

	CBSA	Non-CBSA
1990	1,108	0
2000	1,211	0
2006	1,285	0

Change in population, 2000-2007

Number 71,851
　　percent 5.9%
Natural increase (births minus deaths) 66,781
Net internal migration . . . .-20,583
Net international migration 30,891

Persons by age, 2006

Under 5 years 87,321
5 to 17 years 210,760
18 years and over .987,417
65 years and over .179,370
85 years and over 26,888
　　Median age 37.3

Persons by age, 2010 (projected)

Under 5 years 101,347
18 and over 1,024,411
65 and over 191,065
　　Median age 37.4

Race, 2006

One Race
　　White. 367,230
　　Black or African American 31,761
　　Asian 514,395
　　American Indian/Alaska Native. 6,378
　　Hawaiian Native/Pacific Islander. 116,967
Two or more races. 248,767

Persons of Hispanic origin, 2006

Total Hispanic or Latino 99,664
　　Mexican. 24,385
　　Puerto Rican 37,862
　　Cuban 771

Persons of Asian origin, 2006

Total Asian 512,995
  Asian Indian. 1,722
  Chinese 56,288
  Filipino 182,767
  Japanese 194,208
  Korean. 20,823
  Vietnamese. 9,564

Marital status, 2006

Population 15 years & over 1,039,527
  Never married 332,193
  Married. 544,426
  Separated 12,620
  Widowed. 65,080
  Divorced 97,828

Language spoken at home, 2006

Population 5 years and older. 1,198,319
  English only 917,085
  Spanish 17,442
  French 4,917
  German. 3,875
  Chinese 28,201

Households & families, 2006

Households. 432,632
  with persons under 18 years 149,125
  with persons over 65 years. 121,910
  persons per household 2.88
Families. 301,102
  persons per family. 3.45
Married couples. 222,725
Female householder,
  no husband present. 54,111
One-person households 106,013

Nativity, 2006

Number of residents born in state 709,105
  percent of population. 55.2%

Immigration & naturalization, 2006

Legal permanent residents admitted. 7,501
Persons naturalized .5,276
Non-immigrant admissions 1,669,783

Vital Statistics and Health

Marriages

2004 28,843
2005 29,271
2006 28,662

Divorces

2004 . . . . NA
2005 . . . . NA
2006 . . . . NA

Health risks, 2006

Percent of adults who are:
  Smokers. 17.5%
  Overweight (BMI > 25). 56.1%
  Obese (BMI > 30). 20.6%

Births

2005 17,924
  Birthrate (per 1,000). 14.1
  White. 5,115
  Black 487
  Hispanic 2,789
  Asian/Pacific Islander 12,205
  Amer. Indian/Alaska Native. 117
  Low birth weight (2,500g or less). 8.2%
  Cesarian births 25.6%
  Preterm births 12.2%
  To unmarried mothers. 36.3%
  Twin births (per 1,000) 28.0
  Triplets or higher order (per 100,000). 88.4
2006 (preliminary). 18,982
  rate per 1,000 . . . . .14.8

Deaths

2004
All causes 9,030
  rate per 100,000. . . . . .623.1
Heart disease 2,457
  rate per 100,000. . . . . .167.3
Malignant neoplasms 2,088
  rate per 100,000. . . . . .147.8
Cerebrovascular disease. 714
  rate per 100,000. 47.1
Chronic lower respiratory disease 307
  rate per 100,000. . . . . .21.0
Diabetes. 194
  rate per 100,000. . . . . .13.4
2005 (preliminary). 9,137
  rate per 100,000. . . . . .609.1
2006 (provisional) 9,384

Infant deaths

2004 104
  rate per 1,000 . . . . .5.7
2005 (provisional) 123
  rate per 1,000 . . . . .6.9

Exercise routines, 2005

None. 19.5%
Moderate or greater. 52.2%
Vigorous 30.2%

Abortions, 2004

Total performed in state. 3,467
  rate per 1,000 women age 15-44. 14
  % obtained by out-of-state residents 0.3%

Physicians, 2005

Total. 3,964
  rate per 100,000 persons 311

Community hospitals, 2005

Number of hospitals 25
Beds (x 1,000). 3.0
Patients admitted (x 1,000) 114
Average daily census (x 1,000) 2.3
Average cost per day $1,310
Outpatient visits (x 1 mil) 1.9

Disability status of population, 2006
5 to 15 years 4.9%
16 to 64 years 9.6%
65 years and over 38.2%

Education

Educational attainment, 2006
Population over 25 years 863,019
   Less than 9th grade.................... 5.3%
   High school graduate or more 89.0%
   College graduate or more............. 29.7%
   Graduate or professional degree........ 9.8%

Public school enrollment, 2005-06
Total................................182,818
   Pre-kindergarten through grade 8.....127,379
   Grades 9 through 12................. 55,258

Graduating public high school seniors, 2004-05
Diplomas (incl. GED and others) 11,014

SAT scores, 2007
Average critical reading score.............. 484
Average writing score..................... 473
Average math score....................... 506
Percent of graduates taking test 61%

Public school teachers, 2006-07 (estimate)
Total (x 1,000) 11.5
   Elementary..............................6.1
   Secondary...............................5.3
Average salary $51,922
   Elementary........................ $51,922
   Secondary......................... $51,922

State receipts & expenditures for public schools, 2006-07 (estimate)
Revenue receipts ($ mil) $2,801
Expenditures
Total ($ mil) $2,103
   Per capita $1,466
   Per pupil $11,529

NAEP proficiency scores, 2007

	Reading		Math	
	Basic	Proficient	Basic	Proficient
Grade 4	59.0%	25.7%	76.9%	33.3%
Grade 8	62.5%	20.3%	59.1%	21.2%

Higher education enrollment, fall 2005
Total................................. 16,926
   Full-time men 4,275
   Full-time women....................7,587
   Part-time men 2,274
   Part-time women.................... 2,790

Minority enrollment in institutions of higher education, 2005
Black, non-Hispanic 1,534
Hispanic 2,040
Asian/Pacific Islander 40,352
American Indian/Alaska Native............ 379

Institutions of higher education, 2005-06
Total.................................... 23
   Public................................ 10
   Private................................ 13

Earned degrees conferred, 2004-05
Associate's...........................3,423
Bachelor's 5,300
Master's 2,025
First-professional...................... 155
Doctor's.............................. 172

Public Libraries, 2006
Number of libraries....................... 1
Number of outlets 53
Annual visits per capita 4.4
Circulation per capita.....................5.1

State & local financial support for higher education, FY 2006
Full-time equivalent enrollment (x 1,000).....35.3
Appropriations per FTE............... $10,893

Social Insurance & Welfare Programs

Social Security benefits & beneficiaries, 2005
Beneficiaries (x 1,000) 203
   Retired & dependents................. 157
   Survivors............................. 23
   Disabled & dependents.................. 23
Annual benefit payments ($ mil) $2,162
   Retired & dependents................$1,607
   Survivors........................... $302
   Disabled & dependents................ $253
Average monthly benefit
   Retired & dependents................. $990
   Disabled & dependents................ $964
   Widowed............................ $945

Medicare, July 2005
Enrollment (x 1,000)..................... 182
Payments ($ mil) $628

Medicaid, 2004
Beneficiaries (x 1,000)................... 218
Payments ($ mil) $862

State Children's Health Insurance Program, 2006
Enrollment (x 1,000)....................22.0
Expenditures ($ mil)....................$19.3

Persons without health insurance, 2006
Number (x 1,000)........................ 110
   percent............................8.8%
Number of children (x 1,000) 19
   percent of children 6.4%

Health care expenditures, 2004
Total expenditures.................... $6,222
   per capita $4,941

Federal and state public aid

State unemployment insurance, 2006
Recipients, first payments (x 1,000) 21
Total payments ($ mil) $97
Average weekly benefit $365
Temporary Assistance for Needy Families, 2006
Recipients (x 1,000) 203.4
Families (x 1,000) 81.6
Supplemental Security Income, 2005
Recipients (x 1,000) 22.7
Payments ($ mil) $119.1
Food Stamp Program, 2006
Avg monthly participants (x 1,000) 87.9
Total benefits ($ mil) $147.8

Housing & Construction

Housing units
Total 2005 (estimate) 491,071
Total 2006 (estimate) 500,036
Seasonal or recreational use, 2006 33,334
Owner-occupied, 2006 257,599
   Median home value $529,700
   Homeowner vacancy rate 1.0%
Renter-occupied, 2006 175,033
   Median rent $1,116
   Rental vacancy rate 5.5%
Home ownership rate, 2005 . . . . 59.8%
Home ownership rate, 2006 . . . . 59.9%

New privately-owned housing units
Number authorized, 2006 (x 1,000) 7.5
Value ($ mil) $1,761.2
Started 2005 (x 1,000, estimate) 6.5
Started 2006 (x 1,000, estimate) 6.2

Existing home sales
2005 (x 1,000) 36.8
2006 (x 1,000) 31.5

Government & Elections

State officials 2008
Governor . . . . Linda Lingle
      Republican, term expires 12/10
Lieutenant Governor . . . . James Aiona
Secretary of State . . . . (no secretary of state)
Attorney General . . . . Mark Bennett
Chief Justice . . . . Ronald Moon

Governorship
Minimum age 30
Length of term . . . . 4 years
Consecutive terms permitted 2
Who succeeds . . . . Lieutenant Governor

Local governments by type, 2002
Total 19
   County 3
   Municipal 1
   Township 0
   School District 0
   Special District 15

State legislature
Name . . . . Legislature
Upper chamber . . . . .Senate
   Number of members 25
   Length of term . . . . 4 years
   Party in majority, 2008 . . . . .Democratic
Lower chamber . . . . House of Representatives
   Number of members 51
   Length of term . . . . 2 years
   Party in majority, 2008 . . . . .Democratic

Federal representation, 2008 (110th Congress)
Senator . . . . .Daniel Inouye
   Party . . . . .Democratic
   Year term expires 2011
Senator . . . . Daniel Akaka
   Party . . . . .Democratic
   Year term expires 2013
Representatives, total 2
   Democrats 2
   Republicans 0

Voters in November 2006 election (estimate)
Total 387,520
   Male 178,218
   Female 209,302
   White 97,342
   Black 2,881
   Hispanic 9,187
   Asian 201,645

Presidential election, 2004
Total Popular Vote 429,013
   Kerry 231,708
   Bush 194,191
Total Electoral Votes 4

Votes cast for US Senators
2004
Total vote (x 1,000) 415
Leading party .Democratic
Percent for leading party 75.5%
2006
Total vote (x 1,000) 343
Leading party .Democratic
Percent for leading party 61.3%

Votes cast for US Representatives
2004
Total vote (x 1,000) 417
   Democratic 262
   Republican 148
Leading party .Democratic
Percent for leading party 62.9%
2006
Total vote (x 1,000) 338
   Democratic 220
   Republican 118
Leading party .Democratic
Percent for leading party 65.0%

State government employment, 2006
Full-time equivalent employees 54,958
Payroll ($ mil) $207.3

Local government employment, 2006
Full-time equivalent employees 14,636
Payroll ($ mil) $61.4

Women holding public office, 2008
US Congress 1
Statewide elected office...................... 1
State legislature 25

Black public officials, 2002
Total... 1
   US and state legislatures 1
   City/county/regional offices 0
   Judicial/law enforcement................... 0
   Education/school boards.................. 0

Hispanic public officials, 2006
Total... 1
   State executives & legislators 1
   City/county/regional offices 0
   Judicial/law enforcement................... 0
   Education/school boards.................. 0

Governmental Finance

State government revenues, 2006
Total revenue (x $1,000)............$9,856,552
  per capita $7,708.65
General revenue (x $1,000) $8,551,896
  Intergovernmental 1,834,393
  Taxes 4,918,655
    general sales.....................2,355,316
    individual income tax 1,550,757
    corporate income tax 148,084
  Current charges..................1,142,090
  Miscellaneous 656,758

State government expenditure, 2006
Total expenditure (x $1,000).........$8,913,697
  per capita $6,971.26
General expenditure (x $1,000) $8,090,272
  per capita, total.................. $6,327.27
    Education 2,277.91
    Public welfare 1,116.21
    Health 389.80
    Hospitals.......................... 318.94
    Highways 209.78
    Police protection.................... 11.43
    Corrections 140.24
    Natural resources 93.26
    Parks & recreation 56.81
    Governmental administration...... 303.86
    Interest on general debt........... 338.00

State debt & cash, 2006 ($ per capita)
Debt $4,529.66
Cash/security holdings.............. $14,327.06

Federal government grants to state & local government, 2005 (x $1,000)
Total.............................$2,167,856
by Federal agency
  Defense 37,635
  Education 213,383
  Energy.............................7,986
  Environmental Protection Agency 29,597
  Health & Human Services. 1,022,177
  Homeland Security.................. 10,223
  Housing & Urban Development...... 153,043
  Justice 47,471
  Labor 41,913
  Transportation 309,643
  Veterans Affairs....................20,916

Crime & Law Enforcement

Crime, 2006 (rates per 100,000 residents)
Property crimes 54,382
  Burglary 8,709
  Larceny 37,910
  Motor vehicle theft 7,763
  Property crime rate..................4,230.4
Violent crimes..........................3,615
  Murder 21
  Forcible rape....................... 355
  Robbery...........................1,143
  Aggravated assault 2,096
  Violent crime rate 281.2
Hate crimes........................... NA

Fraud and identity theft, 2006
Fraud complaints...................... 2,020
  rate per 100,000 residents 157.1
Identity theft complaints 615
  rate per 100,000 residents 47.8

Law enforcement agencies, 2006
Total agencies............................ 4
Total employees 3,654
  Officers 2,896
  Civilians 758

Prisoners, probation, and parole, 2006
Total prisoners........................5,967
  percent change, 12/31/05 to 12/31/06 ... -2.9%
  in private facilities 32.1%
  in local jails .... NA
Sentenced to more than one year 4,373
  rate per 100,000 residents 338
Adults on probation 18,598
Adults on parole........................2,316

Prisoner demographics, June 30, 2005 (rate per 100,000 residents)
Male..................................... 787
Female 109
White.................................... 453
Black...................................... 851
Hispanic 185

Arrests, 2006

Total 48,018
   Persons under 18 years of age 10,315

Persons under sentence of death, 1/1/07

Total 0
   White 0
   Black 0
   Hispanic 0

State's highest court

Name . . . . .Supreme Court
Number of members 5
Length of term . . . . 10 years
Intermediate appeals court? . . . . .yes

Labor & Income

Civilian labor force, 2006 (x 1,000)

Total 657
   Men 342
   Women 315
   Persons 16-19 years 23
   White 147
   Black . . . . NA
   Hispanic 40

Civilian labor force as a percent of civilian non-institutional population, 2006

Total 66.5%
   Men 72.6
   Women 61.0
   Persons 16-19 years 42.0
   White 67.1
   Black . . . . NA
   Hispanic 72.5

Employment, 2006 (x 1,000)

Total 639
   Men 333
   Women 307
   Persons 16-19 years 20
   White 144
   Black . . . . NA
   Hispanic 39

Unemployment rate, 2006

Total 2.7%
   Men 2.8
   Women 2.5
   Persons 16-19 years 14.8
   White 2.6
   Black . . . . NA
   Hispanic 4.4

Full-time/part-time labor force, 2003 (x 1,000)

Full-time labor force, employed 487
Part-time labor force, employed 105

Unemployed, looking for

   Full-time work 22
   Part-time work 5

Mean duration of unemployment (weeks) 15.9
   Median 8.9

Labor unions, 2006

Membership (x 1,000) 139
   percent of employed 24.7%

Experienced civilian labor force by private industry, 2006

Total 500,515
   Natural resources & mining 7,587
   Construction 35,723
   Manufacturing 15,149
   Trade, transportation & utilities 120,758
   Information 10,706
   Finance 29,922
   Professional & business 78,275
   Education & health 69,697
   Leisure & hospitality 107,807
   Other 24,686

Experienced civilian labor force by occupation, May 2006

Management 28,520
Business & financial .23,180
Legal 3,860
Sales 62,240
Office & admin. support 103,830
Computers & math 8,500
Architecture & engineering 8,750
Arts & entertainment 9,790
Education 38,710
Social services 9,420
Health care practitioner & technical 24,650
Health care support 13,290
Maintenance & repair 22,570
Construction 30,560
Transportation & moving 41,870
Production 17,930
Farming, fishing & forestry 1,070

Hours and earnings of production workers on manufacturing payrolls, 2006

Average weekly hours .38.6
Average hourly earnings $15.89
Average weekly earnings $613.35

Income and poverty, 2006

Median household income $61,160
Personal income, per capita (current $) . . . $36,299
   in constant (2000) dollars $31,687
Persons below poverty level 9.3%

Average annual pay

2006 . . . .$37,799
   increase from 2005 . . . . 4.0%

Federal individual income tax returns, 2005

Returns filed 621,014
Adjusted gross income ($1,000) $31,284,219
Total tax liability ($1,000) $3,785,802

Charitable contributions, 2004

Number of contributions 178.4
Total amount ($ mil) $560.9

Economy, Business, Industry & Agriculture

Fortune 500 companies, 2007 0
Bankruptcy cases filed, FY 2007 1,281

Patents and trademarks issued, 2007
Patents 83
Trademarks 264

Business firm ownership, 2002
Women-owned 29,943
  Sales ($ mil) $4,594
Black-owned 817
  Sales ($ mil) $81
Hispanic-owned 3,095
  Sales ($ mil) $483
Asian-owned 44,924
  Sales ($ mil) $12,556
Amer. Indian/Alaska Native-owned 953
  Sales ($ mil) $114
Hawaiian/Pacific Islander-owned 8,359
  Sales ($ mil) $1,436

Gross domestic product, 2006 ($ mil)
Total gross domestic product $58,307
  Agriculture, forestry, fishing and
    hunting 348
  Mining 39
  Utilities 997
  Construction 3,465
  Manufacturing, durable goods 330
  Manufacturing, non-durable goods 668
  Wholesale trade 1,998
  Retail trade 4,279
  Transportation & warehousing 1,997
  Information 1,461
  Finance & insurance 2,645
  Real estate, rental & leasing 10,457
  Professional and technical services 2,653
  Educational services 605
  Health care and social assistance 3,902
  Accommodation/food services 4,887
  Other services, except government 1,427
  Government 12,844

Establishments, payroll, employees & receipts, by major industry group, 2005
Total 32,244
  Annual payroll ($1,000) $16,163,137
  Paid employees 490,682
Forestry, fishing & agriculture 46
  Annual payroll ($1,000) $7,001
  Paid employees 350
Mining 9
  Annual payroll ($1,000) . . . . NA
  Paid employees . . . . NA
  Receipts, 2002 ($1,000) $25,581

Utilities 46
  Annual payroll ($1,000) $187,927
  Paid employees 2,730
  Receipts, 2002 ($1,000) . . . . NA
Construction 2,753
  Annual payroll ($1,000) $1,556,880
  Paid employees 29,480
  Receipts, 2002 ($1,000) $5,640,054
Manufacturing 946
  Annual payroll ($1,000) $478,722
  Paid employees 14,923
  Receipts, 2002 ($1,000) $3,460,199
Wholesale trade 1,861
  Annual payroll ($1,000) $763,702
  Paid employees 19,978
  Receipts, 2002 ($1,000) $9,986,355
Retail trade 4,924
  Annual payroll ($1,000) $1,645,587
  Paid employees 69,323
  Receipts, 2002 ($1,000) $13,008,182
Transportation & warehousing 850
  Annual payroll ($1,000) $926,945
  Paid employees 26,490
  Receipts, 2002 ($1,000) $1,293,826
Information 631
  Annual payroll ($1,000) $471,448
  Paid employees 10,291
  Receipts, 2002 ($1,000) . . . . NA
Finance & insurance 1,600
  Annual payroll ($1,000) $1,060,036
  Paid employees 19,707
  Receipts, 2002 ($1,000) . . . . NA
Professional, scientific & technical 3,257
  Annual payroll ($1,000) $1,218,103
  Paid employees 24,724
  Receipts, 2002 ($1,000) $2,290,675
Education 516
  Annual payroll ($1,000) $480,968
  Paid employees 16,801
  Receipts, 2002 ($1,000) $107,844
Health care & social assistance 3,389
  Annual payroll ($1,000) $2,358,932
  Paid employees 61,005
  Receipts, 2002 ($1,000) $4,686,323
Arts and entertainment 490
  Annual payroll ($1,000) $231,148
  Paid employees 11,854
  Receipts, 2002 ($1,000) $605,862
Real estate 2,111
  Annual payroll ($1,000) $564,209
  Paid employees 15,047
  Receipts, 2002 ($1,000) $2,372,266
Accommodation & food service 3,393
  Annual payroll ($1,000) $2,308,858
  Paid employees 99,886
  Receipts, 2002 ($1,000) $5,551,380

Exports, 2006

Value of exported goods ($ mil) $706
   Manufactured $477
   Non-manufactured.................... $91

Foreign direct investment in US affiliates, 2004

Property, plants & equipment ($ mil) $6,948
Employment (x 1,000)..................... 31.6

Agriculture, 2006

Number of farms 5,500
Farm acreage (x 1,000) 1,300
   Acres per farm....................... 236
Farm marketings and income ($ mil)
Total.................................. $554.6
   Crops.............................. $466.9
   Livestock...........................$87.7
Net farm income $105.5

Principal commodities, in order by marketing receipts, 2005

Greenhouse/nursery, Pineapples, Cane for sugar, Macadamia nuts, Coffee

Federal economic activity in state

Expenditures, 2005 ($ mil)
   Total............................. $12,699
      Per capita $9,973.72
   Defense $5,015
   Non-defense........................$7,684
Defense department, 2006 ($ mil)
   Payroll........................... $4,064
   Contract awards $1,963
   Grants $77
Homeland security grants ($1,000)
   2006.............................. $12,935
   2007...............................$12,114

FDIC-insured financial institutions, 2005

Number................................... 9
Assets ($ billion) $37.5
Deposits ($ billion) $27.5

Fishing, 2006

Catch (x 1,000 lbs)..................... 26,021
Value ($1,000)......................... $66,780

Mining, 2006 ($ mil)

Total non-fuel mineral production $107
Percent of U.S. 0.17%

Communication, Energy & Transportation

Communication

Households with computers, 2003........ 63.3%
Households with internet access, 2003 .... 55.0%
High-speed internet providers 14
Total high-speed internet lines..........417,674
   Residential 294,863
   Business......................... 122,811
Wireless phone customers, 12/2006 1,034,788

FCC-licensed stations (as of January 1, 2008)

TV stations 27
FM radio stations......................... 58
AM radio stations 31

Energy

Energy consumption, 2004
   Total (trillion Btu)..................... 324
   Per capita (million Btu) 256.9
By source of production (trillion Btu)
   Coal.................................. 19
   Natural gas 3
   Petroleum............................ 283
   Nuclear electric power 0
   Hydroelectric power...................... 1
By end-use sector (trillion Btu)
   Residential 35
   Commercial 47
   Industrial 69
   Transportation 172
Electric energy, 2005
   Primary source of electricity....... Petroleum
   Net generation (billion kWh) 11.5
      percent from renewable sources....... 5.5%
   Net summer capability (million kW) 2.4
   CO_2 emitted from generation 9.0
Natural gas utilities, 2005
   Customers (x 1,000) 29
   Sales (trillion Btu)........................ 3
   Revenues ($ mil) $70
Nuclear plants, 2007 0
Total CO_2 emitted (million metric tons)......21.5
Energy spending, 2004 ($ mil) $4,038
   per capita $3,207
   Price per million Btu $18.05

Transportation, 2006

Public road & street mileage 4,330
   Urban.............................. 2,290
   Rural 2,040
   Interstate............................ 55
Vehicle miles of travel (millions) 10,182
   per capita 7,963.2
Total motor vehicle registrations.......1,008,540
   Automobiles....................... 538,581
   Trucks 464,288
   Motorcycles 31,223
Licensed drivers 867,375
   19 years & under 29,602
Deaths from motor vehicle accidents 161
Gasoline consumed (x 1,000 gallons) 483,136
   per capita 377.9

Commuting Statistics, 2006

Average commute time (min) 25.5
   Drove to work alone 67.0%
   Carpooled.......................... 16.0%
   Public transit 5.4%
   Walk to work 4.8%
   Work from home...................... 4.3%

State Summary

Capital city . . . . .Boise
Governor . . . . C.L. "Butch" Otter
700 West Jefferson
Second Floor
Boise, ID 83702
208-334-2100
Admitted as a state 1890
Area (square miles) 83,570
Population, 2007 (estimate) 1,499,402
Largest city . . . . .Boise
Population, 2006 198,638
Personal income per capita, 2006
(in current dollars) $29,952
Gross domestic product, 2006 ($ mil) $49,907

Leading industries by payroll, 2005

Manufacturing, Health care/Social assistance,
Retail trade

Leading agricultural commodities by receipts, 2005

Dairy products, Cattle and calves, Potatoes,
Wheat, Hay

Geography & Environment

Total area (square miles) 83,570
land 82,747
water 823
Federally-owned land, 2004 (acres) . . .26,565,412
percent 50.2%
Highest point . . . . .Borah Peak
elevation (feet) 12,662
Lowest point . . . . .Snake River
elevation (feet) 710
General coastline (miles) 0
Tidal shoreline (miles) 0
Cropland, 2003 (x 1,000 acres) 5,453
Forest land, 2003 (x 1,000 acres) 4,007
Capital city . . . . .Boise
Population 2000 185,787
Population 2006 198,638
Largest city . . . . .Boise
Population 2000 185,787
Population 2006 198,638

Number of cities with over 100,000 population

1990 1
2000 1
2006 1

State park and recreation areas, 2005

Area (x 1,000 acres) 46
Number of visitors (x 1,000) . . . . NA
Revenues ($1,000) $3,241
percent of operating expenditures 21.2%

National forest system land, 2007

Acres 20,466,617

Demographics & Population Characteristics

Population

1980 943,935
1990 1,006,749
2000 1,293,956
2006 1,466,465
Male 738,366
Female 728,099
Living in group quarters, 2006 33,801
percent of total 2.3%
2007 (estimate) .1,499,402
persons per square mile of land 18.1
2008 (projected) 1,472,584
2010 (projected) 1,517,291
2020 (projected) 1,741,333
2030 (projected) 1,969,624

Population of Core-Based Statistical Areas (formerly Metropolitan Areas), x 1,000

	CBSA	Non-CBSA
1990	846	161
2000	1,103	191
2006	1,267	200

Change in population, 2000-2007

Number 205,446
percent 15.9%
Natural increase (births minus deaths) 88,483
Net internal migration 100,415
Net international migration 17,520

Persons by age, 2006

Under 5 years 112,963
5 to 17 years 281,317
18 years and over 1,072,185
65 years and over 169,173
85 years and over 23,384
Median age 34.2

Persons by age, 2010 (projected)

Under 5 years 115,880
18 and over 1,117,054
65 and over 181,416
Median age 34.8

Race, 2006

One Race
White 1,396,543
Black or African American 9,534
Asian 15,918
American Indian/Alaska Native 20,897
Hawaiian Native/Pacific Islander 1,841
Two or more races 21,732

Persons of Hispanic origin, 2006

Total Hispanic or Latino 138,871
Mexican 120,107
Puerto Rican 1,607
Cuban 1,011

Persons of Asian origin, 2006

Total Asian 15,335
  Asian Indian. 1,269
  Chinese 4,281
  Filipino 2,077
  Japanese 2,560
  Korean. 1,129
  Vietnamese. 1,671

Marital status, 2006

Population 15 years & over 1,140,486
  Never married 272,985
  Married. 669,856
  Separated 15,659
  Widowed. 60,335
  Divorced 137,310

Language spoken at home, 2006

Population 5 years and older. 1,354,099
  English only 1,217,344
  Spanish 103,686
  French 2,365
  German 5,356
  Chinese 2,488

Households & families, 2006

Households 548,555
  with persons under 18 years 197,141
  with persons over 65 years. 115,908
  persons per household 2.61
Families 382,686
  persons per family. 3.11
Married couples 313,995
Female householder,
  no husband present. 47,130
One-person households 130,887

Nativity, 2006

Number of residents born in state 661,708
  percent of population 45.1%

Immigration & naturalization, 2006

Legal permanent residents admitted 2,377
Persons naturalized 980
Non-immigrant admissions 26,975

Vital Statistics and Health

Marriages

2004 14,997
2005 14,935
2006 14,811

Divorces

2004 6,922
2005 7,126
2006 7,500

Health risks, 2006

Percent of adults who are:
  Smokers. 16.8%
  Overweight (BMI > 25). 59.7%
  Obese (BMI > 30). 24.1%

Births

2005 23,062
  Birthrate (per 1,000). 16.1
  White. 22,112
  Black 146
  Hispanic 3,488
  Asian/Pacific Islander 392
  Amer. Indian/Alaska Native 412
  Low birth weight (2,500g or less) 6.7%
  Cesarian births 22.6%
  Preterm births 11.4%
  To unmarried mothers. 22.9%
  Twin births (per 1,000) 29.5
  Triplets or higher order (per 100,000). . . . 178.1
2006 (preliminary). 24,184
  rate per 1,000 . . . . 16.5

Deaths

2004
All causes 10,028
  rate per 100,000 . . . . 753.5
Heart disease 2,450
  rate per 100,000 . . . . 184.3
Malignant neoplasms 2,227
  rate per 100,000 . . . . 169.3
Cerebrovascular disease. 712
  rate per 100,000 . . . . 53.8
Chronic lower respiratory disease 572
  rate per 100,000 . . . . 44.4
Diabetes. 344
  rate per 100,000 . . . . 26.4
2005 (preliminary). 10,554
  rate per 100,000 . . . . 766.4
2006 (provisional) 10,703

Infant deaths

2004 139
  rate per 1,000 . . . . 6.2
2005 (provisional) 154
  rate per 1,000 . . . . 6.7

Exercise routines, 2005

None. 21.6%
Moderate or greater. 54.0%
Vigorous 31.1%

Abortions, 2004

Total performed in state. 963
  rate per 1,000 women age 15-44. 3
  % obtained by out-of-state residents 3.6%

Physicians, 2005

Total. 2,429
  rate per 100,000 persons 170

Community hospitals, 2005

Number of hospitals 39
Beds (x 1,000). 3.3
Patients admitted (x 1,000) 130
Average daily census (x 1,000) 1.8
Average cost per day $1,484
Outpatient visits (x 1 mil) 2.7

Disability status of population, 2006

5 to 15 years 5.9%
16 to 64 years 12.8%
65 years and over 41.4%

Education

Educational attainment, 2006

Population over 25 years 919,203
   Less than 9th grade. 4.5%
   High school graduate or more 87.3%
   College graduate or more. 23.3%
   Graduate or professional degree. 7.1%

Public school enrollment, 2005-06

Total. 261,982
   Pre-kindergarten through grade 8. . . . 182,829
   Grades 9 through 12 79,153

Graduating public high school seniors, 2004-05

Diplomas (incl. GED and others) 15,877

SAT scores, 2007

Average critical reading score. 541
Average writing score 519
Average math score 539
Percent of graduates taking test 19%

Public school teachers, 2006-07 (estimate)

Total (x 1,000) 14.8
   Elementary 7.7
   Secondary 7.1
Average salary $42,798
   Elementary $42,837
   Secondary $42,756

State receipts & expenditures for public schools, 2006-07 (estimate)

Revenue receipts ($ mil) $1,963
Expenditures
Total ($ mil) $2,130
   Per capita $1,309
   Per pupil $7,649

NAEP proficiency scores, 2007

	Reading		Math	
	Basic	Proficient	Basic	Proficient
Grade 4	70.3%	35.1%	84.5%	40.1%
Grade 8	78.5%	31.6%	74.7%	34.1%

Higher education enrollment, fall 2005

Total. 17,405
   Full-time men 6,860
   Full-time women .8,514
   Part-time men 885
   Part-time women. 1,146

Minority enrollment in institutions of higher education, 2005

Black, non-Hispanic 651
Hispanic 3,594
Asian/Pacific Islander 1,472
American Indian/Alaska Native. 1,022

Institutions of higher education, 2005-06

Total. 14
   Public. 7
   Private 7

Earned degrees conferred, 2004-05

Associate's. 3,189
Bachelor's 7,295
Master's 1,623
First-professional. 163
Doctor's 139

Public Libraries, 2006

Number of libraries. 104
Number of outlets 146
Annual visits per capita 6.0
Circulation per capita 8.3

State & local financial support for higher education, FY 2006

Full-time equivalent enrollment (x 1,000). 44.6
Appropriations per FTE. $7,303

Social Insurance & Welfare Programs

Social Security benefits & beneficiaries, 2005

Beneficiaries (x 1,000) 228
   Retired & dependents. 162
   Survivors. 28
   Disabled & dependents. 37
Annual benefit payments ($ mil) $2,379
   Retired & dependents. $1,618
   Survivors. $388
   Disabled & dependents. $373
Average monthly benefit
   Retired & dependents. $980
   Disabled & dependents. $913
   Widowed. $985

Medicare, July 2005

Enrollment (x 1,000) 192
Payments ($ mil) $1,005

Medicaid, 2004

Beneficiaries (x 1,000). 383
Payments ($ mil) $2,206

State Children's Health Insurance Program, 2006

Enrollment (x 1,000). 24.7
Expenditures ($ mil) $23.0

Persons without health insurance, 2006

Number (x 1,000). 227
   percent. 15.4%
Number of children (x 1,000) 52
   percent of children 12.9%

Health care expenditures, 2004

Total expenditures. $6,197
   per capita $4,444

Federal and state public aid

State unemployment insurance, 2006
Recipients, first payments (x 1,000) 40
Total payments ($ mil) $101
Average weekly benefit $241
Temporary Assistance for Needy Families, 2006
Recipients (x 1,000) 35.3
Families (x 1,000) 21.4
Supplemental Security Income, 2005
Recipients (x 1,000) 22.2
Payments ($ mil) $105.6
Food Stamp Program, 2006
Avg monthly participants (x 1,000) 91.1
Total benefits ($ mil) $100.2

Housing & Construction

Housing units

Total 2005 (estimate) 595,623
Total 2006 (estimate) 615,624
Seasonal or recreational use, 2006 31,591
Owner-occupied, 2006 390,982
    Median home value $163,900
    Homeowner vacancy rate 2.2%
Renter-occupied, 2006 157,573
    Median rent $623
    Rental vacancy rate 7.4%
Home ownership rate, 2005 . . . . 74.2%
Home ownership rate, 2006 . . . . 75.1%

New privately-owned housing units

Number authorized, 2006 (x 1,000) 17.1
    Value ($ mil) $2,987.3
Started 2005 (x 1,000, estimate) 13.1
Started 2006 (x 1,000, estimate) 12.8

Existing home sales

2005 (x 1,000) . . . . NA
2006 (x 1,000) 37.0

Government & Elections

State officials 2008

Governor . . . . C.L. "Butch" Otter
              Republican, term expires 1/11
Lieutenant Governor . . . . Jim Risch
Secretary of State . . . . Ben Ysursa
Attorney General . . . . Lawrence Wasden
Chief Justice . . . . Daniel Eismann

Governorship

Minimum age 30
Length of term . . . . 4 years
Consecutive terms permitted . . . . . . not specified
Who succeeds . . . . Lieutenant Governor

Local governments by type, 2002

Total 1,158
    County 44
    Municipal 200
    Township 0
    School District 116
    Special District 798

State legislature

Name . . . . Legislature
Upper chamber . . . . Senate
    Number of members 35
    Length of term . . . . 2 years
    Party in majority, 2008 . . . . Republican
Lower chamber . . . . House of Representatives
    Number of members 70
    Length of term . . . . 2 years
    Party in majority, 2008 . . . . Republican

Federal representation, 2008 (110th Congress)

Senator . . . . Larry Craig
    Party . . . . Republican
    Year term expires 2009
Senator . . . . Mike Crapo
    Party . . . . Republican
    Year term expires 2011
Representatives, total 2
    Democrats 0
    Republicans 2

Voters in November 2006 election (estimate)

Total 522,807
    Male 249,300
    Female 273,506
    White 515,271
    Black . . . . NA
    Hispanic 5,904
    Asian 2,553

Presidential election, 2004

Total Popular Vote 598,447
    Kerry 181,098
    Bush 409,235
Total Electoral Votes 4

Votes cast for US Senators

2004
Total vote (x 1,000) 504
Leading party . . . . Republican
Percent for leading party 99.2%

2006
Total vote (x 1,000) . . . . NA
Leading party . . . . NA
Percent for leading party . . . . NA

Votes cast for US Representatives

2004
Total vote (x 1,000) 572
    Democratic 171
    Republican 401
Leading party . . . . Republican
Percent for leading party 70.1%

2006
Total vote (x 1,000) 445
    Democratic 177
    Republican 248
Leading party . . . . Republican
Percent for leading party 55.7%

Idaho 5

State government employment, 2006
Full-time equivalent employees 22,259
Payroll ($ mil) $74.5

Local government employment, 2006
Full-time equivalent employees 57,154
Payroll ($ mil) $161.4

Women holding public office, 2008
US Congress 0
Statewide elected office...................... 1
State legislature 25

Black public officials, 2002
Total....................................... 1
  US and state legislatures 0
  City/county/regional offices 1
  Judicial/law enforcement................... 0
  Education/school boards.................. 0

Hispanic public officials, 2006
Total....................................... 2
  State executives & legislators 1
  City/county/regional offices 1
  Judicial/law enforcement................... 0
  Education/school boards.................. 0

Governmental Finance

State government revenues, 2006
Total revenue (x $1,000)............. $7,785,621
  per capita $5,318.49
General revenue (x $1,000) $5,978,897
  Intergovernmental 1,836,357
  Taxes 3,142,663
    general sales....................1,078,543
    individual income tax 1,222,569
    corporate income tax 198,302
  Current charges................... 532,248
  Miscellaneous 467,629

State government expenditure, 2006
Total expenditure (x $1,000).........$6,352,876
  per capita $4,339.76
General expenditure (x $1,000) $5,659,741
  per capita, total.................. $3,866.27
    Education....................... 1,477.30
    Public welfare 982.72
    Health 93.94
    Hospitals.........................31.00
    Highways 410.52
    Police protection...................31.04
    Corrections 136.50
    Natural resources 132.28
    Parks & recreation 24.12
    Governmental administration.......185.97
    Interest on general debt.............83.96

State debt & cash, 2006 ($ per capita)
Debt $1,677.25
Cash/security holdings..............$10,008.78

Federal government grants to state & local government, 2005 (x $1,000)
Total............................ $2,092,900
by Federal agency
  Defense 26,313
  Education 178,209
  Energy...........................17,226
  Environmental Protection Agency 41,443
  Health & Human Services. 1,039,421
  Homeland Security....................8,013
  Housing & Urban Development....... 86,303
  Justice 33,407
  Labor 44,478
  Transportation 335,979
  Veterans Affairs....................6,075

Crime & Law Enforcement

Crime, 2006 (rates per 100,000 residents)
Property crimes 35,471
  Burglary 7,526
  Larceny 25,516
  Motor vehicle theft 2,429
  Property crime rate.................2,418.8
Violent crimes. 3,625
  Murder 36
  Forcible rape........................ 587
  Robbery............................. 301
  Aggravated assault 2,701
  Violent crime rate 247.2
Hate crimes............................. 25

Fraud and identity theft, 2006
Fraud complaints.......................2,012
  rate per 100,000 residents 137.2
Identity theft complaints 718
  rate per 100,000 residents 49.0

Law enforcement agencies, 2006
Total agencies........................... 107
Total employees 3,896
  Officers 2,594
  Civilians 1,302

Prisoners, probation, and parole, 2006
Total prisoners.........................7,124
  percent change, 12/31/05 to 12/31/06 .... 4.5%
  in private facilities 27.0%
  in local jails 6.4%
Sentenced to more than one year 7,124
  rate per 100,000 residents 480
Adults on probation 48,609
Adults on parole.......................2,732

Prisoner demographics, June 30, 2005 (rate per 100,000 residents)
Male...................................1,379
Female 185
White.................................. 675
Black.................................. 2,869
Hispanic 1,654

Arrests, 2006

Total 65,945
  Persons under 18 years of age 14,339

Persons under sentence of death, 1/1/07

Total 20
  White 20
  Black 0
  Hispanic 0

State's highest court

Name . . . . .Supreme Court
Number of members 5
Length of term . . . . 6 years
Intermediate appeals court? . . . . .yes

Labor & Income

Civilian labor force, 2006 (x 1,000)

Total 759
  Men 416
  Women 343
  Persons 16-19 years 48
  White 724
  Black . . . . NA
  Hispanic 63

Civilian labor force as a percent of civilian non-institutional population, 2006

Total 68.9%
  Men 76.4
  Women 61.5
  Persons 16-19 years 52.4
  White 69.1
  Black . . . . NA
  Hispanic 71.3

Employment, 2006 (x 1,000)

Total 732
  Men 403
  Women 329
  Persons 16-19 years 43
  White 699
  Black . . . . NA
  Hispanic 60

Unemployment rate, 2006

Total 3.5%
  Men 3.1
  Women 4.0
  Persons 16-19 years 11.4
  White 3.3
  Black . . . . NA
  Hispanic 4.5

Full-time/part-time labor force, 2003 (x 1,000)

Full-time labor force, employed 510
Part-time labor force, employed 145
Unemployed, looking for
  Full-time work 31
  Part-time work 7
Mean duration of unemployment (weeks) 14.1
  Median 7.0

Labor unions, 2006

Membership (x 1,000) 37
  percent of employed 6.0%

Experienced civilian labor force by private industry, 2006

Total 532,929
  Natural resources & mining 24,096
  Construction 52,113
  Manufacturing. .65,981
  Trade, transportation & utilities 126,344
  Information 10,592
  Finance 29,828
  Professional & business 81,598
  Education & health 66,979
  Leisure & hospitality. 59,727
  Other 15,628

Experienced civilian labor force by occupation, May 2006

Management. 43,590
Business & financial 20,750
Legal. 3,640
Sales 61,090
Office & admin. support. 104,050
Computers & math 10,760
Architecture & engineering. 15,080
Arts & entertainment 7,440
Education 34,830
Social services 9,050
Health care practitioner & technical 28,050
Health care support 16,590
Maintenance & repair. 28,090
Construction 41,440
Transportation & moving 46,990
Production 40,890
Farming, fishing & forestry 6,520

Hours and earnings of production workers on manufacturing payrolls, 2006

Average weekly hours 41.7
Average hourly earnings $16.89
Average weekly earnings $704.31

Income and poverty, 2006

Median household income. $42,865
Personal income, per capita (current $) . . . $29,952
  in constant (2000) dollars $26,146
Persons below poverty level 12.6%

Average annual pay

2006 . . . . $32,580
  increase from 2005 . . . . 5.9%

Federal individual income tax returns, 2005

Returns filed. 613,932
Adjusted gross income ($1,000) $28,226,440
Total tax liability ($1,000) $3,288,355

Charitable contributions, 2004

Number of contributions 175.0
Total amount ($ mil) $707.0

Economy, Business, Industry & Agriculture

Fortune 500 companies, 2007 2
Bankruptcy cases filed, FY 2007 3,716

Patents and trademarks issued, 2007
Patents 1,478
Trademarks 260

Business firm ownership, 2002
Women-owned 28,824
  Sales ($ mil) $3,216
Black-owned 373
  Sales ($ mil) $58
Hispanic-owned 2,775
  Sales ($ mil) $352
Asian-owned 1,111
  Sales ($ mil) $284
Amer. Indian/Alaska Native-owned 1,143
  Sales ($ mil) $204
Hawaiian/Pacific Islander-owned 99
  Sales ($ mil) $9

Gross domestic product, 2006 ($ mil)
Total gross domestic product $49,907
  Agriculture, forestry, fishing and
    hunting 2,253
  Mining 302
  Utilities 903
  Construction 3,357
  Manufacturing, durable goods 5,584
  Manufacturing, non-durable goods 1,609
  Wholesale trade .2,716
  Retail trade 4,307
  Transportation & warehousing 1,393
  Information 1,126
  Finance & insurance 2,283
  Real estate, rental & leasing 5,760
  Professional and technical services 3,444
  Educational services 276
  Health care and social assistance 3,326
  Accommodation/food services 1,248
  Other services, except government 964
  Government 6,303

Establishments, payroll, employees & receipts, by major industry group, 2005
Total 43,346
  Annual payroll ($1,000) $15,397,889
  Paid employees 519,319
Forestry, fishing & agriculture 543
  Annual payroll ($1,000) $110,786
  Paid employees 3,742
Mining 134
  Annual payroll ($1,000) $104,826
  Paid employees 2,071
  Receipts, 2002 ($1,000) $284,619

Utilities 184
  Annual payroll ($1,000) $200,283
  Paid employees 3,451
  Receipts, 2002 ($1,000) . . . . .NA
Construction 7,697
  Annual payroll ($1,000) $1,622,096
  Paid employees 44,658
  Receipts, 2002 ($1,000) $5,507,211
Manufacturing 1,849
  Annual payroll ($1,000) $2,393,039
  Paid employees 61,167
  Receipts, 2002 ($1,000) $15,174,196
Wholesale trade 1,983
  Annual payroll ($1,000) $907,831
  Paid employees 23,602
  Receipts, 2002 ($1,000) $11,458,012
Retail trade 6,064
  Annual payroll ($1,000) $1,673,120
  Paid employees 75,716
  Receipts, 2002 ($1,000) $13,540,952
Transportation & warehousing 1,645
  Annual payroll ($1,000) $455,008
  Paid employees 15,533
  Receipts, 2002 ($1,000) $1,183,968
Information 698
  Annual payroll ($1,000) $458,656
  Paid employees 12,575
  Receipts, 2002 ($1,000) . . . . .NA
Finance & insurance 2,670
  Annual payroll ($1,000) $907,058
  Paid employees 20,924
  Receipts, 2002 ($1,000) . . . . .NA
Professional, scientific & technical 3,805
  Annual payroll ($1,000) $1,411,856
  Paid employees 35,126
  Receipts, 2002 ($1,000) $2,309,182
Education 361
  Annual payroll ($1,000) $147,680
  Paid employees 8,349
  Receipts, 2002 ($1,000) $54,738
Health care & social assistance 4,153
  Annual payroll ($1,000) $2,146,695
  Paid employees 68,820
  Receipts, 2002 ($1,000) $4,251,492
Arts and entertainment 670
  Annual payroll ($1,000) $104,488
  Paid employees 7,326
  Receipts, 2002 ($1,000) $274,384
Real estate 2,133
  Annual payroll ($1,000) $199,311
  Paid employees 7,287
  Receipts, 2002 ($1,000) $700,380
Accommodation & food service 3,256
  Annual payroll ($1,000) $571,584
  Paid employees 51,670
  Receipts, 2002 ($1,000) $1,653,671

Exports, 2006
Value of exported goods ($ mil) $3,721
   Manufactured $2,849
   Non-manufactured $259

Foreign direct investment in US affiliates, 2004
Property, plants & equipment ($ mil) $2,187
Employment (x 1,000). 12.9

Agriculture, 2006
Number of farms 25,000
Farm acreage (x 1,000) 11,800
   Acres per farm 472
Farm marketings and income ($ mil)
Total. $4,415.6
   Crops $1,999.6
   Livestock. $2,416.0
Net farm income $758.4

Principal commodities, in order by marketing receipts, 2005
   Dairy products, Cattle and calves, Potatoes,
           Wheat, Hay

Federal economic activity in state
Expenditures, 2005 ($ mil)
   Total. $9,598
      Per capita $6,714.69
   Defense $678
   Non-defense. $8,920
Defense department, 2006 ($ mil)
   Payroll. $541
   Contract awards $168
   Grants $37
Homeland security grants ($1,000)
   2006. . . . .$11,759
   2007 . . . . $6,701

FDIC-insured financial institutions, 2005
Number 19
Assets ($ billion) $6.9
Deposits ($ billion) $5.4

Fishing, 2006
Catch (x 1,000 lbs). . . . . NA
Value ($1,000). . . . . NA

Mining, 2006 ($ mil)
Total non-fuel mineral production $810
Percent of U.S. 1.26%

Communication, Energy & Transportation

Communication
Households with computers, 2003. . . . . 69.2%
Households with internet access, 2003 . . . .56.4%
High-speed internet providers 45
Total high-speed internet lines. 381,583
   Residential 242,163
   Business. 139,420
Wireless phone customers, 12/2006 972,825

FCC-licensed stations (as of January 1, 2008)
TV stations 21
FM radio stations. 102
AM radio stations 47

Energy
Energy consumption, 2004
   Total (trillion Btu). 500
   Per capita (million Btu) 358.4
By source of production (trillion Btu)
   Coal 12
   Natural gas. 77
   Petroleum. 157
   Nuclear electric power 0
   Hydroelectric power 85
By end-use sector (trillion Btu)
   Residential 110
   Commercial 78
   Industrial 190
   Transportation 122
Electric energy, 2005
   Primary source of electricity. . . . Hydroelectric
   Net generation (billion kWh) 10.8
      percent from renewable sources. 84.2%
   Net summer capability (million kW) 3.2
   CO_2 emitted from generation 1.3
Natural gas utilities, 2005
   Customers (x 1,000) 335
   Sales (trillion Btu). 59
   Revenues ($ mil) $345
Nuclear plants, 2007 0
Total CO_2 emitted (million metric tons). 14.2
Energy spending, 2004 ($ mil) $3,736
   per capita $2,679
   Price per million Btu $11.82

Transportation, 2006
Public road & street mileage 47,105
   Urban. 4,755
   Rural 42,350
   Interstate. 612
Vehicle miles of travel (millions) 15,198
   per capita 10,382.0
Total motor vehicle registrations. 1,275,115
   Automobiles. 541,487
   Trucks 729,861
   Motorcycles 50,536
Licensed drivers .1,008,016
   19 years & under 66,038
Deaths from motor vehicle accidents 267
Gasoline consumed (x 1,000 gallons) 658,019
   per capita 449.5

Commuting Statistics, 2006
Average commute time (min) 20.1
   Drove to work alone 77.2%
   Carpooled. 11.7%
   Public transit 0.8%
   Walk to work 3.4%
   Work from home. 5.0%

State Summary

Capital city . . . . Springfield
Governor . . . . Rod Blagojevich

State Capitol
207 Statehouse
Springfield, IL 62706
217-782-6830

Admitted as a state 1818
Area (square miles) 57,914
Population, 2007 (estimate). 12,852,548
Largest city . . . . Chicago
  Population, 2006 2,833,321
Personal income per capita, 2006
  (in current dollars) $38,215
Gross domestic product, 2006 ($ mil) . . . $589,598

Leading industries by payroll, 2005

Manufacturing, Health care/Social assistance,
Finance & Insurance

**Leading agricultural commodities
by receipts, 2005**

Corn, Soybeans, Hogs, Cattle and calves, Green-
house/nursery

Geography & Environment

Total area (square miles). 57,914
  land 55,584
  water 2,331
Federally-owned land, 2004 (acres) 641,959
  percent 1.8%
Highest point . . . . Charles Mound
  elevation (feet) 1,235
Lowest point . . . . Mississippi River
  elevation (feet) 279
General coastline (miles) 0
Tidal shoreline (miles) 0
Cropland, 2003 (x 1,000 acres) 23,981
Forest land, 2003 (x 1,000 acres). 3,949
Capital city . . . . Springfield
  Population 2000 .111,454
  Population 2006 116,482
Largest city . . . . Chicago
  Population 2000 2,896,016
  Population 2006 2,833,321

Number of cities with over 100,000 population

1990 4
2000 7
2006 8

State park and recreation areas, 2005

Area (x 1,000 acres) 481
Number of visitors (x 1,000) 44,950
Revenues ($1,000) $7,336
  percent of operating expenditures 14.0%

National forest system land, 2007

Acres 297,077

Demographics & Population Characteristics

Population

1980 11,426,518
1990 11,430,602
2000 12,419,647
2006 12,831,970
  Male 6,317,460
  Female 6,514,510
Living in group quarters, 2006 323,647
  percent of total. 2.5%
2007 (estimate). 12,852,548
  persons per square mile of land 231.2
2008 (projected). 12,835,851
2010 (projected) 12,916,894
2020 (projected) 13,236,720
2030 (projected) 13,432,892

**Population of Core-Based Statistical Areas
(formerly Metropolitan Areas), x 1,000**

	CBSA	Non-CBSA
1990	10,809	622
2000	11,796	624
2006	12,218	614

Change in population, 2000-2007

Number 432,901
  percent. 3.5%
Natural increase (births minus deaths) 564,091
Net internal migration . . . . -551,311
Net international migration 420,052

Persons by age, 2006

Under 5 years 887,605
5 to 17 years 2,327,639
18 years and over 9,616,726
65 years and over 1,534,476
85 years and over .227,074
  Median age 35.7

Persons by age, 2010 (projected)

Under 5 years 926,650
18 and over 9,719,988
65 and over 1,600,863
  Median age 36.0

Race, 2006

One Race

  White. 10,169,966
  Black or African American 1,928,153
  Asian 541,218
  American Indian/Alaska Native. 41,231
  Hawaiian Native/Pacific Islander. 8,448
Two or more races. 142,954

Persons of Hispanic origin, 2006

Total Hispanic or Latino 1,888,439
  Mexican. 1,486,386
  Puerto Rican 169,955
  Cuban 19,515

Persons of Asian origin, 2006

Total Asian	536,992
Asian Indian	166,870
Chinese	104,266
Filipino	114,266
Japanese	20,602
Korean	58,026
Vietnamese	24,365

Marital status, 2006

Population 15 years & over	10,169,211
Never married	3,318,202
Married	5,244,153
Separated	189,423
Widowed	657,856
Divorced	949,000

Language spoken at home, 2006

Population 5 years and older	11,942,632
English only	9,341,064
Spanish	1,516,560
French	36,856
German	60,726
Chinese	81,702

Households & families, 2006

Households	4,724,252
with persons under 18 years	1,661,252
with persons over 65 years	1,067,221
persons per household	2.65
Families	3,146,342
persons per family	3.29
Married couples	2,355,451
Female householder, no husband present	587,369
One-person households	1,329,813

Nativity, 2006

Number of residents born in state	8,580,066
percent of population	66.9%

Immigration & naturalization, 2006

Legal permanent residents admitted	52,459
Persons naturalized	30,156
Non-immigrant admissions	791,277

Vital Statistics and Health

Marriages

2004	77,845
2005	74,065
2006	77,981

Divorces

2004	33,076
2005	32,408
2006	32,158

Health risks, 2006

Percent of adults who are:

Smokers	20.5%
Overweight (BMI > 25)	61.7%
Obese (BMI > 30)	25.1%

Births

2005	179,020
Birthrate (per 1,000)	14.0
White	138,884
Black	30,710
Hispanic	43,441
Asian/Pacific Islander	9,139
Amer. Indian/Alaska Native	287
Low birth weight (2,500g or less)	8.5%
Cesarian births	28.8%
Preterm births	13.1%
To unmarried mothers	37.1%
Twin births (per 1,000)	35.9
Triplets or higher order (per 100,000)	234.6
2006 (preliminary)	180,583
rate per 1,000	14.1

Deaths

2004

All causes	102,670
rate per 100,000	801.4
Heart disease	28,284
rate per 100,000	219.1
Malignant neoplasms	24,289
rate per 100,000	193.2
Cerebrovascular disease	6,489
rate per 100,000	50.0
Chronic lower respiratory disease	4,723
rate per 100,000	37.5
Diabetes	3,069
rate per 100,000	24.2
2005 (preliminary)	103,977
rate per 100,000	798.2
2006 (provisional)	101,922

Infant deaths

2004	1,349
rate per 1,000	7.5
2005 (provisional)	1,261
rate per 1,000	7.1

Exercise routines, 2005

None	25.6%
Moderate or greater	47.1%
Vigorous	25.7%

Abortions, 2004

Total performed in state	43,537
rate per 1,000 women age 15-44	16
% obtained by out-of-state residents	7.8%

Physicians, 2005

Total	34,826
rate per 100,000 persons	273

Community hospitals, 2005

Number of hospitals	191
Beds (x 1,000)	34.5
Patients admitted (x 1,000)	1,583
Average daily census (x 1,000)	22.6
Average cost per day	$1,637
Outpatient visits (x 1 mil)	28.7

Disability status of population, 2006
5 to 15 years 5.6%
16 to 64 years 9.9%
65 years and over 39.6%

Education

Educational attainment, 2006
Population over 25 years 8,326,130
   Less than 9th grade..................... 6.6%
   High school graduate or more 85.0%
   College graduate or more............. 28.9%
   Graduate or professional degree....... 10.8%

Public school enrollment, 2005-06
Total............................... 2,111,706
   Pre-kindergarten through grade 8...1,480,047
   Grades 9 through 12................. 631,198

Graduating public high school seniors, 2004-05
Diplomas (incl. GED and others) 123,615

SAT scores, 2007
Average critical reading score.............. 594
Average writing score 588
Average math score 611
Percent of graduates taking test 8%

Public school teachers, 2006-07 (estimate)
Total (x 1,000) 131.9
   Elementary.........................89.8
   Secondary..........................42.2
Average salary $58,246
   Elementary.......................$55,775
   Secondary........................$64,061

State receipts & expenditures for public schools, 2006-07 (estimate)
Revenue receipts ($ mil) $21,566
Expenditures
Total ($ mil) $24,071
   Per capita $1,717
   Per pupil $11,489

NAEP proficiency scores, 2007

	Reading		Math	
	Basic	Proficient	Basic	Proficient
Grade 4	65.0%	32.2%	78.6%	36.3%
Grade 8	74.9%	29.8%	70.3%	30.8%

Higher education enrollment, fall 2005
Total................................277,818
   Full-time men 87,050
   Full-time women....................116,432
   Part-time men 28,458
   Part-time women....................45,878

Minority enrollment in institutions of higher education, 2005
Black, non-Hispanic 118,905
Hispanic 95,542
Asian/Pacific Islander 48,336
American Indian/Alaska Native..........3,109

Institutions of higher education, 2005-06
Total.................................. 172
   Public............................... 60
   Private............................. 112

Earned degrees conferred, 2004-05
Associate's........................... 34,715
Bachelor's 63,913
Master's 35,992
First-professional.....................4,573
Doctor's.............................2,752

Public Libraries, 2006
Number of libraries.................... 623
Number of outlets 811
Annual visits per capita 5.8
Circulation per capita....................8.6

State & local financial support for higher education, FY 2006
Full-time equivalent enrollment (x 1,000)....385.3
Appropriations per FTE............... $6,689

Social Insurance & Welfare Programs

Social Security benefits & beneficiaries, 2005
Beneficiaries (x 1,000) 1,898
   Retired & dependents..................1,347
   Survivors........................... 271
   Disabled & dependents................. 281
Annual benefit payments ($ mil) $21,364
   Retired & dependents............... $14,497
   Survivors......................... $3,899
   Disabled & dependents.............. $2,967
Average monthly benefit
   Retired & dependents.................$1,040
   Disabled & dependents............... $966
   Widowed............................$1,031

Medicare, July 2005
Enrollment (x 1,000).....................1,691
Payments ($ mil) $12,468

Medicaid, 2004
Beneficiaries (x 1,000).................... 206
Payments ($ mil) $990

State Children's Health Insurance Program, 2006
Enrollment (x 1,000)....................316.8
Expenditures ($ mil)...................$312.1

Persons without health insurance, 2006
Number (x 1,000)........................1,776
   percent............................ 14.0%
Number of children (x 1,000) 302
   percent of children 9.5%

Health care expenditures, 2004
Total expenditures.................... $67,292
   per capita $5,293

Federal and state public aid

State unemployment insurance, 2006
Recipients, first payments (x 1,000) 335
Total payments ($ mil) $1,649
Average weekly benefit $292
Temporary Assistance for Needy Families, 2006
Recipients (x 1,000) 1,042.1
Families (x 1,000) 422.0
Supplemental Security Income, 2005
Recipients (x 1,000) 258.6
Payments ($ mil) $1,336.6
Food Stamp Program, 2006
Avg monthly participants (x 1,000) 1,225.1
Total benefits ($ mil) $1,503.2

Housing & Construction

Housing units
Total 2005 (estimate) 5,144,625
Total 2006 (estimate) 5,199,589
Seasonal or recreational use, 2006 36,049
Owner-occupied, 2006 3,301,367
    Median home value $200,200
    Homeowner vacancy rate 2.3%
Renter-occupied, 2006 1,422,885
    Median rent $761
    Rental vacancy rate 12.6%
Home ownership rate, 2005 . . . . 70.9%
Home ownership rate, 2006 . . . . 70.4%

New privately-owned housing units
Number authorized, 2006 (x 1,000) 58.8
    Value ($ mil) $9,470.3
Started 2005 (x 1,000, estimate) 58.5
Started 2006 (x 1,000, estimate) 56.6

Existing home sales
2005 (x 1,000) 315.3
2006 (x 1,000) 289.0

Government & Elections

State officials 2008
Governor . . . . .Rod Blagojevich
    Democratic, term expires 1/11
Lieutenant Governor . . . . Patrick Quinn
Secretary of State . . . . Jesse White
Attorney General . . . . Lisa Madigan
Chief Justice . . . . .Robert Thomas

Governorship
Minimum age 25
Length of term . . . . 4 years
Consecutive terms permitted . . . . . . not specified
Who succeeds . . . . Lieutenant Governor

Local governments by type, 2002
Total 6,903
    County 102
    Municipal 1,291
    Township 1,431
    School District 934
    Special District 3,145

State legislature

Name . . . . General Assembly
Upper chamber . . . . .Senate
    Number of members 59
    Length of term . . . . 4 years
    Party in majority, 2008 . . . . .Democratic
Lower chamber . . . . . . .House of Representatives
    Number of members 118
    Length of term . . . . 2 years
    Party in majority, 2008 . . . . .Democratic

Federal representation, 2008 (110th Congress)
Senator . . . . Richard Durbin
    Party . . . . .Democratic
    Year term expires 2009
Senator . . . . Barack Obama
    Party . . . . .Democratic
    Year term expires 2011
Representatives, total . . . . 19 (1 vacant)
    Democrats 10
    Republicans 8

Voters in November 2006 election (estimate)
Total 3,967,614
    Male 1,805,445
    Female 2,162,169
    White 3,261,613
    Black 601,554
    Hispanic 100,349
    Asian 79,456

Presidential election, 2004
Total Popular Vote 5,274,322
    Kerry 2,891,550
    Bush 2,345,946
Total Electoral Votes 21

Votes cast for US Senators
2004
Total vote (x 1,000) 5,142
Leading party .Democratic
Percent for leading party 70.0%
2006
Total vote (x 1,000) . . . . NA
Leading party . . . . NA
Percent for leading party . . . . NA

Votes cast for US Representatives
2004
Total vote (x 1,000) 4,989
    Democratic 2,675
    Republican 2,272
Leading party .Democratic
Percent for leading party 53.6%
2006
Total vote (x 1,000) 3,453
    Democratic 1,986
    Republican 1,443
Leading party .Democratic
Percent for leading party 57.5%

State government employment, 2006
Full-time equivalent employees 131,859
Payroll ($ mil) $537.3

Local government employment, 2006
Full-time equivalent employees 503,131
Payroll ($ mil) $1,941.6

Women holding public office, 2008
US Congress................................ 3
Statewide elected office...................... 1
State legislature 48

Black public officials, 2002
Total................................... 619
  US and state legislatures 28
  City/county/regional offices 327
  Judicial/law enforcement............... 59
  Education/school boards................ 205

Hispanic public officials, 2006
Total.................................... 96
  State executives & legislators 11
  City/county/regional offices 63
  Judicial/law enforcement.................. 6
  Education/school boards................. 16

Governmental Finance

State government revenues, 2006
Total revenue (x $1,000)........... $62,728,922
  per capita $4,909.50
General revenue (x $1,000) $49,271,484
  Intergovernmental 13,387,270
  Taxes 28,128,749
    general sales....................7,760,590
    individual income tax 8,635,104
    corporate income tax 2,400,270
  Current charges...................3,885,325
  Miscellaneous 3,870,140

State government expenditure, 2006
Total expenditure (x $1,000)........ $55,767,569
  per capita $4,364.67
General expenditure (x $1,000) $48,051,530
  per capita, total.................... $3,760.77
    Education...................... 1,162.93
    Public welfare 1,154.07
    Health 164.70
    Hospitals....................... 72.54
    Highways 285.79
    Police protection....................33.72
    Corrections 90.06
    Natural resources 21.54
    Parks & recreation 20.58
    Governmental administration........89.63
    Interest on general debt............184.74

State debt & cash, 2006 ($ per capita)
Debt $4,199.36
Cash/security holdings..............$9,820.59

Federal government grants to state & local government, 2005 (x $1,000)
Total............................$16,634,795
by Federal agency
  Defense 100,879
  Education 1,531,680
  Energy........................... 94,897
  Environmental Protection Agency ... 129,838
  Health & Human Services. 9,636,578
  Homeland Security..................46,143
  Housing & Urban Development.....1,866,308
  Justice 206,139
  Labor 401,598
  Transportation 1,241,528
  Veterans Affairs.................. 24,619

Crime & Law Enforcement

Crime, 2006 (rates per 100,000 residents)
Property crimes 387,478
  Burglary 77,259
  Larceny 272,578
  Motor vehicle theft 37,641
  Property crime rate................. 3,019.6
Violent crimes......................... 69,498
  Murder 780
  Forcible rape.......................4,078
  Robbery.........................23,782
  Aggravated assault 40,858
  Violent crime rate 541.6
Hate crimes............................. 188

Fraud and identity theft, 2006
Fraud complaints.................... 13,908
  rate per 100,000 residents 108.4
Identity theft complaints 10,080
  rate per 100,000 residents 78.6

Law enforcement agencies, 2006
Total agencies....................... 757
Total employees 52,055
  Officers 37,229
  Civilians 14,826

Prisoners, probation, and parole, 2006
Total prisoners........................45,106
  percent change, 12/31/05 to 12/31/06 .... 0.4%
  in private facilities 0%
  in local jails 0%
Sentenced to more than one year 45,106
  rate per 100,000 residents 350
Adults on probation 141,000
Adults on parole....................... NA

Prisoner demographics, June 30, 2005 (rate per 100,000 residents)
Male................................. 951
Female............................... 79
White................................ 223
Black................................ 2,020
Hispanic 415

Arrests, 2006

Total 191,165
   Persons under 18 years of age 33,775

Persons under sentence of death, 1/1/07

Total 11
   White 5
   Black 3
   Hispanic 3

State's highest court

Name . . . . .Supreme Court
Number of members 7
Length of term . . . . 10 years
Intermediate appeals court? . . . . .yes

Labor & Income

Civilian labor force, 2006 (x 1,000)

Total 6,584
   Men 3,569
   Women 3,015
   Persons 16-19 years 307
   White 5,358
   Black 846
   Hispanic 734

Civilian labor force as a percent of civilian non-institutional population, 2006

Total 67.4%
   Men 75.4
   Women 59.8
   Persons 16-19 years .41.8
   White 68.2
   Black 62.3
   Hispanic 72.3

Employment, 2006 (x 1,000)

Total 6,289
   Men 3,408
   Women 2,882
   Persons 16-19 years 272
   White 5,162
   Black 761
   Hispanic 694

Unemployment rate, 2006

Total 4.5%
   Men 4.5
   Women 4.4
   Persons 16-19 years .11.4
   White 3.7
   Black 10.0
   Hispanic 5.5

Full-time/part-time labor force, 2003 (x 1,000)

Full-time labor force, employed 4,907
Part-time labor force, employed 1,000
Unemployed, looking for
   Full-time work 366
   Part-time work 57
Mean duration of unemployment (weeks) 20.9
   Median 11.5

Labor unions, 2006

Membership (x 1,000) 931
   percent of employed 16.4%

Experienced civilian labor force by private industry, 2006

Total 5,012,850
   Natural resources & mining 25,835
   Construction 275,205
   Manufacturing 682,715
   Trade, transportation & utilities 1,181,726
   Information 116,813
   Finance 399,344
   Professional & business 855,136
   Education & health 750,330
   Leisure & hospitality 522,867
   Other 195,835

Experienced civilian labor force by occupation, May 2006

Management 250,790
Business & financial 305,860
Legal 47,560
Sales 622,590
Office & admin. support 1,004,380
Computers & math 136,450
Architecture & engineering 82,850
Arts & entertainment 66,650
Education 371,910
Social services 66,650
Health care practitioner & technical 297,370
Health care support 137,740
Maintenance & repair 210,810
Construction 240,910
Transportation & moving 478,240
Production 530,540
Farming, fishing & forestry 5,000

Hours and earnings of production workers on manufacturing payrolls, 2006

Average weekly hours .41.1
Average hourly earnings $16.03
Average weekly earnings $658.83

Income and poverty, 2006

Median household income $52,006
Personal income, per capita (current $) . . . $38,215
   in constant (2000) dollars $33,359
Persons below poverty level 12.3%

Average annual pay

2006 . . . . $45,650
   increase from 2005 . . . . 4.4%

Federal individual income tax returns, 2005

Returns filed 5,836,193
Adjusted gross income ($1,000) $335,321,455
Total tax liability ($1,000) $46,753,758

Charitable contributions, 2004

Number of contributions 1,840.4
Total amount ($ mil) $7,054.5

Economy, Business, Industry & Agriculture

Fortune 500 companies, 2007 33
Bankruptcy cases filed, FY 2007 39,147

Patents and trademarks issued, 2007
Patents 3,795
Trademarks 3,910

Business firm ownership, 2002
Women-owned 284,954
   Sales ($ mil) $46,862
Black-owned 68,699
   Sales ($ mil) $4,980
Hispanic-owned 39,539
   Sales ($ mil) $7,389
Asian-owned 44,477
   Sales ($ mil) $14,545
Amer. Indian/Alaska Native-owned 3,393
   Sales ($ mil) $452
Hawaiian/Pacific Islander-owned 656
   Sales ($ mil) . . . . NA

Gross domestic product, 2006 ($ mil)
Total gross domestic product $589,598
   Agriculture, forestry, fishing and
      hunting 1,996
   Mining 1,765
   Utilities 13,223
   Construction 28,041
   Manufacturing, durable goods 44,275
   Manufacturing, non-durable goods . . . 33,366
   Wholesale trade 42,284
   Retail trade 33,874
   Transportation & warehousing 20,691
   Information 21,078
   Finance & insurance 55,049
   Real estate, rental & leasing 77,914
   Professional and technical services 49,639
   Educational services 6,183
   Health care and social assistance 38,404
   Accommodation/food services 13,641
   Other services, except government 13,872
   Government 56,823

Establishments, payroll, employees & receipts, by major industry group, 2005

Total 318,927
   Annual payroll ($1,000) $217,221,786
   Paid employees 5,235,866
Forestry, fishing & agriculture 324
   Annual payroll ($1,000) $56,494
   Paid employees 1,598
Mining 603
   Annual payroll ($1,000) $556,295
   Paid employees 9,934
   Receipts, 2002 ($1,000) $2,276,094

Utilities 481
   Annual payroll ($1,000) $2,437,078
   Paid employees 27,688
   Receipts, 2002 ($1,000) . . . . .NA
Construction 32,551
   Annual payroll ($1,000) $13,615,634
   Paid employees 250,157
   Receipts, 2002 ($1,000) $55,308,836
Manufacturing 16,073
   Annual payroll ($1,000) $30,078,477
   Paid employees 676,298
   Receipts, 2002 ($1,000) $188,365,216
Wholesale trade 20,001
   Annual payroll ($1,000) $17,770,519
   Paid employees 322,342
   Receipts, 2002 ($1,000) $317,467,059
Retail trade 43,169
   Annual payroll ($1,000) $14,365,019
   Paid employees 629,286
   Receipts, 2002 ($1,000) $131,469,518
Transportation & warehousing 10,924
   Annual payroll ($1,000) $8,717,147
   Paid employees 218,771
   Receipts, 2002 ($1,000) $19,329,778
Information 5,697
   Annual payroll ($1,000) $7,685,997
   Paid employees 133,241
   Receipts, 2002 ($1,000) . . . . .NA
Finance & insurance 23,108
   Annual payroll ($1,000) $24,867,356
   Paid employees 341,884
   Receipts, 2002 ($1,000) . . . . .NA
Professional, scientific & technical 38,478
   Annual payroll ($1,000) $22,464,307
   Paid employees 350,082
   Receipts, 2002 ($1,000) $45,533,746
Education 3,294
   Annual payroll ($1,000) $4,239,205
   Paid employees 132,528
   Receipts, 2002 ($1,000) $1,233,194
Health care & social assistance 29,475
   Annual payroll ($1,000) $25,360,320
   Paid employees 677,927
   Receipts, 2002 ($1,000) $52,394,634
Arts and entertainment 4,537
   Annual payroll ($1,000) $1,930,647
   Paid employees 71,638
   Receipts, 2002 ($1,000) $5,737,943
Real estate 13,673
   Annual payroll ($1,000) $3,885,579
   Paid employees 84,839
   Receipts, 2002 ($1,000) $16,942,947
Accommodation & food service 25,595
   Annual payroll ($1,000) $6,277,520
   Paid employees 446,724
   Receipts, 2002 ($1,000) $19,072,168

8   Illinois

Exports, 2006
Value of exported goods ($ mil) $42,085
  Manufactured $36,288
  Non-manufactured................. $2,039

Foreign direct investment in US affiliates, 2004
Property, plants & equipment ($ mil) $39,276
Employment (x 1,000)....................235.6

Agriculture, 2006
Number of farms 72,400
Farm acreage (x 1,000) 27,300
  Acres per farm 377
Farm marketings and income ($ mil)
Total.................................$8,635.7
  Crops.............................$6,840.8
  Livestock...........................$1,794.9
Net farm income $1,511.0

Principal commodities, in order by marketing receipts, 2005
Corn, Soybeans, Hogs, Cattle and calves, Greenhouse/nursery

Federal economic activity in state
Expenditures, 2005 ($ mil)
  Total............................. $80,778
    Per capita $6,327.91
  Defense $6,412
  Non-defense..................... $74,367
Defense department, 2006 ($ mil)
  Payroll............................ $2,838
  Contract awards $3,274
  Grants $107
Homeland security grants ($1,000)
  2006....................... $90,405
  2007....................... $86,248

FDIC-insured financial institutions, 2005
Number 685
Assets ($ billion) $380.9
Deposits ($ billion) $284.0

Fishing, 2006
Catch (x 1,000 lbs)...................... NA
Value ($1,000)......................... NA

Mining, 2006 ($ mil)
Total non-fuel mineral production $1,280
Percent of U.S. 1.99%

Communication, Energy & Transportation

Communication
Households with computers, 2003........60.0%
Households with internet access, 2003 .... 51.1%
High-speed internet providers 121
Total high-speed internet lines........ 3,317,065
  Residential 2,401,478
  Business......................... 915,587
Wireless phone customers, 12/2006 9,588,517

FCC-licensed stations (as of January 1, 2008)
TV stations 47
FM radio stations......................... 334
AM radio stations 135

Energy
Energy consumption, 2004
  Total (trillion Btu).....................3,961
  Per capita (million Btu) 311.5
By source of production (trillion Btu)
  Coal 1,070
  Natural gas........................ 956
  Petroleum..........................1,375
  Nuclear electric power 960
  Hydroelectric power.................... 2
By end-use sector (trillion Btu)
  Residential 958
  Commercial 746
  Industrial 1,253
  Transportation 1,004
Electric energy, 2005
  Primary source of electricity......... Nuclear
  Net generation (billion kWh) 194.1
    percent from renewable sources....... 0.5%
  Net summer capability (million kW) 42.5
  CO_2 emitted from generation 100.8
Natural gas utilities, 2005
  Customers (x 1,000) 4,092
  Sales (trillion Btu)..................... 911
  Revenues ($ mil) $5,620
Nuclear plants, 2007 11
Total CO_2 emitted (million metric tons).....230.0
Energy spending, 2004 ($ mil) $34,067
  per capita $2,680
  Price per million Btu $12.46

Transportation, 2006
Public road & street mileage 138,997
  Urban............................. 40,403
  Rural............................. 98,594
  Interstate...........................2,169
Vehicle miles of travel (millions) 106,869
  per capita 8,364.1
Total motor vehicle registrations.......9,876,246
  Automobiles......................5,947,468
  Trucks 5,965,504
  Motorcycles 293,052
Licensed drivers 8,071,253
  19 years & under 455,823
Deaths from motor vehicle accidents 1,254
Gasoline consumed (x 1,000 gallons) 5,189,824
  per capita 406.2

Commuting Statistics, 2006
Average commute time (min) 27.9
  Drove to work alone 74.3%
  Carpooled.......................... 9.3%
  Public transit 8.4%
  Walk to work 2.9%
  Work from home..................... 3.6%

Indiana 1

State Summary

Capital city . . . . Indianapolis
Governor . . . . Mitch Daniels

State House
Room 206
Indianapolis, IN 46204
317-232-4567

Admitted as a state 1816
Area (square miles) 36,418
Population, 2007 (estimate). 6,345,289
Largest city . . . . Indianapolis
Population, 2006 785,597
Personal income per capita, 2006
(in current dollars) $32,526
Gross domestic product, 2006 ($ mil) . . . $248,915

Leading industries by payroll, 2005

Manufacturing, Health care/Social assistance,
Retail trade

**Leading agricultural commodities
by receipts, 2005**

Corn, Soybeans, Hogs, Dairy products, Cattle
and calves

Geography & Environment

Total area (square miles). 36,418
land 35,867
water 551
Federally-owned land, 2004 (acres) 463,245
percent. 2.0%
Highest point . . . . Hoosier Hill
elevation (feet) .1,257
Lowest point . . . . Ohio River
elevation (feet) 320
General coastline (miles) 0
Tidal shoreline (miles) 0
Cropland, 2003 (x 1,000 acres) 13,316
Forest land, 2003 (x 1,000 acres). 3,817
Capital city . . . . Indianapolis
Population 2000 781,870
Population 2006 785,597
Largest city . . . . Indianapolis
Population 2000 781,870
Population 2006 785,597

Number of cities with over 100,000 population
1990 5
2000 5
2006 4

State park and recreation areas, 2005
Area (x 1,000 acres). 178
Number of visitors (x 1,000) 19,674
Revenues ($1,000) $39,855
percent of operating expenditures. 83.7%

National forest system land, 2007
Acres 201,467

Demographics & Population Characteristics

Population
1980 5,490,224
1990 5,544,159
2000 6,080,517
2006 6,313,520
Male. 3,110,503
Female. 3,203,017
Living in group quarters, 2006. 178,789
percent of total. .2.8%
2007 (estimate). 6,345,289
persons per square mile of land 176.9
2008 (projected) 6,337,404
2010 (projected) 6,392,139
2020 (projected) 6,627,008
2030 (projected). 6,810,108

**Population of Core-Based Statistical Areas
(formerly Metropolitan Areas), x 1,000**

	CBSA	Non-CBSA
1990	5,198	346
2000	5,715	366
2006	5,946	367

Change in population, 2000-2007
Number 264,768
percent. 4.4%
Natural increase (births minus deaths) 229,514
Net internal migration . . . .-16,431
Net international migration 69,836

Persons by age, 2006
Under 5 years 431,089
5 to 17 years 1,146,540
18 years and over 4,735,891
65 years and over 784,219
85 years and over 111,190
Median age 36.3

Persons by age, 2010 (projected)
Under 5 years 436,614
18 and over 4,795,954
65 and over 811,290
Median age 36.5

Race, 2006
One Race
White. 5,575,402
Black or African American 563,037
Asian 83,583
American Indian/Alaska Native. 18,603
Hawaiian Native/Pacific Islander. 2,850
Two or more races. 70,045

Persons of Hispanic origin, 2006
Total Hispanic or Latino 299,398
Mexican. 228,457
Puerto Rican 23,907
Cuban 1,899

Persons of Asian origin, 2006
Total Asian 81,054
  Asian Indian. 16,204
  Chinese 23,020
  Filipino 9,296
  Japanese 5,284
  Korean. 8,351
  Vietnamese. 7,210

Marital status, 2006
Population 15 years & over 5,010,795
  Never married 1,386,975
  Married. 2,694,647
  Separated 79,300
  Widowed 322,019
  Divorced 607,154

Language spoken at home, 2006
Population 5 years and older. 5,879,940
  English only 5,434,897
  Spanish 254,219
  French 17,184
  German 52,813
  Chinese 17,662

Households & families, 2006
Households. 2,435,274
  with persons under 18 years 839,268
  with persons over 65 years. 539,677
  persons per household 2.52
Families. 1,645,031
  persons per family. 3.06
Married couples. .1,248,625
Female householder,
  no husband present. 283,854
One-person households 661,365

Nativity, 2006
Number of residents born in state 4,329,973
  percent of population 68.6%

Immigration & naturalization, 2006
Legal permanent residents admitted 8,125
Persons naturalized 3,885
Non-immigrant admissions 127,523

Vital Statistics and Health

Marriages
2004 48,354
2005 43,496
2006 50,854

Divorces
2004 . . . . NA
2005 . . . . NA
2006 . . . . NA

Health risks, 2006
Percent of adults who are:
  Smokers. 24.1%
  Overweight (BMI > 25). 62.8%
  Obese (BMI > 30). 27.8%

Births
2005 87,193
  Birthrate (per 1,000). 13.9
  White. 75,733
  Black 9,878
  Hispanic 8,039
  Asian/Pacific Islander 1,435
  Amer. Indian/Alaska Native 147
  Low birth weight (2,500g or less). 8.3%
  Cesarian births .28.2%
  Preterm births 13.5%
  To unmarried mothers. 40.2%
  Twin births (per 1,000) 31.9
  Triplets or higher order (per 100,000). . . 234.3
2006 (preliminary). 88,674
  rate per 1,000 . . . . .14.0

Deaths
2004
All causes 54,211
  rate per 100,000. . . . . .849.4
Heart disease 14,636
  rate per 100,000. . . . . 228.0
Malignant neoplasms 12,552
  rate per 100,000. . . . . .198.2
Cerebrovascular disease. 3,454
  rate per 100,000. . . . . .53.7
Chronic lower respiratory disease 3,145
  rate per 100,000. . . . . .49.8
Diabetes. 1,673
  rate per 100,000. . . . . .26.3
2005 (preliminary). 55,676
  rate per 100,000. . . . . .858.7
2006 (provisional) 55,652

Infant deaths
2004 700
  rate per 1,000 . . . . .8.0
2005 (provisional) 676
  rate per 1,000 . . . . .7.7

Exercise routines, 2005
None. 26.9%
Moderate or greater. 47.7%
Vigorous 27.1%

Abortions, 2004
Total performed in state. 10,514
  rate per 1,000 women age 15-44. 8
  % obtained by out-of-state residents 3.9%

Physicians, 2005
Total. 13,448
  rate per 100,000 persons 215

Community hospitals, 2005
Number of hospitals 113
Beds (x 1,000). 17.8
Patients admitted (x 1,000) 717
Average daily census (x 1,000) 10.3
Average cost per day $1,569
Outpatient visits (x 1 mil) 16.5

Disability status of population, 2006
5 to 15 years 7.4%
16 to 64 years 12.7%
65 years and over 41.8%

Education

Educational attainment, 2006
Population over 25 years 4,110,754
    Less than 9th grade. 4.6%
    High school graduate or more 85.2%
    College graduate or more. 21.7%
    Graduate or professional degree. 8.0%

Public school enrollment, 2005-06
Total 1,035,074
    Pre-kindergarten through grade 8. 724,467
    Grades 9 through 12 310,607

Graduating public high school seniors, 2004-05
Diplomas (incl. GED and others) 57,021

SAT scores, 2007
Average critical reading score 497
Average writing score 483
Average math score 507
Percent of graduates taking test 62%

Public school teachers, 2006-07 (estimate)
Total (x 1,000) 61.2
    Elementary 32.8
    Secondary 28.4
Average salary $47,831
    Elementary $49,079
    Secondary $47,744

State receipts & expenditures for public schools, 2006-07 (estimate)
Revenue receipts ($ mil) $10,948
Expenditures
Total ($ mil) $11,575
    Per capita $1,530
    Per pupil $10,044

NAEP proficiency scores, 2007

	Reading		Math	
	Basic	Proficient	Basic	Proficient
Grade 4	68.2%	33.0%	88.9%	46.3%
Grade 8	76.1%	31.1%	75.7%	35.1%

Higher education enrollment, fall 2005
Total 93,955
    Full-time men 34,182
    Full-time women 43,430
    Part-time men 5,817
    Part-time women. 10,526

Minority enrollment in institutions of higher education, 2005
Black, non-Hispanic 30,315
Hispanic 10,366
Asian/Pacific Islander 7,443
American Indian/Alaska Native. 1,343

Institutions of higher education, 2005-06
Total 100
    Public. 29
    Private 71

Earned degrees conferred, 2004-05
Associate's 13,836
Bachelor's 36,655
Master's 11,087
First-professional. 1,764
Doctor's 1,306

Public Libraries, 2006
Number of libraries. 239
Number of outlets 476
Annual visits per capita 6.9
Circulation per capita 12.2

State & local financial support for higher education, FY 2006
Full-time equivalent enrollment (x 1,000) 218.7
Appropriations per FTE $5,390

Social Insurance & Welfare Programs

Social Security benefits & beneficiaries, 2005
Beneficiaries (x 1,000) 1,055
    Retired & dependents. 728
    Survivors. 145
    Disabled & dependents. 182
Annual benefit payments ($ mil) $11,872
    Retired & dependents. $7,937
    Survivors. $2,083
    Disabled & dependents. $1,852
Average monthly benefit
    Retired & dependents. $1,053
    Disabled & dependents. $938
    Widowed. $1,030

Medicare, July 2005
Enrollment (x 1,000) 905
Payments ($ mil) $6,310

Medicaid, 2004
Beneficiaries (x 1,000). 2,032
Payments ($ mil) $10,796

State Children's Health Insurance Program, 2006
Enrollment (x 1,000) 133.7
Expenditures ($ mil) $106.3

Persons without health insurance, 2006
Number (x 1,000). 748
    percent. 11.8%
Number of children (x 1,000) 123
    percent of children 7.8%

Health care expenditures, 2004
Total expenditures. $32,951
    per capita $5,295

4   Indiana

Federal and state public aid

State unemployment insurance, 2006
Recipients, first payments (x 1,000) 187
Total payments ($ mil) $731
Average weekly benefit $286
Temporary Assistance for Needy Families, 2006
Recipients (x 1,000) 1,432.3
Families (x 1,000) 506.4
Supplemental Security Income, 2005
Recipients (x 1,000) 98.6
Payments ($ mil) $488.1
Food Stamp Program, 2006
Avg monthly participants (x 1,000) 574.7
Total benefits ($ mil) $648.1

Housing & Construction

Housing units
Total 2005 (estimate) 2,724,479
Total 2006 (estimate) 2,756,331
Seasonal or recreational use, 2006 38,051
Owner-occupied, 2006 1,756,328
 Median home value $120,700
 Homeowner vacancy rate 3.2%
Renter-occupied, 2006 678,946
 Median rent $638
 Rental vacancy rate 14.0%
Home ownership rate, 2005 . . . . 75.0%
Home ownership rate, 2006 . . . . 74.2%

New privately-owned housing units
Number authorized, 2006 (x 1,000) 29.1
 Value ($ mil) $4,687.9
Started 2005 (x 1,000, estimate) 39.4
Started 2006 (x 1,000, estimate) 38.8

Existing home sales
2005 (x 1,000) 138.3
2006 (x 1,000) 147.4

Government & Elections

State officials 2008
Governor . . . . .Mitch Daniels
        Republican, term expires 1/09
Lieutenant Governor . . . . Becky Skillman
Secretary of State . . . . Todd Rokita
Attorney General . . . . Steve Carter
Chief Justice . . . . Randall Shepard

Governorship
Minimum age 30
Length of term . . . . 4 years
Consecutive terms permitted . 8 out of any 12 yrs
Who succeeds . . . . Lieutenant Governor

Local governments by type, 2002
Total 3,085
 County 91
 Municipal 567
 Township 1,008
 School District 294
 Special District .1,125

State legislature
Name . . . . General Assembly
Upper chamber . . . . .Senate
 Number of members 50
 Length of term . . . . 4 years
 Party in majority, 2008 . . . . Republican
Lower chamber . . . . House of Representatives
 Number of members 100
 Length of term . . . . 2 years
 Party in majority, 2008 . . . . Democratic

Federal representation, 2008 (110th Congress)
Senator . . . . Even Bayh
 Party . . . . Democratic
 Year term expires 2011
Senator . . . . Richard Lugar
 Party . . . . Republican
 Year term expires 2013
Representatives, total . . . . 9 (1 vacant)
 Democrats 4
 Republicans 4

Voters in November 2006 election (estimate)
Total 2,052,579
 Male 1,024,420
 Female 1,028,160
 White 1,901,436
 Black 139,539
 Hispanic 11,356
 Asian 9,074

Presidential election, 2004
Total Popular Vote 2,468,002
 Kerry 969,011
 Bush 1,479,438
Total Electoral Votes 11

Votes cast for US Senators
2004
Total vote (x 1,000) 2,428
Leading party .Democratic
Percent for leading party 61.6%
2006
Total vote (x 1,000) 1,341
Leading party .Democratic
Percent for leading party 87.4%

Votes cast for US Representatives
2004
Total vote (x 1,000) .2,416
 Democratic 999
 Republican 1,382
Leading party . . . . Republican
Percent for leading party 57.2%
2006
Total vote (x 1,000) .1,667
 Democratic 812
 Republican 832
Leading party . . . . Republican
Percent for leading party 49.9%

State government employment, 2006
Full-time equivalent employees 89,799
Payroll ($ mil) $303.7

Local government employment, 2006
Full-time equivalent employees 243,050
Payroll ($ mil) $789.8

Women holding public office, 2008
US Congress 0
Statewide elected office. 2
State legislature 29

Black public officials, 2002
Total. 94
   US and state legislatures 13
   City/county/regional offices 54
   Judicial/law enforcement. 13
   Education/school boards 14

Hispanic public officials, 2006
Total. 13
   State executives & legislators 1
   City/county/regional offices 8
   Judicial/law enforcement. 3
   Education/school boards 1

Governmental Finance

State government revenues, 2006
Total revenue (x $1,000). $32,854,548
   per capita $5,212.82
General revenue (x $1,000) $29,603,636
   Intergovernmental 7,270,493
   Taxes 13,625,667
      general sales. 5,334,275
      individual income tax 4,381,548
      corporate income tax 1,043,873
   Current charges. 6,861,100
   Miscellaneous .1,846,376

State government expenditure, 2006
Total expenditure (x $1,000) $26,958,772
   per capita $4,277.37
General expenditure (x $1,000) $24,955,887
   per capita, total. $3,959.59
      Education 1,568.00
      Public welfare 985.50
      Health 86.05
      Hospitals. 41.56
      Highways 281.34
      Police protection. 31.77
      Corrections 99.58
      Natural resources 46.60
      Parks & recreation 9.47
      Governmental administration. 92.81
      Interest on general debt 120.24

State debt & cash, 2006 ($ per capita)
Debt $2,748.45
Cash/security holdings. $8,804.52

Federal government grants to state & local government, 2005 (x $1,000)
Total. $8,064,847
by Federal agency
   Defense 31,177
   Education 652,897
   Energy. 45,264
   Environmental Protection Agency 67,649
   Health & Human Services. 4,905,919
   Homeland Security. 76,665
   Housing & Urban Development. 526,459
   Justice 76,039
   Labor 156,966
   Transportation 937,807
   Veterans Affairs. 5,891

Crime & Law Enforcement

Crime, 2006 (rates per 100,000 residents)
Property crimes 221,127
   Burglary 46,168
   Larceny 153,093
   Motor vehicle theft 21,866
   Property crime rate. 3,502.4
Violent crimes. 19,876
   Murder 369
   Forcible rape. 1,835
   Robbery. 7,243
   Aggravated assault 10,429
   Violent crime rate 314.8
Hate crimes. 43

Fraud and identity theft, 2006
Fraud complaints. .7,863
   rate per 100,000 residents 124.5
Identity theft complaints 3,928
   rate per 100,000 residents 62.2

Law enforcement agencies, 2006
Total agencies. 208
Total employees 15,934
   Officers 10,197
   Civilians 5,737

Prisoners, probation, and parole, 2006
Total prisoners. 26,091
   percent change, 12/31/05 to 12/31/06 . . . . 6.7%
   in private facilities 4.9%
   in local jails 4.5%
Sentenced to more than one year 26,055
   rate per 100,000 residents 411
Adults on probation 120,421
Adults on parole. 7,950

Prisoner demographics, June 30, 2005 (rate per 100,000 residents)
Male. 1,165
Female. 126
White. 463
Black. 2,526
Hispanic 579

Arrests, 2006

Total.................................. 170,293
  Persons under 18 years of age 27,770

Persons under sentence of death, 1/1/07

Total...................................... 23
  White................................... 16
  Black 7
  Hispanic 0

State's highest court

Name ....Supreme Court
Number of members........................ 5
Length of term..................... 10 years
Intermediate appeals court? ....yes

Labor & Income

Civilian labor force, 2006 (x 1,000)

Total..................................3,253
  Men 1,751
  Women 1,502
  Persons 16-19 years.................... 162
  White..................................2,947
  Black 258
  Hispanic 138

Civilian labor force as a percent of civilian non-institutional population, 2006

Total................................. 67.7%
  Men 74.9
  Women 60.8
  Persons 16-19 years....................45.7
  White..................................67.8
  Black 66.5
  Hispanic 73.6

Employment, 2006 (x 1,000)

Total................................. 3,090
  Men 1,672
  Women 1,417
  Persons 16-19 years................... 137
  White..................................2,815
  Black 230
  Hispanic 130

Unemployment rate, 2006

Total.................................. 5.0%
  Men 4.5
  Women 5.6
  Persons 16-19 years....................15.5
  White...................................4.5
  Black 10.9
  Hispanic 5.3

Full-time/part-time labor force, 2003 (x 1,000)

Full-time labor force, employed 2,488
Part-time labor force, employed............ 537
Unemployed, looking for
  Full-time work......................... 140
  Part-time work......................... 23
Mean duration of unemployment (weeks)......21.7
  Median 12.0

Labor unions, 2006

Membership (x 1,000).................... 334
  percent of employed 12.0%

Experienced civilian labor force by private industry, 2006

Total..........................2,494,391
  Natural resources & mining 18,788
  Construction 150,648
  Manufacturing................... 565,032
  Trade, transportation & utilities 578,299
  Information 39,875
  Finance 136,601
  Professional & business 279,986
  Education & health................359,759
  Leisure & hospitality............... 280,923
  Other...................... 83,846

Experienced civilian labor force by occupation, May 2006

Management....................... 109,250
Business & financial 90,470
Legal............................. 12,630
Sales............................ 289,780
Office & admin. support........... 453,900
Computers & math 38,660
Architecture & engineering........... 45,780
Arts & entertainment 30,150
Education 163,890
Social services 33,720
Health care practitioner & technical.... 154,870
Health care support 67,190
Maintenance & repair.............. 134,980
Construction 142,420
Transportation & moving 263,630
Production 398,820
Farming, fishing & forestry.............2,760

Hours and earnings of production workers on manufacturing payrolls, 2006

Average weekly hours 41.7
Average hourly earnings $18.57
Average weekly earnings $774.37

Income and poverty, 2006

Median household income............. $45,394
Personal income, per capita (current $)... $32,526
  in constant (2000) dollars $28,393
Persons below poverty level............. 12.7%

Average annual pay

2006 .... $36,553
  increase from 2005 .... 3.2%

Federal individual income tax returns, 2005

Returns filed........................2,883,701
Adjusted gross income ($1,000) $134,324,776
Total tax liability ($1,000) $15,673,118

Charitable contributions, 2004

Number of contributions................ 724.5
Total amount ($ mil)..................$2,660.3

Economy, Business, Industry & Agriculture

Fortune 500 companies, 2007 5
Bankruptcy cases filed, FY 2007 29,656

Patents and trademarks issued, 2007
Patents 1,350
Trademarks 1,236

Business firm ownership, 2002
Women-owned 118,857
　Sales ($ mil) $16,481
Black-owned 14,056
　Sales ($ mil) $1,688
Hispanic-owned 5,482
　Sales ($ mil) $792
Asian-owned 6,078
　Sales ($ mil) $2,584
Amer. Indian/Alaska Native-owned 1,974
　Sales ($ mil) $288
Hawaiian/Pacific Islander-owned 114
　Sales ($ mil) $77

Gross domestic product, 2006 ($ mil)
Total gross domestic product $248,915
　Agriculture, forestry, fishing and
　　hunting 1,788
　Mining 898
　Utilities 5,816
　Construction 10,835
　Manufacturing, durable goods 43,930
　Manufacturing, non-durable goods 26,110
　Wholesale trade 14,078
　Retail trade 15,804
　Transportation & warehousing 8,826
　Information 5,328
　Finance & insurance 14,065
　Real estate, rental & leasing 24,351
　Professional and technical services 9,397
　Educational services 1,925
　Health care and social assistance 18,005
　Accommodation/food services 5,358
　Other services, except government 5,664
　Government 24,439

Establishments, payroll, employees & receipts, by major industry group, 2005
Total 149,871
　Annual payroll ($1,000) $88,145,224
　Paid employees 2,610,899
Forestry, fishing & agriculture 250
　Annual payroll ($1,000) $46,597
　Paid employees 1,408
Mining 329
　Annual payroll ($1,000) $300,784
　Paid employees 5,591
　Receipts, 2002 ($1,000) $1,359,560

Utilities 529
　Annual payroll ($1,000) $918,875
　Paid employees 14,401
　Receipts, 2002 ($1,000) . . . . .NA
Construction 16,442
　Annual payroll ($1,000) $5,963,039
　Paid employees 139,661
　Receipts, 2002 ($1,000) $23,435,911
Manufacturing 8,970
　Annual payroll ($1,000) $24,191,908
　Paid employees 554,273
　Receipts, 2002 ($1,000) $160,924,188
Wholesale trade .8,153
　Annual payroll ($1,000) $5,206,097
　Paid employees 117,305
　Receipts, 2002 ($1,000) $79,806,006
Retail trade 23,494
　Annual payroll ($1,000) $6,912,064
　Paid employees 346,073
　Receipts, 2002 ($1,000) $67,261,298
Transportation & warehousing 5,090
　Annual payroll ($1,000) $3,531,963
　Paid employees 106,149
　Receipts, 2002 ($1,000) $10,601,332
Information 2,334
　Annual payroll ($1,000) $2,010,861
　Paid employees 47,493
　Receipts, 2002 ($1,000) . . . . .NA
Finance & insurance 10,077
　Annual payroll ($1,000) $5,324,071
　Paid employees 107,628
　Receipts, 2002 ($1,000) . . . . .NA
Professional, scientific & technical 12,797
　Annual payroll ($1,000) $5,022,670
　Paid employees 110,046
　Receipts, 2002 ($1,000) $9,154,500
Education 1,372
　Annual payroll ($1,000) $1,189,334
　Paid employees 49,491
　Receipts, 2002 ($1,000) $340,184
Health care & social assistance 14,280
　Annual payroll ($1,000) $12,213,877
　Paid employees 354,481
　Receipts, 2002 ($1,000) $25,539,903
Arts and entertainment 2,103
　Annual payroll ($1,000) $839,422
　Paid employees 33,431
　Receipts, 2002 ($1,000) $2,725,191
Real estate 6,121
　Annual payroll ($1,000) $1,047,878
　Paid employees 35,169
　Receipts, 2002 ($1,000) $4,491,668
Accommodation & food service 12,316
　Annual payroll ($1,000) $2,934,176
　Paid employees 245,467
　Receipts, 2002 ($1,000) $9,409,270

Exports, 2006
Value of exported goods ($ mil) $22,620
    Manufactured $20,660
    Non-manufactured................... $460

Foreign direct investment in US affiliates, 2004
Property, plants & equipment ($ mil) ... $30,904
Employment (x 1,000)....................132.5

Agriculture, 2006
Number of farms 59,000
Farm acreage (x 1,000) 15,000
    Acres per farm......................... 254
Farm marketings and income ($ mil)
Total............................... $5,973.2
    Crops............................. $3,918.9
    Livestock.......................... $2,054.3
Net farm income $1,545.4

Principal commodities, in order by
marketing receipts, 2005
    Corn, Soybeans, Hogs, Dairy products, Cattle
       and calves

Federal economic activity in state
Expenditures, 2005 ($ mil)
    Total.............................. $42,347
       Per capita $6,758.14
    Defense $5,633
    Non-defense....................... $36,714
Defense department, 2006 ($ mil)
    Payroll............................. $1,361
    Contract awards $4,627
    Grants $64
Homeland security grants ($1,000)
    2006............................. $21,129
    2007............................. $23,397

FDIC-insured financial institutions, 2005
Number..................................... 172
Assets ($ billion) $71.8
Deposits ($ billion) $54.7

Fishing, 2006
Catch (x 1,000 lbs)........................ NA
Value ($1,000)............................ NA

Mining, 2006 ($ mil)
Total non-fuel mineral production $963
Percent of U.S. 1.50%

Communication, Energy & Transportation

Communication
Households with computers, 2003........ 59.6%
Households with internet access, 2003 .... 51.0%
High-speed internet providers 81
Total high-speed internet lines........ 1,586,501
    Residential 1,077,595
    Business.......................... 508,906
Wireless phone customers, 12/2006 4,271,412

FCC-licensed stations (as of January 1, 2008)
TV stations 40
FM radio stations........................... 256
AM radio stations 86

Energy
Energy consumption, 2004
    Total (trillion Btu)................. 2,946
    Per capita (million Btu) 473.3
By source of production (trillion Btu)
    Coal............................... 1,614
    Natural gas......................... 543
    Petroleum.......................... 885
    Nuclear electric power 0
    Hydroelectric power..................... 4
By end-use sector (trillion Btu)
    Residential 532
    Commercial 373
    Industrial 1,400
    Transportation 641
Electric energy, 2005
    Primary source of electricity........... Coal
    Net generation (billion kWh)........... 130.4
       percent from renewable sources...... 0.4%
    Net summer capability (million kW) 27.0
    CO_2 emitted from generation 122.1
Natural gas utilities, 2005
    Customers (x 1,000) 1,866
    Sales (trillion Btu)..................... 502
    Revenues ($ mil) $2,635
Nuclear plants, 2007 0
Total CO_2 emitted (million metric tons)..... 235.1
Energy spending, 2004 ($ mil) $20,932
    per capita $3,364
    Price per million Btu $10.19

Transportation, 2006
Public road & street mileage 96,250
    Urban............................. 21,780
    Rural............................. 74,470
    Interstate......................... 1,169
Vehicle miles of travel (millions) 71,215
    per capita 11,299.2
Total motor vehicle registrations....... 4,955,434
    Automobiles..................... 2,694,901
    Trucks.......................... 2,228,559
    Motorcycles...................... 147,544
Licensed drivers 4,246,189
    19 years & under 232,326
Deaths from motor vehicle accidents 899
Gasoline consumed (x 1,000 gallons) 3,221,758
    per capita 511.2

Commuting Statistics, 2006
Average commute time (min) 22.3
    Drove to work alone 82.4%
    Carpooled.......................... 9.9%
    Public transit 1.0%
    Walk to work 2.2%
    Work from home..................... 3.2%

State Summary

Capital city . . . . .Des Moines
Governor. . . . . .Chet Culver
State Capitol
Des Moines, IA 50319
515-281-5211
Admitted as a state 1846
Area (square miles) 56,272
Population, 2007 (estimate). 2,988,046
Largest city . . . . Des Moines
Population, 2006. 193,886
Personal income per capita, 2006
(in current dollars) $33,236
Gross domestic product, 2006 ($ mil) . . . $123,970

Leading industries by payroll, 2005

Manufacturing, Health care/Social assistance,
Finance & Insurance

Leading agricultural commodities by receipts, 2005

Corn, Hogs, Soybeans, Cattle and calves, Dairy
products

Geography & Environment

Total area (square miles). 56,272
land 55,869
water 402
Federally-owned land, 2004 (acres) 273,954
percent. 0.8%
Highest point . . . . Hawkeye Point
elevation (feet) 1,670
Lowest point . . . . Mississippi River
elevation (feet) 480
General coastline (miles) 0
Tidal shoreline (miles) 0
Cropland, 2003 (x 1,000 acres) 25,511
Forest land, 2003 (x 1,000 acres). 2,301
Capital city . . . . Des Moines
Population 2000 198,682
Population 2006 193,886
Largest city . . . . Des Moines
Population 2000 198,682
Population 2006 193,886

Number of cities with over 100,000 population

1990 2
2000 2
2006 2

State park and recreation areas, 2005

Area (x 1,000 acres). 68
Number of visitors (x 1,000) 13,580
Revenues ($1,000) $4,070
percent of operating expenditures. 29.6%

National forest system land, 2007

Acres 0

Demographics & Population Characteristics

Population

1980 2,913,808
1990 2,776,755
2000 2,926,382
2006 2,982,085
Male. 1,472,810
Female. 1,509,275
Living in group quarters, 2006. 104,071
percent of total. 3.5%
2007 (estimate). 2,988,046
persons per square mile of land 53.5
2008 (projected) 2,997,608
2010 (projected) 3,009,907
2020 (projected). 3,020,496
2030 (projected). 2,955,172

Population of Core-Based Statistical Areas (formerly Metropolitan Areas), x 1,000

	CBSA	Non-CBSA
1990	1,939	838
2000	2,090	836
2006	2,167	816

Change in population, 2000-2007

Number 61,664
percent 2.1%
Natural increase (births minus deaths) 81,489
Net internal migration . . . .-50,248
Net international migration 36,217

Persons by age, 2006

Under 5 years 192,055
5 to 17 years 518,139
18 years and over 2,271,891
65 years and over 435,657
85 years and over 75,180
Median age 37.8

Persons by age, 2010 (projected)

Under 5 years 193,313
18 and over 2,298,851
65 and over 449,887
Median age 38.3

Race, 2006

One Race
White. 2,820,425
Black or African American 73,086
Asian 46,553
American Indian/Alaska Native. 11,145
Hawaiian Native/Pacific Islander. 1,400
Two or more races. 29,476

Persons of Hispanic origin, 2006

Total Hispanic or Latino 112,987
Mexican. 89,751
Puerto Rican 2,836
Cuban 1,197

Persons of Asian origin, 2006

Total Asian 45,647
   Asian Indian. 8,695
   Chinese 8,093
   Filipino 4,638
   Japanese 1,897
   Korean. 5,105
   Vietnamese. 8,274

Marital status, 2006

Population 15 years & over 2,397,350
   Never married 639,253
   Married. 1,355,795
   Separated 28,739
   Widowed. 162,063
   Divorced 240,239

Language spoken at home, 2006

Population 5 years and older. 2,790,958
   English only 2,612,625
   Spanish 97,876
   French 5,260
   German. 17,127
   Chinese 7,064

Households & families, 2006

Households. 1,208,765
   with persons under 18 years 386,758
   with persons over 65 years. 294,264
   persons per household 2.38
Families. 796,970
   persons per family. 2.92
Married couples. 641,334
Female householder,
   no husband present. 110,569
One-person households 337,390

Nativity, 2006

Number of residents born in state 2,156,469
   percent of population. 72.3%

Immigration & naturalization, 2006

Legal permanent residents admitted. 4,086
Persons naturalized 805
Non-immigrant admissions 43,543

Vital Statistics and Health

Marriages

2004 20,455
2005 20,419
2006 20,024

Divorces

2004 8,305
2005 8,148
2006 8,024

Health risks, 2006

Percent of adults who are:
   Smokers. 21.4%
   Overweight (BMI > 25). 62.9%
   Obese (BMI > 30). 25.7%

Births

2005 39,311
   Birthrate (per 1,000). 13.3
   White. 36,603
   Black 1,508
   Hispanic 3,115
   Asian/Pacific Islander 946
   Amer. Indian/Alaska Native. 254
   Low birth weight (2,500g or less). 7.2%
   Cesarian births 26.7%
   Preterm births 11.8%
   To unmarried mothers. 32.5%
   Twin births (per 1,000) 33.2
   Triplets or higher order (per 100,000). . . .154.4
2006 (preliminary). 40,610
   rate per 1,000 . . . . .13.6

Deaths

2004
All causes 26,897
   rate per 100,000 .729.4
Heart disease 7,299
   rate per 100,000 .191.9
Malignant neoplasms 6,340
   rate per 100,000 .181.8
Cerebrovascular disease. 1,960
   rate per 100,000 .49.5
Chronic lower respiratory disease 1,547
   rate per 100,000 .42.5
Diabetes. 700
   rate per 100,000 .19.4
2005 (preliminary). 27,812
   rate per 100,000 .742.0
2006 (provisional) 27,493

Infant deaths

2004 195
   rate per 1,000 . . . . .5.1
2005 (provisional) 202
   rate per 1,000 . . . . .5.2

Exercise routines, 2005

None. 24.7%
Moderate or greater. 46.2%
Vigorous 22.9%

Abortions, 2004

Total performed in state. 6,022
   rate per 1,000 women age 15-44. 10
   % obtained by out-of-state residents 11.4%

Physicians, 2005

Total. 5,503
   rate per 100,000 persons 186

Community hospitals, 2005

Number of hospitals 116
Beds (x 1,000). 10.8
Patients admitted (x 1,000) 363
Average daily census (x 1,000) 6.4
Average cost per day $1,036
Outpatient visits (x 1 mil) 10.1

Disability status of population, 2006

5 to 15 years 6.7%
16 to 64 years 11.3%
65 years and over 36.0%

Education

Educational attainment, 2006

Population over 25 years 1,952,026
　Less than 9th grade. 4.4%
　High school graduate or more 88.9%
　College graduate or more. 24.0%
　Graduate or professional degree. 7.4%

Public school enrollment, 2005-06

Total. 483,482
　Pre-kindergarten through grade 8. . . . 326,160
　Grades 9 through 12 157,322

Graduating public high school seniors, 2004-05

Diplomas (incl. GED and others) 33,641

SAT scores, 2007

Average critical reading score 608
Average writing score 586
Average math score 613
Percent of graduates taking test 4%

Public school teachers, 2006-07 (estimate)

Total (x 1,000) 35.4
　Elementary 23.3
　Secondary 12.1
Average salary $43,130
　Elementary $43,308
　Secondary $42,787

State receipts & expenditures for public schools, 2006-07 (estimate)

Revenue receipts ($ mil) $4,814
Expenditures
Total ($ mil) $4,580
　Per capita $1,319
　Per pupil $8,684

NAEP proficiency scores, 2007

	Reading		Math	
	Basic	Proficient	Basic	Proficient
Grade 4	73.7%	36.1%	86.6%	43.0%
Grade 8	79.8%	35.7%	77.2%	35.2%

Higher education enrollment, fall 2005

Total 78,815
　Full-time men 21,724
　Full-time women 31,493
　Part-time men 7,434
　Part-time women 18,164

Minority enrollment in institutions of higher education, 2005

Black, non-Hispanic 11,660
Hispanic 6,423
Asian/Pacific Islander 4,804
American Indian/Alaska Native 1,045

Institutions of higher education, 2005-06

Total. 65
　Public. 19
　Private 46

Earned degrees conferred, 2004-05

Associate's. 12,199
Bachelor's 20,786
Master's 4,316
First-professional. 1,683
Doctor's 672

Public Libraries, 2006

Number of libraries. 540
Number of outlets 568
Annual visits per capita 5.8
Circulation per capita. 9.4

State & local financial support for higher education, FY 2006

Full-time equivalent enrollment (x 1,000) 112.3
Appropriations per FTE $5,809

Social Insurance & Welfare Programs

Social Security benefits & beneficiaries, 2005

Beneficiaries (x 1,000) 548
　Retired & dependents 397
　Survivors. 76
　Disabled & dependents. 75
Annual benefit payments ($ mil) $5,946
　Retired & dependents $4,102
　Survivors. $1,087
　Disabled & dependents. $757
Average monthly benefit
　Retired & dependents. $1,000
　Disabled & dependents. $896
　Widowed. $992

Medicare, July 2005

Enrollment (x 1,000) 490
Payments ($ mil) $2,818

Medicaid, 2004

Beneficiaries (x 1,000). 946
Payments ($ mil) $4,343

State Children's Health Insurance Program, 2006

Enrollment (x 1,000) 49.6
Expenditures ($ mil) $64.2

Persons without health insurance, 2006

Number (x 1,000). 307
　percent. 10.5%
Number of children (x 1,000) 44
　percent of children 6.2%

Health care expenditures, 2004

Total expenditures. $15,892
　per capita $5,380

Federal and state public aid

State unemployment insurance, 2006
Recipients, first payments (x 1,000) 93
Total payments ($ mil) $310
Average weekly benefit $282
Temporary Assistance for Needy Families, 2006
Recipients (x 1,000) 470.1
Families (x 1,000) 195.7
Supplemental Security Income, 2005
Recipients (x 1,000) 43.4
Payments ($ mil) $193.2
Food Stamp Program, 2006
Avg monthly participants (x 1,000) 225.7
Total benefits ($ mil) $244.2

Housing & Construction

Housing units
Total 2005 (estimate) 1,306,516
Total 2006 (estimate) 1,320,331
Seasonal or recreational use, 2006 18,443
Owner-occupied, 2006 885,969
  Median home value $112,600
  Homeowner vacancy rate 2.7%
Renter-occupied, 2006 322,796
  Median rent $584
  Rental vacancy rate 13.5%
Home ownership rate, 2005 . . . . 73.9%
Home ownership rate, 2006 . . . . 74.0%

New privately-owned housing units
Number authorized, 2006 (x 1,000) 13.4
  Value ($ mil) $2,006.0
Started 2005 (x 1,000, estimate) 14.6
Started 2006 (x 1,000, estimate) 14.1

Existing home sales
2005 (x 1,000) 74.9
2006 (x 1,000) 74.6

Government & Elections

State officials 2008
Governor . . . . .Chet Culver
   Democratic, term expires 1/11
Lieutenant Governor . . . . Patty Judge
Secretary of State . . . . .Michael Mauro
Attorney General . . . . Tom Miller
Chief Justice . . . . Marsha Ternus

Governorship
Minimum age 30
Length of term . . . . 4 years
Consecutive terms permitted . . . . . . not specified
Who succeeds . . . . Lieutenant Governor

Local governments by type, 2002
Total 1,975
  County 99
  Municipal 948
  Township 0
  School District 386
  Special District 542

State legislature
Name . . . . General Assembly
Upper chamber . . . . .Senate
  Number of members 50
  Length of term . . . . 4 years
  Party in majority, 2008 . . . . .Democratic
Lower chamber . . . . .House of Representatives
  Number of members 100
  Length of term . . . . 2 years
  Party in majority, 2008 . . . . .Democratic

Federal representation, 2008 (110th Congress)
Senator . . . . Tom Harkin
  Party . . . . .Democratic
  Year term expires 2009
Senator . . . . Charles Grassley
  Party . . . . Republican
  Year term expires 2011
Representatives, total 5
  Democrats 3
  Republicans 2

Voters in November 2006 election (estimate)
Total 1,179,795
  Male 544,951
  Female 634,844
  White 1,148,860
  Black 14,313
  Hispanic 2,309
  Asian 10,816

Presidential election, 2004
Total Popular Vote 1,506,908
  Kerry 741,898
  Bush 751,957
Total Electoral Votes 7

Votes cast for US Senators
2004
Total vote (x 1,000) .1,479
Leading party . . . . Republican
Percent for leading party 70.2%
2006
Total vote (x 1,000) . . . . NA
Leading party . . . . NA
Percent for leading party . . . . NA

Votes cast for US Representatives
2004
Total vote (x 1,000) .1,458
  Democratic 625
  Republican 823
Leading party . . . . Republican
Percent for leading party 56.4%
2006
Total vote (x 1,000) .1,033
  Democratic 493
  Republican 522
Leading party . . . . Republican
Percent for leading party 50.6%

State government employment, 2006
Full-time equivalent employees 53,258
Payroll ($ mil) $230.0

Local government employment, 2006
Full-time equivalent employees 132,663
Payroll ($ mil) $398.3

Women holding public office, 2008
US Congress 0
Statewide elected office. 1
State legislature 34

Black public officials, 2002
Total..................................... 12
　　US and state legislatures 1
　　City/county/regional offices 8
　　Judicial/law enforcement.................. 1
　　Education/school boards.................. 2

Hispanic public officials, 2006
Total..................................... 0
　　State executives & legislators 0
　　City/county/regional offices 0
　　Judicial/law enforcement.................. 0
　　Education/school boards.................. 0

Governmental Finance

State government revenues, 2006
Total revenue (x $1,000)............$16,808,578
　　per capita $5,654.57
General revenue (x $1,000) $13,434,028
　　Intergovernmental 4,296,014
　　Taxes 6,118,897
　　　　general sales....................1,800,829
　　　　individual income tax 2,413,775
　　　　corporate income tax 284,976
　　Current charges...................2,017,249
　　Miscellaneous 1,001,868

State government expenditure, 2006
Total expenditure (x $1,000) $14,941,961
　　per capita $5,026.62
General expenditure (x $1,000) $13,470,126
　　per capita, total.................. $4,531.48
　　　　Education 1,741.32
　　　　Public welfare 1,229.15
　　　　Health 65.70
　　　　Hospitals..........................311.19
　　　　Highways 491.46
　　　　Police protection.....................29.31
　　　　Corrections 80.95
　　　　Natural resources 83.44
　　　　Parks & recreation 8.09
　　　　Governmental administration...... 166.85
　　　　Interest on general debt.............87.85

State debt & cash, 2006 ($ per capita)
Debt....................................$2,219.75
Cash/security holdings.............. $11,053.74

Federal government grants to state & local government, 2005 (x $1,000)
Total............................$4,035,419
by Federal agency
　　Defense 36,812
　　Education 329,551
　　Energy............................27,127
　　Environmental Protection Agency 73,047
　　Health & Human Services. 2,358,362
　　Homeland Security..................21,736
　　Housing & Urban Development...... 241,726
　　Justice 59,283
　　Labor 73,056
　　Transportation 392,421
　　Veterans Affairs................. 14,598

Crime & Law Enforcement

Crime, 2006 (rates per 100,000 residents)
Property crimes 83,579
　　Burglary 18,017
　　Larceny 60,556
　　Motor vehicle theft 5,006
　　Property crime rate.................2,802.7
Violent crimes. 8,455
　　Murder 55
　　Forcible rape........................ 828
　　Robbery...........................1,298
　　Aggravated assault 6,274
　　Violent crime rate 283.5
Hate crimes............................ 42

Fraud and identity theft, 2006
Fraud complaints...................... 2,666
　　rate per 100,000 residents 89.4
Identity theft complaints 1,041
　　rate per 100,000 residents 34.9

Law enforcement agencies, 2006
Total agencies........................ 231
Total employees.......................7,615
　　Officers 5,040
　　Civilians 2,575

Prisoners, probation, and parole, 2006
Total prisoners........................8,875
　　percent change, 12/31/05 to 12/31/06 .... 1.6%
　　in private facilities 0%
　　in local jails 0%
Sentenced to more than one year 8,838
　　rate per 100,000 residents 296
Adults on probation 22,622
Adults on parole........................3,578

Prisoner demographics, June 30, 2005 (rate per 100,000 residents)
Male................................... 751
Female................................ 83
White.................................. 309
Black................................. 4,200
Hispanic 764

Arrests, 2006
Total................................ 109,230
    Persons under 18 years of age 19,605

Persons under sentence of death, 1/1/07
Total..................................... 0
    White.................................. 0
    Black 0
    Hispanic 0

State's highest court
Name ....Supreme Court
Number of members........................ 7
Length of term........................ 8 years
Intermediate appeals court? ....yes

Labor & Income

Civilian labor force, 2006 (x 1,000)
Total.................................1,701
    Men 896
    Women 806
    Persons 16-19 years.................... 108
    White................................1,619
    Black 34
    Hispanic 69

Civilian labor force as a percent of civilian non-institutional population, 2006
Total.................................72.7%
    Men 78.4
    Women 67.2
    Persons 16-19 years....................64.6
    White................................72.9
    Black 73.0
    Hispanic 76.9

Employment, 2006 (x 1,000)
Total.................................1,641
    Men 864
    Women 776
    Persons 16-19 years.................... 97
    White................................ 1,566
    Black 28
    Hispanic 65

Unemployment rate, 2006
Total.................................3.6%
    Men 3.5
    Women 3.6
    Persons 16-19 years...................10.1
    White................................3.2
    Black 16.5
    Hispanic 4.8

Full-time/part-time labor force, 2003 (x 1,000)
Full-time labor force, employed 1,217
Part-time labor force, employed............ 323
Unemployed, looking for
    Full-time work.......................... 55
    Part-time work......................... 17
*Mean duration of unemployment (weeks)......*15.4
    Median 8.0

Labor unions, 2006
Membership (x 1,000)................... 161
    percent of employed 11.3%

Experienced civilian labor force by private industry, 2006
Total.............................1,240,335
    Natural resources & mining 16,294
    Construction 74,412
    Manufacturing.......................231,162
    Trade, transportation & utilities 305,731
    Information 32,965
    Finance 100,719
    Professional & business 116,974
    Education & health 187,376
    Leisure & hospitality................ 134,072
    Other............................. 40,631

Experienced civilian labor force by occupation, May 2006
Management........................ 54,900
Business & financial 58,980
Legal.................................6,770
Sales...............................157,080
Office & admin. support............... 232,640
Computers & math 26,130
Architecture & engineering............17,070
Arts & entertainment 17,430
Education 90,290
Social services 22,580
Health care practitioner & technical......74,160
Health care support 43,990
Maintenance & repair.................. 60,720
Construction 68,140
Transportation & moving 126,620
Production 166,660
Farming, fishing & forestry..............4,510

Hours and earnings of production workers on manufacturing payrolls, 2006
Average weekly hours 41.9
Average hourly earnings $16.40
Average weekly earnings $687.16

Income and poverty, 2006
Median household income............ $44,491
Personal income, per capita (current $)... $33,236
    in constant (2000) dollars $29,013
Persons below poverty level.............. 11.0%

Average annual pay
2006 .... $34,320
    increase from 2005 .... 3.8%

Federal individual income tax returns, 2005
Returns filed......................1,346,535
Adjusted gross income ($1,000) $61,643,860
Total tax liability ($1,000) $6,917,573

Charitable contributions, 2004
Number of contributions................ 364.8
Total amount ($ mil).................. $1,159.7

Economy, Business, Industry & Agriculture

Fortune 500 companies, 2007 1
Bankruptcy cases filed, FY 2007 6,660

Patents and trademarks issued, 2007
Patents 665
Trademarks 715

Business firm ownership, 2002
Women-owned 63,821
   Sales ($ mil) $7,399
Black-owned 1,609
   Sales ($ mil) $258
Hispanic-owned 1,536
   Sales ($ mil) $289
Asian-owned 1,786
   Sales ($ mil) $456
Amer. Indian/Alaska Native-owned 644
   Sales ($ mil) $86
Hawaiian/Pacific Islander-owned 17
   Sales ($ mil) $7

Gross domestic product, 2006 ($ mil)
Total gross domestic product $123,970
   Agriculture, forestry, fishing and
      hunting 4,051
   Mining 205
   Utilities 2,451
   Construction 5,191
   Manufacturing, durable goods 15,078
   Manufacturing, non-durable goods 10,991
   Wholesale trade .7,177
   Retail trade 7,537
   Transportation & warehousing 4,429
   Information 3,670
   Finance & insurance 15,055
   Real estate, rental & leasing 11,312
   Professional and technical services 3,764
   Educational services 1,010
   Health care and social assistance 8,184
   Accommodation/food services 2,455
   Other services, except government 2,558
   Government 14,266

Establishments, payroll, employees & receipts, by major industry group, 2005

Total 82,087
   Annual payroll ($1,000) $39,420,961
   Paid employees 1,261,108

Forestry, fishing & agriculture 259
   Annual payroll ($1,000) $55,239
   Paid employees .1,501

Mining 205
   Annual payroll ($1,000) $91,551
   Paid employees .1,942
   Receipts, 2002 ($1,000) $333,227

Utilities 255
   Annual payroll ($1,000) $500,719
   Paid employees .7,963
   Receipts, 2002 ($1,000) . . . . .NA

Construction 9,055
   Annual payroll ($1,000) $2,573,372
   Paid employees 62,855
   Receipts, 2002 ($1,000) $9,940,503

Manufacturing 3,800
   Annual payroll ($1,000) $9,025,961
   Paid employees 225,567
   Receipts, 2002 ($1,000) $65,042,043

Wholesale trade 4,815
   Annual payroll ($1,000) $2,558,534
   Paid employees 63,167
   Receipts, 2002 ($1,000) $33,546,948

Retail trade 13,643
   Annual payroll ($1,000) $3,494,449
   Paid employees 178,216
   Receipts, 2002 ($1,000) $31,195,012

Transportation & warehousing 3,702
   Annual payroll ($1,000) $1,698,170
   Paid employees 49,876
   Receipts, 2002 ($1,000) $5,063,344

Information 1,582
   Annual payroll ($1,000) $1,418,993
   Paid employees 36,695
   Receipts, 2002 ($1,000) . . . . .NA

Finance & insurance 5,945
   Annual payroll ($1,000) $4,380,754
   Paid employees 91,727
   Receipts, 2002 ($1,000) . . . . .NA

Professional, scientific & technical 6,103
   Annual payroll ($1,000) $1,759,551
   Paid employees 42,486
   Receipts, 2002 ($1,000) $3,580,073

Education 700
   Annual payroll ($1,000) $625,473
   Paid employees 33,121
   Receipts, 2002 ($1,000) $263,404

Health care & social assistance 7,513
   Annual payroll ($1,000) $5,921,736
   Paid employees 188,242
   Receipts, 2002 ($1,000) $11,441,141

Arts and entertainment 1,441
   Annual payroll ($1,000) $379,634
   Paid employees 21,811
   Receipts, 2002 ($1,000) $1,229,803

Real estate 2,848
   Annual payroll ($1,000) $387,079
   Paid employees 14,006
   Receipts, 2002 ($1,000) $1,702,144

Accommodation & food service 6,771
   Annual payroll ($1,000) $1,105,219
   Paid employees 108,439
   Receipts, 2002 ($1,000) $3,698,955

8   Iowa

Exports, 2006
Value of exported goods ($ mil) $8,410
  Manufactured $7,559
  Non-manufactured $581

Foreign direct investment in US affiliates, 2004
Property, plants & equipment ($ mil) $6,391
Employment (x 1,000). 36.2

Agriculture, 2006
Number of farms 88,600
Farm acreage (x 1,000) 31,500
  Acres per farm 356
Farm marketings and income ($ mil)
Total. $15,108.3
  Crops $7,229.1
  Livestock $7,879.1
Net farm income $3,274.8

Principal commodities, in order by marketing receipts, 2005
Corn, Hogs, Soybeans, Cattle and calves, Dairy products

Federal economic activity in state
Expenditures, 2005 ($ mil)
  Total. $20,345
    Per capita $6,860.47
  Defense $1,355
  Non-defense $18,990
Defense department, 2006 ($ mil)
  Payroll. $445
  Contract awards $944
  Grants $42
Homeland security grants ($1,000)
  2006 .... $13,480
  2007 .... $7,043

FDIC-insured financial institutions, 2005
Number 401
Assets ($ billion) $56.6
Deposits ($ billion) $44.8

Fishing, 2006
Catch (x 1,000 lbs) .... NA
Value ($1,000). .... NA

Mining, 2006 ($ mil)
Total non-fuel mineral production $704
Percent of U.S. 1.09%

Communication, Energy & Transportation

Communication
Households with computers, 2003 .... 64.7%
Households with internet access, 2003 .... 57.1%
High-speed internet providers 182
Total high-speed internet lines 654,694
  Residential 452,699
  Business. 201,995
Wireless phone customers, 12/2006 2,009,826

FCC-licensed stations (as of January 1, 2008)
TV stations 33
FM radio stations. 186
AM radio stations 84

Energy
Energy consumption, 2004
  Total (trillion Btu). 1,206
  Per capita (million Btu) 408.2
By source of production (trillion Btu)
  Coal 443
  Natural gas 229
  Petroleum 439
  Nuclear electric power 51
  Hydroelectric power 10
By end-use sector (trillion Btu)
  Residential 230
  Commercial 182
  Industrial 496
  Transportation 297
Electric energy, 2005
  Primary source of electricity. .... Coal
  Net generation (billion kWh) 44.2
    percent from renewable sources. 6.2%
  Net summer capability (million kW) 11.1
  CO_2 emitted from generation 40.2
Natural gas utilities, 2005
  Customers (x 1,000) 950
  Sales (trillion Btu). 215
  Revenues ($ mil) $1,299
Nuclear plants, 2007 1
Total CO_2 emitted (million metric tons). 78.9
Energy spending, 2004 ($ mil) $10,111
  per capita $3,423
  Price per million Btu $11.80

Transportation, 2006
Public road & street mileage 114,084
  Urban. 11,197
  Rural 102,887
  Interstate. 781
Vehicle miles of travel (millions) 31,355
  per capita 10,548.1
Total motor vehicle registrations. 3,345,951
  Automobiles. 1,744,519
  Trucks 1,593,003
  Motorcycles 161,106
Licensed drivers 2,040,873
  19 years & under 123,970
Deaths from motor vehicle accidents 439
Gasoline consumed (x 1,000 gallons) 1,673,188
  per capita 562.9

Commuting Statistics, 2006
Average commute time (min) 18.2
  Drove to work alone 78.5%
  Carpooled. 10.8%
  Public transit 1.0%
  Walk to work 3.7%
  Work from home 4.7%

Kansas 1

State Summary

Capital city . . . . Topeka
Governor . . . . Kathleen Sebelius
Capitol
300 SW 10th Ave, Suite 212S
Topeka, KS 66612
785-296-3232
Admitted as a state 1861
Area (square miles) 82,277
Population, 2007 (estimate). 2,775,997
Largest city . . . . Wichita
Population, 2006 .357,698
Personal income per capita, 2006
(in current dollars) $34,743
Gross domestic product, 2006 ($ mil) . . . $111,699

Leading industries by payroll, 2005

Manufacturing, Health care/Social assistance,
Retail trade

Leading agricultural commodities by receipts, 2005

Cattle and calves, Wheat, Corn, Soybeans, Hogs

Geography & Environment

Total area (square miles). 82,277
land 81,815
water 462
Federally-owned land, 2004 (acres) 631,351
percent. 1.2%
Highest point . . . . .Mt. Sunflower
elevation (feet) 4,039
Lowest point . . . . .Verdigris River
elevation (feet) 679
General coastline (miles) 0
Tidal shoreline (miles) 0
Cropland, 2003 (x 1,000 acres) 26,466
Forest land, 2003 (x 1,000 acres). 1,549
Capital city . . . . Topeka
Population 2000 122,377
Population 2006 122,113
Largest city . . . . Wichita
Population 2000 344,284
Population 2006 357,698

Number of cities with over 100,000 population

1990 4
2000 4
2006 5

State park and recreation areas, 2005

Area (x 1,000 acres). 33
Number of visitors (x 1,000) 7,310
Revenues ($1,000) $5,967
percent of operating expenditures. 58.6%

National forest system land, 2007

Acres 108,175

Demographics & Population Characteristics

Population

1980 2,363,679
1990 2,477,574
2000 2,688,824
2006 2,764,075
Male. 1,371,446
Female 1,392,629
Living in group quarters, 2006 82,162
percent of total. 3.0%
2007 (estimate). 2,775,997
persons per square mile of land 33.9
2008 (projected). 2,784,728
2010 (projected). 2,805,470
2020 (projected). 2,890,566
2030 (projected). 2,940,084

Population of Core-Based Statistical Areas (formerly Metropolitan Areas), x 1,000

	CBSA	Non-CBSA
1990	2,029	448
2000	2,248	440
2006	2,349	415

Change in population, 2000-2007

Number 87,173
percent. 3.2%
Natural increase (births minus deaths) 109,842
Net internal migration . . . . -67,315
Net international migration 46,314

Persons by age, 2006

Under 5 years 194,100
5 to 17 years 501,737
18 years and over 2,068,238
65 years and over 357,709
85 years and over 59,518
Median age 36.0

Persons by age, 2010 (projected)

Under 5 years 199,534
18 and over 2,106,474
65 and over 375,315
Median age 36.4

Race, 2006

One Race
White. 2,462,232
Black or African American 164,507
Asian 60,870
American Indian/Alaska Native. 27,374
Hawaiian Native/Pacific Islander. 1,863
Two or more races .47,229

Persons of Hispanic origin, 2006

Total Hispanic or Latino 236,351
Mexican. 193,309
Puerto Rican 6,241
Cuban 785

Persons of Asian origin, 2006

Total Asian 60,646
 Asian Indian....................... 15,295
 Chinese 9,646
 Filipino 3,743
 Japanese 1,352
 Korean............................ 5,068
 Vietnamese........................ 12,525

Marital status, 2006

Population 15 years & over 2,190,376
 Never married 582,595
 Married....................... 1,229,547
 Separated 31,025
 Widowed........................ 138,334
 Divorced 239,900

Language spoken at home, 2006

Population 5 years and older........ 2,569,373
 English only 2,304,997
 Spanish 169,376
 French 4,647
 German.......................... 16,736
 Chinese 8,159

Households & families, 2006

Households.......................1,088,288
 with persons under 18 years 371,279
 with persons over 65 years........... 241,992
 persons per household 2.46
Families......................... 724,553
 persons per family....................3.02
Married couples...................... 571,689
Female householder,
 no husband present.................111,874
One-person households 303,157

Nativity, 2006

Number of residents born in state 1,633,671
 percent of population................. 59.1%

Immigration & naturalization, 2006

Legal permanent residents admitted...... 4,280
Persons naturalized 2,509
Non-immigrant admissions 61,161

Vital Statistics and Health

Marriages

2004 19,072
2005 18,804
2006 18,862

Divorces

2004 9,102
2005 8,512
2006 9,158

Health risks, 2006

Percent of adults who are:
 Smokers.........................20.0%
 Overweight (BMI > 25)................62.3%
 Obese (BMI > 30)....................25.9%

Births

2005 39,888
 Birthrate (per 1,000)...................14.5
 White..............................35,116
 Black 3,127
 Hispanic 6,121
 Asian/Pacific Islander 1,214
 Amer. Indian/Alaska Native............ 431
 Low birth weight (2,500g or less)....... 7.2%
 Cesarian births 28.9%
 Preterm births 12.2%
 To unmarried mothers................34.2%
 Twin births (per 1,000) 30.3
 Triplets or higher order (per 100,000)....158.8
2006 (preliminary)..................... 40,964
 rate per 1,000 ....14.8

Deaths

2004
All causes 23,818
 rate per 100,000......................793.5
Heart disease 6,048
 rate per 100,000......................197.3
Malignant neoplasms 5,312
 rate per 100,000......................183.2
Cerebrovascular disease...................1,611
 rate per 100,000......................51.8
Chronic lower respiratory disease 1,316
 rate per 100,000......................44.9
Diabetes.............................. 690
 rate per 100,000......................23.5
2005 (preliminary) 24,684
 rate per 100,000.................... 806.8
2006 (provisional) 24,473

Infant deaths

2004 284
 rate per 1,000 ....7.2
2005 (provisional) 280
 rate per 1,000 ....6.9

Exercise routines, 2005

None................................24.4%
Moderate or greater..................48.7%
Vigorous 25.0%

Abortions, 2004

Total performed in state.................11,357
 rate per 1,000 women age 15-44........... 20
 % obtained by out-of-state residents 48.2%

Physicians, 2005

Total..................................6,070
 rate per 100,000 persons 221

Community hospitals, 2005

Number of hospitals 131
Beds (x 1,000)........................10.1
Patients admitted (x 1,000) 330
Average daily census (x 1,000) 5.7
Average cost per day $1,055
Outpatient visits (x 1 mil) 5.9

Disability status of population, 2006
5 to 15 years	6.9%
16 to 64 years	11.8%
65 years and over	40.5%

Education

Educational attainment, 2006
Population over 25 years	1,771,185
Less than 9th grade	4.3%
High school graduate or more	88.5%
College graduate or more	28.6%
Graduate or professional degree	9.8%

Public school enrollment, 2005-06
Total	467,285
Pre-kindergarten through grade 8	309,555
Grades 9 through 12	142,349

Graduating public high school seniors, 2004-05
Diplomas (incl. GED and others)	30,355

SAT scores, 2007
Average critical reading score	583
Average writing score	569
Average math score	590
Percent of graduates taking test	8%

Public school teachers, 2006-07 (estimate)
Total (x 1,000)	34.4
Elementary	16.9
Secondary	17.4
Average salary	$43,334
Elementary	$43,334
Secondary	$43,334

State receipts & expenditures for public schools, 2006-07 (estimate)
Revenue receipts ($ mil) ... $4,923
Expenditures
Total ($ mil)	$4,957
Per capita	$1,500
Per pupil	$10,119

NAEP proficiency scores, 2007
	Reading		Math	
	Basic	Proficient	Basic	Proficient
Grade 4	71.8%	36.1%	89.4%	51.1%
Grade 8	80.6%	35.2%	81.4%	40.2%

Higher education enrollment, fall 2005
Total	21,433
Full-time men	6,844
Full-time women	8,206
Part-time men	2,380
Part-time women	4,003

Minority enrollment in institutions of higher education, 2005
Black, non-Hispanic	11,230
Hispanic	8,618
Asian/Pacific Islander	7,279
American Indian/Alaska Native	3,194

Institutions of higher education, 2005-06
Total	62
Public	35
Private	27

Earned degrees conferred, 2004-05
Associate's	7,954
Bachelor's	16,221
Master's	5,668
First-professional	767
Doctor's	413

Public Libraries, 2006
Number of libraries	325
Number of outlets	379
Annual visits per capita	6.4
Circulation per capita	10.9

State & local financial support for higher education, FY 2006
Full-time equivalent enrollment (x 1,000)	127.6
Appropriations per FTE	$5,792

Social Insurance & Welfare Programs

Social Security benefits & beneficiaries, 2005
Beneficiaries (x 1,000)	451
Retired & dependents	320
Survivors	61
Disabled & dependents	70
Annual benefit payments ($ mil)	$4,974
Retired & dependents	$3,406
Survivors	$879
Disabled & dependents	$690
Average monthly benefit	
Retired & dependents	$1,027
Disabled & dependents	$909
Widowed	$1,025

Medicare, July 2005
Enrollment (x 1,000)	402
Payments ($ mil)	$2,661

Medicaid, 2004
Beneficiaries (x 1,000)	365
Payments ($ mil)	$1,860

State Children's Health Insurance Program, 2006
Enrollment (x 1,000)	48.9
Expenditures ($ mil)	$67.2

Persons without health insurance, 2006
Number (x 1,000)	335
percent	12.3%
Number of children (x 1,000)	51
percent of children	7.3%

Health care expenditures, 2004
Total expenditures	$14,736
per capita	$5,382

Federal and state public aid

State unemployment insurance, 2006
Recipients, first payments (x 1,000) 54
Total payments ($ mil) $210
Average weekly benefit $287
Temporary Assistance for Needy Families, 2006
Recipients (x 1,000) 525.5
Families (x 1,000) 201.9
Supplemental Security Income, 2005
Recipients (x 1,000) 39.2
Payments ($ mil) $186.7
Food Stamp Program, 2006
Avg monthly participants (x 1,000) 183.1
Total benefits ($ mil) $188.3

Housing & Construction

Housing units

Total 2005 (estimate) 1,196,732
Total 2006 (estimate) 1,207,987
Seasonal or recreational use, 2006 11,864
Owner-occupied, 2006 761,022
    Median home value $114,400
    Homeowner vacancy rate 2.1%
Renter-occupied, 2006 327,266
    Median rent $609
    Rental vacancy rate 11.3%
Home ownership rate, 2005 . . . . 69.5%
Home ownership rate, 2006 . . . . 70.0%

New privately-owned housing units

Number authorized, 2006 (x 1,000) 14.6
    Value ($ mil) $1,995.5
Started 2005 (x 1,000, estimate) 13.8
Started 2006 (x 1,000, estimate) 13.8

Existing home sales

2005 (x 1,000) 77.9
2006 (x 1,000) 76.1

Government & Elections

State officials 2008

Governor . . . . Kathleen Sebelius
    Democratic, term expires 1/11
Lieutenant Governor . . . . .Mark Parkinson
Secretary of State . . . . Ron Thornburgh
Attorney General . . . . (vacant)
Chief Justice . . . . .Kay McFarland

Governorship

Minimum age . . . . not specified
Length of term . . . . 4 years
Consecutive terms permitted 2
Who succeeds . . . . Lieutenant Governor

Local governments by type, 2002

Total 3,887
    County 104
    Municipal 627
    Township 1,299
    School District 324
    Special District 1,533

State legislature

Name . . . . Legislature
Upper chamber . . . . .Senate
    Number of members 40
    Length of term . . . . 4 years
    Party in majority, 2008 . . . . Republican
Lower chamber . . . . .House of Representatives
    Number of members 125
    Length of term . . . . 2 years
    Party in majority, 2008 . . . . Republican

Federal representation, 2008 (110th Congress)

Senator . . . . Pat Roberts
    Party . . . . Republican
    Year term expires 2009
Senator . . . . Sam Brownback
    Party . . . . Republican
    Year term expires 2011
Representatives, total 4
    Democrats 2
    Republicans 2

Voters in November 2006 election (estimate)

Total 900,638
    Male 417,509
    Female 483,129
    White 854,991
    Black 36,468
    Hispanic 13,112
    Asian . . . . NA

Presidential election, 2004

Total Popular Vote 1,187,756
    Kerry 434,993
    Bush 736,456
Total Electoral Votes 6

Votes cast for US Senators

2004
Total vote (x 1,000) 1,129
Leading party . . . . Republican
Percent for leading party 69.2%
2006
Total vote (x 1,000) . . . . NA
Leading party . . . . NA
Percent for leading party . . . . NA

Votes cast for US Representatives

2004
Total vote (x 1,000) 1,156
    Democratic 387
    Republican 724
Leading party . . . . Republican
Percent for leading party 62.6%
2006
Total vote (x 1,000) 845
    Democratic 369
    Republican 459
Leading party . . . . Republican
Percent for leading party 54.3%

State government employment, 2006
Full-time equivalent employees 44,393
Payroll ($ mil) $153.8

Local government employment, 2006
Full-time equivalent employees 140,550
Payroll ($ mil) $413.3

Women holding public office, 2008
US Congress 1
Statewide elected office..................... 3
State legislature 48

Black public officials, 2002
Total..................................... 16
  US and state legislatures 7
  City/county/regional offices 4
  Judicial/law enforcement.................. 3
  Education/school boards.................. 2

Hispanic public officials, 2006
Total..................................... 11
  State executives & legislators 4
  City/county/regional offices 6
  Judicial/law enforcement.................. 0
  Education/school boards.................. 1

Governmental Finance

State government revenues, 2006
Total revenue (x $1,000)............ $13,615,302
  per capita $4,940.57
General revenue (x $1,000) $11,448,515
  Intergovernmental 3,314,770
  Taxes 6,275,075
    general sales..................... 2,127,597
    individual income tax 2,401,128
    corporate income tax 381,259
  Current charges.................. 1,135,185
  Miscellaneous 723,485

State government expenditure, 2006
Total expenditure (x $1,000) $12,553,494
  per capita $4,555.27
General expenditure (x $1,000) $11,439,941
  per capita, total................... $4,151.20
  Education 1,876.44
  Public welfare 1,020.56
  Health 71.10
  Hospitals......................... 44.35
  Highways 455.24
  Police protection................. 43.64
  Corrections 113.63
  Natural resources 69.19
  Parks & recreation 9.40
  Governmental administration...... 160.49
  Interest on general debt............ 103.35

State debt & cash, 2006 ($ per capita)
Debt $2,084.14
Cash/security holdings............... $6,043.97

Federal government grants to state & local government, 2005 (x $1,000)
Total............................. $3,617,795
by Federal agency
  Defense 26,874
  Education 354,695
  Energy 12,065
  Environmental Protection Agency 44,838
  Health & Human Services. 1,869,708
  Homeland Security................ 101,898
  Housing & Urban Development...... 194,646
  Justice 49,069
  Labor 54,289
  Transportation 401,699
  Veterans Affairs.................... 4,810

Crime & Law Enforcement

Crime, 2006 (rates per 100,000 residents)
Property crimes 103,658
  Burglary 19,992
  Larceny 74,963
  Motor vehicle theft 8,703
  Property crime rate................ 3,750.2
Violent crimes........................ 11,748
  Murder 127
  Forcible rape...................... 1,238
  Robbery.......................... 1,877
  Aggravated assault 8,506
  Violent crime rate 425.0
Hate crimes........................... 135

Fraud and identity theft, 2006
Fraud complaints..................... 3,068
  rate per 100,000 residents 111.0
Identity theft complaints 1,626
  rate per 100,000 residents 58.8

Law enforcement agencies, 2006
Total agencies......................... 327
Total employees 10,451
  Officers 7,085
  Civilians 3,366

Prisoners, probation, and parole, 2006
Total prisoners....................... 8,816
  percent change, 12/31/05 to 12/31/06 ... -2.8%
  in private facilities 0%
  in local jails 0%
Sentenced to more than one year 8,816
  rate per 100,000 residents 318
Adults on probation 15,518
Adults on parole....................... 4,886

Prisoner demographics, June 30, 2005 (rate per 100,000 residents)
Male 1,054
Female 117
White 443
Black................................. 3,096
Hispanic .... NA

Arrests, 2006

Total.............................. 70,057
   Persons under 18 years of age 10,036

Persons under sentence of death, 1/1/07

Total..................................... 9
   White................................. 5
   Black 4
   Hispanic 0

State's highest court

Name ....Supreme Court
Number of members........................ 7
Length of term........................ 6 years
Intermediate appeals court? ....yes

Labor & Income

Civilian labor force, 2006 (x 1,000)

Total..................................1,480
   Men 787
   Women 693
   Persons 16-19 years..................... 84
   White...............................1,338
   Black 67
   Hispanic 90

Civilian labor force as a percent of civilian non-institutional population, 2006

Total..................................70.4%
   Men 76.5
   Women 64.5
   Persons 16-19 years...................51.9
   White...............................70.7
   Black 63.8
   Hispanic 75.8

Employment, 2006 (x 1,000)

Total..................................1,414
   Men 755
   Women 659
   Persons 16-19 years..................... 71
   White............................... 1,288
   Black 59
   Hispanic 85

Unemployment rate, 2006

Total..................................4.4%
   Men 4.0
   Women 4.9
   Persons 16-19 years...................15.3
   White................................3.7
   Black 12.4
   Hispanic 5.6

Full-time/part-time labor force, 2003 (x 1,000)

Full-time labor force, employed 1,073
Part-time labor force, employed............ 284
Unemployed, looking for
   Full-time work........................... 63
   Part-time work........................... 14
*Mean duration of unemployment (weeks)......*15.2
   Median 8.3

Labor unions, 2006

Membership (x 1,000)..................... 99
   percent of employed 8.0%

Experienced civilian labor force by private industry, 2006

Total...............................1,085,952
   Natural resources & mining 18,260
   Construction 64,867
   Manufacturing......................182,714
   Trade, transportation & utilities 256,056
   Information 39,382
   Finance 71,826
   Professional & business 139,661
   Education & health..................161,184
   Leisure & hospitality.............. 115,277
   Other............................. 36,704

Experienced civilian labor force by occupation, May 2006

Management..........................57,470
Business & financial 54,490
Legal................................7,410
Sales 133,930
Office & admin. support.............. 229,540
Computers & math 24,870
Architecture & engineering............. 25,800
Arts & entertainment 16,120
Education 87,860
Social services 16,870
Health care practitioner & technical 65,150
Health care support 39,880
Maintenance & repair................. 56,470
Construction 65,320
Transportation & moving 91,660
Production 126,420
Farming, fishing & forestry............. 2,260

Hours and earnings of production workers on manufacturing payrolls, 2006

Average weekly hours 43.0
Average hourly earnings $17.68
Average weekly earnings $760.24

Income and poverty, 2006

Median household income............. $45,478
Personal income, per capita (current $)... $34,743
   in constant (2000) dollars $30,328
Persons below poverty level............. 12.4%

Average annual pay

2006 .... $35,696
   increase from 2005 .... 5.4%

Federal individual income tax returns, 2005

Returns filed.......................1,241,568
Adjusted gross income ($1,000) $60,483,659
Total tax liability ($1,000) $7,427,755

Charitable contributions, 2004

Number of contributions................ 328.8
Total amount ($ mil)..................$1,347.6

Economy, Business, Industry & Agriculture

Fortune 500 companies, 2007 1
Bankruptcy cases filed, FY 2007 7,730

Patents and trademarks issued, 2007
Patents 544
Trademarks 557

Business firm ownership, 2002
Women-owned 59,635
 Sales ($ mil) $6,949
Black-owned 4,468
 Sales ($ mil) $376
Hispanic-owned 4,176
 Sales ($ mil) $660
Asian-owned 3,547
 Sales ($ mil) $896
Amer. Indian/Alaska Native-owned 1,727
 Sales ($ mil) $353
Hawaiian/Pacific Islander-owned 44
 Sales ($ mil) $20

Gross domestic product, 2006 ($ mil)
Total gross domestic product $111,699
 Agriculture, forestry, fishing and
  hunting 3,092
 Mining 2,578
 Utilities 2,494
 Construction 4,465
 Manufacturing, durable goods 8,757
 Manufacturing, non-durable goods 6,552
 Wholesale trade 7,055
 Retail trade 7,566
 Transportation & warehousing 3,951
 Information 6,798
 Finance & insurance 6,555
 Real estate, rental & leasing 10,775
 Professional and technical services 5,682
 Educational services 622
 Health care and social assistance 7,802
 Accommodation/food services 2,675
 Other services, except government 2,575
 Government 16,622

Establishments, payroll, employees & receipts, by major industry group, 2005
Total 76,173
 Annual payroll ($1,000) $36,646,065
 Paid employees 1,116,216
Forestry, fishing & agriculture 188
 Annual payroll ($1,000) $16,298
 Paid employees 670
Mining 941
 Annual payroll ($1,000) $381,069
 Paid employees 8,004
 Receipts, 2002 ($1,000) $3,247,527

Utilities 254
 Annual payroll ($1,000) $429,864
 Paid employees 6,545
 Receipts, 2002 ($1,000) . . . . .NA
Construction 8,032
 Annual payroll ($1,000) $2,465,977
 Paid employees 62,331
 Receipts, 2002 ($1,000) $10,341,081
Manufacturing 3,128
 Annual payroll ($1,000) $7,221,614
 Paid employees 177,170
 Receipts, 2002 ($1,000) $50,897,796
Wholesale trade 4,541
 Annual payroll ($1,000) $2,345,990
 Paid employees 54,461
 Receipts, 2002 ($1,000) $44,117,100
Retail trade 11,562
 Annual payroll ($1,000) $2,952,196
 Paid employees 148,988
 Receipts, 2002 ($1,000) $26,505,396
Transportation & warehousing 2,632
 Annual payroll ($1,000) $1,393,651
 Paid employees 42,533
 Receipts, 2002 ($1,000) $3,963,169
Information 1,519
 Annual payroll ($1,000) $2,395,081
 Paid employees 43,002
 Receipts, 2002 ($1,000) . . . . .NA
Finance & insurance 5,708
 Annual payroll ($1,000) $2,786,136
 Paid employees 58,675
 Receipts, 2002 ($1,000) . . . . .NA
Professional, scientific & technical 7,087
 Annual payroll ($1,000) $2,418,500
 Paid employees 56,793
 Receipts, 2002 ($1,000) $6,285,201
Education 699
 Annual payroll ($1,000) $375,781
 Paid employees 18,026
 Receipts, 2002 ($1,000) $309,700
Health care & social assistance 7,412
 Annual payroll ($1,000) $5,487,089
 Paid employees 169,777
 Receipts, 2002 ($1,000) $11,162,607
Arts and entertainment 1,109
 Annual payroll ($1,000) $196,594
 Paid employees 13,536
 Receipts, 2002 ($1,000) $694,248
Real estate 3,203
 Annual payroll ($1,000) $465,149
 Paid employees 15,558
 Receipts, 2002 ($1,000) $2,028,027
Accommodation & food service 5,776
 Annual payroll ($1,000) $1,101,854
 Paid employees 101,824
 Receipts, 2002 ($1,000) $3,196,947

Exports, 2006
Value of exported goods ($ mil) $8,626
  Manufactured $7,591
  Non-manufactured. $598

Foreign direct investment in US affiliates, 2004
Property, plants & equipment ($ mil) $5,322
Employment (x 1,000). 32.2

Agriculture, 2006
Number of farms 64,000
Farm acreage (x 1,000) 47,200
  Acres per farm. 738
Farm marketings and income ($ mil)
Total. $10,335.8
  Crops. $3,365.1
  Livestock. $6,970.7
Net farm income $1,614.3

Principal commodities, in order by marketing receipts, 2005
Cattle and calves, Wheat, Corn, Soybeans, Hogs

Federal economic activity in state
Expenditures, 2005 ($ mil)
  Total. $20,492
    Per capita $7,456.72
  Defense $3,269
  Non-defense $17,224
Defense department, 2006 ($ mil)
  Payroll. $1,827
  Contract awards $1,706
  Grants $46
Homeland security grants ($1,000)
  2006. . . . .$14,274
  2007 . . . . $8,375

FDIC-insured financial institutions, 2005
Number 362
Assets ($ billion) $59.2
Deposits ($ billion) $44.0

Fishing, 2006
Catch (x 1,000 lbs) . . . . NA
Value ($1,000). . . . . NA

Mining, 2006 ($ mil)
Total non-fuel mineral production $913
Percent of U.S. 1.42%

Communication, Energy & Transportation

Communication
Households with computers, 2003 . . . . 63.8%
Households with internet access, 2003 . . . . 54.3%
High-speed internet providers 83
Total high-speed internet lines. 755,922
  Residential 600,073
  Business. 155,849
Wireless phone customers, 12/2006 2,046,542

FCC-licensed stations (as of January 1, 2008)
TV stations 25
FM radio stations. 165
AM radio stations 62

Energy
Energy consumption, 2004
  Total (trillion Btu). 1,104
  Per capita (million Btu) 403.0
By source of production (trillion Btu)
  Coal 386
  Natural gas 273
  Petroleum 428
  Nuclear electric power 106
  Hydroelectric power 0
By end-use sector (trillion Btu)
  Residential 217
  Commercial 197
  Industrial 408
  Transportation 281
Electric energy, 2005
  Primary source of electricity. . . . . Coal
  Net generation (billion kWh) 45.9
    percent from renewable sources. 1.0%
  Net summer capability (million kW) 11.0
  CO_2 emitted from generation 37.6
Natural gas utilities, 2005
  Customers (x 1,000) 950
  Sales (trillion Btu). 198
  Revenues ($ mil) $1,059
Nuclear plants, 2007 1
Total CO_2 emitted (million metric tons). 79.9
Energy spending, 2004 ($ mil) $8,954
  per capita $3,270
  Price per million Btu $12.44

Transportation, 2006
Public road & street mileage 140,381
  Urban. 12,790
  Rural. 127,591
  Interstate. 874
Vehicle miles of travel (millions) 30,215
  per capita 10,964.1
Total motor vehicle registrations 2,389,192
  Automobiles. 872,878
  Trucks 1,512,396
  Motorcycles 72,072
Licensed drivers .2,003,112
  19 years & under 166,663
Deaths from motor vehicle accidents 468
Gasoline consumed (x 1,000 gallons) 1,329,522
  per capita 482.4

Commuting Statistics, 2006
Average commute time (min) 18.5
  Drove to work alone 81.8%
  Carpooled. 9.2%
  Public transit 0.6%
  Walk to work 2.6%
  Work from home. 4.3%

State Summary

Capital city . . . . Frankfort
Governor . . . . Steve Beshar
700 Capitol Ave
Suite 100
Frankfort, KY 40601
502-564-2611
Admitted as a state 1792
Area (square miles) 40,409
Population, 2007 (estimate). 4,241,474
Largest city . . . . Louisville
Population, 2006 554,496
Personal income per capita, 2006
(in current dollars) $29,352
Gross domestic product, 2006 ($ mil) . . . $145,959

Leading industries by payroll, 2005

Manufacturing, Health care/Social assistance,
Retail trade

Leading agricultural commodities by receipts, 2005

Horses/mules, Cattle and calves, Broilers, Corn,
Soybeans

Geography & Environment

Total area (square miles). 40,409
land 39,728
water 681
Federally-owned land, 2004 (acres) 1,378,677
percent. 5.4%
Highest point . . . . Black Mountain
elevation (feet) 4,139
Lowest point . . . . Mississippi River
elevation (feet) 257
General coastline (miles) 0
Tidal shoreline (miles) 0
Cropland, 2003 (x 1,000 acres) 5,479
Forest land, 2003 (x 1,000 acres). 10,510
Capital city . . . . Frankfort
Population 2000 27,741
Population 2006 27,077
Largest city . . . . Louisville
Population 2000 551,284
Population 2006 554,496

Number of cities with over 100,000 population

1990 2
2000 2
2006 2

State park and recreation areas, 2005

Area (x 1,000 acres) 58
Number of visitors (x 1,000) 7,037
Revenues ($1,000) $52,143
percent of operating expenditures 61.7%

National forest system land, 2007

Acres 814,045

Demographics & Population Characteristics

Population

1980 3,660,777
1990 3,685,296
2000 4,042,285
2006 4,206,074
Male. 2,061,310
Female 2,144,764
Living in group quarters, 2006 114,777
percent of total. 2.7%
2007 (estimate). .4,241,474
persons per square mile of land 106.8
2008 (projected). 4,226,659
2010 (projected) .4,265,117
2020 (projected) .4,424,431
2030 (projected) .4,554,998

Population of Core-Based Statistical Areas (formerly Metropolitan Areas), x 1,000

	CBSA	Non-CBSA
1990	2,734	953
2000	3,036	1,006
2006	3,184	1,022

Change in population, 2000-2007

Number 199,193
percent. 4.9%
Natural increase (births minus deaths) 110,877
Net internal migration 63,791
Net international migration 30,881

Persons by age, 2006

Under 5 years 275,751
5 to 17 years 723,780
18 years and over 3,206,543
65 years and over .537,294
85 years and over 69,463
Median age 37.2

Persons by age, 2010 (projected)

Under 5 years 275,053
18 and over 3,262,810
65 and over 557,471
Median age 38.0

Race, 2006

One Race
White. 3,793,438
Black or African American 316,945
Asian 41,752
American Indian/Alaska Native. 9,988
Hawaiian Native/Pacific Islander. 1,765
Two or more races. 42,186

Persons of Hispanic origin, 2006

Total Hispanic or Latino 83,015
Mexican. 55,761
Puerto Rican 6,785
Cuban 6,421

Persons of Asian origin, 2006

Total Asian 38,835
  Asian Indian........................10,912
  Chinese 7,306
  Filipino 3,843
  Japanese 5,040
  Korean..............................3,056
  Vietnamese..........................5,394

Marital status, 2006

Population 15 years & over 3,381,302
  Never married 879,970
  Married......................... 1,828,798
  Separated 69,732
  Widowed.......................... 243,830
  Divorced 428,704

Language spoken at home, 2006

Population 5 years and older.......... 3,929,110
  English only 3,769,097
  Spanish 80,450
  French 9,056
  German.......................... 16,243
  Chinese 6,259

Households & families, 2006

Households.......................... 1,651,911
  with persons under 18 years 550,811
  with persons over 65 years.......... 378,261
  persons per household 2.48
Families...........................1,106,404
  persons per family.....................3.04
Married couples...................... 832,504
Female householder,
  no husband present................ 205,540
One-person households 465,843

Nativity, 2006

Number of residents born in state 3,019,808
  percent of population 71.8%

Immigration & naturalization, 2006

Legal permanent residents admitted...... 5,506
Persons naturalized 2,049
Non-immigrant admissions 70,731

Vital Statistics and Health

Marriages

2004 36,391
2005 36,251
2006 36,905

Divorces

2004 20,298
2005 19,342
2006 21,489

Health risks, 2006

Percent of adults who are:
  Smokers..........................28.5%
  Overweight (BMI > 25)................66.4%
  Obese (BMI > 30)....................28.0%

Births

2005 56,444
  Birthrate (per 1,000)...............13.5
  White............................ 50,445
  Black 5,094
  Hispanic 2,509
  Asian/Pacific Islander 823
  Amer. Indian/Alaska Native 82
  Low birth weight (2,500g or less)....... 9.1%
  Cesarian births 33.9%
  Preterm births 15.2%
  To unmarried mothers................ 35.5%
  Twin births (per 1,000) 30.6
  Triplets or higher order (per 100,000)... 234.8
2006 (preliminary).................... 58,291
  rate per 1,000 ....13.9

Deaths

2004
All causes 38,646
  rate per 100,000......................935.1
Heart disease 10,465
  rate per 100,000 .... 254.9
Malignant neoplasms 9,159
  rate per 100,000......................215.4
Cerebrovascular disease.................. 2,339
  rate per 100,000......................58.0
Chronic lower respiratory disease 2,265
  rate per 100,000......................54.7
Diabetes.............................1,195
  rate per 100,000......................28.6
2005 (preliminary).................... 40,223
  rate per 100,000......................958.4
2006 (provisional) 40,066

Infant deaths

2004 378
  rate per 1,000 ....6.8
2005 (provisional) 367
  rate per 1,000 ....6.5

Exercise routines, 2005

None................................. 31.5%
Moderate or greater.................... 34.7%
Vigorous 16.8%

Abortions, 2004

Total performed in state..................3,557
  rate per 1,000 women age 15-44............ 4
  % obtained by out-of-state residents ...... NA

Physicians, 2005

Total..................................9,608
  rate per 100,000 persons 230

Community hospitals, 2005

Number of hospitals 105
Beds (x 1,000)..........................14.9
Patients admitted (x 1,000) 618
Average daily census (x 1,000) 9.3
Average cost per day $1,194
Outpatient visits (x 1 mil) 8.8

Kentucky 3

Disability status of population, 2006
5 to 15 years 8.5%
16 to 64 years 19.2%
65 years and over 47.9%

Education

Educational attainment, 2006
Population over 25 years 2,812,772
   Less than 9th grade. 8.6%
   High school graduate or more 79.6%
   College graduate or more. 20.0%
   Graduate or professional degree. 8.2%

Public school enrollment, 2005-06
Total. 679,878
   Pre-kindergarten through grade 8. . . . 483,797
   Grades 9 through 12 190,975

Graduating public high school seniors, 2004-05
Diplomas (incl. GED and others) 38,782

SAT scores, 2007
Average critical reading score 567
Average writing score 553
Average math score 565
Percent of graduates taking test 10%

Public school teachers, 2006-07 (estimate)
Total (x 1,000) 41.3
   Elementary 29.3
   Secondary 12.0
Average salary $43,646
   Elementary $43,432
   Secondary $44,175

State receipts & expenditures for public schools, 2006-07 (estimate)
Revenue receipts ($ mil) $6,061
Expenditures
Total ($ mil) $5,984
   Per capita $1,300
   Per pupil $9,214

NAEP proficiency scores, 2007

	Reading		Math	
	Basic	Proficient	Basic	Proficient
Grade 4	68.4%	33.5%	79.3%	30.8%
Grade 8	73.3%	27.7%	69.0%	27.3%

Higher education enrollment, fall 2005
Total. 43,390
   Full-time men 12,392
   Full-time women 19,606
   Part-time men 4,024
   Part-time women. 7,368

Minority enrollment in institutions of higher education, 2005
Black, non-Hispanic 21,322
Hispanic 2,834
Asian/Pacific Islander 2,995
American Indian/Alaska Native. 748

Institutions of higher education, 2005-06
Total. 76
   Public. 31
   Private 45

Earned degrees conferred, 2004-05
Associate's. 9,009
Bachelor's 17,862
Master's 6,564
First-professional. 1,111
Doctor's 511

Public Libraries, 2006
Number of libraries. 116
Number of outlets 277
Annual visits per capita 4.0
Circulation per capita. 6.0

State & local financial support for higher education, FY 2006
Full-time equivalent enrollment (x 1,000) 144.3
Appropriations per FTE. $6,753

Social Insurance & Welfare Programs

Social Security benefits & beneficiaries, 2005
Beneficiaries (x 1,000) 799
   Retired & dependents. 468
   Survivors. 123
   Disabled & dependents. 207
Annual benefit payments ($ mil) $8,129
   Retired & dependents. $4,509
   Survivors. $1,547
   Disabled & dependents. $2,073
Average monthly benefit
   Retired & dependents. $949
   Disabled & dependents. $924
   Widowed. $881

Medicare, July 2005
Enrollment (x 1,000) 678
Payments ($ mil) $4,581

Medicaid, 2004
Beneficiaries (x 1,000). 861
Payments ($ mil) $3,924

State Children's Health Insurance Program, 2006
Enrollment (x 1,000) 64.9
Expenditures ($ mil) $98.3

Persons without health insurance, 2006
Number (x 1,000). 639
   percent. 15.6%
Number of children (x 1,000) 98
   percent of children 9.7%

Health care expenditures, 2004
Total expenditures. $22,662
   per capita $5,473

Federal and state public aid

State unemployment insurance, 2006
Recipients, first payments (x 1,000) 111
Total payments ($ mil) $382
Average weekly benefit $271
Temporary Assistance for Needy Families, 2006
Recipients (x 1,000) 816.7
Families (x 1,000) 389.6
Supplemental Security Income, 2005
Recipients (x 1,000) 180.2
Payments ($ mil) $861.9
Food Stamp Program, 2006
Avg monthly participants (x 1,000) 589.1
Total benefits ($ mil) $645.4

Housing & Construction

Housing units
Total 2005 (estimate) 1,865,387
Total 2006 (estimate) 1,888,164
Seasonal or recreational use, 2006 31,449
Owner-occupied, 2006 1,167,081
     Median home value $111,000
     Homeowner vacancy rate 3.4%
Renter-occupied, 2006 484,830
     Median rent $548
     Rental vacancy rate 9.8%
Home ownership rate, 2005 . . . . 71.6%
Home ownership rate, 2006 . . . . 71.7%

New privately-owned housing units
Number authorized, 2006 (x 1,000) 16.6
     Value ($ mil) $2,260.8
Started 2005 (x 1,000, estimate) 20.4
Started 2006 (x 1,000, estimate) 20.5

Existing home sales
2005 (x 1,000) 96.2
2006 (x 1,000) 96.9

Government & Elections

State officials 2008
Governor . . . . Steve Beshar
     Democratic, term expires 12/11
Lieutenant Governor . . . . .Daniel Mongiardo
Secretary of State . . . . Trey Grayson
Attorney General . . . . .Jack Conway
Chief Justice . . . . Joseph Lambert

Governorship
Minimum age 30
Length of term . . . . 4 years
Consecutive terms permitted 2
Who succeeds . . . . Lieutenant Governor

Local governments by type, 2002
Total 1,439
     County 119
     Municipal 424
     Township 0
     School District 176
     Special District 720

State legislature
Name . . . . General Assembly
Upper chamber . . . . .Senate
     Number of members 38
     Length of term . . . . 4 years
     Party in majority, 2008 . . . . Republican
Lower chamber . . . . House of Representatives
     Number of members 100
     Length of term . . . . 2 years
     Party in majority, 2008 . . . . Democratic

Federal representation, 2008 (110th Congress)
Senator . . . . Mitch McConnell
     Party . . . . Republican
     Year term expires 2009
Senator . . . . .Jim Bunning
     Party . . . . Republican
     Year term expires 2011
Representatives, total 6
     Democrats 2
     Republicans 4

Voters in November 2006 election (estimate)
Total 1,508,207
     Male 742,986
     Female 765,220
     White 1,412,696
     Black 86,321
     Hispanic 1,605
     Asian . . . . NA

Presidential election, 2004
Total Popular Vote 1,795,882
     Kerry 712,733
     Bush 1,069,439
Total Electoral Votes 8

Votes cast for US Senators
2004
Total vote (x 1,000) .1,724
Leading party . . . . Republican
Percent for leading party 50.7%
2006
Total vote (x 1,000) . . . . NA
Leading party . . . . NA
Percent for leading party . . . . NA

Votes cast for US Representatives
2004
Total vote (x 1,000) .1,635
     Democratic 602
     Republican 1,017
Leading party . . . . Republican
Percent for leading party 62.2%
2006
Total vote (x 1,000) .1,254
     Democratic 602
     Republican 612
Leading party . . . . Republican
Percent for leading party 48.8%

State government employment, 2006
Full-time equivalent employees 79,266
Payroll ($ mil) $270.8

Local government employment, 2006
Full-time equivalent employees 164,532
Payroll ($ mil) $453.2

Women holding public office, 2008
US Congress 0
Statewide elected office.................... 1
State legislature 17

Black public officials, 2002
Total.................................... 62
  US and state legislatures 5
  City/county/regional offices 45
  Judicial/law enforcement................... 6
  Education/school boards.................... 6

Hispanic public officials, 2006
Total..................................... 0
  State executives & legislators 0
  City/county/regional offices 0
  Judicial/law enforcement................... 0
  Education/school boards.................... 0

Governmental Finance

State government revenues, 2006
Total revenue (x $1,000).......... $23,542,502
  per capita........................$5,599.43
General revenue (x $1,000) $20,061,184
  Intergovernmental 6,374,951
  Taxes 9,953,098
    general sales....................2,748,643
    individual income tax 2,918,536
    corporate income tax 1,001,619
  Current charges...................2,335,402
  Miscellaneous 1,397,733

State government expenditure, 2006
Total expenditure (x $1,000) $21,992,340
  per capita $5,230.74
General expenditure (x $1,000) $19,335,386
  per capita, total...................$4,598.80
    Education.......................1,679.24
    Public welfare 1,368.91
    Health 131.20
    Hospitals.......................206.31
    Highways 400.15
    Police protection................44.52
    Corrections 109.13
    Natural resources...............90.21
    Parks & recreation 34.25
    Governmental administration......189.96
    Interest on general debt...........102.63

State debt & cash, 2006 ($ per capita)
Debt $2,324.93
Cash/security holdings...............$9,319.50

Federal government grants to state & local government, 2005 (x $1,000)
Total...........................$6,633,970
by Federal agency
  Defense 19,895
  Education 562,013
  Energy...........................21,183
  Environmental Protection Agency 52,212
  Health & Human Services. 4,111,657
  Homeland Security...................51,381
  Housing & Urban Development...... 476,266
  Justice 95,194
  Labor 118,606
  Transportation 591,543
  Veterans Affairs...................11,921

Crime & Law Enforcement

Crime, 2006 (rates per 100,000 residents)
Property crimes 107,023
  Burglary 27,122
  Larceny 70,658
  Motor vehicle theft 9,243
  Property crime rate................2,544.5
Violent crimes.........................11,063
  Murder 168
  Forcible rape......................1,297
  Robbery............................3,626
  Aggravated assault 5,972
  Violent crime rate 263.0
Hate crimes.............................. 70

Fraud and identity theft, 2006
Fraud complaints......................4,477
  rate per 100,000 residents 106.4
Identity theft complaints 1,766
  rate per 100,000 residents 42.0

Law enforcement agencies, 2006
Total agencies.......................... 391
Total employees.......................10,194
  Officers 8,028
  Civilians 2,166

Prisoners, probation, and parole, 2006
Total prisoners....................... 20,000
  percent change, 12/31/05 to 12/31/06 .... 1.7%
  in private facilities 12.5%
  in local jails 29.6%
Sentenced to more than one year 19,514
  rate per 100,000 residents 462
Adults on probation 41,162
Adults on parole.......................11,867

Prisoner demographics, June 30, 2005 (rate per 100,000 residents)
Male.................................1,287
Female 173
White................................ 561
Black.................................2,793
Hispanic 757

Arrests, 2006

Total................................. 73,504
  Persons under 18 years of age 8,746

Persons under sentence of death, 1/1/07

Total.................................... 41
  White................................. 31
  Black 9
  Hispanic 1

State's highest court

Name ....Supreme Court
Number of members....................... 7
Length of term........................ 8 years
Intermediate appeals court? ....yes

Labor & Income

Civilian labor force, 2006 (x 1,000)

Total................................. 2,042
  Men 1,077
  Women 965
  Persons 16-19 years.................... 103
  White...............................1,870
  Black 132
  Hispanic 34

Civilian labor force as a percent of civilian non-institutional population, 2006

Total................................62.8%
  Men 68.8
  Women 57.2
  Persons 16-19 years...................45.4
  White...............................62.8
  Black 64.2
  Hispanic 79.3

Employment, 2006 (x 1,000)

Total.................................1,927
  Men 1,017
  Women 910
  Persons 16-19 years.................... 82
  White...............................1,771
  Black 117
  Hispanic 32

Unemployment rate, 2006

Total.................................. 5.6%
  Men 5.5
  Women 5.7
  Persons 16-19 years...................19.8
  White...............................5.3
  Black 10.8
  Hispanic 4.4

Full-time/part-time labor force, 2003 (x 1,000)

Full-time labor force, employed 1,510
Part-time labor force, employed............ 326
Unemployed, looking for
  Full-time work........................... 98
  Part-time work........................... 22
*Mean duration of unemployment (weeks)......*18.0
  Median 9.7

Labor unions, 2006

Membership (x 1,000)................... 172
  percent of employed 9.8%

Experienced civilian labor force by private industry, 2006

Total.............................1,483,314
  Natural resources & mining 30,094
  Construction 83,184
  Manufacturing..................... 260,876
  Trade, transportation & utilities 375,694
  Information 29,707
  Finance 89,973
  Professional & business 178,880
  Education & health 218,722
  Leisure & hospitality............... 168,410
  Other 45,202

Experienced civilian labor force by occupation, May 2006

Management.........................77,480
Business & financial 52,270
Legal................................ 10,000
Sales 180,770
Office & admin. support............... 292,820
Computers & math 23,970
Architecture & engineering..............22,110
Arts & entertainment 16,350
Education 107,220
Social services 21,300
Health care practitioner & technical.... 101,600
Health care support 47,880
Maintenance & repair..................79,610
Construction 84,710
Transportation & moving 158,120
Production 209,360
Farming, fishing & forestry..............4,510

Hours and earnings of production workers on manufacturing payrolls, 2006

Average weekly hours.....................41.1
Average hourly earnings $16.92
Average weekly earnings $695.41

Income and poverty, 2006

Median household income............. $39,372
Personal income, per capita (current $)... $29,352
  in constant (2000) dollars $25,622
Persons below poverty level.............. 17.0%

Average annual pay

2006 .... $35,201
  increase from 2005 .... 3.6%

Federal individual income tax returns, 2005

Returns filed.......................1,779,856
Adjusted gross income ($1,000) $77,639,797
Total tax liability ($1,000) $8,758,762

Charitable contributions, 2004

Number of contributions 461.1
Total amount ($ mil).................$1,642.6

Economy, Business, Industry & Agriculture

Fortune 500 companies, 2007 6
Bankruptcy cases filed, FY 2007 16,216

Patents and trademarks issued, 2007
Patents 500
Trademarks 475

Business firm ownership, 2002
Women-owned 77,159
  Sales ($ mil) $9,451
Black-owned 7,592
  Sales ($ mil) $1,106
Hispanic-owned 2,094
  Sales ($ mil) $770
Asian-owned 3,236
  Sales ($ mil) $1,363
Amer. Indian/Alaska Native-owned 1,324
  Sales ($ mil) $79
Hawaiian/Pacific Islander-owned 60
  Sales ($ mil) . . . . NA

Gross domestic product, 2006 ($ mil)
Total gross domestic product $145,959
  Agriculture, forestry, fishing and
    hunting 2,400
  Mining 3,788
  Utilities 2,460
  Construction 6,118
  Manufacturing, durable goods 16,458
  Manufacturing, non-durable goods 10,870
  Wholesale trade 9,140
  Retail trade 10,115
  Transportation & warehousing 6,734
  Information 3,937
  Finance & insurance 7,145
  Real estate, rental & leasing 13,631
  Professional and technical services 5,923
  Educational services 815
  Health care and social assistance 11,811
  Accommodation/food services 3,818
  Other services, except government 3,167
  Government 21,448

Establishments, payroll, employees & receipts, by major industry group, 2005
Total 92,176
  Annual payroll ($1,000) $47,983,162
  Paid employees 1,514,199
Forestry, fishing & agriculture 299
  Annual payroll ($1,000) $44,803
  Paid employees 1,680
Mining 667
  Annual payroll ($1,000) $1,074,803
  Paid employees 20,198
  Receipts, 2002 ($1,000) $4,948,381

Utilities 330
  Annual payroll ($1,000) $530,266
  Paid employees 8,179
  Receipts, 2002 ($1,000) . . . . .NA
Construction 9,318
  Annual payroll ($1,000) $2,974,769
  Paid employees 82,815
  Receipts, 2002 ($1,000) $12,644,444
Manufacturing 4,152
  Annual payroll ($1,000) $10,625,628
  Paid employees 253,804
  Receipts, 2002 ($1,000) $88,513,497
Wholesale trade 4,560
  Annual payroll ($1,000) $2,992,997
  Paid employees 69,769
  Receipts, 2002 ($1,000) $51,838,719
Retail trade 16,566
  Annual payroll ($1,000) $4,340,765
  Paid employees 223,666
  Receipts, 2002 ($1,000) $40,062,561
Transportation & warehousing 3,167
  Annual payroll ($1,000) $3,071,746
  Paid employees 75,975
  Receipts, 2002 ($1,000) $8,249,830
Information 1,688
  Annual payroll ($1,000) $1,127,912
  Paid employees 31,102
  Receipts, 2002 ($1,000) . . . . .NA
Finance & insurance 6,189
  Annual payroll ($1,000) $2,940,416
  Paid employees 66,124
  Receipts, 2002 ($1,000) . . . . .NA
Professional, scientific & technical 8,004
  Annual payroll ($1,000) $2,395,720
  Paid employees 60,829
  Receipts, 2002 ($1,000) $5,190,416
Education 865
  Annual payroll ($1,000) $564,572
  Paid employees 28,076
  Receipts, 2002 ($1,000) $258,040
Health care & social assistance 10,083
  Annual payroll ($1,000) $7,623,152
  Paid employees 224,193
  Receipts, 2002 ($1,000) $16,633,446
Arts and entertainment 1,301
  Annual payroll ($1,000) $317,393
  Paid employees 17,294
  Receipts, 2002 ($1,000) $1,005,610
Real estate 3,734
  Annual payroll ($1,000) $513,704
  Paid employees 19,162
  Receipts, 2002 ($1,000) $2,470,137
Accommodation & food service 6,965
  Annual payroll ($1,000) $1,676,868
  Paid employees 147,371
  Receipts, 2002 ($1,000) $4,908,331

Exports, 2006

Value of exported goods ($ mil) $17,232
   Manufactured $14,800
   Non-manufactured. $589

Foreign direct investment in US affiliates, 2004

Property, plants & equipment ($ mil) . . . $26,919
Employment (x 1,000). 84.7

Agriculture, 2006

Number of farms 84,000
Farm acreage (x 1,000) 13,700
   Acres per farm 163
Farm marketings and income ($ mil)
Total. $4,007.2
   Crops $1,299.2
   Livestock. $2,708.0
Net farm income $1,741.5

Principal commodities, in order by marketing receipts, 2005

Horses/mules, Cattle and calves, Broilers, Corn, Soybeans

Federal economic activity in state

Expenditures, 2005 ($ mil)
   Total. $34,653
     Per capita $8,304.85
   Defense $6,665
   Non-defense. $27,988
Defense department, 2006 ($ mil)
   Payroll. $2,959
   Contract awards $5,395
   Grants $18
Homeland security grants ($1,000)
   2006. . . . .$24,119
   2007 . . . .$11,757

FDIC-insured financial institutions, 2005

Number 220
Assets ($ billion) $45.7
Deposits ($ billion) $36.0

Fishing, 2006

Catch (x 1,000 lbs). . . . . NA
Value ($1,000). . . . . NA

Mining, 2006 ($ mil)

Total non-fuel mineral production $918
Percent of U.S. 1.43%

Communication, Energy & Transportation

Communication

Households with computers, 2003. . . . . 58.1%
Households with internet access, 2003 . . . . 49.6%
High-speed internet providers 66
Total high-speed internet lines. 774,736
   Residential 612,529
   Business. 162,207
Wireless phone customers, 12/2006 2,966,195

FCC-licensed stations (as of January 1, 2008)

TV stations 38
FM radio stations. 211
AM radio stations 132

Energy

Energy consumption, 2004
   Total (trillion Btu). 1,956
   Per capita (million Btu) 472.5
By source of production (trillion Btu)
   Coal 962
   Natural gas 232
   Petroleum 728
   Nuclear electric power 0
   Hydroelectric power 38
By end-use sector (trillion Btu)
   Residential 354
   Commercial 255
   Industrial 863
   Transportation 485
Electric energy, 2005
   Primary source of electricity. . . . . Coal
   Net generation (billion kWh) 97.8
     percent from renewable sources. 3.5%
   Net summer capability (million kW) 20.0
   CO_2 emitted from generation 90.3
Natural gas utilities, 2005
   Customers (x 1,000) 857
   Sales (trillion Btu). 211
   Revenues ($ mil) $1,246
Nuclear plants, 2007 0
Total CO_2 emitted (million metric tons). 143.0
Energy spending, 2004 ($ mil) $13,882
   per capita $3,353
   Price per million Btu $11.30

Transportation, 2006

Public road & street mileage 78,231
   Urban. 12,325
   Rural 65,906
   Interstate. 762
Vehicle miles of travel (millions) 47,742
   per capita 11,355.1
Total motor vehicle registrations 3,558,122
   Automobiles. .1,969,142
   Trucks 1,574,731
   Motorcycles 58,959
Licensed drivers 2,896,460
   19 years & under 132,217
Deaths from motor vehicle accidents 913
Gasoline consumed (x 1,000 gallons) 2,228,724
   per capita 530.1

Commuting Statistics, 2006

Average commute time (min) 22.4
   Drove to work alone 81.5%
   Carpooled. 11.3%
   Public transit 1.0%
   Walk to work 2.0%
   Work from home. 3.2%

State Summary

Capital city . . . . Baton Rouge
Governor . . . . Bobby Jindal

PO Box 94004
Baton Rouge, LA 70804
225-342-0991

Admitted as a state 1812
Area (square miles) 51,840
Population, 2007 (estimate) 4,293,204
Largest city . . . . Baton Rouge
Population, 2006 229,553
Personal income per capita, 2006
(in current dollars) $30,952
Gross domestic product, 2006 ($ mil) . . . $193,138

Leading industries by payroll, 2005

Health care/Social assistance, Manufacturing,
Retail trade

**Leading agricultural commodities
by receipts, 2005**

Cotton, Cane for sugar, Rice, Cattle and calves,
Soybeans

Geography & Environment

Total area (square miles) 51,840
land 43,562
water 8,278
Federally-owned land, 2004 (acres) 1,474,788
percent 5.1%
Highest point . . . . Driskill Mountain
elevation (feet) 535
Lowest point . . . . New Orleans
elevation (feet) . . . .-8
General coastline (miles) 397
Tidal shoreline (miles) 7,721
Cropland, 2003 (x 1,000 acres) 5,435
Forest land, 2003 (x 1,000 acres) 13,338
Capital city . . . . Baton Rouge
Population 2000 227,818
Population 2006 229,553
Largest city . . . . Baton Rouge
Population 2000 227,818
Population 2006 229,553

Number of cities with over 100,000 population

1990 4
2000 4
2006 4

State park and recreation areas, 2005

Area (x 1,000 acres) 41
Number of visitors (x 1,000) 1,598
Revenues ($1,000) $4,821
percent of operating expenditures 16.8%

National forest system land, 2007

Acres 604,373

Demographics & Population Characteristics

Population

1980 4,205,900
1990 4,219,973
2000 4,468,958
2006 4,287,768
Male 2,085,761
Female 2,202,007
Living in group quarters, 2006 122,467
percent of total 2.9%
2007 (estimate) 4,293,204
persons per square mile of land 98.6
2008 (projected) 4,583,733
2010 (projected) 4,612,679
2020 (projected) 4,719,160
2030 (projected) 4,802,633

**Population of Core-Based Statistical Areas
(formerly Metropolitan Areas), x 1,000**

	CBSA	Non-CBSA
1990	3,917	303
2000	4,156	312
2006	3,979	309

Change in population, 2000-2007

Number . . . .-175,754
percent . . . . -3.9%
Natural increase (births minus deaths) 156,595
Net internal migration . . . . -335,216
Net international migration 22,477

Persons by age, 2006

Under 5 years 301,375
5 to 17 years 788,626
18 years and over 3,197,767
65 years and over 523,346
85 years and over 67,599
Median age 35.7

Persons by age, 2010 (projected)

Under 5 years 337,954
18 and over 3,441,177
65 and over 582,340
Median age 35.7

Race, 2006

One Race
White 2,802,347
Black or African American 1,357,661
Asian 60,455
American Indian/Alaska Native 27,042
Hawaiian Native/Pacific Islander 1,610
Two or more races 38,653

Persons of Hispanic origin, 2006

Total Hispanic or Latino 123,281
Mexican 50,280
Puerto Rican 8,165
Cuban 8,808

Persons of Asian origin, 2006

Total Asian 57,084
Asian Indian. 8,069
Chinese 9,438
Filipino 3,599
Japanese 2,076
Korean. 1,785
Vietnamese. 24,887

Marital status, 2006

Population 15 years & over 3,386,670
Never married 1,069,428
Married. 1,688,642
Separated 84,330
Widowed. 255,167
Divorced 373,433

Language spoken at home, 2006

Population 5 years and older. 3,986,570
English only 3,650,061
Spanish 106,872
French 155,975
German. 6,371
Chinese 7,446

Households & families, 2006

Households. 1,564,978
with persons under 18 years 556,956
with persons over 65 years. 369,047
persons per household 2.66
Families. 1,072,568
persons per family. 3.25
Married couples. 748,396
Female householder,
no husband present. 251,656
One-person households 415,423

Nativity, 2006

Number of residents born in state 3,420,568
percent of population 79.8%

Immigration & naturalization, 2006

Legal permanent residents admitted 2,693
Persons naturalized 1,336
Non-immigrant admissions 87,185

Vital Statistics and Health

Marriages

2004 36,282
2005 36,569
2006 . . . . NA

Divorces

2004 . . . . NA
2005 . . . . NA
2006 . . . . NA

Health risks, 2006

Percent of adults who are:
Smokers. 23.4%
Overweight (BMI > 25). 63.0%
Obese (BMI > 30). 27.1%

Births

2005 60,937
Birthrate (per 1,000). 13.5
White. 35,374
Black 24,145
Hispanic 1,897
Asian/Pacific Islander 1,040
Amer. Indian/Alaska Native 378
Low birth weight (2,500g or less) 11.5%
Cesarian births .36.8%
Preterm births 16.5%
To unmarried mothers. 48.0%
Twin births (per 1,000) 31.3
Triplets or higher order (per 100,000). . . .154.7
2006 (preliminary). 63,399
rate per 1,000 . . . . .14.8

Deaths

2004
All causes 42,215
rate per 100,000 . . . . .986.1
Heart disease 10,852
rate per 100,000 . . . . 256.6
Malignant neoplasms 9,434
rate per 100,000 . . . . .216.7
Cerebrovascular disease. 2,489
rate per 100,000 .59.4
Chronic lower respiratory disease 1,615
rate per 100,000 .38.2
Diabetes. 1,717
rate per 100,000 .39.9
2005 (preliminary). 44,333
rate per 100,000 . . . . .1,020.6
2006 (provisional) 38,376

Infant deaths

2004 684
rate per 1,000 . . . . .10.5
2005 (provisional) 632
rate per 1,000 . . . . .9.7

Exercise routines, 2005

None. 33.4%
Moderate or greater. 38.3%
Vigorous 20.7%

Abortions, 2004

Total performed in state. 11,224
rate per 1,000 women age 15-44 11
% obtained by out-of-state residents . . . . . NA

Physicians, 2005

Total. 11,481
rate per 100,000 persons 255

Community hospitals, 2005

Number of hospitals 128
Beds (x 1,000). 15.5
Patients admitted (x 1,000) 620
Average daily census (x 1,000) 9.5
Average cost per day $1,293
Outpatient visits (x 1 mil) 9.8

Disability status of population, 2006

5 to 15 years 7.8%
16 to 64 years 16.0%
65 years and over 48.1%

Education

Educational attainment, 2006

Population over 25 years 2,734,518
   Less than 9th grade. 7.3%
   High school graduate or more 79.4%
   College graduate or more. 20.3%
   Graduate or professional degree. 6.8%

Public school enrollment, 2005-06

Total. 654,526
   Pre-kindergarten through grade 8. . . . 482,082
   Grades 9 through 12 172,444

Graduating public high school seniors, 2004-05

Diplomas (incl. GED and others) 37,785

SAT scores, 2007

Average critical reading score 569
Average writing score 563
Average math score 567
Percent of graduates taking test 7%

Public school teachers, 2006-07 (estimate)

Total (x 1,000) 46.4
   Elementary 32.7
   Secondary 13.7
Average salary $42,816
   Elementary $42,816
   Secondary $42,816

State receipts & expenditures for public schools, 2006-07 (estimate)

Revenue receipts ($ mil) $7,115
Expenditures
Total ($ mil) $6,849
   Per capita $1,365
   Per pupil $9,355

NAEP proficiency scores, 2007

	Reading		Math	
	Basic	Proficient	Basic	Proficient
Grade 4	51.9%	20.4%	72.9%	24.4%
Grade 8	64.2%	19.4%	63.9%	19.0%

Higher education enrollment, fall 2005

Total. 16,670
   Full-time men 3,949
   Full-time women 10,053
   Part-time men 773
   Part-time women 1,895

Minority enrollment in institutions of higher education, 2005

Black, non-Hispanic 59,974
Hispanic 3,589
Asian/Pacific Islander 3,657
American Indian/Alaska Native. 1,220

Institutions of higher education, 2005-06

Total. 90
   Public. 58
   Private 32

Earned degrees conferred, 2004-05

Associate's. 5,734
Bachelor's 21,494
Master's 6,874
First-professional. 1,651
Doctor's 562

Public Libraries, 2006

Number of libraries. 67
Number of outlets 363
Annual visits per capita 3.1
Circulation per capita. 3.9

State & local financial support for higher education, FY 2006

Full-time equivalent enrollment (x 1,000) 170.8
Appropriations per FTE. $5,583

Social Insurance & Welfare Programs

Social Security benefits & beneficiaries, 2005

Beneficiaries (x 1,000) 716
   Retired & dependents. 429
   Survivors. 140
   Disabled & dependents. 146
Annual benefit payments ($ mil) $7,378
   Retired & dependents. $4,109
   Survivors. $1,782
   Disabled & dependents. $1,488
Average monthly benefit
   Retired & dependents. $937
   Disabled & dependents. $937
   Widowed. $891

Medicare, July 2005

Enrollment (x 1,000). 610
Payments ($ mil) $4,883

Medicaid, 2004

Beneficiaries (x 1,000). 1,108
Payments ($ mil) $4,039

State Children's Health Insurance Program, 2006

Enrollment (x 1,000). 142.4
Expenditures ($ mil) $122.4

Persons without health insurance, 2006

Number (x 1,000). 921
   percent. 21.9%
Number of children (x 1,000) 170
   percent of children 15.9%

Health care expenditures, 2004

Total expenditures. $22,658
   per capita $5,040

Federal and state public aid
State unemployment insurance, 2006
Recipients, first payments (x 1,000) 60
Total payments ($ mil) $294
Average weekly benefit $191
Temporary Assistance for Needy Families, 2006
Recipients (x 1,000). .297.1
Families (x 1,000) 133.3
Supplemental Security Income, 2005
Recipients (x 1,000). .155.8
Payments ($ mil) $771.3
Food Stamp Program, 2006
Avg monthly participants (x 1,000) 829.9
Total benefits ($ mil). $1,031.6

Housing & Construction

Housing units
Total 2005 (estimate) 1,940,006
Total 2006 (estimate) 1,830,073
Seasonal or recreational use, 2006. 42,431
Owner-occupied, 2006 1,071,667
    Median home value. $114,700
    Homeowner vacancy rate. 1.4%
Renter-occupied, 2006 493,311
    Median rent $618
    Rental vacancy rate. 7.9%
Home ownership rate, 2005. . . . . 72.5%
Home ownership rate, 2006. . . . . 71.3%

New privately-owned housing units
Number authorized, 2006 (x 1,000). 28.7
    Value ($ mil). $3,818.3
Started 2005 (x 1,000, estimate) 18.0
Started 2006 (x 1,000, estimate) 17.7

Existing home sales
2005 (x 1,000). 87.7
2006 (x 1,000). 92.3

Government & Elections

State officials 2008
Governor. . . . . .Bobby Jindal
           Republican, term expires 1/12
Lieutenant Governor. . . . . Mitch Landrieu
Secretary of State. . . . . Jay Dardenne
Attorney General. . . . . .James Caldwell
Chief Justice . . . . Pascal Calogero Jr

Governorship
Minimum age. 25
Length of term. . . . . 4 years
Consecutive terms permitted 2
Who succeeds. . . . . Lieutenant Governor

Local governments by type, 2002
Total. 473
    County. 60
    Municipal 302
    Township 0
    School District. 66
    Special District 45

State legislature
Name . . . . Legislature
Upper chamber . . . . .Senate
    Number of members. 39
    Length of term. 4 years
    Party in majority, 2008 . . . . .Democratic
Lower chamber. . . . . . . .House of Representatives
    Number of members. 105
    Length of term. 4 years
    Party in majority, 2008 . . . . .Democratic

Federal representation, 2008 (110th Congress)
Senator. . . . . .Mary Landrieu
    Party . . . . .Democratic
    Year term expires 2009
Senator. . . . . David Vitter
    Party . . . . Republican
    Year term expires 2011
Representatives, total 7
    Democrats. 2
    Republicans 5

Voters in November 2006 election (estimate)
Total. 1,201,499
    Male. 551,100
    Female. 650,399
    White. 864,705
    Black 319,176
    Hispanic 15,008
    Asian 15,474

Presidential election, 2004
Total Popular Vote 1,943,106
    Kerry 820,299
    Bush. 1,102,169
Total Electoral Votes. 9

Votes cast for US Senators
2004
Total vote (x 1,000) 1,848
Leading party. . . . . Republican
Percent for leading party 51.0%
2006
Total vote (x 1,000) . . . . NA
Leading party. . . . . NA
Percent for leading party . . . . NA

Votes cast for US Representatives
2004
Total vote (x 1,000) 1,259
    Democratic. 478
    Republican 780
Leading party. . . . . Republican
Percent for leading party 62.0%
2006
Total vote (x 1,000) 916
    Democratic. 309
    Republican 580
Leading party. . . . . Republican
Percent for leading party 63.3%

State government employment, 2006
Full-time equivalent employees 83,358
Payroll ($ mil) $284.1

Local government employment, 2006
Full-time equivalent employees . . . . NA
Payroll ($ mil) . . . . NA

Women holding public office, 2008
US Congress 1
Statewide elected office. 0
State legislature 25

Black public officials, 2002
Total. 739
   US and state legislatures 32
   City/county/regional offices 408
   Judicial/law enforcement. 132
   Education/school boards 167

Hispanic public officials, 2006
Total. 3
   State executives & legislators 0
   City/county/regional offices 1
   Judicial/law enforcement. 2
   Education/school boards 0

Governmental Finance

State government revenues, 2006
Total revenue (x $1,000) $27,679,632
   per capita $6,523.16
General revenue (x $1,000) $22,925,700
   Intergovernmental 9,079,426
   Taxes 9,651,457
      general sales 3,427,486
      individual income tax 2,501,120
      corporate income tax 506,174
   Current charges 2,360,563
   Miscellaneous .1,834,254

State government expenditure, 2006
Total expenditure (x $1,000) $24,220,667
   per capita $5,708.00
General expenditure (x $1,000) $21,026,980
   per capita, total. *$4,955.35*
      Education 1,618.26
      Public welfare 1,090.67
      Health 131.21
      Hospitals. 364.93
      Highways 373.95
      Police protection 70.73
      Corrections 154.45
      Natural resources 102.01
      Parks & recreation 61.71
      Governmental administration 152.09
      Interest on general debt 156.24

State debt & cash, 2006 ($ per capita)
Debt $2,765.64
Cash/security holdings. $11,505.15

Federal government grants to state & local government, 2005 (x $1,000)
Total. $11,388,684
by Federal agency
   Defense 55,252
   Education 716,375
   Energy 10,417
   Environmental Protection Agency 49,283
   Health & Human Services. 5,082,396
   Homeland Security. 3,380,689
   Housing & Urban Development 468,531
   Justice 109,550
   Labor 140,643
   Transportation 646,107
   Veterans Affairs. 39,657

Crime & Law Enforcement

Crime, 2006 (rates per 100,000 residents)
Property crimes 171,239
   Burglary 44,986
   Larceny 110,613
   Motor vehicle theft 15,640
   Property crime rate. 3,993.7
Violent crimes. 29,919
   Murder 530
   Forcible rape. .1,562
   Robbery. 5,729
   Aggravated assault 22,098
   Violent crime rate 697.8
Hate crimes. 27

Fraud and identity theft, 2006
Fraud complaints. .3,981
   rate per 100,000 residents 92.8
Identity theft complaints 2,256
   rate per 100,000 residents 52.6

Law enforcement agencies, 2006
Total agencies. 171
Total employees 18,969
   Officers 14,779
   Civilians 4,190

Prisoners, probation, and parole, 2006
Total prisoners 37,012
   percent change, 12/31/05 to 12/31/06 . . . . 2.6%
   in private facilities 8.3%
   in local jails 43.9%
Sentenced to more than one year 36,376
   rate per 100,000 residents 846
Adults on probation 38,057
Adults on parole. 24,663

Prisoner demographics, June 30, 2005 (rate per 100,000 residents)
Male 2,134
Female 195
White 523
Black. 2,452
Hispanic 244

Arrests, 2006

Total...................................161,316
  Persons under 18 years of age 22,355

Persons under sentence of death, 1/1/07

Total... 88
  White..................................... 30
  Black 55
  Hispanic 2

State's highest court

Name ....Supreme Court
Number of members........................ 7
Length of term...................... 10 years
Intermediate appeals court? ....yes

Labor & Income

Civilian labor force, 2006 (x 1,000)

Total...................................1,960
  Men 1,041
  Women 919
  Persons 16-19 years.................... 102
  White...................................1,370
  Black 539
  Hispanic 53

Civilian labor force as a percent of civilian non-institutional population, 2006

Total................................... 61.8%
  Men 69.4
  Women 55.0
  Persons 16-19 years....................39.8
  White...................................63.1
  Black 58.5
  Hispanic 69.6

Employment, 2006 (x 1,000)

Total...................................1,870
  Men 995
  Women 875
  Persons 16-19 years.................... 89
  White...................................1,333
  Black 490
  Hispanic 50

Unemployment rate, 2006

Total...................................... 4.6%
  Men 4.4
  Women 4.8
  Persons 16-19 years....................13.0
  White...................................2.7
  Black 9.1
  Hispanic 5.7

Full-time/part-time labor force, 2003 (x 1,000)

Full-time labor force, employed 1,617
Part-time labor force, employed............ 287
Unemployed, looking for
  Full-time work......................... 120
  Part-time work......................... 14
*Mean duration of unemployment (weeks)......*16.7
  Median 9.9

Labor unions, 2006

Membership (x 1,000).................... 107
  percent of employed 6.4%

Experienced civilian labor force by private industry, 2006

Total...........................1,474,800
  Natural resources & mining 56,549
  Construction 130,424
  Manufacturing........................ 152,076
  Trade, transportation & utilities 369,758
  Information 27,012
  Finance 91,285
  Professional & business 194,141
  Education & health 220,252
  Leisure & hospitality.................184,162
  Other............................ 46,441

Experienced civilian labor force by occupation, May 2006

Management......................... 89,060
Business & financial 56,890
Legal............................... 12,530
Sales.............................. 188,670
Office & admin. support.............. 296,390
Computers & math 17,590
Architecture & engineering............. 28,280
Arts & entertainment.................. 16,660
Education 98,460
Social services 22,890
Health care practitioner & technical.... 104,430
Health care support 49,440
Maintenance & repair................. 92,120
Construction 118,900
Transportation & moving 152,880
Production 121,040
Farming, fishing & forestry............ 5,220

Hours and earnings of production workers on manufacturing payrolls, 2006

Average weekly hours 43.0
Average hourly earnings $17.94
Average weekly earnings $771.42

Income and poverty, 2006

Median household income............. $39,337
Personal income, per capita (current $)... $30,952
  in constant (2000) dollars $27,019
Persons below poverty level.............. 19.0%

Average annual pay

2006................................ $36,604
  increase from 2005 .... 9.1%

Federal individual income tax returns, 2005

Returns filed.......................1,770,050
Adjusted gross income ($1,000) $77,629,149
Total tax liability ($1,000) $9,031,225

Charitable contributions, 2004

Number of contributions.................347.9
Total amount ($ mil)..................$1,476.7

Economy, Business, Industry & Agriculture

Fortune 500 companies, 2007 3

Bankruptcy cases filed, FY 2007 13,534

Patents and trademarks issued, 2007

Patents 293
Trademarks 391

Business firm ownership, 2002

Women-owned 86,876
   Sales ($ mil) $12,253
Black-owned 40,243
   Sales ($ mil) $1,934
Hispanic-owned 7,645
   Sales ($ mil) $1,945
Asian-owned 8,218
   Sales ($ mil) $1,794
Amer. Indian/Alaska Native-owned 2,707
   Sales ($ mil) $283
Hawaiian/Pacific Islander-owned 80
   Sales ($ mil) $9

Gross domestic product, 2006 ($ mil)

Total gross domestic product $193,138
   Agriculture, forestry, fishing and
     hunting 1,326
   Mining 27,431
   Utilities 4,915
   Construction 8,939
   Manufacturing, durable goods 8,014
   Manufacturing, non-durable goods . . . 32,500
   Wholesale trade 8,773
   Retail trade 12,826
   Transportation & warehousing 6,318
   Information 4,140
   Finance & insurance 6,261
   Real estate, rental & leasing 15,286
   Professional and technical services 7,338
   Educational services 1,146
   Health care and social assistance 10,404
   Accommodation/food services 4,947
   Other services, except government 3,706
   Government 19,899

Establishments, payroll, employees & receipts, by major industry group, 2005

Total 102,790
   Annual payroll ($1,000) $50,657,624
   Paid employees 1,617,507
Forestry, fishing & agriculture 704
   Annual payroll ($1,000) $138,320
   Paid employees 4,448
Mining 1,390
   Annual payroll ($1,000) $2,743,845
   Paid employees 44,247
   Receipts, 2002 ($1,000) $30,181,037

Utilities 567
   Annual payroll ($1,000) $738,018
   Paid employees 11,382
   Receipts, 2002 ($1,000) . . . . .NA
Construction 8,615
   Annual payroll ($1,000) $4,080,813
   Paid employees 117,564
   Receipts, 2002 ($1,000) $15,288,176
Manufacturing 3,377
   Annual payroll ($1,000) $7,074,264
   Paid employees 145,173
   Receipts, 2002 ($1,000) $89,540,799
Wholesale trade 5,604
   Annual payroll ($1,000) $2,990,452
   Paid employees 72,586
   Receipts, 2002 ($1,000) $47,192,153
Retail trade 17,426
   Annual payroll ($1,000) $4,572,205
   Paid employees 227,856
   Receipts, 2002 ($1,000) $41,885,192
Transportation & warehousing 3,652
   Annual payroll ($1,000) $2,489,818
   Paid employees 62,936
   Receipts, 2002 ($1,000) $7,847,325
Information 1,498
   Annual payroll ($1,000) $1,376,922
   Paid employees 32,639
   Receipts, 2002 ($1,000) . . . . .NA
Finance & insurance 7,618
   Annual payroll ($1,000) $3,054,677
   Paid employees 67,802
   Receipts, 2002 ($1,000) . . . . .NA
Professional, scientific & technical 11,047
   Annual payroll ($1,000) $3,535,206
   Paid employees 85,308
   Receipts, 2002 ($1,000) $8,243,267
Education 981
   Annual payroll ($1,000) $914,885
   Paid employees 36,448
   Receipts, 2002 ($1,000) $230,627
Health care & social assistance 11,332
   Annual payroll ($1,000) $7,940,735
   Paid employees 264,664
   Receipts, 2002 ($1,000) $18,169,655
Arts and entertainment 1,329
   Annual payroll ($1,000) $755,662
   Paid employees 33,279
   Receipts, 2002 ($1,000) $2,248,731
Real estate 4,491
   Annual payroll ($1,000) $1,042,231
   Paid employees 31,196
   Receipts, 2002 ($1,000) $3,942,696
Accommodation & food service 7,886
   Annual payroll ($1,000) $2,194,457
   Paid employees 180,353
   Receipts, 2002 ($1,000) $7,411,702

Exports, 2006

Value of exported goods ($ mil) $23,503
   Manufactured $13,788
   Non-manufactured $9,415

Foreign direct investment in US affiliates, 2004

Property, plants & equipment ($ mil) $27,962
Employment (x 1,000) 49.9

Agriculture, 2006

Number of farms 26,800
Farm acreage (x 1,000) 7,800
   Acres per farm 291
Farm marketings and income ($ mil)
Total $2,186.2
   Crops $1,321.9
   Livestock $864.3
Net farm income $765.7

Principal commodities, in order by marketing receipts, 2005

Cotton, Cane for sugar, Rice, Cattle and calves, Soybeans

Federal economic activity in state

Expenditures, 2005 ($ mil)
   Total $39,628
      Per capita $8,791.94
   Defense $4,693
   Non-defense $34,935
Defense department, 2006 ($ mil)
   Payroll $1,734
   Contract awards $5,154
   Grants $311
Homeland security grants ($1,000)
   2006 . . . . $30,437
   2007 . . . .$21,873

FDIC-insured financial institutions, 2005

Number 166
Assets ($ billion) $76.4
Deposits ($ billion) $59.6

Fishing, 2006

Catch (x 1,000 lbs) 844,027
Value ($1,000) $201,742

Mining, 2006 ($ mil)

Total non-fuel mineral production $362
Percent of U.S. 0.56%

Communication, Energy & Transportation

Communication

Households with computers, 2003 . . . . .52.3%
Households with internet access, 2003 . . . . 44.1%
High-speed internet providers 51
Total high-speed internet lines 892,835
   Residential 689,828
   Business 203,007
Wireless phone customers, 12/2006 3,492,358

FCC-licensed stations (as of January 1, 2008)

TV stations 38
FM radio stations 179
AM radio stations 83

Energy

Energy consumption, 2004
   Total (trillion Btu) 3,816
   Per capita (million Btu) 848.9
By source of production (trillion Btu)
   Coal 257
   Natural gas 1,400
   Petroleum 1,651
   Nuclear electric power 178
   Hydroelectric power 11
By end-use sector (trillion Btu)
   Residential 369
   Commercial 286
   Industrial 2,403
   Transportation 758
Electric energy, 2005
   Primary source of electricity . . . . Gas
   Net generation (billion kWh) 92.6
      percent from renewable sources 3.8%
   Net summer capability (million kW) 26.8
   CO_2 emitted from generation 57.1
Natural gas utilities, 2005
   Customers (x 1,000) 956
   Sales (trillion Btu) 893
   Revenues ($ mil) $3,010
Nuclear plants, 2007 2
Total CO_2 emitted (million metric tons) 179.1
Energy spending, 2004 ($ mil) $24,402
   per capita $5,428
   Price per million Btu $10.09

Transportation, 2006

Public road & street mileage 60,925
   Urban 15,932
   Rural 44,993
   Interstate 903
Vehicle miles of travel (millions) 45,417
   per capita 10,703.3
Total motor vehicle registrations 3,872,744
   Automobiles 1,950,372
   Trucks 1,900,270
   Motorcycles 61,117
Licensed drivers 3,014,191
   19 years & under 120,282
Deaths from motor vehicle accidents 982
Gasoline consumed (x 1,000 gallons) 2,621,024
   per capita 617.7

Commuting Statistics, 2006

Average commute time (min) 25.1
   Drove to work alone 81.6%
   Carpooled 11.6%
   Public transit 1.1%
   Walk to work 1.8%
   Work from home 2.2%

State Summary

Capital city . . . . Augusta
Governor . . . . John Baldacci

#1 State House Station
Augusta, ME 04333
207-287-3531

Admitted as a state 1820
Area (square miles) 35,385
Population, 2007 (estimate). 1,317,207
Largest city . . . . Portland
    Population, 2006 63,011
Personal income per capita, 2006
    (in current dollars) $32,348
Gross domestic product, 2006 ($ mil) $46,973

Leading industries by payroll, 2005

Health care/Social assistance, Manufacturing,
Retail trade

**Leading agricultural commodities
by receipts, 2005**

Potatoes, Dairy products, Blueberries, Chicken
eggs, Greenhouse/nursery

Geography & Environment

Total area (square miles). 35,385
    land 30,862
    water 4,523
Federally-owned land, 2004 (acres) 208,422
    percent 1.1%
Highest point . . . . Mount Katahdin
    elevation (feet) 5,268
Lowest point . . . . Atlantic Ocean
    elevation (feet) . . . . sea level
General coastline (miles) 228
Tidal shoreline (miles) 3,478
Cropland, 2003 (x 1,000 acres) 385
Forest land, 2003 (x 1,000 acres). 17,620
Capital city . . . . Augusta
    Population 2000 18,560
    Population 2006 18,560
Largest city . . . . Portland
    Population 2000 64,249
    Population 2006 63,011

Number of cities with over 100,000 population
1990 0
2000 0
2006 0

State park and recreation areas, 2005
Area (x 1,000 acres) 100
Number of visitors (x 1,000) 2,006
Revenues ($1,000) $3,146
    percent of operating expenditures 37.7%

National forest system land, 2007
Acres 53,042

Demographics & Population Characteristics

Population
1980 1,124,660
1990 1,227,928
2000 1,274,923
2006 1,321,574
    Male 646,427
    Female 675,147
Living in group quarters, 2006 37,484
    percent of total. 2.8%
2007 (estimate). 1,317,207
    persons per square mile of land 42.7
2008 (projected) 1,342,286
2010 (projected) 1,357,134
2020 (projected) 1,408,665
2030 (projected) 1,411,097

**Population of Core-Based Statistical Areas
(formerly Metropolitan Areas), x 1,000**

	CBSA	Non-CBSA
1990	845	383
2000	893	382
2006	931	391

Change in population, 2000-2007
Number 42,286
    percent. 3.3%
Natural increase (births minus deaths) 10,644
Net internal migration 31,390
Net international migration 5,275

Persons by age, 2006
Under 5 years 70,245
5 to 17 years 210,749
18 years and over 1,040,580
65 years and over 192,639
85 years and over 27,012
    Median age 41.1

Persons by age, 2010 (projected)
Under 5 years 72,829
18 and over 1,087,902
65 and over 212,278
    Median age 42.2

Race, 2006
One Race
    White. 1,278,398
    Black or African American 10,918
    Asian 11,490
    American Indian/Alaska Native. 7,582
    Hawaiian Native/Pacific Islander. 433
Two or more races. 12,753

Persons of Hispanic origin, 2006
Total Hispanic or Latino 12,622
    Mexican. 3,262
    Puerto Rican 3,913
    Cuban 447

Persons of Asian origin, 2006

Total Asian 12,004
  Asian Indian. 1,805
  Chinese 2,764
  Filipino 1,990
  Japanese 714
  Korean. 1,843
  Vietnamese. 1,369

Marital status, 2006

Population 15 years & over 1,096,285
  Never married 294,724
  Married. 592,562
  Separated 12,522
  Widowed. 72,887
  Divorced 136,112

Language spoken at home, 2006

Population 5 years and older. 1,251,347
  English only 1,154,615
  Spanish 12,576
  French 58,273
  German. 4,314
  Chinese 2,081

Households & families, 2006

Households. 548,247
  with persons under 18 years 166,980
  with persons over 65 years. 136,742
  persons per household 2.34
Families. 358,314
  persons per family. 2.82
Married couples. 276,972
Female householder,
  no husband present. 57,724
One-person households 149,229

Nativity, 2006

Number of residents born in state 859,105
  percent of population. 65.0%

Immigration & naturalization, 2006

Legal permanent residents admitted. 1,719
Persons naturalized 802
Non-immigrant admissions 46,993

Vital Statistics and Health

Marriages

2004 11,234
2005 10,879
2006 9,740

Divorces

2004 5,677
2005 5,443
2006 4,752

Health risks, 2006

Percent of adults who are:
  Smokers. 20.9%
  Overweight (BMI > 25). 59.7%
  Obese (BMI > 30). 23.1%

Births

2005 14,112
  Birthrate (per 1,000). 10.7
  White. 13,508
  Black 264
  Hispanic 181
  Asian/Pacific Islander 226
  Amer. Indian/Alaska Native 114
  Low birth weight (2,500g or less). 6.8%
  Cesarian births 28.3%
  Preterm births 10.7%
  To unmarried mothers. 35.0%
  Twin births (per 1,000) 32.8
  Triplets or higher order (per 100,000). . . .138.4
2006 (preliminary). 14,151
  rate per 1,000 . . . . .10.7

Deaths

2004
All causes 12,443
  rate per 100,000. . . . . 806.3
Heart disease 2,948
  rate per 100,000. . . . . .188.3
Malignant neoplasms 3,124
  rate per 100,000. . . . . 200.8
Cerebrovascular disease. 801
  rate per 100,000. . . . . .51.0
Chronic lower respiratory disease 766
  rate per 100,000. . . . . .49.3
Diabetes. 382
  rate per 100,000. . . . . .24.5
2005 (preliminary). 12,871
  rate per 100,000. . . . . 813.2
2006 (provisional) 12,280

Infant deaths

2004 79
  rate per 1,000 . . . . .5.7
2005 (provisional) 97
  rate per 1,000 . . . . .6.8

Exercise routines, 2005

None. 22.3%
Moderate or greater. 54.1%
Vigorous 30.8%

Abortions, 2004

Total performed in state. 2,593
  rate per 1,000 women age 15-44. 10
  % obtained by out-of-state residents 4.2%

Physicians, 2005

Total. 3,520
  rate per 100,000 persons 267

Community hospitals, 2005

Number of hospitals 37
Beds (x 1,000). 3.5
Patients admitted (x 1,000) 151
Average daily census (x 1,000) 2.3
Average cost per day $1,528
Outpatient visits (x 1 mil) 4.3

Maine   3

Disability status of population, 2006
5 to 15 years 10.1%
16 to 64 years 16.8%
65 years and over 40.6%

Education

Educational attainment, 2006
Population over 25 years 923,328
　Less than 9ᵗʰ grade. 4.2%
　High school graduate or more 88.7%
　College graduate or more. 25.8%
　Graduate or professional degree. 8.9%

Public school enrollment, 2005-06
Total. 195,498
　Pre-kindergarten through grade 8. 133,491
　Grades 9 through 12 62,007

Graduating public high school seniors, 2004-05
Diplomas (incl. GED and others) 13,407

SAT scores, 2007
Average critical reading score. 466
Average writing score 457
Average math score 465
Percent of graduates taking test 100%

Public school teachers, 2006-07 (estimate)
Total (x 1,000) 16.4
　Elementary. 11.0
　Secondary. 5.4
Average salary $41,596
　Elementary. $41,596
　Secondary. $41,596

State receipts & expenditures for public schools, 2006-07 (estimate)
Revenue receipts ($ mil) $2,425
Expenditures
Total ($ mil) $2,584
　Per capita $1,787
　Per pupil $13,025

NAEP proficiency scores, 2007
	Reading		Math	
	Basic	Proficient	Basic	Proficient
Grade 4	73.1%	35.8%	85.5%	41.8%
Grade 8	82.8%	36.9%	78.3%	34.1%

Higher education enrollment, fall 2005
Total. 18,032
　Full-time men 5,610
　Full-time women. 7,633
　Part-time men 1,359
　Part-time women. 3,430

Minority enrollment in institutions of higher education, 2005
Black, non-Hispanic 1,279
Hispanic 832
Asian/Pacific Islander 1,101
American Indian/Alaska Native. 975

Institutions of higher education, 2005-06
Total. 30
　Public. 15
　Private 15

Earned degrees conferred, 2004-05
Associate's. 2,374
Bachelor's 6,500
Master's 1,648
First-professional. 217
Doctor's. 40

Public Libraries, 2006
Number of libraries. 272
Number of outlets 278
Annual visits per capita 5.7
Circulation per capita. 7.5

State & local financial support for higher education, FY 2006
Full-time equivalent enrollment (x 1,000) 35.2
Appropriations per FTE. $6,096

Social Insurance & Welfare Programs

Social Security benefits & beneficiaries, 2005
Beneficiaries (x 1,000) 269
　Retired & dependents. 178
　Survivors. 33
　Disabled & dependents. 59
Annual benefit payments ($ mil) $2,686
　Retired & dependents. $1,702
　Survivors. $435
　Disabled & dependents. $549
Average monthly benefit
　Retired & dependents. $926
　Disabled & dependents. $863
　Widowed. $924

Medicare, July 2005
Enrollment (x 1,000). 235
Payments ($ mil) $1,429

Medicaid, 2004
Beneficiaries (x 1,000). 1,074
Payments ($ mil) $7,776

State Children's Health Insurance Program, 2006
Enrollment (x 1,000). 31.1
Expenditures ($ mil). $33.1

Persons without health insurance, 2006
Number (x 1,000). 122
　percent. 9.3%
Number of children (x 1,000) 18
　percent of children 6.3%

Health care expenditures, 2004
Total expenditures. $8,593
　per capita $6,540

Federal and state public aid

State unemployment insurance, 2006
Recipients, first payments (x 1,000) 31
Total payments ($ mil) $106
Average weekly benefit $246
Temporary Assistance for Needy Families, 2006
Recipients (x 1,000) 296.4
Families (x 1,000) 111.1
Supplemental Security Income, 2005
Recipients (x 1,000) 32.0
Payments ($ mil) $145.9
Food Stamp Program, 2006
Avg monthly participants (x 1,000) 160.3
Total benefits ($ mil) $169.3

Housing & Construction

Housing units

Total 2005 (estimate) 683,802
Total 2006 (estimate) 691,132
Seasonal or recreational use, 2006 99,118
Owner-occupied, 2006 399,076
   Median home value $170,500
   Homeowner vacancy rate 1.9%
Renter-occupied, 2006 149,171
   Median rent $636
   Rental vacancy rate 6.8%
Home ownership rate, 2005 . . . . 73.9%
Home ownership rate, 2006 . . . . 75.3%

New privately-owned housing units

Number authorized, 2006 (x 1,000) 7.3
   Value ($ mil) $1,125.3
Started 2005 (x 1,000, estimate) 6.8
Started 2006 (x 1,000, estimate) 6.5

Existing home sales

2005 (x 1,000) 33.3
2006 (x 1,000) 30.7

Government & Elections

State officials 2008

Governor . . . . John Baldacci
         Democratic, term expires 1/11
Lieutenant Governor . . . . Beth Edmonds
Secretary of State . . . . Matthew Dunlap
Attorney General . . . . .G. Steven Rowe
Chief Justice . . . . Leigh Saufley

Governorship

Minimum age 30
Length of term . . . . 4 years
Consecutive terms permitted 2
Who succeeds . . . . President of the Senate

Local governments by type, 2002

Total 826
   County 16
   Municipal 22
   Township 467
   School District 99
   Special District 222

State legislature

Name . . . . Legislature
Upper chamber . . . . .Senate
   Number of members 35
   Length of term . . . . 2 years
   Party in majority, 2008 . . . . .Democratic
Lower chamber . . . . .House of Representatives
   Number of members 151
   Length of term . . . . 2 years
   Party in majority, 2008 . . . . .Democratic

Federal representation, 2008 (110th Congress)

Senator . . . . Susan Collins
   Party . . . . Republican
   Year term expires 2009
Senator . . . . Olympia Snowe
   Party . . . . Republican
   Year term expires 2013
Representatives, total 2
   Democrats 2
   Republicans 0

Voters in November 2006 election (estimate)

Total 594,723
   Male 286,075
   Female 308,648
   White 584,519
   Black 1,961
   Hispanic 607
   Asian . . . . NA

Presidential election, 2004

Total Popular Vote 740,752
   Kerry 396,842
   Bush 330,201
Total Electoral Votes 4

Votes cast for US Senators

2004
Total vote (x 1,000) . . . . NA
Leading party . . . . NA
Percent for leading party . . . . NA

2006
Total vote (x 1,000) 545
Leading party . . . . Republican
Percent for leading party 74.4%

Votes cast for US Representatives

2004
Total vote (x 1,000) 710
   Democratic 418
   Republican 283
Leading party . . . . .Democratic
Percent for leading party 58.9%

2006
Total vote (x 1,000) 536
   Democratic 351
   Republican 163
Leading party . . . . .Democratic
Percent for leading party 65.4%

State government employment, 2006
Full-time equivalent employees 21,680
Payroll ($ mil) $78.8

Local government employment, 2006
Full-time equivalent employees 55,925
Payroll ($ mil) $165.8

Women holding public office, 2008
US Congress 2
Statewide elected office. 0
State legislature 56

Black public officials, 2002
Total. 2
US and state legislatures 0
City/county/regional offices 1
Judicial/law enforcement. 0
Education/school boards 1

Hispanic public officials, 2006
Total. 0
State executives & legislators 0
City/county/regional offices 0
Judicial/law enforcement. 0
Education/school boards 0

Governmental Finance

State government revenues, 2006
Total revenue (x $1,000) $8,630,865
per capita $6,563.84
General revenue (x $1,000) $7,565,287
Intergovernmental 2,580,118
Taxes 3,590,334
general sales. 1,041,216
individual income tax 1,368,927
corporate income tax 188,016
Current charges. 649,911
Miscellaneous 744,924

State government expenditure, 2006
Total expenditure (x $1,000) $7,854,687
per capita $5,973.55
General expenditure (x $1,000) $7,231,514
per capita, total. *$5,499.63*
Education 1,419.79
Public welfare 1,893.11
Health 359.43
Hospitals. 40.88
Highways 429.52
Police protection. 50.46
Corrections 96.37
Natural resources 133.40
Parks & recreation 8.98
Governmental administration 215.29
Interest on general debt 173.95

State debt & cash, 2006 ($ per capita)
Debt $3,802.77
Cash/security holdings. $12,038.51

Federal government grants to state & local government, 2005 (x $1,000)
Total. $2,773,126
by Federal agency
Defense 3,340
Education 174,123
Energy 5,161
Environmental Protection Agency 32,484
Health & Human Services. 1,891,964
Homeland Security. 29,992
Housing & Urban Development. 194,443
Justice 32,399
Labor 57,551
Transportation 171,509
Veterans Affairs. 8,671

Crime & Law Enforcement

Crime, 2006 (rates per 100,000 residents)
Property crimes 33,286
Burglary 6,779
Larceny 25,167
Motor vehicle theft 1,340
Property crime rate. 2,518.7
Violent crimes. 1,526
Murder 23
Forcible rape. 339
Robbery. 384
Aggravated assault 780
Violent crime rate 115.5
Hate crimes. 74

Fraud and identity theft, 2006
Fraud complaints. .1,791
rate per 100,000 residents 135.5
Identity theft complaints 525
rate per 100,000 residents 39.7

Law enforcement agencies, 2006
Total agencies. 133
Total employees 2,933
Officers 2,202
Civilians 731

Prisoners, probation, and parole, 2006
Total prisoners 2,120
percent change, 12/31/05 to 12/31/06 . . . . 4.8%
in private facilities 0.9%
in local jails 0%
Sentenced to more than one year 1,997
rate per 100,000 residents 151
Adults on probation 7,919
Adults on parole. 31

Prisoner demographics, June 30, 2005 (rate per 100,000 residents)
Male 513
Female 44
White 262
Black. 1,992
Hispanic . . . . NA

Arrests, 2006
Total................................57,351
   Persons under 18 years of age..........7,765

Persons under sentence of death, 1/1/07
Total.....................................0
   White..................................0
   Black..................................0
   Hispanic...............................0

State's highest court
Name................Supreme Judicial Court
Number of members.........................7
Length of term.......................7 years
Intermediate appeals court?................no

Labor & Income

Civilian labor force, 2006 (x 1,000)
Total...................................715
   Men...................................373
   Women.................................342
   Persons 16-19 years....................42
   White.................................695
   Black..................................NA
   Hispanic...............................NA

Civilian labor force as a percent of civilian non-institutional population, 2006
Total.................................66.7%
   Men..................................72.1
   Women................................61.6
   Persons 16-19 years..................52.4
   White................................67.0
   Black..................................NA
   Hispanic...............................NA

Employment, 2006 (x 1,000)
Total...................................683
   Men...................................355
   Women.................................328
   Persons 16-19 years....................35
   White.................................664
   Black..................................NA
   Hispanic...............................NA

Unemployment rate, 2006
Total..................................4.6%
   Men...................................4.9
   Women.................................4.2
   Persons 16-19 years..................15.0
   White.................................4.5
   Black..................................NA
   Hispanic...............................NA

Full-time/part-time labor force, 2003 (x 1,000)
Full-time labor force, employed............509
Part-time labor force, employed............149
Unemployed, looking for
   Full-time work.........................29
   Part-time work..........................6
Mean duration of unemployment (weeks)......16.0
   Median.................................8.8

Labor unions, 2006
Membership (x 1,000)......................69
   percent of employed..................11.9%

Experienced civilian labor force by private industry, 2006
Total.............................498,942
   Natural resources & mining..........5,842
   Construction.......................31,310
   Manufacturing......................60,188
   Trade, transportation & utilities.....125,001
   Information........................11,267
   Finance............................32,352
   Professional & business.............51,776
   Education & health.................105,170
   Leisure & hospitality..............59,736
   Other..............................16,209

Experienced civilian labor force by occupation, May 2006
Management........................31,130
Business & financial..............21,000
Legal..............................3,380
Sales.............................58,260
Office & admin. support...........102,660
Computers & math..................8,010
Architecture & engineering........8,930
Arts & entertainment..............7,330
Education.........................42,040
Social services...................13,950
Health care practitioner & technical......35,120
Health care support...............19,340
Maintenance & repair..............25,840
Construction......................32,230
Transportation & moving...........42,120
Production........................41,740
Farming, fishing & forestry.......2,900

Hours and earnings of production workers on manufacturing payrolls, 2006
Average weekly hours...................41.4
Average hourly earnings..............$18.57
Average weekly earnings.............$768.80

Income and poverty, 2006
Median household income............$43,439
Personal income, per capita (current $)...$32,348
   in constant (2000) dollars..........$28,238
Persons below poverty level.............12.9%

Average annual pay
2006................................$33,794
   increase from 2005...................3.3%

Federal individual income tax returns, 2005
Returns filed......................621,150
Adjusted gross income ($1,000).....$27,763,882
Total tax liability ($1,000)..........$3,137,737

Charitable contributions, 2004
Number of contributions................163.5
Total amount ($ mil)..................$421.0

Economy, Business, Industry & Agriculture

Fortune 500 companies, 2007 1
Bankruptcy cases filed, FY 2007 2,143

Patents and trademarks issued, 2007
Patents 133
Trademarks 362

Business firm ownership, 2002
Women-owned 32,512
  Sales ($ mil) $3,282
Black-owned 327
  Sales ($ mil) $32
Hispanic-owned 731
  Sales ($ mil) $113
Asian-owned 833
  Sales ($ mil) $205
Amer. Indian/Alaska Native-owned 680
  Sales ($ mil) $47
Hawaiian/Pacific Islander-owned 29
  Sales ($ mil) $5

Gross domestic product, 2006 ($ mil)
Total gross domestic product $46,973
  Agriculture, forestry, fishing and
    hunting 653
  Mining 8
  Utilities 998
  Construction 2,535
  Manufacturing, durable goods 2,726
  Manufacturing, non-durable goods 2,641
  Wholesale trade 2,514
  Retail trade 4,169
  Transportation & warehousing 1,038
  Information 1,236
  Finance & insurance 3,195
  Real estate, rental & leasing 6,484
  Professional and technical services 2,214
  Educational services 483
  Health care and social assistance 5,070
  Accommodation/food services 1,462
  Other services, except government 1,016
  Government 6,603

Establishments, payroll, employees & receipts, by major industry group, 2005

Total 41,933
  Annual payroll ($1,000) $15,873,419
  Paid employees 497,387
Forestry, fishing & agriculture 773
  Annual payroll ($1,000) . . . . NA
  Paid employees . . . . NA
Mining 30
  Annual payroll ($1,000) . . . . NA
  Paid employees . . . . NA
  Receipts, 2002 ($1,000) . . . . NA

Utilities 109
  Annual payroll ($1,000) $130,042
  Paid employees 2,345
  Receipts, 2002 ($1,000) . . . . NA
Construction 5,536
  Annual payroll ($1,000) $1,060,191
  Paid employees 27,065
  Receipts, 2002 ($1,000) $4,256,279
Manufacturing 1,850
  Annual payroll ($1,000) $2,496,875
  Paid employees 60,995
  Receipts, 2002 ($1,000) $13,851,915
Wholesale trade 1,669
  Annual payroll ($1,000) $809,605
  Paid employees 19,456
  Receipts, 2002 ($1,000) $10,371,084
Retail trade 6,980
  Annual payroll ($1,000) $1,850,083
  Paid employees 85,352
  Receipts, 2002 ($1,000) $16,053,515
Transportation & warehousing 1,274
  Annual payroll ($1,000) $463,365
  Paid employees 14,071
  Receipts, 2002 ($1,000) $1,118,787
Information 770
  Annual payroll ($1,000) $467,386
  Paid employees 11,729
  Receipts, 2002 ($1,000) . . . . NA
Finance & insurance 1,921
  Annual payroll ($1,000) $1,293,728
  Paid employees 29,421
  Receipts, 2002 ($1,000) . . . . NA
Professional, scientific & technical 3,503
  Annual payroll ($1,000) $1,028,862
  Paid employees 22,199
  Receipts, 2002 ($1,000) $2,252,787
Education 466
  Annual payroll ($1,000) $337,530
  Paid employees 12,501
  Receipts, 2002 ($1,000) $112,910
Health care & social assistance 4,620
  Annual payroll ($1,000) $3,260,097
  Paid employees 97,973
  Receipts, 2002 ($1,000) $6,237,132
Arts and entertainment 899
  Annual payroll ($1,000) $127,790
  Paid employees 6,783
  Receipts, 2002 ($1,000) $392,456
Real estate 1,744
  Annual payroll ($1,000) $205,083
  Paid employees 6,807
  Receipts, 2002 ($1,000) $761,069
Accommodation & food service 3,909
  Annual payroll ($1,000) $717,503
  Paid employees 45,484
  Receipts, 2002 ($1,000) $2,045,841

Exports, 2006
Value of exported goods ($ mil) $2,627
   Manufactured $2,077
   Non-manufactured $471

Foreign direct investment in US affiliates, 2004
Property, plants & equipment ($ mil) $5,313
Employment (x 1,000) 29.0

Agriculture, 2006
Number of farms 7,100
Farm acreage (x 1,000) 1,360
   Acres per farm 192
Farm marketings and income ($ mil)
Total $591.7
   Crops $302.8
   Livestock $288.9
Net farm income $216.8

Principal commodities, in order by marketing receipts, 2005
Potatoes, Dairy products, Blueberries, Chicken eggs, Greenhouse/nursery

Federal economic activity in state
Expenditures, 2005 ($ mil)
   Total $11,356
      Per capita $8,614.55
   Defense $2,374
   Non-defense $8,982
Defense department, 2006 ($ mil)
   Payroll $827
   Contract awards $1,020
   Grants $19
Homeland security grants ($1,000)
   2006 . . . . $7,785
   2007 . . . . $6,697

FDIC-insured financial institutions, 2005
Number 36
Assets ($ billion) $56.3
Deposits ($ billion) $39.4

Fishing, 2006
Catch (x 1,000 lbs) 234,275
Value ($1,000) $361,862

Mining, 2006 ($ mil)
Total non-fuel mineral production $155
Percent of U.S. 0.24%

Communication, Energy & Transportation

Communication
Households with computers, 2003 . . . . 67.8%
Households with internet access, 2003 . . . . 57.9%
High-speed internet providers 25
Total high-speed internet lines 305,883
   Residential 247,991
   Business 57,892
Wireless phone customers, 12/2006 844,537

FCC-licensed stations (as of January 1, 2008)
TV stations 15
FM radio stations 89
AM radio stations 29

Energy
Energy consumption, 2004
   Total (trillion Btu) 480
   Per capita (million Btu) 365.5
By source of production (trillion Btu)
   Coal 7
   Natural gas 76
   Petroleum 261
   Nuclear electric power 0
   Hydroelectric power 34
By end-use sector (trillion Btu)
   Residential 123
   Commercial 81
   Industrial 154
   Transportation 122
Electric energy, 2005
   Primary source of electricity . . . . Gas
   Net generation (billion kWh) 18.8
      percent from renewable sources 43.3%
   Net summer capability (million kW) 4.2
   CO_2 emitted from generation 7.1
Natural gas utilities, 2005
   Customers (x 1,000) 27
   Sales (trillion Btu) 9
   Revenues ($ mil) $63
Nuclear plants, 2007 0
Total CO_2 emitted (million metric tons) 23.3
Energy spending, 2004 ($ mil) $4,471
   per capita $3,403
   Price per million Btu $12.80

Transportation, 2006
Public road & street mileage 22,783
   Urban 2,972
   Rural 19,811
   Interstate 367
Vehicle miles of travel (millions) 15,044
   per capita 11,441.1
Total motor vehicle registrations 1,071,876
   Automobiles 581,797
   Trucks 486,680
   Motorcycles 45,482
Licensed drivers 1,005,160
   19 years & under 45,890
Deaths from motor vehicle accidents 188
Gasoline consumed (x 1,000 gallons) 704,463
   per capita 535.7

Commuting Statistics, 2006
Average commute time (min) 22.3
   Drove to work alone 77.6%
   Carpooled 11.0%
   Public transit 0.7%
   Walk to work 4.2%
   Work from home 4.9%

State Summary

Capital city .... Annapolis
Governor.................... Martin O'Malley

100 State Circle
Annapolis, MD 21401
410-974-3591

Admitted as a state 1788
Area (square miles) 12,407
Population, 2007 (estimate)........... 5,618,344
Largest city .... Baltimore
  Population, 2006.................. 631,366
Personal income per capita, 2006
  (in current dollars) $44,077
Gross domestic product, 2006 ($ mil) ... $257,815

Leading industries by payroll, 2005

Professional/Scientific/Technical, Health care/
Social assistance, Construction

**Leading agricultural commodities
by receipts, 2005**

Broilers, Greenhouse/nursery, Dairy products,
Corn, Soybeans

Geography & Environment

Total area (square miles)................ 12,407
  land 9,774
  water 2,633
Federally-owned land, 2004 (acres) 178,527
  percent............................. 2.8%
Highest point .. Hoye Crest, Backbone Mountain
  elevation (feet) 3,360
Lowest point................... Atlantic Ocean
  elevation (feet) .... sea level
General coastline (miles) 31
Tidal shoreline (miles) 3,190
Cropland, 2003 (x 1,000 acres) 1,517
Forest land, 2003 (x 1,000 acres)........... 2,370
Capital city .... Annapolis
  Population 2000 35,838
  Population 2006 36,408
Largest city .... Baltimore
  Population 2000 651,154
  Population 2006 631,366

Number of cities with over 100,000 population
1990 1
2000 1
2006 1

State park and recreation areas, 2005
Area (x 1,000 acres)...................... 137
Number of visitors (x 1,000) 11,186
Revenues ($1,000) $13,811
  percent of operating expenditures...... 38.5%

National forest system land, 2007
Acres 0

Demographics & Population Characteristics

Population
1980 4,216,975
1990 4,781,468
2000 5,296,506
2006 5,615,727
  Male.......................... 2,716,854
  Female........................ 2,898,873
Living in group quarters, 2006......... 141,501
  percent of total..................... 2.5%
2007 (estimate)................... 5,618,344
  persons per square mile of land 574.8
2008 (projected)................... 5,783,344
2010 (projected) 5,904,970
2020 (projected)................... 6,497,626
2030 (projected)................... 7,022,251

**Population of Core-Based Statistical Areas
(formerly Metropolitan Areas), x 1,000**

	CBSA	Non-CBSA
1990	4,708	73
2000	5,218	79
2006	5,533	82

Change in population, 2000-2007
Number........................... 321,836
  percent............................ 6.1%
Natural increase (births minus deaths) 227,910
Net internal migration .... -54,415
Net international migration 135,800

Persons by age, 2006
Under 5 years 368,199
5 to 17 years 992,332
18 years and over 4,255,196
65 years and over 650,568
85 years and over 85,783
  Median age 37.2

Persons by age, 2010 (projected)
Under 5 years 412,152
18 and over 4,498,676
65 and over 717,987
  Median age 36.8

Race, 2006
One Race
  White........................... 3,573,922
  Black or African American 1,656,615
  Asian 277,697
  American Indian/Alaska Native....... 18,584
  Hawaiian Native/Pacific Islander........ 3,515
Two or more races..................... 85,394

Persons of Hispanic origin, 2006
Total Hispanic or Latino 336,390
  Mexican........................... 64,374
  Puerto Rican 36,592
  Cuban 7,862

Persons of Asian origin, 2006

Total Asian	276,362
Asian Indian.	64,142
Chinese	67,351
Filipino	33,812
Japanese	8,876
Korean.	48,516
Vietnamese.	22,736

Marital status, 2006

Population 15 years & over	4,501,537
Never married	1,456,369
Married	2,339,736
Separated	135,688
Widowed.	278,321
Divorced	427,111

Language spoken at home, 2006

Population 5 years and older.	5,247,226
English only	4,467,027
Spanish	298,072
French	62,022
German	26,722
Chinese	55,704

Households & families, 2006

Households	2,089,031
with persons under 18 years	744,133
with persons over 65 years	458,675
persons per household	2.62
Families	1,405,655
persons per family.	3.19
Married couples	1,018,096
Female householder, no husband present.	290,453
One-person households	557,622

Nativity, 2006

Number of residents born in state	2,685,350
percent of population	47.8%

Immigration & naturalization, 2006

Legal permanent residents admitted	30,204
Persons naturalized	14,465
Non-immigrant admissions	300,318

Vital Statistics and Health

Marriages

2004	38,318
2005	38,475
2006	36,495

Divorces

2004	17,802
2005	17,233
2006	17,012

Health risks, 2006

Percent of adults who are:

Smokers.	17.7%
Overweight (BMI > 25).	60.7%
Obese (BMI > 30).	24.9%

Births

2005	74,980
Birthrate (per 1,000).	13.4
White.	43,285
Black	26,526
Hispanic	8,681
Asian/Pacific Islander	4,980
Amer. Indian/Alaska Native	189
Low birth weight (2,500g or less)	9.1%
Cesarian births	31.1%
Preterm births	13.3%
To unmarried mothers.	37.1%
Twin births (per 1,000)	37.1
Triplets or higher order (per 100,000).	193.7
2006 (preliminary).	77,478
rate per 1,000	13.8

Deaths

2004

All causes	43,232
rate per 100,000.	806.0
Heart disease	11,346
rate per 100,000.	212.4
Malignant neoplasms	10,168
rate per 100,000.	188.6
Cerebrovascular disease.	2,718
rate per 100,000.	51.5
Chronic lower respiratory disease	1,910
rate per 100,000.	36.5
Diabetes.	1,417
rate per 100,000.	26.4
2005 (preliminary).	43,893
rate per 100,000.	796.4
2006 (provisional)	43,566

Infant deaths

2004	630
rate per 1,000	8.4
2005 (provisional)	602
rate per 1,000	7.9

Exercise routines, 2005

None.	22.9%
Moderate or greater.	49.1%
Vigorous	29.6%

Abortions, 2004

Total performed in state.	10,096
rate per 1,000 women age 15-44	8
% obtained by out-of-state residents	12.6%

Physicians, 2005

Total.	23,128
rate per 100,000 persons	414

Community hospitals, 2005

Number of hospitals	50
Beds (x 1,000).	11.4
Patients admitted (x 1,000)	680
Average daily census (x 1,000)	8.7
Average cost per day	$1,831
Outpatient visits (x 1 mil)	6.8

Maryland   3

Disability status of population, 2006
5 to 15 years 6.0%
16 to 64 years 10.2%
65 years and over 37.7%

Education

Educational attainment, 2006
Population over 25 years 3,717,512
  Less than 9th grade. 4.2%
  High school graduate or more 87.1%
  College graduate or more. 35.1%
  Graduate or professional degree. 15.7%

Public school enrollment, 2005-06
Total. 860,020
  Pre-kindergarten through grade 8. . . . 588,571
  Grades 9 through 12. 271,449

Graduating public high school seniors, 2004-05
Diplomas (incl. GED and others) 54,750

SAT scores, 2007
Average critical reading score. 500
Average writing score 496
Average math score 502
Percent of graduates taking test 70%

Public school teachers, 2006-07 (estimate)
Total (x 1,000) 59.3
  Elementary. 34.4
  Secondary. 24.9
Average salary $56,927
  Elementary. $56,678
  Secondary. $57,228

State receipts & expenditures for public schools, 2006-07 (estimate)
Revenue receipts ($ mil) $10,523
Expenditures
Total ($ mil) $9,771
  Per capita $1,561
  Per pupil $10,824

NAEP proficiency scores, 2007
	Reading		Math	
	Basic	Proficient	Basic	Proficient
Grade 4	68.9%	35.9%	80.0%	40.1%
Grade 8	75.6%	33.2%	73.6%	36.5%

Higher education enrollment, fall 2005
Total. 58,078
  Full-time men 15,076
  Full-time women. 21,168
  Part-time men 8,494
  Part-time women. 13,340

Minority enrollment in institutions of higher education, 2005
Black, non-Hispanic 86,984
Hispanic 12,063
Asian/Pacific Islander 20,185
American Indian/Alaska Native. 1,292

Institutions of higher education, 2005-06
Total. 58
  Public. 29
  Private 29

Earned degrees conferred, 2004-05
Associate's. 9,834
Bachelor's 25,018
Master's 13,163
First-professional. .1,080
Doctor's 1,228

Public Libraries, 2006
Number of libraries. 24
Number of outlets 193
Annual visits per capita 5.0
Circulation per capita. 9.4

State & local financial support for higher education, FY 2006
Full-time equivalent enrollment (x 1,000). . . .192.6
Appropriations per FTE. $6,427

Social Insurance & Welfare Programs

Social Security benefits & beneficiaries, 2005
Beneficiaries (x 1,000) 772
  Retired & dependents. 549
  Survivors. 110
  Disabled & dependents. 113
Annual benefit payments ($ mil) $8,512
  Retired & dependents. $5,766
  Survivors. $1,516
  Disabled & dependents. $1,231
Average monthly benefit
  Retired & dependents. $1,012
  Disabled & dependents. $967
  Widowed. $986

Medicare, July 2005
Enrollment (x 1,000). 695
Payments ($ mil) $5,832

Medicaid, 2004
Beneficiaries (x 1,000). 750
Payments ($ mil) $4,594

State Children's Health Insurance Program, 2006
Enrollment (x 1,000). 136.0
Expenditures ($ mil) $212.4

Persons without health insurance, 2006
Number (x 1,000). 776
  percent. 13.8%
Number of children (x 1,000) 137
  percent of children 9.9%

Health care expenditures, 2004
Total expenditures. $31,044
  per capita $5,590

Federal and state public aid

State unemployment insurance, 2006
Recipients, first payments (x 1,000) 96
Total payments ($ mil) $391
Average weekly benefit $274
Temporary Assistance for Needy Families, 2006
Recipients (x 1,000) 535.1
Families (x 1,000) 234.5
Supplemental Security Income, 2005
Recipients (x 1,000) 94.4
Payments ($ mil) $480.9
Food Stamp Program, 2006
Avg monthly participants (x 1,000) 305.4
Total benefits ($ mil) $336.1

Housing & Construction

Housing units

Total 2005 (estimate) 2,274,307
Total 2006 (estimate) 2,300,567
Seasonal or recreational use, 2006 49,654
Owner-occupied, 2006 1,450,411
   Median home value $334,700
   Homeowner vacancy rate 2.1%
Renter-occupied, 2006 638,620
   Median rent $953
   Rental vacancy rate 10.2%
Home ownership rate, 2005 . . . . 71.2%
Home ownership rate, 2006 . . . . 72.6%

New privately-owned housing units

Number authorized, 2006 (x 1,000) 23.3
   Value ($ mil) $3,889.9
Started 2005 (x 1,000, estimate) 27.1
Started 2006 (x 1,000, estimate) 27.0

Existing home sales

2005 (x 1,000) 135.5
2006 (x 1,000) 113.2

Government & Elections

State officials 2008

Governor . . . . Martin O'Malley
     Democratic, term expires 1/11
Lieutenant Governor . . . . Anthony Brown
Secretary of State . . . . Dennis Schnepfe
Attorney General . . . . Douglas Gansler
Chief Justice . . . . Robert Bell

Governorship

Minimum age 30
Length of term . . . . 4 years
Consecutive terms permitted 2
Who succeeds . . . . Lieutenant Governor

Local governments by type, 2002

Total 265
   County 23
   Municipal 157
   Township 0
   School District 0
   Special District 85

State legislature

Name . . . . General Assembly
Upper chamber . . . . .Senate
   Number of members 47
   Length of term . . . . 4 years
   Party in majority, 2008 . . . . .Democratic
Lower chamber . . . . House of Delegates
   Number of members 141
   Length of term . . . . 4 years
   Party in majority, 2008 . . . . .Democratic

Federal representation, 2008 (110ᵗʰ Congress)

Senator . . . . Barbara Mikulski
   Party . . . . .Democratic
   Year term expires 2011
Senator . . . . Ben Cardin
   Party . . . . .Democratic
   Year term expires 2013
Representatives, total 8
   Democrats 6
   Republicans 2

Voters in November 2006 election (estimate)

Total 2,144,913
   Male 982,029
   Female 1,162,884
   White 1,512,616
   Black 584,152
   Hispanic 35,174
   Asian 25,102

Presidential election, 2004

Total Popular Vote 2,386,678
   Kerry 1,334,493
   Bush 1,024,703
Total Electoral Votes 10

Votes cast for US Senators

2004
Total vote (x 1,000) 2,322
Leading party .Democratic
Percent for leading party 64.8%
2006
Total vote (x 1,000) .1,781
Leading party .Democratic
Percent for leading party 54.2%

Votes cast for US Representatives

2004
Total vote (x 1,000) 2,254
   Democratic 1,311
   Republican 896
Leading party .Democratic
Percent for leading party 58.2%
2006
Total vote (x 1,000) .1,701
   Democratic 1,099
   Republican 547
Leading party .Democratic
Percent for leading party 64.6%

State government employment, 2006
Full-time equivalent employees 90,262
Payroll ($ mil) $379.8

Local government employment, 2006
Full-time equivalent employees 200,878
Payroll ($ mil) $857.1

Women holding public office, 2008
US Congress 1
Statewide elected office. 0
State legislature 61

Black public officials, 2002
Total. 192
US and state legislatures 40
City/county/regional offices 101
Judicial/law enforcement. 41
Education/school boards 10

Hispanic public officials, 2006
Total. 13
State executives & legislators 4
City/county/regional offices 7
Judicial/law enforcement. 0
Education/school boards 2

Governmental Finance

State government revenues, 2006
Total revenue (x $1,000). $31,006,534
per capita $5,534.89
General revenue (x $1,000) $26,272,398
Intergovernmental 6,967,769
Taxes 14,626,889
general sales. 3,381,694
individual income tax 6,151,365
corporate income tax 846,863
Current charges. 2,642,009
Miscellaneous .2,035,731

State government expenditure, 2006
Total expenditure (x $1,000) $28,965,977
per capita $5,170.63
General expenditure (x $1,000) $25,721,600
per capita, total. $4,591.49
Education 1,585.19
Public welfare 1,141.98
Health 307.09
Hospitals. 81.48
Highways 383.88
Police protection. 69.33
Corrections 212.28
Natural resources 72.56
Parks & recreation 28.00
Governmental administration 205.96
Interest on general debt 139.43

State debt & cash, 2006 ($ per capita)
Debt $2,838.58
Cash/security holdings. $9,804.63

Federal government grants to state & local government, 2005 (x $1,000)
Total. $8,643,028
by Federal agency
Defense 206,636
Education 589,413
Energy. 28,233
Environmental Protection Agency 95,172
Health & Human Services. 5,350,761
Homeland Security. 29,555
Housing & Urban Development 683,496
Justice 129,369
Labor 179,134
Transportation 654,638
Veterans Affairs. 4,493

Crime & Law Enforcement

Crime, 2006 (rates per 100,000 residents)
Property crimes 195,476
Burglary 37,457
Larceny 127,497
Motor vehicle theft 30,522
Property crime rate. 3,480.9
Violent crimes. 38,110
Murder 546
Forcible rape. .1,178
Robbery. 14,375
Aggravated assault 22,011
Violent crime rate 678.6
Hate crimes. 218

Fraud and identity theft, 2006
Fraud complaints. .8,653
rate per 100,000 residents 154.1
Identity theft complaints 4,656
rate per 100,000 residents 82.9

Law enforcement agencies, 2006
Total agencies. 149
Total employees 20,097
Officers 15,048
Civilians 5,049

Prisoners, probation, and parole, 2006
Total prisoners. 22,945
percent change, 12/31/05 to 12/31/06 . . . . 0.9%
in private facilities 0.5%
in local jails 0.7%
Sentenced to more than one year 22,316
rate per 100,000 residents 396
Adults on probation 75,698
Adults on parole. .14,351

Prisoner demographics, June 30, 2005 (rate per 100,000 residents)
Male. 1,219
Female 88
White. 288
Black. 1,579
Hispanic . . . . NA

Arrests, 2006

Total 297,530
    Persons under 18 years of age 49,359

Persons under sentence of death, 1/1/07

Total 8
    White 3
    Black 5
    Hispanic 0

State's highest court

Name . . . . Court of Appeals
Number of members 7
Length of term . . . . 10 years
Intermediate appeals court? . . . . yes

Labor & Income

Civilian labor force, 2006 (x 1,000)

Total 3,001
    Men 1,548
    Women 1,453
    Persons 16-19 years 131
    White 1,990
    Black 825
    Hispanic 242

Civilian labor force as a percent of civilian non-institutional population, 2006

Total 69.5%
    Men 76.0
    Women 63.7
    Persons 16-19 years 45.6
    White 69.8
    Black 68.1
    Hispanic 80.4

Employment, 2006 (x 1,000)

Total 2,885
    Men 1,489
    Women 1,395
    Persons 16-19 years 115
    White 1,932
    Black 773
    Hispanic 233

Unemployment rate, 2006

Total 3.9%
    Men 3.8
    Women 4.0
    Persons 16-19 years 12.1
    White 2.9
    Black 6.3
    Hispanic 3.5

Full-time/part-time labor force, 2003 (x 1,000)

Full-time labor force, employed 2,336
Part-time labor force, employed 438
Unemployed, looking for
    Full-time work 111
    Part-time work 20
Mean duration of unemployment (weeks) 18.4
    Median 9.1

Labor unions, 2006

Membership (x 1,000) 342
    percent of employed 13.1%

Experienced civilian labor force by private industry, 2006

Total 2,074,499
    Natural resources & mining 6,825
    Construction 188,310
    Manufacturing 136,253
    Trade, transportation & utilities 470,261
    Information 50,774
    Finance 157,614
    Professional & business 394,712
    Education & health 349,186
    Leisure & hospitality 229,611
    Other 89,690

Experienced civilian labor force by occupation, May 2006

Management 138,520
Business & financial 137,050
Legal 19,280
Sales 265,160
Office & admin. support 439,730
Computers & math 96,090
Architecture & engineering 56,170
Arts & entertainment 31,270
Education 165,270
Social services 33,170
Health care practitioner & technical 133,010
Health care support 63,670
Maintenance & repair 103,270
Construction 148,130
Transportation & moving 150,040
Production 102,080
Farming, fishing & forestry 2,530

Hours and earnings of production workers on manufacturing payrolls, 2006

Average weekly hours 40.6
Average hourly earnings $17.87
Average weekly earnings $725.52

Income and poverty, 2006

Median household income $65,144
Personal income, per capita (current $) . . . $44,077
    in constant (2000) dollars $38,476
Persons below poverty level 7.8%

Average annual pay

2006 . . . . $46,162
    increase from 2005 . . . . 4.0%

Federal individual income tax returns, 2005

Returns filed 2,674,329
Adjusted gross income ($1,000) $170,124,868
Total tax liability ($1,000) $22,826,143

Charitable contributions, 2004

Number of contributions 1,177.5
Total amount ($ mil) $4,887.2

Economy, Business, Industry & Agriculture

Fortune 500 companies, 2007 6
Bankruptcy cases filed, FY 2007 12,509

Patents and trademarks issued, 2007
Patents 1,435
Trademarks 1,511

Business firm ownership, 2002
Women-owned 137,410
   Sales ($ mil) $17,295
Black-owned 69,410
   Sales ($ mil) $4,655
Hispanic-owned 15,353
   Sales ($ mil) $2,398
Asian-owned 26,184
   Sales ($ mil) $7,062
Amer. Indian/Alaska Native-owned 3,634
   Sales ($ mil) $344
Hawaiian/Pacific Islander-owned 83
   Sales ($ mil) . . . . NA

Gross domestic product, 2006 ($ mil)
Total gross domestic product $257,815
   Agriculture, forestry, fishing and
      hunting 760
   Mining 299
   Utilities 7,014
   Construction 15,876
   Manufacturing, durable goods 6,591
   Manufacturing, non-durable goods 7,469
   Wholesale trade .13,231
   Retail trade 16,202
   Transportation & warehousing 5,090
   Information 9,134
   Finance & insurance 16,549
   Real estate, rental & leasing 43,786
   Professional and technical services 26,340
   Educational services 3,204
   Health care and social assistance 18,988
   Accommodation/food services 6,886
   Other services, except government 6,529
   Government 42,428

Establishments, payroll, employees & receipts, by major industry group, 2005
Total 138,481
   Annual payroll ($1,000) $88,964,728
   Paid employees 2,167,999
Forestry, fishing & agriculture 217
   Annual payroll ($1,000) $28,949
   Paid employees 991
Mining 92
   Annual payroll ($1,000) $88,289
   Paid employees .1,999
   Receipts, 2002 ($1,000) $417,336

Utilities 108
   Annual payroll ($1,000) $888,039
   Paid employees 10,181
   Receipts, 2002 ($1,000) . . . . .NA
Construction 16,888
   Annual payroll ($1,000) $8,298,193
   Paid employees 181,735
   Receipts, 2002 ($1,000) $29,735,639
Manufacturing 3,742
   Annual payroll ($1,000) $6,717,027
   Paid employees 135,120
   Receipts, 2002 ($1,000) $36,363,340
Wholesale trade 6,043
   Annual payroll ($1,000) $5,215,987
   Paid employees 97,350
   Receipts, 2002 ($1,000) $60,679,602
Retail trade 19,561
   Annual payroll ($1,000) $7,225,671
   Paid employees 299,658
   Receipts, 2002 ($1,000) $60,039,971
Transportation & warehousing 3,712
   Annual payroll ($1,000) $2,264,039
   Paid employees 62,663
   Receipts, 2002 ($1,000) $4,635,726
Information 2,631
   Annual payroll ($1,000) $3,941,341
   Paid employees 66,195
   Receipts, 2002 ($1,000) . . . . .NA
Finance & insurance 8,130
   Annual payroll ($1,000) $8,071,435
   Paid employees 121,374
   Receipts, 2002 ($1,000) . . . . .NA
Professional, scientific & technical 19,132
   Annual payroll ($1,000) $13,706,692
   Paid employees 221,269
   Receipts, 2002 ($1,000) $28,059,470
Education 1,805
   Annual payroll ($1,000) $2,132,329
   Paid employees 63,413
   Receipts, 2002 ($1,000) $904,718
Health care & social assistance 14,622
   Annual payroll ($1,000) $11,855,818
   Paid employees 300,272
   Receipts, 2002 ($1,000) $23,785,022
Arts and entertainment 2,172
   Annual payroll ($1,000) $864,554
   Paid employees 35,698
   Receipts, 2002 ($1,000) $2,143,001
Real estate 6,549
   Annual payroll ($1,000) $2,123,783
   Paid employees 49,532
   Receipts, 2002 ($1,000) $8,482,853
Accommodation & food service 10,230
   Annual payroll ($1,000) $2,710,753
   Paid employees 188,835
   Receipts, 2002 ($1,000) $7,832,268

Exports, 2006
Value of exported goods ($ mil) $7,598
   Manufactured $6,035
   Non-manufactured................... $907

Foreign direct investment in US affiliates, 2004
Property, plants & equipment ($ mil) $11,172
Employment (x 1,000)................... 101.1

Agriculture, 2006
Number of farms 12,000
Farm acreage (x 1,000) 2,035
   Acres per farm........................ 170
Farm marketings and income ($ mil)
Total............................... $1,597.7
   Crops............................ $725.6
   Livestock........................ $872.1
Net farm income $594.6

Principal commodities, in order by marketing receipts, 2005
   Broilers, Greenhouse/nursery, Dairy products,
        Corn, Soybeans

Federal economic activity in state
Expenditures, 2005 ($ mil)
   Total............................. $66,720
      Per capita $11,936.47
   Defense $15,256
   Non-defense...................... $51,464
Defense department, 2006 ($ mil)
   Payroll........................... $5,334
   Contract awards $10,244
   Grants $215
Homeland security grants ($1,000)
   2006............................ $24,291
   2007............................ $32,670

FDIC-insured financial institutions, 2005
Number 112
Assets ($ billion) $54.2
Deposits ($ billion) $40.7

Fishing, 2006
Catch (x 1,000 lbs).....................51,216
Value ($1,000)....................... $53,546

Mining, 2006 ($ mil)
Total non-fuel mineral production $596
Percent of U.S. 0.93%

Communication, Energy & Transportation

Communication
Households with computers, 2003........ 66.0%
Households with internet access, 2003 .... 59.2%
High-speed internet providers 43
Total high-speed internet lines........ 1,813,960
   Residential 1,347,366
   Business.......................... 466,594
Wireless phone customers, 12/2006 4,691,026

FCC-licensed stations (as of January 1, 2008)
TV stations 16
FM radio stations......................... 75
AM radio stations 53

Energy
Energy consumption, 2004
   Total (trillion Btu)....................1,527
   Per capita (million Btu) 274.9
By source of production (trillion Btu)
   Coal 327
   Natural gas 199
   Petroleum.......................... 582
   Nuclear electric power 152
   Hydroelectric power 25
By end-use sector (trillion Btu)
   Residential 437
   Commercial 281
   Industrial 368
   Transportation 440
Electric energy, 2005
   Primary source of electricity........... Coal
   Net generation (billion kWh) 52.7
      percent from renewable sources....... 4.4%
   Net summer capability (million kW) ...12.5
   CO_2 emitted from generation 33.3
Natural gas utilities, 2005
   Customers (x 1,000) 1,100
   Sales (trillion Btu)..................... 185
   Revenues ($ mil) $1,385
Nuclear plants, 2007 2
Total CO_2 emitted (million metric tons)......78.8
Energy spending, 2004 ($ mil) $14,167
   per capita $2,551
   Price per million Btu $14.11

Transportation, 2006
Public road & street mileage 31,099
   Urban........................17,099
   Rural 14,000
   Interstate........................... 481
Vehicle miles of travel (millions) 56,302
   per capita 10,050.3
Total motor vehicle registrations.......4,488,397
   Automobiles.....................2,656,597
   Trucks 1,819,645
   Motorcycles 72,626
Licensed drivers 3,694,290
   19 years & under 160,482
Deaths from motor vehicle accidents 651
Gasoline consumed (x 1,000 gallons) 2,770,954
   per capita 494.6

Commuting Statistics, 2006
Average commute time (min) 30.6
   Drove to work alone 72.8%
   Carpooled......................... 10.7%
   Public transit 8.8%
   Walk to work 2.6%
   Work from home 3.6%

State Summary

Capital city . . . . Boston
Governor . . . . Deval Patrick

State House
Office of the Governor, Room 360
Boston, MA 02133
617-727-6250

Admitted as a state 1788
Area (square miles) 10,555
Population, 2007 (estimate). 6,449,755
Largest city . . . . Boston
   Population, 2006 590,763
Personal income per capita, 2006
   (in current dollars) $45,877
Gross domestic product, 2006 ($ mil) . . . $337,570

Leading industries by payroll, 2005

Health care/Social assistance, Finance & Insurance, Professional/Scientific/Technical

Leading agricultural commodities by receipts, 2005

Greenhouse/nursery, Cranberries, Dairy products, Sweet corn, Apples

Geography & Environment

Total area (square miles). 10,555
   land 7,840
   water 2,715
Federally-owned land, 2004 (acres) 93,950
   percent. 1.9%
Highest point .Mt. Greylock
   elevation (feet) 3,491
Lowest point . . . . .Atlantic Ocean
   elevation (feet) . . . . sea level
General coastline (miles) 192
Tidal shoreline (miles) 1,519
Cropland, 2003 (x 1,000 acres) 252
Forest land, 2003 (x 1,000 acres). 2,665
Capital city . . . . Boston
   Population 2000 589,141
   Population 2006 590,763
Largest city . . . . Boston
   Population 2000 589,141
   Population 2006 590,763

Number of cities with over 100,000 population
1990 3
2000 5
2006 5

State park and recreation areas, 2005
Area (x 1,000 acres). 336
Number of visitors (x 1,000) 33,162
Revenues ($1,000) $13,898
   percent of operating expenditures. 22.9%

National forest system land, 2007
Acres 0

Demographics & Population Characteristics

Population
1980 5,737,037
1990 6,016,425
2000 6,349,105
2006 6,437,193
   Male. 3,117,205
   Female 3,319,988
Living in group quarters, 2006. 215,883
   percent of total. 3.4%
2007 (estimate) .6,449,755
   persons per square mile of land 822.7
2008 (projected). 6,601,235
2010 (projected) .6,649,441
2020 (projected) .6,855,546
2030 (projected). 7,012,009

Population of Core-Based Statistical Areas (formerly Metropolitan Areas), x 1,000

	CBSA	Non-CBSA
1990	5,999	18
2000	6,325	25
2006	6,411	26

Change in population, 2000-2007
Number 100,650
   percent. 1.6%
Natural increase (births minus deaths) 172,254
Net internal migration . . . .-305,690
Net international migration 206,438

Persons by age, 2006
Under 5 years 387,863
5 to 17 years 1,061,021
18 years and over 4,988,309
65 years and over 855,962
85 years and over 137,022
   Median age 38.2

Persons by age, 2010 (projected)
Under 5 years 400,704
18 and over 5,165,588
65 and over 908,565
   Median age 38.8

Race, 2006
One Race
   White. 5,568,643
   Black or African American 446,721
   Asian 313,942
   American Indian/Alaska Native. 19,044
   Hawaiian Native/Pacific Islander. 5,126
Two or more races. .83,717

Persons of Hispanic origin, 2006
Total Hispanic or Latino 510,482
   Mexican. 35,659
   Puerto Rican 226,892
   Cuban 8,012

Persons of Asian origin, 2006

Total Asian 310,441
- Asian Indian........................ 61,042
- Chinese 114,638
- Filipino 10,823
- Japanese 8,218
- Korean............................ 21,840
- Vietnamese..........................47,121

Marital status, 2006

Population 15 years & over 5,249,776
- Never married 1,804,439
- Married......................... 2,634,715
- Separated 107,866
- Widowed.......................... 341,245
- Divorced 469,377

Language spoken at home, 2006

Population 5 years and older........ 6,049,574
- English only 4,827,632
- Spanish 411,192
- French 125,209
- German......................... 19,443
- Chinese 94,615

Households & families, 2006

Households......................... 2,446,485
- with persons under 18 years 792,164
- with persons over 65 years.......... 590,012
- persons per household 2.54
Families.........................1,565,973
- persons per family.....................3.17
Married couples..................... 1,175,784
Female householder,
- no husband present................ 290,102
One-person households 707,650

Nativity, 2006

Number of residents born in state 4,126,291
- percent of population................ 64.1%

Immigration & naturalization, 2006

Legal permanent residents admitted..... 35,560
Persons naturalized 22,932
Non-immigrant admissions 716,538

Vital Statistics and Health

Marriages

2004................................ 41,549
2005................................ 39,507
2006................................ 38,494

Divorces

2004................................14,148
2005................................ 14,354
2006................................ 14,607

Health risks, 2006

Percent of adults who are:
- Smokers........................... 17.8%
- Overweight (BMI > 25)............... 55.5%
- Obese (BMI > 30)................... 20.3%

Births

2005 76,865
- Birthrate (per 1,000)...................12.0
- White............................. 62,406
- Black 8,800
- Hispanic 10,125
- Asian/Pacific Islander 5,482
- Amer. Indian/Alaska Native............. 177
- Low birth weight (2,500g or less)........ 7.9%
- Cesarian births 32.2%
- Preterm births...................... 11.3%
- To unmarried mothers................. 30.2%
- Twin births (per 1,000) 44.5
- Triplets or higher order (per 100,000)....290.4
2006 (preliminary)...................77,769
- rate per 1,000.....................12.1

Deaths

2004
All causes 54,511
- rate per 100,000......................740.6
Heart disease 13,824
- rate per 100,000......................183.3
Malignant neoplasms 13,337
- rate per 100,000......................188.7
Cerebrovascular disease.................. 3,254
- rate per 100,000......................42.5
Chronic lower respiratory disease 2,574
- rate per 100,000......................35.2
Diabetes...........................1,329
- rate per 100,000......................18.4
2005 (preliminary).................... 53,872
- rate per 100,000......................721.9
2006 (provisional) 53,631

Infant deaths

2004................................. 380
- rate per 1,000 ....4.8
2005 (provisional) 395
- rate per 1,000 ....5.1

Exercise routines, 2005

None................................ 23.3%
Moderate or greater..................... 52.6%
Vigorous 29.7%

Abortions, 2004

Total performed in state................ 24,366
- rate per 1,000 women age 15-44.......... 18
- % obtained by out-of-state residents 4.6%

Physicians, 2005

Total................................ 29,343
- rate per 100,000 persons 456

Community hospitals, 2005

Number of hospitals 80
Beds (x 1,000)...........................16.2
Patients admitted (x 1,000) 800
Average daily census (x 1,000) 12.0
Average cost per day $1,751
Outpatient visits (x 1 mil) 18.9

Disability status of population, 2006
5 to 15 years 6.6%
16 to 64 years 10.9%
65 years and over 37.7%

Education

Educational attainment, 2006
Population over 25 years 4,345,561
   Less than 9th grade...................... 5.0%
   High school graduate or more 87.9%
   College graduate or more.............. 37.0%
   Graduate or professional degree....... 15.6%

Public school enrollment, 2005-06
Total................................. 971,909
   Pre-kindergarten through grade 8.... 675,398
   Grades 9 through 12 296,511

Graduating public high school seniors, 2004-05
Diplomas (incl. GED and others) 60,653

SAT scores, 2007
Average critical reading score.............. 513
Average writing score 511
Average math score 522
Percent of graduates taking test 85%

Public school teachers, 2006-07 (estimate)
Total (x 1,000) 73.2
   Elementary 29.2
   Secondary..............................44.0
Average salary $58,624
   Elementary......................... $58,624
   Secondary.......................... $58,624

State receipts & expenditures for public schools, 2006-07 (estimate)
Revenue receipts ($ mil) $14,585
Expenditures
Total ($ mil) $14,945
   Per capita $1,999
   Per pupil $14,125

NAEP proficiency scores, 2007

	Reading		Math	
	Basic	Proficient	Basic	Proficient
Grade 4	81.1%	49.2%	93.2%	57.6%
Grade 8	83.9%	43.0%	85.0%	50.7%

Higher education enrollment, fall 2005
Total............................... 255,021
   Full-time men 88,824
   Full-time women 109,755
   Part-time men 21,292
   Part-time women.....................35,150

Minority enrollment in institutions of higher education, 2005
Black, non-Hispanic 34,986
Hispanic 27,174
Asian/Pacific Islander 32,061
American Indian/Alaska Native..........1,885

Institutions of higher education, 2005-06
Total.................................. 121
   Public.............................. 31
   Private 90

Earned degrees conferred, 2004-05
Associate's..........................11,595
Bachelor's 45,714
Master's 27,663
First-professional..................... 4,305
Doctor's.............................2,676

Public Libraries, 2006
Number of libraries...................... 370
Number of outlets 488
Annual visits per capita 5.9
Circulation per capita....................7.8

State & local financial support for higher education, FY 2006
Full-time equivalent enrollment (x 1,000)....139.9
Appropriations per FTE................ $8,372

Social Insurance & Welfare Programs

Social Security benefits & beneficiaries, 2005
Beneficiaries (x 1,000) 1,072
   Retired & dependents................... 748
   Survivors............................. 128
   Disabled & dependents................. 196
Annual benefit payments ($ mil) $11,691
   Retired & dependents.................$7,865
   Survivors...........................$1,829
   Disabled & dependents...............$1,997
Average monthly benefit
   Retired & dependents................ $1,009
   Disabled & dependents............... $924
   Widowed............................$1,001

Medicare, July 2005
Enrollment (x 1,000)..................... 971
Payments ($ mil) $6,699

Medicaid, 2004
Beneficiaries (x 1,000).................... 294
Payments ($ mil) $2,366

State Children's Health Insurance Program, 2006
Enrollment (x 1,000)....................190.6
Expenditures ($ mil) $233.5

Persons without health insurance, 2006
Number (x 1,000)....................... 657
   percent............................ 10.4%
Number of children (x 1,000) 103
   percent of children 7.0%

Health care expenditures, 2004
Total expenditures.................... $43,009
   per capita $6,683

4   Massachusetts

Federal and state public aid
State unemployment insurance, 2006
Recipients, first payments (x 1,000)........ 210
Total payments ($ mil) $1,255
Average weekly benefit $366
Temporary Assistance for Needy Families, 2006
Recipients (x 1,000).....................1,104.8
Families (x 1,000) 552.6
Supplemental Security Income, 2005
Recipients (x 1,000).......................171.5
Payments ($ mil) $902.3
Food Stamp Program, 2006
Avg monthly participants (x 1,000) 431.5
Total benefits ($ mil)................. $421.5

Housing & Construction
Housing units
Total 2005 (estimate) 2,691,111
Total 2006 (estimate) 2,708,986
Seasonal or recreational use, 2006...... 103,599
Owner-occupied, 2006...............1,588,359
  Median home value............... $370,400
  Homeowner vacancy rate............... 1.8%
Renter-occupied, 2006 858,126
  Median rent $933
  Rental vacancy rate................. 6.2%
Home ownership rate, 2005............. 63.4%
Home ownership rate, 2006............. 65.2%

New privately-owned housing units
Number authorized, 2006 (x 1,000).........19.6
  Value ($ mil)....................$3,249.2
Started 2005 (x 1,000, estimate)...........16.0
Started 2006 (x 1,000, estimate)...........16.0

Existing home sales
2005 (x 1,000)..........................148.6
2006 (x 1,000)..........................128.1

Government & Elections
State officials 2008
Governor...................... Deval Patrick
  Democratic, term expires 1/11
Lieutenant Governor............. Tim Murray
Secretary of State............. William Galvin
Attorney General.............Martha Coakley
Chief Justice .... Margaret Marshall

Governorship
Minimum age.................... not specified
Length of term .... 4 years
Consecutive terms permitted ..... not specified
Who succeeds........... Lieutenant Governor

Local governments by type, 2002
Total.................................. 841
  County................................. 5
  Municipal 45
  Township 306
  School District....................... 82
  Special District 403

State legislature
Name .... General Court
Upper chamber ....Senate
  Number of members.................... 40
  Length of term..................... 2 years
  Party in majority, 2008 ....Democratic
Lower chamber.......House of Representatives
  Number of members................... 160
  Length of term..................... 2 years
  Party in majority, 2008 ....Democratic

Federal representation, 2008 (110th Congress)
Senator......................... John Kerry
  Party ....Democratic
  Year term expires 2009
Senator.................. Edward M. Kennedy
  Party ....Democratic
  Year term expires 2013
Representatives, total 10
  Democrats............................. 10
  Republicans 0

Voters in November 2006 election (estimate)
Total.........................2,434,432
  Male.........................1,110,863
  Female.......................1,323,569
  White........................2,274,168
  Black 97,096
  Hispanic 44,032
  Asian 42,590

Presidential election, 2004
Total Popular Vote 2,912,388
  Kerry 1,803,800
  Bush.........................1,071,109
Total Electoral Votes........................ 12

Votes cast for US Senators
2004
Total vote (x 1,000) .... NA
Leading party.......................... NA
Percent for leading party .... NA
2006
Total vote (x 1,000) 2,244
Leading party....................Democratic
Percent for leading party 66.9%

Votes cast for US Representatives
2004
Total vote (x 1,000) 2,927
  Democratic....................... 2,060
  Republican 435
Leading party....................Democratic
Percent for leading party 70.4%
2006
Total vote (x 1,000) 2,244
  Democratic.......................1,632
  Republican 199
Leading party....................Democratic
Percent for leading party 72.7%

State government employment, 2006
Full-time equivalent employees 90,989
Payroll ($ mil) $414.9

Local government employment, 2006
Full-time equivalent employees 241,083
Payroll ($ mil) $979.9

Women holding public office, 2008
US Congress 1
Statewide elected office..................... 1
State legislature 49

Black public officials, 2002
Total...................................... 79
   US and state legislatures 6
   City/county/regional offices 60
   Judicial/law enforcement................... 2
   Education/school boards 11

Hispanic public officials, 2006
Total...................................... 19
   State executives & legislators 4
   City/county/regional offices 10
   Judicial/law enforcement................... 0
   Education/school boards 5

Governmental Finance

State government revenues, 2006
Total revenue (x $1,000) $45,499,157
   per capita $7,071.25
General revenue (x $1,000) $36,522,412
   Intergovernmental 8,801,349
   Taxes 19,395,270
      general sales....................4,009,371
      individual income tax 10,483,437
      corporate income tax 1,859,009
   Current charges...................3,265,387
   Miscellaneous 5,060,406

State government expenditure, 2006
Total expenditure (x $1,000) $39,880,324
   per capita $6,198.00
General expenditure (x $1,000) $36,036,961
   per capita, total................... $5,600.68
   Education 1,401.12
   Public welfare 1,843.16
   Health 116.77
   Hospitals.........................70.47
   Highways 261.30
   Police protection....................81.11
   Corrections 166.52
   Natural resources 48.27
   Parks & recreation.................32.70
   Governmental administration...... 233.22
   Interest on general debt........... 486.73

State debt & cash, 2006 ($ per capita)
Debt $10,150.18
Cash/security holdings..............$14,001.75

Federal government grants to state & local government, 2005 (x $1,000)
Total...............................$13,748,662
by Federal agency
   Defense 148,664
   Education 747,337
   Energy 146,497
   Environmental Protection Agency ... 112,379
   Health & Human Services. 8,822,429
   Homeland Security...................72,177
   Housing & Urban Development.....1,674,041
   Justice 112,513
   Labor 183,753
   Transportation 653,233
   Veterans Affairs................... 29,049

Crime & Law Enforcement

Crime, 2006 (rates per 100,000 residents)
Property crimes 153,913
   Burglary 35,181
   Larceny 100,771
   Motor vehicle theft 17,961
   Property crime rate................ 2,391.0
Violent crimes......................... 28,775
   Murder 186
   Forcible rape.......................1,742
   Robbery......................... 8,047
   Aggravated assault 18,800
   Violent crime rate 447.0
Hate crimes............................ 448

Fraud and identity theft, 2006
Fraud complaints.......................7,333
   rate per 100,000 residents 113.9
Identity theft complaints 4,102
   rate per 100,000 residents 63.7

Law enforcement agencies, 2006
Total agencies............................ 340
Total employees 20,410
   Officers 17,032
   Civilians 3,378

Prisoners, probation, and parole, 2006
Total prisoners........................11,032
   percent change, 12/31/05 to 12/31/06 .... 3.1%
   in private facilities 0%
   in local jails 1.6%
Sentenced to more than one year 9,472
   rate per 100,000 residents 243
Adults on probation 169,522
Adults on parole.......................3,223

Prisoner demographics, June 30, 2005 (rate per 100,000 residents)
Male................................. 687
Female 45
White 201
Black................................1,635
Hispanic 1,229

Arrests, 2006
Total............................... 130,219
  Persons under 18 years of age.........17,862

Persons under sentence of death, 1/1/07
Total...................................... 0
  White..................................... 0
  Black..................................... 0
  Hispanic.................................. 0

State's highest court
Name................ Supreme Judicial Court
Number of members........................ 7
Length of term.......................to age 70
Intermediate appeals court?................yes

Labor & Income

Civilian labor force, 2006 (x 1,000)
Total................................. 3,368
  Men 1,770
  Women 1,598
  Persons 16-19 years................... 163
  White................................2,976
  Black................................. 192
  Hispanic.............................. 215

Civilian labor force as a percent of civilian non-institutional population, 2006
Total................................. 67.0%
  Men 73.5
  Women 61.0
  Persons 16-19 years..................44.0
  White................................67.4
  Black................................61.9
  Hispanic.............................66.4

Employment, 2006 (x 1,000)
Total.................................3,198
  Men 1,670
  Women 1,528
  Persons 16-19 years................... 144
  White............................... 2,836
  Black................................. 175
  Hispanic.............................. 192

Unemployment rate, 2006
Total................................. 5.1%
  Men 5.6
  Women 4.4
  Persons 16-19 years..................11.4
  White.................................4.7
  Black.................................9.0
  Hispanic.............................10.9

Full-time/part-time labor force, 2003 (x 1,000)
Full-time labor force, employed.......... 2,558
Part-time labor force, employed............ 659
Unemployed, looking for
  Full-time work......................... 163
  Part-time work.......................... 35
*Mean duration of unemployment (weeks)......*21.5
  Median 11.5

Labor unions, 2006
Membership (x 1,000).................... 414
  percent of employed 14.5%

Experienced civilian labor force by private industry, 2006
Total.............................2,789,469
  Natural resources & mining.......... 8,360
  Construction 140,883
  Manufacturing..................... 299,389
  Trade, transportation & utilities 566,900
  Information 87,184
  Finance 224,146
  Professional & business 472,670
  Education & health................ 571,561
  Leisure & hospitality................ 296,219
  Other 122,157

Experienced civilian labor force by occupation, May 2006
Management........................ 185,530
Business & financial 169,230
Legal............................... 24,210
Sales.............................. 327,560
Office & admin. support..............547,190
Computers & math 113,890
Architecture & engineering...........74,130
Arts & entertainment 47,630
Education 213,600
Social services 58,500
Health care practitioner & technical.....197,320
Health care support 94,700
Maintenance & repair................101,130
Construction 115,860
Transportation & moving 165,900
Production 177,060
Farming, fishing & forestry............. 2,900

Hours and earnings of production workers on manufacturing payrolls, 2006
Average weekly hours 40.7
Average hourly earnings $18.26
Average weekly earnings $743.18

Income and poverty, 2006
Median household income............ $59,963
Personal income, per capita (current $)... $45,877
  in constant (2000) dollars $40,048
Persons below poverty level............... 9.9%

Average annual pay
2006................................ $52,435
  increase from 2005 .... 4.7%

Federal individual income tax returns, 2005
Returns filed.......................3,083,021
Adjusted gross income ($1,000) ... $206,948,515
Total tax liability ($1,000) $30,926,389

Charitable contributions, 2004
Number of contributions............... 1,134.3
Total amount ($ mil).................. $3,930.4

Economy, Business, Industry & Agriculture

Fortune 500 companies, 2007 10
Bankruptcy cases filed, FY 2007 13,011

Patents and trademarks issued, 2007
Patents 3,876
Trademarks 2,056

Business firm ownership, 2002
Women-owned 161,918
   Sales ($ mil) $23,134
Black-owned 12,819
   Sales ($ mil) $1,239
Hispanic-owned 15,933
   Sales ($ mil) $2,068
Asian-owned 18,081
   Sales ($ mil) $5,020
Amer. Indian/Alaska Native-owned 2,220
   Sales ($ mil) $340
Hawaiian/Pacific Islander-owned 208
   Sales ($ mil) $24

Gross domestic product, 2006 ($ mil)
Total gross domestic product $337,570
   Agriculture, forestry, fishing and
     hunting 821
   Mining 191
   Utilities 4,571
   Construction 14,745
   Manufacturing, durable goods 23,204
   Manufacturing, non-durable goods 10,116
   Wholesale trade 20,715
   Retail trade 17,826
   Transportation & warehousing 5,280
   Information 16,619
   Finance & insurance 33,316
   Real estate, rental & leasing 50,186
   Professional and technical services 36,855
   Educational services 8,267
   Health care and social assistance 30,229
   Accommodation/food services 8,395
   Other services, except government ... 7,017
   Government 29,588

Establishments, payroll, employees & receipts, by major industry group, 2005

Total 175,291
   Annual payroll ($1,000) $140,580,627
   Paid employees 2,996,347

Forestry, fishing & agriculture 425
   Annual payroll ($1,000) $30,052
   Paid employees 1,115

Mining 103
   Annual payroll ($1,000) $92,120
   Paid employees 1,400
   Receipts, 2002 ($1,000) $297,738

Utilities 251
   Annual payroll ($1,000) $949,020
   Paid employees 11,601
   Receipts, 2002 ($1,000) .... NA

Construction 19,326
   Annual payroll ($1,000) $7,118,084
   Paid employees 126,481
   Receipts, 2002 ($1,000) $31,547,604

Manufacturing 7,915
   Annual payroll ($1,000) $15,570,158
   Paid employees 285,916
   Receipts, 2002 ($1,000) $77,996,586

Wholesale trade 8,818
   Annual payroll ($1,000) $9,591,832
   Paid employees 149,283
   Receipts, 2002 ($1,000) $127,129,789

Retail trade 25,839
   Annual payroll ($1,000) $8,908,761
   Paid employees 369,290
   Receipts, 2002 ($1,000) $73,903,837

Transportation & warehousing 3,675
   Annual payroll ($1,000) $2,857,806
   Paid employees 77,335
   Receipts, 2002 ($1,000) $5,919,533

Information 3,720
   Annual payroll ($1,000) $7,335,491
   Paid employees 118,772
   Receipts, 2002 ($1,000) .... NA

Finance & insurance 9,731
   Annual payroll ($1,000) $19,344,901
   Paid employees 206,327
   Receipts, 2002 ($1,000) .... NA

Professional, scientific & technical 22,073
   Annual payroll ($1,000) $18,513,912
   Paid employees 243,889
   Receipts, 2002 ($1,000) $37,329,788

Education 2,482
   Annual payroll ($1,000) $5,922,084
   Paid employees 185,539
   Receipts, 2002 ($1,000) $1,130,911

Health care & social assistance 17,298
   Annual payroll ($1,000) $19,545,348
   Paid employees 485,617
   Receipts, 2002 ($1,000) $37,307,723

Arts and entertainment 3,058
   Annual payroll ($1,000) $1,437,862
   Paid employees 47,509
   Receipts, 2002 ($1,000) $3,310,135

Real estate 6,962
   Annual payroll ($1,000) $2,344,568
   Paid employees 48,932
   Receipts, 2002 ($1,000) $8,440,569

Accommodation & food service 15,562
   Annual payroll ($1,000) $4,045,039
   Paid employees 241,077
   Receipts, 2002 ($1,000) $11,789,582

Exports, 2006
Value of exported goods ($ mil) $24,047
    Manufactured $20,910
    Non-manufactured...................$1,383

Foreign direct investment in US affiliates, 2004
Property, plants & equipment ($ mil) ... $22,834
Employment (x 1,000)....................182.9

Agriculture, 2006
Number of farms 6,100
Farm acreage (x 1,000) 520
    Acres per farm 85
Farm marketings and income ($ mil)
Total................................. $433.0
    Crops............................. $343.6
    Livestock...........................$89.4
Net farm income $115.4

Principal commodities, in order by marketing receipts, 2005
    Greenhouse/nursery, Cranberries, Dairy products, Sweet corn, Apples

Federal economic activity in state
Expenditures, 2005 ($ mil)
    Total............................. $55,830
        Per capita $8,678.17
    Defense $9,457
    Non-defense $46,373
Defense department, 2006 ($ mil)
    Payroll............................$1,098
    Contract awards $9,077
    Grants $155
Homeland security grants ($1,000)
    2006............................ $41,246
    2007 .... $35,509

FDIC-insured financial institutions, 2005
Number 194
Assets ($ billion) $244.7
Deposits ($ billion) $173.9

Fishing, 2006
Catch (x 1,000 lbs)................... 383,466
Value ($1,000)....................... $436,903

Mining, 2006 ($ mil)
Total non-fuel mineral production $262
Percent of U.S. 0.41%

Communication, Energy & Transportation

Communication
Households with computers, 2003........ 64.1%
Households with internet access, 2003 .... 58.1%
High-speed internet providers 37
Total high-speed internet lines.......2,243,743
    Residential 1,577,555
    Business........................... 666,188
Wireless phone customers, 12/2006 5,128,860

FCC-licensed stations (as of January 1, 2008)
TV stations 22
FM radio stations......................... 125
AM radio stations 73

Energy
Energy consumption, 2004
    Total (trillion Btu)....................1,543
    Per capita (million Btu)...............239.7
By source of production (trillion Btu)
    Coal 105
    Natural gas............................ 387
    Petroleum............................. 749
    Nuclear electric power 62
    Hydroelectric power 10
By end-use sector (trillion Btu)
    Residential 468
    Commercial 395
    Industrial 205
    Transportation 475
Electric energy, 2005
    Primary source of electricity............ Gas
    Net generation (billion kWh) 47.5
        percent from renewable sources....... 4.8%
    Net summer capability (million kW) 14.0
    CO_2 emitted from generation 26.8
Natural gas utilities, 2005
    Customers (x 1,000) 1,430
    Sales (trillion Btu)..................... 230
    Revenues ($ mil) $2,637
Nuclear plants, 2007 1
Total CO_2 emitted (million metric tons).....87.0
Energy spending, 2004 ($ mil) $17,855
    per capita $2,774
    Price per million Btu $16.18

Transportation, 2006
Public road & street mileage 35,938
    Urban...............................27,977
    Rural 7,961
    Interstate........................... 573
Vehicle miles of travel (millions) 55,136
    per capita 8,569.0
Total motor vehicle registrations.......5,385,215
    Automobiles........................3,310,725
    Trucks 2,063,283
    Motorcycles 143,853
Licensed drivers 4,711,735
    19 years & under 197,165
Deaths from motor vehicle accidents 430
Gasoline consumed (x 1,000 gallons) ... 2,826,663
    per capita 439.3

Commuting Statistics, 2006
Average commute time (min) 26.6
    Drove to work alone 73.7%
    Carpooled............................ 8.5%
    Public transit 8.6%
    Walk to work 4.2%
    Work from home...................... 3.6%

Michigan 1

State Summary

Capital city . . . . Lansing
Governor . . . . Jennifer Granholm

PO Box 30013
Lansing, MI 48909
517-335-7858

Admitted as a state 1837
Area (square miles) .96,716
Population, 2007 (estimate). 10,071,822
Largest city . . . . .Detroit
    Population, 2006 .871,121
Personal income per capita, 2006
    (in current dollars) $33,847
Gross domestic product, 2006 ($ mil) . . . $381,003

Leading industries by payroll, 2005

Manufacturing, Health care/Social assistance,
    Professional/Scientific/Technical

Leading agricultural commodities by receipts, 2005

Dairy products, Greenhouse/nursery, Corn,
    Soybeans, Cattle and calves

Geography & Environment

Total area (square miles). 96,716
    land 56,804
    water 39,912
Federally-owned land, 2004 (acres) 3,637,873
    percent. 10.0%
Highest point . . . . Mt. Avron
    elevation (feet) 1,979
Lowest point . . . . Lake Erie
    elevation (feet) 571
General coastline (miles) 0
Tidal shoreline (miles) 0
Cropland, 2003 (x 1,000 acres) 8,097
Forest land, 2003 (x 1,000 acres). 16,708
Capital city . . . . Lansing
    Population 2000 119,128
    Population 2006 114,276
Largest city . . . . .Detroit
    Population 2000 951,270
    Population 2006 871,121

Number of cities with over 100,000 population

1990 7
2000 8
2006 7

State park and recreation areas, 2005

Area (x 1,000 acres). 273
Number of visitors (x 1,000) 23,057
Revenues ($1,000) $36,095
    percent of operating expenditures. 81.7%

National forest system land, 2007

Acres 2,872,833

Demographics & Population Characteristics

Population

1980 9,262,078
1990 9,295,297
2000 9,938,480
2006 10,095,643
    Male. 4,969,692
    Female 5,125,951
Living in group quarters, 2006 255,247
    percent of total. 2.5%
2007 (estimate) .10,071,822
    persons per square mile of land 177.3
2008 (projected). 10,345,033
2010 (projected) 10,428,683
2020 (projected) 10,695,993
2030 (projected) 10,694,172

Population of Core-Based Statistical Areas (formerly Metropolitan Areas), x 1,000

	CBSA	Non-CBSA
1990	8,601	694
2000	9,153	785
2006	9,302	794

Change in population, 2000-2007

Number 133,340
    percent 1.3%
Natural increase (births minus deaths) 319,389
Net internal migration . . . . -359,758
Net international migration 155,686

Persons by age, 2006

Under 5 years 638,195
5 to 17 years 1,840,161
18 years and over 7,617,287
65 years and over 1,260,864
85 years and over 174,758
    Median age 37.2

Persons by age, 2010 (projected)

Under 5 years 681,154
18 and over 7,941,625
65 and over 1,334,491
    Median age 37.4

Race, 2006

One Race
    White. 8,198,927
    Black or African American 1,444,451
    Asian 237,389
    American Indian/Alaska Native. 60,820
    Hawaiian Native/Pacific Islander. 3,757
Two or more races. 150,299

Persons of Hispanic origin, 2006

Total Hispanic or Latino 392,770
    Mexican. 281,856
    Puerto Rican 34,284
    Cuban 10,197

Persons of Asian origin, 2006

Total Asian	236,972
Asian Indian	71,757
Chinese	41,810
Filipino	23,718
Japanese	14,711
Korean	26,291
Vietnamese	21,854

Marital status, 2006

Population 15 years & over	8,076,640
Never married	2,478,408
Married	4,192,545
Separated	119,967
Widowed	505,129
Divorced	900,558

Language spoken at home, 2006

Population 5 years and older	9,456,404
English only	8,607,334
Spanish	292,996
French	33,089
German	53,317
Chinese	35,232

Households & families, 2006

Households	3,869,117
with persons under 18 years	1,301,031
with persons over 65 years	887,504
persons per household	2.54
Families	2,579,201
persons per family	3.13
Married couples	1,938,688
Female householder, no husband present	475,035
One-person households	1,082,712

Nativity, 2006

Number of residents born in state	7,638,467
percent of population	75.7%

Immigration & naturalization, 2006

Legal permanent residents admitted	20,911
Persons naturalized	11,675
Non-immigrant admissions	373,108

Vital Statistics and Health

Marriages

2004	61,932
2005	61,108
2006	59,162

Divorces

2004	34,701
2005	34,580
2006	35,596

Health risks, 2006

Percent of adults who are:

Smokers	22.4%
Overweight (BMI > 25)	64.8%
Obese (BMI > 30)	28.8%

Births

2005	127,706
Birthrate (per 1,000)	12.6
White	100,039
Black	22,509
Hispanic	8,611
Asian/Pacific Islander	4,429
Amer. Indian/Alaska Native	729
Low birth weight (2,500g or less)	8.3%
Cesarian births	28.8%
Preterm births	12.5%
To unmarried mothers	36.6%
Twin births (per 1,000)	34.2
Triplets or higher order (per 100,000)	229.0
2006 (preliminary)	127,476
rate per 1,000	12.6

Deaths

2004	
All causes	85,169
rate per 100,000	812.6
Heart disease	24,825
rate per 100,000	234.3
Malignant neoplasms	19,653
rate per 100,000	189.5
Cerebrovascular disease	5,290
rate per 100,000	49.9
Chronic lower respiratory disease	4,252
rate per 100,000	41.0
Diabetes	2,953
rate per 100,000	28.4
2005 (preliminary)	86,868
rate per 100,000	812.3
2006 (provisional)	84,716

Infant deaths

2004	984
rate per 1,000	7.6
2005 (provisional)	1,014
rate per 1,000	7.9

Exercise routines, 2005

None	22.5%
Moderate or greater	49.5%
Vigorous	28.1%

Abortions, 2004

Total performed in state	26,269
rate per 1,000 women age 15-44	12
% obtained by out-of-state residents	2.9%

Physicians, 2005

Total	24,387
rate per 100,000 persons	241

Community hospitals, 2005

Number of hospitals	146
Beds (x 1,000)	26.2
Patients admitted (x 1,000)	1,198
Average daily census (x 1,000)	17.6
Average cost per day	$1,460
Outpatient visits (x 1 mil)	26.1

Disability status of population, 2006
5 to 15 years 7.3%
16 to 64 years 13.5%
65 years and over 40.2%

Education

Educational attainment, 2006
Population over 25 years 6,638,666
    Less than 9th grade..................... 3.8%
    High school graduate or more 87.2%
    College graduate or more.............. 24.5%
    Graduate or professional degree........ 9.2%

Public school enrollment, 2005-06
Total............................... 1,741,845
    Pre-kindergarten through grade 8... 1,165,704
    Grades 9 through 12................ 538,642

Graduating public high school seniors, 2004-05
Diplomas (incl. GED and others) 101,835

SAT scores, 2007
Average critical reading score.............. 568
Average writing score 553
Average math score 579
Percent of graduates taking test 9%

Public school teachers, 2006-07 (estimate)
Total (x 1,000) 109.9
    Elementary............................60.9
    Secondary.............................49.0
Average salary $54,895
    Elementary....................... $54,895
    Secondary........................ $54,895

State receipts & expenditures for public schools, 2006-07 (estimate)
Revenue receipts ($ mil) $19,580
Expenditures
Total ($ mil) $19,010
    Per capita $1,754
    Per pupil $11,149

NAEP proficiency scores, 2007
	Reading		Math	
	Basic	Proficient	Basic	Proficient
Grade 4	66.2%	32.4%	79.9%	37.1%
Grade 8	72.1%	28.2%	66.4%	28.9%

Higher education enrollment, fall 2005
Total................................121,165
    Full-time men 29,917
    Full-time women.................... 42,762
    Part-time men 17,315
    Part-time women....................31,171

Minority enrollment in institutions of higher education, 2005
Black, non-Hispanic 83,007
Hispanic 17,520
Asian/Pacific Islander 20,819
American Indian/Alaska Native..........5,271

Institutions of higher education, 2005-06
Total................................... 104
    Public................................. 45
    Private 59

Earned degrees conferred, 2004-05
Associate's........................... 23,509
Bachelor's 51,207
Master's 22,834
First-professional..................... 2,942
Doctor's.............................1,634

Public Libraries, 2006
Number of libraries.................... 383
Number of outlets 672
Annual visits per capita 4.8
Circulation per capita....................6.6

State & local financial support for higher education, FY 2006
Full-time equivalent enrollment (x 1,000) 377.7
Appropriations per FTE................ $5,799

Social Insurance & Welfare Programs

Social Security benefits & beneficiaries, 2005
Beneficiaries (x 1,000) 1,743
    Retired & dependents...................1,189
    Survivors............................ 247
    Disabled & dependents................. 306
Annual benefit payments ($ mil) $20,106
    Retired & dependents.................$13,193
    Survivors........................... $3,599
    Disabled & dependents................$3,315
Average monthly benefit
    Retired & dependents.................$1,080
    Disabled & dependents................ $994
    Widowed.............................$1,043

Medicare, July 2005
Enrollment (x 1,000)....................1,483
Payments ($ mil) $11,693

Medicaid, 2004
Beneficiaries (x 1,000)..................1,799
Payments ($ mil) $7,697

State Children's Health Insurance Program, 2006
Enrollment (x 1,000) 118.5
Expenditures ($ mil) $95.5

Persons without health insurance, 2006
Number (x 1,000)......................1,043
    percent 10.5%
Number of children (x 1,000) 116
    percent of children 4.7%

Health care expenditures, 2004
Total expenditures $51,048
    per capita $5,058

Federal and state public aid

State unemployment insurance, 2006
Recipients, first payments (x 1,000) 476
Total payments ($ mil) $1,960
Average weekly benefit $294
Temporary Assistance for Needy Families, 2006
Recipients (x 1,000) .2,560.0
Families (x 1,000) 970.4
Supplemental Security Income, 2005
Recipients (x 1,000) 222.1
Payments ($ mil) $1,157.3
Food Stamp Program, 2006
Avg monthly participants (x 1,000) 1,133.8
Total benefits ($ mil) $1,238.8

Housing & Construction

Housing units
Total 2005 (estimate) 4,478,354
Total 2006 (estimate) 4,513,726
Seasonal or recreational use, 2006 246,759
Owner-occupied, 2006 2,908,273
    Median home value $153,300
    Homeowner vacancy rate 3.4%
Renter-occupied, 2006 960,844
    Median rent $675
    Rental vacancy rate 18.1%
Home ownership rate, 2005 . . . . 76.4%
Home ownership rate, 2006 . . . . 77.4%

New privately-owned housing units
Number authorized, 2006 (x 1,000) 29.2
    Value ($ mil) $4,492.9
Started 2005 (x 1,000, estimate) 51.7
Started 2006 (x 1,000, estimate) 50.7

Existing home sales
2005 (x 1,000) 208.6
2006 (x 1,000) 182.4

Government & Elections

State officials 2008
Governor . . . . Jennifer Granholm
        Democratic, term expires 1/11
Lieutenant Governor . . . . John Cherry
Secretary of State . . . . .Terri Lynn Land
Attorney General . . . . .Mike Cox
Chief Justice . . . . Clifford Taylor

Governorship
Minimum age 30
Length of term . . . . 4 years
Consecutive terms permitted 2
Who succeeds . . . . Lieutenant Governor

Local governments by type, 2002
Total 2,804
    County 83
    Municipal 533
    Township 1,242
    School District 580
    Special District 366

State legislature
Name . . . . Legislature
Upper chamber . . . . .Senate
    Number of members 38
    Length of term . . . . 4 years
    Party in majority, 2008 . . . . Republican
Lower chamber . . . . House of Representatives
    Number of members 110
    Length of term . . . . 2 years
    Party in majority, 2008 . . . . .Democratic

Federal representation, 2008 (110th Congress)
Senator . . . . .Carl Levin
    Party . . . . .Democratic
    Year term expires 2009
Senator . . . . Debbie Stabenow
    Party . . . . .Democratic
    Year term expires 2013
Representatives, total 15
    Democrats 6
    Republicans 9

Voters in November 2006 election (estimate)
Total 4,087,790
    Male 1,945,650
    Female 2,142,140
    White 3,412,356
    Black 545,729
    Hispanic 43,137
    Asian 53,652

Presidential election, 2004
Total Popular Vote 4,839,252
    Kerry 2,479,183
    Bush 2,313,746
Total Electoral Votes 17

Votes cast for US Senators
2004
Total vote (x 1,000) . . . . NA
Leading party . . . . NA
Percent for leading party . . . . NA
2006
Total vote (x 1,000) 3,780
Leading party .Democratic
Percent for leading party 56.9%

Votes cast for US Representatives
2004
Total vote (x 1,000) 4,631
    Democratic 2,242
    Republican 2,289
Leading party . . . . Republican
Percent for leading party 49.4%
2006
Total vote (x 1,000) 3,646
    Democratic 1,923
    Republican 1,625
Leading party .Democratic
Percent for leading party 52.7%

Michigan 5

State government employment, 2006
Full-time equivalent employees 134,918
Payroll ($ mil) $560.3

Local government employment, 2006
Full-time equivalent employees 351,779
Payroll ($ mil) $1,328.2

Women holding public office, 2008
US Congress 3
Statewide elected office. 2
State legislature 29

Black public officials, 2002
Total. 353
   US and state legislatures 24
   City/county/regional offices 153
   Judicial/law enforcement. 62
   Education/school boards 114

Hispanic public officials, 2006
Total. 16
   State executives & legislators 3
   City/county/regional offices 3
   Judicial/law enforcement. 3
   Education/school boards 7

Governmental Finance

State government revenues, 2006
Total revenue (x $1,000) $62,087,004
   per capita $6,145.82
General revenue (x $1,000) $46,001,404
   Intergovernmental 12,551,526
   Taxes 23,714,514
      general sales. 8,080,905
      individual income tax 6,226,304
      corporate income tax 1,886,168
   Current charges. 5,896,047
   Miscellaneous 3,839,317

State government expenditure, 2006
Total expenditure (x $1,000) $53,087,424
   per capita $5,254.97
General expenditure (x $1,000) $46,793,387
   per capita, total. $4,631.94
      Education 2,107.34
      Public welfare 1,174.22
      Health 97.92
      Hospitals. 201.75
      Highways 274.27
      Police protection. 32.55
      Corrections 170.34
      Natural resources 35.45
      Parks & recreation 8.51
      Governmental administration 117.43
      Interest on general debt 105.85

State debt & cash, 2006 ($ per capita)
Debt $2,869.22
Cash/security holdings. $9,909.08

Federal government grants to state & local government, 2005 (x $1,000)
Total. $13,313,206
by Federal agency
   Defense 37,876
   Education 1,168,870
   Energy 117,557
   Environmental Protection Agency . . . 166,638
   Health & Human Services. 8,220,031
   Homeland Security. 25,671
   Housing & Urban Development. 882,237
   Justice 148,169
   Labor 351,787
   Transportation 1,185,101
   Veterans Affairs. 17,199

Crime & Law Enforcement

Crime, 2006 (rates per 100,000 residents)
Property crimes 324,351
   Burglary 76,107
   Larceny 198,227
   Motor vehicle theft 50,017
   Property crime rate. 3,212.8
Violent crimes. 56,778
   Murder 713
   Forcible rape. 5,269
   Robbery. 14,208
   Aggravated assault 36,588
   Violent crime rate 562.4
Hate crimes. 739

Fraud and identity theft, 2006
Fraud complaints. 11,665
   rate per 100,000 residents 115.5
Identity theft complaints 6,784
   rate per 100,000 residents 67.2

Law enforcement agencies, 2006
Total agencies. 600
Total employees 25,896
   Officers 19,228
   Civilians 6,668

Prisoners, probation, and parole, 2006
Total prisoners. 51,577
   percent change, 12/31/05 to 12/31/06 . . . . 4.1%
   in private facilities 0%
   in local jails 0.1%
Sentenced to more than one year 51,577
   rate per 100,000 residents 511
Adults on probation 182,650
Adults on parole. 18,486

Prisoner demographics, June 30, 2005 (rate per 100,000 residents)
Male 1,262
Female 85
White 412
Black. 2,262
Hispanic 397

Arrests, 2006

Total................................ 324,698
    Persons under 18 years of age 44,002

Persons under sentence of death, 1/1/07

Total...................................... 0
    White.................................... 0
    Black 0
    Hispanic 0

State's highest court

Name ....Supreme Court
Number of members........................ 7
Length of term........................ 8 years
Intermediate appeals court? ....yes

Labor & Income

Civilian labor force, 2006 (x 1,000)

Total................................ 5,086
    Men 2,699
    Women 2,387
    Persons 16-19 years.................... 272
    White................................ 4,232
    Black 610
    Hispanic 178

Civilian labor force as a percent of civilian non-institutional population, 2006

Total................................ 65.1%
    Men 71.4
    Women 59.2
    Persons 16-19 years...................46.5
    White................................65.7
    Black 59.3
    Hispanic 69.9

Employment, 2006 (x 1,000)

Total................................4,732
    Men 2,502
    Women 2,230
    Persons 16-19 years.................... 220
    White................................3,970
    Black 532
    Hispanic 168

Unemployment rate, 2006

Total................................ 7.0%
    Men 7.3
    Women 6.6
    Persons 16-19 years...................19.2
    White................................6.2
    Black 12.8
    Hispanic 5.5

Full-time/part-time labor force, 2003 (x 1,000)

Full-time labor force, employed 3,694
Part-time labor force, employed............ 980
Unemployed, looking for
    Full-time work.......................... 304
    Part-time work......................... 64
Mean duration of unemployment (weeks)......20.1
    Median 10.4

Labor unions, 2006

Membership (x 1,000).................... 842
    percent of employed 19.6%

Experienced civilian labor force by private industry, 2006

Total..........................3,613,440
    Natural resources & mining 31,028
    Construction 175,278
    Manufacturing.................... 649,203
    Trade, transportation & utilities 786,053
    Information 65,252
    Finance 210,249
    Professional & business 581,769
    Education & health 562,870
    Leisure & hospitality............... 403,143
    Other 130,914

Experienced civilian labor force by occupation, May 2006

Management........................ 175,640
Business & financial 197,100
Legal............................... 22,970
Sales............................ 448,050
Office & admin. support............... 687,690
Computers & math 94,090
Architecture & engineering.......... 134,900
Arts & entertainment 53,150
Education 261,730
Social services 51,700
Health care practitioner & technical.... 233,860
Health care support 124,550
Maintenance & repair................. 173,840
Construction 162,550
Transportation & moving 295,220
Production 462,350
Farming, fishing & forestry............5,770

Hours and earnings of production workers on manufacturing payrolls, 2006

Average weekly hours 42.2
Average hourly earnings $21.83
Average weekly earnings $921.23

Income and poverty, 2006

Median household income.............$47,182
Personal income, per capita (current $)... $33,847
    in constant (2000) dollars $29,546
Persons below poverty level.............. 13.5%

Average annual pay

2006 .... $42,157
    increase from 2005 .... 2.3%

Federal individual income tax returns, 2005

Returns filed........................4,562,770
Adjusted gross income ($1,000) ... $226,438,921
Total tax liability ($1,000) $27,538,094

Charitable contributions, 2004

Number of contributions............... 1,483.1
Total amount ($ mil)................$5,273.9

Economy, Business, Industry & Agriculture

Fortune 500 companies, 2007 22
Bankruptcy cases filed, FY 2007 43,806

Patents and trademarks issued, 2007

Patents 3,797
Trademarks 2,140

Business firm ownership, 2002

Women-owned 217,673
  Sales ($ mil) $29,217
Black-owned 44,366
  Sales ($ mil) $4,294
Hispanic-owned 9,841
  Sales ($ mil) $3,184
Asian-owned 15,337
  Sales ($ mil) $5,111
Amer. Indian/Alaska Native-owned 5,365
  Sales ($ mil) $773
Hawaiian/Pacific Islander-owned 196
  Sales ($ mil) $37

Gross domestic product, 2006 ($ mil)

Total gross domestic product $381,003
  Agriculture, forestry, fishing and
    hunting 2,123
  Mining 1,585
  Utilities 8,754
  Construction 15,958
  Manufacturing, durable goods 53,768
  Manufacturing, non-durable goods . . . 14,587
  Wholesale trade 23,441
  Retail trade 25,881
  Transportation & warehousing 9,102
  Information 10,837
  Finance & insurance 23,336
  Real estate, rental & leasing 47,141
  Professional and technical services 29,644
  Educational services 2,470
  Health care and social assistance 29,649
  Accommodation/food services 8,603
  Other services, except government 8,780
  Government 41,127

Establishments, payroll, employees & receipts, by major industry group, 2005

Total 237,523
  Annual payroll ($1,000) $148,456,286
  Paid employees 3,796,876

Forestry, fishing & agriculture 604
  Annual payroll ($1,000) $93,514
  Paid employees 3,103

Mining 442
  Annual payroll ($1,000) $327,428
  Paid employees 5,464
  Receipts, 2002 ($1,000) $1,427,350

Utilities 401
  Annual payroll ($1,000) $1,608,841
  Paid employees 23,935
  Receipts, 2002 ($1,000) . . . . .NA

Construction 26,168
  Annual payroll ($1,000) $7,589,911
  Paid employees 160,493
  Receipts, 2002 ($1,000) $36,536,275

Manufacturing 14,033
  Annual payroll ($1,000) $31,631,273
  Paid employees 635,234
  Receipts, 2002 ($1,000) $221,433,262

Wholesale trade 11,981
  Annual payroll ($1,000) $9,277,616
  Paid employees 172,853
  Receipts, 2002 ($1,000) $165,958,945

Retail trade 38,675
  Annual payroll ($1,000) $10,364,568
  Paid employees .499,121
  Receipts, 2002 ($1,000) $109,350,139

Transportation & warehousing 5,557
  Annual payroll ($1,000) $4,040,167
  Paid employees 99,822
  Receipts, 2002 ($1,000) $9,189,132

Information 3,895
  Annual payroll ($1,000) $4,514,440
  Paid employees 84,575
  Receipts, 2002 ($1,000) . . . . .NA

Finance & insurance 13,915
  Annual payroll ($1,000) $8,744,903
  Paid employees 163,807
  Receipts, 2002 ($1,000) . . . . .NA

Professional, scientific & technical 22,701
  Annual payroll ($1,000) $18,336,119
  Paid employees 291,171
  Receipts, 2002 ($1,000) $24,220,096

Education 2,081
  Annual payroll ($1,000) $1,445,064
  Paid employees 64,882
  Receipts, 2002 ($1,000) $687,578

Health care & social assistance 25,348
  Annual payroll ($1,000) $19,567,164
  Paid employees 528,673
  Receipts, 2002 ($1,000) $39,441,794

Arts and entertainment 3,647
  Annual payroll ($1,000) $1,525,685
  Paid employees 55,389
  Receipts, 2002 ($1,000) $4,715,019

Real estate 9,200
  Annual payroll ($1,000) $1,813,884
  Paid employees .59,018
  Receipts, 2002 ($1,000) . . . . .NA

Accommodation & food service 19,297
  Annual payroll ($1,000) $3,861,399
  Paid employees .331,065
  Receipts, 2002 ($1,000) $12,248,269

8   Michigan

Exports, 2006
Value of exported goods ($ mil) $40,405
  Manufactured $35,342
  Non-manufactured $2,738

Foreign direct investment in US affiliates, 2004
Property, plants & equipment ($ mil) ... $38,886
Employment (x 1,000)................... 201.0

Agriculture, 2006
Number of farms 53,000
Farm acreage (x 1,000) 10,100
  Acres per farm 191
Farm marketings and income ($ mil)
Total $4,487.8
  Crops $2,833.4
  Livestock $1,654.4
Net farm income $1,321.2

Principal commodities, in order by marketing receipts, 2005
  Dairy products, Greenhouse/nursery, Corn, Soybeans, Cattle and calves

Federal economic activity in state
Expenditures, 2005 ($ mil)
  Total $64,787
    Per capita $6,414.02
  Defense $5,026
  Non-defense $59,760
Defense department, 2006 ($ mil)
  Payroll $1,307
  Contract awards $3,898
  Grants $98
Homeland security grants ($1,000)
  2006 .... $46,899
  2007 .... $39,237

FDIC-insured financial institutions, 2005
Number 171
Assets ($ billion) $231.5
Deposits ($ billion) $163.1

Fishing, 2006
Catch (x 1,000 lbs) 9,351
Value ($1,000) $5,977

Mining, 2006 ($ mil)
Total non-fuel mineral production $2,010
Percent of U.S. 3.12%

Communication, Energy & Transportation

Communication
Households with computers, 2003 .... 59.9%
Households with internet access, 2003 .... 52.0%
High-speed internet providers 67
Total high-speed internet lines 2,416,451
  Residential 1,734,686
  Business 681,765
Wireless phone customers, 12/2006 7,093,721

FCC-licensed stations (as of January 1, 2008)
TV stations 54
FM radio stations 304
AM radio stations 133

Energy
Energy consumption, 2004
  Total (trillion Btu) 3,119
  Per capita (million Btu) 309.1
By source of production (trillion Btu)
  Coal 774
  Natural gas 918
  Petroleum 1,034
  Nuclear electric power 319
  Hydroelectric power 15
By end-use sector (trillion Btu)
  Residential 799
  Commercial 629
  Industrial 885
  Transportation 807
Electric energy, 2005
  Primary source of electricity .... Coal
  Net generation (billion kWh) 121.6
    percent from renewable sources 3.3%
  Net summer capability (million kW) 30.4
  CO_2 emitted from generation 78.7
Natural gas utilities, 2005
  Customers (x 1,000) 3,451
  Sales (trillion Btu) 767
  Revenues ($ mil) $4,947
Nuclear plants, 2007 4
Total CO_2 emitted (million metric tons) 184.9
Energy spending, 2004 ($ mil) $27,063
  per capita $2,681
  Price per million Btu $12.24

Transportation, 2006
Public road & street mileage 121,722
  Urban 35,619
  Rural 86,103
  Interstate 1,241
Vehicle miles of travel (millions) 104,184
  per capita 10,312.9
Total motor vehicle registrations 8,154,235
  Automobiles 4,765,547
  Trucks 3,362,440
  Motorcycles 247,988
Licensed drivers 7,112,992
  19 years & under 373,957
Deaths from motor vehicle accidents 1,085
Gasoline consumed (x 1,000 gallons) 4,879,874
  per capita 483.0

Commuting Statistics, 2006
Average commute time (min) 23.4
  Drove to work alone 82.9%
  Carpooled 9.1%
  Public transit 1.2%
  Walk to work 2.2%
  Work from home 3.4%

Minnesota   1

State Summary

Capital city . . . . St. Paul
Governor . . . . Tim Pawlenty
130 State Capitol
75 Rev Dr MLK Jr Blvd
St Paul, MN 55155
651-296-3391
Admitted as a state 1858
Area (square miles) 86,939
Population, 2007 (estimate). 5,197,621
Largest city . . . . Minneapolis
Population, 2006 372,833
Personal income per capita, 2006
(in current dollars) $38,712
Gross domestic product, 2006 ($ mil) . . .$244,546

Leading industries by payroll, 2005
Manufacturing, Health care/Social assistance,
Finance & Insurance

**Leading agricultural commodities
by receipts, 2005**
Corn, Hogs, Soybeans, Dairy products, Cattle
and calves

Geography & Environment

Total area (square miles). 86,939
land 79,610
water 7,329
Federally-owned land, 2004 (acres) 2,873,517
percent. 5.6%
Highest point . . . . Eagle Mountain
elevation (feet) 2,301
Lowest point . . . . .Lake Superior
elevation (feet) 601
General coastline (miles) 0
Tidal shoreline (miles) 0
Cropland, 2003 (x 1,000 acres) 21,100
Forest land, 2003 (x 1,000 acres). 16,357
Capital city . . . . .St. Paul
Population 2000 .287,151
Population 2006 273,535
Largest city . . . . Minneapolis
Population 2000 382,618
Population 2006 372,833

Number of cities with over 100,000 population
1990 2
2000 2
2006 2

State park and recreation areas, 2005
Area (x 1,000 acres) 220
Number of visitors (x 1,000) 8,245
Revenues ($1,000) $15,025
percent of operating expenditures. 46.0%

National forest system land, 2007
Acres 2,840,746

Demographics & Population Characteristics

Population
1980 4,075,970
1990 4,375,099
2000 4,919,492
2006 5,167,101
Male. 2,568,869
Female 2,598,232
Living in group quarters, 2006 141,703
percent of total. 2.7%
2007 (estimate). 5,197,621
persons per square mile of land 65.3
2008 (projected). 5,321,587
2010 (projected). 5,420,636
2020 (projected) 5,900,769
2030 (projected). 6,306,130

**Population of Core-Based Statistical Areas
(formerly Metropolitan Areas), x 1,000**

	CBSA	Non-CBSA
1990	3,750	626
2000	4,266	654
2006	4,510	657

Change in population, 2000-2007
Number 278,129
percent. 5.7%
Natural increase (births minus deaths) 238,111
Net internal migration . . . . -34,997
Net international migration 89,636

Persons by age, 2006
Under 5 years 345,250
5 to 17 years 912,014
18 years and over 3,909,837
65 years and over 627,394
85 years and over 101,634
Median age 36.8

Persons by age, 2010 (projected)
Under 5 years 369,571
18 and over 4,130,673
65 and over 670,429
Median age 36.5

Race, 2006
One Race
White. 4,615,613
Black or African American 231,053
Asian 181,065
American Indian/Alaska Native. 60,491
Hawaiian Native/Pacific Islander. 2,766
Two or more races. .76,113

Persons of Hispanic origin, 2006
Total Hispanic or Latino 195,138
Mexican. 138,368
Puerto Rican 8,813
Cuban 1,902

Persons of Asian origin, 2006

Total Asian	179,295
Asian Indian.	28,669
Chinese	20,540
Filipino	7,828
Japanese	2,936
Korean.	14,450
Vietnamese.	23,563

Marital status, 2006

Population 15 years & over	4,134,380
Never married	1,251,658
Married.	2,267,495
Separated	48,648
Widowed.	230,610
Divorced	384,617

Language spoken at home, 2006

Population 5 years and older	4,819,697
English only	4,356,565
Spanish	171,042
French	15,622
German	29,438
Chinese	15,296

Households & families, 2006

Households	2,042,297
with persons under 18 years	679,983
with persons over 65 years	426,838
persons per household	2.46
Families	1,330,451
persons per family	3.03
Married couples	1,064,699
Female householder,	
no husband present	185,465
One-person households	573,640

Nativity, 2006

Number of residents born in state	3,570,653
percent of population	69.1%

Immigration & naturalization, 2006

Legal permanent residents admitted	18,254
Persons naturalized	9,137
Non-immigrant admissions	158,805

Vital Statistics and Health

Marriages

2004	30,359
2005	30,515
2006	30,916

Divorces

2004	14,235
2005	NA
2006	NA

Health risks, 2006

Percent of adults who are:

Smokers.	18.3%
Overweight (BMI > 25).	62.7%
Obese (BMI > 30).	24.7%

Births

2005	70,919
Birthrate (per 1,000).	13.8
White.	57,776
Black	6,898
Hispanic	5,509
Asian/Pacific Islander	4,777
Amer. Indian/Alaska Native	1,468
Low birth weight (2,500g or less)	6.5%
Cesarian births	25.3%
Preterm births	10.7%
To unmarried mothers	29.8%
Twin births (per 1,000)	33.5
Triplets or higher order (per 100,000).	208.9
2006 (preliminary)	73,559
rate per 1,000	14.2

Deaths

2004

All causes	37,034
rate per 100,000	691.2
Heart disease	7,891
rate per 100,000	144.3
Malignant neoplasms	9,093
rate per 100,000	176.4
Cerebrovascular disease.	2,542
rate per 100,000	46.2
Chronic lower respiratory disease	1,839
rate per 100,000	35.4
Diabetes.	1,130
rate per 100,000	21.4
2005 (preliminary).	37,537
rate per 100,000	683.9
2006 (provisional)	36,982

Infant deaths

2004	332
rate per 1,000	4.7
2005 (provisional)	370
rate per 1,000	5.2

Exercise routines, 2005

None.	16.2%
Moderate or greater.	51.0%
Vigorous	28.3%

Abortions, 2004

Total performed in state.	13,791
rate per 1,000 women age 15-44	13
% obtained by out-of-state residents	7.5%

Physicians, 2005

Total.	14,595
rate per 100,000 persons	285

Community hospitals, 2005

Number of hospitals	133
Beds (x 1,000).	16.0
Patients admitted (x 1,000)	635
Average daily census (x 1,000)	11.0
Average cost per day	$1,300
Outpatient visits (x 1 mil)	9.4

Disability status of population, 2006
5 to 15 years 6.1%
16 to 64 years 10.1%
65 years and over 34.8%

Education

Educational attainment, 2006
Population over 25 years 3,387,448
    Less than 9th grade. 3.8%
    High school graduate or more 90.7%
    College graduate or more. 30.4%
    Graduate or professional degree. 9.6%

Public school enrollment, 2005-06
Total. 839,243
    Pre-kindergarten through grade 8. 557,493
    Grades 9 through 12 281,486

Graduating public high school seniors, 2004-05
Diplomas (incl. GED and others) 58,391

SAT scores, 2007
Average critical reading score 596
Average writing score 577
Average math score 603
Percent of graduates taking test 9%

Public school teachers, 2006-07 (estimate)
Total (x 1,000) 50.2
    Elementary. 25.1
    Secondary. 25.1
Average salary $49,634
    Elementary $49,634
    Secondary. $49,634

State receipts & expenditures for public schools, 2006-07 (estimate)
Revenue receipts ($ mil) $9,429
Expenditures
Total ($ mil) $10,623
    Per capita $1,627
    Per pupil $10,809

NAEP proficiency scores, 2007

	Reading		Math	
	Basic	Proficient	Basic	Proficient
Grade 4	72.8%	36.9%	87.5%	50.6%
Grade 8	80.2%	36.6%	81.0%	43.1%

Higher education enrollment, fall 2005
Total. 120,848
    Full-time men 30,471
    Full-time women. 50,523
    Part-time men 13,865
    Part-time women. 25,989

Minority enrollment in institutions of higher education, 2005
Black, non-Hispanic 24,452
Hispanic 8,368
Asian/Pacific Islander 15,670
American Indian/Alaska Native. 4,253

Institutions of higher education, 2005-06
Total. 109
    Public. 42
    Private 67

Earned degrees conferred, 2004-05
Associate's. 15,469
Bachelor's 28,275
Master's 13,052
First-professional. 1,759
Doctor's. 1,239

Public Libraries, 2006
Number of libraries. 140
Number of outlets 373
Annual visits per capita 5.2
Circulation per capita. 9.9

State & local financial support for higher education, FY 2006
Full-time equivalent enrollment (x 1,000) 189.0
Appropriations per FTE. $5,907

Social Insurance & Welfare Programs

Social Security benefits & beneficiaries, 2005
Beneficiaries (x 1,000) 786
    Retired & dependents. 575
    Survivors. 100
    Disabled & dependents. 112
Annual benefit payments ($ mil) $8,525
    Retired & dependents. $5,959
    Survivors. $1,425
    Disabled & dependents. $1,140
Average monthly benefit
    Retired & dependents. $1,004
    Disabled & dependents. $922
    Widowed. $988

Medicare, July 2005
Enrollment (x 1,000). 698
Payments ($ mil) $3,861

Medicaid, 2004
Beneficiaries (x 1,000). 698
Payments ($ mil) $4,575

State Children's Health Insurance Program, 2006
Enrollment (x 1,000). 5.3
Expenditures ($ mil) $39.4

Persons without health insurance, 2006
Number (x 1,000). 475
    percent. 9.2%
Number of children (x 1,000) 104
    percent of children 8.3%

Health care expenditures, 2004
Total expenditures. $29,524
    per capita $5,795

Federal and state public aid

State unemployment insurance, 2006
Recipients, first payments (x 1,000) 141
Total payments ($ mil) $663
Average weekly benefit $333
Temporary Assistance for Needy Families, 2006
Recipients (x 1,000) 790.9
Families (x 1,000) 326.9
Supplemental Security Income, 2005
Recipients (x 1,000) 72.9
Payments ($ mil) $354.5
Food Stamp Program, 2006
Avg monthly participants (x 1,000) 264.0
Total benefits ($ mil) $282.4

Housing & Construction

Housing units
Total 2005 (estimate) 2,251,975
Total 2006 (estimate) 2,283,453
Seasonal or recreational use, 2006 110,451
Owner-occupied, 2006 1,558,206
  Median home value $208,200
  Homeowner vacancy rate 2.0%
Renter-occupied, 2006 484,091
  Median rent $701
  Rental vacancy rate 8.9%
Home ownership rate, 2005 . . . . 76.5%
Home ownership rate, 2006 . . . . 75.6%

New privately-owned housing units
Number authorized, 2006 (x 1,000) 26.4
  Value ($ mil) $4,842.7
Started 2005 (x 1,000, estimate) 39.0
Started 2006 (x 1,000, estimate) 37.1

Existing home sales
2005 (x 1,000) 134.9
2006 (x 1,000) 115.4

Government & Elections

State officials 2008
Governor . . . . Tim Pawlenty
  Republican, term expires 1/11
Lieutenant Governor . . . . Carol Molnau
Secretary of State . . . . .Mark Ritchie
Attorney General . . . . Lori Swanson
Chief Justice . . . . .Russell Anderson

Governorship
Minimum age 25
Length of term . . . . 4 years
Consecutive terms permitted . . . . . . not specified
Who succeeds . . . . Lieutenant Governor

Local governments by type, 2002
Total 3,482
  County 87
  Municipal 854
  Township 1,793
  School District 345
  Special District 403

State legislature
Name . . . . Legislature
Upper chamber . . . . .Senate
  Number of members 67
  Length of term . . . . 4 years
  Party in majority, 2008 . . . . .Democratic
Lower chamber . . . . .House of Representatives
  Number of members 134
  Length of term . . . . 2 years
  Party in majority, 2008 . . . . .Democratic

Federal representation, 2008 (110th Congress)
Senator . . . . Norm Coleman
  Party . . . . Republican
  Year term expires 2009
Senator . . . . Amy Klobuchar
  Party . . . . .Democratic
  Year term expires 2013
Representatives, total 8
  Democrats 5
  Republicans 3

Voters in November 2006 election (estimate)
Total 2,374,680
  Male 1,173,376
  Female 1,201,304
  White 2,287,760
  Black 53,199
  Hispanic 11,895
  Asian 16,222

Presidential election, 2004
Total Popular Vote 2,828,387
  Kerry 1,445,014
  Bush 1,346,695
Total Electoral Votes 10

Votes cast for US Senators
2004
Total vote (x 1,000) . . . . NA
Leading party . . . . NA
Percent for leading party . . . . NA
2006
Total vote (x 1,000) 2,203
Leading party .Democratic
Percent for leading party 58.1%

Votes cast for US Representatives
2004
Total vote (x 1,000) .2,722
  Democratic 1,400
  Republican 1,236
Leading party .Democratic
Percent for leading party 51.4%
2006
Total vote (x 1,000) .2,179
  Democratic 1,153
  Republican 925
Leading party .Democratic
Percent for leading party 52.9%

State government employment, 2006
Full-time equivalent employees 76,795
Payroll ($ mil) $338.2

Local government employment, 2006
Full-time equivalent employees 195,599
Payroll ($ mil) $734.2

Women holding public office, 2008
US Congress 3
Statewide elected office...................... 3
State legislature 70

Black public officials, 2002
Total.................................... 20
    US and state legislatures 2
    City/county/regional offices 4
    Judicial/law enforcement................. 10
    Education/school boards............... 4

Hispanic public officials, 2006
Total..................................... 3
    State executives & legislators 1
    City/county/regional offices 1
    Judicial/law enforcement................. 1
    Education/school boards................. 0

Governmental Finance

State government revenues, 2006
Total revenue (x $1,000).......... $34,772,988
    per capita $6,746.03
General revenue (x $1,000) $27,690,770
    Intergovernmental 6,660,890
    Taxes 17,331,413
        general sales................... 4,437,407
        individual income tax 6,862,953
        corporate income tax 1,071,884
    Current charges................... 2,213,701
    Miscellaneous 1,484,766

State government expenditure, 2006
Total expenditure (x $1,000) $30,988,533
    per capita $6,011.84
General expenditure (x $1,000) $27,449,035
    per capita, total................... $5,325.17
        Education 2,236.41
        Public welfare 1,604.47
        Health 99.60
        Hospitals....................... 56.91
        Highways 370.11
        Police protection................. 50.94
        Corrections 85.76
        Natural resources 86.31
        Parks & recreation 31.74
        Governmental administration.......167.35
        Interest on general debt 82.68

State debt & cash, 2006 ($ per capita)
Debt $1,442.40
Cash/security holdings..............$11,491.48

Federal government grants to state & local government, 2005 (x $1,000)
Total.............................$7,483,670
by Federal agency
    Defense 67,750
    Education 545,652
    Energy........................... 48,126
    Environmental Protection Agency 71,294
    Health & Human Services. 4,708,816
    Homeland Security.................. 33,689
    Housing & Urban Development...... 583,328
    Justice 84,958
    Labor 130,405
    Transportation 529,678
    Veterans Affairs.................. 14,268

Crime & Law Enforcement

Crime, 2006 (rates per 100,000 residents)
Property crimes 159,119
    Burglary 30,173
    Larceny 115,567
    Motor vehicle theft 13,379
    Property crime rate................. 3,079.5
Violent crimes.........................16,123
    Murder 125
    Forcible rape....................... 1,645
    Robbery........................... 5,433
    Aggravated assault 8,920
    Violent crime rate 312.0
Hate crimes............................ 162

Fraud and identity theft, 2006
Fraud complaints....................... 5,860
    rate per 100,000 residents 113.4
Identity theft complaints 2,872
    rate per 100,000 residents 55.6

Law enforcement agencies, 2006
Total agencies........................... 317
Total employees 13,179
    Officers 8,493
    Civilians 4,686

Prisoners, probation, and parole, 2006
Total prisoners......................... 9,108
    percent change, 12/31/05 to 12/31/06 ... -1.9%
    in private facilities 10.7%
    in local jails 5.6%
Sentenced to more than one year 9,108
    rate per 100,000 residents 176
Adults on probation 127,289
Adults on parole........................ 4,431

Prisoner demographics, June 30, 2005 (rate per 100,000 residents)
Male................................. 553
Female................................ 52
White................................ 212
Black................................. 1,937
Hispanic .... NA

Arrests, 2006

Total..................................... NA
   Persons under 18 years of age .... NA

Persons under sentence of death, 1/1/07

Total...................................... 0
   White...................................... 0
   Black 0
   Hispanic 0

State's highest court

Name ....Supreme Court
Number of members...................... 7
Length of term........................ 6 years
Intermediate appeals court? ....yes

Labor & Income

Civilian labor force, 2006 (x 1,000)

Total.................................2,933
   Men 1,534
   Women 1,399
   Persons 16-19 years.................... 187
   White............................. 2,667
   Black 107
   Hispanic 115

Civilian labor force as a percent of civilian non-institutional population, 2006

Total..................................72.9%
   Men 77.5
   Women 68.3
   Persons 16-19 years....................59.3
   White.................................72.8
   Black 71.3
   Hispanic 79.9

Employment, 2006 (x 1,000)

Total.................................2,815
   Men 1,462
   Women 1,353
   Persons 16-19 years................... 160
   White.............................2,571
   Black 95
   Hispanic 110

Unemployment rate, 2006

Total...................................4.0%
   Men 4.7
   Women 3.3
   Persons 16-19 years...................14.7
   White..................................3.6
   Black 10.7
   Hispanic 4.7

Full-time/part-time labor force, 2003 (x 1,000)

Full-time labor force, employed 2,175
Part-time labor force, employed............ 602
Unemployed, looking for
   Full-time work......................... 114
   Part-time work......................... 32
*Mean duration of unemployment (weeks)......*14.4
   Median 8.0

Labor unions, 2006

Membership (x 1,000).................... 395
   percent of employed 16.0%

Experienced civilian labor force by private industry, 2006

Total............................2,296,367
   Natural resources & mining 22,401
   Construction 126,393
   Manufacturing..................... 345,757
   Trade, transportation & utilities 522,327
   Information 58,009
   Finance 178,417
   Professional & business 320,928
   Education & health 390,104
   Leisure & hospitality................ 244,200
   Other 87,129

Experienced civilian labor force by occupation, May 2006

Management....................... 132,070
Business & financial 150,620
Legal...............................17,950
Sales 280,330
Office & admin. support.............. 434,080
Computers & math 74,630
Architecture & engineering............ 52,390
Arts & entertainment 35,540
Education 148,290
Social services 49,280
Health care practitioner & technical.... 142,160
Health care support 77,290
Maintenance & repair................. 92,770
Construction 116,700
Transportation & moving 174,660
Production 236,940
Farming, fishing & forestry.............. 4,300

Hours and earnings of production workers on manufacturing payrolls, 2006

Average weekly hours 41.0
Average hourly earnings $17.23
Average weekly earnings $706.43

Income and poverty, 2006

Median household income............ $54,023
Personal income, per capita (current $)... $38,712
   in constant (2000) dollars $33,793
Persons below poverty level............... 9.8%

Average annual pay

2006 .... $42,185
   increase from 2005 .... 3.4%

Federal individual income tax returns, 2005

Returns filed.......................2,445,599
Adjusted gross income ($1,000) $137,232,136
Total tax liability ($1,000) $17,597,364

Charitable contributions, 2004

Number of contributions................896.1
Total amount ($ mil)................. $3,161.7

Economy, Business, Industry & Agriculture

Fortune 500 companies, 2007 20
Bankruptcy cases filed, FY 2007 11,139

Patents and trademarks issued, 2007
Patents 2,992
Trademarks 2,289

Business firm ownership, 2002
Women-owned 123,905
    Sales ($ mil) $16,252
Black-owned 7,837
    Sales ($ mil) $682
Hispanic-owned 3,984
    Sales ($ mil) $463
Asian-owned 7,700
    Sales ($ mil) $1,776
Amer. Indian/Alaska Native-owned 2,742
    Sales ($ mil) $321
Hawaiian/Pacific Islander-owned 119
    Sales ($ mil) $11

Gross domestic product, 2006 ($ mil)
Total gross domestic product $244,546
    Agriculture, forestry, fishing and
        hunting 3,724
    Mining 1,094
    Utilities 3,419
    Construction 11,275
    Manufacturing, durable goods 21,232
    Manufacturing, non-durable goods . . . 12,644
    Wholesale trade 17,719
    Retail trade 14,738
    Transportation & warehousing 6,408
    Information 8,441
    Finance & insurance 22,937
    Real estate, rental & leasing 32,014
    Professional and technical services 14,591
    Educational services 2,086
    Health care and social assistance 20,300
    Accommodation/food services 5,317
    Other services, except government 5,697
    Government 25,509

Establishments, payroll, employees & receipts, by major industry group, 2005

Total 150,231
    Annual payroll ($1,000) $96,992,711
    Paid employees 2,430,853

Forestry, fishing & agriculture 446
    Annual payroll ($1,000) $61,339
    Paid employees 2,211

Mining 156
    Annual payroll ($1,000) $373,043
    Paid employees 5,372
    Receipts, 2002 ($1,000) $1,649,882

Utilities 276
    Annual payroll ($1,000) $866,279
    Paid employees 11,988
    Receipts, 2002 ($1,000) . . . . NA

Construction 18,284
    Annual payroll ($1,000) $6,555,958
    Paid employees 123,782
    Receipts, 2002 ($1,000) $29,296,756

Manufacturing 7,957
    Annual payroll ($1,000) $15,434,841
    Paid employees 336,311
    Receipts, 2002 ($1,000) $80,623,873

Wholesale trade 8,743
    Annual payroll ($1,000) $8,262,854
    Paid employees 141,320
    Receipts, 2002 ($1,000) $108,388,816

Retail trade 20,950
    Annual payroll ($1,000) $7,063,822
    Paid employees 308,231
    Receipts, 2002 ($1,000) $60,015,531

Transportation & warehousing 4,666
    Annual payroll ($1,000) $3,125,684
    Paid employees 78,428
    Receipts, 2002 ($1,000) $6,735,513

Information 2,725
    Annual payroll ($1,000) $3,385,894
    Paid employees 64,407
    Receipts, 2002 ($1,000) . . . . NA

Finance & insurance 9,949
    Annual payroll ($1,000) $10,175,833
    Paid employees 150,673
    Receipts, 2002 ($1,000) . . . . NA

Professional, scientific & technical 16,534
    Annual payroll ($1,000) $7,495,145
    Paid employees 127,953
    Receipts, 2002 ($1,000) $14,652,614

Education 1,676
    Annual payroll ($1,000) $1,268,128
    Paid employees 56,757
    Receipts, 2002 ($1,000) $645,269

Health care & social assistance 13,408
    Annual payroll ($1,000) $13,297,478
    Paid employees 377,267
    Receipts, 2002 ($1,000) $24,337,547

Arts and entertainment 2,668
    Annual payroll ($1,000) $1,004,347
    Paid employees 38,352
    Receipts, 2002 ($1,000) $2,252,664

Real estate 7,035
    Annual payroll ($1,000) $1,259,089
    Paid employees 37,646
    Receipts, 2002 ($1,000) $5,912,883

Accommodation & food service 10,812
    Annual payroll ($1,000) $2,768,082
    Paid employees 214,543
    Receipts, 2002 ($1,000) $7,959,590

8   Minnesota

Exports, 2006
Value of exported goods ($ mil) $16,309
  Manufactured $13,970
  Non-manufactured $1,047

Foreign direct investment in US affiliates, 2004
Property, plants & equipment ($ mil) . . . $10,926
Employment (x 1,000) 83.2

Agriculture, 2006
Number of farms 79,300
Farm acreage (x 1,000) 27,400
  Acres per farm 346
Farm marketings and income ($ mil)
Total $9,769.5
  Crops $5,127.6
  Livestock $4,641.9
Net farm income $2,493.6

Principal commodities, in order by marketing receipts, 2005
  Corn, Hogs, Soybeans, Dairy products, Cattle
            and calves

Federal economic activity in state
Expenditures, 2005 ($ mil)
  Total $31,067
    Per capita $6,059.76
  Defense $2,437
  Non-defense $28,630
Defense department, 2006 ($ mil)
  Payroll $762
  Contract awards $1,526
  Grants $70
Homeland security grants ($1,000)
  2006 . . . . $13,395
  2007 . . . . $20,504

FDIC-insured financial institutions, 2005
Number 448
Assets ($ billion) $80.0
Deposits ($ billion) $60.6

Fishing, 2006
Catch (x 1,000 lbs) 308
Value ($1,000) $178

Mining, 2006 ($ mil)
Total non-fuel mineral production $2,740
Percent of U.S. 4.25%

Communication, Energy & Transportation

Communication
Households with computers, 2003 . . . . 67.9%
Households with internet access, 2003 . . . . 61.6%
High-speed internet providers 101
Total high-speed internet lines 1,312,911
  Residential 952,244
  Business 360,667
Wireless phone customers, 12/2006 3,701,515

FCC-licensed stations (as of January 1, 2008)
TV stations 31
FM radio stations 235
AM radio stations 103

Energy
Energy consumption, 2004
  Total (trillion Btu) 1,826
  Per capita (million Btu) 358.5
By source of production (trillion Btu)
  Coal 379
  Natural gas 363
  Petroleum 715
  Nuclear electric power 139
  Hydroelectric power 7
By end-use sector (trillion Btu)
  Residential 402
  Commercial 335
  Industrial 559
  Transportation 530
Electric energy, 2005
  Primary source of electricity . . . . Coal
  Net generation (billion kWh) 53.0
    percent from renewable sources 6.5%
  Net summer capability (million kW) 12.1
  CO_2 emitted from generation 38.9
Natural gas utilities, 2005
  Customers (x 1,000) 1,492
  Sales (trillion Btu) 329
  Revenues ($ mil) $2,734
Nuclear plants, 2007 3
Total CO_2 emitted (million metric tons) 102.4
Energy spending, 2004 ($ mil) $15,229
  per capita $2,989
  Price per million Btu $12.17

Transportation, 2006
Public road & street mileage 132,309
  Urban 16,756
  Rural 115,553
  Interstate 913
Vehicle miles of travel (millions) 56,518
  per capita 10,964.6
Total motor vehicle registrations 4,704,914
  Automobiles 2,512,491
  Trucks 2,174,813
  Motorcycles 215,665
Licensed drivers 3,086,610
  19 years & under 182,918
Deaths from motor vehicle accidents 494
Gasoline consumed (x 1,000 gallons) 2,691,672
  per capita 522.2

Commuting Statistics, 2006
Average commute time (min) 22.0
  Drove to work alone 78.1%
  Carpooled 9.3%
  Public transit 3.0%
  Walk to work 3.1%
  Work from home 4.9%

State Summary

Capital city . . . . Jackson
Governor . . . . Haley Barbour
PO Box 139
Jackson, MS 39205
601-359-3100
Admitted as a state 1817
Area (square miles) 48,430
Population, 2007 (estimate). 2,918,785
Largest city . . . . Jackson
Population, 2006 .176,614
Personal income per capita, 2006
(in current dollars) $26,535
Gross domestic product, 2006 ($ mil) $84,225

Leading industries by payroll, 2005
Manufacturing, Health care/Social assistance,
Retail trade

**Leading agricultural commodities
by receipts, 2005**
Broilers, Cotton, Soybeans, Aquaculture, Cattle
and calves

Geography & Environment

Total area (square miles). 48,430
land 46,907
water 1,523
Federally-owned land, 2004 (acres) 2,196,940
percent. 7.3%
Highest point . . . . Woodall Mountain
elevation (feet) 806
Lowest point . . . . Gulf of Mexico
elevation (feet) . . . . sea level
General coastline (miles) 44
Tidal shoreline (miles) 359
Cropland, 2003 (x 1,000 acres) 4,976
Forest land, 2003 (x 1,000 acres). 16,755
Capital city . . . . Jackson
Population 2000 184,256
Population 2006 176,614
Largest city . . . . Jackson
Population 2000 184,256
Population 2006 176,614

Number of cities with over 100,000 population
1990 1
2000 1
2006 1

State park and recreation areas, 2005
Area (x 1,000 acres) 24
Number of visitors (x 1,000) 2,256
Revenues ($1,000) $7,865
percent of operating expenditures. 74.4%

National forest system land, 2007
Acres 1,174,079

Demographics & Population Characteristics

Population
1980 2,520,638
1990 2,573,216
2000 2,844,656
2006 2,910,540
Male 1,409,348
Female 1,501,192
Living in group quarters, 2006 94,247
percent of total. 3.2%
2007 (estimate) 2,918,785
persons per square mile of land 62.2
2008 (projected). .2,950,652
2010 (projected) 2,971,412
2020 (projected) 3,044,812
2030 (projected) 3,092,410

**Population of Core-Based Statistical Areas
(formerly Metropolitan Areas), x 1,000**

	CBSA	Non-CBSA
1990	1,969	606
2000	2,196	648
2006	2,263	647

Change in population, 2000-2007
Number 74,129
percent. 2.6%
Natural increase (births minus deaths) 106,023
Net internal migration . . . . -30,039
Net international migration 10,429

Persons by age, 2006
Under 5 years 209,457
5 to 17 years 549,948
18 years and over 2,151,135
65 years and over 362,172
85 years and over 49,582
Median age 35.3

Persons by age, 2010 (projected)
Under 5 years 211,215
18 and over 2,211,962
65 and over 379,025
Median age 36.5

Race, 2006
One Race
White. 1,771,596
Black or African American 1,080,796
Asian 22,399
American Indian/Alaska Native. 13,816
Hawaiian Native/Pacific Islander. 935
Two or more races. 20,998

Persons of Hispanic origin, 2006
Total Hispanic or Latino 46,348
Mexican. 30,399
Puerto Rican 2,205
Cuban 1,182

Persons of Asian origin, 2006

Total Asian	22,116
Asian Indian	5,220
Chinese	4,325
Filipino	3,391
Japanese	1,261
Korean	1,218
Vietnamese	4,835

Marital status, 2006

Population 15 years & over	2,284,716
Never married	712,155
Married	1,147,068
Separated	75,574
Widowed	180,352
Divorced	245,141

Language spoken at home, 2006

Population 5 years and older	2,704,451
English only	2,619,420
Spanish	46,561
French	4,860
German	4,198
Chinese	3,352

Households & families, 2006

Households	1,075,521
with persons under 18 years	401,497
with persons over 65 years	257,854
persons per household	2.62
Families	741,988
persons per family	3.19
Married couples	497,649
Female householder, no husband present	192,667
One-person households	294,381

Nativity, 2006

Number of residents born in state	2,115,526
percent of population	72.7%

Immigration & naturalization, 2006

Legal permanent residents admitted	1,480
Persons naturalized	495
Non-immigrant admissions	25,197

Vital Statistics and Health

Marriages

2004	17,705
2005	16,868
2006	16,861

Divorces

2004	13,077
2005	12,798
2006	13,658

Health risks, 2006

Percent of adults who are:

Smokers	25.1%
Overweight (BMI > 25)	66.7%
Obese (BMI > 30)	31.4%

Births

2005	42,395
Birthrate (per 1,000)	14.5
White	23,045
Black	18,659
Hispanic	1,170
Asian/Pacific Islander	408
Amer. Indian/Alaska Native	283
Low birth weight (2,500g or less)	11.8%
Cesarian births	35.1%
Preterm births	18.8%
To unmarried mothers	49.4%
Twin births (per 1,000)	31.9
Triplets or higher order (per 100,000)	130.9
2006 (preliminary)	46,069
rate per 1,000	15.8

Deaths

2004

All causes	27,871
rate per 100,000	998.2
Heart disease	8,282
rate per 100,000	300.1
Malignant neoplasms	5,983
rate per 100,000	209.8
Cerebrovascular disease	1,651
rate per 100,000	60.1
Chronic lower respiratory disease	1,350
rate per 100,000	48.4
Diabetes	665
rate per 100,000	23.6
2005 (preliminary)	29,198
rate per 100,000	1,026.9
2006 (provisional)	28,656

Infant deaths

2004	420
rate per 1,000	9.8
2005 (provisional)	465
rate per 1,000	11.0

Exercise routines, 2005

None	32.4%
Moderate or greater	40.0%
Vigorous	20.9%

Abortions, 2004

Total performed in state	3,500
rate per 1,000 women age 15-44	6
% obtained by out-of-state residents	2.8%

Physicians, 2005

Total	5,168
rate per 100,000 persons	178

Community hospitals, 2005

Number of hospitals	94
Beds (x 1,000)	12.8
Patients admitted (x 1,000)	414
Average daily census (x 1,000)	7.3
Average cost per day	$1,021
Outpatient visits (x 1 mil)	4.1

Disability status of population, 2006
5 to 15 years 8.1%
16 to 64 years 19.0%
65 years and over 52.0%

Education

Educational attainment, 2006
Population over 25 years 1,839,682
   Less than 9th grade. 7.8%
   High school graduate or more 77.9%
   College graduate or more. 18.8%
   Graduate or professional degree. 6.1%

Public school enrollment, 2005-06
Total. 494,954
   Pre-kindergarten through grade 8. ... 350,983
   Grades 9 through 12 132,192

Graduating public high school seniors, 2004-05
Diplomas (incl. GED and others) 25,180

SAT scores, 2007
Average critical reading score 568
Average writing score 560
Average math score 549
Percent of graduates taking test 4%

Public school teachers, 2006-07 (estimate)
Total (x 1,000) 33.5
   Elementary 19.8
   Secondary 13.7
Average salary $40,182
   Elementary $39,636
   Secondary $40,851

State receipts & expenditures for public schools, 2006-07 (estimate)
Revenue receipts ($ mil) $3,933
Expenditures
Total ($ mil) $3,803
   Per capita $1,166
   Per pupil $7,189

NAEP proficiency scores, 2007
	Reading		Math	
	Basic	Proficient	Basic	Proficient
Grade 4	51.5%	18.7%	69.9%	21.3%
Grade 8	60.3%	17.4%	53.8%	13.6%

Higher education enrollment, fall 2005
Total. 14,561
   Full-time men 4,371
   Full-time women 7,663
   Part-time men 684
   Part-time women. 1,843

Minority enrollment in institutions of higher education, 2005
Black, non-Hispanic 58,758
Hispanic 1,203
Asian/Pacific Islander 1,252
American Indian/Alaska Native. 648

Institutions of higher education, 2005-06
Total. 41
   Public. 26
   Private. 15

Earned degrees conferred, 2004-05
Associate's. 8,630
Bachelor's 11,681
Master's. 3,877
First-professional. 607
Doctor's. 373

Public Libraries, 2006
Number of libraries. 50
Number of outlets. 243
Annual visits per capita 2.9
Circulation per capita. 3.2

State & local financial support for higher education, FY 2006
Full-time equivalent enrollment (x 1,000). ... 117.7
Appropriations per FTE. $5,053

Social Insurance & Welfare Programs

Social Security benefits & beneficiaries, 2005
Beneficiaries (x 1,000) 552
   Retired & dependents. 322
   Survivors. 88
   Disabled & dependents. 142
Annual benefit payments ($ mil) $5,395
   Retired & dependents. $3,052
   Survivors. $998
   Disabled & dependents. $1,344
Average monthly benefit
   Retired & dependents. $920
   Disabled & dependents. $880
   Widowed. $838

Medicare, July 2005
Enrollment (x 1,000). 454
Payments ($ mil) $3,488

Medicaid, 2004
Beneficiaries (x 1,000). 1,140
Payments ($ mil) $4,887

State Children's Health Insurance Program, 2006
Enrollment (x 1,000). 83.4
Expenditures ($ mil). $124.2

Persons without health insurance, 2006
Number (x 1,000). 600
   percent. 20.7%
Number of children (x 1,000) 146
   percent of children 18.9%

Health care expenditures, 2004
Total expenditures. $14,634
   per capita $5,059

Federal and state public aid

State unemployment insurance, 2006
Recipients, first payments (x 1,000) 53
Total payments ($ mil) $161
Average weekly benefit $186
Temporary Assistance for Needy Families, 2006
Recipients (x 1,000) 316.3
Families (x 1,000) 153.6
Supplemental Security Income, 2005
Recipients (x 1,000) 124.6
Payments ($ mil) $571.8
Food Stamp Program, 2006
Avg monthly participants (x 1,000) 447.7
Total benefits ($ mil) $507.1

Housing & Construction

Housing units
Total 2005 (estimate) 1,235,377
Total 2006 (estimate) 1,241,489
Seasonal or recreational use, 2006 29,187
Owner-occupied, 2006 760,318
  Median home value $88,600
  Homeowner vacancy rate 1.6%
Renter-occupied, 2006 315,203
  Median rent $584
  Rental vacancy rate 12.9%
Home ownership rate, 2005 . . . . 78.8%
Home ownership rate, 2006 . . . . 76.2%

New privately-owned housing units
Number authorized, 2006 (x 1,000) 16.6
  Value ($ mil) $2,011.2
Started 2005 (x 1,000, estimate) 12.8
Started 2006 (x 1,000, estimate) 12.9

Existing home sales
2005 (x 1,000) 61.2
2006 (x 1,000) 63.8

Government & Elections

State officials 2008
Governor . . . . Haley Barbour
      Republican, term expires 1/08
Lieutenant Governor . . . . Phil Bryant
Secretary of State . . . . Delbert Hosemann
Attorney General . . . . .Jim Hood
Chief Justice . . . . James Smith Jr

Governorship
Minimum age 30
Length of term . . . . 4 years
Consecutive terms permitted 2
Who succeeds . . . . Lieutenant Governor

Local governments by type, 2002
Total 1,000
  County 82
  Municipal 296
  Township 0
  School District 164
  Special District 458

State legislature
Name . . . . Legislature
Upper chamber . . . . .Senate
  Number of members 52
  Length of term . . . . 4 years
  Party in majority, 2008 . . . . Democratic
Lower chamber . . . . House of Representatives
  Number of members 122
  Length of term . . . . 4 years
  Party in majority, 2008 . . . . Democratic

Federal representation, 2008 (110th Congress)
Senator . . . . Roger Wicker
  Party . . . . Republican
  Year term expires . . . . . 2008 (special election)
Senator . . . . Thad Cochran
  Party . . . . Republican
  Year term expires 2009
Representatives, total . . . . 4 (1 vacant)
  Democrats 2
  Republicans 1

Voters in November 2006 election (estimate)
Total 878,567
  Male 378,883
  Female 499,684
  White 510,205
  Black 362,465
  Hispanic . . . . NA
  Asian . . . . NA

Presidential election, 2004
Total Popular Vote 1,152,145
  Kerry 458,094
  Bush 684,981
Total Electoral Votes 6

Votes cast for US Senators
2004
Total vote (x 1,000) . . . . NA
Leading party . . . . NA
Percent for leading party . . . . NA
2006
Total vote (x 1,000) 611
Leading party . . . . Republican
Percent for leading party 63.6%

Votes cast for US Representatives
2004
Total vote (x 1,000) .1,116
  Democratic 335
  Republican 659
Leading party . . . . Republican
Percent for leading party 59.0%
2006
Total vote (x 1,000) 601
  Democratic 260
  Republican 304
Leading party . . . . Republican
Percent for leading party 50.7%

State government employment, 2006
Full-time equivalent employees 55,036
Payroll ($ mil) $169.5

Local government employment, 2006
Full-time equivalent employees . . . . NA
Payroll ($ mil) . . . . NA

Women holding public office, 2008
US Congress 0
Statewide elected office. 0
State legislature 26

Black public officials, 2002
Total. 950
    US and state legislatures 46
    City/county/regional offices 646
    Judicial/law enforcement. 121
    Education/school boards 137

Hispanic public officials, 2006
Total. 0
    State executives & legislators 0
    City/county/regional offices 0
    Judicial/law enforcement. 0
    Education/school boards 0

Governmental Finance

State government revenues, 2006
Total revenue (x $1,000) $17,743,579
    per capita $6,120.35
General revenue (x $1,000) $14,604,494
    Intergovernmental 6,973,204
    Taxes 5,989,603
        general sales. 3,047,837
        individual income tax 1,254,733
        corporate income tax 316,981
    Current charges. 1,174,397
    Miscellaneous 467,290

State government expenditure, 2006
Total expenditure (x $1,000) $16,293,095
    per capita $5,620.03
General expenditure (x $1,000) $14,554,388
    per capita, total. $5,020.29
    Education 1,690.51
    Public welfare 1,334.74
    Health 105.13
    Hospitals. 264.16
    Highways 468.01
    Police protection. 35.04
    Corrections 106.84
    Natural resources 77.41
    Parks & recreation 13.40
    Governmental administration 83.14
    Interest on general debt 73.20

State debt & cash, 2006 ($ per capita)
Debt $1,679.99
Cash/security holdings. $10,054.72

Federal government grants to state & local government, 2005 (x $1,000)
Total. $6,567,356
by Federal agency
    Defense 51,914
    Education 467,203
    Energy 19,243
    Environmental Protection Agency 46,294
    Health & Human Services. 3,533,567
    Homeland Security. 834,082
    Housing & Urban Development 274,465
    Justice 53,704
    Labor 109,356
    Transportation 588,248
    Veterans Affairs. 13,988

Crime & Law Enforcement

Crime, 2006 (rates per 100,000 residents)
Property crimes 93,393
    Burglary 27,239
    Larceny 57,807
    Motor vehicle theft 8,347
    Property crime rate. 3,208.8
Violent crimes. 8,691
    Murder 223
    Forcible rape. 1,000
    Robbery. 3,118
    Aggravated assault 4,350
    Violent crime rate 298.6
Hate crimes. 0

Fraud and identity theft, 2006
Fraud complaints. .2,318
    rate per 100,000 residents 79.6
Identity theft complaints 1,494
    rate per 100,000 residents 51.3

Law enforcement agencies, 2006
Total agencies. 193
Total employees 9,200
    Officers 5,624
    Civilians 3,576

Prisoners, probation, and parole, 2006
Total prisoners. 21,068
    percent change, 12/31/05 to 12/31/06 . . . . 2.7%
    in private facilities 23.1%
    in local jails 22.2%
Sentenced to more than one year 19,219
    rate per 100,000 residents 658
Adults on probation 24,107
Adults on parole. 1,899

Prisoner demographics, June 30, 2005 (rate per 100,000 residents)
Male 1,790
Female 168
White 503
Black. 1,742
Hispanic 611

Arrests, 2006
Total................................ 119,506
  Persons under 18 years of age.........11,802

Persons under sentence of death, 1/1/07
Total.................................... 66
  White................................. 30
  Black 35
  Hispanic 0

State's highest court
Name.......................Supreme Court
Number of members........................ 9
Length of term........................ 8 years
Intermediate appeals court?................yes

Labor & Income

Civilian labor force, 2006 (x 1,000)
Total....................................1,296
  Men 681
  Women 615
  Persons 16-19 years.................... 67
  White................................. 841
  Black 424
  Hispanic 43

Civilian labor force as a percent of civilian non-institutional population, 2006
Total.................................. 59.6%
  Men 66.4
  Women 53.6
  Persons 16-19 years...................36.7
  White................................61.2
  Black 56.0
  Hispanic 76.5

Employment, 2006 (x 1,000)
Total....................................1,213
  Men 635
  Women 577
  Persons 16-19 years.................... 56
  White................................. 807
  Black 376
  Hispanic 42

Unemployment rate, 2006
Total................................... 6.4%
  Men 6.6
  Women 6.2
  Persons 16-19 years...................17.4
  White.................................4.0
  Black 11.3
  Hispanic 4.5

Full-time/part-time labor force, 2003 (x 1,000)
Full-time labor force, employed...........1,051
Part-time labor force, employed............ 178
Unemployed, looking for
  Full-time work......................... 73
  Part-time work......................... 11
Mean duration of unemployment (weeks)......24.1
  Median 12.0

Labor unions, 2006
Membership (x 1,000).................... 60
  percent of employed 5.6%

Experienced civilian labor force by private industry, 2006
Total.............................890,161
  Natural resources & mining.......... 20,669
  Construction 57,448
  Manufacturing......................175,718
  Trade, transportation & utilities 224,844
  Information 13,701
  Finance 45,724
  Professional & business 93,880
  Education & health 115,313
  Leisure & hospitality................119,135
  Other........................... 23,728

Experienced civilian labor force by occupation, May 2006
Management.........................47,580
Business & financial 24,900
Legal............................. 5,850
Sales............................. 118,040
Office & admin. support.............. 172,270
Computers & math 8,960
Architecture & engineering............. NA
Arts & entertainment...................8,780
Education 73,490
Social services 10,570
Health care practitioner & technical..... 65,380
Health care support 30,190
Maintenance & repair.................47,330
Construction 57,230
Transportation & moving 95,900
Production 130,850
Farming, fishing & forestry..............5,330

Hours and earnings of production workers on manufacturing payrolls, 2006
Average weekly hours.....................39.4
Average hourly earnings $13.78
Average weekly earnings $542.93

Income and poverty, 2006
Median household income............. $34,473
Personal income, per capita (current $)... $26,535
  in constant (2000) dollars $23,163
Persons below poverty level.............. 21.1%

Average annual pay
2006 ....$31,194
  increase from 2005 ....4.8%

Federal individual income tax returns, 2005
Returns filed.......................1,169,598
Adjusted gross income ($1,000) $45,340,179
Total tax liability ($1,000) $4,712,723

Charitable contributions, 2004
Number of contributions.................235.5
Total amount ($ mil).................. $1,128.1

Economy, Business, Industry & Agriculture

Fortune 500 companies, 2007 0
Bankruptcy cases filed, FY 2007 10,789

Patents and trademarks issued, 2007
Patents 169
Trademarks. 176

Business firm ownership, 2002
Women-owned. 47,102
   Sales ($ mil) $6,728
Black-owned. 25,002
   Sales ($ mil) $1,314
Hispanic-owned. 1,326
   Sales ($ mil) $213
Asian-owned 2,921
   Sales ($ mil) $1,216
Amer. Indian/Alaska Native-owned 689
   Sales ($ mil) $64
Hawaiian/Pacific Islander-owned 126
   Sales ($ mil) $7

Gross domestic product, 2006 ($ mil)
Total gross domestic product $84,225
   Agriculture, forestry, fishing and
     hunting 2,003
   Mining. 2,225
   Utilities 2,242
   Construction 4,281
   Manufacturing, durable goods. 7,847
   Manufacturing, non-durable goods 5,039
   Wholesale trade. 4,624
   Retail trade. 7,505
   Transportation & warehousing 3,034
   Information 2,035
   Finance & insurance 3,550
   Real estate, rental & leasing 7,570
   Professional and technical services 2,954
   Educational services. 483
   Health care and social assistance 6,080
   Accommodation/food services. 3,122
   Other services, except government 2,026
   Government 14,230

Establishments, payroll, employees & receipts, by major industry group, 2005
Total 60,542
   Annual payroll ($1,000) $25,796,066
   Paid employees 926,952
Forestry, fishing & agriculture 820
   Annual payroll ($1,000) $153,849
   Paid employees 5,276
Mining 309
   Annual payroll ($1,000) $214,896
   Paid employees 4,246
   Receipts, 2002 ($1,000) $988,177

Utilities 576
   Annual payroll ($1,000). $496,075
   Paid employees 8,693
   Receipts, 2002 ($1,000) . . . . .NA
Construction. 4,976
   Annual payroll ($1,000). $1,665,301
   Paid employees 49,735
   Receipts, 2002 ($1,000) $7,212,182
Manufacturing 2,629
   Annual payroll ($1,000). $5,792,877
   Paid employees 176,767
   Receipts, 2002 ($1,000) $38,276,054
Wholesale trade 2,853
   Annual payroll ($1,000). $1,307,500
   Paid employees 35,256
   Receipts, 2002 ($1,000) $19,215,751
Retail trade 12,429
   Annual payroll ($1,000). $2,692,884
   Paid employees 140,119
   Receipts, 2002 ($1,000) $25,017,531
Transportation & warehousing 2,342
   Annual payroll ($1,000). $1,067,633
   Paid employees 33,548
   Receipts, 2002 ($1,000) $2,801,650
Information. 1,106
   Annual payroll ($1,000). $642,136
   Paid employees 17,519
   Receipts, 2002 ($1,000) . . . . .NA
Finance & insurance 4,707
   Annual payroll ($1,000). $1,388,034
   Paid employees 35,616
   Receipts, 2002 ($1,000) . . . . .NA
Professional, scientific & technical 4,597
   Annual payroll ($1,000). $1,256,427
   Paid employees 31,689
   Receipts, 2002 ($1,000) $2,922,664
Education 570
   Annual payroll ($1,000). $296,439
   Paid employees 16,435
   Receipts, 2002 ($1,000) $79,757
Health care & social assistance 5,599
   Annual payroll ($1,000). $4,674,594
   Paid employees 141,936
   Receipts, 2002 ($1,000) $10,092,701
Arts and entertainment 660
   Annual payroll ($1,000). $168,254
   Paid employees 10,021
   Receipts, 2002 ($1,000) $529,276
Real estate 2,347
   Annual payroll ($1,000). $256,194
   Paid employees 10,396
   Receipts, 2002 ($1,000) $1,296,752
Accommodation & food service 4,649
   Annual payroll ($1,000). $1,598,053
   Paid employees 114,571
   Receipts, 2002 ($1,000) $5,486,105

Exports, 2006
Value of exported goods ($ mil) $4,674
    Manufactured $3,696
    Non-manufactured................... $424

Foreign direct investment in US affiliates, 2004
Property, plants & equipment ($ mil) $6,777
Employment (x 1,000)................... 25.5

Agriculture, 2006
Number of farms 42,000
Farm acreage (x 1,000) 11,000
    Acres per farm 262
Farm marketings and income ($ mil)
Total.............................. $3,788.5
    Crops............................ $1,245.0
    Livestock......................... $2,543.5
Net farm income $1,230.3

Principal commodities, in order by marketing receipts, 2005
Broilers, Cotton, Soybeans, Aquaculture, Cattle and calves

Federal economic activity in state
Expenditures, 2005 ($ mil)
    Total.............................. $26,181
      Per capita $9,001.47
    Defense $4,869
    Non-defense....................... $21,311
Defense department, 2006 ($ mil)
    Payroll............................ $1,702
    Contract awards $5,477
    Grants $126
Homeland security grants ($1,000)
    2006.............................. $8,528
    2007.............................. $7,002

FDIC-insured financial institutions, 2005
Number 98
Assets ($ billion) $50.6
Deposits ($ billion) $40.7

Fishing, 2006
Catch (x 1,000 lbs)................... 221,838
Value ($1,000)....................... $21,751

Mining, 2006 ($ mil)
Total non-fuel mineral production $212
Percent of U.S. 0.33%

Communication, Energy & Transportation

Communication
Households with computers, 2003........ 48.3%
Households with internet access, 2003 .... 38.9%
High-speed internet providers 51
Total high-speed internet lines......... 332,307
    Residential 275,423
    Business.......................... 56,884
Wireless phone customers, 12/2006 2,029,916

FCC-licensed stations (as of January 1, 2008)
TV stations 29
FM radio stations........................ 191
AM radio stations 92

Energy
Energy consumption, 2004
    Total (trillion Btu).................... 1,214
    Per capita (million Btu)............... 419.8
By source of production (trillion Btu)
    Coal 185
    Natural gas.......................... 294
    Petroleum........................... 488
    Nuclear electric power 107
    Hydroelectric power.................... 0
By end-use sector (trillion Btu)
    Residential 230
    Commercial 167
    Industrial 452
    Transportation 365
Electric energy, 2005
    Primary source of electricity............ Coal
    Net generation (billion kWh) 45.1
      percent from renewable sources....... 3.4%
    Net summer capability (million kW) 16.9
    CO_2 emitted from generation 25.1
Natural gas utilities, 2005
    Customers (x 1,000) 495
    Sales (trillion Btu)..................... 142
    Revenues ($ mil) $912
Nuclear plants, 2007 1
Total CO_2 emitted (million metric tons)...... 62.1
Energy spending, 2004 ($ mil) $9,453
    per capita $3,268
    Price per million Btu $12.51

Transportation, 2006
Public road & street mileage 74,408
    Urban............................. 10,681
    Rural.............................. 63,727
    Interstate........................... 685
Vehicle miles of travel (millions) 41,498
    per capita 14,314.0
Total motor vehicle registrations....... 1,997,581
    Automobiles...................... 1,118,200
    Trucks 869,860
    Motorcycles....................... 27,553
Licensed drivers 1,929,636
    19 years & under 123,579
Deaths from motor vehicle accidents 911
Gasoline consumed (x 1,000 gallons) 1,678,003
    per capita 578.8

Commuting Statistics, 2006
Average commute time (min) 24.0
    Drove to work alone 82.2%
    Carpooled......................... 12.1%
    Public transit 0.4%
    Walk to work 1.8%
    Work from home..................... 2.1%

State Summary

Capital city . . . . Jefferson City
Governor. . . . . .Matt Blunt

Capitol Building
Room 218, PO Box 720
Jefferson City, MO 65102
573-751-3222

Admitted as a state 1821
Area (square miles). 69,704
Population, 2007 (estimate). 5,878,415
Largest city . . . . .Kansas City
    Population, 2006. 447,306
Personal income per capita, 2006
    (in current dollars) $32,705
Gross domestic product, 2006 ($ mil) . . . $225,876

Leading industries by payroll, 2005

Health care/Social assistance, Manufacturing,
Finance & Insurance

**Leading agricultural commodities
by receipts, 2005**

Cattle and calves, Soybeans, Corn, Hogs, Turkeys

Geography & Environment

Total area (square miles). 69,704
    land 68,886
    water 818
Federally-owned land, 2004 (acres) 2,224,788
    percent. 5.0%
Highest point . . . . .Taum Sauk Mountain
    elevation (feet) 1,772
Lowest point . . . . .St. Francis River
    elevation (feet) 230
General coastline (miles) 0
Tidal shoreline (miles) 0
Cropland, 2003 (x 1,000 acres) 13,678
Forest land, 2003 (x 1,000 acres). 12,550
Capital city . . . . Jefferson City
    Population 2000 .39,636
    Population 2006 .39,274
Largest city . . . . .Kansas City
    Population 2000 441,545
    Population 2006 447,306

Number of cities with over 100,000 population

1990 4
2000 4
2006 4

State park and recreation areas, 2005

Area (x 1,000 acres). 202
Number of visitors (x 1,000) 16,695
Revenues ($1,000) $7,406
    percent of operating expenditures. 26.6%

National forest system land, 2007

Acres 1,491,811

Demographics & Population Characteristics

Population

1980 4,916,686
1990 5,117,073
2000 5,596,683
2006 5,842,713
    Male. 2,854,715
    Female 2,987,998
Living in group quarters, 2006. 167,076
    percent of total. 2.9%
2007 (estimate). .5,878,415
    persons per square mile of land 85.3
2008 (projected). 5,860,326
2010 (projected) .5,922,078
2020 (projected) .6,199,882
2030 (projected) .6,430,173

**Population of Core-Based Statistical Areas
(formerly Metropolitan Areas), x 1,000**

	CBSA	Non-CBSA
1990	4,392	725
2000	4,810	787
2006	5,043	800

Change in population, 2000-2007

Number 281,732
    percent. 5.0%
Natural increase (births minus deaths) 168,856
Net internal migration 41,079
Net international migration 51,809

Persons by age, 2006

Under 5 years 386,752
5 to 17 years 1,029,840
18 years and over 4,426,121
65 years and over 778,891
85 years and over 113,789
    Median age. 37.1

Persons by age, 2010 (projected)

Under 5 years 394,878
18 and over 4,510,684
65 and over 821,645
    Median age. 37.6

Race, 2006

One Race
    White. 4,974,983
    Black or African American 673,075
    Asian 83,216
    American Indian/Alaska Native. 28,332
    Hawaiian Native/Pacific Islander. 4,373
Two or more races. 78,734

Persons of Hispanic origin, 2006

Total Hispanic or Latino 160,898
    Mexican. 110,119
    Puerto Rican 10,033
    Cuban 3,129

Persons of Asian origin, 2006

Total Asian 86,010
   Asian Indian. 18,152
   Chinese 19,513
   Filipino 11,858
   Japanese 2,620
   Korean............................... 9,256
   Vietnamese.......................... 16,849

Marital status, 2006

Population 15 years & over 4,674,246
   Never married 1,300,189
   Married........................... 2,513,178
   Separated 91,782
   Widowed........................... 316,307
   Divorced 544,572

Language spoken at home, 2006

Population 5 years and older......... 5,451,998
   English only 5,146,967
   Spanish 129,329
   French 16,725
   German........................... 32,547
   Chinese 15,890

Households & families, 2006

Households........................... 2,305,027
   with persons under 18 years 769,181
   with persons over 65 years........... 541,314
   persons per household 2.46
Families............................. 1,518,860
   persons per family................. 3.04
Married couples...................... 1,154,259
Female householder,
   no husband present................. 273,870
One-person households 662,944

Nativity, 2006

Number of residents born in state 3,875,492
   percent of population 66.3%

Immigration & naturalization, 2006

Legal permanent residents admitted 6,857
Persons naturalized 3,711
Non-immigrant admissions 101,566

Vital Statistics and Health

Marriages

2004 40,824
2005 40,675
2006 40,746

Divorces

2004 21,700
2005 21,013
2006 22,935

Health risks, 2006

Percent of adults who are:
   Smokers.......................... 23.2%
   Overweight (BMI > 25)............. 62.9%
   Obese (BMI > 30).................. 27.2%

Births

2005 78,618
   Birthrate (per 1,000).................... 13.6
   White.......................... 64,729
   Black.......................... 11,686
   Hispanic 4,271
   Asian/Pacific Islander 1,760
   Amer. Indian/Alaska Native 443
   Low birth weight (2,500g or less)....... 8.1%
   Cesarian births 29.7%
   Preterm births 13.3%
   To unmarried mothers................ 37.8%
   Twin births (per 1,000) 32.5
   Triplets or higher order (per 100,000).... 170.1
2006 (preliminary)..................... 81,388
   rate per 1,000 .... 13.9

Deaths

2004
All causes 53,950
   rate per 100,000..................... 872.0
Heart disease 15,500
   rate per 100,000.................... 248.4
Malignant neoplasms 12,450
   rate per 100,000.................... 201.2
Cerebrovascular disease............... 3,503
   rate per 100,000.................... 56.0
Chronic lower respiratory disease 2,731
   rate per 100,000.................... 44.1
Diabetes............................. 1,461
   rate per 100,000.................... 23.6
2005 (preliminary)................... 54,658
   rate per 100,000.................... 869.4
2006 (provisional) 54,913

Infant deaths

2004 584
   rate per 1,000 .... 7.5
2005 (provisional) 580
   rate per 1,000 .... 7.4

Exercise routines, 2005

None................................ 25.4%
Moderate or greater.................. 46.4%
Vigorous 25.3%

Abortions, 2004

Total performed in state................ 8,072
   rate per 1,000 women age 15-44........... 7
   % obtained by out-of-state residents 10.0%

Physicians, 2005

Total................................ 13,965
   rate per 100,000 persons 241

Community hospitals, 2005

Number of hospitals 119
Beds (x 1,000)......................... 19.1
Patients admitted (x 1,000) 836
Average daily census (x 1,000) 12.0
Average cost per day $1,560
Outpatient visits (x 1 mil) 17.2

Disability status of population, 2006
5 to 15 years 7.0%
16 to 64 years 14.2%
65 years and over 43.3%

Education

Educational attainment, 2006
Population over 25 years 3,849,275
  Less than 9th grade..................... 5.2%
  High school graduate or more 84.8%
  College graduate or more.............. 24.3%
  Graduate or professional degree........ 8.7%

Public school enrollment, 2005-06
Total...............................917,705
  Pre-kindergarten through grade 8.....635,142
  Grades 9 through 12................ 282,563

Graduating public high school seniors, 2004-05
Diplomas (incl. GED and others) 57,841

SAT scores, 2007
Average critical reading score.............. 594
Average writing score..................... 587
Average math score..................... 594
Percent of graduates taking test 6%

Public school teachers, 2006-07 (estimate)
Total (x 1,000) 66.8
  Elementary...........................34.4
  Secondary...........................32.4
Average salary $41,839
  Elementary....................... $41,879
  Secondary....................... $41,797

State receipts & expenditures for public schools, 2006-07 (estimate)
Revenue receipts ($ mil) $9,242
Expenditures
Total ($ mil) $8,540
  Per capita $1,256
  Per pupil $8,857

NAEP proficiency scores, 2007

	Reading		Math	
	Basic	Proficient	Basic	Proficient
Grade 4	67.1%	31.8%	82.0%	38.4%
Grade 8	74.9%	31.0%	72.2%	29.9%

Higher education enrollment, fall 2005
Total................................ 156,723
  Full-time men 40,125
  Full-time women.................... 53,442
  Part-time men 26,708
  Part-time women.................... 36,448

Minority enrollment in institutions of higher education, 2005
Black, non-Hispanic 46,582
Hispanic 10,624
Asian/Pacific Islander 9,516
American Indian/Alaska Native.......... 2,293

Institutions of higher education, 2005-06
Total................................. 128
  Public............................. 33
  Private............................ 95

Earned degrees conferred, 2004-05
Associate's...........................13,451
Bachelor's 34,352
Master's 17,180
First-professional..................... 2,625
Doctor's.............................1,363

Public Libraries, 2006
Number of libraries...................... 149
Number of outlets 387
Annual visits per capita....................5.0
Circulation per capita....................8.9

State & local financial support for higher education, FY 2006
Full-time equivalent enrollment (x 1,000)....170.7
Appropriations per FTE............... $5,846

Social Insurance & Welfare Programs

Social Security benefits & beneficiaries, 2005
Beneficiaries (x 1,000) 1,064
  Retired & dependents................... 712
  Survivors........................... 144
  Disabled & dependents.................. 207
Annual benefit payments ($ mil) $11,281
  Retired & dependents.................$7,289
  Survivors...........................$1,929
  Disabled & dependents.............. $2,063
Average monthly benefit
  Retired & dependents.................. $990
  Disabled & dependents.............. $913
  Widowed........................... $968

Medicare, July 2005
Enrollment (x 1,000).................... 912
Payments ($ mil) $5,734

Medicaid, 2004
Beneficiaries (x 1,000)................. 726
Payments ($ mil) $3,312

State Children's Health Insurance Program, 2006
Enrollment (x 1,000)...................106.6
Expenditures ($ mil)...................$106.4

Persons without health insurance, 2006
Number (x 1,000)....................... 772
  percent............................ 13.3%
Number of children (x 1,000) 127
  percent of children 9.1%

Health care expenditures, 2004
Total expenditures....................$31,317
  per capita $5,444

4   Missouri

Federal and state public aid

State unemployment insurance, 2006
Recipients, first payments (x 1,000) 135
Total payments ($ mil) $411
Average weekly benefit $212
Temporary Assistance for Needy Families, 2006
Recipients (x 1,000) 1,110.9
Families (x 1,000) 459.9
Supplemental Security Income, 2005
Recipients (x 1,000) 117.6
Payments ($ mil) $573.1
Food Stamp Program, 2006
Avg monthly participants (x 1,000) 796.4
Total benefits ($ mil) $740.1

Housing & Construction

Housing units
Total 2005 (estimate) 2,595,306
Total 2006 (estimate) 2,623,094
Seasonal or recreational use, 2006 70,472
Owner-occupied, 2006 1,628,838
    Median home value. $131,900
    Homeowner vacancy rate. 2.8%
Renter-occupied, 2006 676,189
    Median rent $607
    Rental vacancy rate. 11.3%
Home ownership rate, 2005. . . . . .72.3%
Home ownership rate, 2006. . . . . .71.9%

New privately-owned housing units
Number authorized, 2006 (x 1,000) 29.2
    Value ($ mil) $4,086.7
Started 2005 (x 1,000, estimate) 27.5
Started 2006 (x 1,000, estimate) 27.5

Existing home sales
2005 (x 1,000). 142.9
2006 (x 1,000). 135.3

Government & Elections

State officials 2008
Governor. . . . . .Matt Blunt
        Republican, term expires 1/09
Lieutenant Governor. . . . . .Peter Kinder
Secretary of State. . . . . Robin Carnahan
Attorney General. . . . . Jeremiah Nixon
Chief Justice . . . . Laura Denvir Stith

Governorship
Minimum age. 30
Length of term . . . . 4 years
Consecutive terms permitted 2
Who succeeds. . . . . Lieutenant Governor

Local governments by type, 2002
Total. 3,422
    County. 114
    Municipal 946
    Township 312
    School District. 536
    Special District 1,514

State legislature
Name . . . . General Assembly
Upper chamber . . . . .Senate
    Number of members. 34
    Length of term. . . . . 4 years
    Party in majority, 2008 . . . . Republican
Lower chamber. . . . . . . .House of Representatives
    Number of members. 163
    Length of term. . . . . 2 years
    Party in majority, 2008 . . . . Republican

Federal representation, 2008 (110th Congress)
Senator. . . . . Christopher Bond
    Party . . . . Republican
    Year term expires 2011
Senator. Claire McCaskill
    Party . . . . .Democratic
    Year term expires 2013
Representatives, total 9
    Democrats. 4
    Republicans 5

Voters in November 2006 election (estimate)
Total. 2,310,214
    Male. 1,094,660
    Female. 1,215,554
    White. 2,052,974
    Black 208,591
    Hispanic 14,568
    Asian 8,421

Presidential election, 2004
Total Popular Vote 2,731,364
    Kerry 1,259,171
    Bush. 1,455,713
Total Electoral Votes. 11

Votes cast for US Senators
2004
Total vote (x 1,000) 2,706
Leading party. . . . . Republican
Percent for leading party 56.1%
2006
Total vote (x 1,000) 2,128
Leading party. . . . . .Democratic
Percent for leading party 49.6%

Votes cast for US Representatives
2004
Total vote (x 1,000) 2,667
    Democratic. 1,193
    Republican 1,430
Leading party. . . . . Republican
Percent for leading party 53.6%
2006
Total vote (x 1,000) 2,097
    Democratic. 992
    Republican 1,049
Leading party. . . . . Republican
Percent for leading party 50.0%

State government employment, 2006
Full-time equivalent employees 90,228
Payroll ($ mil) $271.9

Local government employment, 2006
Full-time equivalent employees 229,855
Payroll ($ mil) $689.7

Women holding public office, 2008
US Congress 2
Statewide elected office...................... 3
State legislature 38

Black public officials, 2002
Total.................................. 206
  US and state legislatures 19
  City/county/regional offices 145
  Judicial/law enforcement................. 17
  Education/school boards 25

Hispanic public officials, 2006
Total....................................... 1
  State executives & legislators 0
  City/county/regional offices 1
  Judicial/law enforcement.................. 0
  Education/school boards.................. 0

Governmental Finance

State government revenues, 2006
Total revenue (x $1,000) $28,760,284
  per capita $4,926.70
General revenue (x $1,000) $22,372,539
  Intergovernmental 7,936,489
  Taxes 10,180,045
    general sales....................3,100,045
    individual income tax 4,491,428
    corporate income tax 343,689
  Current charges..................2,166,823
  Miscellaneous 2,089,182

State government expenditure, 2006
Total expenditure (x $1,000) $24,355,850
  per capita $4,172.21
General expenditure (x $1,000) $21,721,267
  per capita, total.................... $3,720.90
    Education......................1,294.61
    Public welfare 1,027.15
    Health 179.98
    Hospitals.........................197.86
    Highways 341.55
    Police protection................... 32.56
    Corrections 103.74
    Natural resources 59.55
    Parks & recreation 7.09
    Governmental administration.......92.75
    Interest on general debt...........159.18

State debt & cash, 2006 ($ per capita)
Debt $3,026.67
Cash/security holdings.............$12,236.65

Federal government grants to state & local government, 2005 (x $1,000)
Total........................... $8,930,488
by Federal agency
  Defense 35,476
  Education 645,758
  Energy............................ 30,594
  Environmental Protection Agency 101,748
  Health & Human Services. 5,799,930
  Homeland Security.................. 34,853
  Housing & Urban Development...... 518,222
  Justice 99,156
  Labor 129,596
  Transportation 880,629
  Veterans Affairs...................31,942

Crime & Law Enforcement

Crime, 2006 (rates per 100,000 residents)
Property crimes 223,570
  Burglary 44,647
  Larceny 153,490
  Motor vehicle theft 25,433
  Property crime rate.................3,826.5
Violent crimes........................ 31,880
  Murder 368
  Forcible rape........................1,764
  Robbery...........................7,587
  Aggravated assault 22,161
  Violent crime rate 545.6
Hate crimes............................. 97

Fraud and identity theft, 2006
Fraud complaints.......................7,331
  rate per 100,000 residents 125.5
Identity theft complaints 3,753
  rate per 100,000 residents 64.2

Law enforcement agencies, 2006
Total agencies........................ 552
Total employees 19,378
  Officers 13,584
  Civilians 5,794

Prisoners, probation, and parole, 2006
Total prisoners........................30,167
  percent change, 12/31/05 to 12/31/06 ... -2.1%
  in private facilities 0%
  in local jails 0%
Sentenced to more than one year 30,146
  rate per 100,000 residents 514
Adults on probation 54,963
Adults on parole.......................19,063

Prisoner demographics, June 30, 2005 (rate per 100,000 residents)
Male..................................1,323
Female 133
White................................. 487
Black................................. 2,556
Hispanic 587

Arrests, 2006

Total 372,182
   Persons under 18 years of age 49,659

Persons under sentence of death, 1/1/07

Total 51
   White 30
   Black 21
   Hispanic 0

State's highest court

Name .... Supreme Court
Number of members 7
Length of term .... 12 years
Intermediate appeals court? .... yes

Labor & Income

Civilian labor force, 2006 (x 1,000)

Total 3,069
   Men 1,604
   Women 1,465
   Persons 16-19 years 169
   White 2,634
   Black 339
   Hispanic 79

Civilian labor force as a percent of civilian non-institutional population, 2006

Total 67.8%
   Men 73.8
   Women 62.3
   Persons 16-19 years 51.4
   White 67.4
   Black 71.9
   Hispanic 71.7

Employment, 2006 (x 1,000)

Total 2,921
   Men 1,529
   Women 1,391
   Persons 16-19 years 144
   White 2,532
   Black 298
   Hispanic 74

Unemployment rate, 2006

Total 4.8%
   Men 4.6
   Women 5.0
   Persons 16-19 years 14.6
   White 3.9
   Black 12.2
   Hispanic 7.3

Full-time/part-time labor force, 2003 (x 1,000)

Full-time labor force, employed 2,351
Part-time labor force, employed 500
Unemployed, looking for
   Full-time work 147
   Part-time work 23
Mean duration of unemployment (weeks) 19.0
   Median 8.6

Labor unions, 2006

Membership (x 1,000) 284
   percent of employed 10.9%

Experienced civilian labor force by private industry, 2006

Total 2,280,566
   Natural resources & mining 16,619
   Construction 147,806
   Manufacturing 306,961
   Trade, transportation & utilities 540,284
   Information 62,984
   Finance 158,719
   Professional & business 331,395
   Education & health 353,375
   Leisure & hospitality 278,385
   Other 84,038

Experienced civilian labor force by occupation, May 2006

Management 84,290
Business & financial 108,800
Legal 17,340
Sales 297,480
Office & admin. support 478,600
Computers & math 62,880
Architecture & engineering 37,270
Arts & entertainment 32,970
Education 155,260
Social services 30,060
Health care practitioner & technical 160,030
Health care support 72,730
Maintenance & repair 115,740
Construction 133,820
Transportation & moving 204,350
Production 229,100
Farming, fishing & forestry 4,550

Hours and earnings of production workers on manufacturing payrolls, 2006

Average weekly hours 39.3
Average hourly earnings $17.16
Average weekly earnings $674.39

Income and poverty, 2006

Median household income $42,841
Personal income, per capita (current $) ... $32,705
   in constant (2000) dollars $28,549
Persons below poverty level 13.6%

Average annual pay

2006 .... $37,143
   increase from 2005 .... 3.3%

Federal individual income tax returns, 2005

Returns filed 2,610,839
Adjusted gross income ($1,000) $122,774,783
Total tax liability ($1,000) $14,859,837

Charitable contributions, 2004

Number of contributions 687.9
Total amount ($ mil) $2,595.7

Economy, Business, Industry & Agriculture

Fortune 500 companies, 2007 10
Bankruptcy cases filed, FY 2007 20,141

Patents and trademarks issued, 2007
Patents 858
Trademarks 1,543

Business firm ownership, 2002
Women-owned 120,443
  Sales ($ mil) $18,605
Black-owned 16,750
  Sales ($ mil) $1,345
Hispanic-owned 3,652
  Sales ($ mil) $682
Asian-owned 6,376
  Sales ($ mil) $1,883
Amer. Indian/Alaska Native-owned 3,298
  Sales ($ mil) $340
Hawaiian/Pacific Islander-owned 96
  Sales ($ mil) $34

Gross domestic product, 2006 ($ mil)
Total gross domestic product $225,876
  Agriculture, forestry, fishing and
    hunting 1,946
  Mining 945
  Utilities 3,968
  Construction 10,835
  Manufacturing, durable goods 18,543
  Manufacturing, non-durable goods 15,742
  Wholesale trade 14,749
  Retail trade 15,527
  Transportation & warehousing 7,795
  Information 10,802
  Finance & insurance 13,541
  Real estate, rental & leasing 24,077
  Professional and technical services 13,416
  Educational services 2,864
  Health care and social assistance 16,858
  Accommodation/food services 5,792
  Other services, except government 5,551
  Government 26,133

Establishments, payroll, employees & receipts, by major industry group, 2005

Total 154,306
  Annual payroll ($1,000) $82,340,359
  Paid employees 2,425,403
Forestry, fishing & agriculture 261
  Annual payroll ($1,000) $32,435
  Paid employees 1,386
Mining 257
  Annual payroll ($1,000) $183,533
  Paid employees 4,257
  Receipts, 2002 ($1,000) $773,258

Utilities 384
  Annual payroll ($1,000) $1,065,504
  Paid employees 15,112
  Receipts, 2002 ($1,000) .... NA
Construction 17,050
  Annual payroll ($1,000) $6,218,667
  Paid employees 148,881
  Receipts, 2002 ($1,000) $26,103,729
Manufacturing 6,935
  Annual payroll ($1,000) $11,640,421
  Paid employees 298,117
  Receipts, 2002 ($1,000) $92,909,173
Wholesale trade 8,276
  Annual payroll ($1,000) $5,291,381
  Paid employees 130,004
  Receipts, 2002 ($1,000) $95,603,561
Retail trade 23,507
  Annual payroll ($1,000) $6,780,597
  Paid employees 321,615
  Receipts, 2002 ($1,000) $61,861,163
Transportation & warehousing 5,114
  Annual payroll ($1,000) $3,046,865
  Paid employees 87,366
  Receipts, 2002 ($1,000) $9,216,811
Information 2,570
  Annual payroll ($1,000) $3,612,077
  Paid employees 74,233
  Receipts, 2002 ($1,000) .... NA
Finance & insurance 10,742
  Annual payroll ($1,000) $7,067,143
  Paid employees 136,316
  Receipts, 2002 ($1,000) .... NA
Professional, scientific & technical 13,570
  Annual payroll ($1,000) $6,968,986
  Paid employees 133,171
  Receipts, 2002 ($1,000) $14,379,844
Education 1,460
  Annual payroll ($1,000) $1,874,297
  Paid employees 66,197
  Receipts, 2002 ($1,000) $335,325
Health care & social assistance 15,229
  Annual payroll ($1,000) $11,730,526
  Paid employees 355,301
  Receipts, 2002 ($1,000) $24,944,155
Arts and entertainment 2,134
  Annual payroll ($1,000) $1,119,419
  Paid employees 36,856
  Receipts, 2002 ($1,000) $2,747,690
Real estate 6,873
  Annual payroll ($1,000) $1,330,721
  Paid employees 41,101
  Receipts, 2002 ($1,000) $5,654,672
Accommodation & food service 11,811
  Annual payroll ($1,000) $2,867,580
  Paid employees 234,662
  Receipts, 2002 ($1,000) $8,607,025

8   Missouri

Exports, 2006
Value of exported goods ($ mil) $12,776
   Manufactured $11,361
   Non-manufactured $1,087

Foreign direct investment in US affiliates, 2004
Property, plants & equipment ($ mil) $16,027
Employment (x 1,000). 84.2

Agriculture, 2006
Number of farms 105,000
Farm acreage (x 1,000) 30,100
   Acres per farm 287
Farm marketings and income ($ mil)
Total. $5,621.3
   Crops $2,627.6
   Livestock. $2,993.7
Net farm income $1,697.3

Principal commodities, in order by marketing receipts, 2005
Cattle and calves, Soybeans, Corn, Hogs, Turkeys

Federal economic activity in state
Expenditures, 2005 ($ mil)
   Total. $48,273
      Per capita $8,326.24
   Defense $8,975
   Non-defense $39,298
Defense department, 2006 ($ mil)
   Payroll $2,432
   Contract awards $9,393
   Grants $46
Homeland security grants ($1,000)
   2006 . . . . $42,861
   2007 . . . . $31,244

FDIC-insured financial institutions, 2005
Number 368
Assets ($ billion) $106.9
Deposits ($ billion) $83.8

Fishing, 2006
Catch (x 1,000 lbs) . . . . NA
Value ($1,000). . . . . NA

Mining, 2006 ($ mil)
Total non-fuel mineral production $2,130
Percent of U.S. 3.31%

Communication, Energy & Transportation

Communication
Households with computers, 2003 . . . . .60.7%
Households with internet access, 2003 . . . .53.0%
High-speed internet providers 83
Total high-speed internet lines 1,266,504
   Residential 1,024,388
   Business. 242,116
Wireless phone customers, 12/2006 4,322,458

FCC-licensed stations (as of January 1, 2008)
TV stations 35
FM radio stations. 253
AM radio stations 117

Energy
Energy consumption, 2004
   Total (trillion Btu). 1,849
   Per capita (million Btu) 321.5
By source of production (trillion Btu)
   Coal 808
   Natural gas 268
   Petroleum 747
   Nuclear electric power 82
   Hydroelectric power 15
By end-use sector (trillion Btu)
   Residential 489
   Commercial 391
   Industrial 390
   Transportation 578
Electric energy, 2005
   Primary source of electricity. . . . . Coal
   Net generation (billion kWh) 90.8
      percent from renewable sources. 1.3%
   Net summer capability (million kW) 20.5
   CO_2 emitted from generation 79.8
Natural gas utilities, 2005
   Customers (x 1,000) 1,494
   Sales (trillion Btu). 241
   Revenues ($ mil) $2,006
Nuclear plants, 2007 1
*Total CO_2 emitted (million metric tons). 137.2
Energy spending, 2004 ($ mil) $16,370
   per capita $2,846
   Price per million Btu $12.89

Transportation, 2006
Public road & street mileage 127,205
   Urban. 19,244
   Rural 107,961
   Interstate. 1,181
Vehicle miles of travel (millions) 68,834
   per capita 11,791.4
Total motor vehicle registrations 4,957,172
   Automobiles 2,715,297
   Trucks 2,230,390
   Motorcycles 85,464
Licensed drivers .4,139,632
   19 years & under 226,221
Deaths from motor vehicle accidents 1,096
Gasoline consumed (x 1,000 gallons) 3,221,159
   per capita 551.8

Commuting Statistics, 2006
Average commute time (min) 22.9
   Drove to work alone 80.8%
   Carpooled. 10.4%
   Public transit 1.4%
   Walk to work 2.1%
   Work from home 4.1%

Montana　1

State Summary

Capital city . . . . Helena
Governor . . . . Brian Schweitzer
State Capitol
Helena, MT 59620
406-444-3111
Admitted as a state 1889
Area (square miles) 147,042
Population, 2007 (estimate). 957,861
Largest city . . . . Billings
Population, 2006 100,148
Personal income per capita, 2006
(in current dollars) $30,688
Gross domestic product, 2006 ($ mil) $32,322

Leading industries by payroll, 2005
Health care/Social assistance, Retail trade,
Construction

**Leading agricultural commodities
by receipts, 2005**
Cattle and calves, Wheat, Barley, Hay, Sugar
beets

Geography & Environment

Total area (square miles). 147,042
land 145,552
water 1,490
Federally-owned land, 2004 (acres) . . . 27,910,152
percent. 29.9%
Highest point . . . . .Granite Peak
elevation (feet) 12,799
Lowest point . . . . .Kootenai River
elevation (feet) 1,800
General coastline (miles) 0
Tidal shoreline (miles) 0
Cropland, 2003 (x 1,000 acres) 14,527
Forest land, 2003 (x 1,000 acres). 5,402
Capital city . . . . Helena
Population 2000 25,780
Population 2006 27,885
Largest city . . . . Billings
Population 2000 89,847
Population 2006 100,148

Number of cities with over 100,000 population
1990 0
2000 0
2006 1

State park and recreation areas, 2005
Area (x 1,000 acres). 55
Number of visitors (x 1,000) 5,671
Revenues ($1,000) $5,214
percent of operating expenditures. 66.4%

National forest system land, 2007
Acres 1,692,737

Demographics & Population Characteristics

Population
1980 786,690
1990 799,065
2000 902,195
2006 944,632
Male. 472,660
Female 471,972
Living in group quarters, 2006. 25,102
percent of total. 2.7%
2007 (estimate). .957,861
persons per square mile of land 6.6
2008 (projected). 954,653
2010 (projected) 968,598
2020 (projected). 1,022,735
2030 (projected). 1,044,898

**Population of Core-Based Statistical Areas
(formerly Metropolitan Areas), x 1,000**

	CBSA	Non-CBSA
1990	495	304
2000	574	328
2006	615	330

Change in population, 2000-2007
Number 55,666
percent 6.2%
Natural increase (births minus deaths) 23,847
Net internal migration 30,446
Net international migration 2,099

Persons by age, 2006
Under 5 years 57,916
5 to 17 years 159,932
18 years and over 726,784
65 years and over 130,592
85 years and over 19,000
Median age 39.2

Persons by age, 2010 (projected)
Under 5 years 59,714
18 and over 756,286
65 and over 144,961
Median age 40.4

Race, 2006
One Race
White. 858,140
Black or African American 4,094
Asian 5,699
American Indian/Alaska Native. 60,725
Hawaiian Native/Pacific Islander. 527
Two or more races. 15,447

Persons of Hispanic origin, 2006
Total Hispanic or Latino 20,513
Mexican. 12,835
Puerto Rican 2,429
Cuban 929

Persons of Asian origin, 2006
Total Asian 5,525
  Asian Indian. 473
  Chinese 646
  Filipino 1,433
  Japanese 923
  Korean. 1,208
  Vietnamese. 581

Marital status, 2006
Population 15 years & over 769,036
  Never married 206,878
  Married. 424,273
  Separated 10,318
  Widowed. 48,890
  Divorced 88,995

Language spoken at home, 2006
Population 5 years and older. 887,055
  English only 845,089
  Spanish 13,458
  French 2,018
  German. 9,671
  Chinese 303

Households & families, 2006
Households. 372,190
  with persons under 18 years 112,207
  with persons over 65 years. 90,662
  persons per household 2.47
Families. 240,412
  persons per family. 3.05
Married couples. 197,345
Female householder,
  no husband present. 30,098
One-person households 107,392

Nativity, 2006
Number of residents born in state 505,296
  percent of population 53.5%

Immigration & naturalization, 2006
Legal permanent residents admitted 505
Persons naturalized 225
Non-immigrant admissions 34,791

Vital Statistics and Health

Marriages
2004 6,946
2005 6,964
2006 6,757

Divorces
2004 3,516
2005 4,203
2006 3,372

Health risks, 2006
Percent of adults who are:
  Smokers. 18.9%
  Overweight (BMI > 25). 59.3%
  Obese (BMI > 30). 21.2%

Births
2005 11,583
  Birthrate (per 1,000). 12.4
  White. 9,914
  Black 63
  Hispanic 396
  Asian/Pacific Islander 119
  Amer. Indian/Alaska Native 1,487
  Low birth weight (2,500g or less). 6.6%
  Cesarian births 25.8%
  Preterm births 11.4%
  To unmarried mothers. 34.6%
  Twin births (per 1,000). 27.6
  Triplets or higher order (per 100,000). 95.6
2006 (preliminary). 12,506
  rate per 1,000 . . . . .13.2

Deaths
2004
All causes 8,094
  rate per 100,000. . . . . .778.6
Heart disease 1,838
  rate per 100,000. . . . . .173.6
Malignant neoplasms 1,867
  rate per 100,000. . . . . .180.2
Cerebrovascular disease. 484
  rate per 100,000. . . . . .45.7
Chronic lower respiratory disease 578
  rate per 100,000. . . . . .56.1
Diabetes. 237
  rate per 100,000. . . . . .22.6
2005 (preliminary). 8,529
  rate per 100,000. . . . . .798.4
2006 (provisional) 8,488

Infant deaths
2004 52
  rate per 1,000 . . . . .4.5
2005 (provisional) 71
  rate per 1,000 . . . . .6.3

Exercise routines, 2005
None. 22.4%
Moderate or greater. 56.5%
Vigorous 33.1%

Abortions, 2004
Total performed in state. 2,256
  rate per 1,000 women age 15-44. 12
  % obtained by out-of-state residents 8.6%

Physicians, 2005
Total. 2,084
  rate per 100,000 persons 223

Community hospitals, 2005
Number of hospitals 54
Beds (x 1,000). 4.3
Patients admitted (x 1,000) 106
Average daily census (x 1,000) 2.8
Average cost per day $814
Outpatient visits (x 1 mil) 2.9

Disability status of population, 2006
5 to 15 years 6.6%
16 to 64 years 14.6%
65 years and over 42.1%

Education

Educational attainment, 2006
Population over 25 years 630,680
   Less than 9th grade. 3.6%
   High school graduate or more 90.1%
   College graduate or more. 27.4%
   Graduate or professional degree. 8.4%

Public school enrollment, 2005-06
Total 145,416
   Pre-kindergarten through grade 8. 97,575
   Grades 9 through 12 47,562

Graduating public high school seniors, 2004-05
Diplomas (incl. GED and others) 10,335

SAT scores, 2007
Average critical reading score 538
Average writing score 522
Average math score 543
Percent of graduates taking test 28%

Public school teachers, 2006-07 (estimate)
Total (x 1,000) 10.5
   Elementary 7.0
   Secondary 3.6
Average salary $41,225
   Elementary $41,225
   Secondary $41,225

State receipts & expenditures for public schools, 2006-07 (estimate)
Revenue receipts ($ mil) $1,372
Expenditures
Total ($ mil) $1,306
   Per capita $1,327
   Per pupil $10,119

NAEP proficiency scores, 2007

	Reading		Math	
	Basic	Proficient	Basic	Proficient
Grade 4	75.0%	38.5%	87.7%	44.4%
Grade 8	84.5%	38.9%	79.1%	37.6%

Higher education enrollment, fall 2005
Total 4,853
   Full-time men 1,585
   Full-time women 2,215
   Part-time men 360
   Part-time women. 693

Minority enrollment in institutions of higher education, 2005
Black, non-Hispanic 270
Hispanic 791
Asian/Pacific Islander 536
American Indian/Alaska Native. 4,588

Institutions of higher education, 2005-06
Total 23
   Public. 18
   Private 5

Earned degrees conferred, 2004-05
Associate's 1,782
Bachelor's 5,177
Master's 1,122
First-professional. 129
Doctor's 117

Public Libraries, 2006
Number of libraries. 79
Number of outlets 112
Annual visits per capita 4.1
Circulation per capita 6.2

State & local financial support for higher education, FY 2006
Full-time equivalent enrollment (x 1,000) 35.4
Appropriations per FTE $4,409

Social Insurance & Welfare Programs

Social Security benefits & beneficiaries, 2005
Beneficiaries (x 1,000) 169
   Retired & dependents 122
   Survivors. 23
   Disabled & dependents. 25
Annual benefit payments ($ mil) $1,748
   Retired & dependents $1,193
   Survivors $305
   Disabled & dependents. $250
Average monthly benefit
   Retired & dependents $959
   Disabled & dependents. $903
   Widowed $955

Medicare, July 2005
Enrollment (x 1,000) 148
Payments ($ mil) $847

Medicaid, 2004
Beneficiaries (x 1,000). 113
Payments ($ mil) $585

State Children's Health Insurance Program, 2006
Enrollment (x 1,000) 17.3
Expenditures ($ mil) $21.8

Persons without health insurance, 2006
Number (x 1,000) 160
   percent. 17.2%
Number of children (x 1,000) 31
   percent of children 14.6%

Health care expenditures, 2004
Total expenditures. $4,706
   per capita $5,080

Federal and state public aid

State unemployment insurance, 2006
Recipients, first payments (x 1,000) 20
Total payments ($ mil) $63
Average weekly benefit $204
Temporary Assistance for Needy Families, 2006
Recipients (x 1,000) .112.7
Families (x 1,000) 43.7
Supplemental Security Income, 2005
Recipients (x 1,000) .14.8
Payments ($ mil) $69.9
Food Stamp Program, 2006
Avg monthly participants (x 1,000) 81.6
Total benefits ($ mil) $90.0

Housing & Construction

Housing units
Total 2005 (estimate) 428,300
Total 2006 (estimate) 432,023
Seasonal or recreational use, 2006 27,992
Owner-occupied, 2006 260,137
   Median home value $155,500
   Homeowner vacancy rate 1.9%
Renter-occupied, 2006 112,053
   Median rent $571
   Rental vacancy rate 7.9%
Home ownership rate, 2005 . . . . 70.4%
Home ownership rate, 2006 . . . . 69.5%

New privately-owned housing units
Number authorized, 2006 (x 1,000) 4.5
   Value ($ mil) $723.1
Started 2005 (x 1,000, estimate) 2.9
Started 2006 (x 1,000, estimate) 2.8

Existing home sales
2005 (x 1,000) 25.4
2006 (x 1,000) 26.8

Government & Elections

State officials 2008
Governor . . . . Brian Schweitzer
          Democratic, term expires 1/09
Lieutenant Governor . . . . .John Bohlinger
Secretary of State . . . . Brad Johnson
Attorney General . . . . Mike McGrath
Chief Justice . . . . Karla Gray

Governorship
Minimum age 25
Length of term . . . . 4 years
Consecutive terms permitted . . . . . 8 out of 16 yrs
Who succeeds . . . . Lieutenant Governor

Local governments by type, 2002
Total 1,127
   County 54
   Municipal 129
   Township 0
   School District 352
   Special District 592

State legislature
Name . . . . Legislature
Upper chamber . . . . .Senate
   Number of members 50
   Length of term . . . . 4 years
   Party in majority, 2008 . . . . .Democratic
Lower chamber . . . . .House of Representatives
   Number of members 100
   Length of term . . . . 2 years
   Party in majority, 2008 . . . . Republican

Federal representation, 2008 (110th Congress)
Senator . . . . Max Baucus
   Party . . . . .Democratic
   Year term expires 2009
Senator . . . . Jon Tester
   Party . . . . .Democratic
   Year term expires 2013
Representatives, total 1
   Democrats 0
   Republicans 1

Voters in November 2006 election (estimate)
Total 435,025
   Male 220,871
   Female 214,154
   White 413,480
   Black 393
   Hispanic 1,524
   Asian 1,571

Presidential election, 2004
Total Popular Vote 450,445
   Kerry 173,710
   Bush 266,063
Total Electoral Votes 3

Votes cast for US Senators
2004
Total vote (x 1,000) . . . . NA
Leading party . . . . NA
Percent for leading party . . . . NA
2006
Total vote (x 1,000) 407
Leading party . . . . .Democratic
Percent for leading party 49.2%

Votes cast for US Representatives
2004
Total vote (x 1,000) 444
   Democratic 146
   Republican 286
Leading party . . . . Republican
Percent for leading party 64.4%
2006
Total vote (x 1,000) 406
   Democratic 159
   Republican 239
Leading party . . . . Republican
Percent for leading party 58.9%

State government employment, 2006
Full-time equivalent employees 18,933
Payroll ($ mil) $64.2

Local government employment, 2006
Full-time equivalent employees 35,255
Payroll ($ mil) $100.5

Women holding public office, 2008
US Congress 0
Statewide elected office..................... 1
State legislature 38

Black public officials, 2002
Total....................................... 0
  US and state legislatures 0
  City/county/regional offices 0
  Judicial/law enforcement.................. 0
  Education/school boards 0

Hispanic public officials, 2006
Total....................................... 1
  State executives & legislators 0
  City/county/regional offices 0
  Judicial/law enforcement.................. 1
  Education/school boards 0

Governmental Finance

State government revenues, 2006
Total revenue (x $1,000)............$6,130,467
  per capita $6,474.97
General revenue (x $1,000) $4,935,220
  Intergovernmental 1,825,693
  Taxes 2,126,324
    general sales........................... 0
    individual income tax 768,911
    corporate income tax 153,675
  Current charges.................... 476,860
  Miscellaneous 506,343

State government expenditure, 2006
Total expenditure (x $1,000) $5,194,561
  per capita $5,486.47
General expenditure (x $1,000) $4,583,636
  per capita, total.................... $4,841.21
  Education 1,607.32
  Public welfare 900.26
  Health 306.03
  Hospitals....................... 42.82
  Highways 616.01
  Police protection................ 42.47
  Corrections 151.53
  Natural resources 215.99
  Parks & recreation 16.15
  Governmental administration 298.78
  Interest on general debt........... 165.03

State debt & cash, 2006 ($ per capita)
Debt...............................$4,598.43
Cash/security holdings.............$15,249.00

Federal government grants to state & local government, 2005 (x $1,000)
Total.............................$2,139,765
by Federal agency
  Defense 47,326
  Education 213,571
  Energy............................8,415
  Environmental Protection Agency 44,436
  Health & Human Services. 883,416
  Homeland Security.................10,731
  Housing & Urban Development...... 106,990
  Justice 34,289
  Labor 32,473
  Transportation 404,448
  Veterans Affairs.....................3,539

Crime & Law Enforcement

Crime, 2006 (rates per 100,000 residents)
Property crimes 25,387
  Burglary 2,935
  Larceny 20,704
  Motor vehicle theft 1,748
  Property crime rate................2,687.5
Violent crimes......................... 2,397
  Murder 17
  Forcible rape....................... 269
  Robbery 164
  Aggravated assault 1,947
  Violent crime rate 253.7
Hate crimes........................... 29

Fraud and identity theft, 2006
Fraud complaints......................1,289
  rate per 100,000 residents 136.5
Identity theft complaints 434
  rate per 100,000 residents 45.9

Law enforcement agencies, 2006
Total agencies........................... 109
Total employees 2,753
  Officers 1,679
  Civilians 1,074

Prisoners, probation, and parole, 2006
Total prisoners.........................3,572
  percent change, 12/31/05 to 12/31/06 .... 1.1%
  in private facilities 26.9%
  in local jails 19.1%
Sentenced to more than one year 3,547
  rate per 100,000 residents 374
Adults on probation 8,770
Adults on parole........................ 844

Prisoner demographics, June 30, 2005 (rate per 100,000 residents)
Male...................................... 926
Female 129
White.................................. 433
Black................................... 3,569
Hispanic 846

Arrests, 2006
Total . . . . NA
  Persons under 18 years of age . . . . NA

Persons under sentence of death, 1/1/07
Total 2
  White 2
  Black 0
  Hispanic 0

State's highest court
Name . . . . .Supreme Court
Number of members 7
Length of term . . . . 8 years
Intermediate appeals court? . . . . no

Labor & Income

Civilian labor force, 2006 (x 1,000)
Total 505
  Men 265
  Women 240
  Persons 16-19 years 29
  White 475
  Black . . . . NA
  Hispanic 10

Civilian labor force as a percent of civilian non-institutional population, 2006
Total 67.2%
  Men 71.5
  Women 63.1
  Persons 16-19 years 53.1
  White 67.6
  Black . . . . NA
  Hispanic 76.4

Employment, 2006 (x 1,000)
Total 487
  Men 255
  Women 232
  Persons 16-19 years 26
  White 460
  Black . . . . NA
  Hispanic 9

Unemployment rate, 2006
Total 3.6%
  Men 3.7
  Women 3.5
  Persons 16-19 years 10.5
  White 3.2
  Black . . . . NA
  Hispanic 5.1

Full-time/part-time labor force, 2003 (x 1,000)
Full-time labor force, employed 354
Part-time labor force, employed 99
Unemployed, looking for
  Full-time work 18
  Part-time work 5
Mean duration of unemployment (weeks) 15.1
  Median 8.3

Labor unions, 2006
Membership (x 1,000) 48
  percent of employed 12.2%

Experienced civilian labor force by private industry, 2006
Total 346,275
  Natural resources & mining 11,726
  Construction 30,136
  Manufacturing 20,168
  Trade, transportation & utilities 86,444
  Information 7,736
  Finance 22,008
  Professional & business 38,016
  Education & health 57,184
  Leisure & hospitality 56,759
  Other 15,833

Experienced civilian labor force by occupation, May 2006
Management 19,210
Business & financial 14,290
Legal 2,970
Sales 43,990
Office & admin. support 72,280
Computers & math 6,000
Architecture & engineering 6,210
Arts & entertainment 5,980
Education 27,460
Social services 7,240
Health care practitioner & technical 21,710
Health care support 10,960
Maintenance & repair 19,050
Construction 29,210
Transportation & moving 29,400
Production 18,450
Farming, fishing & forestry 2,560

Hours and earnings of production workers on manufacturing payrolls, 2006
Average weekly hours 40.0
Average hourly earnings $15.90
Average weekly earnings $636.00

Income and poverty, 2006
Median household income $40,627
Personal income, per capita (current $) . . . $30,688
  in constant (2000) dollars $26,789
Persons below poverty level 13.6%

Average annual pay
2006 . . . . $30,596
  increase from 2005 . . . . 5.0%

Federal individual income tax returns, 2005
Returns filed 448,050
Adjusted gross income ($1,000) $18,315,335
Total tax liability ($1,000) $2,063,735

Charitable contributions, 2004
Number of contributions 111.8
Total amount ($ mil) $348.8

Economy, Business, Industry & Agriculture

Fortune 500 companies, 2007 0
Bankruptcy cases filed, FY 2007 1,934

Patents and trademarks issued, 2007
Patents 123
Trademarks 198

Business firm ownership, 2002
Women-owned 24,519
　Sales ($ mil) $2,139
Black-owned 220
　Sales ($ mil) $12
Hispanic-owned 964
　Sales ($ mil) $99
Asian-owned 511
　Sales ($ mil) $100
Amer. Indian/Alaska Native-owned 1,990
　Sales ($ mil) $215
Hawaiian/Pacific Islander-owned 40
　Sales ($ mil) $2

Gross domestic product, 2006 ($ mil)
Total gross domestic product $32,322
　Agriculture, forestry, fishing and
　　hunting 1,281
　Mining 1,838
　Utilities 1,181
　Construction 2,160
　Manufacturing, durable goods 907
　Manufacturing, non-durable goods 566
　Wholesale trade 1,729
　Retail trade 2,296
　Transportation & warehousing 1,364
　Information 907
　Finance & insurance 1,601
　Real estate, rental & leasing 3,800
　Professional and technical services 1,511
　Educational services 137
　Health care and social assistance 2,923
　Accommodation/food services 1,034
　Other services, except government 725
　Government 5,166

Establishments, payroll, employees & receipts, by major industry group, 2005
Total 35,736
　Annual payroll ($1,000) $8,950,520
　Paid employees 326,887
Forestry, fishing & agriculture 405
　Annual payroll ($1,000) $50,741
　Paid employees 1,602
Mining 294
　Annual payroll ($1,000) $325,011
　Paid employees 5,552
　Receipts, 2002 ($1,000) $1,226,555

Utilities 217
　Annual payroll ($1,000) $170,688
　Paid employees 2,645
　Receipts, 2002 ($1,000) . . . . NA
Construction 5,367
　Annual payroll ($1,000) $876,686
　Paid employees 23,795
　Receipts, 2002 ($1,000) $3,372,837
Manufacturing 1,283
　Annual payroll ($1,000) $739,644
　Paid employees 19,470
　Receipts, 2002 ($1,000) $4,987,577
Wholesale trade 1,491
　Annual payroll ($1,000) $488,131
　Paid employees 13,931
　Receipts, 2002 ($1,000) $7,223,420
Retail trade 5,192
　Annual payroll ($1,000) $1,165,388
　Paid employees 56,287
　Receipts, 2002 ($1,000) $10,122,625
Transportation & warehousing 1,237
　Annual payroll ($1,000) $311,031
　Paid employees 10,647
　Receipts, 2002 ($1,000) $996,647
Information 613
　Annual payroll ($1,000) $295,958
　Paid employees 7,915
　Receipts, 2002 ($1,000) . . . . NA
Finance & insurance 1,937
　Annual payroll ($1,000) $618,820
　Paid employees 16,096
　Receipts, 2002 ($1,000) . . . . NA
Professional, scientific & technical 3,274
　Annual payroll ($1,000) $727,538
　Paid employees 21,555
　Receipts, 2002 ($1,000) $1,249,057
Education 278
　Annual payroll ($1,000) $96,852
　Paid employees 5,342
　Receipts, 2002 ($1,000) $39,674
Health care & social assistance 3,216
　Annual payroll ($1,000) $1,665,581
　Paid employees 54,114
　Receipts, 2002 ($1,000) $3,432,698
Arts and entertainment 1,034
　Annual payroll ($1,000) $135,631
　Paid employees 9,723
　Receipts, 2002 ($1,000) $486,116
Real estate 1,727
　Annual payroll ($1,000) $149,727
　Paid employees 5,933
　Receipts, 2002 ($1,000) $520,932
Accommodation & food service 3,375
　Annual payroll ($1,000) $474,679
　Paid employees 42,447
　Receipts, 2002 ($1,000) $1,537,986

8 Montana

Exports, 2006

Value of exported goods ($ mil) $887
  Manufactured $685
  Non-manufactured. $176

Foreign direct investment in US affiliates, 2004

Property, plants & equipment ($ mil) $2,233
Employment (x 1,000). .6.4

Agriculture, 2006

Number of farms 28,100
Farm acreage (x 1,000) 60,100
  Acres per farm 2,139
Farm marketings and income ($ mil)
Total. $2,349.2
  Crops $1,070.0
  Livestock. $1,279.2
Net farm income $256.8

Principal commodities, in order by
  marketing receipts, 2005
  Cattle and calves, Wheat, Barley, Hay, Sugar
    beets

Federal economic activity in state

Expenditures, 2005 ($ mil)
  Total. $7,814
    Per capita $8,359.11
  Defense $663
  Non-defense $7,151
Defense department, 2006 ($ mil)
  Payroll. $407
  Contract awards $247
  Grants $32
Homeland security grants ($1,000)
  2006 . . . .$7,930
  2007 . . . . $6,686

FDIC-insured financial institutions, 2005

Number 83
Assets ($ billion) $17.1
Deposits ($ billion) $13.2

Fishing, 2006

Catch (x 1,000 lbs) . . . . NA
Value ($1,000). . . . . NA

Mining, 2006 ($ mil)

Total non-fuel mineral production $1,040
Percent of U.S. 1.61%

Communication, Energy & Transportation

Communication

Households with computers, 2003 . . . . 59.5%
Households with internet access, 2003 . . . . 50.4%
High-speed internet providers 38
Total high-speed internet lines. 264,121
  Residential 146,276
  Business. 117,845
Wireless phone customers, 12/2006 619,620

FCC-licensed stations (as of January 1, 2008)

TV stations 26
FM radio stations. 123
AM radio stations 52

Energy

Energy consumption, 2004
  Total (trillion Btu). 403
  Per capita (million Btu) 434.9
By source of production (trillion Btu)
  Coal 196
  Natural gas 67
  Petroleum 186
  Nuclear electric power 0
  Hydroelectric power. 89
By end-use sector (trillion Btu)
  Residential 74
  Commercial 66
  Industrial 153
  Transportation 110
Electric energy, 2005
  Primary source of electricity. . . . . Coal
  Net generation (billion kWh) 27.9
    percent from renewable sources. 34.5%
  Net summer capability (million kW) 5.3
  CO_2 emitted from generation 19.5
Natural gas utilities, 2005
  Customers (x 1,000) 273
  Sales (trillion Btu). 57
  Revenues ($ mil) $325
Nuclear plants, 2007 0
Total CO_2 emitted (million metric tons). 32.7
Energy spending, 2004 ($ mil) $3,182
  per capita $3,435
  Price per million Btu $12.12

Transportation, 2006

Public road & street mileage 73,148
  Urban. 2,973
  Rural 70,175
  Interstate. 1,192
Vehicle miles of travel (millions) 11,265
  per capita 11,898.0
Total motor vehicle registrations. 1,066,562
  Automobiles. 447,446
  Trucks 616,613
  Motorcycles 85,873
Licensed drivers 723,976
  19 years & under 46,810
Deaths from motor vehicle accidents 263
Gasoline consumed (x 1,000 gallons) 498,343
  per capita 526.3

Commuting Statistics, 2006

Average commute time (min) 17.6
  Drove to work alone 72.7%
  Carpooled. 12.0%
  Public transit 0.9%
  Walk to work 5.3%
  Work from home 6.7%

State Summary

Capital city . . . . Lincoln
Governor . . . . Dave Heineman
PO Box 94848
Lincoln, NE 68509
402-471-2244
Admitted as a state 1867
Area (square miles) 77,354
Population, 2007 (estimate). 1,774,571
Largest city . . . . .Omaha
Population, 2006 419,545
Personal income per capita, 2006
(in current dollars) $34,397
Gross domestic product, 2006 ($ mil) $75,700

Leading industries by payroll, 2005

Manufacturing, Health care/Social assistance,
Finance & Insurance

**Leading agricultural commodities
by receipts, 2005**

Cattle and calves, Corn, Soybeans, Hogs, Wheat

Geography & Environment

Total area (square miles). 77,354
land 76,872
water 481
Federally-owned land, 2004 (acres) 665,481
percent. 1.4%
Highest point . . . . .Panorama Point
elevation (feet) 5,424
Lowest point . . . Missouri River (Richardson Co.)
elevation (feet) 840
General coastline (miles) 0
Tidal shoreline (miles) 0
Cropland, 2003 (x 1,000 acres) 19,552
Forest land, 2003 (x 1,000 acres). 812
Capital city . . . . Lincoln
Population 2000 225,581
Population 2006 241,167
Largest city . . . . .Omaha
Population 2000 390,007
Population 2006 419,545

Number of cities with over 100,000 population

1990 2
2000 2
2006 2

State park and recreation areas, 2005

Area (x 1,000 acres) 135
Number of visitors (x 1,000) 9,998
Revenues ($1,000) $16,044
percent of operating expenditures 86.8%

National forest system land, 2007

Acres 352,289

Demographics & Population Characteristics

Population

1980 1,569,825
1990 1,578,385
2000 1,711,265
2006 1,768,331
Male. 876,754
Female 891,577
Living in group quarters, 2006 52,087
percent of total. 2.9%
2007 (estimate). 1,774,571
persons per square mile of land 23.1
2008 (projected) 1,759,829
2010 (projected) 1,768,997
2020 (projected). 1,802,678
2030 (projected). 1,820,247

**Population of Core-Based Statistical Areas
(formerly Metropolitan Areas), x 1,000**

	CBSA	Non-CBSA
1990	1,198	381
2000	1,339	373
2006	1,415	354

Change in population, 2000-2007

Number 63,306
percent. 3.7%
Natural increase (births minus deaths) 77,995
Net internal migration . . . . -36,717
Net international migration 27,398

Persons by age, 2006

Under 5 years 127,665
5 to 17 years 317,368
18 years and over 1,323,298
65 years and over 234,655
85 years and over 39,128
Median age 36.0

Persons by age, 2010 (projected)

Under 5 years 127,806
18 and over 1,322,741
65 and over 243,313
Median age 36.7

Race, 2006

One Race

White. 1,622,682
Black or African American 77,636
Asian 29,253
American Indian/Alaska Native. 17,103
Hawaiian Native/Pacific Islander. 1,225
Two or more races. 20,432

Persons of Hispanic origin, 2006

Total Hispanic or Latino 130,230
Mexican. 102,180
Puerto Rican 2,645
Cuban 625

Persons of Asian origin, 2006

Total Asian 29,815
  Asian Indian..........................5,558
  Chinese 6,465
  Filipino 1,667
  Japanese 1,626
  Korean..............................1,917
  Vietnamese..........................9,163

Marital status, 2006

Population 15 years & over 1,400,725
  Never married 384,010
  Married........................ 790,764
  Separated 18,404
  Widowed........................ 89,291
  Divorced 136,660

Language spoken at home, 2006

Population 5 years and older......... 1,640,024
  English only 1,491,321
  Spanish 98,211
  French 4,576
  German.......................... 6,614
  Chinese 5,553

Households & families, 2006

Households......................... 700,888
  with persons under 18 years 235,508
  with persons over 65 years........... 158,988
  persons per household 2.45
Families........................... 462,408
  persons per family.....................3.02
Married couples......................371,052
Female householder,
  no husband present.................. 65,408
One-person households 198,674

Nativity, 2006

Number of residents born in state 1,158,794
  percent of population 65.5%

Immigration & naturalization, 2006

Legal permanent residents admitted.......3,795
Persons naturalized 1,797
Non-immigrant admissions 25,483

Vital Statistics and Health

Marriages

2004 12,489
2005 12,256
2006 12,037

Divorces

2004 5,962
2005 5,864
2006 6,173

Health risks, 2006

Percent of adults who are:
  Smokers........................ 18.7%
  Overweight (BMI > 25).............. 63.9%
  Obese (BMI > 30)..................... 26.9%

Births

2005 .... .26,145
  Birthrate (per 1,000)................... .14.9
  White.......................... 23,233
  Black 1,718
  Hispanic 3,854
  Asian/Pacific Islander 697
  Amer. Indian/Alaska Native 497
  Low birth weight (2,500g or less)....... 7.0%
  Cesarian births 28.6%
  Preterm births 12.2%
  To unmarried mothers............... 30.9%
  Twin births (per 1,000) 32.1
  Triplets or higher order (per 100,000)....269.2
2006 (preliminary).................. 26,733
  rate per 1,000 ....15.1

Deaths

2004
All causes 14,657
  rate per 100,000......................746.9
Heart disease 3,738
  rate per 100,000......................185.3
Malignant neoplasms 3,270
  rate per 100,000......................173.6
Cerebrovascular disease............ 978
  rate per 100,000......................48.0
Chronic lower respiratory disease 815
  rate per 100,000......................42.0
Diabetes........................... 395
  rate per 100,000......................20.4
2005 (preliminary)............... 14,964
  rate per 100,000......................749.5
2006 (provisional) 14,952

Infant deaths

2004 173
  rate per 1,000 ....6.6
2005 (provisional) 149
  rate per 1,000 ....5.7

Exercise routines, 2005

None................................23.8%
Moderate or greater..................... 47.3%
Vigorous 24.7%

Abortions, 2004

Total performed in state................. 3,584
  rate per 1,000 women age 15-44.......... 10
  % obtained by out-of-state residents 14.3%

Physicians, 2005

Total.................................. 4,209
  rate per 100,000 persons 239

Community hospitals, 2005

Number of hospitals 87
Beds (x 1,000)...........................7.6
Patients admitted (x 1,000) 214
Average daily census (x 1,000) 4.8
Average cost per day $1,066
Outpatient visits (x 1 mil) 3.9

Disability status of population, 2006
5 to 15 years 6.0%
16 to 64 years 10.7%
65 years and over 37.3%

Education

Educational attainment, 2006
Population over 25 years 1,135,868
    Less than 9th grade. 4.2%
    High school graduate or more 89.5%
    College graduate or more. 26.9%
    Graduate or professional degree. 8.4%

Public school enrollment, 2005-06
Total. 286,646
    Pre-kindergarten through grade 8. . . . 195,055
    Grades 9 through 12 91,591

Graduating public high school seniors, 2004-05
Diplomas (incl. GED and others) 20,089

SAT scores, 2007
Average critical reading score 579
Average writing score 562
Average math score 585
Percent of graduates taking test 6%

Public school teachers, 2006-07 (estimate)
Total (x 1,000) 21.3
    Elementary 13.6
    Secondary 7.7
Average salary $42,044
    Elementary $42,044
    Secondary $42,044

State receipts & expenditures for public schools, 2006-07 (estimate)
Revenue receipts ($ mil) $2,620
Expenditures
Total ($ mil) $2,577
    Per capita $1,349
    Per pupil $9,028

NAEP proficiency scores, 2007

	Reading		Math	
	Basic	Proficient	Basic	Proficient
Grade 4	70.8%	34.6%	80.1%	37.9%
Grade 8	78.8%	35.0%	74.3%	34.6%

Higher education enrollment, fall 2005
Total. 28,055
    Full-time men 9,449
    Full-time women 12,828
    Part-time men 2,016
    Part-time women. 3,762

Minority enrollment in institutions of higher education, 2005
Black, non-Hispanic 5,094
Hispanic 4,224
Asian/Pacific Islander 2,827
American Indian/Alaska Native. 908

Institutions of higher education, 2005-06
Total. 39
    Public. 15
    Private 24

Earned degrees conferred, 2004-05
Associate's. 4,630
Bachelor's 11,999
Master's 3,936
First-professional. 864
Doctor's. 492

Public Libraries, 2006
Number of libraries. 270
Number of outlets 294
Annual visits per capita 6.5
Circulation per capita. 10.1

State & local financial support for higher education, FY 2006
Full-time equivalent enrollment (x 1,000) 72.6
Appropriations per FTE. $6,999

Social Insurance & Welfare Programs

Social Security benefits & beneficiaries, 2005
Beneficiaries (x 1,000) 294
    Retired & dependents. 212
    Survivors. 39
    Disabled & dependents. 43
Annual benefit payments ($ mil) $3,120
    Retired & dependents. $2,153
    Survivors. $549
    Disabled & dependents. $418
Average monthly benefit
    Retired & dependents. $985
    Disabled & dependents. $889
    Widowed. $994

Medicare, July 2005
Enrollment (x 1,000). 261
Payments ($ mil) $1,716

Medicaid, 2004
Beneficiaries (x 1,000). 1,513
Payments ($ mil) $7,388

State Children's Health Insurance Program, 2006
Enrollment (x 1,000). 45.0
Expenditures ($ mil) $29.9

Persons without health insurance, 2006
Number (x 1,000). 217
    percent. 12.3%
Number of children (x 1,000) 45
    percent of children 10.1%

Health care expenditures, 2004
Total expenditures. $9,782
    per capita $5,599

Federal and state public aid

State unemployment insurance, 2006
Recipients, first payments (x 1,000) 33
Total payments ($ mil) $93
Average weekly benefit $231
Temporary Assistance for Needy Families, 2006
Recipients (x 1,000) 283.7
Families (x 1,000) 118.1
Supplemental Security Income, 2005
Recipients (x 1,000) .22.3
Payments ($ mil) $103.2
Food Stamp Program, 2006
Avg monthly participants (x 1,000) 119.7
Total benefits ($ mil) $124.3

Housing & Construction

Housing units
Total 2005 (estimate) 767,070
Total 2006 (estimate) 774,843
Seasonal or recreational use, 2006 14,506
Owner-occupied, 2006 475,899
    Median home value $119,200
    Homeowner vacancy rate 2.6%
Renter-occupied, 2006 224,989
    Median rent $593
    Rental vacancy rate 10.2%
Home ownership rate, 2005 . . . . 70.2%
Home ownership rate, 2006 . . . . 67.6%

New privately-owned housing units
Number authorized, 2006 (x 1,000) 8.2
    Value ($ mil) $1,064.9
Started 2005 (x 1,000, estimate) 10.0
Started 2006 (x 1,000, estimate) 9.7

Existing home sales
2005 (x 1,000) 41.2
2006 (x 1,000) 38.7

Government & Elections

State officials 2008
Governor . . . . Dave Heineman
    Republican, term expires 1/11
Lieutenant Governor . . . . Rick Sheehy
Secretary of State . . . . John Gale
Attorney General . . . . Jon Bruning
Chief Justice . . . . Michael Heavican

Governorship
Minimum age 30
Length of term . . . . 4 years
Consecutive terms permitted 2
Who succeeds . . . . Lieutenant Governor

Local governments by type, 2002
Total 2,791
    County 93
    Municipal 531
    Township 446
    School District 575
    Special District 1,146

State legislature
Name . . . . Unicameral Legislature
Upper chamber . . . . NA
    Number of members 49
    Length of term . . . . 4 year
    Party in majority, 2008 . . . . Nonpartisan
Lower chamber . . . . NA
    Number of members . . . . NA
    Length of term . . . . NA
    Party in majority, 2008 . . . . Nonpartisan

Federal representation, 2008 (110th Congress)
Senator . . . . .Charles Hagel
    Party . . . . Republican
    Year term expires 2009
Senator . . . . Benjamin Nelson
    Party . . . . Democratic
    Year term expires 2013
Representatives, total 3
    Democrats 0
    Republicans 3

Voters in November 2006 election (estimate)
Total 634,194
    Male 295,008
    Female 339,186
    White 614,024
    Black 12,381
    Hispanic 6,243
    Asian . . . . NA

Presidential election, 2004
Total Popular Vote 778,186
    Kerry 254,328
    Bush 512,814
Total Electoral Votes 5

Votes cast for US Senators
2004
Total vote (x 1,000) . . . . NA
Leading party . . . . NA
Percent for leading party . . . . NA
2006
Total vote (x 1,000) 592
Leading party . . . . .Democratic
Percent for leading party 63.9%

Votes cast for US Representatives
2004
Total vote (x 1,000) 765
    Democratic 231
    Republican 515
Leading party . . . . Republican
Percent for leading party 67.3%
2006
Total vote (x 1,000) 596
    Democratic 262
    Republican 334
Leading party . . . . Republican
Percent for leading party 56.1%

State government employment, 2006
Full-time equivalent employees 32,904
Payroll ($ mil) $101.8

Local government employment, 2006
Full-time equivalent employees 84,592
Payroll ($ mil) $285.9

Women holding public office, 2008
US Congress 0
Statewide elected office...................... 1
State legislature 9

Black public officials, 2002
Total....................................... 9
  US and state legislatures 1
  City/county/regional offices 5
  Judicial/law enforcement.................. 0
  Education/school boards.................. 3

Hispanic public officials, 2006
Total....................................... 3
  State executives & legislators 1
  City/county/regional offices 1
  Judicial/law enforcement.................. 0
  Education/school boards.................. 1

Governmental Finance

State government revenues, 2006
Total revenue (x $1,000) $9,103,340
  per capita $5,161.31
General revenue (x $1,000) $8,045,282
  Intergovernmental 2,472,030
  Taxes 3,961,093
    general sales....................1,409,015
    individual income tax 1,545,024
    corporate income tax............. 262,296
  Current charges.................... 769,908
  Miscellaneous 842,251

State government expenditure, 2006
Total expenditure (x $1,000) $7,702,325
  per capita $4,366.98
General expenditure (x $1,000) $7,357,894
  per capita, total. *$4,171.70*
    Education 1,456.47
    Public welfare 1,117.40
    Health 239.98
    Hospitals....................... 124.59
    Highways 365.00
    Police protection....................43.63
    Corrections 112.74
    Natural resources 89.70
    Parks & recreation 16.66
    Governmental administration...... 104.09
    Interest on general debt..............45.33

State debt & cash, 2006 ($ per capita)
Debt $1,045.69
Cash/security holdings...............$6,788.04

Federal government grants to state & local government, 2005 (x $1,000)
Total............................$2,595,784
by Federal agency
  Defense 23,349
  Education 220,723
  Energy...........................6,195
  Environmental Protection Agency 31,951
  Health & Human Services. 1,428,059
  Homeland Security...................19,512
  Housing & Urban Development...... 146,764
  Justice 43,590
  Labor 34,888
  Transportation 293,236
  Veterans Affairs.................. 24,423

Crime & Law Enforcement

Crime, 2006 (rates per 100,000 residents)
Property crimes 59,075
  Burglary 9,452
  Larceny 44,585
  Motor vehicle theft 5,038
  Property crime rate..................3,340.7
Violent crimes. 4,983
  Murder 50
  Forcible rape........................ 548
  Robbery...........................1,129
  Aggravated assault 3,256
  Violent crime rate 281.8
Hate crimes............................. 62

Fraud and identity theft, 2006
Fraud complaints.....................1,968
  rate per 100,000 residents 111.3
Identity theft complaints 868
  rate per 100,000 residents 49.1

Law enforcement agencies, 2006
Total agencies........................ 156
Total employees 4,774
  Officers 3,453
  Civilians 1,321

Prisoners, probation, and parole, 2006
Total prisoners........................ 4,407
  percent change, 12/31/05 to 12/31/06 ....-1.1%
  in private facilities 0%
  in local jails 0%
Sentenced to more than one year 4,204
  rate per 100,000 residents 237
Adults on probation 18,731
Adults on parole........................ 797

Prisoner demographics, June 30, 2005 (rate per 100,000 residents)
Male.................................... 756
Female 93
White................................... 290
Black....................................2,418
Hispanic 739

Arrests, 2006

Total................................. 88,602
   Persons under 18 years of age..........14,967

Persons under sentence of death, 1/1/07

Total..................................... 9
   White.................................... 5
   Black 1
   Hispanic 3

State's highest court

Name ....Supreme Court
Number of members....................... 7
Length of term........................ 6 years
Intermediate appeals court? ....yes

Labor & Income

Civilian labor force, 2006 (x 1,000)

Total.................................... 982
   Men 524
   Women 458
   Persons 16-19 years...................... 59
   White.................................. 906
   Black 34
   Hispanic 69

Civilian labor force as a percent of civilian non-institutional population, 2006

Total...................................72.5%
   Men 79.2
   Women 66.1
   Persons 16-19 years.....................58.3
   White..................................72.8
   Black 63.8
   Hispanic 70.6

Employment, 2006 (x 1,000)

Total.................................... 951
   Men 506
   Women 446
   Persons 16-19 years...................... 53
   White.................................. 882
   Black 31
   Hispanic 66

Unemployment rate, 2006

Total.................................... 3.1%
   Men 3.5
   Women 2.7
   Persons 16-19 years.....................9.5
   White...................................2.7
   Black 9.2
   Hispanic 4.5

Full-time/part-time labor force, 2003 (x 1,000)

Full-time labor force, employed 750
Part-time labor force, employed........... 187
Unemployed, looking for
   Full-time work.......................... 31
   Part-time work.......................... 8
Mean duration of unemployment (weeks)......16.4
   Median 8.1

Labor unions, 2006

Membership (x 1,000)................... 66
   percent of employed 7.9%

Experienced civilian labor force by private industry, 2006

Total............................... $748,399
   Natural resources & mining 11,852
   Construction 47,201
   Manufacturing..................... 101,484
   Trade, transportation & utilities 188,043
   Information 19,502
   Finance 62,814
   Professional & business 101,326
   Education & health 110,267
   Leisure & hospitality................. 80,553
   Other 25,359

Experienced civilian labor force by occupation, May 2006

Management......................... 29,590
Business & financial 38,110
Legal................................. 4,470
Sales.................................95,210
Office & admin. support............... 159,330
Computers & math 21,240
Architecture & engineering............10,870
Arts & entertainment 10,900
Education 53,660
Social services 12,960
Health care practitioner & technical..... 48,680
Health care support 25,090
Maintenance & repair................. 41,850
Construction 43,490
Transportation & moving 79,450
Production 80,910
Farming, fishing & forestry.............. 2,860

Hours and earnings of production workers on manufacturing payrolls, 2006

Average weekly hours....................40.9
Average hourly earnings $15.04
Average weekly earnings $615.14

Income and poverty, 2006

Median household income............. $45,474
Personal income, per capita (current $)... $34,397
   in constant (2000) dollars $30,026
Persons below poverty level.............. 11.5%

Average annual pay

2006 ....$33,814
   increase from 2005 .... 4.3%

Federal individual income tax returns, 2005

Returns filed......................... 816,053
Adjusted gross income ($1,000) $37,830,701
Total tax liability ($1,000) $4,433,778

Charitable contributions, 2004

Number of contributions 218.6
Total amount ($ mil)................. $848.8

Economy, Business, Industry & Agriculture

Fortune 500 companies, 2007 5
Bankruptcy cases filed, FY 2007 5,204

Patents and trademarks issued, 2007
Patents 245
Trademarks 429

Business firm ownership, 2002
Women-owned 38,679
   Sales ($ mil) $5,765
Black-owned 2,091
   Sales ($ mil) $141
Hispanic-owned 1,966
   Sales ($ mil) $434
Asian-owned 1,456
   Sales ($ mil) $686
Amer. Indian/Alaska Native-owned 425
   Sales ($ mil) $47
Hawaiian/Pacific Islander-owned 9
   Sales ($ mil) . . . . NA

Gross domestic product, 2006 ($ mil)
Total gross domestic product $75,700
   Agriculture, forestry, fishing and
      hunting 3,496
   Mining 113
   Utilities 1,425
   Construction 3,270
   Manufacturing, durable goods 4,857
   Manufacturing, non-durable goods 4,065
   Wholesale trade 4,458
   Retail trade 4,775
   Transportation & warehousing 5,635
   Information 2,323
   Finance & insurance 7,514
   Real estate, rental & leasing 7,102
   Professional and technical services 3,484
   Educational services 624
   Health care and social assistance 5,461
   Accommodation/food services 1,502
   Other services, except government 1,665
   Government 10,427

Establishments, payroll, employees & receipts, by major industry group, 2005

Total 51,440
   Annual payroll ($1,000) $24,180,753
   Paid employees 773,082
Forestry, fishing & agriculture 162
   Annual payroll ($1,000) . . . . NA
   Paid employees . . . . NA
Mining 128
   Annual payroll ($1,000) $37,616
   Paid employees 943
   Receipts, 2002 ($1,000) $163,244

Utilities 128
   Annual payroll ($1,000) $93,103
   Paid employees 1,172
   Receipts, 2002 ($1,000) . . . . NA
Construction 6,078
   Annual payroll ($1,000) $1,576,751
   Paid employees 43,088
   Receipts, 2002 ($1,000) $6,700,924
Manufacturing 1,985
   Annual payroll ($1,000) $3,662,922
   Paid employees 102,367
   Receipts, 2002 ($1,000) $30,610,970
Wholesale trade 2,905
   Annual payroll ($1,000) $1,625,672
   Paid employees .37,932
   Receipts, 2002 ($1,000) $26,155,770
Retail trade 8,080
   Annual payroll ($1,000) $2,134,208
   Paid employees .107,366
   Receipts, 2002 ($1,000) $20,249,200
Transportation & warehousing 2,330
   Annual payroll ($1,000) $1,102,031
   Paid employees 30,150
   Receipts, 2002 ($1,000) $4,452,719
Information 899
   Annual payroll ($1,000) $812,644
   Paid employees .19,818
   Receipts, 2002 ($1,000) . . . . .NA
Finance & insurance 3,993
   Annual payroll ($1,000) $2,915,960
   Paid employees 59,858
   Receipts, 2002 ($1,000) . . . . .NA
Professional, scientific & technical 4,139
   Annual payroll ($1,000) $1,997,798
   Paid employees 44,813
   Receipts, 2002 ($1,000) $3,020,944
Education 483
   Annual payroll ($1,000) $378,634
   Paid employees .16,136
   Receipts, 2002 ($1,000) $74,932
Health care & social assistance 4,634
   Annual payroll ($1,000) $3,633,981
   Paid employees .109,104
   Receipts, 2002 ($1,000) $7,492,496
Arts and entertainment 839
   Annual payroll ($1,000) $149,189
   Paid employees 10,528
   Receipts, 2002 ($1,000) $468,527
Real estate 1,971
   Annual payroll ($1,000) $287,835
   Paid employees 10,049
   Receipts, 2002 ($1,000) $1,194,332
Accommodation & food service 4,108
   Annual payroll ($1,000) $696,713
   Paid employees 66,768
   Receipts, 2002 ($1,000) $2,088,710

Exports, 2006

Value of exported goods ($ mil) $3,625
  Manufactured $2,903
  Non-manufactured.................... $584

Foreign direct investment in US affiliates, 2004

Property, plants & equipment ($ mil) $2,021
Employment (x 1,000)....................20.0

Agriculture, 2006

Number of farms 47,600
Farm acreage (x 1,000) 45,700
  Acres per farm........................ 960
Farm marketings and income ($ mil)
Total...............................$12,042.3
  Crops............................$4,359.0
  Livestock........................$7,683.4
Net farm income $2,297.0

Principal commodities, in order by marketing receipts, 2005

Cattle and calves, Corn, Soybeans, Hogs, Wheat

Federal economic activity in state

Expenditures, 2005 ($ mil)
  Total........................... $12,785
    Per capita $7,272.04
  Defense $1,351
  Non-defense........................$11,434
Defense department, 2006 ($ mil)
  Payroll............................. $961
  Contract awards $718
  Grants $11
Homeland security grants ($1,000)
  2006................................$21,746
  2007................................$7,226

FDIC-insured financial institutions, 2005

Number 254
Assets ($ billion) $39.6
Deposits ($ billion) $30.4

Fishing, 2006

Catch (x 1,000 lbs)...................... NA
Value ($1,000)......................... NA

Mining, 2006 ($ mil)

Total non-fuel mineral production $112
Percent of U.S. 0.17%

Communication, Energy & Transportation

Communication

Households with computers, 2003........ 66.1%
Households with internet access, 2003 .... 55.4%
High-speed internet providers 67
Total high-speed internet lines..........470,118
  Residential 352,387
  Business........................... 117,731
Wireless phone customers, 12/2006 1,272,067

FCC-licensed stations (as of January 1, 2008)

TV stations 27
FM radio stations.......................... 109
AM radio stations 53

Energy

Energy consumption, 2004
  Total (trillion Btu)..................... 652
  Per capita (million Btu) 373.2
By source of production (trillion Btu)
  Coal 224
  Natural gas 115
  Petroleum............................. 238
  Nuclear electric power 107
  Hydroelectric power.................... 9
By end-use sector (trillion Btu)
  Residential 144
  Commercial 128
  Industrial 206
  Transportation 174
Electric energy, 2005
  Primary source of electricity............ Coal
  Net generation (billion kWh) 31.5
    percent from renewable sources........ 3.2%
  Net summer capability (million kW) 7.0
  CO_2 emitted from generation 22.1
Natural gas utilities, 2005
  Customers (x 1,000) 567
  Sales (trillion Btu)..................... 110
  Revenues ($ mil) $586
Nuclear plants, 2007 2
Total CO_2 emitted (million metric tons).....43.2
Energy spending, 2004 ($ mil) $5,404
  per capita $3,093
  Price per million Btu $12.18

Transportation, 2006

Public road & street mileage 93,379
  Urban...............................6,191
  Rural 87,188
  Interstate........................... 482
Vehicle miles of travel (millions) 19,415
  per capita 11,007.7
Total motor vehicle registrations....... 1,733,133
  Automobiles........................ 832,511
  Trucks 893,627
  Motorcycles 36,951
Licensed drivers 1,327,916
  19 years & under 85,217
Deaths from motor vehicle accidents 269
Gasoline consumed (x 1,000 gallons) 836,683
  per capita 474.4

Commuting Statistics, 2006

Average commute time (min) 17.7
  Drove to work alone 79.1%
  Carpooled........................... 10.4%
  Public transit 0.5%
  Walk to work 3.5%
  Work from home...................... 5.0%

State Summary

Capital city . . . . .Carson City
Governor . . . . Jim Gibbons

Capitol Building
Carson City, NV 89701
775-684-5670

Admitted as a state 1864
Area (square miles) 110,561
Population, 2007 (estimate). 2,565,382
Largest city . . . . .Las Vegas
   Population, 2006 552,539
Personal income per capita, 2006
   (in current dollars) $37,089
Gross domestic product, 2006 ($ mil) . . . $118,399

Leading industries by payroll, 2005

Accommodation & Food services, Construction,
Health care/Social assistance

Leading agricultural commodities by receipts, 2005

Cattle and calves, Hay, Dairy products, Onions,
Potatoes

Geography & Environment

Total area (square miles). 110,561
   land 109,826
   water 735
Federally-owned land, 2004 (acres) . . .59,362,643
   percent. 84.5%
Highest point . . . . Boundary Peak
   elevation (feet) 13,140
Lowest point . . . . .Colorado River
   elevation (feet) 479
General coastline (miles) 0
Tidal shoreline (miles) 0
Cropland, 2003 (x 1,000 acres) 636
Forest land, 2003 (x 1,000 acres). 314
Capital city . . . . .Carson City
   Population 2000 52,457
   Population 2006 55,289
Largest city . . . . .Las Vegas
   Population 2000 478,434
   Population 2006 552,539

Number of cities with over 100,000 population

1990 3
2000 4
2006 4

State park and recreation areas, 2005

Area (x 1,000 acres) 133
Number of visitors (x 1,000) 3,178
Revenues ($1,000) $2,565
   percent of operating expenditures 23.9%

National forest system land, 2007

Acres 5,853,963

Demographics & Population Characteristics

Population

1980 800,493
1990 1,201,833
2000 1,998,257
2006 2,495,529
   Male 1,268,894
   Female 1,226,635
Living in group quarters, 2006 33,434
   percent of total. 1.3%
2007 (estimate). 2,565,382
   persons per square mile of land 23.4
2008 (projected). 2,551,889
2010 (projected) .2,690,531
2020 (projected) .3,452,283
2030 (projected) .4,282,102

Population of Core-Based Statistical Areas (formerly Metropolitan Areas), x 1,000

	CBSA	Non-CBSA
1990	1,157	44
2000	1,950	48
2006	2,447	49

Change in population, 2000-2007

Number 567,125
   percent. 28.4%
Natural increase (births minus deaths) 124,490
Net internal migration 364,683
Net international migration 84,578

Persons by age, 2006

Under 5 years 183,588
5 to 17 years 450,932
18 years and over 1,861,009
65 years and over 276,943
85 years and over .27,841
   Median age 35.5

Persons by age, 2010 (projected)

Under 5 years 196,094
18 and over 2,025,446
65 and over 329,621
   Median age 37.8

Race, 2006

One Race
   White. 2,038,372
   Black or African American 196,075
   Asian 149,621
   American Indian/Alaska Native. 34,813
   Hawaiian Native/Pacific Islander. 12,441
Two or more races. 64,207

Persons of Hispanic origin, 2006

Total Hispanic or Latino 610,051
   Mexican. 475,390
   Puerto Rican 19,020
   Cuban 15,120

Persons of Asian origin, 2006

Total Asian 147,363
  Asian Indian. 6,524
  Chinese 23,700
  Filipino 73,261
  Japanese 12,678
  Korean. 8,886
  Vietnamese. 9,238

Marital status, 2006

Population 15 years & over 1,965,437
  Never married 566,781
  Married. 1,026,022
  Separated 42,362
  Widowed. 111,826
  Divorced 260,808

Language spoken at home, 2006

Population 5 years and older. 2,312,092
  English only 1,691,109
  Spanish 445,622
  French 7,654
  German. 11,722
  Chinese 18,553

Households & families, 2006

Households. 936,828
  with persons under 18 years 325,947
  with persons over 65 years. 199,099
  persons per household 2.63
Families. 612,349
  persons per family. 3.20
Married couples. 443,841
Female householder,
  no husband present. 108,682
One-person households 248,784

Nativity, 2006

Number of residents born in state 575,422
  percent of population. 23.1%

Immigration & naturalization, 2006

Legal permanent residents admitted. 14,714
Persons naturalized 8,202
Non-immigrant admissions 1,067,921

Vital Statistics and Health

Marriages

2004 145,763
2005 139,572
2006 131,826

Divorces

2004 14,828
2005 18,084
2006 16,737

Health risks, 2006

Percent of adults who are:
  Smokers. 22.2%
  Overweight (BMI > 25). 63.6%
  Obese (BMI > 30). 25.0%

Births

2005 37,268
  Birthrate (per 1,000). 15.4
  White. 30,664
  Black. 3,219
  Hispanic 14,090
  Asian/Pacific Islander 2,906
  Amer. Indian/Alaska Native. 479
  Low birth weight (2,500g or less). 8.3%
  Cesarian births 31.0%
  Preterm births 13.9%
  To unmarried mothers. 40.9%
  Twin births (per 1,000) 29.0
  Triplets or higher order (per 100,000). . . .147.0
2006 (preliminary). 40,085
  rate per 1,000 . . . . .16.1

Deaths

2004
All causes 17,929
  rate per 100,000. . . . . 880.5
Heart disease 4,693
  rate per 100,000. . . . . 236.6
Malignant neoplasms 4,119
  rate per 100,000. . . . . .193.4
Cerebrovascular disease. 1,030
  rate per 100,000. . . . . .53.4
Chronic lower respiratory disease 1,124
  rate per 100,000. . . . . .56.8
Diabetes. 290
  rate per 100,000. . . . . .13.9
2005 (preliminary). 19,037
  rate per 100,000. . . . . 892.3
2006 (provisional) 18,295

Infant deaths

2004 225
  rate per 1,000 . . . . .6.4
2005 (provisional) 210
  rate per 1,000 . . . . .5.8

Exercise routines, 2005

None. 26.8%
Moderate or greater. 50.7%
Vigorous 32.6%

Abortions, 2004

Total performed in state. 9,856
  rate per 1,000 women age 15-44. 20
  % obtained by out-of-state residents 6.6%

Physicians, 2005

Total. 4,519
  rate per 100,000 persons 187

Community hospitals, 2005

Number of hospitals 32
Beds (x 1,000). 4.7
Patients admitted (x 1,000) 241
Average daily census (x 1,000) 3.5
Average cost per day $1,685
Outpatient visits (x 1 mil) 2.6

Disability status of population, 2006
5 to 15 years 3.7%
16 to 64 years 10.4%
65 years and over 38.7%

Education

Educational attainment, 2006
Population over 25 years 1,644,320
Less than 9th grade.....................6.3%
High school graduate or more 83.9%
College graduate or more............. 20.8%
Graduate or professional degree........ 7.2%

Public school enrollment, 2005-06
Total............................... 412,395
Pre-kindergarten through grade 8.....295,011
Grades 9 through 12.................116,375

Graduating public high school seniors, 2004-05
Diplomas (incl. GED and others) 18,236

SAT scores, 2007
Average critical reading score.............. 500
Average writing score..................... 480
Average math score...................... 506
Percent of graduates taking test 41%

Public school teachers, 2006-07 (estimate)
Total (x 1,000) 22.1
Elementary...........................12.9
Secondary.............................9.2
Average salary $45,342
Elementary....................... $45,342
Secondary....................... $45,342

State receipts & expenditures for public schools, 2006-07 (estimate)
Revenue receipts ($ mil) $3,104
Expenditures
Total ($ mil) $3,912
Per capita $1,190
Per pupil $7,060

NAEP proficiency scores, 2007
	Reading		Math	
	Basic	Proficient	Basic	Proficient
Grade 4	57.1%	24.4%	73.7%	30.1%
Grade 8	63.1%	21.5%	60.2%	23.0%

Higher education enrollment, fall 2005
Total................................ 10,662
Full-time men 4,102
Full-time women..................... 5,906
Part-time men 276
Part-time women...................... 378

Minority enrollment in institutions of higher education, 2005
Black, non-Hispanic 8,651
Hispanic 15,515
Asian/Pacific Islander 11,877
American Indian/Alaska Native..........1,658

Institutions of higher education, 2005-06
Total..................................... 23
Public.................................. 7
Private................................ 16

Earned degrees conferred, 2004-05
Associate's............................. 3,236
Bachelor's 5,608
Master's 2,042
First-professional....................... 180
Doctor's................................ 126

Public Libraries, 2006
Number of libraries.................... 22
Number of outlets 89
Annual visits per capita 4.1
Circulation per capita...................6.2

State & local financial support for higher education, FY 2006
Full-time equivalent enrollment (x 1,000).....60.9
Appropriations per FTE................$8,919

Social Insurance & Welfare Programs

Social Security benefits & beneficiaries, 2005
Beneficiaries (x 1,000) 348
Retired & dependents................... 254
Survivors............................. 38
Disabled & dependents.................. 55
Annual benefit payments ($ mil) $3,830
Retired & dependents.................. $2,666
Survivors............................. $538
Disabled & dependents................. $626
Average monthly benefit
Retired & dependents.................. $1,008
Disabled & dependents................. $1,008
Widowed........................... $1,012

Medicare, July 2005
Enrollment (x 1,000)..................... 297
Payments ($ mil) $1,539

Medicaid, 2004
Beneficiaries (x 1,000).................. 78
Payments ($ mil) $477

State Children's Health Insurance Program, 2006
Enrollment (x 1,000)....................39.3
Expenditures ($ mil)................... $40.2

Persons without health insurance, 2006
Number (x 1,000)........................ 496
percent........................... 19.6%
Number of children (x 1,000) 122
percent of children 18.8%

Health care expenditures, 2004
Total expenditures.................... $10,656
per capita $4,569

4   Nevada

Federal and state public aid

State unemployment insurance, 2006
Recipients, first payments (x 1,000) 64
Total payments ($ mil) $246
Average weekly benefit $274
Temporary Assistance for Needy Families, 2006
Recipients (x 1,000) 153.1
Families (x 1,000) 66.6
Supplemental Security Income, 2005
Recipients (x 1,000) 33.0
Payments ($ mil) $163.0
Food Stamp Program, 2006
Avg monthly participants (x 1,000) 117.9
Total benefits ($ mil) $124.3

Housing & Construction

Housing units
Total 2005 (estimate) 1,019,435
Total 2006 (estimate) 1,065,197
Seasonal or recreational use, 2006 30,879
Owner-occupied, 2006 580,705
    Median home value $315,200
    Homeowner vacancy rate 3.0%
Renter-occupied, 2006 356,123
    Median rent $917
    Rental vacancy rate 9.1%
Home ownership rate, 2005 . . . . 63.4%
Home ownership rate, 2006 . . . . 65.7%

New privately-owned housing units
Number authorized, 2006 (x 1,000) 39.4
    Value ($ mil) $5,383.2
Started 2005 (x 1,000, estimate) 36.1
Started 2006 (x 1,000, estimate) 35.0

Existing home sales
2005 (x 1,000) 98.0
2006 (x 1,000) 70.2

Government & Elections

State officials 2008
Governor . . . . Jim Gibbons
        Republican, term expires 1/11
Lieutenant Governor . . . . Brian Krolicki
Secretary of State . . . . Ross Miller
Attorney General . . . . Catherine Masto
Chief Justice . . . . A. William Maupin

Governorship
Minimum age 25
Length of term . . . . 4 years
Consecutive terms permitted 2
Who succeeds . . . . Lieutenant Governor

Local governments by type, 2002
Total 210
    County 16
    Municipal 19
    Township 0
    School District 17
    Special District 158

State legislature
Name . . . . Legislature
Upper chamber . . . . .Senate
    Number of members 21
    Length of term . . . . 4 years
    Party in majority, 2008 . . . . Republican
Lower chamber . . . . Assembly
    Number of members 42
    Length of term . . . . 2 years
    Party in majority, 2008 . . . . Democratic

Federal representation, 2008 (110th Congress)
Senator . . . . Harry Reid
    Party . . . . Democratic
    Year term expires 2011
Senator . . . . John Ensign
    Party . . . . Republican
    Year term expires 2013
Representatives, total 3
    Democrats 1
    Republicans 2

Voters in November 2006 election (estimate)
Total 686,199
    Male 331,614
    Female 354,584
    White 595,064
    Black 41,124
    Hispanic 27,210
    Asian 37,267

Presidential election, 2004
Total Popular Vote 829,587
    Kerry 397,190
    Bush 418,690
Total Electoral Votes 5

Votes cast for US Senators
2004
Total vote (x 1,000) 810
Leading party . . . . Democratic
Percent for leading party 61.1%
2006
Total vote (x 1,000) 583
Leading party . . . . Republican
Percent for leading party 55.4%

Votes cast for US Representatives
2004
Total vote (x 1,000) 791
    Democratic 334
    Republican 421
Leading party . . . . Republican
Percent for leading party 53.2%
2006
Total vote (x 1,000) 575
    Democratic 288
    Republican 260
Leading party . . . . Democratic
Percent for leading party 50.1%

Nevada 5

State government employment, 2006
Full-time equivalent employees 25,859
Payroll ($ mil) $104.5

Local government employment, 2006
Full-time equivalent employees 77,445
Payroll ($ mil) $331.3

Women holding public office, 2008
US Congress 1
Statewide elected office.................... 3
State legislature 19

Black public officials, 2002
Total..................................... 13
  US and state legislatures 5
  City/county/regional offices 4
  Judicial/law enforcement................... 2
  Education/school boards................... 2

Hispanic public officials, 2006
Total..................................... 11
  State executives & legislators 2
  City/county/regional offices 5
  Judicial/law enforcement................... 3
  Education/school boards................... 1

Governmental Finance

State government revenues, 2006
Total revenue (x $1,000)............$12,341,503
  per capita $4,951.60
General revenue (x $1,000) $9,461,111
  Intergovernmental 1,980,326
  Taxes 6,152,980
    general sales.....................3,163,832
    individual income tax 0
    corporate income tax 0
  Current charges.................... 632,196
  Miscellaneous 695,609

State government expenditure, 2006
Total expenditure (x $1,000) $10,341,683
  per capita $4,149.24
General expenditure (x $1,000) $9,152,975
  per capita, total................... $3,672.31
  Education 1,420.13
  Public welfare 654.10
  Health 75.55
  Hospitals..........................83.31
  Highways 303.87
  Police protection..................39.26
  Corrections 105.47
  Natural resources 57.43
  Parks & recreation 9.73
  Governmental administration...... 134.86
  Interest on general debt.............72.51

State debt & cash, 2006 ($ per capita)
Debt $1,625.01
Cash/security holdings..............$10,867.20

Federal government grants to state & local government, 2005 (x $1,000)
Total.............................$2,925,545
by Federal agency
  Defense 32,254
  Education 231,079
  Energy........................... 86,742
  Environmental Protection Agency 49,961
  Health & Human Services. 1,079,572
  Homeland Security................ 22,047
  Housing & Urban Development.......159,706
  Justice 66,360
  Labor 53,895
  Transportation 275,037
  Veterans Affairs.....................9,608

Crime & Law Enforcement

Crime, 2006 (rates per 100,000 residents)
Property crimes 102,036
  Burglary 24,820
  Larceny 50,255
  Motor vehicle theft 26,961
  Property crime rate................4,088.8
Violent crimes........................ 18,508
  Murder 224
  Forcible rape......................1,079
  Robbery..........................7,027
  Aggravated assault 10,178
  Violent crime rate 741.6
Hate crimes......................... 142

Fraud and identity theft, 2006
Fraud complaints.................... 4,222
  rate per 100,000 residents 169.2
Identity theft complaints 2,994
  rate per 100,000 residents 120.0

Law enforcement agencies, 2006
Total agencies............................ 37
Total employees 9,080
  Officers 5,262
  Civilians 3,818

Prisoners, probation, and parole, 2006
Total prisoners....................... 12,901
  percent change, 12/31/05 to 12/31/06 .... 9.5%
  in private facilities 0%
  in local jails 1.1%
Sentenced to more than one year 12,753
  rate per 100,000 residents 503
Adults on probation 13,208
Adults on parole...................... 3,824

Prisoner demographics, June 30, 2005 (rate per 100,000 residents)
Male................................1,319
Female 173
White............................... 627
Black................................2,916
Hispanic 621

Arrests, 2006
Total................................163,109
   Persons under 18 years of age......... 20,725

Persons under sentence of death, 1/1/07
Total....................................... 80
   White.................................... 42
   Black.................................... 29
   Hispanic................................. 8

State's highest court
Name.........................Supreme Court
Number of members......................... 7
Length of term......................... 6 years
Intermediate appeals court?................ no

Labor & Income

Civilian labor force, 2006 (x 1,000)
Total...................................1,296
   Men.................................... 716
   Women.................................. 580
   Persons 16-19 years..................... 62
   White...................................1,052
   Black.................................... 92
   Hispanic................................ 300

Civilian labor force as a percent of civilian non-institutional population, 2006
Total....................................68.3%
   Men....................................74.9
   Women..................................61.5
   Persons 16-19 years....................45.7
   White..................................67.9
   Black..................................68.3
   Hispanic...............................76.5

Employment, 2006 (x 1,000)
Total................................... 1,243
   Men.................................... 686
   Women.................................. 557
   Persons 16-19 years..................... 52
   White...................................1,012
   Black.................................... 86
   Hispanic................................ 285

Unemployment rate, 2006
Total.................................... 4.1%
   Men.....................................4.2
   Women...................................4.0
   Persons 16-19 years....................16.2
   White...................................3.8
   Black...................................6.8
   Hispanic................................4.9

Full-time/part-time labor force, 2003 (x 1,000)
Full-time labor force, employed............ 941
Part-time labor force, employed............ 141
Unemployed, looking for
   Full-time work.......................... 51
   Part-time work.......................... 8
Mean duration of unemployment (weeks)......16.3
   Median.................................8.5

Labor unions, 2006
Membership (x 1,000).................... 167
   percent of employed................... 14.8%

Experienced civilian labor force by private industry, 2006
Total...........................$1,125,197
   Natural resources & mining...........13,812
   Construction...................... 142,815
   Manufacturing..................... 50,252
   Trade, transportation & utilities..... 225,743
   Information.........................15,161
   Finance............................65,576
   Professional & business............. 158,250
   Education & health..................87,356
   Leisure & hospitality............... 336,970
   Other.............................. 28,465

Experienced civilian labor force by occupation, May 2006
Management........................ 50,570
Business & financial.................. 38,760
Legal................................8,410
Sales............................. 131,840
Office & admin. support..............197,350
Computers & math.................. 13,260
Architecture & engineering...........17,010
Arts & entertainment................ 16,680
Education...........................47,750
Social services..................... 8,430
Health care practitioner & technical..... 39,540
Health care support.................. 19,440
Maintenance & repair................. 51,380
Construction...................... 121,920
Transportation & moving............. 100,300
Production.......................... 45,370
Farming, fishing & forestry........... 790

Hours and earnings of production workers on manufacturing payrolls, 2006
Average weekly hours.................39.4
Average hourly earnings.............$15.47
Average weekly earnings............. $609.52

Income and poverty, 2006
Median household income............ $52,998
Personal income, per capita (current $)... $37,089
   in constant (2000) dollars........... $32,376
Persons below poverty level............. 10.3%

Average annual pay
2006................................. $40,070
   increase from 2005................... 3.4%

Federal individual income tax returns, 2005
Returns filed.......................1,150,204
Adjusted gross income ($1,000).....$72,209,472
Total tax liability ($1,000).........$10,495,210

Charitable contributions, 2004
Number of contributions................ 346.7
Total amount ($ mil)..................$1,500.6

Economy, Business, Industry & Agriculture

Fortune 500 companies, 2007 2
Bankruptcy cases filed, FY 2007 9,445

Patents and trademarks issued, 2007
Patents 451
Trademarks 2,777

Business firm ownership, 2002
Women-owned 47,675
  Sales ($ mil) $8,643
Black-owned 4,343
  Sales ($ mil) $434
Hispanic-owned 9,741
  Sales ($ mil) $1,643
Asian-owned 8,872
  Sales ($ mil) $1,989
Amer. Indian/Alaska Native-owned 1,915
  Sales ($ mil) $218
Hawaiian/Pacific Islander-owned 313
  Sales ($ mil) $55

Gross domestic product, 2006 ($ mil)
Total gross domestic product $118,399
  Agriculture, forestry, fishing and
    hunting 243
  Mining 2,047
  Utilities 1,969
  Construction 11,881
  Manufacturing, durable goods 4,307
  Manufacturing, non-durable goods 1,453
  Wholesale trade 5,005
  Retail trade 9,067
  Transportation & warehousing 3,268
  Information 2,161
  Finance & insurance 8,134
  Real estate, rental & leasing 17,611
  Professional and technical services 6,042
  Educational services 303
  Health care and social assistance 5,724
  Accommodation/food services 16,506
  Other services, except government 2,080
  Government 11,776

Establishments, payroll, employees & receipts, by major industry group, 2005
Total 58,561
  Annual payroll ($1,000) $39,261,902
  Paid employees 1,089,422
Forestry, fishing & agriculture 52
  Annual payroll ($1,000) $5,608
  Paid employees 210
Mining 198
  Annual payroll ($1,000) $570,033
  Paid employees 9,483
  Receipts, 2002 ($1,000) $2,570,066

Utilities 103
  Annual payroll ($1,000) $448,209
  Paid employees 5,324
  Receipts, 2002 ($1,000) . . . . .NA
Construction 5,713
  Annual payroll ($1,000) $5,267,935
  Paid employees 122,231
  Receipts, 2002 ($1,000) $16,100,809
Manufacturing 1,863
  Annual payroll ($1,000) $1,897,233
  Paid employees 45,068
  Receipts, 2002 ($1,000) $8,466,212
Wholesale trade 2,812
  Annual payroll ($1,000) $1,726,773
  Paid employees 36,417
  Receipts, 2002 ($1,000) $16,513,814
Retail trade 8,006
  Annual payroll ($1,000) $3,583,275
  Paid employees 135,522
  Receipts, 2002 ($1,000) $26,999,899
Transportation & warehousing 1,447
  Annual payroll ($1,000) $1,159,454
  Paid employees 39,281
  Receipts, 2002 ($1,000) $1,842,072
Information 1,155
  Annual payroll ($1,000) $757,260
  Paid employees 15,689
  Receipts, 2002 ($1,000) . . . . .NA
Finance & insurance 4,444
  Annual payroll ($1,000) $1,946,376
  Paid employees 38,672
  Receipts, 2002 ($1,000) . . . . .NA
Professional, scientific & technical 7,477
  Annual payroll ($1,000) $2,854,612
  Paid employees 53,317
  Receipts, 2002 ($1,000) $5,665,309
Education 552
  Annual payroll ($1,000) $188,865
  Paid employees 6,649
  Receipts, 2002 ($1,000) $159,673
Health care & social assistance 5,256
  Annual payroll ($1,000) $3,649,668
  Paid employees 88,200
  Receipts, 2002 ($1,000) $7,553,145
Arts and entertainment 1,286
  Annual payroll ($1,000) $726,470
  Paid employees 28,290
  Receipts, 2002 ($1,000) $2,392,612
Real estate 4,426
  Annual payroll ($1,000) $1,050,710
  Paid employees 28,812
  Receipts, 2002 ($1,000) $3,432,258
Accommodation & food service 4,915
  Annual payroll ($1,000) $7,733,195
  Paid employees 290,919
  Receipts, 2002 ($1,000) $19,537,592

Exports, 2006
Value of exported goods ($ mil) $5,493
  Manufactured $4,475
  Non-manufactured................... $463

Foreign direct investment in US affiliates, 2004
Property, plants & equipment ($ mil) $6,530
Employment (x 1,000)....................27.0

Agriculture, 2006
Number of farms 3,000
Farm acreage (x 1,000) 6,300
  Acres per farm........................2,100
Farm marketings and income ($ mil)
Total................................. $446.6
  Crops...............................$166.2
  Livestock........................... $280.4
Net farm income $84.6

Principal commodities, in order by marketing receipts, 2005
Cattle and calves, Hay, Dairy products, Onions, Potatoes

Federal economic activity in state
Expenditures, 2005 ($ mil)
  Total............................. $14,089
    Per capita $5,840.47
  Defense $1,625
  Non-defense....................... $12,464
Defense department, 2006 ($ mil)
  Payroll.............................$1,146
  Contract awards $750
  Grants $20
Homeland security grants ($1,000)
  2006............................. $20,509
  2007.............................$19,357

FDIC-insured financial institutions, 2005
Number 38
Assets ($ billion) $1,416.3
Deposits ($ billion) $917.8

Fishing, 2006
Catch (x 1,000 lbs)...................... NA
Value ($1,000)........................... NA

Mining, 2006 ($ mil)
Total non-fuel mineral production $5,240
Percent of U.S. 8.14%

Communication, Energy & Transportation

Communication
Households with computers, 2003........ 61.3%
Households with internet access, 2003 .... 55.2%
High-speed internet providers 32
Total high-speed internet lines......... 782,840
  Residential 550,643
  Business.......................... 232,197
Wireless phone customers, 12/2006 1,990,215

FCC-licensed stations (as of January 1, 2008)
TV stations 21
FM radio stations......................... 66
AM radio stations 30

Energy
Energy consumption, 2004
  Total (trillion Btu)..................... 694
  Per capita (million Btu) 297.4
By source of production (trillion Btu)
  Coal.................................. 194
  Natural gas........................... 220
  Petroleum............................ 264
  Nuclear electric power 0
  Hydroelectric power 16
By end-use sector (trillion Btu)
  Residential 159
  Commercial 121
  Industrial 186
  Transportation 228
Electric energy, 2005
  Primary source of electricity............. Gas
  Net generation (billion kWh) 40.2
    percent from renewable sources...... 7.4%
  Net summer capability (million kW) 8.7
  CO_2 emitted from generation 26.0
Natural gas utilities, 2005
  Customers (x 1,000) 725
  Sales (trillion Btu)...................... 79
  Revenues ($ mil) $872
Nuclear plants, 2007 0
Total CO_2 emitted (million metric tons)......43.3
Energy spending, 2004 ($ mil) $6,878
  per capita $2,949
  Price per million Btu $15.43

Transportation, 2006
Public road & street mileage 33,703
  Urban.............................7,143
  Rural 26,560
  Interstate.......................... 571
Vehicle miles of travel (millions) 21,824
  per capita 8,756.1
Total motor vehicle registrations......1,366,557
  Automobiles........................ 679,828
  Trucks 684,806
  Motorcycles 56,971
Licensed drivers 1,626,021
  19 years & under 58,743
Deaths from motor vehicle accidents 432
Gasoline consumed (x 1,000 gallons) 1,173,077
  per capita 470.7

Commuting Statistics, 2006
Average commute time (min) 24.2
  Drove to work alone 76.7%
  Carpooled........................... 12.3%
  Public transit 3.6%
  Walk to work 2.1%
  Work from home 3.1%

State Summary

Capital city . . . . Concord
Governor. . . . . John Lynch

Office of the Governor
25 Capitol St, Room 212
Concord, NH 03301
603-271-7532

Admitted as a state 1788
Area (square miles) 9,350
Population, 2007 (estimate). 1,315,828
Largest city . . . . Manchester
  Population, 2006. 109,497
Personal income per capita, 2006
  (in current dollars) $39,311
Gross domestic product, 2006 ($ mil) $56,276

Leading industries by payroll, 2005

Manufacturing, Health care/Social assistance,
Retail trade

**Leading agricultural commodities
by receipts, 2005**

Greenhouse/nursery, Dairy products, Cattle and
calves, Apples, Hay

Geography & Environment

Total area (square miles). 9,350
  land 8,968
  water 382
Federally-owned land, 2004 (acres) 775,665
  percent. 13.5%
Highest point . . . . .Mt. Washington
  elevation (feet) 6,288
Lowest point. . . . . .Atlantic Ocean
  elevation (feet) . . . . sea level
General coastline (miles) 13
Tidal shoreline (miles) 131
Cropland, 2003 (x 1,000 acres) 125
Forest land, 2003 (x 1,000 acres). 3,899
Capital city . . . . .Concord
  Population 2000 40,687
  Population 2006 42,378
Largest city . . . . Manchester
  Population 2000 107,006
  Population 2006 109,497

Number of cities with over 100,000 population

1990 0
2000 1
2006 1

State park and recreation areas, 2005

Area (x 1,000 acres) 232
Number of visitors (x 1,000) . . . . NA
Revenues ($1,000) . . . . NA
  percent of operating expenditures. . . . . . . NA

National forest system land, 2007

Acres 734,798

Demographics & Population Characteristics

Population

1980 920,610
1990 1,109,252
2000 1,235,786
2006 1,314,895
  Male. 648,568
  Female. 666,327
Living in group quarters, 2006. 37,347
  percent of total. 2.8%
2007 (estimate). .1,315,828
  persons per square mile of land 146.7
2008 (projected). 1,357,216
2010 (projected) 1,385,560
2020 (projected) 1,524,751
2030 (projected) 1,646,471

**Population of Core-Based Statistical Areas
(formerly Metropolitan Areas), x 1,000**

	CBSA	Non-CBSA
1990	1,074	35
2000	1,192	44
2006	1,267	47

Change in population, 2000-2007

Number 80,042
  percent. 6.5%
Natural increase (births minus deaths) 35,461
Net internal migration 35,682
Net international migration 13,928

Persons by age, 2006

Under 5 years 73,575
5 to 17 years 224,050
18 years and over 1,017,270
65 years and over 162,629
85 years and over 23,118
  Median age 39.4

Persons by age, 2010 (projected)

Under 5 years 82,238
18 and over 1,081,396
65 and over 178,823
  Median age. 39.6

Race, 2006

One Race
  White. 1,259,738
  Black or African American 13,905
  Asian 24,389
  American Indian/Alaska Native. 3,458
  Hawaiian Native/Pacific Islander. 514
Two or more races. 12,891

Persons of Hispanic origin, 2006

Total Hispanic or Latino 29,721
  Mexican. 5,354
  Puerto Rican 11,123
  Cuban 783

Persons of Asian origin, 2006

Total Asian 26,136
  Asian Indian 6,823
  Chinese 6,267
  Filipino 1,535
  Japanese 1,486
  Korean 2,996
  Vietnamese 2,720

Marital status, 2006

Population 15 years & over 1,075,279
  Never married 308,733
  Married 584,486
  Separated 14,698
  Widowed 62,527
  Divorced 119,533

Language spoken at home, 2006

Population 5 years and older 1,241,415
  English only 1,139,278
  Spanish 26,607
  French 28,134
  German 4,207
  Chinese 5,144

Households & families, 2006

Households 504,503
  with persons under 18 years 162,731
  with persons over 65 years.......... 110,236
  persons per household 2.53
Families 335,509
  persons per family 3.05
Married couples 267,935
Female householder,
  no husband present 45,983
One-person households 129,310

Nativity, 2006

Number of residents born in state 549,491
  percent of population 41.8%

Immigration & naturalization, 2006

Legal permanent residents admitted 2,990
Persons naturalized 2,483
Non-immigrant admissions 57,196

Vital Statistics and Health

Marriages

2004 10,383
2005 9,488
2006 9,328

Divorces

2004 5,131
2005 5,028
2006 5,258

Health risks, 2006

Percent of adults who are:
  Smokers 18.7%
  Overweight (BMI > 25) 60.7%
  Obese (BMI > 30) 22.4%

Births

2005 14,420
  Birthrate (per 1,000) 11.0
  White 13,572
  Black 232
  Hispanic 522
  Asian/Pacific Islander 587
  Amer. Indian/Alaska Native 29
  Low birth weight (2,500g or less) 7.0%
  Cesarian births 28.0%
  Preterm births 10.5%
  To unmarried mothers 27.3%
  Twin births (per 1,000) 37.2
  Triplets or higher order (per 100,000)....214.4
2006 (preliminary).................... 14,380
  rate per 1,000 ....10.9

Deaths

2004
All causes 10,111
  rate per 100,000 ....761.1
Heart disease 2,639
  rate per 100,000 ....197.6
Malignant neoplasms 2,554
  rate per 100,000 ....192.1
Cerebrovascular disease.................. 586
  rate per 100,000 .... 44.2
Chronic lower respiratory disease 600
  rate per 100,000 ....45.8
Diabetes 313
  rate per 100,000 ....23.5
2005 (preliminary)....................10,194
  rate per 100,000 ....732.3
2006 (provisional) 9,901

Infant deaths

2004 81
  rate per 1,000 ....5.6
2005 (provisional) 75
  rate per 1,000 ....5.2

Exercise routines, 2005

None 21.6%
Moderate or greater 56.0%
Vigorous 32.9%

Abortions, 2004

Total performed in state.................. NA
  rate per 1,000 women age 15-44 .... NA
  % obtained by out-of-state residents ...... NA

Physicians, 2005

Total 3,440
  rate per 100,000 persons 263

Community hospitals, 2005

Number of hospitals 28
Beds (x 1,000) 2.8
Patients admitted (x 1,000) 117
Average daily census (x 1,000) 1.8
Average cost per day $1,627
Outpatient visits (x 1 mil) 3.8

Disability status of population, 2006
5 to 15 years 6.6%
16 to 64 years 11.5%
65 years and over 37.9%

Education

Educational attainment, 2006
Population over 25 years 896,872
   Less than 9th grade. 3.2%
   High school graduate or more 89.9%
   College graduate or more. 31.9%
   Graduate or professional degree. 11.2%

Public school enrollment, 2005-06
Total. 205,767
   Pre-kindergarten through grade 8. . . . 138,043
   Grades 9 through 12 67,112

Graduating public high school seniors, 2004-05
Diplomas (incl. GED and others) 13,847

SAT scores, 2007
Average critical reading score 521
Average writing score 512
Average math score 521
Percent of graduates taking test 83%

Public school teachers, 2006-07 (estimate)
Total (x 1,000) 15.8
   Elementary 10.9
   Secondary 4.9
Average salary $46,527
   Elementary $46,527
   Secondary $46,527

State receipts & expenditures for
public schools, 2006-07 (estimate)
Revenue receipts ($ mil) $2,401
Expenditures
Total ($ mil) $2,438
   Per capita $1,690
   Per pupil $11,879

NAEP proficiency scores, 2007

	Reading		Math	
	Basic	Proficient	Basic	Proficient
Grade 4	76.0%	41.1%	91.3%	51.8%
Grade 8	81.9%	37.2%	77.6%	37.9%

Higher education enrollment, fall 2005
Total. 28,886
   Full-time men 9,891
   Full-time women .12,166
   Part-time men 2,171
   Part-time women. 4,658

Minority enrollment in institutions
of higher education, 2005
Black, non-Hispanic .1,418
Hispanic 1,742
Asian/Pacific Islander 1,775
American Indian/Alaska Native. 382

Institutions of higher education, 2005-06
Total. 26
   Public. 9
   Private 17

Earned degrees conferred, 2004-05
Associate's. 3,498
Bachelor's 8,107
Master's 2,751
First-professional. 183
Doctor's 167

Public Libraries, 2006
Number of libraries. 230
Number of outlets 238
Annual visits per capita 4.9
Circulation per capita. 7.7

State & local financial support for
higher education, FY 2006
Full-time equivalent enrollment (x 1,000) 31.7
Appropriations per FTE. $3,193

Social Insurance & Welfare Programs

Social Security benefits & beneficiaries, 2005
Beneficiaries (x 1,000) 226
   Retired & dependents. 157
   Survivors. 26
   Disabled & dependents. 42
Annual benefit payments ($ mil) $2,485
   Retired & dependents. $1,686
   Survivors. $369
   Disabled & dependents. $430
Average monthly benefit
   Retired & dependents. $1,028
   Disabled & dependents. $943
   Widowed. $1,023

Medicare, July 2005
Enrollment (x 1,000). 192
Payments ($ mil) $1,206

Medicaid, 2004
Beneficiaries (x 1,000). 244
Payments ($ mil) $1,346

State Children's Health Insurance Program, 2006
Enrollment (x 1,000). 12.4
Expenditures ($ mil) $11.6

Persons without health insurance, 2006
Number (x 1,000). 150
   percent. 11.5%
Number of children (x 1,000) 22
   percent of children 7.3%

Health care expenditures, 2004
Total expenditures. $7,050
   per capita $5,432

Federal and state public aid

State unemployment insurance, 2006
Recipients, first payments (x 1,000) 25
Total payments ($ mil) $78
Average weekly benefit $256
Temporary Assistance for Needy Families, 2006
Recipients (x 1,000) 159.3
Families (x 1,000) 71.4
Supplemental Security Income, 2005
Recipients (x 1,000) 13.6
Payments ($ mil) $66.5
Food Stamp Program, 2006
Avg monthly participants (x 1,000) 56.3
Total benefits ($ mil) $57.9

Housing & Construction

Housing units

Total 2005 (estimate) 583,318
Total 2006 (estimate) 589,812
Seasonal or recreational use, 2006 56,722
Owner-occupied, 2006 363,652
  Median home value $253,200
  Homeowner vacancy rate 1.4%
Renter-occupied, 2006 140,851
  Median rent $861
  Rental vacancy rate 6.0%
Home ownership rate, 2005 . . . . 74.0%
Home ownership rate, 2006 . . . . 74.2%

New privately-owned housing units

Number authorized, 2006 (x 1,000) 5.7
  Value ($ mil) $1,036.6
Started 2005 (x 1,000, estimate) 7.0
Started 2006 (x 1,000, estimate) 6.6

Existing home sales

2005 (x 1,000) . . . . NA
2006 (x 1,000) . . . . NA

Government & Elections

State officials 2008

Governor . . . . John Lynch
        Democratic, term expires 1/09
Lieutenant Governor . . (no Lieutenant Governor)
Secretary of State . . . . William Gardner
Attorney General . . . . Kelly Ayotte
Chief Justice . . . . .John Broderick Jr

Governorship

Minimum age 30
Length of term . . . . 2 years
Consecutive terms permitted . . . . . . not specified
Who succeeds . . . . President of Senate

Local governments by type, 2002

Total 559
  County 10
  Municipal 13
  Township 221
  School District 167
  Special District 148

State legislature

Name . . . . General Court
Upper chamber . . . . .Senate
  Number of members 24
  Length of term . . . . 2 years
  Party in majority, 2008 . . . . Democratic
Lower chamber . . . . House of Representatives
  Number of members 400
  Length of term . . . . 2 years
  Party in majority, 2008 . . . . .Democratic

Federal representation, 2008 (110th Congress)

Senator . . . . .John Sununu
  Party . . . . Republican
  Year term expires 2009
Senator . . . . Judd Gregg
  Party . . . . Republican
  Year term expires 2011
Representatives, total 2
  Democrats 2
  Republicans 0

Voters in November 2006 election (estimate)

Total 477,037
  Male 229,479
  Female 247,557
  White 462,517
  Black 2,979
  Hispanic 1,500
  Asian 5,602

Presidential election, 2004

Total Popular Vote 677,738
  Kerry 340,511
  Bush 331,237
Total Electoral Votes 4

Votes cast for US Senators

2004
Total vote (x 1,000) 657
Leading party . . . . Republican
Percent for leading party 66.2%
2006
Total vote (x 1,000) . . . . NA
Leading party . . . . NA
Percent for leading party . . . . NA

Votes cast for US Representatives

2004
Total vote (x 1,000) 652
  Democratic 244
  Republican 396
Leading party . . . . Republican
Percent for leading party 60.8%
2006
Total vote (x 1,000) 403
  Democratic 209
  Republican 190
Leading party .Democratic
Percent for leading party 52.0%

State government employment, 2006
Full-time equivalent employees 19,076
Payroll ($ mil) $70.4

Local government employment, 2006
Full-time equivalent employees 50,701
Payroll ($ mil) $163.9

Women holding public office, 2008
US Congress 1
Statewide elected office 0
State legislature 152

Black public officials, 2002
Total 5
  US and state legislatures 5
  City/county/regional offices 0
  Judicial/law enforcement 0
  Education/school boards 0

Hispanic public officials, 2006
Total 3
  State executives & legislators 2
  City/county/regional offices 1
  Judicial/law enforcement 0
  Education/school boards 0

Governmental Finance

State government revenues, 2006
Total revenue (x $1,000) $6,373,151
  per capita $4,858.25
General revenue (x $1,000) $5,186,159
  Intergovernmental 1,717,500
  Taxes 2,080,573
    general sales 0
    individual income tax 80,931
    corporate income tax 542,644
  Current charges 689,445
  Miscellaneous 698,641

State government expenditure, 2006
Total expenditure (x $1,000) $5,987,952
  per capita $4,564.61
General expenditure (x $1,000) $5,212,161
  per capita, total $3,973.23
    Education 1,440.06
    Public welfare 1,066.19
    Health 100.60
    Hospitals 41.81
    Highways 340.26
    Police protection 34.85
    Corrections 89.04
    Natural resources 48.58
    Parks & recreation 10.62
    Governmental administration 149.74
    Interest on general debt 262.51

State debt & cash, 2006 ($ per capita)
Debt $5,666.35
Cash/security holdings $9,040.18

Federal government grants to state & local government, 2005 (x $1,000)
Total $1,795,266
by Federal agency
  Defense 20,176
  Education 147,320
  Energy 6,469
  Environmental Protection Agency 37,510
  Health & Human Services 981,105
  Homeland Security 14,131
  Housing & Urban Development 143,170
  Justice 52,624
  Labor 27,795
  Transportation 171,780
  Veterans Affairs 5,759

Crime & Law Enforcement

Crime, 2006 (rates per 100,000 residents)
Property crimes 24,642
  Burglary 4,358
  Larceny 18,862
  Motor vehicle theft 1,422
  Property crime rate 1,874.1
Violent crimes 1,824
  Murder 13
  Forcible rape 344
  Robbery 423
  Aggravated assault 1,044
  Violent crime rate 138.7
Hate crimes 39

Fraud and identity theft, 2006
Fraud complaints 1,964
  rate per 100,000 residents 149.4
Identity theft complaints 606
  rate per 100,000 residents 46.1

Law enforcement agencies, 2006
Total agencies 148
Total employees 3,197
  Officers 2,414
  Civilians 783

Prisoners, probation, and parole, 2006
Total prisoners 2,805
  percent change, 12/31/05 to 12/31/06 . . . 10.9%
  in private facilities 0%
  in local jails 0.5%
Sentenced to more than one year 2,737
  rate per 100,000 residents 207
Adults on probation 4,590
Adults on parole 1,621

Prisoner demographics, June 30, 2005 (rate per 100,000 residents)
Male 590
Female 56
White 289
Black 2,666
Hispanic 1,063

Arrests, 2006

Total................................. 46,100
  Persons under 18 years of age 8,314

Persons under sentence of death, 1/1/07

Total..................................... 0
  White.................................. 0
  Black.................................. 0
  Hispanic 0

State's highest court

Name ....Supreme Court
Number of members........................ 5
Length of term........................ 5 years
Intermediate appeals court? .... no

Labor & Income

Civilian labor force, 2006 (x 1,000)

Total.................................. 741
  Men 392
  Women 349
  Persons 16-19 years.................... 38
  White............................... 710
  Black .... NA
  Hispanic 13

Civilian labor force as a percent of civilian non-institutional population, 2006

Total.................................70.9%
  Men 76.9
  Women 65.3
  Persons 16-19 years...................52.2
  White................................70.8
  Black .... NA
  Hispanic 76.8

Employment, 2006 (x 1,000)

Total.................................. 716
  Men 378
  Women 338
  Persons 16-19 years.................... 34
  White............................... 687
  Black .... NA
  Hispanic 12

Unemployment rate, 2006

Total.................................. 3.4%
  Men 3.5
  Women 3.1
  Persons 16-19 years...................11.8
  White................................. 3.3
  Black .... NA
  Hispanic 3.6

Full-time/part-time labor force, 2003 (x 1,000)

Full-time labor force, employed 550
Part-time labor force, employed............ 139
Unemployed, looking for
  Full-time work........................... 23
  Part-time work........................... 7
Mean duration of unemployment (weeks)......20.6
  Median 10.0

Labor unions, 2006

Membership (x 1,000).................... 63
  percent of employed 10.1%

Experienced civilian labor force by private industry, 2006

Total............................. 541,506
  Natural resources & mining 2,416
  Construction 29,443
  Manufacturing...................... 78,363
  Trade, transportation & utilities 141,903
  Information 12,531
  Finance 37,541
  Professional & business 61,507
  Education & health 94,072
  Leisure & hospitality.................63,975
  Other 19,274

Experienced civilian labor force by occupation, May 2006

Management........................ 32,890
Business & financial 27,490
Legal.............................. 3,280
Sales.............................. 80,560
Office & admin. support.............. 108,740
Computers & math 16,620
Architecture & engineering............ 12,420
Arts & entertainment 5,700
Education 45,530
Social services 7,560
Health care practitioner & technical......31,900
Health care support 14,860
Maintenance & repair................. 26,390
Construction 25,950
Transportation & moving 35,820
Production 49,780
Farming, fishing & forestry................ 840

Hours and earnings of production workers on manufacturing payrolls, 2006

Average weekly hours 41.2
Average hourly earnings $16.56
Average weekly earnings $682.27

Income and poverty, 2006

Median household income............ $59,683
Personal income, per capita (current $)... $39,311
  in constant (2000) dollars $34,316
Persons below poverty level............... 8.0%

Average annual pay

2006................................. $42,447
  increase from 2005 .... 4.7%

Federal individual income tax returns, 2005

Returns filed........................ 650,233
Adjusted gross income ($1,000) $37,533,740
Total tax liability ($1,000) $5,094,192

Charitable contributions, 2004

Number of contributions.................196.9
Total amount ($ mil)...................$547.5

Economy, Business, Industry & Agriculture

Fortune 500 companies, 2007 0
Bankruptcy cases filed, FY 2007 2,804

Patents and trademarks issued, 2007

Patents 609
Trademarks 334

Business firm ownership, 2002

Women-owned 31,024
   Sales ($ mil) $4,665
Black-owned 470
   Sales ($ mil) $68
Hispanic-owned 913
   Sales ($ mil) $194
Asian-owned 1,528
   Sales ($ mil) $404
Amer. Indian/Alaska Native-owned 535
   Sales ($ mil) $59
Hawaiian/Pacific Islander-owned 17
   Sales ($ mil) . . . . NA

Gross domestic product, 2006 ($ mil)

Total gross domestic product $56,276
   Agriculture, forestry, fishing and
     hunting 221
   Mining 63
   Utilities 2,089
   Construction 2,733
   Manufacturing, durable goods 4,924
   Manufacturing, non-durable goods 1,678
   Wholesale trade .3,634
   Retail trade 4,714
   Transportation & warehousing 872
   Information 1,958
   Finance & insurance 4,607
   Real estate, rental & leasing 8,251
   Professional and technical services 3,739
   Educational services 1,041
   Health care and social assistance 4,808
   Accommodation/food services 1,664
   Other services, except government 1,349
   Government 5,182

Establishments, payroll, employees & receipts, by major industry group, 2005

Total 39,224
   Annual payroll ($1,000) $21,026,773
   Paid employees 562,398

Forestry, fishing & agriculture 153
   Annual payroll ($1,000) $19,217
   Paid employees 691

Mining 46
   Annual payroll ($1,000) $18,910
   Paid employees 326
   Receipts, 2002 ($1,000) *$61,093*

Utilities 103
   Annual payroll ($1,000) $233,759
   Paid employees 3,434
   Receipts, 2002 ($1,000) . . . .*NA*

Construction 4,913
   Annual payroll ($1,000) $1,349,971
   Paid employees 27,877
   Receipts, 2002 ($1,000) *$5,222,133*

Manufacturing 2,155
   Annual payroll ($1,000) $3,549,995
   Paid employees 75,837
   Receipts, 2002 ($1,000) *$15,235,144*

Wholesale trade 2,018
   Annual payroll ($1,000) $1,383,024
   Paid employees 24,728
   Receipts, 2002 ($1,000) *$13,741,876*

Retail trade 6,687
   Annual payroll ($1,000) $2,359,255
   Paid employees 99,693
   Receipts, 2002 ($1,000) *$20,830,057*

Transportation & warehousing 839
   Annual payroll ($1,000) $389,185
   Paid employees 12,244
   Receipts, 2002 ($1,000) *$1,297,644*

Information 777
   Annual payroll ($1,000) $785,703
   Paid employees 13,392
   Receipts, 2002 ($1,000) . . . .*NA*

Finance & insurance 1,942
   Annual payroll ($1,000) $1,678,378
   Paid employees 28,136
   Receipts, 2002 ($1,000) . . . .*NA*

Professional, scientific & technical 4,032
   Annual payroll ($1,000) $1,715,627
   Paid employees 29,619
   Receipts, 2002 ($1,000) *$2,866,611*

Education 588
   Annual payroll ($1,000) $702,695
   Paid employees 21,659
   Receipts, 2002 ($1,000) *$200,819*

Health care & social assistance 3,334
   Annual payroll ($1,000) $2,936,765
   Paid employees 79,240
   Receipts, 2002 ($1,000) *$5,518,477*

Arts and entertainment 747
   Annual payroll ($1,000) $199,301
   Paid employees 10,530
   Receipts, 2002 ($1,000) *$601,029*

Real estate 1,592
   Annual payroll ($1,000) $278,452
   Paid employees 7,943
   Receipts, 2002 ($1,000) *$1,117,115*

Accommodation & food service 3,369
   Annual payroll ($1,000) $803,288
   Paid employees 56,070
   Receipts, 2002 ($1,000) *$2,082,145*

8　New Hampshire

Exports, 2006
Value of exported goods ($ mil) $2,811
　Manufactured $2,307
　Non-manufactured................... $258

Foreign direct investment in US affiliates, 2004
Property, plants & equipment ($ mil) $4,693
Employment (x 1,000)....................41.0

Agriculture, 2006
Number of farms 3,400
Farm acreage (x 1,000) 450
　Acres per farm........................ 132
Farm marketings and income ($ mil)
Total................................$161.8
　Crops...............................$97.8
　Livestock........................... $64.0
Net farm income $42.6

Principal commodities, in order by marketing receipts, 2005
Greenhouse/nursery, Dairy products, Cattle and calves, Apples, Hay

Federal economic activity in state
Expenditures, 2005 ($ mil)
　Total.............................. $8,331
　　Per capita $6,374.82
　Defense $1,293
　Non-defense.........................$7,038
Defense department, 2006 ($ mil)
　Payroll............................. $324
　Contract awards $1,106
　Grants $32
Homeland security grants ($1,000)
　2006..............................$7,887
　2007 .... $6,955

FDIC-insured financial institutions, 2005
Number 26
Assets ($ billion) $19.7
Deposits ($ billion) $13.4

Fishing, 2006
Catch (x 1,000 lbs).................... 10,295
Value ($1,000)........................$18,970

Mining, 2006 ($ mil)
Total non-fuel mineral production $100
Percent of U.S. 0.16%

Communication, Energy & Transportation

Communication
Households with computers, 2003........ 71.5%
Households with internet access, 2003 .... 65.2%
High-speed internet providers 36
Total high-speed internet lines......... 443,137
　Residential 304,594
　Business........................... 138,543
Wireless phone customers, 12/2006 943,330

FCC-licensed stations (as of January 1, 2008)
TV stations 7
FM radio stations......................... 59
AM radio stations 27

Energy
Energy consumption, 2004
　Total (trillion Btu)..................... 341
　Per capita (million Btu) 262.5
By source of production (trillion Btu)
　Coal 43
　Natural gas 65
　Petroleum............................ 205
　Nuclear electric power 106
　Hydroelectric power 13
By end-use sector (trillion Btu)
　Residential 100
　Commercial 76
　Industrial 56
　Transportation 109
Electric energy, 2005
　Primary source of electricity......... Nuclear
　Net generation (billion kWh) 24.5
　　percent from renewable sources...... 11.2%
　Net summer capability (million kW) 4.3
　CO$_2$ emitted from generation 8.2
Natural gas utilities, 2005
　Customers (x 1,000) 111
　Sales (trillion Btu)...................... 25
　Revenues ($ mil) $228
Nuclear plants, 2007 1
Total CO$_2$ emitted (million metric tons)......20.5
Energy spending, 2004 ($ mil) $3,928
　per capita $3,026
　Price per million Btu $15.52

Transportation, 2006
Public road & street mileage 15,647
　Urban...............................4,733
　Rural 10,914
　Interstate........................... 225
Vehicle miles of travel (millions) 13,614
　per capita 10,377.9
Total motor vehicle registrations.......1,059,963
　Automobiles....................... 585,455
　Trucks 472,635
　Motorcycles 70,778
Licensed drivers 1,027,582
　19 years & under 57,114
Deaths from motor vehicle accidents 127
Gasoline consumed (x 1,000 gallons) 717,750
　per capita 547.1

Commuting Statistics, 2006
Average commute time (min) 24.6
　Drove to work alone 81.7%
　Carpooled........................... 8.6%
　Public transit 0.7%
　Walk to work 3.4%
　Work from home...................... 4.3%

State Summary

Capital city . . . . Trenton
Governor . . . . Jon Corzine

The State House
PO Box 001
Trenton, NJ 08625
609-292-6000

Admitted as a state 1787
Area (square miles) 8,721
Population, 2007 (estimate). 8,685,920
Largest city . . . . Newark
  Population, 2006 281,402
Personal income per capita, 2006
  (in current dollars) $46,344
Gross domestic product, 2006 ($ mil) . . . $453,177

Leading industries by payroll, 2005

Professional/Scientific/Technical, Health care/
  Social assistance, Wholesale trade

Leading agricultural commodities by receipts, 2005

Greenhouse/nursery, Horses/mules, Blueberries,
  Peaches, Dairy products

Geography & Environment

Total area (square miles). 8,721
  land 7,417
  water 1,304
Federally-owned land, 2004 (acres) 148,441
  percent. 3.1%
Highest point . . . . High Point
  elevation (feet) .1,803
Lowest point . . . . Atlantic Ocean
  elevation (feet) . . . . sea level
General coastline (miles) 130
Tidal shoreline (miles) 1,792
Cropland, 2003 (x 1,000 acres) 528
Forest land, 2003 (x 1,000 acres). 1,605
Capital city . . . . Trenton
  Population 2000 85,403
  Population 2006 83,923
Largest city . . . . Newark
  Population 2000 273,546
  Population 2006 281,402

Number of cities with over 100,000 population

1990 4
2000 4
2006 4

State park and recreation areas, 2005

Area (x 1,000 acres) 397
Number of visitors (x 1,000) 15,791
Revenues ($1,000) $10,176
  percent of operating expenditures. 27.6%

National forest system land, 2007

Acres 0

Demographics & Population Characteristics

Population

1980 7,364,823
1990 7,730,188
2000 8,414,347
2006 8,724,560
  Male 4,262,291
  Female 4,462,269
Living in group quarters, 2006 197,712
  percent of total. 2.3%
2007 (estimate) .8,685,920
  persons per square mile of land 1,171.1
2008 (projected). 8,915,495
2010 (projected) 9,018,231
2020 (projected) 9,461,635
2030 (projected) 9,802,440

Population of Core-Based Statistical Areas (formerly Metropolitan Areas), x 1,000

	CBSA	Non-CBSA
1990	7,730	0
2000	8,414	0
2006	8,725	0

Change in population, 2000-2007

Number 271,573
  percent 3.2%
Natural increase (births minus deaths) 291,260
Net internal migration . . . . -377,159
Net international migration 376,519

Persons by age, 2006

Under 5 years 558,994
5 to 17 years 1,530,344
18 years and over 6,635,222
65 years and over 1,127,742
85 years and over 166,529
  Median age 38.2

Persons by age, 2010 (projected)

Under 5 years 587,220
18 and over 6,930,007
65 and over 1,231,585
  Median age 38.9

Race, 2006

One Race
  White. 6,665,390
  Black or African American 1,264,681
  Asian 647,986
  American Indian/Alaska Native. 27,970
  Hawaiian Native/Pacific Islander. 6,878
Two or more races. .111,655

Persons of Hispanic origin, 2006

Total Hispanic or Latino 1,364,699
  Mexican. 186,918
  Puerto Rican 392,619
  Cuban 73,024

Persons of Asian origin, 2006

Total Asian 652,378
  Asian Indian. 256,965
  Chinese 129,896
  Filipino 105,806
  Japanese 16,681
  Korean. 86,356
  Vietnamese. 24,251

Marital status, 2006

Population 15 years & over 7,006,178
  Never married 2,222,005
  Married. 3,723,172
  Separated 160,006
  Widowed. 483,310
  Divorced 577,691

Language spoken at home, 2006

Population 5 years and older. 8,164,688
  English only 5,907,177
  Spanish 1,134,033
  French 68,457
  German. 32,276
  Chinese 104,226

Households & families, 2006

Households. 3,135,490
  with persons under 18 years 1,146,672
  with persons over 65 years. 783,466
  persons per household 2.72
Families. 2,180,404
  persons per family. 3.29
Married couples. 1,631,340
Female householder,
  no husband present. 404,348
One-person households 803,445

Nativity, 2006

Number of residents born in state 4,573,613
  percent of population. 52.4%

Immigration & naturalization, 2006

Legal permanent residents admitted. 65,934
Persons naturalized 39,801
Non-immigrant admissions 771,060

Vital Statistics and Health

Marriages

2004 50,662
2005 49,305
2006 42,398

Divorces

2004 25,981
2005 25,343
2006 25,794

Health risks, 2006

Percent of adults who are:
  Smokers. 18.0%
  Overweight (BMI > 25). 59.9%
  Obese (BMI > 30). 22.6%

Births

2005 113,776
  Birthrate (per 1,000). 13.1
  White. 82,659
  Black 19,990
  Hispanic 27,959
  Asian/Pacific Islander 10,949
  Amer. Indian/Alaska Native 178
  Low birth weight (2,500g or less). 8.2%
  Cesarian births 36.3%
  Preterm births 12.5%
  To unmarried mothers. 31.4%
  Twin births (per 1,000) 41.8
  Triplets or higher order (per 100,000). . . 288.7
2006 (preliminary). 115,006
  rate per 1,000 . . . . .13.2

Deaths

2004
All causes 71,371
  rate per 100,000. . . . . .752.7
Heart disease 20,560
  rate per 100,000. . . . . .213.0
Malignant neoplasms 17,208
  rate per 100,000. . . . . .184.4
Cerebrovascular disease. 3,781
  rate per 100,000. .39.2
Chronic lower respiratory disease 3,031
  rate per 100,000. .32.1
Diabetes. 2,595
  rate per 100,000. .27.6
2005 (preliminary). 71,970
  rate per 100,000. . . . . .745.9
2006 (provisional) 71,809

Infant deaths

2004 651
  rate per 1,000 . . . . .5.7
2005 (provisional) 586
  rate per 1,000 . . . . .5.1

Exercise routines, 2005

None. 29.2%
Moderate or greater. 45.9%
Vigorous 25.5%

Abortions, 2004

Total performed in state. 32,642
  rate per 1,000 women age 15-44. 18
  % obtained by out-of-state residents 4.8%

Physicians, 2005

Total. 26,918
  rate per 100,000 persons 309

Community hospitals, 2005

Number of hospitals 80
Beds (x 1,000). 22.1
Patients admitted (x 1,000) 1,110
Average daily census (x 1,000) 16.2
Average cost per day $1,797
Outpatient visits (x 1 mil) 16.8

Disability status of population, 2006
5 to 15 years 5.3%
16 to 64 years 9.3%
65 years and over 36.5%

Education

Educational attainment, 2006
Population over 25 years 5,871,240
   Less than 9th grade. 5.9%
   High school graduate or more 86.1%
   College graduate or more. 33.4%
   Graduate or professional degree. 12.4%

Public school enrollment, 2005-06
Total 1,395,602
   Pre-kindergarten through grade 8. 926,870
   Grades 9 through 12 407,314

Graduating public high school seniors, 2004-05
Diplomas (incl. GED and others) 86,502

SAT scores, 2007
Average critical reading score 495
Average writing score 494
Average math score 510
Percent of graduates taking test 82%

Public school teachers, 2006-07 (estimate)
Total (x 1,000) 115.0
   Elementary 44.4
   Secondary 70.6
Average salary $59,920
   Elementary $58,866
   Secondary $61,373

State receipts & expenditures for public schools, 2006-07 (estimate)
Revenue receipts ($ mil) $21,167
Expenditures
Total ($ mil) $21,096
   Per capita $2,336
   Per pupil $14,824

NAEP proficiency scores, 2007

	Reading		Math	
	Basic	Proficient	Basic	Proficient
Grade 4	77.2%	43.1%	89.6%	51.8%
Grade 8	81.1%	39.0%	77.5%	40.4%

Higher education enrollment, fall 2005
Total 75,443
   Full-time men 25,388
   Full-time women 26,707
   Part-time men 9,601
   Part-time women 13,747

Minority enrollment in institutions of higher education, 2005
Black, non-Hispanic 53,971
Hispanic 50,502
Asian/Pacific Islander 32,409
American Indian/Alaska Native 1,170

Institutions of higher education, 2005-06
Total 59
   Public 33
   Private 26

Earned degrees conferred, 2004-05
Associate's 14,726
Bachelor's 31,987
Master's 12,386
First-professional 1,817
Doctor's 1,142

Public Libraries, 2006
Number of libraries 306
Number of outlets 467
Annual visits per capita 5.4
Circulation per capita 6.4

State & local financial support for higher education, FY 2006
Full-time equivalent enrollment (x 1,000) 228.1
Appropriations per FTE $8,145

Social Insurance & Welfare Programs

Social Security benefits & beneficiaries, 2005
Beneficiaries (x 1,000) 1,379
   Retired & dependents 1,012
   Survivors 169
   Disabled & dependents 197
Annual benefit payments ($ mil) $16,474
   Retired & dependents $11,675
   Survivors $2,565
   Disabled & dependents $2,234
Average monthly benefit
   Retired & dependents $1,105
   Disabled & dependents $1,023
   Widowed $1,065

Medicare, July 2005
Enrollment (x 1,000) 1,227
Payments ($ mil) $9,860

Medicaid, 2004
Beneficiaries (x 1,000) 119
Payments ($ mil) $822

State Children's Health Insurance Program, 2006
Enrollment (x 1,000) 120.9
Expenditures ($ mil) $190.6

Persons without health insurance, 2006
Number (x 1,000) 1,341
   percent 15.5%
Number of children (x 1,000) 277
   percent of children 13.3%

Health care expenditures, 2004
Total expenditures $50,384
   per capita $5,807

Federal and state public aid

State unemployment insurance, 2006
Recipients, first payments (x 1,000) 305
Total payments ($ mil) $1,775
Average weekly benefit $344
Temporary Assistance for Needy Families, 2006
Recipients (x 1,000). 1,157.4
Families (x 1,000) 472.1
Supplemental Security Income, 2005
Recipients (x 1,000). 152.4
Payments ($ mil) $763.4
Food Stamp Program, 2006
Avg monthly participants (x 1,000) 405.7
Total benefits ($ mil). $455.9

Housing & Construction

Housing units

Total 2005 (estimate) 3,443,194
Total 2006 (estimate) 3,472,643
Seasonal or recreational use, 2006 119,636
Owner-occupied, 2006 2,110,308
  Median home value. $366,600
  Homeowner vacancy rate. 1.6%
Renter-occupied, 2006 1,025,182
  Median rent $974
  Rental vacancy rate. 7.3%
Home ownership rate, 2005. . . . . 70.1%
Home ownership rate, 2006. . . . . 69.0%

New privately-owned housing units

Number authorized, 2006 (x 1,000) 34.3
  Value ($ mil). $4,382.7
Started 2005 (x 1,000, estimate) 26.5
Started 2006 (x 1,000, estimate) 26.1

Existing home sales

2005 (x 1,000). 184.4
2006 (x 1,000). 154.1

Government & Elections

State officials 2008

Governor . . . . .Jon Corzine
  Democratic, term expires 1/10
Lieutenant Governor. . (no Lieutenant Governor)
Secretary of State. . . . . Nina Wells
Attorney General. . . . . Anne Milgram
Chief Justice . . . . .Stuart Rabner

Governorship

Minimum age. 30
Length of term . . . . 4 years
Consecutive terms permitted 2
Who succeeds. . . . . President of Senate

Local governments by type, 2002

Total. 1,412
  County. 21
  Municipal 324
  Township 242
  School District. 549
  Special District 276

State legislature

Name . . . . Legislature
Upper chamber . . . . .Senate
  Number of members. 40
  Length of term . . . . 4 years
  Party in majority, 2008 . . . . .Democratic
Lower chamber. . . . . General Assembly
  Number of members. 80
  Length of term. 2 years
  Party in majority, 2008 . . . . .Democratic

Federal representation, 2008 (110th Congress)

Senator. Frank Lautenberg
  Party . . . . .Democratic
  Year term expires 2009
Senator. Robert Menendez
  Party . . . . .Democratic
  Year term expires 2013
Representatives, total 13
  Democrats. 7
  Republicans 6

Voters in November 2006 election (estimate)

Total 2,406,132
  Male. 1,121,355
  Female. 1,284,777
  White. 2,036,979
  Black 266,563
  Hispanic 83,157
  Asian 96,283

Presidential election, 2004

Total Popular Vote 3,611,691
  Kerry 1,911,430
  Bush. 1,670,003
Total Electoral Votes. 15

Votes cast for US Senators

2004
Total vote (x 1,000) . . . . NA
Leading party. . . . . NA
Percent for leading party . . . . NA

2006
Total vote (x 1,000) 102
Leading party. . . . . .Democratic
Percent for leading party 57.2%

Votes cast for US Representatives

2004
Total vote (x 1,000) 3,285
  Democratic. 1,721
  Republican 1,515
Leading party. . . . . .Democratic
Percent for leading party 52.4%

2006
Total vote (x 1,000) 2,137
  Democratic. 1,208
  Republican 903
Leading party. . . . . .Democratic
Percent for leading party 56.5%

State government employment, 2006
Full-time equivalent employees 156,768
Payroll ($ mil) $767.5

Local government employment, 2006
Full-time equivalent employees 354,987
Payroll ($ mil) $1,608.8

Women holding public office, 2008
US Congress 0
Statewide elected office.................. 0
State legislature 34

Black public officials, 2002
Total.................................. 269
  US and state legislatures 18
  City/county/regional offices 162
  Judicial/law enforcement................. 0
  Education/school boards 89

Hispanic public officials, 2006
Total.................................. 109
  State executives & legislators 5
  City/county/regional offices 61
  Judicial/law enforcement................. 0
  Education/school boards 43

Governmental Finance

State government revenues, 2006
Total revenue (x $1,000) $57,610,331
  per capita $6,647.80
General revenue (x $1,000) $46,445,905
  Intergovernmental 11,378,454
  Taxes 26,266,187
    general sales.................... 6,853,418
    individual income tax 10,506,565
    corporate income tax 2,508,428
  Current charges................... 4,682,195
  Miscellaneous 4,119,069

State government expenditure, 2006
Total expenditure (x $1,000) $54,073,301
  per capita $6,239.65
General expenditure (x $1,000) $43,349,868
  per capita, total.................. $5,002.25
    Education 1,632.60
    Public welfare 1,442.60
    Health 92.11
    Hospitals...................... 197.67
    Highways 301.83
    Police protection.............. 61.54
    Corrections 164.02
    Natural resources 66.60
    Parks & recreation 52.12
    Governmental administration...... 204.17
    Interest on general debt........... 175.17

State debt & cash, 2006 ($ per capita)
Debt $5,515.84
Cash/security holdings............. $11,192.67

Federal government grants to state & local government, 2005 (x $1,000)
Total........................... $11,124,122
by Federal agency
  Defense 68,094
  Education 890,179
  Energy........................... 39,441
  Environmental Protection Agency 89,819
  Health & Human Services. 6,397,656
  Homeland Security................. 33,108
  Housing & Urban Development..... 1,273,098
  Justice 130,135
  Labor 243,616
  Transportation 1,216,468
  Veterans Affairs.................. 22,569

Crime & Law Enforcement

Crime, 2006 (rates per 100,000 residents)
Property crimes 199,958
  Burglary 39,433
  Larceny 135,801
  Motor vehicle theft 24,724
  Property crime rate.............. 2,291.9
Violent crimes........................ 30,672
  Murder 428
  Forcible rape..................... 1,237
  Robbery.......................... 13,357
  Aggravated assault 15,650
  Violent crime rate 351.6
Hate crimes. 802

Fraud and identity theft, 2006
Fraud complaints..................... 11,284
  rate per 100,000 residents 129.3
Identity theft complaints 6,394
  rate per 100,000 residents 73.3

Law enforcement agencies, 2006
Total agencies........................ 529
Total employees 36,456
  Officers 29,013
  Civilians 7,443

Prisoners, probation, and parole, 2006
Total prisoners....................... 27,371
  percent change, 12/31/05 to 12/31/06 .... 0.0%
  in private facilities 9.5%
  in local jails 6.7%
Sentenced to more than one year 27,371
  rate per 100,000 residents 313
Adults on probation 132,636
Adults on parole...................... 14,405

Prisoner demographics, June 30, 2005 (rate per 100,000 residents)
Male................................. 1,019
Female 70
White................................ 190
Black................................ 2,352
Hispanic 630

Arrests, 2006
Total 388,116
    Persons under 18 years of age 60,840

Persons under sentence of death, 1/1/07
Total 11
    White 5
    Black 6
    Hispanic 0

State's highest court
Name .... Supreme Court
Number of members 7
Length of term .... 7 years
Intermediate appeals court? .... yes

Labor & Income

Civilian labor force, 2006 (x 1,000)
Total 4,490
    Men 2,428
    Women 2,063
    Persons 16-19 years 187
    White 3,473
    Black 599
    Hispanic 722

Civilian labor force as a percent of civilian non-institutional population, 2006
Total 66.6%
    Men 75.2
    Women 58.7
    Persons 16-19 years 38.1
    White 66.2
    Black 66.5
    Hispanic 70.6

Employment, 2006 (x 1,000)
Total 4,273
    Men 2,312
    Women 1,961
    Persons 16-19 years 162
    White 3,328
    Black 541
    Hispanic 676

Unemployment rate, 2006
Total 4.8%
    Men 4.8
    Women 4.9
    Persons 16-19 years 13.3
    White 4.2
    Black 9.7
    Hispanic 6.4

Full-time/part-time labor force, 2003 (x 1,000)
Full-time labor force, employed 3,454
Part-time labor force, employed 664
Unemployed, looking for
    Full-time work 222
    Part-time work 35
Mean duration of unemployment (weeks) 20.4
    Median 12.0

Labor unions, 2006
Membership (x 1,000) 770
    percent of employed 20.1%

Experienced civilian labor force by private industry, 2006
Total 3,340,229
    Natural resources & mining 12,073
    Construction 172,909
    Manufacturing 321,825
    Trade, transportation & utilities 864,235
    Information 97,150
    Finance 266,608
    Professional & business 596,296
    Education & health 522,312
    Leisure & hospitality 335,325
    Other 124,190

Experienced civilian labor force by occupation, May 2006
Management 185,110
Business & financial 200,310
Legal 32,750
Sales 418,290
Office & admin. support 761,070
Computers & math 119,890
Architecture & engineering 56,210
Arts & entertainment 44,720
Education 265,780
Social services 54,890
Health care practitioner & technical 201,670
Health care support 106,650
Maintenance & repair 147,460
Construction 144,050
Transportation & moving 318,750
Production 223,550
Farming, fishing & forestry 4,620

Hours and earnings of production workers on manufacturing payrolls, 2006
Average weekly hours 42.1
Average hourly earnings $16.55
Average weekly earnings $696.76

Income and poverty, 2006
Median household income $64,470
Personal income, per capita (current $) ... $46,344
    in constant (2000) dollars $40,455
Persons below poverty level 8.7%

Average annual pay
2006 .... $51,645
    increase from 2005 .... 4.4%

Federal individual income tax returns, 2005
Returns filed 4,152,741
Adjusted gross income ($1,000) ... $282,306,218
Total tax liability ($1,000) $42,460,858

Charitable contributions, 2004
Number of contributions 1,683.8
Total amount ($ mil) $5,533.7

Economy, Business, Industry & Agriculture

Fortune 500 companies, 2007 24
Bankruptcy cases filed, FY 2007 18,702

Patents and trademarks issued, 2007
Patents 3,185
Trademarks 2,691

Business firm ownership, 2002
Women-owned 185,197
  Sales ($ mil) $35,573
Black-owned 36,280
  Sales ($ mil) $3,202
Hispanic-owned 49,841
  Sales ($ mil) $7,245
Asian-owned 51,957
  Sales ($ mil) $18,495
Amer. Indian/Alaska Native-owned 2,645
  Sales ($ mil) $284
Hawaiian/Pacific Islander-owned 448
  Sales ($ mil) $37

Gross domestic product, 2006 ($ mil)
Total gross domestic product $453,177
  Agriculture, forestry, fishing and
    hunting 642
  Mining 226
  Utilities 8,917
  Construction 19,068
  Manufacturing, durable goods 13,915
  Manufacturing, non-durable goods 27,644
  Wholesale trade 36,464
  Retail trade 28,413
  Transportation & warehousing 13,119
  Information 21,541
  Finance & insurance 37,327
  Real estate, rental & leasing 78,182
  Professional and technical services 38,536
  Educational services 3,994
  Health care and social assistance 32,062
  Accommodation/food services 11,176
  Other services, except government 9,208
  Government 45,003

Establishments, payroll, employees & receipts, by major industry group, 2005

Total 242,128
  Annual payroll ($1,000) $166,018,238
  Paid employees 3,594,862
Forestry, fishing & agriculture 243
  Annual payroll ($1,000) $26,847
  Paid employees 751
Mining 110
  Annual payroll ($1,000) $137,556
  Paid employees 2,305
  Receipts, 2002 ($1,000) $379,558

Utilities 340
  Annual payroll ($1,000) $1,545,619
  Paid employees 18,164
  Receipts, 2002 ($1,000) . . . . .NA
Construction 25,455
  Annual payroll ($1,000) $9,240,445
  Paid employees 175,322
  Receipts, 2002 ($1,000) $37,867,759
Manufacturing 9,575
  Annual payroll ($1,000) $15,352,555
  Paid employees 304,976
  Receipts, 2002 ($1,000) $96,599,807
Wholesale trade 16,347
  Annual payroll ($1,000) $17,375,975
  Paid employees 274,063
  Receipts, 2002 ($1,000) $256,925,492
Retail trade 35,263
  Annual payroll ($1,000) $11,303,325
  Paid employees 454,878
  Receipts, 2002 ($1,000) $102,153,833
Transportation & warehousing 7,228
  Annual payroll ($1,000) $6,443,091
  Paid employees 169,118
  Receipts, 2002 ($1,000) $16,421,043
Information 4,059
  Annual payroll ($1,000) $7,846,435
  Paid employees 122,177
  Receipts, 2002 ($1,000) . . . . .NA
Finance & insurance 12,543
  Annual payroll ($1,000) $16,995,391
  Paid employees 216,384
  Receipts, 2002 ($1,000) . . . . .NA
Professional, scientific & technical 31,669
  Annual payroll ($1,000) $20,504,746
  Paid employees 304,803
  Receipts, 2002 ($1,000) $36,005,523
Education 3,021
  Annual payroll ($1,000) $2,702,816
  Paid employees 84,880
  Receipts, 2002 ($1,000) $1,662,096
Health care & social assistance 24,772
  Annual payroll ($1,000) $19,367,540
  Paid employees 479,536
  Receipts, 2002 ($1,000) $38,708,974
Arts and entertainment 3,601
  Annual payroll ($1,000) $1,162,942
  Paid employees 46,240
  Receipts, 2002 ($1,000) $3,303,069
Real estate 9,584
  Annual payroll ($1,000) $2,841,714
  Paid employees 61,965
  Receipts, 2002 ($1,000) $12,262,786
Accommodation & food service 18,872
  Annual payroll ($1,000) $4,978,755
  Paid employees 274,639
  Receipts, 2002 ($1,000) $15,715,595

Exports, 2006

Value of exported goods ($ mil) $27,002
- Manufactured $20,112
- Non-manufactured $1,862

Foreign direct investment in US affiliates, 2004

Property, plants & equipment ($ mil) . . . $33,846
Employment (x 1,000) 219.7

Agriculture, 2006

Number of farms 9,800
Farm acreage (x 1,000) 790
- Acres per farm 81

Farm marketings and income ($ mil)
Total $923.9
- Crops $762.6
- Livestock $161.3
Net farm income $305.4

Principal commodities, in order by marketing receipts, 2005

Greenhouse/nursery, Horses/mules, Blueberries, Peaches, Dairy products

Federal economic activity in state

Expenditures, 2005 ($ mil)
Total $58,617
- Per capita $6,735.11
- Defense $7,645
- Non-defense $50,972

Defense department, 2006 ($ mil)
- Payroll $2,004
- Contract awards $6,151
- Grants $77

Homeland security grants ($1,000)
- 2006 . . . . $51,983
- 2007 . . . . $61,109

FDIC-insured financial institutions, 2005

Number 131
Assets ($ billion) $139.7
Deposits ($ billion) $90.8

Fishing, 2006

Catch (x 1,000 lbs) 175,759
Value ($1,000) $145,850

Mining, 2006 ($ mil)

Total non-fuel mineral production $369
Percent of U.S. 0.57%

Communication, Energy & Transportation

Communication

Households with computers, 2003 . . . . 65.5%
Households with internet access, 2003 . . . . 60.5%
High-speed internet providers 41
Total high-speed internet lines 3,392,607
- Residential 2,109,126
- Business 1,283,481
Wireless phone customers, 12/2006 7,207,018

FCC-licensed stations (as of January 1, 2008)

TV stations 15
FM radio stations 97
AM radio stations 41

Energy

Energy consumption, 2004
Total (trillion Btu) 2,630
Per capita (million Btu) 303.2

By source of production (trillion Btu)
- Coal 113
- Natural gas 647
- Petroleum 1,270
- Nuclear electric power 282
- Hydroelectric power 0

By end-use sector (trillion Btu)
- Residential 626
- Commercial 617
- Industrial 484
- Transportation 903

Electric energy, 2005
Primary source of electricity . . . . Nuclear
Net generation (billion kWh) 60.5
- percent from renewable sources 1.5%
Net summer capability (million kW) 17.5
CO_2 emitted from generation 21.1

Natural gas utilities, 2005
Customers (x 1,000) 2,775
Sales (trillion Btu) 490
Revenues ($ mil) $4,795

Nuclear plants, 2007 4
Total CO_2 emitted (million metric tons) 123.7
Energy spending, 2004 ($ mil) $27,060
per capita $3,119
Price per million Btu $14.07

Transportation, 2006

Public road & street mileage 38,561
- Urban 31,252
- Rural 7,309
- Interstate 431
Vehicle miles of travel (millions) 75,371
per capita 8,697.2
Total motor vehicle registrations 5,957,988
- Automobiles 3,692,966
- Trucks 2,241,195
- Motorcycles 163,609
Licensed drivers 5,834,227
- 19 years & under 244,542
Deaths from motor vehicle accidents 772
Gasoline consumed (x 1,000 gallons) 4,281,216
per capita 494.0

Commuting Statistics, 2006

Average commute time (min) 29.1
- Drove to work alone 71.9%
- Carpooled 9.3%
- Public transit 10.3%
- Walk to work 3.4%
- Work from home 3.2%

State Summary

Capital city . . . . Santa Fe
Governor . . . . Bill Richardson
State Capitol
Fourth Floor
Santa Fe, NM 87300
505-827-3000
Admitted as a state 1912
Area (square miles) 121,590
Population, 2007 (estimate) 1,969,915
Largest city . . . . Albuquerque
Population, 2006 504,949
Personal income per capita, 2006
(in current dollars) $29,673
Gross domestic product, 2006 ($ mil) $75,910

Leading industries by payroll, 2005

Health care/Social assistance, Retail trade, Professional/Scientific/Technical

Leading agricultural commodities by receipts, 2005

Dairy products, Cattle and calves, Hay, Pecans, Greenhouse/nursery

Geography & Environment

Total area (square miles) 121,590
  land 121,356
  water 234
Federally-owned land, 2004 (acres) . . . 32,483,877
  percent 41.8%
Highest point . . . . Wheeler Peak
  elevation (feet) 13,161
Lowest point . . . . Red Bluff Reservoir
  elevation (feet) 2,842
General coastline (miles) 0
Tidal shoreline (miles) 0
Cropland, 2003 (x 1,000 acres) 1,549
Forest land, 2003 (x 1,000 acres) 5,478
Capital city . . . . Santa Fe
  Population 2000 62,203
  Population 2006 72,056
Largest city . . . . Albuquerque
  Population 2000 448,607
  Population 2006 504,949

Number of cities with over 100,000 population

1990 1
2000 1
2006 1

State park and recreation areas, 2005

Area (x 1,000 acres) 93
Number of visitors (x 1,000) 4,157
Revenues ($1,000) $4,097
  percent of operating expenditures . . . . NA

National forest system land, 2007

Acres 9,413,211

Demographics & Population Characteristics

Population

1980 1,302,894
1990 1,515,069
2000 1,819,046
2006 1,954,599
  Male 964,808
  Female 989,791
Living in group quarters, 2006 40,752
  percent of total 2.1%
2007 (estimate) 1,969,915
  persons per square mile of land 16.2
2008 (projected) 1,951,229
2010 (projected) 1,980,225
2020 (projected) 2,084,341
2030 (projected) 2,099,708

Population of Core-Based Statistical Areas (formerly Metropolitan Areas), x 1,000

	CBSA	Non-CBSA
1990	1,442	73
2000	1,737	82
2006	1,876	78

Change in population, 2000-2007

Number 150,869
  percent 8.3%
Natural increase (births minus deaths) 99,615
Net internal migration 24,955
Net international migration 33,790

Persons by age, 2006

Under 5 years 141,969
5 to 17 years 366,961
18 years and over 1,445,669
65 years and over 242,600
85 years and over 31,309
  Median age 35.3

Persons by age, 2010 (projected)

Under 5 years 145,063
18 and over 1,500,820
65 and over 278,967
  Median age 38.3

Race, 2006

One Race
  White 1,653,876
  Black or African American 49,161
  Asian 26,140
  American Indian/Alaska Native 190,826
  Hawaiian Native/Pacific Islander 2,655
Two or more races 31,941

Persons of Hispanic origin, 2006

Total Hispanic or Latino 860,687
  Mexican 448,714
  Puerto Rican 9,632
  Cuban 4,352

Persons of Asian origin, 2006

Total Asian 25,983
  Asian Indian. 4,883
  Chinese 5,798
  Filipino 3,285
  Japanese 3,072
  Korean. 3,269
  Vietnamese. 3,834

Marital status, 2006

Population 15 years & over 1,533,025
  Never married 483,436
  Married. 777,336
  Separated 29,699
  Widowed. 89,626
  Divorced 182,627

Language spoken at home, 2006

Population 5 years and older. 1,812,867
  English only 1,150,760
  Spanish 521,599
  French 4,673
  German. 8,606
  Chinese 4,227

Households & families, 2006

Households. 726,033
  with persons under 18 years 251,407
  with persons over 65 years. 168,577
  persons per household 2.64
Families. 477,430
  persons per family. 3.26
Married couples. 345,376
Female householder,
  no husband present. 92,088
One-person households 206,276

Nativity, 2006

Number of residents born in state 994,202
  percent of population 50.9%

Immigration & naturalization, 2006

Legal permanent residents admitted. 3,805
Persons naturalized 1,538
Non-immigrant admissions 176,951

Vital Statistics and Health

Marriages

2004 14,067
2005 12,821
2006 13,423

Divorces

2004 8,829
2005 8,837
2006 8,383

Health risks, 2006

Percent of adults who are:
  Smokers. 20.1%
  Overweight (BMI > 25). 59.8%
  Obese (BMI > 30). 22.9%

Births

2005 28,835
  Birthrate (per 1,000). 15.0
  White. 24,119
  Black 540
  Hispanic 15,823
  Asian/Pacific Islander 460
  Amer. Indian/Alaska Native 3,716
  Low birth weight (2,500g or less). 8.5%
  Cesarian births 22.2%
  Preterm births 13.1%
  To unmarried mothers. 50.8%
  Twin births (per 1,000) 24.2
  Triplets or higher order (per 100,000). 65.9
2006 (preliminary). 29,937
  rate per 1,000 . . . . .15.3

Deaths

2004
All causes 14,298
  rate per 100,000. . . . . .778.9
Heart disease 3,264
  rate per 100,000. . . . . .180.4
Malignant neoplasms 3,036
  rate per 100,000. . . . . .161.9
Cerebrovascular disease. 721
  rate per 100,000. . . . . .40.5
Chronic lower respiratory disease 753
  rate per 100,000. . . . . .41.7
Diabetes. 590
  rate per 100,000. . . . . .31.7
2005 (preliminary). 14,984
  rate per 100,000. . . . . .795.0
2006 (provisional) 14,962

Infant deaths

2004 179
  rate per 1,000 . . . . .6.3
2005 (provisional) 177
  rate per 1,000 . . . . .6.2

Exercise routines, 2005

None. 23.3%
Moderate or greater. 51.0%
Vigorous 29.0%

Abortions, 2004

Total performed in state. 6,070
  rate per 1,000 women age 15-44. 15
  % obtained by out-of-state residents 6.2%

Physicians, 2005

Total. 4,622
  rate per 100,000 persons 240

Community hospitals, 2005

Number of hospitals 37
Beds (x 1,000). 3.5
Patients admitted (x 1,000) 172
Average daily census (x 1,000) 2.2
Average cost per day $1,780
Outpatient visits (x 1 mil) 4.7

Disability status of population, 2006

5 to 15 years 6.3%
16 to 64 years 14.0%
65 years and over 43.1%

Education

Educational attainment, 2006

Population over 25 years 1,239,433
   Less than 9th grade. 8.3%
   High school graduate or more 81.5%
   College graduate or more. 25.3%
   Graduate or professional degree. 10.9%

Public school enrollment, 2005-06

Total. 326,758
   Pre-kindergarten through grade 8. . . . 229,552
   Grades 9 through 12 97,206

Graduating public high school seniors, 2004-05

Diplomas (incl. GED and others) 17,837

SAT scores, 2007

Average critical reading score. 555
Average writing score 540
Average math score 546
Percent of graduates taking test 12%

Public school teachers, 2006-07 (estimate)

Total (x 1,000) 21.7
   Elementary. 14.8
   Secondary 6.9
Average salary $42,780
   Elementary $42,634
   Secondary $43,130

**State receipts & expenditures for
public schools, 2006-07 (estimate)**

Revenue receipts ($ mil) $3,277
Expenditures
Total ($ mil) $3,426
   Per capita $1,519
   Per pupil $10,106

NAEP proficiency scores, 2007

	Reading		Math	
	Basic	Proficient	Basic	Proficient
Grade 4	57.6%	24.0%	70.3%	24.5%
Grade 8	62.5%	17.3%	56.6%	17.4%

Higher education enrollment, fall 2005

Total 10,361
   Full-time men 3,329
   Full-time women 5,305
   Part-time men 665
   Part-time women. 1,062

**Minority enrollment in institutions
of higher education, 2005**

Black, non-Hispanic 3,844
Hispanic 54,271
Asian/Pacific Islander 2,602
American Indian/Alaska Native. 11,272

Institutions of higher education, 2005-06

Total. 42
   Public. 28
   Private 14

Earned degrees conferred, 2004-05

Associate's. 4,590
Bachelor's 7,342
Master's 3,219
First-professional. 250
Doctor's. 313

Public Libraries, 2006

Number of libraries. 87
Number of outlets 117
Annual visits per capita 4.6
Circulation per capita. 6.5

**State & local financial support for
higher education, FY 2006**

Full-time equivalent enrollment (x 1,000) 79.5
Appropriations per FTE. $9,299

Social Insurance &
Welfare Programs

Social Security benefits & beneficiaries, 2005

Beneficiaries (x 1,000) 311
   Retired & dependents. 209
   Survivors. 44
   Disabled & dependents. 58
Annual benefit payments ($ mil) $3,079
   Retired & dependents. $1,983
   Survivors. $526
   Disabled & dependents. $570
Average monthly benefit
   Retired & dependents. $935
   Disabled & dependents. $902
   Widowed. $895

Medicare, July 2005

Enrollment (x 1,000) 267
Payments ($ mil) $1,279

Medicaid, 2004

Beneficiaries (x 1,000). 960
Payments ($ mil) $6,623

State Children's Health Insurance Program, 2006

Enrollment (x 1,000). 25.2
Expenditures ($ mil) $23.8

Persons without health insurance, 2006

Number (x 1,000). 445
   percent. 22.9%
Number of children (x 1,000) 93
   percent of children 17.9%

Health care expenditures, 2004

Total expenditures. $8,498
   per capita $4,471

Federal and state public aid

State unemployment insurance, 2006
Recipients, first payments (x 1,000) 25
Total payments ($ mil) $105
Average weekly benefit $238
Temporary Assistance for Needy Families, 2006
Recipients (x 1,000) 497.4
Families (x 1,000) 196.1
Supplemental Security Income, 2005
Recipients (x 1,000) 53.8
Payments ($ mil) $247.9
Food Stamp Program, 2006
Avg monthly participants (x 1,000) 244.7
Total benefits ($ mil) $253.4

Housing & Construction

Housing units

Total 2005 (estimate) 838,050
Total 2006 (estimate) 850,095
Seasonal or recreational use, 2006 42,091
Owner-occupied, 2006 505,915
    Median home value $141,200
    Homeowner vacancy rate 1.7%
Renter-occupied, 2006 220,118
    Median rent $617
    Rental vacancy rate 8.1%
Home ownership rate, 2005 . . . . 71.4%
Home ownership rate, 2006 . . . . 72.0%

New privately-owned housing units

Number authorized, 2006 (x 1,000) 13.6
    Value ($ mil) $2,315.5
Started 2005 (x 1,000, estimate) 10.3
Started 2006 (x 1,000, estimate) 10.1

Existing home sales

2005 (x 1,000) 57.5
2006 (x 1,000) 58.2

Government & Elections

State officials 2008

Governor . . . . Bill Richardson
        Democratic, term expires 1/11
Lieutenant Governor . . . . Diane Denish
Secretary of State . . . . Mary Herrera
Attorney General . . . . Gary King
Chief Justice . . . . Edward Chávez

Governorship

Minimum age 30
Length of term . . . . 4 years
Consecutive terms permitted 2
Who succeeds . . . . Lieutenant Governor

Local governments by type, 2002

Total 858
    County 33
    Municipal 101
    Township 0
    School District 96
    Special District 628

State legislature

Name . . . . Legislature
Upper chamber . . . . .Senate
    Number of members 42
    Length of term . . . . 4 years
    Party in majority, 2008 . . . . .Democratic
Lower chamber . . . . .House of Representatives
    Number of members 70
    Length of term . . . . 2 years
    Party in majority, 2008 . . . . .Democratic

Federal representation, 2008 (110th Congress)

Senator . . . . Pete V. Dolmenici
    Party . . . . Republican
    Year term expires 2009
Senator . . . . .Jeff Bingaman
    Party . . . . .Democratic
    Year term expires 2013
Representatives, total 3
    Democrats 1
    Republicans 2

Voters in November 2006 election (estimate)

Total 730,909
    Male 343,429
    Female 387,481
    White 641,173
    Black 10,040
    Hispanic 117,873
    Asian 6,141

Presidential election, 2004

Total Popular Vote 756,304
    Kerry 370,942
    Bush 376,930
Total Electoral Votes 5

Votes cast for US Senators

2004
Total vote (x 1,000) . . . . NA
Leading party . . . . NA
Percent for leading party . . . . NA

2006
Total vote (x 1,000) 559
Leading party . . . . .Democratic
Percent for leading party 70.6%

Votes cast for US Representatives

2004
Total vote (x 1,000) 743
    Democratic 385
    Republican 358
Leading party . . . . .Democratic
Percent for leading party 51.8%
2006
Total vote (x 1,000) 561
    Democratic 313
    Republican 248
Leading party . . . . .Democratic
Percent for leading party 55.8%

New Mexico   5

State government employment, 2006
Full-time equivalent employees 50,783
Payroll ($ mil) $162.8

Local government employment, 2006
Full-time equivalent employees 77,146
Payroll ($ mil) $223.6

Women holding public office, 2008
US Congress 1
Statewide elected office...................... 3
State legislature 34

Black public officials, 2002
Total....................................... 4
  US and state legislatures 1
  City/county/regional offices 0
  Judicial/law enforcement.................. 2
  Education/school boards 1

Hispanic public officials, 2006
Total....................................... 649
  State executives & legislators 48
  City/county/regional offices 337
  Judicial/law enforcement................. 111
  Education/school boards 144

Governmental Finance

State government revenues, 2006
Total revenue (x $1,000)............$14,733,656
  per capita $7,585.67
General revenue (x $1,000) $12,116,954
  Intergovernmental 3,854,734
  Taxes 5,110,683
    general sales.....................1,741,673
    individual income tax 1,123,954
    corporate income tax 377,185
  Current charges.....................911,084
  Miscellaneous 2,240,453

State government expenditure, 2006
Total expenditure (x $1,000).......$13,399,021
  per capita $6,898.53
General expenditure (x $1,000) $12,278,379
  per capita, total....................$6,321.56
    Education.......................2,305.87
    Public welfare 1,436.18
    Health 180.87
    Hospitals.........................353.12
    Highways 457.42
    Police protection...................59.82
    Corrections 149.91
    Natural resources 114.48
    Parks & recreation 29.26
    Governmental administration...... 236.83
    Interest on general debt............. 160.26

State debt & cash, 2006 ($ per capita)
Debt $3,251.83
Cash/security holdings.............. $21,277.77

Federal government grants to state & local government, 2005 (x $1,000)
Total............................. $4,564,332
by Federal agency
  Defense 20,223
  Education 508,571
  Energy...........................62,125
  Environmental Protection Agency 38,779
  Health & Human Services. 2,473,963
  Homeland Security.................. 8,982
  Housing & Urban Development......159,018
  Justice 69,063
  Labor 61,116
  Transportation 305,766
  Veterans Affairs.................... 3,608

Crime & Law Enforcement
Crime, 2006 (rates per 100,000 residents)
Property crimes 76,956
  Burglary 20,909
  Larceny 46,822
  Motor vehicle theft 9,225
  Property crime rate................ 3,937.2
Violent crimes........................ 12,572
  Murder 132
  Forcible rape......................1,094
  Robbery..........................2,105
  Aggravated assault 9,241
  Violent crime rate 643.2
Hate crimes........................... 22

Fraud and identity theft, 2006
Fraud complaints...................... 2,406
  rate per 100,000 residents 123.1
Identity theft complaints 1,621
  rate per 100,000 residents 82.9

Law enforcement agencies, 2006
Total agencies......................... 75
Total employees 4,731
  Officers 3,421
  Civilians 1,310

Prisoners, probation, and parole, 2006
Total prisoners........................6,639
  percent change, 12/31/05 to 12/31/06 .... 1.0%
  in private facilities 44.1%
  in local jails 2.1%
Sentenced to more than one year 6,361
  rate per 100,000 residents 323
Adults on probation 16,493
Adults on parole....................... 2,922

Prisoner demographics, June 30, 2005 (rate per 100,000 residents)
Male...................................1,421
Female 163
White................................. NA
Black.................................. NA
Hispanic .... NA

Arrests, 2006
Total.................................72,114
    Persons under 18 years of age.........8,466

Persons under sentence of death, 1/1/07
Total......................................2
    White..................................2
    Black..................................0
    Hispanic...............................0

State's highest court
Name.....................Supreme Court
Number of members.........................5
Length of term.......................8 years
Intermediate appeals court?................yes

Labor & Income

Civilian labor force, 2006 (x 1,000)
Total....................................944
    Men...................................499
    Women.................................445
    Persons 16-19 years....................51
    White.................................814
    Black..................................24
    Hispanic..............................354

Civilian labor force as a percent of civilian non-institutional population, 2006
Total..................................63.1%
    Men..................................69.2
    Women................................57.5
    Persons 16-19 years..................43.1
    White................................63.8
    Black................................70.7
    Hispanic.............................61.9

Employment, 2006 (x 1,000)
Total....................................903
    Men...................................477
    Women.................................425
    Persons 16-19 years....................45
    White.................................779
    Black..................................23
    Hispanic..............................335

Unemployment rate, 2006
Total...................................4.4%
    Men...................................4.3
    Women.................................4.4
    Persons 16-19 years..................13.0
    White.................................4.3
    Black.................................5.5
    Hispanic..............................5.3

Full-time/part-time labor force, 2003 (x 1,000)
Full-time labor force, employed............666
Part-time labor force, employed............174
Unemployed, looking for
    Full-time work.........................48
    Part-time work..........................9
Mean duration of unemployment (weeks)......16.5
    Median................................9.0

Labor unions, 2006
Membership (x 1,000)......................62
    percent of employed..................7.8%

Experienced civilian labor force by private industry, 2006
Total................................623,628
    Natural resources & mining.........29,966
    Construction.......................59,191
    Manufacturing......................37,659
    Trade, transportation & utilities....139,875
    Information........................15,859
    Finance............................33,870
    Professional & business...........102,361
    Education & health.................96,060
    Leisure & hospitality..............86,621
    Other..............................21,817

Experienced civilian labor force by occupation, May 2006
Management...............................39,890
Business & financial.....................23,750
Legal.....................................5,270
Sales....................................80,960
Office & admin. support.................132,970
Computers & math.........................11,790
Architecture & engineering...............21,170
Arts & entertainment......................7,780
Education................................54,630
Social services..........................13,920
Health care practitioner & technical.....39,150
Health care support......................20,640
Maintenance & repair.....................33,140
Construction.............................62,110
Transportation & moving..................45,520
Production...............................33,940
Farming, fishing & forestry...............4,250

Hours and earnings of production workers on manufacturing payrolls, 2006
Average weekly hours......................39.2
Average hourly earnings................$14.06
Average weekly earnings...............$551.15

Income and poverty, 2006
Median household income.............$40,629
Personal income, per capita (current $)...$29,673
    in constant (2000) dollars...........$25,903
Persons below poverty level..............18.5%

Average annual pay
2006...................................$34,567
    increase from 2005....................6.0%

Federal individual income tax returns, 2005
Returns filed...........................843,476
Adjusted gross income ($1,000).....$35,785,778
Total tax liability ($1,000)..........$4,119,263

Charitable contributions, 2004
Number of contributions.................182.6
Total amount ($ mil)...................$597.8

Economy, Business, Industry & Agriculture

Fortune 500 companies, 2007 0
Bankruptcy cases filed, FY 2007 3,232

Patents and trademarks issued, 2007
Patents 313
Trademarks 246

Business firm ownership, 2002
Women-owned 42,254
  Sales ($ mil) $4,714
Black-owned 1,541
  Sales ($ mil) $255
Hispanic-owned .29,708
  Sales ($ mil) $4,678
Asian-owned 2,364
  Sales ($ mil) $631
Amer. Indian/Alaska Native-owned 6,819
  Sales ($ mil) $792
Hawaiian/Pacific Islander-owned 140
  Sales ($ mil) $17

Gross domestic product, 2006 ($ mil)
Total gross domestic product $75,910
  Agriculture, forestry, fishing and
    hunting 1,187
  Mining 12,040
  Utilities 1,632
  Construction 3,637
  Manufacturing, durable goods 6,257
  Manufacturing, non-durable goods 1,080
  Wholesale trade .2,581
  Retail trade 4,683
  Transportation & warehousing 1,802
  Information 1,917
  Finance & insurance 2,323
  Real estate, rental & leasing 7,136
  Professional and technical services 5,276
  Educational services 365
  Health care and social assistance 4,722
  Accommodation/food services 2,068
  Other services, except government 1,453
  Government 12,984

Establishments, payroll, employees & receipts, by major industry group, 2005

Total 45,006
  Annual payroll ($1,000) $18,171,120
  Paid employees 595,249
Forestry, fishing & agriculture 93
  Annual payroll ($1,000) $9,897
  Paid employees 378
Mining 629
  Annual payroll ($1,000) $835,555
  Paid employees .15,516
  Receipts, 2002 ($1,000) $9,803,360

Utilities 225
  Annual payroll ($1,000) $255,416
  Paid employees .4,134
  Receipts, 2002 ($1,000) . . . . .NA
Construction 5,456
  Annual payroll ($1,000) $1,691,385
  Paid employees 50,027
  Receipts, 2002 ($1,000) $6,017,501
Manufacturing 1,531
  Annual payroll ($1,000) $1,391,868
  Paid employees 34,520
  Receipts, 2002 ($1,000) $10,168,130
Wholesale trade 1,960
  Annual payroll ($1,000) $824,284
  Paid employees 20,589
  Receipts, 2002 ($1,000) $8,993,729
Retail trade 7,232
  Annual payroll ($1,000) $2,132,370
  Paid employees 95,043
  Receipts, 2002 ($1,000) $18,328,637
Transportation & warehousing 1,281
  Annual payroll ($1,000) $502,221
  Paid employees .15,710
  Receipts, 2002 ($1,000) $1,655,584
Information 793
  Annual payroll ($1,000) $471,028
  Paid employees 13,054
  Receipts, 2002 ($1,000) . . . . .NA
Finance & insurance 2,779
  Annual payroll ($1,000) $1,022,546
  Paid employees 24,666
  Receipts, 2002 ($1,000) . . . . .NA
Professional, scientific & technical 4,704
  Annual payroll ($1,000) $1,719,953
  Paid employees .35,769
  Receipts, 2002 ($1,000) $3,272,378
Education 543
  Annual payroll ($1,000) $229,797
  Paid employees .9,445
  Receipts, 2002 ($1,000) $138,081
Health care & social assistance 4,439
  Annual payroll ($1,000) $3,332,669
  Paid employees 95,623
  Receipts, 2002 ($1,000) $6,103,864
Arts and entertainment 666
  Annual payroll ($1,000) $284,729
  Paid employees 14,445
  Receipts, 2002 ($1,000) $1,228,882
Real estate 2,399
  Annual payroll ($1,000) $287,554
  Paid employees .10,216
  Receipts, 2002 ($1,000) $1,269,230
Accommodation & food service 3,944
  Annual payroll ($1,000) $933,609
  Paid employees .77,487
  Receipts, 2002 ($1,000) $2,771,474

8 New Mexico

Exports, 2006
Value of exported goods ($ mil) $2,892
  Manufactured $2,605
  Non-manufactured................... $117

Foreign direct investment in US affiliates, 2004
Property, plants & equipment ($ mil) $3,792
Employment (x 1,000)....................12.6

Agriculture, 2006
Number of farms 17,500
Farm acreage (x 1,000) 44,500
  Acres per farm...................... 2,543
Farm marketings and income ($ mil)
Total....................................$2,463.5
  Crops............................. $602.4
  Livestock.......................... $1,861.1
Net farm income $423.0

Principal commodities, in order by marketing receipts, 2005
Dairy products, Cattle and calves, Hay, Pecans, Greenhouse/nursery

Federal economic activity in state
Expenditures, 2005 ($ mil)
  Total............................. $20,604
    Per capita $10,697.88
  Defense $2,451
  Non-defense.......................$18,152
Defense department, 2006 ($ mil)
  Payroll............................$1,466
  Contract awards $1,075
  Grants $30
Homeland security grants ($1,000)
  2006.............................. $8,270
  2007.............................. $6,973

FDIC-insured financial institutions, 2005
Number.................................. 54
Assets ($ billion) $17.7
Deposits ($ billion) $13.9

Fishing, 2006
Catch (x 1,000 lbs)...................... NA
Value ($1,000)........................... NA

Mining, 2006 ($ mil)
Total non-fuel mineral production $1,460
Percent of U.S. 2.27%

Communication, Energy & Transportation

Communication
Households with computers, 2003........ 53.9%
Households with internet access, 2003 ....44.5%
High-speed internet providers 38
Total high-speed internet lines......... 422,964
  Residential 264,814
  Business.......................... 158,150
Wireless phone customers, 12/2006 1,333,210

FCC-licensed stations (as of January 1, 2008)
TV stations 26
FM radio stations......................... 139
AM radio stations 63

Energy
Energy consumption, 2004
  Total (trillion Btu)................. 682
  Per capita (million Btu) 359.0
By source of production (trillion Btu)
  Coal 309
  Natural gas........................ 230
  Petroleum.......................... 260
  Nuclear electric power 0
  Hydroelectric power....................... 1
By end-use sector (trillion Btu)
  Residential 107
  Commercial 121
  Industrial 228
  Transportation 226
Electric energy, 2005
  Primary source of electricity........... Coal
  Net generation (billion kWh) 35.1
    percent from renewable sources....... 2.7%
  Net summer capability (million kW) 6.5
  CO_2 emitted from generation 32.7
Natural gas utilities, 2005
  Customers (x 1,000) 579
  Sales (trillion Btu)................... 85
  Revenues ($ mil) $544
Nuclear plants, 2007 0
*Total CO_2 emitted (million metric tons)......57.6
Energy spending, 2004 ($ mil) $5,217
  per capita $2,745
  Price per million Btu $13.48

Transportation, 2006
Public road & street mileage 63,796
  Urban.............................7,996
  Rural 55,800
  Interstate......................... 1,000
Vehicle miles of travel (millions) 25,787
  per capita 13,276.5
Total motor vehicle registrations.......1,580,820
  Automobiles....................... 699,312
  Trucks 877,956
  Motorcycles 43,489
Licensed drivers 1,338,246
  19 years & under 49,485
Deaths from motor vehicle accidents 484
Gasoline consumed (x 1,000 gallons) 966,209
  per capita 497.5

Commuting Statistics, 2006
Average commute time (min) 20.9
  Drove to work alone 78.2%
  Carpooled..........................12.5%
  Public transit 0.9%
  Walk to work 2.2%
  Work from home..................... 4.6%

State Summary

Capital city . . . . Albany
Governor. . . . . Eliot Spitzer
State Capitol
Albany, NY 12224
518-474-7516

Admitted as a state 1788
Area (square miles) 54,556
Population, 2007 (estimate). 19,297,729
Largest city . . . . .New York
   Population, 2006. 8,214,426
Personal income per capita, 2006
   (in current dollars) $42,392
Gross domestic product, 2006 ($ mil) . .$1,021,944

Leading industries by payroll, 2005

Finance & Insurance, Health care/Social assistance, Professional/Scientific/Technical

Leading agricultural commodities by receipts, 2005

Dairy products, Greenhouse/nursery, Apples, Cattle and calves, Hay

Geography & Environment

Total area (square miles). 54,556
   land 47,214
   water 7,342
Federally-owned land, 2004 (acres) 233,533
   percent. 0.8%
Highest point . . . . Mt. Marcy
   elevation (feet) 5,344
Lowest point . . . . .Atlantic Ocean
   elevation (feet) . . . . sea level
General coastline (miles) 127
Tidal shoreline (miles) 1,850
Cropland, 2003 (x 1,000 acres) 5,359
Forest land, 2003 (x 1,000 acres). 17,599
Capital city . . . . .Albany
   Population 2000 95,658
   Population 2006 93,963
Largest city . . . . .New York
   Population 2000 8,008,278
   Population 2006 8,214,426

Number of cities with over 100,000 population

1990 5
2000 5
2006 5

State park and recreation areas, 2005

Area (x 1,000 acres). 1,367
Number of visitors (x 1,000) 56,405
Revenues ($1,000) $83,000
   percent of operating expenditures. 41.3%

National forest system land, 2007

Acres 16,211

Demographics & Population Characteristics

Population

1980 17,558,072
1990 17,990,455
2000 18,976,821
2006 19,306,183
   Male. 9,355,020
   Female. 9,951,163
Living in group quarters, 2006. 603,275
   percent of total. 3.1%
2007 (estimate). 19,297,729
   persons per square mile of land 408.7
2008 (projected). 19,383,109
2010 (projected) 19,443,672
2020 (projected). 19,576,920
2030 (projected). 19,477,429

Population of Core-Based Statistical Areas (formerly Metropolitan Areas), x 1,000

	CBSA	Non-CBSA
1990	17,574	417
2000	18,547	430
2006	18,873	433

Change in population, 2000-2007

Number 320,908
   percent. 1.7%
Natural increase (births minus deaths) 698,971
Net internal migration . . . . -1,449,169
Net international migration 859,994

Persons by age, 2006

Under 5 years 1,220,468
5 to 17 years 3,293,874
18 years and over 14,791,841
65 years and over 2,522,686
85 years and over 371,667
   Median age 37.3

Persons by age, 2010 (projected)

Under 5 years 1,250,867
18 and over 15,022,796
65 and over 2,651,655
   Median age 37.9

Race, 2006

One Race
   White. 14,220,047
   Black or African American 3,352,874
   Asian 1,326,089
   American Indian/Alaska Native. 104,936
   Hawaiian Native/Pacific Islander. 19,163
Two or more races. 283,074

Persons of Hispanic origin, 2006

Total Hispanic or Latino 3,139,590
   Mexican. 373,247
   Puerto Rican 1,071,394
   Cuban 64,899

Persons of Asian origin, 2006

Total Asian	1,322,971
Asian Indian	349,290
Chinese	519,672
Filipino	107,418
Japanese	39,350
Korean	139,282
Vietnamese	40,523

Marital status, 2006

Population 15 years & over	15,606,628
Never married	5,566,776
Married	7,674,884
Separated	465,872
Widowed	1,049,212
Divorced	1,315,756

Language spoken at home, 2006

Population 5 years and older	18,085,173
English only	12,875,365
Spanish	2,574,121
French	270,131
German	84,763
Chinese	447,602

Households & families, 2006

Households	7,088,376
with persons under 18 years	2,362,278
with persons over 65 years	1,775,976
persons per household	2.64
Families	4,573,941
persons per family	3.31
Married couples	3,200,366
Female householder, no husband present	1,035,127
One-person households	2,086,857

Nativity, 2006

Number of residents born in state	12,446,607
percent of population	64.5%

Immigration & naturalization, 2006

Legal permanent residents admitted	180,165
Persons naturalized	103,870
Non-immigrant admissions	4,243,472

Vital Statistics and Health

Marriages

2004	130,813
2005	130,409
2006	127,401

Divorces

2004	57,830
2005	54,708
2006	55,627

Health risks, 2006

Percent of adults who are:

Smokers	18.2%
Overweight (BMI > 25)	58.3%
Obese (BMI > 30)	22.9%

Births

2005	246,351
Birthrate (per 1,000)	12.8
White	170,021
Black	54,360
Hispanic	57,419
Asian/Pacific Islander	21,297
Amer. Indian/Alaska Native	673
Low birth weight (2,500g or less)	8.3%
Cesarian births	31.5%
Preterm births	12.1%
To unmarried mothers	38.7%
Twin births (per 1,000)	36.0
Triplets or higher order (per 100,000)	229.9
2006 (preliminary)	250,091
rate per 1,000	13.0

Deaths

2004

All causes	152,681
rate per 100,000	733.9
Heart disease	52,480
rate per 100,000	247.9
Malignant neoplasms	36,100
rate per 100,000	176.2
Cerebrovascular disease	6,927
rate per 100,000	32.9
Chronic lower respiratory disease	6,786
rate per 100,000	32.8
Diabetes	3,913
rate per 100,000	19.0
2005 (preliminary)	152,427
rate per 100,000	718.0
2006 (provisional)	150,329

Infant deaths

2004	1,518
rate per 1,000	6.1
2005 (provisional)	1,499
rate per 1,000	6.0

Exercise routines, 2005

None	27.1%
Moderate or greater	48.1%
Vigorous	27.3%

Abortions, 2004

Total performed in state	126,002
rate per 1,000 women age 15-44	30
% obtained by out-of-state residents	NA

Physicians, 2005

Total	74,945
rate per 100,000 persons	388

Community hospitals, 2005

Number of hospitals	203
Beds (x 1,000)	63.1
Patients admitted (x 1,000)	2,538
Average daily census (x 1,000)	50.1
Average cost per day	$1,539
Outpatient visits (x 1 mil)	51.5

Disability status of population, 2006
5 to 15 years 6.1%
16 to 64 years 10.9%
65 years and over 38.7%

Education

Educational attainment, 2006
Population over 25 years 12,845,882
    Less than 9th grade. 6.9%
    High school graduate or more 84.1%
    College graduate or more. 31.2%
    Graduate or professional degree. 13.3%

Public school enrollment, 2005-06
Total 2,815,581
    Pre-kindergarten through grade 8. . . 1,857,165
    Grades 9 through 12 851,404

Graduating public high school seniors, 2004-05
Diplomas (incl. GED and others) 158,880

SAT scores, 2007
Average critical reading score 491
Average writing score 482
Average math score 505
Percent of graduates taking test 89%

Public school teachers, 2006-07 (estimate)
Total (x 1,000) 229.3
    Elementary 112.9
    Secondary 116.4
Average salary $58,537
    Elementary $58,537
    Secondary $58,537

State receipts & expenditures for
public schools, 2006-07 (estimate)
Revenue receipts ($ mil) $43,033
Expenditures
Total ($ mil) $44,833
    Per capita $2,067
    Per pupil $15,263

NAEP proficiency scores, 2007

	Reading		Math	
	Basic	Proficient	Basic	Proficient
Grade 4	69.3%	36.0%	85.1%	43.3%
Grade 8	75.1%	32.2%	70.3%	30.2%

Higher education enrollment, fall 2005
Total 525,859
    Full-time men 175,479
    Full-time women 230,204
    Part-time men 42,938
    Part-time women 77,238

Minority enrollment in institutions
of higher education, 2005
Black, non-Hispanic 160,007
Hispanic 130,198
Asian/Pacific Islander 89,927
American Indian/Alaska Native. 4,144

Institutions of higher education, 2005-06
Total 308
    Public 78
    Private 230

Earned degrees conferred, 2004-05
Associate's 56,877
Bachelor's 109,852
Master's 60,505
First-professional. 8,732
Doctor's 4,350

Public Libraries, 2006
Number of libraries. 754
Number of outlets 1,076
Annual visits per capita 5.7
Circulation per capita. 7.5

State & local financial support for
higher education, FY 2006
Full-time equivalent enrollment (x 1,000) . . . 501.8
Appropriations per FTE. $7,784

Social Insurance & Welfare Programs

Social Security benefits & beneficiaries, 2005
Beneficiaries (x 1,000) 3,064
    Retired & dependents. 2,170
    Survivors. 378
    Disabled & dependents. 516
Annual benefit payments ($ mil) $34,797
    Retired & dependents. $23,800
    Survivors. $5,427
    Disabled & dependents. $5,570
Average monthly benefit
    Retired & dependents. $1,059
    Disabled & dependents. $989
    Widowed. $1,020

Medicare, July 2005
Enrollment (x 1,000) 2,776
Payments ($ mil) $19,430

Medicaid, 2004
Beneficiaries (x 1,000). 474
Payments ($ mil) $2,278

State Children's Health Insurance Program, 2006
Enrollment (x 1,000). 688.4
Expenditures ($ mil) $505.4

Persons without health insurance, 2006
Number (x 1,000) 2,662
    percent. 14.0%
Number of children (x 1,000) 380
    percent of children 8.4%

Health care expenditures, 2004
Total expenditures. $126,076
    per capita $6,535

Federal and state public aid

State unemployment insurance, 2006
Recipients, first payments (x 1,000) 454
Total payments ($ mil) $2,278
Average weekly benefit $277
Temporary Assistance for Needy Families, 2006
Recipients (x 1,000) 3,570.9
Families (x 1,000) 1,578.9
Supplemental Security Income, 2005
Recipients (x 1,000) 635.1
Payments ($ mil) $3,561.2
Food Stamp Program, 2006
Avg monthly participants (x 1,000) 1,785.9
Total benefits ($ mil) $2,240.0

Housing & Construction

Housing units

Total 2005 (estimate) 7,866,117
Total 2006 (estimate) 7,907,420
Seasonal or recreational use, 2006 255,667
Owner-occupied, 2006 3,940,942
   Median home value $303,400
   Homeowner vacancy rate 1.8%
Renter-occupied, 2006 3,147,434
   Median rent $875
   Rental vacancy rate 5.8%
Home ownership rate, 2005 .... 55.9%
Home ownership rate, 2006 .... 55.7%

New privately-owned housing units

Number authorized, 2006 (x 1,000) 54.4
   Value ($ mil) $7,078.0
Started 2005 (x 1,000, estimate) 38.8
Started 2006 (x 1,000, estimate) 37.5

Existing home sales

2005 (x 1,000) 319.8
2006 (x 1,000) 303.4

Government & Elections

State officials 2008

Governor .... Eliot Spitzer
   Democratic, term expires 1/11
Lieutenant Governor .... David Paterson
Secretary of State ..... Lorraine Cortes-Vasquez
Attorney General .... Andrew Cuomo
Chief Justice .... Judith Kaye

Governorship

Minimum age 25
Length of term .... 4 years
Consecutive terms permitted ...... not specified
Who succeeds .... Lieutenant Governor

Local governments by type, 2002

Total 3,420
   County 57
   Municipal 616
   Township 929
   School District 683
   Special District 1,135

State legislature

Name .... Legislature
Upper chamber .... Senate
   Number of members 62
   Length of term .... 2 years
   Party in majority, 2008 .... Republican
Lower chamber .... Assembly
   Number of members 150
   Length of term .... 2 years
   Party in majority, 2008 .... Democratic

Federal representation, 2008 (110th Congress)

Senator .... Charles Schumer
   Party .... Democratic
   Year term expires 2011
Senator .... Hillary Rodham Clinton
   Party .... Democratic
   Year term expires 2013
Representatives, total 29
   Democrats 23
   Republicans 6

Voters in November 2006 election (estimate)

Total 5,402,247
   Male 2,494,729
   Female 2,907,517
   White 4,397,320
   Black 742,073
   Hispanic 246,015
   Asian 217,105

Presidential election, 2004

Total Popular Vote 7,391,036
   Kerry 4,314,280
   Bush 2,962,567
Total Electoral Votes 31

Votes cast for US Senators

2004
Total vote (x 1,000) 7,448
Leading party .... Democratic
Percent for leading party 58.9%
2006
Total vote (x 1,000) 4,701
Leading party .... Democratic
Percent for leading party 57.4%

Votes cast for US Representatives

2004
Total vote (x 1,000) 7,448
   Democratic 3,457
   Republican 2,209
Leading party .... Democratic
Percent for leading party 46.4%
2006
Total vote (x 1,000) 4,687
   Democratic 2,538
   Republican 1,160
Leading party .... Democratic
Percent for leading party 54.1%

State government employment, 2006
Full-time equivalent employees 249,208
Payroll ($ mil) $1,183.8

Local government employment, 2006
Full-time equivalent employees 941,079
Payroll ($ mil) $4,222.4

Women holding public office, 2008
US Congress 8
Statewide elected office..................... 0
State legislature 51

Black public officials, 2002
Total..................................... 328
   US and state legislatures 34
   City/county/regional offices 90
   Judicial/law enforcement................. 84
   Education/school boards 120

Hispanic public officials, 2006
Total..................................... 63
   State executives & legislators 16
   City/county/regional offices 30
   Judicial/law enforcement................. 15
   Education/school boards................. 2

Governmental Finance

State government revenues, 2006
Total revenue (x $1,000)........... $166,001,915
   per capita $8,609.17
General revenue (x $1,000) $123,484,906
   Intergovernmental 45,772,844
   Taxes 57,326,481
      general sales.................... 11,263,576
      individual income tax 30,812,924
      corporate income tax 4,018,199
   Current charges.................. 8,051,582
   Miscellaneous 12,333,999

State government expenditure, 2006
Total expenditure (x $1,000) $142,853,305
   per capita $7,408.64
General expenditure (x $1,000) $115,453,948
   per capita, total.................... $5,987.66
      Education 1,744.60
      Public welfare 2,268.57
      Health 310.55
      Hospitals...................... 225.48
      Highways 200.46
      Police protection................ 41.05
      Corrections 140.64
      Natural resources 21.83
      Parks & recreation 28.17
      Governmental administration...... 246.37
      Interest on general debt............ 184.91

State debt & cash, 2006 ($ per capita)
Debt.............................. $5,461.38
Cash/security holdings.............. $15,799.31

Federal government grants to state & local government, 2005 (x $1,000)
Total............................. $45,631,397
by Federal agency
   Defense 150,766
   Education 2,674,829
   Energy........................... 173,620
   Environmental Protection Agency ... 293,632
   Health & Human Services. 32,364,871
   Homeland Security................. 160,435
   Housing & Urban Development..... 3,720,291
   Justice 555,099
   Labor 391,649
   Transportation 2,642,815
   Veterans Affairs.................. 25,382

Crime & Law Enforcement

Crime, 2006 (rates per 100,000 residents)
Property crimes 396,304
   Burglary 68,565
   Larceny 295,605
   Motor vehicle theft 32,134
   Property crime rate............... 2,052.7
Violent crimes........................ 83,966
   Murder 921
   Forcible rape....................... 3,169
   Robbery.......................... 34,489
   Aggravated assault 45,387
   Violent crime rate 434.9
Hate crimes 537

Fraud and identity theft, 2006
Fraud complaints...................... 21,129
   rate per 100,000 residents 109.4
Identity theft complaints 16,452
   rate per 100,000 residents 85.2

Law enforcement agencies, 2006
Total agencies......................... 402
Total employees 86,053
   Officers 62,176
   Civilians 23,877

Prisoners, probation, and parole, 2006
Total prisoners........................ 63,315
   percent change, 12/31/05 to 12/31/06 .... 0.9%
   in private facilities 0%
   in local jails 0%
Sentenced to more than one year 62,974
   rate per 100,000 residents 326
Adults on probation 123,418
Adults on parole....................... 53,001

Prisoner demographics, June 30, 2005 (rate per 100,000 residents)
Male.................................. 935
Female 57
White................................. 174
Black................................. 1,627
Hispanic 778

Arrests, 2006
Total 345,357
   Persons under 18 years of age 48,209

Persons under sentence of death, 1/1/07
Total 1
   White 0
   Black 1
   Hispanic 0

State's highest court
Name .... Court of Appeals
Number of members 7
Length of term .... 14 years
Intermediate appeals court? .... yes

Labor & Income

Civilian labor force, 2006 (x 1,000)
Total 9,464
   Men 4,967
   Women 4,497
   Persons 16-19 years 367
   White 7,187
   Black 1,451
   Hispanic 1,379

Civilian labor force as a percent of civilian non-institutional population, 2006
Total 63.2%
   Men 69.6
   Women 57.3
   Persons 16-19 years 34.7
   White 64.2
   Black 59.6
   Hispanic 62.2

Employment, 2006 (x 1,000)
Total 9,043
   Men 4,726
   Women 4,317
   Persons 16-19 years 296
   White 6,905
   Black 1,338
   Hispanic 1,300

Unemployment rate, 2006
Total 4.4%
   Men 4.8
   Women 4.0
   Persons 16-19 years 19.2
   White 3.9
   Black 7.8
   Hispanic 5.7

Full-time/part-time labor force, 2003 (x 1,000)
Full-time labor force, employed 7,215
Part-time labor force, employed 1,511
Unemployed, looking for
   Full-time work 502
   Part-time work 87
Mean duration of unemployment (weeks) 23.4
   Median 12.8

Labor unions, 2006
Membership (x 1,000) 1,981
   percent of employed 24.4%

Experienced civilian labor force by private industry, 2006
Total 7,011,126
   Natural resources & mining 26,838
   Construction 335,333
   Manufacturing 564,564
   Trade, transportation & utilities 1,493,355
   Information 266,721
   Finance 721,725
   Professional & business 1,100,828
   Education & health 1,462,019
   Leisure & hospitality 675,009
   Other 315,962

Experienced civilian labor force by occupation, May 2006
Management 391,110
Business & financial 385,840
Legal 104,430
Sales 884,170
Office & admin. support 1,616,450
Computers & math 193,190
Architecture & engineering 108,130
Arts & entertainment 169,990
Education 654,000
Social services 175,030
Health care practitioner & technical 444,180
Health care support 308,290
Maintenance & repair 304,930
Construction 314,280
Transportation & moving 451,870
Production 420,220
Farming, fishing & forestry 7,420

Hours and earnings of production workers on manufacturing payrolls, 2006
Average weekly hours 41.1
Average hourly earnings $18.29
Average weekly earnings $751.72

Income and poverty, 2006
Median household income $51,384
Personal income, per capita (current $) ... $42,392
   in constant (2000) dollars $37,005
Persons below poverty level 14.2%

Average annual pay
2006 .... $55,479
   increase from 2005 .... 6.8%

Federal individual income tax returns, 2005
Returns filed 8,715,913
Adjusted gross income ($1,000) ... $552,244,486
Total tax liability ($1,000) $84,125,598

Charitable contributions, 2004
Number of contributions 3,059.6
Total amount ($ mil) $14,454.8

Economy, Business, Industry & Agriculture

Fortune 500 companies, 2007 57
Bankruptcy cases filed, FY 2007 38,823

Patents and trademarks issued, 2007
Patents 6,007
Trademarks 7,064

Business firm ownership, 2002
Women-owned 505,077
    Sales ($ mil) $70,838
Black-owned 129,329
    Sales ($ mil) $7,481
Hispanic-owned 163,588
    Sales ($ mil) $12,326
Asian-owned 145,108
    Sales ($ mil) $30,408
Amer. Indian/Alaska Native-owned 12,307
    Sales ($ mil) $897
Hawaiian/Pacific Islander-owned 3,005
    Sales ($ mil) $123

Gross domestic product, 2006 ($ mil)
Total gross domestic product $1,021,944
    Agriculture, forestry, fishing and
        hunting 2,093
    Mining 955
    Utilities 18,670
    Construction 32,181
    Manufacturing, durable goods 30,132
    Manufacturing, non-durable goods 34,010
    Wholesale trade 51,691
    Retail trade 54,378
    Transportation & warehousing 17,041
    Information 73,142
    Finance & insurance 158,598
    Real estate, rental & leasing 156,865
    Professional and technical services 88,137
    Educational services 15,665
    Health care and social assistance 77,127
    Accommodation/food services 23,044
    Other services, except government 21,074
    Government 101,956

Establishments, payroll, employees & receipts, by major industry group, 2005
Total 514,265
    Annual payroll ($1,000) $370,842,630
    Paid employees 7,417,463
Forestry, fishing & agriculture 608
    Annual payroll ($1,000) $147,297
    Paid employees .4,983
Mining 390
    Annual payroll ($1,000) $234,876
    Paid employees 4,095
    Receipts, 2002 ($1,000) $813,202

Utilities 584
    Annual payroll ($1,000) $3,296,369
    Paid employees 40,341
    Receipts, 2002 ($1,000) . . . . .NA
Construction 46,448
    Annual payroll ($1,000) $15,792,641
    Paid employees 308,934
    Receipts, 2002 ($1,000) $65,368,319
Manufacturing 19,349
    Annual payroll ($1,000) $24,908,069
    Paid employees 571,986
    Receipts, 2002 ($1,000) $147,317,463
Wholesale trade 35,437
    Annual payroll ($1,000) $22,824,939
    Paid employees 409,023
    Receipts, 2002 ($1,000) $343,663,041
Retail trade 78,134
    Annual payroll ($1,000) $21,139,844
    Paid employees 877,803
    Receipts, 2002 ($1,000) $178,067,530
Transportation & warehousing 12,004
    Annual payroll ($1,000) $8,140,912
    Paid employees 228,585
    Receipts, 2002 ($1,000) $18,845,179
Information 11,199
    Annual payroll ($1,000) $20,214,888
    Paid employees 287,231
    Receipts, 2002 ($1,000) . . . . .NA
Finance & insurance 27,567
    Annual payroll ($1,000) $83,556,622
    Paid employees 579,827
    Receipts, 2002 ($1,000) . . . . .NA
Professional, scientific & technical 58,105
    Annual payroll ($1,000) $39,540,151
    Paid employees 578,103
    Receipts, 2002 ($1,000) $83,549,043
Education 6,214
    Annual payroll ($1,000) $10,861,885
    Paid employees 340,497
    Receipts, 2002 ($1,000) $3,040,735
Health care & social assistance 52,246
    Annual payroll ($1,000) $50,393,418
    Paid employees 1,297,637
    Receipts, 2002 ($1,000) $98,966,149
Arts and entertainment 10,837
    Annual payroll ($1,000) $5,039,508
    Paid employees 138,313
    Receipts, 2002 ($1,000) $13,738,916
Real estate 32,262
    Annual payroll ($1,000) $7,535,087
    Paid employees 170,820
    Receipts, 2002 ($1,000) $35,629,134
Accommodation & food service 42,300
    Annual payroll ($1,000) $10,007,371
    Paid employees 558,057
    Receipts, 2002 ($1,000) $27,835,952

Exports, 2006
Value of exported goods ($ mil) $57,369
   Manufactured $38,091
   Non-manufactured $7,260

Foreign direct investment in US affiliates, 2004
Property, plants & equipment ($ mil) . . . $60,572
Employment (x 1,000). 377.0

Agriculture, 2006
Number of farms 35,000
Farm acreage (x 1,000) 7,500
   Acres per farm 214
Farm marketings and income ($ mil)
Total. $3,509.0
   Crops $1,527.3
   Livestock. $1,981.7
Net farm income $868.7

Principal commodities, in order by marketing receipts, 2005
   Dairy products, Greenhouse/nursery, Apples,
         Cattle and calves, Hay

Federal economic activity in state
Expenditures, 2005 ($ mil)
  Total. $144,876
     Per capita $7,500.42
  Defense $8,568
  Non-defense $136,308
Defense department, 2006 ($ mil)
  Payroll. $2,669
  Contract awards $8,020
  Grants $150
Homeland security grants ($1,000)
  2006. . . . .$183,674
  2007 . . . . $208,039

FDIC-insured financial institutions, 2005
Number 199
Assets ($ billion) $523.5
Deposits ($ billion) $362.5

Fishing, 2006
Catch (x 1,000 lbs) 32,834
Value ($1,000). $57,668

Mining, 2006 ($ mil)
Total non-fuel mineral production $1,330
Percent of U.S. 2.07%

Communication, Energy & Transportation

Communication
Households with computers, 2003 . . . . 60.0%
Households with internet access, 2003 . . . . 53.3%
High-speed internet providers 72
Total high-speed internet lines. 5,669,523
   Residential 4,129,160
   Business. 1,540,363
Wireless phone customers, 12/2006 . . . 15,261,760

FCC-licensed stations (as of January 1, 2008)
TV stations 55
FM radio stations. 377
AM radio stations 169

Energy
Energy consumption, 2004
  Total (trillion Btu). 4,254
  Per capita (million Btu) 220.5
By source of production (trillion Btu)
  Coal 277
  Natural gas 1,120
  Petroleum. 1,885
  Nuclear electric power 424
  Hydroelectric power 240
By end-use sector (trillion Btu)
  Residential 1,215
  Commercial 1,399
  Industrial 535
  Transportation .1,105
Electric energy, 2005
  Primary source of electricity. . . . . Nuclear
  Net generation (billion kWh) 146.9
    percent from renewable sources. 18.9%
  Net summer capability (million kW) 39.1
  CO_2 emitted from generation 60.4
Natural gas utilities, 2005
  Customers (x 1,000) 4,611
  Sales (trillion Btu). 867
  Revenues ($ mil) $7,304
Nuclear plants, 2007 6
Total CO_2 emitted (million metric tons). 214.3
Energy spending, 2004 ($ mil) $48,504
  per capita $2,514
  Price per million Btu $15.65

Transportation, 2006
Public road & street mileage 113,617
  Urban. 47,744
  Rural 65,873
  Interstate. 1,697
Vehicle miles of travel (millions) 141,348
  per capita 7,330.6
Total motor vehicle registrations. 11,283,896
  Automobiles. .8,528,457
  Trucks 2,685,424
  Motorcycles 203,207
Licensed drivers .11,146,367
  19 years & under 413,587
Deaths from motor vehicle accidents 1,456
Gasoline consumed (x 1,000 gallons) 5,784,552
  per capita 300.0

Commuting Statistics, 2006
Average commute time (min) 30.9
  Drove to work alone 54.4%
  Carpooled. 7.6%
  Public transit 26.1%
  Walk to work 6.3%
  Work from home. 3.8%

State Summary

Capital city . . . . Raleigh
Governor . . . . Michael Easley

Office of the Governor
20301 Mail Service Center
Raleigh, NC 27699
919-733-4240

Admitted as a state 1789
Area (square miles) .53,819
Population, 2007 (estimate). 9,061,032
Largest city . . . . .Charlotte
   Population, 2006 630,478
Personal income per capita, 2006
   (in current dollars) $32,234
Gross domestic product, 2006 ($ mil) . . . $374,525

Leading industries by payroll, 2005
   Manufacturing, Health care/Social assistance,
      Finance & Insurance

**Leading agricultural commodities
by receipts, 2005**
   Broilers, Hogs, Greenhouse/nursery, Turkeys,
      Tobacco

Geography & Environment

Total area (square miles). 53,819
   land 48,711
   water 5,108
Federally-owned land, 2004 (acres) 3,710,338
   percent. 11.8%
Highest point . . . . Mt. Mitchell
   elevation (feet) 6,684
Lowest point . . . . .Atlantic Ocean
   elevation (feet) . . . . sea level
General coastline (miles) 301
Tidal shoreline (miles) 3,375
Cropland, 2003 (x 1,000 acres) 5,513
Forest land, 2003 (x 1,000 acres). 15,456
Capital city . . . . Raleigh
   Population 2000 276,093
   Population 2006 356,321
Largest city . . . . .Charlotte
   Population 2000 540,828
   Population 2006 630,478

Number of cities with over 100,000 population
1990 5
2000 6
2006 7

State park and recreation areas, 2005
Area (x 1,000 acres) 187
Number of visitors (x 1,000) 12,674
Revenues ($1,000) $5,132
   percent of operating expenditures 16.5%

National forest system land, 2007
Acres 1,255,167

Demographics & Population Characteristics

Population
1980 5,881,766
1990 6,628,637
2000 8,046,491
2006 8,856,505
   Male 4,341,298
   Female 4,515,207
Living in group quarters, 2006 270,572
   percent of total. 3.1%
2007 (estimate). 9,061,032
   persons per square mile of land 186.0
2008 (projected). 9,086,527
2010 (projected) .9,345,823
2020 (projected) 10,709,289
2030 (projected) 12,227,739

**Population of Core-Based Statistical Areas
(formerly Metropolitan Areas), x 1,000**

	CBSA	Non-CBSA
1990	6,030	602
2000	7,352	695
2006	8,135	722

Change in population, 2000-2007
Number 1,014,541
   percent. 12.6%
Natural increase (births minus deaths) 352,899
Net internal migration 490,907
Net international migration 188,925

Persons by age, 2006
Under 5 years 611,110
5 to 17 years 1,544,277
18 years and over 6,701,118
65 years and over 1,076,951
85 years and over 136,229
   Median age 36.6

Persons by age, 2010 (projected)
Under 5 years 645,144
18 and over 7,076,985
65 and over 1,161,164
   Median age 36.9

Race, 2006
One Race
   White 6,558,154
   Black or African American 1,921,307
   Asian 164,111
   American Indian/Alaska Native. 111,148
   Hawaiian Native/Pacific Islander. 5,755
Two or more races. 96,030

Persons of Hispanic origin, 2006
Total Hispanic or Latino 597,382
   Mexican. 397,971
   Puerto Rican 44,707
   Cuban 10,530

Persons of Asian origin, 2006

Total Asian 162,578
  Asian Indian....................... 45,291
  Chinese 23,780
  Filipino 16,721
  Japanese 7,958
  Korean.............................14,107
  Vietnamese........................ 22,698

Marital status, 2006

Population 15 years & over 7,072,249
  Never married 2,021,960
  Married......................... 3,878,605
  Separated 236,344
  Widowed.......................... 456,182
  Divorced 715,502

Language spoken at home, 2006

Population 5 years and older......... 8,253,772
  English only 7,465,526
  Spanish 532,553
  French 29,080
  German........................... 23,168
  Chinese 19,170

Households & families, 2006

Households........................3,454,068
  with persons under 18 years 1,170,646
  with persons over 65 years........... 755,875
  persons per household 2.49
Families.........................2,310,456
  persons per family..................3.04
Married couples.....................1,706,840
Female householder,
  no husband present................ 454,809
One-person households 959,166

Nativity, 2006

Number of residents born in state 5,286,411
  percent of population................. 59.7%

Immigration & naturalization, 2006

Legal permanent residents admitted..... 18,989
Persons naturalized 12,592
Non-immigrant admissions 235,417

Vital Statistics and Health

Marriages

2004 62,235
2005 63,384
2006 55,343

Divorces

2004 35,926
2005 35,684
2006 36,378

Health risks, 2006

Percent of adults who are:
  Smokers.......................... 22.1%
  Overweight (BMI > 25)................. 62.8%
  Obese (BMI > 30)..................... 26.6%

Births

2005 123,096
  Birthrate (per 1,000)...................14.2
  White........................... 89,636
  Black 28,433
  Hispanic 19,519
  Asian/Pacific Islander 3,342
  Amer. Indian/Alaska Native 1,685
  Low birth weight (2,500g or less)........ 9.2%
  Cesarian births 29.3%
  Preterm births 13.7%
  To unmarried mothers................. 38.4%
  Twin births (per 1,000) 31.9
  Triplets or higher order (per 100,000)....150.0
2006 (preliminary).....................127,841
  rate per 1,000 ....14.4

Deaths

2004
All causes 72,384
  rate per 100,000......................874.9
Heart disease 17,607
  rate per 100,000......................214.4
Malignant neoplasms 16,477
  rate per 100,000......................195.4
Cerebrovascular disease..................4,955
  rate per 100,000......................61.1
Chronic lower respiratory disease 3,625
  rate per 100,000......................44.0
Diabetes............................. 2,253
  rate per 100,000......................27.0
2005 (preliminary).....................74,639
  rate per 100,000......................876.0
2006 (provisional) 74,734

Infant deaths

2004 1,053
  rate per 1,000 ....8.8
2005 (provisional) 1,058
  rate per 1,000 ....8.6

Exercise routines, 2005

None................................ 25.6%
Moderate or greater..................... 42.1%
Vigorous 22.2%

Abortions, 2004

Total performed in state............... 33,954
  rate per 1,000 women age 15-44.......... 19
  % obtained by out-of-state residents 15.5%

Physicians, 2005

Total................................21,972
  rate per 100,000 persons 253

Community hospitals, 2005

Number of hospitals 115
Beds (x 1,000)..........................23.3
Patients admitted (x 1,000) 1,013
Average daily census (x 1,000) 16.7
Average cost per day $1,320
Outpatient visits (x 1 mil) 16.8

Disability status of population, 2006
5 to 15 years 7.2%
16 to 64 years 14.4%
65 years and over 43.5%

Education

Educational attainment, 2006
Population over 25 years 5,845,235
   Less than 9th grade.................... 6.6%
   High school graduate or more 82.0%
   College graduate or more............. 24.8%
   Graduate or professional degree........ 8.3%

Public school enrollment, 2005-06
Total.............................1,416,436
   Pre-kindergarten through grade 8...1,003,118
   Grades 9 through 12.................413,318

Graduating public high school seniors, 2004-05
Diplomas (incl. GED and others) 76,663

SAT scores, 2007
Average critical reading score............. 495
Average writing score 482
Average math score 509
Percent of graduates taking test 71%

Public school teachers, 2006-07 (estimate)
Total (x 1,000) 95.5
   Elementary...........................71.8
   Secondary............................23.7
Average salary $46,410
   Elementary........................ $46,410
   Secondary......................... $46,410

State receipts & expenditures for public schools, 2006-07 (estimate)
Revenue receipts ($ mil) $11,281
Expenditures
Total ($ mil) $12,940
   Per capita $1,267
   Per pupil $8,544

NAEP proficiency scores, 2007

	Reading		Math	
	Basic	Proficient	Basic	Proficient
Grade 4	63.9%	29.1%	84.9%	41.0%
Grade 8	71.0%	28.0%	72.9%	34.5%

Higher education enrollment, fall 2005
Total....................................87,637
   Full-time men 31,956
   Full-time women.................... 42,309
   Part-time men 4,731
   Part-time women.................... 8,641

Minority enrollment in institutions of higher education, 2005
Black, non-Hispanic 116,786
Hispanic 12,052
Asian/Pacific Islander 11,740
American Indian/Alaska Native.......... 6,096

Institutions of higher education, 2005-06
Total................................... 128
   Public................................ 75
   Private............................... 53

Earned degrees conferred, 2004-05
Associate's........................... 18,460
Bachelor's 39,303
Master's 11,534
First-professional.....................1,925
Doctor's...............................1,355

Public Libraries, 2006
Number of libraries.................... 75
Number of outlets 423
Annual visits per capita 4.0
Circulation per capita....................5.5

State & local financial support for higher education, FY 2006
Full-time equivalent enrollment (x 1,000)....338.6
Appropriations per FTE................$7,522

Social Insurance & Welfare Programs

Social Security benefits & beneficiaries, 2005
Beneficiaries (x 1,000) 1,511
   Retired & dependents................. 1,006
   Survivors............................ 192
   Disabled & dependents................ 313
Annual benefit payments ($ mil) $15,856
   Retired & dependents............... $10,269
   Survivors.......................... $2,400
   Disabled & dependents...............$3,187
Average monthly benefit
   Retired & dependents.................. $984
   Disabled & dependents................. $921
   Widowed.............................. $907

Medicare, July 2005
Enrollment (x 1,000).....................1,277
Payments ($ mil) $8,551

Medicaid, 2004
Beneficiaries (x 1,000)................. 237
Payments ($ mil) $806

State Children's Health Insurance Program, 2006
Enrollment (x 1,000).................... 248.0
Expenditures ($ mil)...................$271.9

Persons without health insurance, 2006
Number (x 1,000).......................1,585
   percent............................ 17.9%
Number of children (x 1,000) 307
   percent of children 14.0%

Health care expenditures, 2004
Total expenditures.................... $44,281
   per capita $5,191

Federal and state public aid

State unemployment insurance, 2006
Recipients, first payments (x 1,000) 239
Total payments ($ mil) $720
Average weekly benefit $265
Temporary Assistance for Needy Families, 2006
Recipients (x 1,000) 677.8
Families (x 1,000) 350.3
Supplemental Security Income, 2005
Recipients (x 1,000) 199.3
Payments ($ mil) $894.2
Food Stamp Program, 2006
Avg monthly participants (x 1,000) 854.4
Total benefits ($ mil) $921.0

Housing & Construction

Housing units
Total 2005 (estimate) 3,940,154
Total 2006 (estimate) 4,028,959
Seasonal or recreational use, 2006 166,866
Owner-occupied, 2006 2,350,798
　　Median home value $137,200
　　Homeowner vacancy rate 2.2%
Renter-occupied, 2006 1,103,270
　　Median rent $656
　　Rental vacancy rate 11.7%
Home ownership rate, 2005 . . . . 70.9%
Home ownership rate, 2006 . . . . 70.2%

New privately-owned housing units
Number authorized, 2006 (x 1,000) 100.0
　　Value ($ mil) $16,074.3
Started 2005 (x 1,000, estimate) 71.1
Started 2006 (x 1,000, estimate) 70.2

Existing home sales
2005 (x 1,000) 215.7
2006 (x 1,000) 234.8

Government & Elections

State officials 2008
Governor . . . . Michael Easley
　　　　Democratic, term expires 1/09
Lieutenant Governor . . . . Beverly Perdue
Secretary of State . . . . Elaine Marshall
Attorney General . . . . .Roy Cooper
Chief Justice .Sarah Parker

Governorship
Minimum age 30
Length of term . . . . 4 years
Consecutive terms permitted 2
Who succeeds . . . . Lieutenant Governor

Local governments by type, 2002
Total 960
　　County 100
　　Municipal 541
　　Township 0
　　School District 0
　　Special District 319

State legislature
Name . . . . General Assembly
Upper chamber . . . . .Senate
　　Number of members 50
　　Length of term . . . . 2 years
　　Party in majority, 2008 . . . . .Democratic
Lower chamber . . . . .House of Representatives
　　Number of members 120
　　Length of term . . . . 2 years
　　Party in majority, 2008 . . . . .Democratic

Federal representation, 2008 (110th Congress)
Senator . . . . Elizabeth Dole
　　Party . . . . Republican
　　Year term expires 2009
Senator . . . . Richard Burr
　　Party . . . . Republican
　　Year term expires 2011
Representatives, total 13
　　Democrats 7
　　Republicans 6

Voters in November 2006 election (estimate)
Total 2,422,170
　　Male 1,180,136
　　Female 1,242,034
　　White 1,994,343
　　Black 407,932
　　Hispanic 5,874
　　Asian 8,936

Presidential election, 2004
Total Popular Vote 3,501,007
　　Kerry 1,525,849
　　Bush 1,961,166
Total Electoral Votes 15

Votes cast for US Senators
2004
Total vote (x 1,000) .3,472
Leading party . . . . Republican
Percent for leading party 51.6%
2006
Total vote (x 1,000) . . . . NA
Leading party . . . . NA
Percent for leading party . . . . NA

Votes cast for US Representatives
2004
Total vote (x 1,000) .3,413
　　Democratic 1,670
　　Republican 1,743
Leading party . . . . Republican
Percent for leading party 51.1%
2006
Total vote (x 1,000) .1,941
　　Democratic 1,027
　　Republican 914
Leading party . . . . .Democratic
Percent for leading party 52.9%

State government employment, 2006
Full-time equivalent employees 139,117
Payroll ($ mil) $495.4

Local government employment, 2006
Full-time equivalent employees 372,146
Payroll ($ mil) $1,154.0

Women holding public office, 2008
US Congress 3
Statewide elected office.................... 4
State legislature 44

Black public officials, 2002
Total................................... 523
   US and state legislatures 28
   City/county/regional offices 369
   Judicial/law enforcement................ 31
   Education/school boards 95

Hispanic public officials, 2006
Total..................................... 3
   State executives & legislators 2
   City/county/regional offices 1
   Judicial/law enforcement................ 0
   Education/school boards................. 0

Governmental Finance

State government revenues, 2006
Total revenue (x $1,000)........... $45,473,975
   per capita $5,127.04
General revenue (x $1,000) $38,883,961
   Intergovernmental 12,905,941
   Taxes 20,602,549
     general sales.................... 5,021,648
     individual income tax 9,467,278
     corporate income tax 1,308,022
   Current charges................... 3,285,975
   Miscellaneous 2,089,496

State government expenditure, 2006
Total expenditure (x $1,000) $41,107,916
   per capita $4,634.78
General expenditure (x $1,000) $37,179,612
   per capita, total.................. *$4,191.88*
     Education...................... 1,715.53
     Public welfare 1,131.94
     Health 166.88
     Hospitals....................... 142.19
     Highways 343.81
     Police protection.................. 64.16
     Corrections 129.72
     Natural resources 53.39
     Parks & recreation 23.84
     Governmental administration....... 107.13
     Interest on general debt............. 63.47

State debt & cash, 2006 ($ per capita)
Debt $2,001.18
Cash/security holdings.............. $9,678.41

Federal government grants to state & local government, 2005 (x $1,000)
Total............................. $12,958,870
by Federal agency
   Defense 75,636
   Education 951,450
   Energy.......................... 29,755
   Environmental Protection Agency 82,040
   Health & Human Services. 8,428,677
   Homeland Security................. 117,937
   Housing & Urban Development...... 707,344
   Justice 118,814
   Labor 305,327
   Transportation 1,032,462
   Veterans Affairs.................. 4,813

Crime & Law Enforcement

Crime, 2006 (rates per 100,000 residents)
Property crimes 364,960
   Burglary 107,407
   Larceny 227,427
   Motor vehicle theft 30,126
   Property crime rate................. 4,120.8
Violent crimes....................... 42,124
   Murder 540
   Forcible rape...................... 2,495
   Robbery......................... 13,484
   Aggravated assault 25,605
   Violent crime rate 475.6
Hate crimes........................... 141

Fraud and identity theft, 2006
Fraud complaints.................... 10,300
   rate per 100,000 residents 116.3
Identity theft complaints 5,748
   rate per 100,000 residents 64.9

Law enforcement agencies, 2006
Total agencies........................ 512
Total employees 30,671
   Officers 21,419
   Civilians 9,252

Prisoners, probation, and parole, 2006
Total prisoners........................ 37,460
   percent change, 12/31/05 to 12/31/06 .... 3.0%
   in private facilities 0.5%
   in local jails 0%
Sentenced to more than one year 32,219
   rate per 100,000 residents 360
Adults on probation 110,419
Adults on parole....................... 3,236

Prisoner demographics, June 30, 2005 (rate per 100,000 residents)
Male.................................. 1,154
Female 104
White 320
Black.................................. 1,727
Hispanic .... NA

Arrests, 2006

Total.............................. 436,676
    Persons under 18 years of age 44,691

Persons under sentence of death, 1/1/07

Total.................................. 185
    White................................. 72
    Black 98
    Hispanic 4

State's highest court

Name ....Supreme Court
Number of members........................ 7
Length of term...................... 8 years
Intermediate appeals court? ....yes

Labor & Income

Civilian labor force, 2006 (x 1,000)

Total.............................. 4,426
    Men 2,353
    Women 2,073
    Persons 16-19 years.................. 204
    White.............................. 3,344
    Black 902
    Hispanic 362

Civilian labor force as a percent of civilian non-institutional population, 2006

Total.............................. 66.1%
    Men 73.4
    Women 59.5
    Persons 16-19 years................. 43.6
    White.............................. 66.3
    Black 66.0
    Hispanic 81.1

Employment, 2006 (x 1,000)

Total.............................. 4,218
    Men 2,250
    Women 1,967
    Persons 16-19 years................. 163
    White.............................. 3,228
    Black 821
    Hispanic 351

Unemployment rate, 2006

Total.............................. 4.7%
    Men 4.4
    Women 5.1
    Persons 16-19 years................. 20.0
    White.............................. 3.5
    Black 9.0
    Hispanic 3.1

Full-time/part-time labor force, 2003 (x 1,000)

Full-time labor force, employed 3,286
Part-time labor force, employed........... 671
Unemployed, looking for
    Full-time work........................ 238
    Part-time work........................ 35
Mean duration of unemployment (weeks)...... 20.6
    Median 11.3

Labor unions, 2006

Membership (x 1,000)................... 126
    percent of employed 3.3%

Experienced civilian labor force by private industry, 2006

Total..........................3,305,395
    Natural resources & mining 32,999
    Construction 244,888
    Manufacturing.................... 553,483
    Trade, transportation & utilities 756,723
    Information 73,172
    Finance 202,415
    Professional & business 477,384
    Education & health 467,884
    Leisure & hospitality.............. 376,394
    Other 99,206

Experienced civilian labor force by occupation, May 2006

Management........................ 178,650
Business & financial 138,000
Legal.............................. 19,410
Sales.............................. 415,100
Office & admin. support.............. 612,240
Computers & math 82,190
Architecture & engineering............ 53,420
Arts & entertainment 35,260
Education 250,300
Social services 47,540
Health care practitioner & technical.... 198,840
Health care support 126,360
Maintenance & repair................ 172,200
Construction 192,160
Transportation & moving 307,430
Production 407,640
Farming, fishing & forestry.............. 8,270

Hours and earnings of production workers on manufacturing payrolls, 2006

Average weekly hours.................... 40.0
Average hourly earnings $14.57
Average weekly earnings $582.80

Income and poverty, 2006

Median household income............. $42,625
Personal income, per capita (current $)... $32,234
    in constant (2000) dollars $28,138
Persons below poverty level.............. 14.7%

Average annual pay

2006................................. $37,439
    increase from 2005 .... 4.3%

Federal individual income tax returns, 2005

Returns filed........................ 3,879,609
Adjusted gross income ($1,000) $186,047,795
Total tax liability ($1,000) $22,000,566

Charitable contributions, 2004

Number of contributions.............. 1,202.0
Total amount ($ mil)................. $4,951.1

Economy, Business, Industry & Agriculture

Fortune 500 companies, 2007 14
Bankruptcy cases filed, FY 2007 19,420

Patents and trademarks issued, 2007

Patents 1,935
Trademarks 1,492

Business firm ownership, 2002

Women-owned 173,874
   Sales ($ mil) $26,743
Black-owned 52,122
   Sales ($ mil) $3,549
Hispanic-owned 9,043
   Sales ($ mil) $1,789
Asian-owned 13,695
   Sales ($ mil) $3,506
Amer. Indian/Alaska Native-owned 5,973
   Sales ($ mil) $592
Hawaiian/Pacific Islander-owned 191
   Sales ($ mil) $13

Gross domestic product, 2006 ($ mil)

Total gross domestic product $374,525
   Agriculture, forestry, fishing and
      hunting 3,570
   Mining 426
   Utilities 6,587
   Construction 18,703
   Manufacturing, durable goods 27,743
   Manufacturing, non-durable goods . . . 46,271
   Wholesale trade 20,833
   Retail trade 23,992
   Transportation & warehousing 8,238
   Information 12,684
   Finance & insurance 41,736
   Real estate, rental & leasing 36,656
   Professional and technical services 17,764
   Educational services 3,030
   Health care and social assistance 23,097
   Accommodation/food services 8,450
   Other services, except government 7,389
   Government 46,827

Establishments, payroll, employees & receipts, by major industry group, 2005

Total 216,994
   Annual payroll ($1,000) $115,740,410
   Paid employees 3,409,968
Forestry, fishing & agriculture 917
   Annual payroll ($1,000) . . . . NA
   Paid employees . . . . NA
Mining 210
   Annual payroll ($1,000) $173,076
   Paid employees 3,518
   Receipts, 2002 ($1,000) $815,465

Utilities 368
   Annual payroll ($1,000) $1,383,746
   Paid employees 19,722
   Receipts, 2002 ($1,000) . . . . .NA
Construction 27,202
   Annual payroll ($1,000) $7,970,603
   Paid employees 221,783
   Receipts, 2002 ($1,000) $34,385,593
Manufacturing 10,138
   Annual payroll ($1,000) $20,681,882
   Paid employees 554,442
   Receipts, 2002 ($1,000) $156,821,943
Wholesale trade 11,866
   Annual payroll ($1,000) $7,794,777
   Paid employees 163,867
   Receipts, 2002 ($1,000) $104,331,152
Retail trade 35,875
   Annual payroll ($1,000) $9,707,125
   Paid employees 449,870
   Receipts, 2002 ($1,000) $88,821,486
Transportation & warehousing 5,819
   Annual payroll ($1,000) $3,924,521
   Paid employees 115,901
   Receipts, 2002 ($1,000) $7,895,233
Information 3,356
   Annual payroll ($1,000) $3,812,515
   Paid employees 74,729
   Receipts, 2002 ($1,000) . . . . .NA
Finance & insurance 12,930
   Annual payroll ($1,000) $10,265,446
   Paid employees 178,306
   Receipts, 2002 ($1,000) . . . . .NA
Professional, scientific & technical 21,169
   Annual payroll ($1,000) $9,503,601
   Paid employees 174,892
   Receipts, 2002 ($1,000) $17,622,547
Education 2,054
   Annual payroll ($1,000) $2,311,554
   Paid employees 75,013
   Receipts, 2002 ($1,000) $747,826
Health care & social assistance 19,846
   Annual payroll ($1,000) $16,282,077
   Paid employees 470,820
   Receipts, 2002 ($1,000) $32,026,359
Arts and entertainment 3,232
   Annual payroll ($1,000) $1,196,776
   Paid employees 48,713
   Receipts, 2002 ($1,000) $3,058,898
Real estate 10,059
   Annual payroll ($1,000) $1,772,769
   Paid employees 50,364
   Receipts, 2002 ($1,000) $7,088,267
Accommodation & food service 16,903
   Annual payroll ($1,000) $3,894,008
   Paid employees 315,212
   Receipts, 2002 ($1,000) $11,237,386

Exports, 2006

Value of exported goods ($ mil) $21,218
   Manufactured $18,320
   Non-manufactured $1,236

Foreign direct investment in US affiliates, 2004

Property, plants & equipment ($ mil) $23,917
Employment (x 1,000). 198.0

Agriculture, 2006

Number of farms 48,000
Farm acreage (x 1,000) 8,800
   Acres per farm 183
Farm marketings and income ($ mil)
Total. $8,199.3
   Crops. $2,925.3
   Livestock. $5,274.0
Net farm income $3,702.2

Principal commodities, in order by marketing receipts, 2005

   Broilers, Hogs, Greenhouse/nursery, Turkeys,
                Tobacco

Federal economic activity in state

Expenditures, 2005 ($ mil)
Total. $59,162
   Per capita $6,821.87
   Defense $9,404
   Non-defense $49,758
Defense department, 2006 ($ mil)
   Payroll. $7,132
   Contract awards $2,690
   Grants $100
Homeland security grants ($1,000)
   2006. . . . . $30,484
   2007 . . . . $25,256

FDIC-insured financial institutions, 2005

Number 110
Assets ($ billion) $1,913.6
Deposits ($ billion) $1,258.8

Fishing, 2006

Catch (x 1,000 lbs). 68,641
Value ($1,000). $71,886

Mining, 2006 ($ mil)

Total non-fuel mineral production $872
Percent of U.S. 1.35%

Communication, Energy & Transportation

Communication

Households with computers, 2003 . . . . 57.7%
Households with internet access, 2003 . . . . 51.1%
High-speed internet providers 60
Total high-speed internet lines. 2,366,079
   Residential 1,659,657
   Business. 706,422
Wireless phone customers, 12/2006 6,626,582

FCC-licensed stations (as of January 1, 2008)

TV stations 50
FM radio stations. 222
AM radio stations 219

Energy

Energy consumption, 2004
   Total (trillion Btu). 2,716
   Per capita (million Btu) 318.3
By source of production (trillion Btu)
   Coal 783
   Natural gas 233
   Petroleum 993
   Nuclear electric power 418
   Hydroelectric power 55
By end-use sector (trillion Btu)
   Residential 702
   Commercial 554
   Industrial 723
   Transportation 738
Electric energy, 2005
   Primary source of electricity. . . . . Coal
   Net generation (billion kWh) 129.7
      percent from renewable sources. 5.6%
   Net summer capability (million kW) 27.1
   CO_2 emitted from generation 75.9
Natural gas utilities, 2005
   Customers (x 1,000) 1,105
   Sales (trillion Btu). 204
   Revenues ($ mil) $1,782
Nuclear plants, 2007 5
Total CO_2 emitted (million metric tons). 146.2
Energy spending, 2004 ($ mil) $23,225
   per capita $2,722
   Price per million Btu $13.60

Transportation, 2006

Public road & street mileage 103,500
   Urban. 32,310
   Rural. 71,190
   Interstate. 1,082
Vehicle miles of travel (millions) 101,515
   per capita 11,445.5
Total motor vehicle registrations. 6,301,436
   Automobiles. .3,659,926
   Trucks 2,607,790
   Motorcycles 110,628
Licensed drivers 6,315,667
   19 years & under 214,442
Deaths from motor vehicle accidents 1,559
Gasoline consumed (x 1,000 gallons) 4,443,067
   per capita 500.9

Commuting Statistics, 2006

Average commute time (min) 23.4
   Drove to work alone 79.8%
   Carpooled. 12.5%
   Public transit 1.0%
   Walk to work 1.8%
   Work from home 3.6%

State Summary

Capital city . . . . Bismarck
Governor . . . . John Hoeven

Dept 101
600 E Boulevard Ave
Bismarck, ND 58505
701-328-2200

Admitted as a state 1889
Area (square miles) 70,700
Population, 2007 (estimate). 639,715
Largest city . . . . Fargo
    Population, 2006 90,056
Personal income per capita, 2006
    (in current dollars) $32,552
Gross domestic product, 2006 ($ mil) $26,385

Leading industries by payroll, 2005

Health care/Social assistance, Retail trade,
Manufacturing

**Leading agricultural commodities
by receipts, 2005**

Wheat, Cattle and calves, Soybeans, Corn, Sugar
beets

Geography & Environment

Total area (square miles). 70,700
    land 68,976
    water 1,724
Federally-owned land, 2004 (acres) 1,185,777
    percent. 2.7%
Highest point . . . . White Butte
    elevation (feet) 3,506
Lowest point . . . . .Red River
    elevation (feet) 750
General coastline (miles) 0
Tidal shoreline (miles) 0
Cropland, 2003 (x 1,000 acres) 24,267
Forest land, 2003 (x 1,000 acres). 467
Capital city . . . . Bismarck
    Population 2000 55,532
    Population 2006 58,333
Largest city . . . . Fargo
    Population 2000 90,599
    Population 2006 90,056

Number of cities with over 100,000 population

1990 0
2000 0
2006 0

State park and recreation areas, 2005

Area (x 1,000 acres). 18
Number of visitors (x 1,000) 948
Revenues ($1,000) $1,514
    percent of operating expenditures. 47.3%

National forest system land, 2007

Acres 1,111,177

Demographics & Population Characteristics

Population

1980 652,717
1990 638,800
2000 642,204
2006 635,867
    Male. 319,427
    Female. 316,440
Living in group quarters, 2006. 27,521
    percent of total. 4.3%
2007 (estimate). 639,715
    persons per square mile of land 9.3
2008 (projected). 636,452
2010 (projected) 636,623
2020 (projected). 630,112
2030 (projected). 606,566

**Population of Core-Based Statistical Areas
(formerly Metropolitan Areas), x 1,000**

	CBSA	Non-CBSA
1990	410	228
2000	435	208
2006	442	194

Change in population, 2000-2007

Number . . . .-2,485
    percent. . . . . -0.4%
Natural increase (births minus deaths) 16,608
Net internal migration . . . . -19,531
Net international migration 3,184

Persons by age, 2006

Under 5 years 39,556
5 to 17 years 105,378
18 years and over 490,933
65 years and over 92,874
85 years and over .16,797
    Median age 37.2

Persons by age, 2010 (projected)

Under 5 years 38,869
18 and over 494,659
65 and over 97,108
    Median age 38.4

Race, 2006

One Race
    White. 584,116
    Black or African American 5,262
    Asian 4,743
    American Indian/Alaska Native. 34,190
    Hawaiian Native/Pacific Islander. 297
Two or more races. .7,259

Persons of Hispanic origin, 2006

Total Hispanic or Latino 9,332
    Mexican. 6,072
    Puerto Rican 667
    Cuban 80

Persons of Asian origin, 2006

Total Asian	4,348
Asian Indian	536
Chinese	573
Filipino	776
Japanese	194
Korean	653
Vietnamese	291

Marital status, 2006

Population 15 years & over	519,296
Never married	153,251
Married	285,270
Separated	3,469
Widowed	36,278
Divorced	44,497

Language spoken at home, 2006

Population 5 years and older	596,773
English only	565,565
Spanish	8,853
French	1,204
German	10,299
Chinese	449

Households & families, 2006

Households	272,352
with persons under 18 years	80,213
with persons over 65 years	63,993
persons per household	2.23
Families	169,022
persons per family	2.82
Married couples	138,355
Female householder, no husband present	21,352
One-person households	83,357

Nativity, 2006

Number of residents born in state	451,804
percent of population	71.1%

Immigration & naturalization, 2006

Legal permanent residents admitted	649
Persons naturalized	329
Non-immigrant admissions	14,643

Vital Statistics and Health

Marriages

2004	4,424
2005	4,388
2006	4,331

Divorces

2004	1,979
2005	1,905
2006	1,673

Health risks, 2006

Percent of adults who are:

Smokers	19.5%
Overweight (BMI > 25)	64.5%
Obese (BMI > 30)	25.4%

Births

2005	8,390
Birthrate (per 1,000)	13.2
White	7,195
Black	129
Hispanic	179
Asian/Pacific Islander	106
Amer. Indian/Alaska Native	960
Low birth weight (2,500g or less)	6.4%
Cesarian births	26.4%
Preterm births	11.5%
To unmarried mothers	32.2%
Twin births (per 1,000)	32.6
Triplets or higher order (per 100,000)	240.3
2006 (preliminary)	8,622
rate per 1,000	13.6

Deaths

2004

All causes	5,601
rate per 100,000	697.1
Heart disease	1,470
rate per 100,000	175.8
Malignant neoplasms	1,265
rate per 100,000	166.9
Cerebrovascular disease	475
rate per 100,000	54.6
Chronic lower respiratory disease	273
rate per 100,000	34.7
Diabetes	209
rate per 100,000	26.5
2005 (preliminary)	5,744
rate per 100,000	699.1
2006 (provisional)	5,917

Infant deaths

2004	46
rate per 1,000	5.6
2005 (provisional)	53
rate per 1,000	6.3

Exercise routines, 2005

None	23.1%
Moderate or greater	48.4%
Vigorous	27.5%

Abortions, 2004

Total performed in state	1,357
rate per 1,000 women age 15-44	10
% obtained by out-of-state residents	37.5%

Physicians, 2005

Total	1,523
rate per 100,000 persons	240

Community hospitals, 2005

Number of hospitals	40
Beds (x 1,000)	3.5
Patients admitted (x 1,000)	87
Average daily census (x 1,000)	2.1
Average cost per day	$898
Outpatient visits (x 1 mil)	1.9

Disability status of population, 2006
5 to 15 years 6.7%
16 to 64 years 10.1%
65 years and over 40.1%

Education

Educational attainment, 2006
Population over 25 years 409,865
   Less than 9th grade. 6.2%
   High school graduate or more 88.1%
   College graduate or more. 25.6%
   Graduate or professional degree. 6.5%

Public school enrollment, 2005-06
Total. 98,283
   Pre-kindergarten through grade 8. 65,638
   Grades 9 through 12 32,645

Graduating public high school seniors, 2004-05
Diplomas (incl. GED and others) 7,555

SAT scores, 2007
Average critical reading score 584
Average writing score 562
Average math score 596
Percent of graduates taking test 4%

Public school teachers, 2006-07 (estimate)
Total (x 1,000) 7.6
   Elementary 5.1
   Secondary 2.4
Average salary $38,822
   Elementary $39,141
   Secondary $38,144

State receipts & expenditures for public schools, 2006-07 (estimate)
Revenue receipts ($ mil) $967
Expenditures
Total ($ mil) $973
   Per capita $1,237
   Per pupil $9,036

NAEP proficiency scores, 2007

	Reading		Math	
	Basic	Proficient	Basic	Proficient
Grade 4	75.3%	35.3%	90.8%	45.7%
Grade 8	83.6%	32.2%	85.5%	41.0%

Higher education enrollment, fall 2005
Total. 6,581
   Full-time men 2,017
   Full-time women .3,362
   Part-time men 323
   Part-time women. 879

Minority enrollment in institutions of higher education, 2005
Black, non-Hispanic 682
Hispanic 489
Asian/Pacific Islander 530
American Indian/Alaska Native. 3,075

Institutions of higher education, 2005-06
Total. 22
   Public. 14
   Private 8

Earned degrees conferred, 2004-05
Associate's. 2,213
Bachelor's 5,161
Master's 1,104
First-professional. 178
Doctor's 189

Public Libraries, 2006
Number of libraries. 83
Number of outlets 105
Annual visits per capita 4.8
Circulation per capita. 7.4

State & local financial support for higher education, FY 2006
Full-time equivalent enrollment (x 1,000) 35.9
Appropriations per FTE. $4,683

Social Insurance & Welfare Programs

Social Security benefits & beneficiaries, 2005
Beneficiaries (x 1,000) 115
   Retired & dependents. 82
   Survivors. 19
   Disabled & dependents. 14
Annual benefit payments ($ mil) $1,174
   Retired & dependents. $780
   Survivors. $257
   Disabled & dependents. $137
Average monthly benefit
   Retired & dependents. $935
   Disabled & dependents. $873
   Widowed. $927

Medicare, July 2005
Enrollment (x 1,000) 104
Payments ($ mil) $615

Medicaid, 2004
Beneficiaries (x 1,000). 4,712
Payments ($ mil) $37,273

State Children's Health Insurance Program, 2006
Enrollment (x 1,000). .6.3
Expenditures ($ mil) $14.1

Persons without health insurance, 2006
Number (x 1,000). 75
   percent. 12.2%
Number of children (x 1,000) 15
   percent of children 10.4%

Health care expenditures, 2004
Total expenditures. $3,693
   per capita $5,808

Federal and state public aid

State unemployment insurance, 2006
Recipients, first payments (x 1,000) 14
Total payments ($ mil) $42
Average weekly benefit $255
Temporary Assistance for Needy Families, 2006
Recipients (x 1,000) 76.9
Families (x 1,000) 30.4
Supplemental Security Income, 2005
Recipients (x 1,000) 7.9
Payments ($ mil) $33.5
Food Stamp Program, 2006
Avg monthly participants (x 1,000) 42.6
Total benefits ($ mil) $46.2

Housing & Construction

Housing units

Total 2005 (estimate) 304,477
Total 2006 (estimate) 307,802
Seasonal or recreational use, 2006 11,805
Owner-occupied, 2006 181,666
  Median home value $99,700
  Homeowner vacancy rate 1.1%
Renter-occupied, 2006 90,686
  Median rent $497
  Rental vacancy rate 8.9%
Home ownership rate, 2005 . . . . .68.5%
Home ownership rate, 2006 . . . . .68.3%

New privately-owned housing units

Number authorized, 2006 (x 1,000) 3.5
  Value ($ mil) $462.3
Started 2005 (x 1,000, estimate) 3.4
Started 2006 (x 1,000, estimate) 3.3

Existing home sales

2005 (x 1,000) 15.8
2006 (x 1,000) 14.1

Government & Elections

State officials 2008

Governor . . . . .John Hoeven
    Republican, term expires 12/08
Lieutenant Governor . . . . Jack Dalrymple
Secretary of State . . . . Al Jaeger
Attorney General . . . . Wayne Stenehjem
Chief Justice . . . . Gerald VandeWalle

Governorship

Minimum age 30
Length of term . . . . 4 years
Consecutive terms permitted . . . . . . not specified
Who succeeds . . . . Lieutenant Governor

Local governments by type, 2002

Total 2,735
  County 53
  Municipal 360
  Township 1,332
  School District 226
  Special District 764

State legislature

Name .Legislative Assembly
Upper chamber . . . . .Senate
  Number of members 47
  Length of term . . . . 4 years
  Party in majority, 2008 . . . . Republican
Lower chamber . . . . . .House of Representatives
  Number of members 94
  Length of term . . . . 4 years
  Party in majority, 2008 . . . . Republican

Federal representation, 2008 (110th Congress)

Senator . . . . Byron Dorgan
  Party . . . . .Democratic
  Year term expires 2011
Senator . . . . .Kent Conrad
  Party . . . . .Democratic
  Year term expires 2013
Representatives, total 1
  Democrats 1
  Republicans 0

Voters in November 2006 election (estimate)

Total 258,566
  Male 126,807
  Female 131,759
  White 240,170
  Black 405
  Hispanic 562
  Asian 341

Presidential election, 2004

Total Popular Vote 312,833
  Kerry 111,052
  Bush 196,651
Total Electoral Votes 3

Votes cast for US Senators

2004
Total vote (x 1,000) 311
Leading party .Democratic
Percent for leading party 68.3%
2006
Total vote (x 1,000) 218
Leading party .Democratic
Percent for leading party 68.8%

Votes cast for US Representatives

2004
Total vote (x 1,000) 311
  Democratic 185
  Republican 126
Leading party .Democratic
Percent for leading party 59.6%
2006
Total vote (x 1,000) 218
  Democratic 143
  Republican 75
Leading party .Democratic
Percent for leading party 65.7%

State government employment, 2006
Full-time equivalent employees 18,127
Payroll ($ mil) $57.6

Local government employment, 2006
Full-time equivalent employees 23,046
Payroll ($ mil) $75.7

Women holding public office, 2008
US Congress 0
Statewide elected office. 2
State legislature 25

Black public officials, 2002
Total. 1
  US and state legislatures 0
  City/county/regional offices 1
  Judicial/law enforcement. 0
  Education/school boards 0

Hispanic public officials, 2006
Total. 1
  State executives & legislators 0
  City/county/regional offices 1
  Judicial/law enforcement. 0
  Education/school boards 0

Governmental Finance

State government revenues, 2006
Total revenue (x $1,000). $4,369,763
  per capita $6,854.96
General revenue (x $1,000) $3,667,407
  Intergovernmental 1,213,472
  Taxes 1,621,912
    general sales. 427,487
    individual income tax 275,630
    corporate income tax 120,113
  Current charges. 532,676
  Miscellaneous 299,347

State government expenditure, 2006
Total expenditure (x $1,000) $3,633,349
  per capita $5,699.73
General expenditure (x $1,000) $3,360,266
  per capita, total. $5,271.34
    Education 1,850.26
    Public welfare 1,103.83
    Health 90.53
    Hospitals. 35.49
    Highways 745.56
    Police protection. 39.22
    Corrections 89.13
    Natural resources 236.83
    Parks & recreation 25.50
    Governmental administration 202.67
    Interest on general debt 162.59

State debt & cash, 2006 ($ per capita)
Debt $2,777.16
Cash/security holdings. $15,550.53

Federal government grants to state & local government, 2005 (x $1,000)
Total. $1,666,287
by Federal agency
  Defense 24,304
  Education 138,017
  Energy 17,124
  Environmental Protection Agency 40,308
  Health & Human Services. 570,013
  Homeland Security. 18,631
  Housing & Urban Development. 102,556
  Justice 34,050
  Labor 25,973
  Transportation 257,349
  Veterans Affairs. 4,476

Crime & Law Enforcement

Crime, 2006 (rates per 100,000 residents)
Property crimes 12,719
  Burglary 2,393
  Larceny 9,314
  Motor vehicle theft 1,012
  Property crime rate. 2,000.3
Violent crimes. 813
  Murder 8
  Forcible rape. 193
  Robbery. 72
  Aggravated assault 540
  Violent crime rate 127.9
Hate crimes. 16

Fraud and identity theft, 2006
Fraud complaints. 544
  rate per 100,000 residents 85.6
Identity theft complaints 189
  rate per 100,000 residents 29.7

Law enforcement agencies, 2006
Total agencies. 93
Total employees 1,619
  Officers 1,178
  Civilians 441

Prisoners, probation, and parole, 2006
Total prisoners. 1,363
  percent change, 12/31/05 to 12/31/06 . . . -1.6%
  in private facilities .0%
  in local jails 3.5%
Sentenced to more than one year 1,363
  rate per 100,000 residents 214
Adults on probation 4,303
Adults on parole. 370

Prisoner demographics, June 30, 2005 (rate per 100,000 residents)
Male 632
Female 87
White 267
Black. 2,683
Hispanic 848

Arrests, 2006
Total................................ 28,597
  Persons under 18 years of age 6,769

Persons under sentence of death, 1/1/07
Total..................................... 0
  White.................................. 0
  Black 0
  Hispanic 0

State's highest court
Name ....Supreme Court
Number of members........................ 5
Length of term...................... 10 years
Intermediate appeals court? .... no

Labor & Income

Civilian labor force, 2006 (x 1,000)
Total.................................. 368
  Men 192
  Women 176
  Persons 16-19 years................... 21
  White................................ 338
  Black .... NA
  Hispanic .... NA

Civilian labor force as a percent of civilian non-institutional population, 2006
Total................................73.2%
  Men 77.4
  Women 69.0
  Persons 16-19 years..................56.3
  White................................73.9
  Black .... NA
  Hispanic .... NA

Employment, 2006 (x 1,000)
Total.................................. 355
  Men 185
  Women 171
  Persons 16-19 years................... 19
  White................................ 329
  Black .... NA
  Hispanic .... NA

Unemployment rate, 2006
Total.................................3.3%
  Men 3.8
  Women 2.9
  Persons 16-19 years..................10.6
  White................................2.6
  Black .... NA
  Hispanic .... NA

Full-time/part-time labor force, 2003 (x 1,000)
Full-time labor force, employed 264
Part-time labor force, employed............. 69
Unemployed, looking for
  Full-time work........................... 11
  Part-time work........................... 2
Mean duration of unemployment (weeks)......13.5
  Median 7.8

Labor unions, 2006
Membership (x 1,000)..................... 20
  percent of employed 6.8%

Experienced civilian labor force by private industry, 2006
Total............................. 271,603
  Natural resources & mining 7,574
  Construction 18,265
  Manufacturing........................ 26,009
  Trade, transportation & utilities 74,431
  Information 7,489
  Finance 18,707
  Professional & business 28,323
  Education & health................... 48,078
  Leisure & hospitality.................31,573
  Other...............................11,154

Experienced civilian labor force by occupation, May 2006
Management......................... 13,520
Business & financial 11,070
Legal.................................1,410
Sales.................................37,210
Office & admin. support................ 56,420
Computers & math 4,760
Architecture & engineering............. 4,960
Arts & entertainment 3,980
Education 20,900
Social services 4,840
Health care practitioner & technical......19,160
Health care support 11,590
Maintenance & repair................. 15,580
Construction 19,620
Transportation & moving 26,460
Production 21,590
Farming, fishing & forestry...............1,140

Hours and earnings of production workers on manufacturing payrolls, 2006
Average weekly hours 39.0
Average hourly earnings $14.97
Average weekly earnings $583.83

Income and poverty, 2006
Median household income..............$41,919
Personal income, per capita (current $)... $32,552
  in constant (2000) dollars $28,416
Persons below poverty level.............. 11.4%

Average annual pay
2006 ....$31,316
  increase from 2005 .... 4.5%

Federal individual income tax returns, 2005
Returns filed........................ 307,235
Adjusted gross income ($1,000) $12,970,269
Total tax liability ($1,000) $1,515,289

Charitable contributions, 2004
Number of contributions.................47.5
Total amount ($ mil).................$177.3

Economy, Business, Industry & Agriculture

Fortune 500 companies, 2007 0
Bankruptcy cases filed, FY 2007 1,090

Patents and trademarks issued, 2007
Patents 92
Trademarks 91

Business firm ownership, 2002
Women-owned 13,203
    Sales ($ mil) $1,318
Black-owned 78
    Sales ($ mil) $14
Hispanic-owned 230
    Sales ($ mil) $16
Asian-owned 277
    Sales ($ mil) $108
Amer. Indian/Alaska Native-owned 853
    Sales ($ mil) $121
Hawaiian/Pacific Islander-owned 2
    Sales ($ mil) . . . . NA

Gross domestic product, 2006 ($ mil)
Total gross domestic product $26,385
    Agriculture, forestry, fishing and
       hunting 1,655
    Mining 1,020
    Utilities 679
    Construction 1,250
    Manufacturing, durable goods 1,801
    Manufacturing, non-durable goods 697
    Wholesale trade 2,076
    Retail trade 1,883
    Transportation & warehousing 1,063
    Information 904
    Finance & insurance 1,567
    Real estate, rental & leasing 2,458
    Professional and technical services 933
    Educational services 116
    Health care and social assistance 2,238
    Accommodation/food services 615
    Other services, except government 564
    Government 4,046

Establishments, payroll, employees & receipts, by major industry group, 2005

Total 21,061
    Annual payroll ($1,000) $7,779,322
    Paid employees 270,479
Forestry, fishing & agriculture 144
    Annual payroll ($1,000) . . . . NA
    Paid employees . . . . NA
Mining 182
    Annual payroll ($1,000) $273,613
    Paid employees 4,368
    Receipts, 2002 ($1,000) $1,250,027

Utilities 115
    Annual payroll ($1,000) $230,061
    Paid employees 3,250
    Receipts, 2002 ($1,000) . . . . NA
Construction 2,299
    Annual payroll ($1,000) $641,985
    Paid employees 15,128
    Receipts, 2002 ($1,000) $2,338,220
Manufacturing 748
    Annual payroll ($1,000) $827,442
    Paid employees 24,604
    Receipts, 2002 ($1,000) $6,856,653
Wholesale trade 1,452
    Annual payroll ($1,000) $668,191
    Paid employees 17,233
    Receipts, 2002 ($1,000) $8,806,340
Retail trade 3,435
    Annual payroll ($1,000) $854,201
    Paid employees 43,548
    Receipts, 2002 ($1,000) $7,723,945
Transportation & warehousing 1,040
    Annual payroll ($1,000) $296,518
    Paid employees 9,473
    Receipts, 2002 ($1,000) $1,021,195
Information 374
    Annual payroll ($1,000) $292,650
    Paid employees 7,409
    Receipts, 2002 ($1,000) . . . . NA
Finance & insurance 1,582
    Annual payroll ($1,000) $563,818
    Paid employees 14,990
    Receipts, 2002 ($1,000) . . . . NA
Professional, scientific & technical 1,397
    Annual payroll ($1,000) $417,841
    Paid employees 11,561
    Receipts, 2002 ($1,000) $871,152
Education 147
    Annual payroll ($1,000) $79,618
    Paid employees 4,659
    Receipts, 2002 ($1,000) $41,636
Health care & social assistance 1,691
    Annual payroll ($1,000) $1,609,606
    Paid employees 50,372
    Receipts, 2002 ($1,000) $3,027,796
Arts and entertainment 395
    Annual payroll ($1,000) . . . . NA
    Paid employees . . . . NA
    Receipts, 2002 ($1,000) $242,898
Real estate 751
    Annual payroll ($1,000) $82,551
    Paid employees 3,664
    Receipts, 2002 ($1,000) $463,572
Accommodation & food service 1,795
    Annual payroll ($1,000) $290,993
    Paid employees 28,662
    Receipts, 2002 ($1,000) $854,656

Exports, 2006

Value of exported goods ($ mil) $1,509
   Manufactured $1,206
   Non-manufactured $243

Foreign direct investment in US affiliates, 2004

Property, plants & equipment ($ mil) $1,416
Employment (x 1,000) . . . . NA

Agriculture, 2006

Number of farms 30,300
Farm acreage (x 1,000) 39,400
   Acres per farm 1,300
Farm marketings and income ($ mil)
Total $3,980.7
   Crops $3,088.4
   Livestock $892.4
Net farm income $605.9

Principal commodities, in order by
   marketing receipts, 2005

Wheat, Cattle and calves, Soybeans, Corn, Sugar
beets

Federal economic activity in state

Expenditures, 2005 ($ mil)
   Total $6,608
      Per capita $10,412.83
   Defense $776
   Non-defense $5,832
Defense department, 2006 ($ mil)
   Payroll $501
   Contract awards $240
   Grants $37
Homeland security grants ($1,000)
   2006 . . . .$10,788
   2007 . . . . $6,678

FDIC-insured financial institutions, 2005

Number 96
Assets ($ billion) $18.4
Deposits ($ billion) $11.4

Fishing, 2006

Catch (x 1,000 lbs) . . . . NA
Value ($1,000) . . . . NA

Mining, 2006 ($ mil)

Total non-fuel mineral production $56
Percent of U.S. 0.09%

Communication, Energy & Transportation

Communication

Households with computers, 2003 . . . . 61.2%
Households with internet access, 2003 . . . . 53.2%
High-speed internet providers 40
Total high-speed internet lines 131,348
   Residential 116,643
   Business 14,705
Wireless phone customers, 12/2006 472,799

FCC-licensed stations (as of January 1, 2008)

TV stations 27
FM radio stations 63
AM radio stations 34

Energy

Energy consumption, 2004
   Total (trillion Btu) 402
   Per capita (million Btu) 632.7
By source of production (trillion Btu)
   Coal 398
   Natural gas 60
   Petroleum 134
   Nuclear electric power 0
   Hydroelectric power 16
By end-use sector (trillion Btu)
   Residential 63
   Commercial 59
   Industrial 188
   Transportation 92
Electric energy, 2005
   Primary source of electricity . . . . Coal
   Net generation (billion kWh) 31.9
      percent from renewable sources 4.9%
   Net summer capability (million kW) 4.8
   CO_2 emitted from generation 32.8
Natural gas utilities, 2005
   Customers (x 1,000) 131
   Sales (trillion Btu) 33
   Revenues ($ mil) $247
Nuclear plants, 2007 0
Total CO_2 emitted (million metric tons) 50.7
Energy spending, 2004 ($ mil) $2,650
   per capita $4,167
   Price per million Btu $9.18

Transportation, 2006

Public road & street mileage 86,839
   Urban 1,870
   Rural 84,969
   Interstate 571
Vehicle miles of travel (millions) 7,890
   per capita 12,377.2
Total motor vehicle registrations 712,169
   Automobiles 345,502
   Trucks 364,080
   Motorcycles 25,353
Licensed drivers 468,711
   19 years & under 33,533
Deaths from motor vehicle accidents 111
Gasoline consumed (x 1,000 gallons) 352,308
   per capita 552.7

Commuting Statistics, 2006

Average commute time (min) 15.5
   Drove to work alone 79.3%
   Carpooled 9.2%
   Public transit 0.4%
   Walk to work 4.1%
   Work from home 5.8%

State Summary

Capital city .... Columbus
Governor...................... Ted Strickland

30th Floor
77 South High St
Columbus, OH 43215
614-466-3555

Admitted as a state 1803
Area (square miles) 44,825
Population, 2007 (estimate)......... 11,466,917
Largest city .... Columbus
   Population, 2006................... 733,203
Personal income per capita, 2006
   (in current dollars) $33,338
Gross domestic product, 2006 ($ mil) ... $461,302

Leading industries by payroll, 2005

Manufacturing, Health care/Social assistance,
Finance & Insurance

Leading agricultural commodities by receipts, 2005

Soybeans, Corn, Dairy products, Greenhouse/
nursery, Cattle and calves

Geography & Environment

Total area (square miles)............... 44,825
   land 40,948
   water 3,877
Federally-owned land, 2004 (acres) 448,381
   percent............................... 1.7%
Highest point .... Campbell Hill
   elevation (feet) 1,550
Lowest point .... Ohio River
   elevation (feet) 455
General coastline (miles) 0
Tidal shoreline (miles) 0
Cropland, 2003 (x 1,000 acres) 11,243
Forest land, 2003 (x 1,000 acres)...........7,225
Capital city .... Columbus
   Population 2000 711,470
   Population 2006 733,203
Largest city .... Columbus
   Population 2000 711,470
   Population 2006 733,203

Number of cities with over 100,000 population

1990 6
2000 6
2006 6

State park and recreation areas, 2005

Area (x 1,000 acres)...................... 174
Number of visitors (x 1,000) 50,166
Revenues ($1,000) $27,667
   percent of operating expenditures...... 40.1%

National forest system land, 2007

Acres 238,984

Demographics & Population Characteristics

Population

1980 10,797,630
1990 10,847,115
2000 11,353,145
2006 11,478,006
   Male.............................5,597,677
   Female..........................5,880,329
Living in group quarters, 2006......... 308,323
   percent of total....................... 2.7%
2007 (estimate).....................11,466,917
   persons per square mile of land 280.0
2008 (projected)....................11,541,279
2010 (projected)....................11,576,181
2020 (projected)....................11,644,058
2030 (projected)....................11,550,528

Population of Core-Based Statistical Areas (formerly Metropolitan Areas), x 1,000

	CBSA	Non-CBSA
1990	10,377	470
2000	10,849	504
2006	10,966	512

Change in population, 2000-2007

Number 113,772
   percent................................ 1.0%
Natural increase (births minus deaths) 302,012
Net internal migration ....-301,848
Net international migration 94,461

Persons by age, 2006

Under 5 years 734,735
5 to 17 years 2,035,300
18 years and over 8,707,971
65 years and over 1,531,994
85 years and over 216,992
   Median age 37.6

Persons by age, 2010 (projected)

Under 5 years 760,100
18 and over 8,831,750
65 and over 1,586,981
   Median age..........................38.1

Race, 2006

One Race
   White............................ 9,747,752
   Black or African American 1,377,161
   Asian 177,215
   American Indian/Alaska Native.......27,546
   Hawaiian Native/Pacific Islander.......3,787
Two or more races.................... 144,545

Persons of Hispanic origin, 2006

Total Hispanic or Latino 265,762
   Mexican............................ 137,456
   Puerto Rican 69,657
   Cuban 4,296

Persons of Asian origin, 2006

Total Asian 175,000
  Asian Indian 56,619
  Chinese 43,167
  Filipino 14,528
  Japanese 9,117
  Korean 12,036
  Vietnamese 18,635

Marital status, 2006

Population 15 years & over 9,205,208
  Never married 2,705,608
  Married 4,797,458
  Separated 164,304
  Widowed 634,611
  Divorced 1,067,531

Language spoken at home, 2006

Population 5 years and older 10,741,831
  English only 10,079,739
  Spanish 230,476
  French 31,279
  German 90,179
  Chinese 35,071

Households & families, 2006

Households 4,499,506
  with persons under 18 years 1,481,163
  with persons over 65 years 1,068,490
  persons per household 2.48
Families 2,953,361
  persons per family .3.08
Married couples 2,202,145
Female householder,
  no husband present 563,407
One-person households 1,311,490

Nativity, 2006

Number of residents born in state 8,622,617
  percent of population 75.1%

Immigration & naturalization, 2006

Legal permanent residents admitted 16,592
Persons naturalized 8,796
Non-immigrant admissions 243,902

Vital Statistics and Health

Marriages

2004 75,287
2005 74,453
2006 73,100

Divorces

2004 40,770
2005 40,181
2006 41,035

Health risks, 2006

Percent of adults who are:
  Smokers 22.4%
  Overweight (BMI > 25) 63.9%
  Obese (BMI > 30) 28.4%

Births

2005 148,388
  Birthrate (per 1,000) 12.9
  White 120,507
  Black 24,120
  Hispanic 6,070
  Asian/Pacific Islander 3,468
  Amer. Indian/Alaska Native 293
  Low birth weight (2,500g or less) 8.7%
  Cesarian births 28.1%
  Preterm births 13.0%
  To unmarried mothers 38.9%
  Twin births (per 1,000) 33.4
  Triplets or higher order (per 100,000) . . . 238.2
2006 (preliminary) 150,590
  rate per 1,000 . . . . .13.1

Deaths

2004
All causes 106,288
  rate per 100,000 . . . . 848.0
Heart disease 29,078
  rate per 100,000 . . . . .229.0
Malignant neoplasms 24,940
  rate per 100,000 . . . . 200.6
Cerebrovascular disease 6,501
  rate per 100,000 . . . . .50.9
Chronic lower respiratory disease 5,896
  rate per 100,000 . . . . .47.0
Diabetes 3,615
  rate per 100,000 . . . . .28.9
2005 (preliminary) 109,030
  rate per 100,000 . . . . 856.8
2006 (provisional) 106,977

Infant deaths

2004 1,143
  rate per 1,000 . . . . .7.7
2005 (provisional) 1,208
  rate per 1,000 . . . . .8.2

Exercise routines, 2005

None 25.6%
Moderate or greater 49.2%
Vigorous 27.2%

Abortions, 2004

Total performed in state 34,242
  rate per 1,000 women age 15-44 14
  % obtained by out-of-state residents 7.9%

Physicians, 2005

Total 30,096
  rate per 100,000 persons 262

Community hospitals, 2005

Number of hospitals 170
Beds (x 1,000) 33.3
Patients admitted (x 1,000) 1,511
Average daily census (x 1,000) 21.4
Average cost per day $1,673
Outpatient visits (x 1 mil) 31.3

Ohio 3

Disability status of population, 2006
5 to 15 years 7.4%
16 to 64 years 13.4%
65 years and over 39.8%

Education

Educational attainment, 2006
Population over 25 years 7,602,462
  Less than 9th grade. 3.6%
  High school graduate or more 86.2%
  College graduate or more. 23.0%
  Graduate or professional degree. 8.3%

Public school enrollment, 2005-06
Total. 1,839,683
  Pre-kindergarten through grade 8. . . 1,261,331
  Grades 9 through 12 578,352

Graduating public high school seniors, 2004-05
Diplomas (incl. GED and others) 116,702

SAT scores, 2007
Average critical reading score 536
Average writing score 522
Average math score 542
Percent of graduates taking test 27%

Public school teachers, 2006-07 (estimate)
Total (x 1,000) 119.3
  Elementary 81.2
  Secondary 38.0
Average salary $51,937
  Elementary $51,937
  Secondary $51,937

State receipts & expenditures for public schools, 2006-07 (estimate)
Revenue receipts ($ mil) $21,510
Expenditures
Total ($ mil) $22,393
  Per capita $1,717
  Per pupil $11,947

NAEP proficiency scores, 2007

	Reading		Math	
	Basic	Proficient	Basic	Proficient
Grade 4	73.3%	36.3%	87.5%	45.9%
Grade 8	79.4%	35.9%	76.4%	35.4%

Higher education enrollment, fall 2005
Total. 163,349
  Full-time men 53,803
  Full-time women. 71,345
  Part-time men 13,676
  Part-time women. 24,525

Minority enrollment in institutions of higher education, 2005
Black, non-Hispanic 74,590
Hispanic 12,361
Asian/Pacific Islander 13,008
American Indian/Alaska Native. 2,439

Institutions of higher education, 2005-06
Total. 200
  Public. 61
  Private 139

Earned degrees conferred, 2004-05
Associate's. 22,674
Bachelor's 56,969
Master's 20,360
First-professional. 3,398
Doctor's 2,018

Public Libraries, 2006
Number of libraries. 251
Number of outlets 788
Annual visits per capita 7.2
Circulation per capita. 15.0

State & local financial support for higher education, FY 2006
Full-time equivalent enrollment (x 1,000) 381.9
Appropriations per FTE. $4,690

Social Insurance & Welfare Programs

Social Security benefits & beneficiaries, 2005
Beneficiaries (x 1,000) 1,965
  Retired & dependents. 1,352
  Survivors. 308
  Disabled & dependents. 305
Annual benefit payments ($ mil) $21,546
  Retired & dependents. $14,077
  Survivors. $4,377
  Disabled & dependents. $3,091
Average monthly benefit
  Retired & dependents. $1,016
  Disabled & dependents. $914
  Widowed $1,000

Medicare, July 2005
Enrollment (x 1,000). 1,754
Payments ($ mil) $11,698

Medicaid, 2004
Beneficiaries (x 1,000). 1,896
Payments ($ mil) $11,375

State Children's Health Insurance Program, 2006
Enrollment (x 1,000). 218.5
Expenditures ($ mil) $236.1

Persons without health insurance, 2006
Number (x 1,000). .1,138
  percent. 10.1%
Number of children (x 1,000) 157
  percent of children 5.6%

Health care expenditures, 2004
Total expenditures. $65,622
  per capita $5,725

Federal and state public aid

State unemployment insurance, 2006
Recipients, first payments (x 1,000) 275
Total payments ($ mil) $1,096
Average weekly benefit $287
Temporary Assistance for Needy Families, 2006
Recipients (x 1,000). 2,025.5
Families (x 1,000) .949.2
Supplemental Security Income, 2005
Recipients (x 1,000). 250.3
Payments ($ mil) $1,295.0
Food Stamp Program, 2006
Avg monthly participants (x 1,000) 1,063.9
Total benefits ($ mil). $1,266.2

Housing & Construction

Housing units
Total 2005 (estimate) 5,008,801
Total 2006 (estimate) 5,044,709
Seasonal or recreational use, 2006 47,088
Owner-occupied, 2006. 3,150,239
    Median home value. $135,200
    Homeowner vacancy rate. 2.7%
Renter-occupied, 2006 1,349,267
    Median rent $627
    Rental vacancy rate. 12.3%
Home ownership rate, 2005. . . . . 73.3%
Home ownership rate, 2006. . . . . 72.1%

New privately-owned housing units
Number authorized, 2006 (x 1,000). 34.4
    Value ($ mil). $5,920.0
Started 2005 (x 1,000, estimate) 49.7
Started 2006 (x 1,000, estimate) 48.8

Existing home sales
2005 (x 1,000). 286.9
2006 (x 1,000). 275.4

Government & Elections

State officials 2008
Governor . . . . Ted Strickland
        Democratic, term expires 1/11
Lieutenant Governor. . . . . Lee Fisher
Secretary of State. . . . . Jennifer Brunner
Attorney General. . . . . Marc Dann
Chief Justice . . . . Thomas Moyer

Governorship
Minimum age. 18
Length of term . . . . 4 years
Consecutive terms permitted . 8 out of any 12 yrs
Who succeeds. . . . . Lieutenant Governor

Local governments by type, 2002
Total. 3,636
    County. 88
    Municipal 942
    Township 1,308
    School District. 667
    Special District 631

State legislature
Name . . . . General Assembly
Upper chamber . . . . .Senate
    Number of members. 33
    Length of term. 4 years
    Party in majority, 2008 . . . . Republican
Lower chamber. . . . . . . .House of Representatives
    Number of members. 99
    Length of term. 2 years
    Party in majority, 2008 . . . . Republican

Federal representation, 2008 (110th Congress)
Senator. George Voinovich
    Party . . . . Republican
    Year term expires 2011
Senator. . . . . .Sherrod Brown
    Party . . . . .Democratic
    Year term expires 2013
Representatives, total 18
    Democrats. 7
    Republicans 11

Voters in November 2006 election (estimate)
Total. 4,408,448
    Male. 2,051,155
    Female. 2,357,293
    White. 3,935,906
    Black 396,929
    Hispanic 38,736
    Asian 24,911

Presidential election, 2004
Total Popular Vote 5,627,908
    Kerry 2,741,167
    Bush 2,859,768
Total Electoral Votes. 20

Votes cast for US Senators
2004
Total vote (x 1,000) 5,426
Leading party. . . . . Republican
Percent for leading party 63.8%
2006
Total vote (x 1,000) 4,019
Leading party. . . . . .Democratic
Percent for leading party 56.2%

Votes cast for US Representatives
2004
Total vote (x 1,000) 5,184
    Democratic. 2,515
    Republican 2,650
Leading party. . . . . Republican
Percent for leading party 51.1%
2006
Total vote (x 1,000) 3,961
    Democratic. 2,082
    Republican 1,870
Leading party. . . . . .Democratic
Percent for leading party 52.6%

State government employment, 2006
Full-time equivalent employees 136,840
Payroll ($ mil) $520.5

Local government employment, 2006
Full-time equivalent employees 479,899
Payroll ($ mil) $1,680.1

Women holding public office, 2008
US Congress 5
Statewide elected office...................... 2
State legislature 22

Black public officials, 2002
Total.. 305
   US and state legislatures 21
   City/county/regional offices 197
   Judicial/law enforcement.................. 35
   Education/school boards 52

Hispanic public officials, 2006
Total.. 4
   State executives & legislators 0
   City/county/regional offices 3
   Judicial/law enforcement.................. 1
   Education/school boards.................. 0

Governmental Finance

State government revenues, 2006
Total revenue (x $1,000) $75,405,477
   per capita $6,577.87
General revenue (x $1,000) $51,349,846
   Intergovernmental 16,524,695
   Taxes 24,636,910
      general sales.................... 7,733,133
      individual income tax 9,859,712
      corporate income tax 1,102,351
   Current charges................... 6,210,835
   Miscellaneous 3,977,406

State government expenditure, 2006
Total expenditure (x $1,000) $64,928,716
   per capita $5,663.95
General expenditure (x $1,000) $52,719,823
   per capita, total.................. $4,598.92
      Education 1,633.78
      Public welfare 1,397.69
      Health 213.02
      Hospitals..................... 170.18
      Highways 295.36
      Police protection................ 20.97
      Corrections 140.01
      Natural resources 33.55
      Parks & recreation 9.38
      Governmental administration...... 170.62
      Interest on general debt........... 112.68

State debt & cash, 2006 ($ per capita)
Debt $2,155.80
Cash/security holdings.............. $15,983.00

Federal government grants to state & local government, 2005 (x $1,000)
Total........................... $17,151,707
by Federal agency
   Defense 89,030
   Education 1,239,866
   Energy 79,687
   Environmental Protection Agency 157,037
   Health & Human Services. 11,057,199
   Homeland Security................ 212,049
   Housing & Urban Development..... 1,323,892
   Justice 159,344
   Labor 324,831
   Transportation 1,363,161
   Veterans Affairs...................... 17,134

Crime & Law Enforcement

Crime, 2006 (rates per 100,000 residents)
Property crimes 422,235
   Burglary 104,426
   Larceny 280,384
   Motor vehicle theft 37,425
   Property crime rate.................. 3,678.6
Violent crimes........................ 40,209
   Murder 539
   Forcible rape...................... 4,548
   Robbery.......................... 19,149
   Aggravated assault 15,973
   Violent crime rate 350.3
Hate crimes........................... 350

Fraud and identity theft, 2006
Fraud complaints..................... 14,241
   rate per 100,000 residents 124.1
Identity theft complaints 6,878
   rate per 100,000 residents 59.9

Law enforcement agencies, 2006
Total agencies......................... 563
Total employees 29,607
   Officers 21,289
   Civilians 8,318

Prisoners, probation, and parole, 2006
Total prisoners....................... 49,166
   percent change, 12/31/05 to 12/31/06 .... 7.2%
   in private facilities 4.2%
   in local jails 0%
Sentenced to more than one year 49,166
   rate per 100,000 residents 428
Adults on probation 243,956
Adults on parole....................... 17,603

Prisoner demographics, June 30, 2005
(rate per 100,000 residents)
Male.................................. 1,040
Female 103
White................................. 344
Black................................. 2,196
Hispanic 613

Arrests, 2006

Total............................. 235,005
   Persons under 18 years of age........ 38,509

Persons under sentence of death, 1/1/07

Total.................................. 191
   White.................................. 88
   Black.................................. 96
   Hispanic................................ 3

State's highest court

Name......................Supreme Court
Number of members...................... 7
Length of term..................... 6 years
Intermediate appeals court?..............yes

Labor & Income

Civilian labor force, 2006 (x 1,000)

Total...............................5,975
   Men.................................3,121
   Women............................. 2,854
   Persons 16-19 years.................... 344
   White...............................5,163
   Black................................. 649
   Hispanic.............................. 155

Civilian labor force as a percent of civilian non-institutional population, 2006

Total................................. 67.2%
   Men.................................73.1
   Women..............................61.7
   Persons 16-19 years..................53.0
   White...............................67.3
   Black................................66.7
   Hispanic.............................70.6

Employment, 2006 (x 1,000)

Total...............................5,652
   Men.................................2,938
   Women..............................2,714
   Persons 16-19 years.................... 284
   White...............................4,929
   Black................................. 569
   Hispanic.............................. 144

Unemployment rate, 2006

Total................................. 5.4%
   Men.................................5.9
   Women..............................4.9
   Persons 16-19 years..................17.6
   White................................4.5
   Black................................12.3
   Hispanic.............................7.2

Full-time/part-time labor force, 2003 (x 1,000)

Full-time labor force, employed.......... 4,402
Part-time labor force, employed...........1,149
Unemployed, looking for
   Full-time work......................... 287
   Part-time work......................... 76
*Mean duration of unemployment (weeks)......*18.7
   Median.................................9.7

Labor unions, 2006

Membership (x 1,000).................... 734
   percent of employed.................. 14.2%

Experienced civilian labor force by private industry, 2006

Total...........................4,562,713
   Natural resources & mining.......... 24,906
   Construction......................230,174
   Manufacturing.....................795,610
   Trade, transportation & utilities.... 1,037,823
   Information........................ 88,633
   Finance.......................... 298,788
   Professional & business.............. 655,844
   Education & health................ 764,367
   Leisure & hospitality............... 500,612
   Other............................. 163,682

Experienced civilian labor force by occupation, May 2006

Management........................196,910
Business & financial.................. 228,210
Legal............................. 32,050
Sales.............................547,770
Office & admin. support.............. 892,490
Computers & math....................104,110
Architecture & engineering.............89,730
Arts & entertainment................. 53,560
Education.........................316,110
Social services.................... 58,530
Health care practitioner & technical.... 299,840
Health care support................ 175,320
Maintenance & repair.................216,170
Construction.......................211,660
Transportation & moving..............439,170
Production......................... 589,000
Farming, fishing & forestry..............6,190

Hours and earnings of production workers on manufacturing payrolls, 2006

Average weekly hours.....................41.4
Average hourly earnings...............$19.16
Average weekly earnings.............. $793.22

Income and poverty, 2006

Median household income............ $44,532
Personal income, per capita (current $)... $33,338
   in constant (2000) dollars...........$29,102
Persons below poverty level.............. 13.3%

Average annual pay

2006.............................. $38,568
   increase from 2005.................... 3.3%

Federal individual income tax returns, 2005

Returns filed.......................5,459,548
Adjusted gross income ($1,000)... $252,434,762
Total tax liability ($1,000).........$29,798,934

Charitable contributions, 2004

Number of contributions...............1,549.0
Total amount ($ mil).................$4,899.6

Economy, Business, Industry & Agriculture

Fortune 500 companies, 2007.............. 28
Bankruptcy cases filed, FY 2007......... 48,527

Patents and trademarks issued, 2007
Patents............................3,058
Trademarks............................ 2,869

Business firm ownership, 2002
Women-owned....................... 229,972
  Sales ($ mil) $32,315
Black-owned....................... 35,658
  Sales ($ mil) $3,600
Hispanic-owned.......................7,109
  Sales ($ mil) $1,263
Asian-owned 13,740
  Sales ($ mil) $5,106
Amer. Indian/Alaska Native-owned 3,123
  Sales ($ mil) $500
Hawaiian/Pacific Islander-owned 229
  Sales ($ mil) $28

Gross domestic product, 2006 ($ mil)
Total gross domestic product $461,302
  Agriculture, forestry, fishing and
    hunting 2,023
  Mining............................2,173
  Utilities............................9,822
  Construction 18,230
  Manufacturing, durable goods....... 60,493
  Manufacturing, non-durable goods ... 28,827
  Wholesale trade..................... 28,561
  Retail trade......................... 30,957
  Transportation & warehousing 14,675
  Information 12,076
  Finance & insurance................. 38,331
  Real estate, rental & leasing 49,137
  Professional and technical services 25,444
  Educational services...................3,521
  Health care and social assistance.......37,037
  Accommodation/food services..........9,979
  Other services, except government 10,579
  Government....................... 49,507

Establishments, payroll, employees & receipts, by major industry group, 2005

Total............................. 270,968
  Annual payroll ($1,000)........ $168,350,499
  Paid employees 4,762,618
Forestry, fishing & agriculture.............. 298
  Annual payroll ($1,000)................. NA
  Paid employees .... NA
Mining............................. 789
  Annual payroll ($1,000)........... $495,414
  Paid employees 10,051
  Receipts, 2002 ($1,000) $2,421,333

Utilities 593
  Annual payroll ($1,000)..........$2,039,541
  Paid employees 27,291
  Receipts, 2002 ($1,000) ....NA
Construction........................... 26,322
  Annual payroll ($1,000)...........$9,261,274
  Paid employees 214,948
  Receipts, 2002 ($1,000) $40,273,765
Manufacturing.......................16,617
  Annual payroll ($1,000)..........$35,677,361
  Paid employees 792,783
  Receipts, 2002 ($1,000) $243,903,865
Wholesale trade 15,545
  Annual payroll ($1,000).......... $11,276,311
  Paid employees 237,889
  Receipts, 2002 ($1,000) $166,446,529
Retail trade 40,949
  Annual payroll ($1,000)..........$12,465,820
  Paid employees 620,869
  Receipts, 2002 ($1,000) $119,778,409
Transportation & warehousing 7,583
  Annual payroll ($1,000)..........$6,118,482
  Paid employees 166,815
  Receipts, 2002 ($1,000) $15,546,563
Information............................4,216
  Annual payroll ($1,000)..........$5,107,245
  Paid employees 99,458
  Receipts, 2002 ($1,000) ....NA
Finance & insurance 18,403
  Annual payroll ($1,000)..........$13,685,220
  Paid employees 263,129
  Receipts, 2002 ($1,000) ....NA
Professional, scientific & technical 25,597
  Annual payroll ($1,000)..........$12,704,427
  Paid employees 244,577
  Receipts, 2002 ($1,000) $24,241,958
Education 2,825
  Annual payroll ($1,000)......... $2,486,828
  Paid employees 103,175
  Receipts, 2002 ($1,000) $776,310
Health care & social assistance 26,961
  Annual payroll ($1,000)......... $24,680,904
  Paid employees 715,021
  Receipts, 2002 ($1,000) $50,262,849
Arts and entertainment 4,080
  Annual payroll ($1,000)..........$1,613,178
  Paid employees 59,680
  Receipts, 2002 ($1,000) $4,544,038
Real estate 10,581
  Annual payroll ($1,000)..........$2,272,201
  Paid employees 68,081
  Receipts, 2002 ($1,000) $9,768,869
Accommodation & food service.......... 23,337
  Annual payroll ($1,000)..........$4,799,826
  Paid employees 430,134
  Receipts, 2002 ($1,000) $14,875,890

Exports, 2006

Value of exported goods ($ mil) $37,833
   Manufactured $34,588
   Non-manufactured . . . . . / $1,257

Foreign direct investment in US affiliates, 2004

Property, plants & equipment ($ mil) . . . $32,898
Employment (x 1,000) 203.6

Agriculture, 2006

Number of farms 76,200
Farm acreage (x 1,000) 14,300
   Acres per farm 188
Farm marketings and income ($ mil)
Total $5,479.7
   Crops $3,448.4
   Livestock $2,031.3
Net farm income $1,614.4

Principal commodities, in order by marketing receipts, 2005

   Soybeans, Corn, Dairy products, Greenhouse/
   nursery, Cattle and calves

Federal economic activity in state

Expenditures, 2005 ($ mil)
   Total $77,881
      Per capita $6,789.55
   Defense $8,243
   Non-defense $69,638
Defense department, 2006 ($ mil)
   Payroll $3,030
   Contract awards $5,980
   Grants $97
Homeland security grants ($1,000)
   2006 . . . . $41,347
   2007 . . . . $46,321

FDIC-insured financial institutions, 2005

Number 276
Assets ($ billion) $1,874.7
Deposits ($ billion) $1,105.5

Fishing, 2006

Catch (x 1,000 lbs) 4,242
Value ($1,000) $4,169

Mining, 2006 ($ mil)

Total non-fuel mineral production $1,260
Percent of U.S. 1.96%

Communication, Energy & Transportation

Communication

Households with computers, 2003 . . . . .58.8%
Households with internet access, 2003 . . . .52.5%
High-speed internet providers 81
Total high-speed internet lines 3,186,537
   Residential 2,141,752
   Business 1,044,785
Wireless phone customers, 12/2006 8,380,138

FCC-licensed stations (as of January 1, 2008)

TV stations 52
FM radio stations 307
AM radio stations 124

Energy

Energy consumption, 2004
   Total (trillion Btu) 4,023
   Per capita (million Btu) 351.0
By source of production (trillion Btu)
   Coal 1,391
   Natural gas 845
   Petroleum 1,368
   Nuclear electric power 166
   Hydroelectric power 7
By end-use sector (trillion Btu)
   Residential 942
   Commercial 705
   Industrial 1,360
   Transportation 1,016
Electric energy, 2005
   Primary source of electricity . . . . Coal
   Net generation (billion kWh) 157.0
      percent from renewable sources 0.6%
   Net summer capability (million kW) 33.9
   CO_2 emitted from generation 131.8
Natural gas utilities, 2005
   Customers (x 1,000) 3,558
   Sales (trillion Btu) 807
   Revenues ($ mil) $3,605
Nuclear plants, 2007 2
Total CO_2 emitted (million metric tons) 265.5
Energy spending, 2004 ($ mil) $34,944
   per capita $3,049
   Price per million Btu $12.85

Transportation, 2006

Public road & street mileage 125,107
   Urban 44,594
   Rural 80,513
   Interstate 1,574
Vehicle miles of travel (millions) 111,247
   per capita 9,704.4
Total motor vehicle registrations 10,828,843
   Automobiles 6,438,988
   Trucks 4,345,371
   Motorcycles 332,275
Licensed drivers 7,739,410
   19 years & under 379,645
Deaths from motor vehicle accidents 1,238
Gasoline consumed (x 1,000 gallons) . . . 5,204,068
   per capita 454.0

Commuting Statistics, 2006

Average commute time (min) 22.1
   Drove to work alone 83.1%
   Carpooled 8.3%
   Public transit 2.0%
   Walk to work 2.5%
   Work from home 3.1%

State Summary

Capital city .Oklahoma City
Governor . . . . .Brad Henry
Capitol Building
2300 N Lincoln Blvd, Room 212
Oklahoma City, OK 73105
405-521-2342
Admitted as a state 1907
Area (square miles) 69,898
Population, 2007 (estimate) 3,617,316
Largest city .Oklahoma City
Population, 2006 .537,734
Personal income per capita, 2006
(in current dollars) $32,210
Gross domestic product, 2006 ($ mil) . . . $134,651

Leading industries by payroll, 2005

Health care/Social assistance, Manufacturing,
Retail trade

Leading agricultural commodities by receipts, 2005

Cattle and calves, Hogs, Broilers, Wheat, Dairy
products

Geography & Environment

Total area (square miles) 69,898
land 68,667
water 1,231
Federally-owned land, 2004 (acres) 1,586,148
percent 3.6%
Highest point . . . . Black Mesa
elevation (feet) 4,973
Lowest point . . . . Little River
elevation (feet) 289
General coastline (miles) 0
Tidal shoreline (miles) 0
Cropland, 2003 (x 1,000 acres) 8,971
Forest land, 2003 (x 1,000 acres) 7,368
Capital city .Oklahoma City
Population 2000 506,132
Population 2006 537,734
Largest city .Oklahoma City
Population 2000 506,132
Population 2006 537,734

Number of cities with over 100,000 population

1990 2
2000 2
2006 3

State park and recreation areas, 2005

Area (x 1,000 acres) 72
Number of visitors (x 1,000) 13,282
Revenues ($1,000) $23,260
percent of operating expenditures 58.9%

National forest system land, 2007

Acres 400,768

Demographics & Population Characteristics

Population

1980 3,025,290
1990 3,145,585
2000 3,450,652
2006 3,579,212
Male 1,764,514
Female 1,814,698
Living in group quarters, 2006 111,393
percent of total 3.1%
2007 (estimate) 3,617,316
persons per square mile of land 52.7
2008 (projected) .3,563,865
2010 (projected) .3,591,516
2020 (projected) .3,735,690
2030 (projected) .3,913,251

Population of Core-Based Statistical Areas (formerly Metropolitan Areas), x 1,000

	CBSA	Non-CBSA
1990	2,610	536
2000	2,891	560
2006	3,018	561

Change in population, 2000-2007

Number 166,662
percent 4.8%
Natural increase (births minus deaths) 120,981
Net internal migration 11,901
Net international migration 42,146

Persons by age, 2006

Under 5 years 254,718
5 to 17 years 639,316
18 years and over 2,685,178
65 years and over 473,545
85 years and over 65,571
Median age 36.0

Persons by age, 2010 (projected)

Under 5 years 254,682
18 and over 2,696,443
65 and over 494,966
Median age 36.8

Race, 2006

One Race
White 2,803,755
Black or African American 278,849
Asian 60,201
American Indian/Alaska Native 287,728
Hawaiian Native/Pacific Islander 3,429
Two or more races 145,250

Persons of Hispanic origin, 2006

Total Hispanic or Latino 244,822
Mexican 201,317
Puerto Rican 8,349
Cuban 1,727

Persons of Asian origin, 2006

Total Asian 59,164
  Asian Indian. 11,196
  Chinese 8,292
  Filipino 5,142
  Japanese 2,694
  Korean 5,812
  Vietnamese. 16,678

Marital status, 2006

Population 15 years & over 2,839,257
  Never married 721,736
  Married. 1,551,528
  Separated 62,155
  Widowed. 201,617
  Divorced 364,376

Language spoken at home, 2006

Population 5 years and older. 3,327,159
  English only 3,050,113
  Spanish 173,552
  French 5,359
  German 11,900
  Chinese 6,325

Households & families, 2006

Households. 1,385,300
  with persons under 18 years 474,844
  with persons over 65 years. 334,153
  persons per household 2.50
Families. 927,086
  persons per family. 3.07
Married couples. 699,421
Female householder,
  no husband present. 164,547
One-person households 392,304

Nativity, 2006

Number of residents born in state 2,207,194
  percent of population. 61.7%

Immigration & naturalization, 2006

Legal permanent residents admitted 4,591
Persons naturalized 2,246
Non-immigrant admissions 65,802

Vital Statistics and Health

Marriages

2004 22,812
2005 25,755
2006 26,266

Divorces

2004 17,146
2005 19,966
2006 19,023

Health risks, 2006

Percent of adults who are:
  Smokers. 25.1%
  Overweight (BMI > 25). 64.8%
  Obese (BMI > 30). 28.8%

Births

2005 51,801
  Birthrate (per 1,000). 14.6
  White. 40,036
  Black 4,821
  Hispanic 6,275
  Asian/Pacific Islander 1,090
  Amer. Indian/Alaska Native 5,854
  Low birth weight (2,500g or less). 8.0%
  Cesarian births 32.5%
  Preterm births. 13.1%
  To unmarried mothers. 39.1%
  Twin births (per 1,000) 27.4
  Triplets or higher order (per 100,000). 92.8
2006 (preliminary). 54,018
  rate per 1,000 . . . . .15.1

Deaths

2004
All causes 34,483
  rate per 100,000. .947.7
Heart disease 10,335
  rate per 100,000. 284.3
Malignant neoplasms 7,269
  rate per 100,000. .196.2
Cerebrovascular disease. 2,183
  rate per 100,000. .60.6
Chronic lower respiratory disease 1,985
  rate per 100,000. .54.0
Diabetes. 1,139
  rate per 100,000. .31.0
2005 (preliminary). 36,181
  rate per 100,000. 980.8
2006 (provisional) 35,585

Infant deaths

2004 411
  rate per 1,000 . . . . .8.0
2005 (provisional) 422
  rate per 1,000 . . . . .8.1

Exercise routines, 2005

None. 30.6%
Moderate or greater. 42.3%
Vigorous 22.5%

Abortions, 2004

Total performed in state. 6,712
  rate per 1,000 women age 15-44. 9
  % obtained by out-of-state residents 7.2%

Physicians, 2005

Total. 6,041
  rate per 100,000 persons 170

Community hospitals, 2005

Number of hospitals 110
Beds (x 1,000). 10.8
Patients admitted (x 1,000) 457
Average daily census (x 1,000) 6.4
Average cost per day $1,332
Outpatient visits (x 1 mil) 5.4

Disability status of population, 2006
5 to 15 years 7.5%
16 to 64 years 17.0%
65 years and over 46.8%

Education

Educational attainment, 2006
Population over 25 years 2,312,121
    Less than 9th grade..................... 5.2%
    High school graduate or more 84.3%
    College graduate or more............. 22.1%
    Graduate or professional degree........ 7.2%

Public school enrollment, 2005-06
Total................................ 634,739
    Pre-kindergarten through grade 8.... 454,254
    Grades 9 through 12................ 176,683

Graduating public high school seniors, 2004-05
Diplomas (incl. GED and others) 36,227

SAT scores, 2007
Average critical reading score............. 578
Average writing score 559
Average math score 571
Percent of graduates taking test 6%

Public school teachers, 2006-07 (estimate)
Total (x 1,000) 42.2
    Elementary..........................21.2
    Secondary...........................21.0
Average salary $42,379
    Elementary...................... $41,597
    Secondary....................... $43,166

State receipts & expenditures for public schools, 2006-07 (estimate)
Revenue receipts ($ mil) $5,054
Expenditures
Total ($ mil) $5,041
    Per capita $1,265
    Per pupil $7,593

NAEP proficiency scores, 2007

	Reading		Math	
	Basic	Proficient	Basic	Proficient
Grade 4	65.0%	26.8%	82.4%	32.6%
Grade 8	72.1%	26.1%	66.1%	21.3%

Higher education enrollment, fall 2005
Total............................... 28,828
    Full-time men 11,370
    Full-time women....................12,717
    Part-time men 2,142
    Part-time women.................... 2,599

Minority enrollment in institutions of higher education, 2005
Black, non-Hispanic 19,039
Hispanic 7,272
Asian/Pacific Islander 4,742
American Indian/Alaska Native.........21,158

Institutions of higher education, 2005-06
Total.................................. 57
    Public................................ 29
    Private............................... 28

Earned degrees conferred, 2004-05
Associate's...........................9,243
Bachelor's 18,266
Master's 5,719
First-professional.....................1,094
Doctor's.............................. 413

Public Libraries, 2006
Number of libraries...................... 113
Number of outlets 208
Annual visits per capita 4.6
Circulation per capita....................6.9

State & local financial support for higher education, FY 2006
Full-time equivalent enrollment (x 1,000)....134.9
Appropriations per FTE................ $5,638

Social Insurance & Welfare Programs

Social Security benefits & beneficiaries, 2005
Beneficiaries (x 1,000) 635
    Retired & dependents................. 427
    Survivors............................ 94
    Disabled & dependents............... 114
Annual benefit payments ($ mil) $6,606
    Retired & dependents................. $4,226
    Survivors........................... $1,227
    Disabled & dependents............... $1,152
Average monthly benefit
    Retired & dependents................. $962
    Disabled & dependents............... $924
    Widowed........................... $939

Medicare, July 2005
Enrollment (x 1,000)..................... 541
Payments ($ mil) $3,769

Medicaid, 2004
Beneficiaries (x 1,000)................... 654
Payments ($ mil) $2,335

State Children's Health Insurance Program, 2006
Enrollment (x 1,000)....................116.0
Expenditures ($ mil)...................$105.0

Persons without health insurance, 2006
Number (x 1,000)........................ 661
    percent............................. 18.9%
Number of children (x 1,000) 114
    percent of children 12.5%

Health care expenditures, 2004
Total expenditures..................... $17,323
    per capita $4,917

Federal and state public aid

State unemployment insurance, 2006
Recipients, first payments (x 1,000) 41
Total payments ($ mil) $140
Average weekly benefit $233
Temporary Assistance for Needy Families, 2006
Recipients (x 1,000) 257.8
Families (x 1,000) 118.1
Supplemental Security Income, 2005
Recipients (x 1,000) 79.6
Payments ($ mil) $380.6
Food Stamp Program, 2006
Avg monthly participants (x 1,000) 435.5
Total benefits ($ mil) $467.3

Housing & Construction

Housing units

Total 2005 (estimate) 1,589,349
Total 2006 (estimate) 1,607,349
Seasonal or recreational use, 2006 34,345
Owner-occupied, 2006 950,407
　　Median home value $94,500
　　Homeowner vacancy rate 2.4%
Renter-occupied, 2006 434,893
　　Median rent $580
　　Rental vacancy rate 11.2%
Home ownership rate, 2005 . . . . .72.9%
Home ownership rate, 2006 . . . . 71.6%

New privately-owned housing units

Number authorized, 2006 (x 1,000) 15.8
　　Value ($ mil) $2,322.2
Started 2005 (x 1,000, estimate) 14.3
Started 2006 (x 1,000, estimate) 14.2

Existing home sales

2005 (x 1,000) 104.6
2006 (x 1,000) 106.0

Government & Elections

State officials 2008

Governor . . . . .Brad Henry
　　　　Democratic, term expires 1/11
Lieutenant Governor . . . . Jari Askins
Secretary of State . . . . M. Susan Savage
Attorney General . . . . . . W. A. Drew Edmondson
Chief Justice . . . . James Winchester

Governorship

Minimum age 31
Length of term . . . . 4 years
Consecutive terms permitted 2
Who succeeds . . . . Lieutenant Governor

Local governments by type, 2002

Total 1,798
　　County 77
　　Municipal 590
　　Township 0
　　School District 571
　　Special District 560

State legislature

Name . . . . Legislature
Upper chamber . . . . .Senate
　　Number of members 48
　　Length of term . . . . 4 years
　　Party in majority, 2008 . . . . 50/50
Lower chamber . . . . .House of Representatives
　　Number of members 101
　　Length of term . . . . 2 years
　　Party in majority, 2008 . . . . Republican

Federal representation, 2008 (110th Congress)

Senator . . . . .James Inhofe
　　Party . . . . Republican
　　Year term expires 2009
Senator . . . . .Tom Coburn
　　Party . . . . Republican
　　Year term expires 2011
Representatives, total 5
　　Democrats 1
　　Republicans 4

Voters in November 2006 election (estimate)

Total 1,173,627
　　Male 560,684
　　Female 612,943
　　White 994,791
　　Black 71,533
　　Hispanic 14,169
　　Asian 2,411

Presidential election, 2004

Total Popular Vote 1,463,758
　　Kerry 503,966
　　Bush 959,792
Total Electoral Votes 7

Votes cast for US Senators

2004
Total vote (x 1,000) .1,447
Leading party . . . . Republican
Percent for leading party 52.8%
2006
Total vote (x 1,000) . . . . NA
Leading party . . . . NA
Percent for leading party . . . . NA

Votes cast for US Representatives

2004
Total vote (x 1,000) .1,375
　　Democratic 389
　　Republican 875
Leading party . . . . Republican
Percent for leading party 63.7%
2006
Total vote (x 1,000) 905
　　Democratic 373
　　Republican 518
Leading party . . . . Republican
Percent for leading party 57.2%

State government employment, 2006
Full-time equivalent employees 67,424
Payroll ($ mil) $217.8

Local government employment, 2006
Full-time equivalent employees 146,919
Payroll ($ mil) $389.9

Women holding public office, 2008
US Congress 1
Statewide elected office. 3
State legislature 19

Black public officials, 2002
Total. 115
  US and state legislatures 6
  City/county/regional offices 85
  Judicial/law enforcement. 4
  Education/school boards 20

Hispanic public officials, 2006
Total. 1
  State executives & legislators 0
  City/county/regional offices 0
  Judicial/law enforcement. 0
  Education/school boards 1

Governmental Finance

State government revenues, 2006
Total revenue (x $1,000) $19,617,971
  per capita $5,483.65
General revenue (x $1,000) $16,233,400
  Intergovernmental 5,150,393
  Taxes 7,784,453
    general sales. 1,799,947
    individual income tax 2,658,272
    corporate income tax 231,206
  Current charges. 1,813,668
  Miscellaneous .1,484,886

State government expenditure, 2006
Total expenditure (x $1,000) $16,882,365
  per capita $4,718.99
General expenditure (x $1,000) $14,766,688
  per capita, total. *$4,127.61*
    Education 1,708.78
    Public welfare 1,146.91
    Health 167.52
    Hospitals. 48.06
    Highways 333.43
    Police protection. 40.72
    Corrections 156.32
    Natural resources 61.17
    Parks & recreation 27.51
    Governmental administration 133.99
    Interest on general debt 139.62

State debt & cash, 2006 ($ per capita)
Debt $2,274.76
Cash/security holdings. $9,026.85

Federal government grants to state & local government, 2005 (x $1,000)
Total. $5,501,741
by Federal agency
  Defense 31,135
  Education 538,914
  Energy. 10,508
  Environmental Protection Agency 79,502
  Health & Human Services. 2,947,723
  Homeland Security. 21,093
  Housing & Urban Development. 391,628
  Justice 87,181
  Labor 72,326
  Transportation .731,787
  Veterans Affairs. 30,470

Crime & Law Enforcement

Crime, 2006 (rates per 100,000 residents)
Property crimes 129,002
  Burglary 34,377
  Larceny. 81,267
  Motor vehicle theft 13,358
  Property crime rate. 3,604.2
Violent crimes. 17,803
  Murder 207
  Forcible rape. 1,488
  Robbery. 3,133
  Aggravated assault 12,975
  Violent crime rate 497.4
Hate crimes. 76

Fraud and identity theft, 2006
Fraud complaints. .3,711
  rate per 100,000 residents 103.7
Identity theft complaints 2,254
  rate per 100,000 residents 63.0

Law enforcement agencies, 2006
Total agencies. 296
Total employees 11,001
  Officers 7,058
  Civilians 3,943

Prisoners, probation, and parole, 2006
Total prisoners. 26,243
  percent change, 12/31/05 to 12/31/06 . . . -1.6%
  in private facilities 21.8%
  in local jails 7.4%
Sentenced to more than one year 23,889
  rate per 100,000 residents 664
Adults on probation 27,415
Adults on parole. 3,072

Prisoner demographics, June 30, 2005 (rate per 100,000 residents)
Male. 1,645
Female. 209
White. 740
Black. 3,252
Hispanic 832

Arrests, 2006

Total 145,171
    Persons under 18 years of age 20,192

Persons under sentence of death, 1/1/07

Total 88
    White 48
    Black 33
    Hispanic 3

State's highest court

Name .... Supreme Court
Number of members 9
Length of term .... 6 years
Intermediate appeals court? .... yes

Labor & Income

Civilian labor force, 2006 (x 1,000)

Total 1,733
    Men 936
    Women 797
    Persons 16-19 years 98
    White 1,380
    Black 113
    Hispanic 91

Civilian labor force as a percent of civilian non-institutional population, 2006

Total 63.4%
    Men 70.8
    Women 56.4
    Persons 16-19 years 43.8
    White 64.3
    Black 58.9
    Hispanic 71.9

Employment, 2006 (x 1,000)

Total 1,666
    Men 894
    Women 771
    Persons 16-19 years 86
    White 1,334
    Black 104
    Hispanic 85

Unemployment rate, 2006

Total 3.9%
    Men 4.4
    Women 3.2
    Persons 16-19 years 12.1
    White 3.3
    Black 8.2
    Hispanic 6.2

Full-time/part-time labor force, 2003 (x 1,000)

Full-time labor force, employed 1,324
Part-time labor force, employed 276

Unemployed, looking for
    Full-time work 82
    Part-time work 14
Mean duration of unemployment (weeks) 18.0
    Median 9.0

Labor unions, 2006

Membership (x 1,000) 93
    percent of employed 6.4%

Experienced civilian labor force by private industry, 2006

Total 1,192,548
    Natural resources & mining 49,326
    Construction 70,437
    Manufacturing 149,313
    Trade, transportation & utilities 282,549
    Information 29,884
    Finance 80,656
    Professional & business 175,854
    Education & health 180,309
    Leisure & hospitality 137,104
    Other 36,164

Experienced civilian labor force by occupation, May 2006

Management 80,110
Business & financial 56,130
Legal 10,180
Sales 149,190
Office & admin. support 261,290
Computers & math 26,760
Architecture & engineering 22,810
Arts & entertainment 14,350
Education 99,830
Social services 17,540
Health care practitioner & technical 82,680
Health care support 45,060
Maintenance & repair 72,460
Construction 82,550
Transportation & moving 104,700
Production 121,690
Farming, fishing & forestry 4,980

Hours and earnings of production workers on manufacturing payrolls, 2006

Average weekly hours 39.9
Average hourly earnings $14.77
Average weekly earnings $589.32

Income and poverty, 2006

Median household income $38,770
Personal income, per capita (current $) ... $32,210
    in constant (2000) dollars $28,117
Persons below poverty level 17.0%

Average annual pay

2006 .... $34,022
    increase from 2005 .... 7.3%

Federal individual income tax returns, 2005

Returns filed 1,495,579
Adjusted gross income ($1,000) $66,783,183
Total tax liability ($1,000) $8,223,215

Charitable contributions, 2004

Number of contributions 384.8
Total amount ($ mil) $1,848.9

Economy, Business, Industry & Agriculture

Fortune 500 companies, 2007 4
Bankruptcy cases filed, FY 2007 8,966

Patents and trademarks issued, 2007
Patents 578
Trademarks 525

Business firm ownership, 2002
Women-owned 75,025
 Sales ($ mil) $9,255
Black-owned 7,441
 Sales ($ mil) $458
Hispanic-owned 5,442
 Sales ($ mil) $1,140
Asian-owned 4,583
 Sales ($ mil) $929
Amer. Indian/Alaska Native-owned 17,112
 Sales ($ mil) $2,531
Hawaiian/Pacific Islander-owned 282
 Sales ($ mil) $9

Gross domestic product, 2006 ($ mil)
Total gross domestic product $134,651
 Agriculture, forestry, fishing and
  hunting 2,035
 Mining 20,882
 Utilities 3,404
 Construction 5,162
 Manufacturing, durable goods 9,090
 Manufacturing, non-durable goods 4,909
 Wholesale trade 6,430
 Retail trade 8,967
 Transportation & warehousing 3,834
 Information 4,111
 Finance & insurance 5,818
 Real estate, rental & leasing 12,509
 Professional and technical services 5,478
 Educational services 647
 Health care and social assistance 8,545
 Accommodation/food services 2,852
 Other services, except government 2,849
 Government 20,551

Establishments, payroll, employees & receipts, by major industry group, 2005

Total 88,548
 Annual payroll ($1,000) $37,620,071
 Paid employees 1,220,285
Forestry, fishing & agriculture 179
 Annual payroll ($1,000) $26,964
 Paid employees .1,025
Mining 2,363
 Annual payroll ($1,000) $1,899,124
 Paid employees .31,155
 Receipts, 2002 ($1,000) $9,123,846

Utilities 390
 Annual payroll ($1,000) $513,603
 Paid employees .8,833
 Receipts, 2002 ($1,000) . . . . .NA
Construction 8,255
 Annual payroll ($1,000) $2,036,409
 Paid employees .61,415
 Receipts, 2002 ($1,000) $9,590,154
Manufacturing 3,865
 Annual payroll ($1,000) $5,556,517
 Paid employees 140,428
 Receipts, 2002 ($1,000) $39,924,050
Wholesale trade 4,616
 Annual payroll ($1,000) $2,311,890
 Paid employees .55,771
 Receipts, 2002 ($1,000) $30,799,789
Retail trade 13,727
 Annual payroll ($1,000) $3,350,298
 Paid employees 168,914
 Receipts, 2002 ($1,000) $32,112,960
Transportation & warehousing 2,591
 Annual payroll ($1,000) $1,280,244
 Paid employees 36,737
 Receipts, 2002 ($1,000) $4,649,332
Information 1,540
 Annual payroll ($1,000) $1,431,092
 Paid employees 34,298
 Receipts, 2002 ($1,000) . . . . .NA
Finance & insurance 6,309
 Annual payroll ($1,000) $2,359,868
 Paid employees 58,568
 Receipts, 2002 ($1,000) . . . . .NA
Professional, scientific & technical 8,926
 Annual payroll ($1,000) $2,718,604
 Paid employees .65,621
 Receipts, 2002 ($1,000) $5,833,528
Education 680
 Annual payroll ($1,000) $374,652
 Paid employees .17,960
 Receipts, 2002 ($1,000) $257,581
Health care & social assistance 9,753
 Annual payroll ($1,000) $5,821,233
 Paid employees 187,899
 Receipts, 2002 ($1,000) $12,432,870
Arts and entertainment 1,057
 Annual payroll ($1,000) $287,639
 Paid employees .15,758
 Receipts, 2002 ($1,000) $1,055,444
Real estate 3,795
 Annual payroll ($1,000) $641,194
 Paid employees 21,343
 Receipts, 2002 ($1,000) $2,381,396
Accommodation & food service 6,676
 Annual payroll ($1,000) $1,279,470
 Paid employees 121,362
 Receipts, 2002 ($1,000) $3,901,754

Exports, 2006
Value of exported goods ($ mil) $4,375
   Manufactured $3,803
   Non-manufactured.................... $247

Foreign direct investment in US affiliates, 2004
Property, plants & equipment ($ mil) $8,222
Employment (x 1,000)..................... 31.7

Agriculture, 2006
Number of farms 83,000
Farm acreage (x 1,000) 33,700
   Acres per farm 406
Farm marketings and income ($ mil)
Total............................... $5,093.6
   Crops $974.1
   Livestock......................... $4,119.5
Net farm income $876.5

Principal commodities, in order by marketing receipts, 2005
Cattle and calves, Hogs, Broilers, Wheat, Dairy
products

Federal economic activity in state
Expenditures, 2005 ($ mil)
   Total............................... $27,637
      Per capita $7,799.37
   Defense $4,674
   Non-defense...................... $22,963
Defense department, 2006 ($ mil)
   Payroll............................. $3,260
   Contract awards $2,070
   Grants $33
Homeland security grants ($1,000)
   2006.............................. $19,497
   2007.............................. $14,198

FDIC-insured financial institutions, 2005
Number 264
Assets ($ billion) $67.3
Deposits ($ billion) $46.3

Fishing, 2006
Catch (x 1,000 lbs)....................... NA
Value ($1,000)............................ NA

Mining, 2006 ($ mil)
Total non-fuel mineral production $622
Percent of U.S. 0.97%

Communication, Energy & Transportation

Communication
Households with computers, 2003........ 55.4%
Households with internet access, 2003 .... 48.4%
High-speed internet providers 69
Total high-speed internet lines........ 652,296
   Residential 585,745
   Business.......................... 66,551
Wireless phone customers, 12/2006 2,479,877

FCC-licensed stations (as of January 1, 2008)
TV stations 27
FM radio stations......................... 169
AM radio stations 68

Energy
Energy consumption, 2004
   Total (trillion Btu)...................1,486
   Per capita (million Btu)..............421.8
By source of production (trillion Btu)
   Coal 372
   Natural gas............................ 556
   Petroleum............................. 533
   Nuclear electric power 0
   Hydroelectric power 30
By end-use sector (trillion Btu)
   Residential 289
   Commercial 230
   Industrial 554
   Transportation 413
Electric energy, 2005
   Primary source of electricity............ Coal
   Net generation (billion kWh) 68.6
      percent from renewable sources....... 5.5%
   Net summer capability (million kW) 19.8
   CO_2 emitted from generation 51.5
Natural gas utilities, 2005
   Customers (x 1,000) 962
   Sales (trillion Btu).................... 253
   Revenues ($ mil) $1,023
Nuclear plants, 2007 0
Total CO_2 emitted (million metric tons).....103.3
Energy spending, 2004 ($ mil) $11,274
   per capita $3,200
   Price per million Btu $12.24

Transportation, 2006
Public road & street mileage 113,085
   Urban............................. 15,640
   Rural 97,445
   Interstate.......................... 933
Vehicle miles of travel (millions) 48,689
   per capita 13,609.6
Total motor vehicle registrations.......3,201,831
   Automobiles......................1,606,517
   Trucks 1,576,680
   Motorcycles 94,280
Licensed drivers 2,264,151
   19 years & under 159,696
Deaths from motor vehicle accidents 765
Gasoline consumed (x 1,000 gallons) 1,868,948
   per capita 522.4

Commuting Statistics, 2006
Average commute time (min) 20.0
   Drove to work alone 80.4%
   Carpooled.......................... 11.6%
   Public transit 0.5%
   Walk to work 2.1%
   Work from home..................... 3.7%

Oregon 1

State Summary

Capital city . . . . Salem
Governor . . . . Ted Kulongoski

State Capitol
Room 160, 900 Court St N
Salem, OR 97301
503-378-4582

Admitted as a state 1859
Area (square miles) 98,381
Population, 2007 (estimate). 3,747,455
Largest city . . . . Portland
Population, 2006 .537,081
Personal income per capita, 2006
(in current dollars) $33,666
Gross domestic product, 2006 ($ mil) . . . $151,301

Leading industries by payroll, 2005

Manufacturing, Health care/Social assistance,
Retail trade

**Leading agricultural commodities
by receipts, 2005**

Greenhouse/nursery, Cattle and calves, Dairy
products, Hay, Ryegrass

Geography & Environment

Total area (square miles). 98,381
land 95,997
water 2,384
Federally-owned land, 2004 (acres) . . . 32,715,514
percent. 53.1%
Highest point . . . . .Mt. Hood
elevation (feet) .11,239
Lowest point . . . . Pacific Ocean
elevation (feet) . . . . sea level
General coastline (miles) 26
Tidal shoreline (miles) 1,410
Cropland, 2003 (x 1,000 acres) 3,701
Forest land, 2003 (x 1,000 acres). 12,734
Capital city . . . . Salem
Population 2000 136,924
Population 2006 152,239
Largest city . . . . Portland
Population 2000 .529,121
Population 2006 .537,081

Number of cities with over 100,000 population

1990 3
2000 3
2006 3

State park and recreation areas, 2005

Area (x 1,000 acres) 97
Number of visitors (x 1,000) 42,420
Revenues ($1,000) $15,384
percent of operating expenditures 37.0%

National forest system land, 2007

Acres 15,667,657

Demographics & Population Characteristics

Population

1980 2,633,105
1990 2,842,321
2000 3,421,436
2006 3,700,758
Male 1,839,688
Female 1,861,070
Living in group quarters, 2006 79,987
percent of total. 2.2%
2007 (estimate). 3,747,455
persons per square mile of land 39.0
2008 (projected). 3,709,778
2010 (projected) .3,790,996
2020 (projected) .4,260,393
2030 (projected) .4,833,918

**Population of Core-Based Statistical Areas
(formerly Metropolitan Areas), x 1,000**

	CBSA	Non-CBSA
1990	2,719	123
2000	3,281	140
2006	3,559	142

Change in population, 2000-2007

Number 326,019
percent. 9.5%
Natural increase (births minus deaths) 113,876
Net internal migration 136,376
Net international migration 91,629

Persons by age, 2006

Under 5 years 230,660
5 to 17 years 625,599
18 years and over 2,844,499
65 years and over 478,180
85 years and over 70,969
Median age 37.5

Persons by age, 2010 (projected)

Under 5 years 249,899
18 and over 2,927,830
65 and over 494,328
Median age 37.6

Race, 2006

One Race
White. 3,348,473
Black or African American 68,610
Asian 133,740
American Indian/Alaska Native. 51,209
Hawaiian Native/Pacific Islander. 10,277
Two or more races. 88,449

Persons of Hispanic origin, 2006

Total Hispanic or Latino 379,034
Mexican. 317,961
Puerto Rican 5,811
Cuban 2,320

Persons of Asian origin, 2006

Total Asian 135,746
  Asian Indian. 13,454
  Chinese 29,717
  Filipino 17,776
  Japanese 14,254
  Korean. 19,910
  Vietnamese. 23,875

Marital status, 2006

Population 15 years & over 2,998,516
  Never married 854,994
  Married. 1,586,184
  Separated 55,623
  Widowed. 172,577
  Divorced 384,761

Language spoken at home, 2006

Population 5 years and older. 3,470,802
  English only 2,979,226
  Spanish 293,840
  French 10,909
  German. 21,410
  Chinese 24,046

Households & families, 2006

Households. 1,449,662
  with persons under 18 years 452,328
  with persons over 65 years. 330,756
  persons per household 2.50
Families. 927,071
  persons per family. 3.07
Married couples. 719,045
Female householder,
  no husband present. 147,864
One-person households 405,897

Nativity, 2006

Number of residents born in state 1,666,564
  percent of population 45.0%

Immigration & naturalization, 2006

Legal permanent residents admitted. 9,192
Persons naturalized .4,332
Non-immigrant admissions 127,637

Vital Statistics and Health

Marriages

2004 29,040
2005 26,471
2006 26,888

Divorces

2004 14,774
2005 15,033
2006 14,214

Health risks, 2006

Percent of adults who are:
  Smokers. 18.5%
  Overweight (BMI > 25). 60.7%
  Obese (BMI > 30). 24.8%

Births

2005 45,922
  Birthrate (per 1,000). 12.6
  White. 41,561
  Black 1,011
  Hispanic 9,165
  Asian/Pacific Islander 2,502
  Amer. Indian/Alaska Native 848
  Low birth weight (2,500g or less). 6.1%
  Cesarian births 27.6%
  Preterm births 10.2%
  To unmarried mothers. 33.3%
  Twin births (per 1,000) 29.8
  Triplets or higher order (per 100,000). . . .104.0
2006 (preliminary). 48,717
  rate per 1,000 . . . . .13.2

Deaths

2004
All causes 30,313
  rate per 100,000. . . . . .777.7
Heart disease 6,725
  rate per 100,000. . . . . .169.3
Malignant neoplasms 7,236
  rate per 100,000. . . . . .189.6
Cerebrovascular disease. 2,328
  rate per 100,000. . . . . .58.2
Chronic lower respiratory disease 1,778
  rate per 100,000. . . . . .46.7
Diabetes. 1,073
  rate per 100,000. . . . . .27.9
2005 (preliminary). 31,099
  rate per 100,000. . . . . .773.7
2006 (provisional) 31,361

Infant deaths

2004 251
  rate per 1,000 . . . . .5.5
2005 (provisional) 265
  rate per 1,000 . . . . .5.8

Exercise routines, 2005

None. 18.6%
Moderate or greater. 56.4%
Vigorous 30.7%

Abortions, 2004

Total performed in state. 11,443
  rate per 1,000 women age 15-44. 16
  % obtained by out-of-state residents 10.9%

Physicians, 2005

Total. 9,684
  rate per 100,000 persons 266

Community hospitals, 2005

Number of hospitals 58
Beds (x 1,000). 6.5
Patients admitted (x 1,000) 336
Average daily census (x 1,000) 4.1
Average cost per day $2,062
Outpatient visits (x 1 mil) 8.0

Disability status of population, 2006
5 to 15 years 6.5%
16 to 64 years 13.8%
65 years and over 41.0%

Education

Educational attainment, 2006
Population over 25 years 2,501,372
   Less than 9th grade..................... 4.7%
   High school graduate or more 87.6%
   College graduate or more.............. 27.5%
   Graduate or professional degree....... 10.0%

Public school enrollment, 2005-06
Total............................... 552,194
   Pre-kindergarten through grade 8.... 378,892
   Grades 9 through 12 172,185

Graduating public high school seniors, 2004-05
Diplomas (incl. GED and others) 36,868

SAT scores, 2007
Average critical reading score 522
Average writing score 502
Average math score 526
Percent of graduates taking test 54%

Public school teachers, 2006-07 (estimate)
Total (x 1,000) 29.3
   Elementary...........................18.9
   Secondary...........................10.4
Average salary $50,911
   Elementary...................... $50,679
   Secondary....................... $51,349

**State receipts & expenditures for
  public schools, 2006-07 (estimate)**
Revenue receipts ($ mil) $5,742
Expenditures
Total ($ mil) $5,839
   Per capita $1,367
   Per pupil $10,251

NAEP proficiency scores, 2007

	Reading		Math	
	Basic	Proficient	Basic	Proficient
Grade 4	61.9%	28.3%	78.6%	35.0%
Grade 8	77.2%	34.0%	73.0%	34.8%

Higher education enrollment, fall 2005
Total............................... 36,281
   Full-time men 12,147
   Full-time women.....................16,798
   Part-time men 2,965
   Part-time women.....................4,371

**Minority enrollment in institutions
  of higher education, 2005**
Black, non-Hispanic 4,788
Hispanic 11,103
Asian/Pacific Islander 12,591
American Indian/Alaska Native..........3,330

Institutions of higher education, 2005-06
Total.................................... 60
   Public.............................. 26
   Private............................. 34

Earned degrees conferred, 2004-05
Associate's........................... 8,506
Bachelor's 16,867
Master's...............................6,148
First-professional......................1,147
Doctor's 477

Public Libraries, 2006
Number of libraries.................... 125
Number of outlets 223
Annual visits per capita 6.2
Circulation per capita....................14.9

**State & local financial support for
  higher education, FY 2006**
Full-time equivalent enrollment (x 1,000)....126.4
Appropriations per FTE............... $4,466

Social Insurance & Welfare Programs

Social Security benefits & beneficiaries, 2005
Beneficiaries (x 1,000) 625
   Retired & dependents................... 455
   Survivors............................. 76
   Disabled & dependents.................. 94
Annual benefit payments ($ mil) $6,837
   Retired & dependents...............$4,741
   Survivors.........................$1,095
   Disabled & dependents..............$1,001
Average monthly benefit
   Retired & dependents...............$1,011
   Disabled & dependents................. $939
   Widowed...........................$1,017

Medicare, July 2005
Enrollment (x 1,000) 540
Payments ($ mil) $2,216

Medicaid, 2004
Beneficiaries (x 1,000)................. 559
Payments ($ mil) $2,153

State Children's Health Insurance Program, 2006
Enrollment (x 1,000).....................59.0
Expenditures ($ mil)................... $72.5

Persons without health insurance, 2006
Number (x 1,000)........................ 665
   percent......................... 17.9%
Number of children (x 1,000) 114
   percent of children 13.1%

Health care expenditures, 2004
Total expenditures..................... $17,516
   per capita $4,880

Federal and state public aid

State unemployment insurance, 2006
Recipients, first payments (x 1,000) 126
Total payments ($ mil) $470
Average weekly benefit $270
Temporary Assistance for Needy Families, 2006
Recipients (x 1,000) 495.8
Families (x 1,000) 218.9
Supplemental Security Income, 2005
Recipients (x 1,000) 60.6
Payments ($ mil) $297.5
Food Stamp Program, 2006
Avg monthly participants (x 1,000) 434.2
Total benefits ($ mil) $463.3

Housing & Construction

Housing units

Total 2005 (estimate) 1,558,414
Total 2006 (estimate) 1,586,498
Seasonal or recreational use, 2006 47,959
Owner-occupied, 2006 939,123
   Median home value $236,600
   Homeowner vacancy rate 1.7%
Renter-occupied, 2006 510,539
   Median rent $714
   Rental vacancy rate 7.5%
Home ownership rate, 2005 . . . . .68.2%
Home ownership rate, 2006 . . . . .68.1%

New privately-owned housing units

Number authorized, 2006 (x 1,000) 26.6
   Value ($ mil) $4,941.6
Started 2005 (x 1,000, estimate) 19.6
Started 2006 (x 1,000, estimate) 20.0

Existing home sales

2005 (x 1,000) 100.5
2006 (x 1,000) 85.8

Government & Elections

State officials 2008

Governor . . . . Ted Kulongoski
   Democratic, term expires 1/11
Lieutenant Governor . . (no Lieutenant Governor)
Secretary of State . . . . Bill Bradbury
Attorney General . . . . .Hardy Meyers
Chief Justice . . . . .Paul De Muniz

Governorship

Minimum age 30
Length of term . . . . 4 years
Consecutive terms permitted 2
Who succeeds . . . . .Secretary of State

Local governments by type, 2002

Total 1,439
   County 36
   Municipal 240
   Township 0
   School District 236
   Special District 927

State legislature

Name . . . . Legislature Assembly
Upper chamber . . . . .Senate
   Number of members 30
   Length of term . . . . 4 years
   Party in majority, 2008 . . . . .Democratic
Lower chamber . . . . . . .House of Representatives
   Number of members 60
   Length of term . . . . 2 years
   Party in majority, 2008 . . . . .Democratic

Federal representation, 2008 (110ᵗʰ Congress)

Senator . . . . Gordon Smith
   Party . . . . Republican
   Year term expires 2009
Senator . . . . .Ron Wyden
   Party . . . . .Democratic
   Year term expires 2011
Representatives, total 5
   Democrats 4
   Republicans 1

Voters in November 2006 election (estimate)

Total 1,600,533
   Male 749,052
   Female 851,482
   White 1,517,739
   Black 16,337
   Hispanic 24,798
   Asian 17,940

Presidential election, 2004

Total Popular Vote 1,836,782
   Kerry 943,163
   Bush 866,831
Total Electoral Votes 7

Votes cast for US Senators

2004
Total vote (x 1,000) 1,781
Leading party . . . . .Democratic
Percent for leading party 63.4%
2006
Total vote (x 1,000) . . . . NA
Leading party . . . . NA
Percent for leading party . . . . NA

Votes cast for US Representatives

2004
Total vote (x 1,000) 1,772
   Democratic 952
   Republican 762
Leading party . . . . .Democratic
Percent for leading party 53.7%
2006
Total vote (x 1,000) 1,357
   Democratic 766
   Republican 557
Leading party . . . . .Democratic
Percent for leading party 56.4%

State government employment, 2006
Full-time equivalent employees 57,485
Payroll ($ mil) $219.2

Local government employment, 2006
Full-time equivalent employees 124,226
Payroll ($ mil) $463.7

Women holding public office, 2008
US Congress 1
Statewide elected office 1
State legislature 28

Black public officials, 2002
Total 5
  US and state legislatures 3
  City/county/regional offices 1
  Judicial/law enforcement 1
  Education/school boards 0

Hispanic public officials, 2006
Total 17
  State executives & legislators 3
  City/county/regional offices 9
  Judicial/law enforcement 5
  Education/school boards 0

Governmental Finance

State government revenues, 2006
Total revenue (x $1,000) $25,742,792
  per capita $6,974.32
General revenue (x $1,000) $16,495,371
  Intergovernmental 4,639,898
  Taxes 7,590,306
    general sales 0
    individual income tax 5,416,466
    corporate income tax 438,255
  Current charges 2,430,684
  Miscellaneous 1,834,483

State government expenditure, 2006
Total expenditure (x $1,000) $20,070,629
  per capita $5,437.60
General expenditure (x $1,000) $16,564,827
  per capita, total $4,487.79
    Education 1,605.37
    Public welfare 1,073.00
    Health 107.47
    Hospitals 294.81
    Highways 390.94
    Police protection 72.85
    Corrections 173.28
    Natural resources 109.08
    Parks & recreation 23.24
    Governmental administration 237.36
    Interest on general debt 129.64

State debt & cash, 2006 ($ per capita)
Debt $2,981.99
Cash/security holdings $18,681.64

Federal government grants to state & local government, 2005 (x $1,000)
Total $5,466,310
by Federal agency
  Defense 58,429
  Education 454,015
  Energy 24,183
  Environmental Protection Agency 68,276
  Health & Human Services 2,945,329
  Homeland Security 27,327
  Housing & Urban Development 355,169
  Justice 74,803
  Labor 148,528
  Transportation 399,255
  Veterans Affairs 3,889

Crime & Law Enforcement

Crime, 2006 (rates per 100,000 residents)
Property crimes 135,895
  Burglary 23,879
  Larceny 97,556
  Motor vehicle theft 14,460
  Property crime rate 3,672.1
Violent crimes 10,373
  Murder 86
  Forcible rape 1,195
  Robbery 2,689
  Aggravated assault 6,403
  Violent crime rate 280.3
Hate crimes 174

Fraud and identity theft, 2006
Fraud complaints 5,583
  rate per 100,000 residents 150.9
Identity theft complaints 2,815
  rate per 100,000 residents 76.1

Law enforcement agencies, 2006
Total agencies 171
Total employees 7,471
  Officers 4,556
  Civilians 2,915

Prisoners, probation, and parole, 2006
Total prisoners 13,707
  percent change, 12/31/05 to 12/31/06 .... 2.2%
  in private facilities 0%
  in local jails 0.4%
Sentenced to more than one year 13,667
  rate per 100,000 residents 367
Adults on probation 45,250
Adults on parole 22,396

Prisoner demographics, June 30, 2005 (rate per 100,000 residents)
Male 965
Female 101
White 502
Black 2,930
Hispanic 573

Arrests, 2006

Total............................... 124,612
   Persons under 18 years of age......... 24,723

Persons under sentence of death, 1/1/07

Total................................... 33
   White................................. 26
   Black................................. 3
   Hispanic.............................. 2

State's highest court

Name.......................Supreme Court
Number of members......................... 7
Length of term....................... 6 years
Intermediate appeals court?...............yes

Labor & Income

Civilian labor force, 2006 (x 1,000)

Total...............................1,897
   Men 1,033
   Women 865
   Persons 16-19 years..................... 93
   White..............................1,719
   Black................................. 28
   Hispanic............................. 148

Civilian labor force as a percent of civilian non-institutional population, 2006

Total................................ 65.6%
   Men 72.7
   Women 58.7
   Persons 16-19 years.....................47.3
   White................................65.5
   Black................................62.5
   Hispanic.............................73.7

Employment, 2006 (x 1,000)

Total...............................1,795
   Men 978
   Women 816
   Persons 16-19 years..................... 77
   White..............................1,631
   Black................................. 23
   Hispanic............................. 139

Unemployment rate, 2006

Total................................. 5.4%
   Men 5.2
   Women 5.6
   Persons 16-19 years....................17.3
   White................................5.1
   Black................................16.1
   Hispanic.............................6.3

Full-time/part-time labor force, 2003 (x 1,000)

Full-time labor force, employed...........1,360
Part-time labor force, employed............ 347
Unemployed, looking for
   Full-time work......................... 126
   Part-time work......................... 26
Mean duration of unemployment (weeks)......18.1
   Median 9.7

Labor unions, 2006

Membership (x 1,000)................... 211
   percent of employed 13.8%

Experienced civilian labor force by private industry, 2006

Total..............................1,433,342
   Natural resources & mining.......... 49,945
   Construction 99,825
   Manufacturing..................... 206,697
   Trade, transportation & utilities 332,890
   Information 34,846
   Finance 89,239
   Professional & business 194,271
   Education & health................. 198,677
   Leisure & hospitality.............. 164,615
   Other 61,659

Experienced civilian labor force by occupation, May 2006

Management.........................73,510
Business & financial 69,450
Legal..............................9,250
Sales.............................. 176,950
Office & admin. support...............277,520
Computers & math 35,180
Architecture & engineering............. 33,830
Arts & entertainment 21,100
Education 103,910
Social services 31,530
Health care practitioner & technical..... 72,260
Health care support 40,640
Maintenance & repair................. 65,850
Construction 79,640
Transportation & moving 134,370
Production 135,470
Farming, fishing & forestry.............12,810

Hours and earnings of production workers on manufacturing payrolls, 2006

Average weekly hours 40.5
Average hourly earnings $15.57
Average weekly earnings $630.59

Income and poverty, 2006

Median household income............ $46,230
Personal income, per capita (current $)... $33,666
   in constant (2000) dollars $29,388
Persons below poverty level.............. 13.3%

Average annual pay

2006................................ $38,077
   increase from 2005 .... 4.1%

Federal individual income tax returns, 2005

Returns filed.........................1,645,481
Adjusted gross income ($1,000) $81,023,741
Total tax liability ($1,000) $9,585,060

Charitable contributions, 2004

Number of contributions.................558.1
Total amount ($ mil)................. $1,837.0

Economy, Business, Industry & Agriculture

Fortune 500 companies, 2007 1
Bankruptcy cases filed, FY 2007 8,993

Patents and trademarks issued, 2007
Patents 2,398
Trademarks 1,196

Business firm ownership, 2002
Women-owned 88,317
  Sales ($ mil) $10,608
Black-owned 2,222
  Sales ($ mil) $371
Hispanic-owned 6,360
  Sales ($ mil) $1,416
Asian-owned 9,046
  Sales ($ mil) $2,182
Amer. Indian/Alaska Native-owned 3,070
  Sales ($ mil) $302
Hawaiian/Pacific Islander-owned 350
  Sales ($ mil) $52

Gross domestic product, 2006 ($ mil)
Total gross domestic product $151,301
  Agriculture, forestry, fishing and
    hunting 3,768
  Mining 162
  Utilities 2,232
  Construction 7,273
  Manufacturing, durable goods 21,627
  Manufacturing, non-durable goods 4,867
  Wholesale trade .10,161
  Retail trade 8,662
  Transportation & warehousing 4,196
  Information 4,776
  Finance & insurance 8,493
  Real estate, rental & leasing 20,402
  Professional and technical services 7,156
  Educational services 1,007
  Health care and social assistance 11,309
  Accommodation/food services 3,702
  Other services, except government 3,264
  Government 20,529

Establishments, payroll, employees & receipts, by major industry group, 2005
Total 108,571
  Annual payroll ($1,000) $50,019,294
  Paid employees 1,409,576
Forestry, fishing & agriculture 1,472
  Annual payroll ($1,000) $445,133
  Paid employees .13,106
Mining 161
  Annual payroll ($1,000) . . . . NA
  Paid employees . . . . NA
  Receipts, 2002 ($1,000) $270,239

Utilities 263
  Annual payroll ($1,000) $559,805
  Paid employees .8,051
  Receipts, 2002 ($1,000) . . . . .NA
Construction 13,818
  Annual payroll ($1,000) $3,532,998
  Paid employees .85,319
  Receipts, 2002 ($1,000) $13,772,785
Manufacturing 5,559
  Annual payroll ($1,000) $7,987,583
  Paid employees 184,708
  Receipts, 2002 ($1,000) $45,864,552
Wholesale trade 5,637
  Annual payroll ($1,000) $3,629,651
  Paid employees 75,899
  Receipts, 2002 ($1,000) $56,855,958
Retail trade 14,488
  Annual payroll ($1,000) $4,708,601
  Paid employees 199,261
  Receipts, 2002 ($1,000) $37,896,022
Transportation & warehousing 3,106
  Annual payroll ($1,000) $1,996,733
  Paid employees 55,229
  Receipts, 2002 ($1,000) $4,892,472
Information 1,953
  Annual payroll ($1,000) $1,819,915
  Paid employees 35,185
  Receipts, 2002 ($1,000) . . . . .NA
Finance & insurance 6,382
  Annual payroll ($1,000) $3,586,248
  Paid employees 68,114
  Receipts, 2002 ($1,000) . . . . .NA
Professional, scientific & technical 10,983
  Annual payroll ($1,000) $3,692,635
  Paid employees 75,596
  Receipts, 2002 ($1,000) $6,956,805
Education 1,210
  Annual payroll ($1,000) $903,163
  Paid employees 36,795
  Receipts, 2002 ($1,000) $279,716
Health care & social assistance 10,601
  Annual payroll ($1,000) $6,773,806
  Paid employees 180,291
  Receipts, 2002 ($1,000) $13,860,847
Arts and entertainment 1,564
  Annual payroll ($1,000) $483,181
  Paid employees 23,234
  Receipts, 2002 ($1,000) $1,186,835
Real estate 6,055
  Annual payroll ($1,000) $965,246
  Paid employees 31,269
  Receipts, 2002 ($1,000) $3,561,488
Accommodation & food service 9,433
  Annual payroll ($1,000) $1,944,540
  Paid employees 140,934
  Receipts, 2002 ($1,000) $5,527,223

Exports, 2006
Value of exported goods ($ mil) $15,288
  Manufactured $12,032
  Non-manufactured................... $1,953

Foreign direct investment in US affiliates, 2004
Property, plants & equipment ($ mil) $11,749
Employment (x 1,000)...................... 47.6

Agriculture, 2006
Number of farms 39,300
Farm acreage (x 1,000) 17,100
  Acres per farm 435
Farm marketings and income ($ mil)
Total................................. $3,990.6
  Crops $2,960.6
  Livestock......................... $1,030.0
Net farm income $875.6

Principal commodities, in order by marketing receipts, 2005
  Greenhouse/nursery, Cattle and calves, Dairy products, Hay, Ryegrass

Federal economic activity in state
Expenditures, 2005 ($ mil)
  Total............................. $22,792
    Per capita $6,263.47
  Defense $1,316
  Non-defense $21,476
Defense department, 2006 ($ mil)
  Payroll........................... $760
  Contract awards $562
  Grants $47
Homeland security grants ($1,000)
  2006.............................. $17,956
  2007.............................. $16,033

FDIC-insured financial institutions, 2005
Number 40
Assets ($ billion) $35.4
Deposits ($ billion) $17.1

Fishing, 2006
Catch (x 1,000 lbs)................... 300,670
Value ($1,000)....................... $107,421

Mining, 2006 ($ mil)
Total non-fuel mineral production $428
Percent of U.S. 0.66%

Communication, Energy & Transportation

Communication
Households with computers, 2003........ 67.0%
Households with internet access, 2003 .... 61.0%
High-speed internet providers 61
Total high-speed internet lines........ 1,055,986
  Residential 775,041
  Business............................ 280,945
Wireless phone customers, 12/2006 2,655,905

FCC-licensed stations (as of January 1, 2008)
TV stations 33
FM radio stations......................... 184
AM radio stations 95

Energy
Energy consumption, 2004
  Total (trillion Btu)................... 1,094
  Per capita (million Btu) 304.7
By source of production (trillion Btu)
  Coal 37
  Natural gas 243
  Petroleum 391
  Nuclear electric power 0
  Hydroelectric power 332
By end-use sector (trillion Btu)
  Residential 261
  Commercial 207
  Industrial 301
  Transportation 324
Electric energy, 2005
  Primary source of electricity.... Hydroelectric
  Net generation (billion kWh) 49.3
    percent from renewable sources...... 66.1%
  Net summer capability (million kW) 12.2
  CO_2 emitted from generation 9.0
Natural gas utilities, 2005
  Customers (x 1,000) 701
  Sales (trillion Btu).................. 141
  Revenues ($ mil) $975
Nuclear plants, 2007 0
Total CO_2 emitted (million metric tons)..... 40.4
Energy spending, 2004 ($ mil) $9,129
  per capita $2,544
  Price per million Btu $12.85

Transportation, 2006
Public road & street mileage 64,358
  Urban................................ 12,698
  Rural 51,660
  Interstate........................... 728
Vehicle miles of travel (millions) 35,483
  per capita 9,613.2
Total motor vehicle registrations...... 2,981,379
  Automobiles....................... 1,427,597
  Trucks 1,538,960
  Motorcycles 83,983
Licensed drivers 2,767,591
  19 years & under 108,571
Deaths from motor vehicle accidents 477
Gasoline consumed (x 1,000 gallons) 1,577,746
  per capita 427.4

Commuting Statistics, 2006
Average commute time (min) 21.8
  Drove to work alone 71.4%
  Carpooled............................ 11.7%
  Public transit 4.4%
  Walk to work 3.9%
  Work from home....................... 6.0%

State Summary

Capital city . . . . Harrisburg
Governor . . . . Ed Rendell

Room 225
Main Capitol Building
Harrisburg, PA 17120
717-787-2500

Admitted as a state 1787
Area (square miles) 46,055
Population, 2007 (estimate) 12,432,792
Largest city . . . . Philadelphia
    Population, 2006 1,448,394
Personal income per capita, 2006
    (in current dollars) $36,680
Gross domestic product, 2006 ($ mil) . . . $510,293

Leading industries by payroll, 2005

Health care/Social assistance, Manufacturing,
Professional/Scientific/Technical

**Leading agricultural commodities
by receipts, 2005**

Dairy products, Cattle and calves, Greenhouse/
nursery, Agaricus mushrooms, Broilers

Geography & Environment

Total area (square miles) 46,055
    land 44,817
    water 1,239
Federally-owned land, 2004 (acres) 719,864
    percent 2.5%
Highest point . . . . Mt. Davis
    elevation (feet) 3,213
Lowest point . . . . Delaware River
    elevation (feet) . . . . sea level
General coastline (miles) 0
Tidal shoreline (miles) 83
Cropland, 2003 (x 1,000 acres) 5,124
Forest land, 2003 (x 1,000 acres) 15,631
Capital city . . . . Harrisburg
    Population 2000 48,950
    Population 2006 47,164
Largest city . . . . Philadelphia
    Population 2000 1,517,550
    Population 2006 1,448,394

Number of cities with over 100,000 population

1990 4
2000 4
2006 4

State park and recreation areas, 2005

Area (x 1,000 acres) 291
Number of visitors (x 1,000) 36,263
Revenues ($1,000) $13,893
    percent of operating expenditures 17.9%

National forest system land, 2007

Acres 513,428

Demographics & Population Characteristics

Population

1980 11,863,895
1990 11,881,643
2000 12,281,054
2006 12,440,621
    Male 6,047,537
    Female 6,393,084
Living in group quarters, 2006 455,673
    percent of total 3.7%
2007 (estimate) 12,432,792
    persons per square mile of land 277.4
2008 (projected) 12,525,118
2010 (projected) 12,584,487
2020 (projected) 12,787,354
2030 (projected) 12,768,184

**Population of Core-Based Statistical Areas
(formerly Metropolitan Areas), x 1,000**

	CBSA	Non-CBSA
1990	11,518	365
2000	11,899	382
2006	12,056	385

Change in population, 2000-2007

Number 151,738
    percent 1.2%
Natural increase (births minus deaths) 114,795
Net internal migration . . . . -44,416
Net international migration 128,305

Persons by age, 2006

Under 5 years 724,687
5 to 17 years 2,080,186
18 years and over 9,635,748
65 years and over 1,885,323
85 years and over 294,824
    Median age 39.5

Persons by age, 2010 (projected)

Under 5 years 746,518
18 and over 9,836,892
65 and over 1,956,235
    Median age 40.0

Race, 2006

One Race
    White 10,660,136
    Black or African American 1,336,278
    Asian 292,507
    American Indian/Alaska Native 24,077
    Hawaiian Native/Pacific Islander 5,446
Two or more races 122,177

Persons of Hispanic origin, 2006

Total Hispanic or Latino 527,142
    Mexican 85,699
    Puerto Rican 290,568
    Cuban 11,704

Persons of Asian origin, 2006
Total Asian 289,289
  Asian Indian. 84,111
  Chinese 72,622
  Filipino 18,671
  Japanese 6,959
  Korean. 36,228
  Vietnamese. 35,004

Marital status, 2006
Population 15 years & over 10,164,450
  Never married 3,150,116
  Married. 5,300,946
  Separated 226,797
  Widowed. 793,730
  Divorced 919,658

Language spoken at home, 2006
Population 5 years and older. 11,716,171
  English only 10,639,372
  Spanish 436,254
  French 55,002
  German. 106,931
  Chinese 62,241

Households & families, 2006
Households. 4,845,603
  with persons under 18 years 1,498,721
  with persons over 65 years. 1,294,224
  persons per household 2.47
Families. 3,174,335
  persons per family. 3.07
Married couples. 2,402,123
Female householder,
  no husband present. 567,179
One-person households 1,421,285

Nativity, 2006
Number of residents born in state 9,399,122
  percent of population. 75.6%

Immigration & naturalization, 2006
Legal permanent residents admitted. 25,958
Persons naturalized 15,846
Non-immigrant admissions 386,193

Vital Statistics and Health

Marriages
2004 73,599
2005 71,933
2006 68,584

Divorces
2004 36,692
2005 29,143
2006 27,357

Health risks, 2006
Percent of adults who are:
  Smokers. 21.5%
  Overweight (BMI > 25). 61.3%
  Obese (BMI > 30). 24.0%

Births
2005 145,383
  Birthrate (per 1,000). 11.7
  White. 115,899
  Black 23,294
  Hispanic 12,208
  Asian/Pacific Islander 5,829
  Amer. Indian/Alaska Native. 361
  Low birth weight (2,500g or less). 8.4%
  Cesarian births .28.9%
  Preterm births 11.9%
  To unmarried mothers. 36.5%
  Twin births (per 1,000) 33.7
  Triplets or higher order (per 100,000). . . .192.9
2006 (preliminary). 149,082
  rate per 1,000 . . . . .12.0

Deaths
2004
All causes 127,640
  rate per 100,000. . . . . .814.6
Heart disease 36,434
  rate per 100,000. . . . . .223.7
Malignant neoplasms 29,424
  rate per 100,000. . . . . .193.8
Cerebrovascular disease. 7,792
  rate per 100,000. 47.1
Chronic lower respiratory disease 5,978
  rate per 100,000. 37.6
Diabetes. 3,579
  rate per 100,000. . . . . .23.1
2005 (preliminary). 129,536
  rate per 100,000. . . . . .814.8
2006 (provisional) .125,151

Infant deaths
2004 1,049
  rate per 1,000 . . . . .7.3
2005 (provisional) .1,036
  rate per 1,000 . . . . .7.2

Exercise routines, 2005
None. 25.8%
Moderate or greater. 48.7%
Vigorous 27.4%

Abortions, 2004
Total performed in state. 36,030
  rate per 1,000 women age 15-44. 14
  % obtained by out-of-state residents 4.2%

Physicians, 2005
Total. 36,429
  rate per 100,000 persons 294

Community hospitals, 2005
Number of hospitals 191
Beds (x 1,000). 39.6
Patients admitted (x 1,000) 1,863
Average daily census (x 1,000) 27.9
Average cost per day $1,500
Outpatient visits (x 1 mil) 34.9

Disability status of population, 2006
5 to 15 years 7.3%
16 to 64 years 13.0%
65 years and over 39.3%

Education

Educational attainment, 2006
Population over 25 years 8,431,859
   Less than 9th grade...................... 4.2%
   High school graduate or more 86.2%
   College graduate or more............. 25.4%
   Graduate or professional degree......... 9.6%

Public school enrollment, 2005-06
Total...............................1,830,684
   Pre-kindergarten through grade 8...1,225,383
   Grades 9 through 12 600,857

Graduating public high school seniors, 2004-05
Diplomas (incl. GED and others) 124,758

SAT scores, 2007
Average critical reading score.............. 493
Average writing score 482
Average math score 499
Percent of graduates taking test 75%

Public school teachers, 2006-07 (estimate)
Total (x 1,000) 123.2
   Elementary..............................60.1
   Secondary...............................63.0
Average salary $54,970
   Elementary........................ $54,970
   Secondary......................... $54,970

State receipts & expenditures for public schools, 2006-07 (estimate)
Revenue receipts ($ mil) $23,871
Expenditures
Total ($ mil) $23,836
   Per capita $1,655
   Per pupil $12,121

NAEP proficiency scores, 2007

	Reading		Math	
	Basic	Proficient	Basic	Proficient
Grade 4	72.6%	40.2%	85.1%	47.0%
Grade 8	78.6%	36.4%	76.9%	38.3%

Higher education enrollment, fall 2005
Total............................... 312,069
   Full-time men 107,097
   Full-time women.................... 130,337
   Part-time men 26,626
   Part-time women.................... 48,009

Minority enrollment in institutions of higher education, 2005
Black, non-Hispanic 71,463
Hispanic 20,824
Asian/Pacific Islander 29,203
American Indian/Alaska Native..........1,839

Institutions of higher education, 2005-06
Total................................... 259
   Public................................. 65
   Private............................... 194

Earned degrees conferred, 2004-05
Associate's............................25,619
Bachelor's 77,765
Master's 26,450
First-professional...................... 4,890
Doctor's..............................2,959

Public Libraries, 2006
Number of libraries...................... 458
Number of outlets 670
Annual visits per capita 3.6
Circulation per capita......................5.3

State & local financial support for higher education, FY 2006
Full-time equivalent enrollment (x 1,000)....327.2
Appropriations per FTE............... $5,660

Social Insurance & Welfare Programs

Social Security benefits & beneficiaries, 2005
Beneficiaries (x 1,000) 2,425
   Retired & dependents..................1,708
   Survivors............................. 341
   Disabled & dependents................. 375
Annual benefit payments ($ mil) $27,072
   Retired & dependents............... $18,227
   Survivors......................... $4,953
   Disabled & dependents.............. $3,892
Average monthly benefit
   Retired & dependents................$1,030
   Disabled & dependents............. $954
   Widowed...........................$1,014

Medicare, July 2005
Enrollment (x 1,000)...................2,132
Payments ($ mil) $12,179

Medicaid, 2004
Beneficiaries (x 1,000)...................1,835
Payments ($ mil) $10,055

State Children's Health Insurance Program, 2006
Enrollment (x 1,000)...................188.8
Expenditures ($ mil) $239.8

Persons without health insurance, 2006
Number (x 1,000).......................1,237
   percent........................... 10.0%
Number of children (x 1,000) 203
   percent of children 7.3%

Health care expenditures, 2004
Total expenditures................... $73,441
   per capita $5,933

Federal and state public aid

State unemployment insurance, 2006
Recipients, first payments (x 1,000) 447
Total payments ($ mil) $2,030
Average weekly benefit $301
Temporary Assistance for Needy Families, 2006
Recipients (x 1,000) .2,824.8
Families (x 1,000) 1,097.2
Supplemental Security Income, 2005
Recipients (x 1,000) 317.5
Payments ($ mil) $1,658.8
Food Stamp Program, 2006
Avg monthly participants (x 1,000) 1,092.3
Total benefits ($ mil) $1,182.2

Housing & Construction

Housing units
Total 2005 (estimate) 5,422,584
Total 2006 (estimate) 5,453,228
Seasonal or recreational use, 2006 160,989
Owner-occupied, 2006 3,475,105
   Median home value $145,200
   Homeowner vacancy rate 1.6%
Renter-occupied, 2006 1,370,498
   Median rent $664
   Rental vacancy rate 10.6%
Home ownership rate, 2005 . . . . 73.3%
Home ownership rate, 2006 . . . . 73.2%

New privately-owned housing units
Number authorized, 2006 (x 1,000) 39.1
   Value ($ mil) $6,354.2
Started 2005 (x 1,000, estimate) 39.4
Started 2006 (x 1,000, estimate) 39.0

Existing home sales
2005 (x 1,000) 255.2
2006 (x 1,000) 234.5

Government & Elections

State officials 2008
Governor . . . . .Ed Rendell
   Democratic, term expires 1/11
Lieutenant Governor . . . . . Catherine Baker Knoll
Secretary of State . . . . .Pedro Cortes
Attorney General . . . . .Tom Corbett
Chief Justice .Ralph Cappy

Governorship
Minimum age 30
Length of term . . . . 4 years
Consecutive terms permitted 2
Who succeeds . . . . Lieutenant Governor

Local governments by type, 2002
Total 5,031
   County 66
   Municipal 1,018
   Township 1,546
   School District 516
   Special District 1,885

State legislature
Name . . . . General Assembly
Upper chamber . . . . .Senate
   Number of members 50
   Length of term . . . . 4 years
   Party in majority, 2008 . . . . Republican
Lower chamber . . . . House of Representatives
   Number of members 203
   Length of term . . . . 2 years
   Party in majority, 2008 . . . . Democratic

Federal representation, 2008 (110th Congress)
Senator . . . . Arlen Specter
   Party . . . . Republican
   Year term expires 2011
Senator . . . . Bob Casey Jr
   Party . . . . .Democratic
   Year term expires 2013
Representatives, total 19
   Democrats 11
   Republicans 8

Voters in November 2006 election (estimate)
Total 4,393,536
   Male 2,091,398
   Female 2,302,138
   White 4,026,589
   Black 304,598
   Hispanic 49,349
   Asian 36,490

Presidential election, 2004
Total Popular Vote 5,769,590
   Kerry 2,938,095
   Bush 2,793,847
Total Electoral Votes 21

Votes cast for US Senators
2004
Total vote (x 1,000) 5,559
Leading party . . . . Republican
Percent for leading party 52.6%
2006
Total vote (x 1,000) 4,081
Leading party .Democratic
Percent for leading party 58.6%

Votes cast for US Representatives
2004
Total vote (x 1,000) 5,151
   Democratic 2,478
   Republican 2,565
Leading party . . . . Republican
Percent for leading party 49.8%
2006
Total vote (x 1,000) 4,013
   Democratic 2,229
   Republican 1,732
Leading party .Democratic
Percent for leading party 55.5%

State government employment, 2006
Full-time equivalent employees 161,136
Payroll ($ mil) $622.5

Local government employment, 2006
Full-time equivalent employees 407,214
Payroll ($ mil) $1,548.1

Women holding public office, 2008
US Congress 1
Statewide elected office. 2
State legislature 37

Black public officials, 2002
Total. 215
　　US and state legislatures 19
　　City/county/regional offices 85
　　Judicial/law enforcement. 75
　　Education/school boards 36

Hispanic public officials, 2006
Total. 12
　　State executives & legislators 1
　　City/county/regional offices 7
　　Judicial/law enforcement. 2
　　Education/school boards 2

Governmental Finance

State government revenues, 2006
Total revenue (x $1,000). $73,134,243
　　per capita $5,896.58
General revenue (x $1,000) $55,418,674
　　Intergovernmental 15,326,716
　　Taxes 29,050,577
　　　　general sales .8,403,283
　　　　individual income tax 9,021,917
　　　　corporate income tax 2,116,954
　　Current charges 6,426,381
　　Miscellaneous .4,615,000

State government expenditure, 2006
Total expenditure (x $1,000) $64,917,023
　　per capita $5,234.05
General expenditure (x $1,000) $55,565,739
　　per capita, total. $4,480.09
　　　　Education 1,378.46
　　　　Public welfare 1,535.03
　　　　Health 137.69
　　　　Hospitals. 196.92
　　　　Highways 465.47
　　　　Police protection 53.51
　　　　Corrections 126.38
　　　　Natural resources 46.62
　　　　Parks & recreation 18.60
　　　　Governmental administration 185.81
　　　　Interest on general debt 114.19

State debt & cash, 2006 ($ per capita)
Debt $2,589.85
Cash/security holdings. $10,167.92

Federal government grants to state & local government, 2005 (x $1,000)
Total. $19,868,667
by Federal agency
　　Defense 189,076
　　Education 1,338,208
　　Energy 138,266
　　Environmental Protection Agency 55,599
　　Health & Human Services. 12,866,514
　　Homeland Security 230,647
　　Housing & Urban Development 1,524,175
　　Justice 206,035
　　Labor 304,300
　　Transportation 1,777,051
　　Veterans Affairs. 33,669

Crime & Law Enforcement

Crime, 2006 (rates per 100,000 residents)
Property crimes 303,988
　　Burglary 57,623
　　Larceny 216,825
　　Motor vehicle theft 29,540
　　Property crime rate. 2,443.5
Violent crimes. 54,665
　　Murder 736
　　Forcible rape. 3,401
　　Robbery. 20,974
　　Aggravated assault 29,554
　　Violent crime rate 439.4
Hate crimes 113

Fraud and identity theft, 2006
Fraud complaints. 16,242
　　rate per 100,000 residents 130.6
Identity theft complaints 8,080
　　rate per 100,000 residents 64.9

Law enforcement agencies, 2006
Total agencies. 783
Total employees 27,811
　　Officers 23,414
　　Civilians 4,397

Prisoners, probation, and parole, 2006
Total prisoners. 44,397
　　percent change, 12/31/05 to 12/31/06 . . . . 4.8%
　　in private facilities 2.2%
　　in local jails 0%
Sentenced to more than one year 43,998
　　rate per 100,000 residents 353
Adults on probation 172,184
Adults on parole. 76,386

Prisoner demographics, June 30, 2005 (rate per 100,000 residents)
Male 1,155
Female 92
White 305
Black. 2,792
Hispanic 1,714

Arrests, 2006

Total 457,514
   Persons under 18 years of age 106,572

Persons under sentence of death, 1/1/07

Total 226
   White 68
   Black 137
   Hispanic 19

State's highest court

Name . . . . .Supreme Court
Number of members 7
Length of term . . . . 10 years
Intermediate appeals court? . . . . .yes

Labor & Income

Civilian labor force, 2006 (x 1,000)

Total 6,308
   Men 3,360
   Women 2,948
   Persons 16-19 years 311
   White 5,606
   Black 558
   Hispanic 213

Civilian labor force as a percent of civilian non-institutional population, 2006

Total 64.4%
   Men 71.8
   Women 57.6
   Persons 16-19 years 45.2
   White 65.0
   Black 59.8
   Hispanic 64.4

Employment, 2006 (x 1,000)

Total 6,015
   Men 3,200
   Women 2,814
   Persons 16-19 years 268
   White 5,367
   Black 512
   Hispanic 194

Unemployment rate, 2006

Total 4.7%
   Men 4.7
   Women 4.5
   Persons 16-19 years 13.9
   White 4.3
   Black 8.2
   Hispanic 8.8

Full-time/part-time labor force, 2003 (x 1,000)

Full-time labor force, employed 4,707
Part-time labor force, employed 1,119
Unemployed, looking for
   Full-time work 276
   Part-time work 68
Mean duration of unemployment (weeks) 18.7
   Median 11.2

Labor unions, 2006

Membership (x 1,000) 745
   percent of employed 13.6%

Experienced civilian labor force by private industry, 2006

Total 4,890,795
   Natural resources & mining 42,999
   Construction 261,541
   Manufacturing 672,365
   Trade, transportation & utilities 1,117,725
   Information 108,596
   Finance 335,179
   Professional & business 677,753
   Education & health 994,934
   Leisure & hospitality 491,168
   Other 188,338

Experienced civilian labor force by occupation, May 2006

Management 190,620
Business & financial 251,170
Legal 40,630
Sales 606,190
Office & admin. support 981,000
Computers & math 114,090
Architecture & engineering 93,950
Arts & entertainment 59,380
Education 343,020
Social services 102,090
Health care practitioner & technical 342,010
Health care support 175,450
Maintenance & repair 232,360
Construction 239,160
Transportation & moving 437,710
Production 467,590
Farming, fishing & forestry 5,720

Hours and earnings of production workers on manufacturing payrolls, 2006

Average weekly hours 40.8
Average hourly earnings $15.37
Average weekly earnings $627.10

Income and poverty, 2006

Median household income $46,259
Personal income, per capita (current $) . . . $36,680
   in constant (2000) dollars $32,019
Persons below poverty level 12.1%

Average annual pay

2006 . . . . $41,349
   increase from 2005 . . . . 4.3%

Federal individual income tax returns, 2005

Returns filed 5,867,052
Adjusted gross income ($1,000) $299,493,501
Total tax liability ($1,000) $38,771,971

Charitable contributions, 2004

Number of contributions 1,640.8
Total amount ($ mil) $5,687.3

Economy, Business, Industry & Agriculture

Fortune 500 companies, 2007............... 25
Bankruptcy cases filed, FY 2007..........29,111

Patents and trademarks issued, 2007
Patents................................. 2,980
Trademarks............................. 2,452

Business firm ownership, 2002
Women-owned.........................227,117
   Sales ($ mil) $38,998
Black-owned........................... 24,757
   Sales ($ mil) $2,118
Hispanic-owned........................11,023
   Sales ($ mil) $1,729
Asian-owned 22,631
   Sales ($ mil) $6,540
Amer. Indian/Alaska Native-owned 2,362
   Sales ($ mil) .... NA
Hawaiian/Pacific Islander-owned 291
   Sales ($ mil) $41

Gross domestic product, 2006 ($ mil)
Total gross domestic product $510,293
   Agriculture, forestry, fishing and
      hunting 2,809
   Mining................................3,659
   Utilities.............................12,819
   Construction 23,957
   Manufacturing, durable goods........ 38,949
   Manufacturing, non-durable goods ... 36,423
   Wholesale trade......................30,915
   Retail trade........................ 32,475
   Transportation & warehousing 15,930
   Information 17,799
   Finance & insurance..................37,155
   Real estate, rental & leasing 60,361
   Professional and technical services.....37,387
   Educational services...................9,813
   Health care and social assistance...... 48,035
   Accommodation/food services........ 10,954
   Other services, except government 12,598
   Government 49,752

Establishments, payroll, employees & receipts, by major industry group, 2005

Total............................... 303,333
   Annual payroll ($1,000)........ $189,692,284
   Paid employees 5,082,630
Forestry, fishing & agriculture............. 563
   Annual payroll ($1,000)............. $68,327
   Paid employees 2,538
Mining............................... 882
   Annual payroll ($1,000)............. $905,500
   Paid employees 17,451
   Receipts, 2002 ($1,000) $3,408,913

Utilities 709
   Annual payroll ($1,000)..........$2,724,637
   Paid employees 33,510
   Receipts, 2002 ($1,000) ....NA
Construction....................... 29,828
   Annual payroll ($1,000).........$11,463,841
   Paid employees 242,100
   Receipts, 2002 ($1,000) $46,642,336
Manufacturing...................... 15,624
   Annual payroll ($1,000)...... $28,643,809
   Paid employees 663,605
   Receipts, 2002 ($1,000) $181,462,443
Wholesale trade 15,890
   Annual payroll ($1,000)........$11,945,383
   Paid employees 238,710
   Receipts, 2002 ($1,000) $183,741,873
Retail trade 47,223
   Annual payroll ($1,000).........$14,205,271
   Paid employees 668,973
   Receipts, 2002 ($1,000) $130,713,197
Transportation & warehousing 7,779
   Annual payroll ($1,000)..........$6,288,931
   Paid employees 195,581
   Receipts, 2002 ($1,000) $13,774,754
Information...........................5,315
   Annual payroll ($1,000).........$6,965,474
   Paid employees 133,519
   Receipts, 2002 ($1,000) ....NA
Finance & insurance 18,645
   Annual payroll ($1,000).......$17,612,704
   Paid employees 295,538
   Receipts, 2002 ($1,000) ....NA
Professional, scientific & technical........29,777
   Annual payroll ($1,000).........$18,452,450
   Paid employees 304,291
   Receipts, 2002 ($1,000) $36,708,036
Education 3,242
   Annual payroll ($1,000)........... $6,634,848
   Paid employees 220,531
   Receipts, 2002 ($1,000) $1,444,570
Health care & social assistance 34,222
   Annual payroll ($1,000).........$29,533,070
   Paid employees 837,643
   Receipts, 2002 ($1,000) $59,086,822
Arts and entertainment 4,749
   Annual payroll ($1,000).........$1,902,342
   Paid employees 74,435
   Receipts, 2002 ($1,000) $4,702,320
Real estate...........................9,747
   Annual payroll ($1,000)......... $2,506,857
   Paid employees 69,248
   Receipts, 2002 ($1,000) $9,830,222
Accommodation & food service.........26,115
   Annual payroll ($1,000).........$5,053,740
   Paid employees 404,683
   Receipts, 2002 ($1,000) $15,305,402

Exports, 2006

Value of exported goods ($ mil) $26,334
  Manufactured $23,339
  Non-manufactured...................$1,333

Foreign direct investment in US affiliates, 2004

Property, plants & equipment ($ mil) ... $30,237
Employment (x 1,000)....................225.6

Agriculture, 2006

Number of farms 58,200
Farm acreage (x 1,000) 7,650
  Acres per farm........................ 131
Farm marketings and income ($ mil)
Total................................$4,691.7
  Crops..............................$1,723.3
  Livestock..........................$2,968.3
Net farm income $1,516.4

Principal commodities, in order by marketing receipts, 2005

Dairy products, Cattle and calves, Greenhouse/
nursery, Agaricus mushrooms, Broilers

Federal economic activity in state

Expenditures, 2005 ($ mil)
  Total............................... $99,503
    Per capita $8,020.94
  Defense $10,244
  Non-defense...................... $89,259
Defense department, 2006 ($ mil)
  Payroll............................. $3,077
  Contract awards $7,515
  Grants $300
Homeland security grants ($1,000)
  2006.............................. $49,335
  2007.............................. $61,306

FDIC-insured financial institutions, 2005

Number 251
Assets ($ billion) $415.2
Deposits ($ billion) $294.9

Fishing, 2006

Catch (x 1,000 lbs)........................ 38
Value ($1,000)............................ $96

Mining, 2006 ($ mil)

Total non-fuel mineral production $1,670
Percent of U.S. 2.59%

Communication, Energy & Transportation

Communication

Households with computers, 2003........60.2%
Households with internet access, 2003 ....54.7%
High-speed internet providers 75
Total high-speed internet lines........3,374,313
  Residential 2,279,971
  Business..........................1,094,342
Wireless phone customers, 12/2006 8,831,238

FCC-licensed stations (as of January 1, 2008)

TV stations 46
FM radio stations......................... 325
AM radio stations 181

Energy

Energy consumption, 2004
  Total (trillion Btu)................. 4,049
  Per capita (million Btu) 327.2
By source of production (trillion Btu)
  Coal 1,474
  Natural gas........................ 733
  Petroleum..........................1,519
  Nuclear electric power 808
  Hydroelectric power................... 32
By end-use sector (trillion Btu)
  Residential 995
  Commercial 707
  Industrial 1,328
  Transportation 1,019
Electric energy, 2005
  Primary source of electricity............ Coal
  Net generation (billion kWh) 218.1
    percent from renewable sources....... 2.1%
  Net summer capability (million kW) 44.9
  CO_2 emitted from generation 126.7
Natural gas utilities, 2005
  Customers (x 1,000) 2,839
  Sales (trillion Btu)..................... 592
  Revenues ($ mil) $4,572
Nuclear plants, 2007 9
Total CO_2 emitted (million metric tons).....271.4
Energy spending, 2004 ($ mil) $36,069
  per capita $2,914
  Price per million Btu $13.05

Transportation, 2006

Public road & street mileage 121,292
  Urban............................. 44,923
  Rural............................. 76,369
  Interstate...........................1,758
Vehicle miles of travel (millions) 108,278
  per capita 8,730.1
Total motor vehicle registrations.......9,894,163
  Automobiles......................5,842,819
  Trucks 4,013,315
  Motorcycles 330,938
Licensed drivers 8,526,204
  19 years & under 348,567
Deaths from motor vehicle accidents 1,525
Gasoline consumed (x 1,000 gallons) 5,102,928
  per capita 411.4

Commuting Statistics, 2006

Average commute time (min) 25.0
  Drove to work alone 76.4%
  Carpooled.......................... 9.9%
  Public transit 5.2%
  Walk to work 4.1%
  Work from home..................... 3.2%

State Summary

Capital city . . . . Providence
Governor . . . . .Don Carcieri
State House
Providence, RI 02903
401-222-2080
Admitted as a state 1790
Area (square miles) 1,545
Population, 2007 (estimate). 1,057,832
Largest city . . . . Providence
Population, 2006 175,255
Personal income per capita, 2006
(in current dollars) $37,388
Gross domestic product, 2006 ($ mil) $45,660

Leading industries by payroll, 2005

Health care/Social assistance, Manufacturing,
Finance & Insurance

Leading agricultural commodities by receipts, 2005

Greenhouse/nursery, Dairy products, Sweet corn,
Aquaculture, Potatoes

Geography & Environment

Total area (square miles) 1,545
land 1,045
water 500
Federally-owned land, 2004 (acres) 2,923
percent. 0.4%
Highest point . . . . Jerimoth Hill
elevation (feet) 812
Lowest point .Atlantic Ocean
elevation (feet) . . . . sea level
General coastline (miles) 40
Tidal shoreline (miles) 384
Cropland, 2003 (x 1,000 acres) 20
Forest land, 2003 (x 1,000 acres). 374
Capital city . . . . Providence
Population 2000 173,618
Population 2006 175,255
Largest city . . . . Providence
Population 2000 173,618
Population 2006 175,255

Number of cities with over 100,000 population

1990 1
2000 1
2006 1

State park and recreation areas, 2005

Area (x 1,000 acres). 9
Number of visitors (x 1,000) 5,853
Revenues ($1,000) $3,515
percent of operating expenditures. 39.3%

National forest system land, 2007

Acres 0

Demographics & Population Characteristics

Population

1980 947,154
1990 1,003,464
2000 1,048,319
2006 1,067,610
Male 516,213
Female 551,397
Living in group quarters, 2006 43,088
percent of total. 4.0%
2007 (estimate). 1,057,832
persons per square mile of land 1,012.3
2008 (projected) 1,105,525
2010 (projected) 1,116,652
2020 (projected) .1,154,230
2030 (projected) 1,152,941

Population of Core-Based Statistical Areas (formerly Metropolitan Areas), x 1,000

	CBSA	Non-CBSA
1990	1,003	0
2000	1,048	0
2006	1,068	0

Change in population, 2000-2007

Number 9,513
percent 0.9%
Natural increase (births minus deaths) 20,554
Net internal migration . . . .-30,249
Net international migration 23,874

Persons by age, 2006

Under 5 years 61,961
5 to 17 years 175,490
18 years and over 830,159
65 years and over 147,966
85 years and over 25,123
Median age 38.2

Persons by age, 2010 (projected)

Under 5 years 66,193
18 and over 867,379
65 and over 157,358
Median age 38.2

Race, 2006

One Race
White. 947,030
Black or African American 67,328
Asian 29,177
American Indian/Alaska Native. 6,574
Hawaiian Native/Pacific Islander. 1,287
Two or more races. 16,214

Persons of Hispanic origin, 2006

Total Hispanic or Latino 117,708
Mexican. 8,313
Puerto Rican 33,685
Cuban 2,502

Persons of Asian origin, 2006

Total Asian 29,406
    Asian Indian. 5,545
    Chinese 7,869
    Filipino 3,558
    Japanese 483
    Korean. 1,883
    Vietnamese. 1,017

Marital status, 2006

Population 15 years & over 873,859
    Never married 299,121
    Married. 423,737
    Separated 15,172
    Widowed. 59,563
    Divorced 91,438

Language spoken at home, 2006

Population 5 years and older. 1,005,812
    English only 800,162
    Spanish 100,227
    French 23,281
    German 2,774
    Chinese 6,266

Households & families, 2006

Households. 405,627
    with persons under 18 years 130,032
    with persons over 65 years. 101,089
    persons per household 2.53
Families. 262,352
    persons per family. 3.13
Married couples. 190,694
Female householder,
    no husband present. 54,502
One-person households 116,234

Nativity, 2006

Number of residents born in state 631,785
    percent of population 59.2%

Immigration & naturalization, 2006

Legal permanent residents admitted 4,778
Persons naturalized 2,266
Non-immigrant admissions 45,648

Vital Statistics and Health

Marriages

2004 8,243
2005 7,525
2006 6,916

Divorces

2004 3,287
2005 3,159
2006 3,115

Health risks, 2006

Percent of adults who are:
    Smokers. 19.2%
    Overweight (BMI > 25). 61.0%
    Obese (BMI > 30). 21.4%

Births

2005 12,697
    Birthrate (per 1,000). 11.8
    White. 10,705
    Black 1,288
    Hispanic 2,559
    Asian/Pacific Islander 555
    Amer. Indian/Alaska Native 149
    Low birth weight (2,500g or less). 7.8%
    Cesarian births 30.3%
    Preterm births 12.1%
    To unmarried mothers. 38.5%
    Twin births (per 1,000) 38.9
    Triplets or higher order (per 100,000). . . .178.4
2006 (preliminary). 12,379
    rate per 1,000 . . . . .11.6

Deaths

2004
All causes 9,769
    rate per 100,000 . . . . .741.1
Heart disease 2,969
    rate per 100,000 . . . . .216.0
Malignant neoplasms 2,418
    rate per 100,000 . . . . .194.1
Cerebrovascular disease. 522
    rate per 100,000 .38.1
Chronic lower respiratory disease 463
    rate per 100,000 .35.3
Diabetes. 280
    rate per 100,000 .21.9
2005 (preliminary). 10,007
    rate per 100,000 . . . . .747.3
2006 (provisional) .9,731

Infant deaths

2004 68
    rate per 1,000 . . . . .5.3
2005 (provisional) 74
    rate per 1,000 . . . . .5.9

Exercise routines, 2005

None. 25.9%
Moderate or greater. 51.1%
Vigorous 29.9%

Abortions, 2004

Total performed in state. 5,587
    rate per 1,000 women age 15-44 24
    % obtained by out-of-state residents 23.9%

Physicians, 2005

Total. 3,866
    rate per 100,000 persons 360

Community hospitals, 2005

Number of hospitals 11
Beds (x 1,000). 2.4
Patients admitted (x 1,000) 127
Average daily census (x 1,000) 1.9
Average cost per day $1,719
Outpatient visits (x 1 mil) 2.5

Rhode Island   3

Disability status of population, 2006
5 to 15 years 7.2%
16 to 64 years 12.9%
65 years and over 39.4%

Education

Educational attainment, 2006
Population over 25 years 712,984
Less than 9th grade. 7.3%
High school graduate or more 82.4%
College graduate or more. 29.6%
Graduate or professional degree. 11.3%

Public school enrollment, 2005-06
Total. 153,422
Pre-kindergarten through grade 8. . . . 103,870
Grades 9 through 12 49,552

Graduating public high school seniors, 2004-05
Diplomas (incl. GED and others) 9,903

SAT scores, 2007
Average critical reading score. 496
Average writing score 492
Average math score 498
Percent of graduates taking test 68%

Public school teachers, 2006-07 (estimate)
Total (x 1,000) 14.9
Elementary 9.3
Secondary 5.6
Average salary $55,956
Elementary $55,956
Secondary $55,956

State receipts & expenditures for public schools, 2006-07 (estimate)
Revenue receipts ($ mil) $1,636
Expenditures
Total ($ mil) $1,952
Per capita $1,748
Per pupil $12,095

NAEP proficiency scores, 2007
	Reading		Math	
	Basic	Proficient	Basic	Proficient
Grade 4	65.4%	30.8%	79.6%	34.0%
Grade 8	69.3%	27.2%	65.5%	27.7%

Higher education enrollment, fall 2005
Total. 41,374
Full-time men 17,731
Full-time women. 18,460
Part-time men 2,434
Part-time women. 2,749

Minority enrollment in institutions of higher education, 2005
Black, non-Hispanic 4,897
Hispanic 5,246
Asian/Pacific Islander 3,468
American Indian/Alaska Native. 351

Institutions of higher education, 2005-06
Total. 14
Public. 3
Private 11

Earned degrees conferred, 2004-05
Associate's. 3,573
Bachelor's 9,472
Master's 2,223
First-professional. 318
Doctor's 243

Public Libraries, 2006
Number of libraries. 49
Number of outlets 75
Annual visits per capita 5.9
Circulation per capita. 6.8

State & local financial support for higher education, FY 2006
Full-time equivalent enrollment (x 1,000) 28.1
Appropriations per FTE. $6,413

Social Insurance & Welfare Programs

Social Security benefits & beneficiaries, 2005
Beneficiaries (x 1,000) 192
Retired & dependents. 134
Survivors. 21
Disabled & dependents. 36
Annual benefit payments ($ mil) $2,089
Retired & dependents. $1,418
Survivors. $302
Disabled & dependents. $368
Average monthly benefit
Retired & dependents. $1,006
Disabled & dependents. $913
Widowed. $1,013

Medicare, July 2005
Enrollment (x 1,000). 172
Payments ($ mil) $832

Medicaid, 2004
Beneficiaries (x 1,000). 208
Payments ($ mil) $1,531

State Children's Health Insurance Program, 2006
Enrollment (x 1,000). 25.5
Expenditures ($ mil) $42.1

Persons without health insurance, 2006
Number (x 1,000). 91
percent. 8.6%
Number of children (x 1,000) 10
percent of children 4.2%

Health care expenditures, 2004
Total expenditures. $6,682
per capita $6,193

Federal and state public aid

State unemployment insurance, 2006
Recipients, first payments (x 1,000) 38
Total payments ($ mil) $196
Average weekly benefit $342
Temporary Assistance for Needy Families, 2006
Recipients (x 1,000) 275.0
Families (x 1,000) 112.3
Supplemental Security Income, 2005
Recipients (x 1,000) 30.2
Payments ($ mil) $160.8
Food Stamp Program, 2006
Avg monthly participants (x 1,000) 73.2
Total benefits ($ mil) $80.9

Housing & Construction

Housing units

Total 2005 (estimate) 447,810
Total 2006 (estimate) 449,582
Seasonal or recreational use, 2006 14,856
Owner-occupied, 2006 255,495
    Median home value $295,700
    Homeowner vacancy rate 1.3%
Renter-occupied, 2006 150,132
    Median rent $840
    Rental vacancy rate 7.5%
Home ownership rate, 2005 . . . . 63.1%
Home ownership rate, 2006 . . . . 64.6%

New privately-owned housing units

Number authorized, 2006 (x 1,000) 2.4
    Value ($ mil) $383.8
Started 2005 (x 1,000, estimate) 2.4
Started 2006 (x 1,000, estimate) 2.4

Existing home sales

2005 (x 1,000) 19.8
2006 (x 1,000) 17.4

Government & Elections

State officials 2008

Governor . . . . .Don Carcieri
                Republican, term expires 1/11
Lieutenant Governor . . . . Elizabeth Roberts
Secretary of State . . . . .Ralph Mollis
Attorney General . . . . Patrick Lynch
Chief Justice . . . . Frank Williams

Governorship

Minimum age 18
Length of term . . . . 4 years
Consecutive terms permitted 2
Who succeeds . . . . Lieutenant Governor

Local governments by type, 2002

Total 118
    County 0
    Municipal 8
    Township 31
    School District 4
    Special District 75

State legislature

Name . . . . General Assembly
Upper chamber . . . . .Senate
    Number of members 38
    Length of term . . . . 2 years
    Party in majority, 2008 . . . . Democratic
Lower chamber . . . . House of Representatives
    Number of members 75
    Length of term . . . . 2 years
    Party in majority, 2008 . . . . .Democratic

Federal representation, 2008 (110th Congress)

Senator . . . . John Reed
    Party . . . . .Democratic
    Year term expires 2009
Senator . . . . .Sheldon Whitehouse
    Party . . . . .Democratic
    Year term expires 2013
Representatives, total 2
    Democrats 2
    Republicans 0

Voters in November 2006 election (estimate)

Total 430,706
    Male 197,035
    Female 233,672
    White 400,636
    Black 17,165
    Hispanic 12,059
    Asian 4,455

Presidential election, 2004

Total Popular Vote 437,134
    Kerry 259,765
    Bush 169,046
Total Electoral Votes 4

Votes cast for US Senators

2004
Total vote (x 1,000) . . . . NA
Leading party . . . . NA
Percent for leading party . . . . NA
2006
Total vote (x 1,000) 385
Leading party . . . . .Democratic
Percent for leading party 53.5%

Votes cast for US Representatives

2004
Total vote (x 1,000) 402
    Democratic 279
    Republican 113
Leading party . . . . .Democratic
Percent for leading party 69.5%
2006
Total vote (x 1,000) 373
    Democratic 265
    Republican 42
Leading party . . . . .Democratic
Percent for leading party 71.0%

State government employment, 2006
Full-time equivalent employees 20,594
Payroll ($ mil) $93.3

Local government employment, 2006
Full-time equivalent employees 30,638
Payroll ($ mil) $133.5

Women holding public office, 2008
US Congress 0
Statewide elected office...................... 1
State legislature 22

Black public officials, 2002
Total..................................... 8
   US and state legislatures 7
   City/county/regional offices 1
   Judicial/law enforcement.................. 0
   Education/school boards.................. 0

Hispanic public officials, 2006
Total..................................... 7
   State executives & legislators 4
   City/county/regional offices 3
   Judicial/law enforcement.................. 0
   Education/school boards.................. 0

Governmental Finance

State government revenues, 2006
Total revenue (x $1,000)............$7,670,233
   per capita $7,224.88
General revenue (x $1,000) $6,194,471
   Intergovernmental 2,148,174
   Taxes 2,741,734
      general sales..................... 854,257
      individual income tax 1,019,482
      corporate income tax 169,865
   Current charges.....................511,429
   Miscellaneous 793,134

State government expenditure, 2006
Total expenditure (x $1,000) $6,955,860
   per capita $6,551.99
General expenditure (x $1,000) $5,872,054
   per capita, total................. *$5,531.11*
      Education.....................1,560.49
      Public welfare 2,048.86
      Health 143.44
      Hospitals...................... 108.22
      Highways 284.15
      Police protection..................52.27
      Corrections 162.17
      Natural resources 37.53
      Parks & recreation 13.73
      Governmental administration...... 336.54
      Interest on general debt............ 260.04

State debt & cash, 2006 ($ per capita)
Debt $6,559.82
Cash/security holdings..............$13,777.71

Federal government grants to state & local government, 2005 (x $1,000)
Total.............................$2,325,111
by Federal agency
   Defense 17,441
   Education 146,373
   Energy 6,054
   Environmental Protection Agency 29,749
   Health & Human Services. 1,467,433
   Homeland Security.................... 8,946
   Housing & Urban Development.......233,411
   Justice 37,889
   Labor 37,320
   Transportation 190,408
   Veterans Affairs.................... 3,999

Crime & Law Enforcement

Crime, 2006 (rates per 100,000 residents)
Property crimes 27,618
   Burglary 5,415
   Larceny 18,621
   Motor vehicle theft 3,582
   Property crime rate.................2,586.9
Violent crimes......................... 2,429
   Murder 28
   Forcible rape...................... 285
   Robbery.......................... 735
   Aggravated assault 1,381
   Violent crime rate 227.5
Hate crimes........................... 20

Fraud and identity theft, 2006
Fraud complaints......................1,153
   rate per 100,000 residents 108.0
Identity theft complaints 615
   rate per 100,000 residents 57.6

Law enforcement agencies, 2006
Total agencies........................... 47
Total employees 3,223
   Officers 2,561
   Civilians 662

Prisoners, probation, and parole, 2006
Total prisoners........................3,996
   percent change, 12/31/05 to 12/31/06 .... 9.4%
   in private facilities 0%
   in local jails .... NA
Sentenced to more than one year 2,149
   rate per 100,000 residents 202
Adults on probation 26,017
Adults on parole........................ 364

Prisoner demographics, June 30, 2005 (rate per 100,000 residents)
Male................................... 607
Female 38
White 191
Black...................................1,838
Hispanic 631

Arrests, 2006

Total. 35,999
  Persons under 18 years of age 4,900

Persons under sentence of death, 1/1/07

Total. 0
  White. 0
  Black 0
  Hispanic 0

State's highest court

Name . . . . .Supreme Court
Number of members. 5
Length of term . . . . .life
Intermediate appeals court? . . . . no

Labor & Income

Civilian labor force, 2006 (x 1,000)

Total. 577
  Men 300
  Women 278
  Persons 16-19 years. 32
  White. 519
  Black 33
  Hispanic 56

Civilian labor force as a percent of civilian non-institutional population, 2006

Total. 68.6%
  Men 74.8
  Women 63.0
  Persons 16-19 years. 53.0
  White. 68.3
  Black 71.9
  Hispanic 67.7

Employment, 2006 (x 1,000)

Total. 547
  Men 284
  Women 263
  Persons 16-19 years. 27
  White. 493
  Black 30
  Hispanic 51

Unemployment rate, 2006

Total. 5.2%
  Men 5.1
  Women 5.3
  Persons 16-19 years. 14.9
  White. 4.9
  Black 7.2
  Hispanic 8.5

Full-time/part-time labor force, 2003 (x 1,000)

Full-time labor force, employed 422
Part-time labor force, employed. 121
Unemployed, looking for
  Full-time work. 25
  Part-time work. 6
*Mean duration of unemployment (weeks). *18.6
  Median 9.7

Labor unions, 2006

Membership (x 1,000). 76
  percent of employed 15.3%

Experienced civilian labor force by private industry, 2006

Total. 417,683
  Natural resources & mining 1,121
  Construction 22,791
  Manufacturing. 52,730
  Trade, transportation & utilities 79,256
  Information 10,995
  Finance 33,368
  Professional & business 56,141
  Education & health 92,656
  Leisure & hospitality. 50,234
  Other 18,140

Experienced civilian labor force by occupation, May 2006

Management. 23,270
Business & financial 20,950
Legal. 3,410
Sales 45,370
Office & admin. support. 84,260
Computers & math 9,770
Architecture & engineering. 8,320
Arts & entertainment 6,730
Education 33,630
Social services 9,990
Health care practitioner & technical 29,010
Health care support 17,520
Maintenance & repair. 15,410
Construction 22,000
Transportation & moving 27,630
Production 37,910
Farming, fishing & forestry. 210

Hours and earnings of production workers on manufacturing payrolls, 2006

Average weekly hours 38.9
Average hourly earnings $13.42
Average weekly earnings $522.04

Income and poverty, 2006

Median household income. $51,814
Personal income, per capita (current $). . . $37,388
  in constant (2000) dollars $32,637
Persons below poverty level. 11.1%

Average annual pay

2006 . . . . $40,454
  increase from 2005 . . . . 4.4%

Federal individual income tax returns, 2005

Returns filed. 502,440
Adjusted gross income ($1,000) $26,529,043
Total tax liability ($1,000) $3,414,395

Charitable contributions, 2004

Number of contributions 170.4
Total amount ($ mil). $463.2

Economy, Business, Industry & Agriculture

Fortune 500 companies, 2007 2
Bankruptcy cases filed, FY 2007 2,521

Patents and trademarks issued, 2007
Patents 381
Trademarks 348

Business firm ownership, 2002
Women-owned 23,195
  Sales ($ mil) $3,641
Black-owned . . . . NA
  Sales ($ mil) . . . . NA
Hispanic-owned 3,415
  Sales ($ mil) $214
Asian-owned 1,529
  Sales ($ mil) $326
Amer. Indian/Alaska Native-owned 446
  Sales ($ mil) $27
Hawaiian/Pacific Islander-owned 45
  Sales ($ mil) $3

Gross domestic product, 2006 ($ mil)
Total gross domestic product $45,660
  Agriculture, forestry, fishing and
    hunting 96
  Mining 24
  Utilities 917
  Construction 2,307
  Manufacturing, durable goods 3,270
  Manufacturing, non-durable goods 1,234
  Wholesale trade .2,319
  Retail trade 2,832
  Transportation & warehousing 630
  Information 1,700
  Finance & insurance 5,319
  Real estate, rental & leasing 6,856
  Professional and technical services 2,612
  Educational services 997
  Health care and social assistance 4,241
  Accommodation/food services 1,250
  Other services, except government 979
  Government 5,511

Establishments, payroll, employees & receipts, by major industry group, 2005

Total 30,331
  Annual payroll ($1,000) $15,756,079
  Paid employees 442,291
Forestry, fishing & agriculture 54
  Annual payroll ($1,000) . . . . NA
  Paid employees . . . . NA
Mining 25
  Annual payroll ($1,000) . . . . NA
  Paid employees . . . . NA
  Receipts, 2002 ($1,000) $34,173

Utilities 34
  Annual payroll ($1,000) $110,220
  Paid employees 1,444
  Receipts, 2002 ($1,000) . . . . .NA
Construction 3,697
  Annual payroll ($1,000) $993,532
  Paid employees 20,041
  Receipts, 2002 ($1,000) $4,356,409
Manufacturing 1,956
  Annual payroll ($1,000) $2,366,601
  Paid employees 58,738
  Receipts, 2002 ($1,000) $10,818,058
Wholesale trade 1,419
  Annual payroll ($1,000) $857,371
  Paid employees 18,260
  Receipts, 2002 ($1,000) $8,566,430
Retail trade 4,201
  Annual payroll ($1,000) $1,284,483
  Paid employees 54,724
  Receipts, 2002 ($1,000) $10,342,351
Transportation & warehousing 703
  Annual payroll ($1,000) $300,350
  Paid employees 11,531
  Receipts, 2002 ($1,000) $723,864
Information 403
  Annual payroll ($1,000) $398,220
  Paid employees 8,164
  Receipts, 2002 ($1,000) . . . . .NA
Finance & insurance 1,560
  Annual payroll ($1,000) $1,989,292
  Paid employees 33,032
  Receipts, 2002 ($1,000) . . . . .NA
Professional, scientific & technical 3,114
  Annual payroll ($1,000) $1,141,686
  Paid employees 22,718
  Receipts, 2002 ($1,000) $2,158,832
Education 375
  Annual payroll ($1,000) $688,237
  Paid employees 22,070
  Receipts, 2002 ($1,000) $76,337
Health care & social assistance 3,118
  Annual payroll ($1,000) $2,825,111
  Paid employees 82,286
  Receipts, 2002 ($1,000) $5,186,163
Arts and entertainment 536
  Annual payroll ($1,000) $181,748
  Paid employees 6,909
  Receipts, 2002 ($1,000) $489,588
Real estate 1,218
  Annual payroll ($1,000) $235,339
  Paid employees 6,866
  Receipts, 2002 ($1,000) $849,718
Accommodation & food service 2,901
  Annual payroll ($1,000) $611,147
  Paid employees 42,638
  Receipts, 2002 ($1,000) $1,731,799

8   Rhode Island

Exports, 2006
Value of exported goods ($ mil) $1,531
   Manufactured $1,028
   Non-manufactured....................$329

Foreign direct investment in US affiliates, 2004
Property, plants & equipment ($ mil) $3,381
Employment (x 1,000).....................26.1

Agriculture, 2006
Number of farms 850
Farm acreage (x 1,000) 60
   Acres per farm........................ 71
Farm marketings and income ($ mil)
Total.................................$65.6
   Crops...............................$55.6
   Livestock............................$10.1
Net farm income $26.0

Principal commodities, in order by marketing receipts, 2005
Greenhouse/nursery, Dairy products, Sweet corn, Aquaculture, Potatoes

Federal economic activity in state
Expenditures, 2005 ($ mil)
   Total............................. $8,423
     Per capita $7,846.07
   Defense $959
   Non-defense........................$7,464
Defense department, 2006 ($ mil)
   Payroll.............................. $678
   Contract awards $431
   Grants $17
Homeland security grants ($1,000)
   2006.................................$7,838
   2007.................................$12,119

FDIC-insured financial institutions, 2005
Number 13
Assets ($ billion) $29.6
Deposits ($ billion) $13.9

Fishing, 2006
Catch (x 1,000 lbs).................... 112,605
Value ($1,000)....................... $100,049

Mining, 2006 ($ mil)
Total non-fuel mineral production $38
Percent of U.S. 0.06%

Communication, Energy & Transportation

Communication
Households with computers, 2003........ 62.3%
Households with internet access, 2003 .... 55.7%
High-speed internet providers 19
Total high-speed internet lines........ 349,994
   Residential 235,663
   Business........................... 114,331
Wireless phone customers, 12/2006 797,603

FCC-licensed stations (as of January 1, 2008)
TV stations 5
FM radio stations........................... 21
AM radio stations 15

Energy
Energy consumption, 2004
   Total (trillion Btu)..................... 226
   Per capita (million Btu) 209.8
By source of production (trillion Btu)
   Coal 0
   Natural gas........................... 75
   Petroleum............................ 99
   Nuclear electric power 0
   Hydroelectric power................... 0
By end-use sector (trillion Btu)
   Residential 79
   Commercial 59
   Industrial 26
   Transportation 62
Electric energy, 2005
   Primary source of electricity............. Gas
   Net generation (billion kWh) 6.1
     percent from renewable sources....... 0.1%
   Net summer capability (million kW) 1.7
   CO_2 emitted from generation 2.6
Natural gas utilities, 2005
   Customers (x 1,000) 248
   Sales (trillion Btu)...................... 37
   Revenues ($ mil) $402
Nuclear plants, 2007 0
Total CO_2 emitted (million metric tons)......11.4
Energy spending, 2004 ($ mil) $2,634
   per capita $2,442
   Price per million Btu $15.95

Transportation, 2006
Public road & street mileage 6,528
   Urban...............................5,261
   Rural 1,267
   Interstate............................ 71
Vehicle miles of travel (millions) 8,300
   per capita 7,818.1
Total motor vehicle registrations........ 805,548
   Automobiles........................ 508,389
   Trucks 295,433
   Motorcycles 31,125
Licensed drivers 741,921
   19 years & under 30,695
Deaths from motor vehicle accidents 81
Gasoline consumed (x 1,000 gallons) 418,396
   per capita 394.1

Commuting Statistics, 2006
Average commute time (min) 22.3
   Drove to work alone 81.1%
   Carpooled............................8.9%
   Public transit 2.6%
   Walk to work 3.0%
   Work from home......................2.7%

State Summary

Capital city .... Columbia
Governor....................... Mark Sanford
PO Box 11829
Columbia, SC 29211
803-734-9400
Admitted as a state 1788
Area (square miles) 32,020
Population, 2007 (estimate)........... 4,407,709
Largest city .... Columbia
Population, 2006 119,961
Personal income per capita, 2006
(in current dollars) $29,515
Gross domestic product, 2006 ($ mil) ... $149,214

Leading industries by payroll, 2005

Manufacturing, Health care/Social assistance,
Retail trade

**Leading agricultural commodities
by receipts, 2005**

Broilers, Greenhouse/nursery, Turkeys, Cattle
and calves, Cotton

Geography & Environment

Total area (square miles)............... 32,020
land 30,110
water 1,911
Federally-owned land, 2004 (acres) 560,956
percent...............................2.9%
Highest point .... Sassafras Mountain
elevation (feet) 3,560
Lowest point .... Atlantic Ocean
elevation (feet) .... sea level
General coastline (miles) 187
Tidal shoreline (miles) 2,876
Cropland, 2003 (x 1,000 acres) 2,368
Forest land, 2003 (x 1,000 acres)......... 11,161
Capital city .... Columbia
Population 2000 116,278
Population 2006 119,961
Largest city .... Columbia
Population 2000 116,278
Population 2006 119,961

Number of cities with over 100,000 population

1990 0
2000 1
2006 2

State park and recreation areas, 2005

Area (x 1,000 acres)...................... 81
Number of visitors (x 1,000) 6,707
Revenues ($1,000) $18,304
percent of operating expenditures...... 73.5%

National forest system land, 2007

Acres 629,565

Demographics & Population Characteristics

Population

1980 3,121,820
1990 3,486,703
2000 4,011,816
2006 4,321,249
Male.............................2,103,713
Female...........................2,217,536
Living in group quarters, 2006........ 142,974
percent of total...................... 3.3%
2007 (estimate).....................4,407,709
persons per square mile of land 146.4
2008 (projected).....................4,365,055
2010 (projected)....................4,446,704
2020 (projected)....................4,822,577
2030 (projected)....................5,148,569

**Population of Core-Based Statistical Areas
(formerly Metropolitan Areas), x 1,000**

	CBSA	Non-CBSA
1990	3,230	256
2000	3,735	277
2006	4,046	275

Change in population, 2000-2007

Number............................. 395,893
percent............................. 9.9%
Natural increase (births minus deaths) 132,891
Net internal migration................ 228,133
Net international migration 40,959

Persons by age, 2006

Under 5 years 283,481
5 to 17 years 756,172
18 years and over 3,281,596
65 years and over 553,396
85 years and over 68,701
Median age 37.1

Persons by age, 2010 (projected)

Under 5 years 287,544
18 and over 3,410,355
65 and over 605,660
Median age...........................38.4

Race, 2006

One Race

White...........................2,958,982
Black or African American 1,253,131
Asian 49,681
American Indian/Alaska Native....... 16,849
Hawaiian Native/Pacific Islander....... 2,287
Two or more races......................40,319

Persons of Hispanic origin, 2006

Total Hispanic or Latino 148,632
Mexican........................... 93,660
Puerto Rican 15,083
Cuban 2,493

Persons of Asian origin, 2006

Total Asian	46,939
Asian Indian	10,699
Chinese	9,142
Filipino	9,127
Japanese	3,046
Korean	2,585
Vietnamese	6,493

Marital status, 2006

Population 15 years & over	3,470,748
Never married	1,044,564
Married	1,829,675
Separated	126,529
Widowed	253,598
Divorced	342,911

Language spoken at home, 2006

Population 5 years and older	4,036,541
English only	3,795,110
Spanish	148,345
French	14,435
German	14,706
Chinese	6,586

Households & families, 2006

Households	1,656,978
with persons under 18 years	567,601
with persons over 65 years	390,775
persons per household	2.52
Families	1,122,724
persons per family	3.07
Married couples	798,196
Female householder, no husband present	253,002
One-person households	451,584

Nativity, 2006

Number of residents born in state	2,627,072
percent of population	60.8%

Immigration & naturalization, 2006

Legal permanent residents admitted	5,292
Persons naturalized	2,940
Non-immigrant admissions	108,650

Vital Statistics and Health

Marriages

2004	34,546
2005	35,351
2006	32,846

Divorces

2004	13,448
2005	12,423
2006	12,821

Health risks, 2006

Percent of adults who are:

Smokers	22.3%
Overweight (BMI > 25)	65.4%
Obese (BMI > 30)	29.4%

Births

2005	57,711
Birthrate (per 1,000)	13.6
White	36,098
Black	20,369
Hispanic	4,990
Asian/Pacific Islander	1,028
Amer. Indian/Alaska Native	216
Low birth weight (2,500g or less)	10.2%
Cesarian births	32.7%
Preterm births	15.6%
To unmarried mothers	43.3%
Twin births (per 1,000)	31.5
Triplets or higher order (per 100,000)	141.8
2006 (preliminary)	62,271
rate per 1,000	14.4

Deaths

2004

All causes	37,276
rate per 100,000	898.0
Heart disease	9,182
rate per 100,000	222.0
Malignant neoplasms	8,348
rate per 100,000	195.5
Cerebrovascular disease	2,643
rate per 100,000	65.2
Chronic lower respiratory disease	1,792
rate per 100,000	43.1
Diabetes	1,165
rate per 100,000	27.6
2005 (preliminary)	38,483
rate per 100,000	899.1
2006 (provisional)	36,652

Infant deaths

2004	525
rate per 1,000	9.3
2005 (provisional)	516
rate per 1,000	8.9

Exercise routines, 2005

None	26.3%
Moderate or greater	45.3%
Vigorous	24.6%

Abortions, 2004

Total performed in state	6,565
rate per 1,000 women age 15-44	7
% obtained by out-of-state residents	3.9%

Physicians, 2005

Total	9,769
rate per 100,000 persons	230

Community hospitals, 2005

Number of hospitals	63
Beds (x 1,000)	11.5
Patients admitted (x 1,000)	528
Average daily census (x 1,000)	8.4
Average cost per day	$1,465
Outpatient visits (x 1 mil)	5.8

South Carolina 3

Disability status of population, 2006
5 to 15 years 6.5%
16 to 64 years 14.9%
65 years and over 43.7%

Education

Educational attainment, 2006
Population over 25 years 2,845,744
  Less than 9ᵗʰ grade. 6.4%
  High school graduate or more 81.3%
  College graduate or more. 22.7%
  Graduate or professional degree. 7.9%

Public school enrollment, 2005-06
Total. 701,544
  Pre-kindergarten through grade 8. ... 498,030
  Grades 9 through 12. 203,514

Graduating public high school seniors, 2004-05
Diplomas (incl. GED and others) 36,192

SAT scores, 2007
Average critical reading score 488
Average writing score 475
Average math score 496
Percent of graduates taking test 62%

Public school teachers, 2006-07 (estimate)
Total (x 1,000) 47.0
  Elementary 33.2
  Secondary 13.8
Average salary $44,133
  Elementary $44,133
  Secondary $44,133

State receipts & expenditures for public schools, 2006-07 (estimate)
Revenue receipts ($ mil) $6,870
Expenditures
Total ($ mil) $7,897
  Per capita $1,480
  Per pupil $9,891

NAEP proficiency scores, 2007
	Reading		Math	
	Basic	Proficient	Basic	Proficient
Grade 4	58.9%	25.8%	79.7%	35.9%
Grade 8	68.7%	24.6%	70.9%	31.9%

Higher education enrollment, fall 2005
Total. 35,758
  Full-time men 11,957
  Full-time women 17,477
  Part-time men 1,966
  Part-time women. 4,358

Minority enrollment in institutions of higher education, 2005
Black, non-Hispanic 57,941
Hispanic 3,374
Asian/Pacific Islander 3,272
American Indian/Alaska Native 868

Institutions of higher education, 2005-06
Total. 64
  Public. 33
  Private 31

Earned degrees conferred, 2004-05
Associate's. 8,123
Bachelor's 18,795
Master's 5,007
First-professional. 857
Doctor's. 466

Public Libraries, 2006
Number of libraries. 42
Number of outlets 220
Annual visits per capita 3.6
Circulation per capita. 5.0

State & local financial support for higher education, FY 2006
Full-time equivalent enrollment (x 1,000) 144.0
Appropriations per FTE. $5,822

Social Insurance & Welfare Programs

Social Security benefits & beneficiaries, 2005
Beneficiaries (x 1,000) 774
  Retired & dependents. 505
  Survivors. 104
  Disabled & dependents. 164
Annual benefit payments ($ mil) $8,100
  Retired & dependents. $5,139
  Survivors. $1,283
  Disabled & dependents. $1,677
Average monthly benefit
  Retired & dependents. $982
  Disabled & dependents. $932
  Widowed. $904

Medicare, July 2005
Enrollment (x 1,000) 651
Payments ($ mil) $4,541

Medicaid, 2004
Beneficiaries (x 1,000). 857
Payments ($ mil) $4,015

State Children's Health Insurance Program, 2006
Enrollment (x 1,000). 68.9
Expenditures ($ mil) $62.6

Persons without health insurance, 2006
Number (x 1,000). 672
  percent. 15.9%
Number of children (x 1,000) 112
  percent of children 10.7%

Health care expenditures, 2004
Total expenditures. $21,450
  per capita $5,114

Federal and state public aid

State unemployment insurance, 2006
Recipients, first payments (x 1,000) 112
Total payments ($ mil) $326
Average weekly benefit $223
Temporary Assistance for Needy Families, 2006
Recipients (x 1,000)..................... 432.5
Families (x 1,000) 190.2
Supplemental Security Income, 2005
Recipients (x 1,000)..................... 105.3
Payments ($ mil) $488.2
Food Stamp Program, 2006
Avg monthly participants (x 1,000) 534.3
Total benefits ($ mil).................... $589.4

Housing & Construction

Housing units
Total 2005 (estimate) 1,927,864
Total 2006 (estimate) 1,975,638
Seasonal or recreational use, 2006....... 93,096
Owner-occupied, 2006............... 1,165,464
    Median home value............... $122,400
    Homeowner vacancy rate............... 2.4%
Renter-occupied, 2006 491,514
    Median rent $640
    Rental vacancy rate.................. 10.6%
Home ownership rate, 2005............. 73.9%
Home ownership rate, 2006............. 74.2%

New privately-owned housing units
Number authorized, 2006 (x 1,000)........ 50.8
Value ($ mil)....................... $7,592.1
Started 2005 (x 1,000, estimate) 33.4
Started 2006 (x 1,000, estimate) 32.3

Existing home sales
2005 (x 1,000).......................... 114.6
2006 (x 1,000).......................... 115.2

Government & Elections

State officials 2008
Governor....................... Mark Sanford
        Republican, term expires 1/11
Lieutenant Governor.......... R. André Bauer
Secretary of State............. Mark Hammond
Attorney General............. Henry McMaster
Chief Justice .... Jean Hoefer Toal

Governorship
Minimum age............................ 30
Length of term .... 4 years
Consecutive terms permitted 2
Who succeeds........... Lieutenant Governor

Local governments by type, 2002
Total.................................... 701
    County................................. 46
    Municipal 269
    Township 0
    School District.......................... 85
    Special District 301

State legislature
Name .... General Assembly
Upper chamber .... Senate
    Number of members.................... 46
    Length of term..................... 4 years
    Party in majority, 2008 .... Republican
Lower chamber........ House of Representatives
    Number of members................... 124
    Length of term..................... 2 years
    Party in majority, 2008 .... Republican

Federal representation, 2008 (110th Congress)
Senator.................... Lindsay Graham
    Party .... Republican
    Year term expires 2009
Senator........................... Jim DeMint
    Party .... Republican
    Year term expires 2011
Representatives, total 6
    Democrats............................. 2
    Republicans 4

Voters in November 2006 election (estimate)
Total.............................. 1,375,545
    Male........................... 604,681
    Female.......................... 770,864
    White 935,354
    Black 419,066
    Hispanic 2,388
    Asian 1,638

Presidential election, 2004
Total Popular Vote 1,617,730
    Kerry 661,699
    Bush........................... 937,974
Total Electoral Votes........................ 8

Votes cast for US Senators
2004
Total vote (x 1,000) 1,597
Leading party..................... Republican
Percent for leading party 53.7%
2006
Total vote (x 1,000) .... NA
Leading party....................... NA
Percent for leading party .... NA

Votes cast for US Representatives
2004
Total vote (x 1,000) 1,439
    Democratic........................... 486
    Republican 913
Leading party..................... Republican
Percent for leading party 63.5%
2006
Total vote (x 1,000) 1,086
    Democratic........................... 473
    Republican 600
Leading party..................... Republican
Percent for leading party 55.2%

South Carolina 5

State government employment, 2006
Full-time equivalent employees 76,468
Payroll ($ mil) $245.8

Local government employment, 2006
Full-time equivalent employees 172,498
Payroll ($ mil) $517.3

Women holding public office, 2008
US Congress 0
Statewide elected office.................. 0
State legislature 15

Black public officials, 2002
Total.................................... 547
  US and state legislatures 32
  City/county/regional offices 345
  Judicial/law enforcement................. 12
  Education/school boards............... 158

Hispanic public officials, 2006
Total..................................... 1
  State executives & legislators 1
  City/county/regional offices 0
  Judicial/law enforcement.................. 0
  Education/school boards.................. 0

Governmental Finance

State government revenues, 2006
Total revenue (x $1,000)........... $23,719,970
  per capita $5,477.92
General revenue (x $1,000) $19,435,908
  Intergovernmental 6,867,415
  Taxes 7,759,797
    general sales.................... 3,186,306
    individual income tax 2,727,251
    corporate income tax 296,753
  Current charges.................. 3,305,309
  Miscellaneous 1,503,387

State government expenditure, 2006
Total expenditure (x $1,000) $23,430,743
  per capita $5,411.12
General expenditure (x $1,000) $19,785,364
  per capita, total.................. $4,569.25
    Education 1,633.33
    Public welfare 1,116.46
    Health 198.06
    Hospitals........................ 280.93
    Highways 345.87
    Police protection................. 45.08
    Corrections 101.76
    Natural resources 47.53
    Parks & recreation 21.13
    Governmental administration...... 214.85
    Interest on general debt.......... 120.30

State debt & cash, 2006 ($ per capita)
Debt $3,172.47
Cash/security holdings.............. $8,956.94

Federal government grants to state & local government, 2005 (x $1,000)
Total............................... $6,323,699
by Federal agency
  Defense 61,136
  Education 543,606
  Energy 33,300
  Environmental Protection Agency 48,379
  Health & Human Services. 3,810,768
  Homeland Security................. 43,945
  Housing & Urban Development...... 337,899
  Justice 105,121
  Labor 126,872
  Transportation 675,414
  Veterans Affairs 5,569

Crime & Law Enforcement

Crime, 2006 (rates per 100,000 residents)
Property crimes 183,322
  Burglary 42,772
  Larceny 124,148
  Motor vehicle theft 16,402
  Property crime rate............... 4,242.3
Violent crimes....................... 33,078
  Murder 359
  Forcible rape..................... 1,762
  Robbery.......................... 5,899
  Aggravated assault 25,058
  Violent crime rate 765.5
Hate crimes........................... 128

Fraud and identity theft, 2006
Fraud complaints...................... 4,841
  rate per 100,000 residents 112.0
Identity theft complaints 2,408
  rate per 100,000 residents 55.7

Law enforcement agencies, 2006
Total agencies........................ 365
Total employees...................... 14,332
  Officers 10,597
  Civilians 3,735

Prisoners, probation, and parole, 2006
Total prisoners....................... 23,616
  percent change, 12/31/05 to 12/31/06 .... 2.0%
  in private facilities 0.1%
  in local jails 1.6%
Sentenced to more than one year 22,861
  rate per 100,000 residents 525
Adults on probation 38,353
Adults on parole...................... 2,735

Prisoner demographics, June 30, 2005 (rate per 100,000 residents)
Male.................................. 1,558
Female 137
White 415
Black................................. 1,856
Hispanic 476

Arrests, 2006
Total.....................................187,578
   Persons under 18 years of age.........23,565

Persons under sentence of death, 1/1/07
Total...67
   White.....................................29
   Black.....................................38
   Hispanic...................................0

State's highest court
Name.........................Supreme Court
Number of members............................5
Length of term.........................10 years
Intermediate appeals court?.................yes

Labor & Income

Civilian labor force, 2006 (x 1,000)
Total......................................2,124
   Men....................................1,115
   Women.................................1,009
   Persons 16-19 years......................101
   White..................................1,492
   Black....................................592
   Hispanic..................................82

Civilian labor force as a percent of civilian non-institutional population, 2006
Total......................................64.2%
   Men.....................................71.3
   Women..................................57.9
   Persons 16-19 years.....................44.2
   White...................................63.9
   Black...................................65.7
   Hispanic................................72.2

Employment, 2006 (x 1,000)
Total......................................1,987
   Men....................................1,043
   Women...................................944
   Persons 16-19 years.......................78
   White..................................1,417
   Black....................................532
   Hispanic..................................78

Unemployment rate, 2006
Total.......................................6.5%
   Men......................................6.5
   Women....................................6.5
   Persons 16-19 years.....................22.7
   White....................................5.0
   Black...................................10.2
   Hispanic.................................5.5

Full-time/part-time labor force, 2003 (x 1,000)
Full-time labor force, employed..........1,566
Part-time labor force, employed............300
Unemployed, looking for
   Full-time work..........................112
   Part-time work...........................24
Mean duration of unemployment (weeks)......19.4
   Median..................................10.6

Labor unions, 2006
Membership (x 1,000)........................59
   percent of employed......................3.3%

Experienced civilian labor force by private industry, 2006
Total....................................1,534,903
   Natural resources & mining............14,111
   Construction.........................126,275
   Manufacturing........................253,811
   Trade, transportation & utilities.....368,720
   Information...........................27,631
   Finance...............................97,552
   Professional & business..............214,788
   Education & health...................170,190
   Leisure & hospitality................209,467
   Other.................................48,908

Experienced civilian labor force by occupation, May 2006
Management................................84,000
Business & financial.......................55,470
Legal......................................11,420
Sales.....................................196,950
Office & admin. support..................288,670
Computers & math..........................24,280
Architecture & engineering................35,960
Arts & entertainment......................15,210
Education.................................108,030
Social services...........................21,260
Health care practitioner & technical......91,210
Health care support.......................43,310
Maintenance & repair......................87,930
Construction..............................97,300
Transportation & moving..................145,750
Production...............................202,980
Farming, fishing & forestry...............4,720

Hours and earnings of production workers on manufacturing payrolls, 2006
Average weekly hours.......................41.0
Average hourly earnings..................$15.03
Average weekly earnings.................$616.23

Income and poverty, 2006
Median household income..................$41,100
Personal income, per capita (current $)...$29,515
   in constant (2000) dollars...........$25,765
Persons below poverty level...............15.7%

Average annual pay
2006....................................$34,281
   increase from 2005.......................4.1%

Federal individual income tax returns, 2005
Returns filed..........................1,885,351
Adjusted gross income ($1,000).....$84,321,938
Total tax liability ($1,000)..........$9,567,240

Charitable contributions, 2004
Number of contributions...................533.0
Total amount ($ mil).....................$2,360.2

Economy, Business, Industry & Agriculture

Fortune 500 companies, 2007 1
Bankruptcy cases filed, FY 2007 7,139

Patents and trademarks issued, 2007
Patents 588
Trademarks 552

Business firm ownership, 2002
Women-owned 76,831
   Sales ($ mil) $10,891
Black-owned 28,613
   Sales ($ mil) $1,597
Hispanic-owned 3,015
   Sales ($ mil) $691
Asian-owned 4,414
   Sales ($ mil) $2,061
Amer. Indian/Alaska Native-owned 1,445
   Sales ($ mil) $157
Hawaiian/Pacific Islander-owned 41
   Sales ($ mil) $10

Gross domestic product, 2006 ($ mil)
Total gross domestic product $149,214
   Agriculture, forestry, fishing and
      hunting 1,152
   Mining 242
   Utilities 4,086
   Construction 9,146
   Manufacturing, durable goods 14,693
   Manufacturing, non-durable goods 11,561
   Wholesale trade 9,056
   Retail trade 11,996
   Transportation & warehousing 3,596
   Information 4,098
   Finance & insurance 7,431
   Real estate, rental & leasing 16,901
   Professional and technical services 6,624
   Educational services 786
   Health care and social assistance 8,663
   Accommodation/food services 5,025
   Other services, except government 3,436
   Government 23,357

Establishments, payroll, employees & receipts, by major industry group, 2005
Total 103,416
   Annual payroll ($1,000) $49,450,267
   Paid employees 1,584,914
Forestry, fishing & agriculture 608
   Annual payroll ($1,000) $174,973
   Paid employees 4,971
Mining 79
   Annual payroll ($1,000) $55,707
   Paid employees 1,266
   Receipts, 2002 ($1,000) $266,806

Utilities 302
   Annual payroll ($1,000) $664,361
   Paid employees 11,279
   Receipts, 2002 ($1,000) . . . . .NA
Construction 12,285
   Annual payroll ($1,000) $3,594,290
   Paid employees 108,276
   Receipts, 2002 ($1,000) $15,285,860
Manufacturing 4,289
   Annual payroll ($1,000) $10,958,564
   Paid employees 271,326
   Receipts, 2002 ($1,000) $81,132,781
Wholesale trade 4,795
   Annual payroll ($1,000) $2,822,820
   Paid employees 63,718
   Receipts, 2002 ($1,000) $32,988,974
Retail trade 18,590
   Annual payroll ($1,000) $4,511,411
   Paid employees 220,737
   Receipts, 2002 ($1,000) $40,629,089
Transportation & warehousing 2,688
   Annual payroll ($1,000) $1,693,198
   Paid employees 51,146
   Receipts, 2002 ($1,000) $4,296,475
Information 1,354
   Annual payroll ($1,000) $1,276,632
   Paid employees 29,044
   Receipts, 2002 ($1,000) . . . . .NA
Finance & insurance 6,827
   Annual payroll ($1,000) $2,784,533
   Paid employees 65,591
   Receipts, 2002 ($1,000) . . . . .NA
Professional, scientific & technical 9,140
   Annual payroll ($1,000) $3,778,332
   Paid employees 76,896
   Receipts, 2002 ($1,000) $7,494,425
Education 917
   Annual payroll ($1,000) $505,894
   Paid employees 24,797
   Receipts, 2002 ($1,000) $144,059
Health care & social assistance 8,908
   Annual payroll ($1,000) $6,935,358
   Paid employees 196,457
   Receipts, 2002 ($1,000) $14,823,456
Arts and entertainment 1,512
   Annual payroll ($1,000) $356,010
   Paid employees 22,115
   Receipts, 2002 ($1,000) $1,114,283
Real estate 4,918
   Annual payroll ($1,000) $874,069
   Paid employees 27,204
   Receipts, 2002 ($1,000) $3,138,683
Accommodation & food service 8,913
   Annual payroll ($1,000) $2,150,063
   Paid employees 173,653
   Receipts, 2002 ($1,000) $6,104,316

8   South Carolina

Exports, 2006
Value of exported goods ($ mil) $13,615
    Manufactured $11,889
    Non-manufactured. $495

Foreign direct investment in US affiliates, 2004
Property, plants & equipment ($ mil) . . . $21,844
Employment (x 1,000). 121.7

Agriculture, 2006
Number of farms 24,600
Farm acreage (x 1,000) 4,850
    Acres per farm 197
Farm marketings and income ($ mil)
Total. $1,890.7
    Crops $788.1
    Livestock. $1,102.6
Net farm income $722.2

Principal commodities, in order by marketing receipts, 2005
    Broilers, Greenhouse/nursery, Turkeys, Cattle
        and calves, Cotton

Federal economic activity in state
Expenditures, 2005 ($ mil)
    Total. $32,044
        Per capita $7,545.10
    Defense $5,105
    Non-defense. $26,939
Defense department, 2006 ($ mil)
    Payroll. $3,431
    Contract awards $2,197
    Grants $45
Homeland security grants ($1,000)
    2006. . . . .$14,679
    2007 . . . .$11,001

FDIC-insured financial institutions, 2005
Number 95
Assets ($ billion) $45.5
Deposits ($ billion) $35.1

Fishing, 2006
Catch (x 1,000 lbs). 11,112
Value ($1,000). $24,088

Mining, 2006 ($ mil)
Total non-fuel mineral production $730
Percent of U.S. 1.13%

Communication, Energy & Transportation

Communication
Households with computers, 2003. . . . . 54.9%
Households with internet access, 2003 . . . . 45.6%
High-speed internet providers 42
Total high-speed internet lines. 1,041,762
    Residential 673,468
    Business. 368,294
Wireless phone customers, 12/2006 3,208,504

FCC-licensed stations (as of January 1, 2008)
TV stations 34
FM radio stations. 145
AM radio stations 101

Energy
Energy consumption, 2004
    Total (trillion Btu). 1,718
    Per capita (million Btu) 409.4
By source of production (trillion Btu)
    Coal 434
    Natural gas 164
    Petroleum. 595
    Nuclear electric power 534
    Hydroelectric power. 25
By end-use sector (trillion Btu)
    Residential 354
    Commercial 252
    Industrial 663
    Transportation 449
Electric energy, 2005
    Primary source of electricity. . . . . Nuclear
    Net generation (billion kWh) 102.5
        percent from renewable sources. 4.6%
    Net summer capability (million kW) 22.6
    CO_2 emitted from generation 40.9
Natural gas utilities, 2005
    Customers (x 1,000) 600
    Sales (trillion Btu). 128
    Revenues ($ mil) $1,302
Nuclear plants, 2007 7
Total CO_2 emitted (million metric tons). 79.2
Energy spending, 2004 ($ mil) $13,397
    per capita $3,194
    Price per million Btu $12.53

Transportation, 2006
Public road & street mileage 66,242
    Urban. 16,444
    Rural 49,798
    Interstate. 843
Vehicle miles of travel (millions) 50,199
    per capita 11,593.0
Total motor vehicle registrations. 3,453,843
    Automobiles. .1,964,994
    Trucks 1,470,771
    Motorcycles 87,769
Licensed drivers 3,067,747
    19 years & under 216,125
Deaths from motor vehicle accidents 1,037
Gasoline consumed (x 1,000 gallons) 2,556,418
    per capita 590.4

Commuting Statistics, 2006
Average commute time (min) 22.9
    Drove to work alone 81.1%
    Carpooled. 11.3%
    Public transit 0.6%
    Walk to work 1.8%
    Work from home. 3.4%

South Dakota   1

State Summary

Capital city . . . . Pierre
Governor . . . . Michael Rounds

500 East Capitol St
Pierre, SD 57501
605-773-3212

Admitted as a state 1889
Area (square miles) 77,117
Population, 2007 (estimate). 796,214
Largest city . . . . Sioux Falls
  Population, 2006 142,396
Personal income per capita, 2006
  (in current dollars) $33,929
Gross domestic product, 2006 ($ mil) $32,330

Leading industries by payroll, 2005

  Health care/Social assistance, Manufacturing,
Retail trade

**Leading agricultural commodities
by receipts, 2005**

  Cattle and calves, Corn, Soybeans, Hogs, Wheat

Geography & Environment

Total area (square miles). 77,117
  land 75,885
  water 1,232
Federally-owned land, 2004 (acres) 3,028,003
  percent. 6.2%
Highest point . . . . Harney Peak
  elevation (feet) 7,242
Lowest point . . . . Big Stone Lake
  elevation (feet) 966
General coastline (miles) 0
Tidal shoreline (miles) 0
Cropland, 2003 (x 1,000 acres) 17,087
Forest land, 2003 (x 1,000 acres). 503
Capital city . . . . Pierre
  Population 2000 .13,876
  Population 2006 14,095
Largest city . . . . Sioux Falls
  Population 2000 123,975
  Population 2006 142,396

Number of cities with over 100,000 population

1990 0
2000 1
2006 1

State park and recreation areas, 2005

Area (x 1,000 acres) 103
Number of visitors (x 1,000) 7,399
Revenues ($1,000) $9,951
  percent of operating expenditures 77.4%

National forest system land, 2007

Acres 2,016,889

Demographics & Population Characteristics

Population

1980 690,768
1990 696,004
2000 754,840
2006 781,919
  Male. 390,578
  Female 391,341
Living in group quarters, 2006 29,816
  percent of total. 3.8%
2007 (estimate) 796,214
  persons per square mile of land 10.5
2008 (projected). 780,947
2010 (projected) 786,399
2020 (projected) 801,939
2030 (projected) 800,462

**Population of Core-Based Statistical Areas
(formerly Metropolitan Areas), x 1,000**

	CBSA	Non-CBSA
1990	469	227
2000	527	228
2006	560	222

Change in population, 2000-2007

Number 41,370
  percent 5.5%
Natural increase (births minus deaths) 31,062
Net internal migration 2,516
Net international migration 4,461

Persons by age, 2006

Under 5 years 54,828
5 to 17 years 139,853
18 years and over 587,238
65 years and over 111,183
85 years and over 19,075
  Median age 36.9

Persons by age, 2010 (projected)

Under 5 years 54,618
18 and over 592,247
65 and over 114,459
  Median age 37.5

Race, 2006

One Race
  White. 691,100
  Black or African American 7,389
  Asian 5,808
  American Indian/Alaska Native. 66,665
  Hawaiian Native/Pacific Islander. 381
Two or more races. .10,576

Persons of Hispanic origin, 2006

Total Hispanic or Latino 15,544
  Mexican. 9,444
  Puerto Rican 1,152
  Cuban 205

Persons of Asian origin, 2006

Total Asian	7,064
Asian Indian	742
Chinese	1,187
Filipino	978
Japanese	583
Korean	856
Vietnamese	1,883

Marital status, 2006

Population 15 years & over	621,618
Never married	173,914
Married	349,648
Separated	5,983
Widowed	40,118
Divorced	57,938

Language spoken at home, 2006

Population 5 years and older	728,218
English only	680,816
Spanish	14,403
French	699
German	11,841
Chinese	1,152

Households & families, 2006

Households	312,477
with persons under 18 years	98,546
with persons over 65 years	74,690
persons per household	2.41
Families	205,964
persons per family	2.97
Married couples	166,211
Female householder, no husband present	27,788
One-person households	88,494

Nativity, 2006

Number of residents born in state	509,909
percent of population	65.2%

Immigration & naturalization, 2006

Legal permanent residents admitted	1,013
Persons naturalized	342
Non-immigrant admissions	10,120

Vital Statistics and Health

Marriages

2004	6,485
2005	6,551
2006	6,272

Divorces

2004	2,364
2005	2,159
2006	2,502

Health risks, 2006

Percent of adults who are:

Smokers	20.3%
Overweight (BMI > 25)	64.1%
Obese (BMI > 30)	25.4%

Births

2005	11,462
Birthrate (per 1,000)	14.8
White	9,267
Black	145
Hispanic	392
Asian/Pacific Islander	111
Amer. Indian/Alaska Native	1,939
Low birth weight (2,500g or less)	6.6%
Cesarian births	25.1%
Preterm births	11.5%
To unmarried mothers	36.2%
Twin births (per 1,000)	28.9
Triplets or higher order (per 100,000)	91.6
2006 (preliminary)	11,917
rate per 1,000	15.2

Deaths

2004

All causes	6,833
rate per 100,000	746.4
Heart disease	1,783
rate per 100,000	187.1
Malignant neoplasms	1,555
rate per 100,000	176.8
Cerebrovascular disease	469
rate per 100,000	48.1
Chronic lower respiratory disease	391
rate per 100,000	42.7
Diabetes	229
rate per 100,000	25.2
2005 (preliminary)	7,087
rate per 100,000	757.0
2006 (provisional)	7,043

Infant deaths

2004	93
rate per 1,000	8.2
2005 (provisional)	75
rate per 1,000	6.5

Exercise routines, 2005

None	22.5%
Moderate or greater	47.6%
Vigorous	23.5%

Abortions, 2004

Total performed in state	814
rate per 1,000 women age 15-44	5
% obtained by out-of-state residents	17.7%

Physicians, 2005

Total	1,698
rate per 100,000 persons	219

Community hospitals, 2005

Number of hospitals	52
Beds (x 1,000)	4.3
Patients admitted (x 1,000)	102
Average daily census (x 1,000)	2.8
Average cost per day	$733
Outpatient visits (x 1 mil)	1.6

Disability status of population, 2006
5 to 15 years 5.5%
16 to 64 years 10.3%
65 years and over 38.1%

Education

Educational attainment, 2006
Population over 25 years 505,237
   Less than 9th grade..................... 5.5%
   High school graduate or more 88.3%
   College graduate or more............. 24.8%
   Graduate or professional degree........ 7.2%

Public school enrollment, 2005-06
Total............................... 122,012
   Pre-kindergarten through grade 8..... 83,530
   Grades 9 through 12 38,482

Graduating public high school seniors, 2004-05
Diplomas (incl. GED and others) 8,585

SAT scores, 2007
Average critical reading score.............. 589
Average writing score 567
Average math score 602
Percent of graduates taking test 3%

Public school teachers, 2006-07 (estimate)
Total (x 1,000) 9.0
   Elementary............................ 6.3
   Secondary............................. 2.7
Average salary $35,378
   Elementary....................... $35,473
   Secondary........................ $35,156

State receipts & expenditures for public schools, 2006-07 (estimate)
Revenue receipts ($ mil) $1,144
Expenditures
Total ($ mil) $1,121
   Per capita $1,267
   Per pupil $8,741

NAEP proficiency scores, 2007

	Reading		Math	
	Basic	Proficient	Basic	Proficient
Grade 4	70.9%	33.7%	86.1%	40.6%
Grade 8	83.5%	36.8%	81.2%	39.1%

Higher education enrollment, fall 2005
Total................................. 11,220
   Full-time men 2,564
   Full-time women.................... 4,283
   Part-time men 1,559
   Part-time women..................... 2,814

Minority enrollment in institutions of higher education, 2005
Black, non-Hispanic 642
Hispanic 518
Asian/Pacific Islander 592
American Indian/Alaska Native........... 3,196

Institutions of higher education, 2005-06
Total.................................... 24
   Public................................ 12
   Private............................... 12

Earned degrees conferred, 2004-05
Associate's........................... 2,225
Bachelor's 4,771
Master's 1,217
First-professional........................ 210
Doctor's 89

Public Libraries, 2006
Number of libraries...................... 124
Number of outlets 152
Annual visits per capita 6.2
Circulation per capita..................... 9.1

State & local financial support for higher education, FY 2006
Full-time equivalent enrollment (x 1,000)..... 29.3
Appropriations per FTE................ $4,499

Social Insurance & Welfare Programs

Social Security benefits & beneficiaries, 2005
Beneficiaries (x 1,000) 142
   Retired & dependents................. 103
   Survivors............................. 21
   Disabled & dependents.................. 19
Annual benefit payments ($ mil) $1,415
   Retired & dependents................. $966
   Survivors............................ $269
   Disabled & dependents................. $180
Average monthly benefit
   Retired & dependents................. $920
   Disabled & dependents................ $877
   Widowed............................ $916

Medicare, July 2005
Enrollment (x 1,000).................... 125
Payments ($ mil) $687

Medicaid, 2004
Beneficiaries (x 1,000)................... 128
Payments ($ mil) $580

State Children's Health Insurance Program, 2006
Enrollment (x 1,000).................... 14.6
Expenditures ($ mil)................... $14.0

Persons without health insurance, 2006
Number (x 1,000)........................ 91
   percent............................ 11.8%
Number of children (x 1,000) 18
   percent of children 9.3%

Health care expenditures, 2004
Total expenditures.................... $4,103
   per capita $5,327

Federal and state public aid

State unemployment insurance, 2006
Recipients, first payments (x 1,000) 8
Total payments ($ mil) $22
Average weekly benefit $219
Temporary Assistance for Needy Families, 2006
Recipients (x 1,000) 73.6
Families (x 1,000) 34.2
Supplemental Security Income, 2005
Recipients (x 1,000) 12.6
Payments ($ mil) $54.7
Food Stamp Program, 2006
Avg monthly participants (x 1,000) 58.5
Total benefits ($ mil) $66.2

Housing & Construction

Housing units

Total 2005 (estimate) 347,952
Total 2006 (estimate) 352,813
Seasonal or recreational use, 2006 12,362
Owner-occupied, 2006 216,212
   Median home value $112,600
   Homeowner vacancy rate 2.0%
Renter-occupied, 2006 96,265
   Median rent $522
   Rental vacancy rate 8.3%
Home ownership rate, 2005 . . . . 68.4%
Home ownership rate, 2006 . . . . 70.6%

New privately-owned housing units

Number authorized, 2006 (x 1,000) 5.3
   Value ($ mil) $658.8
Started 2005 (x 1,000, estimate) 4.9
Started 2006 (x 1,000, estimate) 4.8

Existing home sales

2005 (x 1,000) 18.3
2006 (x 1,000) 18.3

Government & Elections

State officials 2008

Governor . . . . .Michael Rounds
          Republican, term expires 1/11
Lieutenant Governor . . . . Dennis Daugaard
Secretary of State . . . . .Chris Nelson
Attorney General . . . . Larry Long
Chief Justice . . . . .David Gilbertson

Governorship

Minimum age 18
Length of term . . . . 4 years
Consecutive terms permitted 2
Who succeeds . . . . Lieutenant Governor

Local governments by type, 2002

Total 1,866
   County 66
   Municipal 308
   Township 940
   School District 176
   Special District 376

State legislature

Name . . . . Legislature
Upper chamber . . . . .Senate
   Number of members 35
   Length of term . . . . 2 years
   Party in majority, 2008 . . . . Republican
Lower chamber . . . . .House of Representatives
   Number of members 70
   Length of term . . . . 2 years
   Party in majority, 2008 . . . . Republican

Federal representation, 2008 (110th Congress)

Senator . . . . .Tim Johnson
   Party . . . . .Democratic
   Year term expires 2009
Senator . . . . .John Thune
   Party . . . . Republican
   Year term expires 2011
Representatives, total 1
   Democrats 1
   Republicans 0

Voters in November 2006 election (estimate)

Total 358,388
   Male 166,916
   Female 191,472
   White 345,890
   Black 404
   Hispanic 1,753
   Asian . . . . NA

Presidential election, 2004

Total Popular Vote 388,215
   Kerry 149,244
   Bush 232,584
Total Electoral Votes 3

Votes cast for US Senators

2004
Total vote (x 1,000) 391
Leading party . . . . Republican
Percent for leading party 50.6%
2006
Total vote (x 1,000) . . . . NA
Leading party . . . . NA
Percent for leading party . . . . NA

Votes cast for US Representatives

2004
Total vote (x 1,000) 389
   Democratic 208
   Republican 179
Leading party .Democratic
Percent for leading party 53.4%
2006
Total vote (x 1,000) 334
   Democratic 230
   Republican 98
Leading party .Democratic
Percent for leading party 69.1%

State government employment, 2006
Full-time equivalent employees 13,905
Payroll ($ mil) $44.2

Local government employment, 2006
Full-time equivalent employees 31,281
Payroll ($ mil) $90.5

Women holding public office, 2008
US Congress 1
Statewide elected office.................... 0
State legislature 18

Black public officials, 2002
Total..................................... 0
  US and state legislatures 0
  City/county/regional offices 0
  Judicial/law enforcement.................. 0
  Education/school boards.................. 0

Hispanic public officials, 2006
Total..................................... 0
  State executives & legislators 0
  City/county/regional offices 0
  Judicial/law enforcement................. 0
  Education/school boards.................. 0

Governmental Finance

State government revenues, 2006
Total revenue (x $1,000)............$4,175,073
  per capita $5,295.18
General revenue (x $1,000) $3,212,568
  Intergovernmental 1,251,314
  Taxes 1,182,027
    general sales......................679,162
    individual income tax 0
    corporate income tax 61,865
  Current charges.................... 245,597
  Miscellaneous 533,630

State government expenditure, 2006
Total expenditure (x $1,000) $3,465,272
  per capita $4,394.95
General expenditure (x $1,000) $3,175,403
  per capita, total................... $4,027.31
    Education.......................1,226.77
    Public welfare 949.03
    Health 127.18
    Hospitals.........................67.10
    Highways 639.18
    Police protection....................38.81
    Corrections 135.83
    Natural resources 151.90
    Parks & recreation 33.77
    Governmental administration...... 192.66
    Interest on general debt............143.98

State debt & cash, 2006 ($ per capita)
Debt $3,990.10
Cash/security holdings.............$14,560.47

Federal government grants to state & local government, 2005 (x $1,000)
Total.............................$1,741,877
by Federal agency
  Defense 26,964
  Education 173,836
  Energy............................ 4,040
  Environmental Protection Agency 28,481
  Health & Human Services. 664,026
  Homeland Security...................7,501
  Housing & Urban Development.......114,485
  Justice 33,087
  Labor 27,542
  Transportation 292,855
  Veterans Affairs....................3,704

Crime & Law Enforcement

Crime, 2006 (rates per 100,000 residents)
Property crimes 12,664
  Burglary 2,650
  Larceny 9,296
  Motor vehicle theft 718
  Property crime rate................. 1,619.6
Violent crimes........................ 1,340
  Murder 9
  Forcible rape....................... 336
  Robbery........................... 119
  Aggravated assault 876
  Violent crime rate 171.4
Hate crimes............................ 79

Fraud and identity theft, 2006
Fraud complaints........................ 618
  rate per 100,000 residents 79.0
Identity theft complaints 236
  rate per 100,000 residents 30.2

Law enforcement agencies, 2006
Total agencies......................... 141
Total employees 2,070
  Officers 1,231
  Civilians 839

Prisoners, probation, and parole, 2006
Total prisoners.........................3,359
  percent change, 12/31/05 to 12/31/06 .... -3.0%
  in private facilities 0.4%
  in local jails 1.8%
Sentenced to more than one year 3,350
  rate per 100,000 residents 426
Adults on probation 5,661
Adults on parole........................2,767

Prisoner demographics, June 30, 2005 (rate per 100,000 residents)
Male...................................1,092
Female 157
White.................................. 470
Black..................................4,710
Hispanic .... NA

6   South Dakota

Arrests, 2006
Total 13,677
    Persons under 18 years of age 2,214

Persons under sentence of death, 1/1/07
Total 4
    White 4
    Black 0
    Hispanic 0

State's highest court
Name .... Supreme Court
Number of members 5
Length of term .... 8 years
Intermediate appeals court? .... no

Labor & Income

Civilian labor force, 2006 (x 1,000)
Total 434
    Men 229
    Women 206
    Persons 16-19 years 28
    White 408
    Black .... NA
    Hispanic 9

Civilian labor force as a percent of civilian non-institutional population, 2006
Total 72.5%
    Men 78.2
    Women 67.1
    Persons 16-19 years 63.2
    White 73.2
    Black .... NA
    Hispanic 72.6

Employment, 2006 (x 1,000)
Total 421
    Men 222
    Women 199
    Persons 16-19 years 25
    White 398
    Black .... NA
    Hispanic 8

Unemployment rate, 2006
Total 3.1%
    Men 2.9
    Women 3.3
    Persons 16-19 years 8.9
    White 2.4
    Black .... NA
    Hispanic 6.7

Full-time/part-time labor force, 2003 (x 1,000)
Full-time labor force, employed 332
Part-time labor force, employed 77
Unemployed, looking for
    Full-time work 13
    Part-time work 3
Mean duration of unemployment (weeks) 15.1
    Median 7.3

Labor unions, 2006
Membership (x 1,000) 21
    percent of employed 5.9%

Experienced civilian labor force by private industry, 2006
Total 314,784
    Natural resources & mining 4,099
    Construction 21,833
    Manufacturing 41,395
    Trade, transportation & utilities 79,334
    Information 6,953
    Finance 29,158
    Professional & business 25,633
    Education & health 53,601
    Leisure & hospitality 42,467
    Other 10,312

Experienced civilian labor force by occupation, May 2006
Management 11,430
Business & financial 14,020
Legal 1,580
Sales 41,370
Office & admin. support 66,640
Computers & math 5,290
Architecture & engineering 4,340
Arts & entertainment 4,920
Education 22,030
Social services 4,940
Health care practitioner & technical 23,310
Health care support 10,500
Maintenance & repair 15,290
Construction 21,260
Transportation & moving 28,750
Production 30,130
Farming, fishing & forestry 1,450

Hours and earnings of production workers on manufacturing payrolls, 2006
Average weekly hours 42.1
Average hourly earnings $13.75
Average weekly earnings $578.88

Income and poverty, 2006
Median household income $42,791
Personal income, per capita (current $) ... $33,929
    in constant (2000) dollars $29,618
Persons below poverty level 13.6%

Average annual pay
2006 .... $30,291
    increase from 2005 .... 3.9%

Federal individual income tax returns, 2005
Returns filed 367,105
Adjusted gross income ($1,000) $16,165,957
Total tax liability ($1,000) $2,032,903

Charitable contributions, 2004
Number of contributions 55.5
Total amount ($ mil) $262.7

Economy, Business, Industry & Agriculture

Fortune 500 companies, 2007 0

Bankruptcy cases filed, FY 2007 1,302

Patents and trademarks issued, 2007

Patents 72

Trademarks 175

Business firm ownership, 2002

Women-owned 15,573

    Sales ($ mil) $1,547

Black-owned 122

    Sales ($ mil) $61

Hispanic-owned 355

    Sales ($ mil) $122

Asian-owned 300

    Sales ($ mil) $88

Amer. Indian/Alaska Native-owned 1,304

    Sales ($ mil) $137

Hawaiian/Pacific Islander-owned 13

    Sales ($ mil) . . . . NA

Gross domestic product, 2006 ($ mil)

Total gross domestic product $32,330

    Agriculture, forestry, fishing and

        hunting 1,947

    Mining 119

    Utilities 582

    Construction 1,371

    Manufacturing, durable goods 2,509

    Manufacturing, non-durable goods 866

    Wholesale trade 1,817

    Retail trade 2,317

    Transportation & warehousing 894

    Information 887

    Finance & insurance 5,544

    Real estate, rental & leasing 2,811

    Professional and technical services 830

    Educational services 239

    Health care and social assistance 2,817

    Accommodation/food services 843

    Other services, except government 734

    Government 4,156

Establishments, payroll, employees & receipts, by major industry group, 2005

Total 25,205

    Annual payroll ($1,000) $8,860,458

    Paid employees 310,802

Forestry, fishing & agriculture 137

    Annual payroll ($1,000) . . . . NA

    Paid employees . . . . NA

Mining 63

    Annual payroll ($1,000) . . . . NA

    Paid employees . . . . NA

    Receipts, 2002 ($1,000) $206,689

Utilities 155

    Annual payroll ($1,000) $108,961

    Paid employees 2,018

    Receipts, 2002 ($1,000) . . . . .NA

Construction 3,251

    Annual payroll ($1,000) $628,966

    Paid employees .17,683

    Receipts, 2002 ($1,000) $2,643,417

Manufacturing 964

    Annual payroll ($1,000) $1,313,973

    Paid employees 39,397

    Receipts, 2002 ($1,000) $10,710,187

Wholesale trade 1,278

    Annual payroll ($1,000) $520,909

    Paid employees .14,318

    Receipts, 2002 ($1,000) $7,845,096

Retail trade 4,282

    Annual payroll ($1,000) $982,171

    Paid employees 49,526

    Receipts, 2002 ($1,000) $9,601,175

Transportation & warehousing 1,055

    Annual payroll ($1,000) $242,009

    Paid employees .8,110

    Receipts, 2002 ($1,000) $904,994

Information 422

    Annual payroll ($1,000) $240,919

    Paid employees 6,868

    Receipts, 2002 ($1,000) . . . . .NA

Finance & insurance 1,843

    Annual payroll ($1,000) $907,331

    Paid employees 23,964

    Receipts, 2002 ($1,000) . . . . .NA

Professional, scientific & technical 1,703

    Annual payroll ($1,000) $331,875

    Paid employees .9,716

    Receipts, 2002 ($1,000) $934,637

Education 201

    Annual payroll ($1,000) $149,156

    Paid employees .8,024

    Receipts, 2002 ($1,000) $15,790

Health care & social assistance 2,172

    Annual payroll ($1,000) $1,947,125

    Paid employees 55,631

    Receipts, 2002 ($1,000) $3,467,289

Arts and entertainment 643

    Annual payroll ($1,000) $96,698

    Paid employees 6,245

    Receipts, 2002 ($1,000) $361,537

Real estate 892

    Annual payroll ($1,000) $92,243

    Paid employees .4,057

    Receipts, 2002 ($1,000) $377,363

Accommodation & food service 2,285

    Annual payroll ($1,000) $383,876

    Paid employees 34,689

    Receipts, 2002 ($1,000) $1,226,459

Exports, 2006
Value of exported goods ($ mil) $1,185
   Manufactured $1,088
   Non-manufactured.................... $67

Foreign direct investment in US affiliates, 2004
Property, plants & equipment ($ mil) $750
Employment (x 1,000)....................5.5

Agriculture, 2006
Number of farms 31,300
Farm acreage (x 1,000) 43,700
   Acres per farm.......................1,396
Farm marketings and income ($ mil)
Total................................$4,716.2
   Crops............................$2,064.6
   Livestock.........................$2,651.6
Net farm income $741.5

Principal commodities, in order by
   marketing receipts, 2005
  Cattle and calves, Corn, Soybeans, Hogs, Wheat

Federal economic activity in state
Expenditures, 2005 ($ mil)
  Total...............................$7,481
    Per capita $9,654.69
  Defense $777
  Non-defense........................ $6,704
Defense department, 2006 ($ mil)
  Payroll............................. $358
  Contract awards $372
  Grants $21
Homeland security grants ($1,000)
  2006...............................$7,734
  2007............................... $6,682

FDIC-insured financial institutions, 2005
Number.............................. 89
Assets ($ billion) $499.0
Deposits ($ billion) $352.5

Fishing, 2006
Catch (x 1,000 lbs)...................... NA
Value ($1,000)......................... NA

Mining, 2006 ($ mil)
Total non-fuel mineral production $204
Percent of U.S. 0.32%

Communication, Energy & Transportation

Communication
Households with computers, 2003........ 62.1%
Households with internet access, 2003 .... 53.6%
High-speed internet providers 42
Total high-speed internet lines......... 154,738
  Residential 137,156
  Business...........................17,582
Wireless phone customers, 12/2006 547,812

FCC-licensed stations (as of January 1, 2008)
TV stations 26
FM radio stations......................... 79
AM radio stations 36

Energy
Energy consumption, 2004
  Total (trillion Btu)..................... 264
  Per capita (million Btu) 342.3
By source of production (trillion Btu)
  Coal 44
  Natural gas............................ 43
  Petroleum............................ 115
  Nuclear electric power 0
  Hydroelectric power.................... 36
By end-use sector (trillion Btu)
  Residential 61
  Commercial 53
  Industrial 63
  Transportation 87
Electric energy, 2005
  Primary source of electricity.... Hydroelectric
  Net generation (billion kWh) 6.5
    percent from renewable sources...... 49.6%
  Net summer capability (million kW) 2.8
  CO_2 emitted from generation 3.3
Natural gas utilities, 2005
  Customers (x 1,000) 179
  Sales (trillion Btu)...................... 34
  Revenues ($ mil) $253
Nuclear plants, 2007 0
Total CO_2 emitted (million metric tons)......13.7
Energy spending, 2004 ($ mil) $2,317
  per capita $3,008
  Price per million Btu $12.54

Transportation, 2006
Public road & street mileage 84,229
  Urban............................. 2,828
  Rural 81,401
  Interstate............................ 679
Vehicle miles of travel (millions) 9,168
  per capita 11,627.6
Total motor vehicle registrations........ 843,984
  Automobiles.......................375,760
  Trucks 465,580
  Motorcycles 53,477
Licensed drivers 582,517
  19 years & under 47,517
Deaths from motor vehicle accidents 191
Gasoline consumed (x 1,000 gallons) 428,785
  per capita 543.8

Commuting Statistics, 2006
Average commute time (min) 15.9
  Drove to work alone 77.5%
  Carpooled........................... 9.6%
  Public transit 0.4%
  Walk to work 4.3%
  Work from home..................... 6.6%

State Summary

Capital city . . . . Nashville
Governor . . . . Phil Bredesen

Tennessee State Capitol
Nashville, TN 37243
615-741-2001

Admitted as a state 1796
Area (square miles) 42,143
Population, 2007 (estimate). 6,156,719
Largest city . . . . Memphis
    Population, 2006 670,902
Personal income per capita, 2006
    (in current dollars) $32,304
Gross domestic product, 2006 ($ mil) . . . $238,029

Leading industries by payroll, 2005

Manufacturing, Health care/Social assistance,
Retail trade

Leading agricultural commodities by receipts, 2005

Cattle and calves, Broilers, Cotton, Greenhouse/
nursery, Soybeans

Geography & Environment

Total area (square miles) 42,143
    land 41,217
    water 926
Federally-owned land, 2004 (acres) 865,837
    percent 3.2%
Highest point . . . . Clingmans Dome
    elevation (feet) 6,643
Lowest point . . . . Mississippi River
    elevation (feet) 178
General coastline (miles) 0
Tidal shoreline (miles) 0
Cropland, 2003 (x 1,000 acres) 4,750
Forest land, 2003 (x 1,000 acres). 11,959
Capital city . . . . Nashville
    Population 2000 545,524
    Population 2006 552,120
Largest city . . . . Memphis
    Population 2000 650,100
    Population 2006 670,902

Number of cities with over 100,000 population

1990 4
2000 5
2006 5

State park and recreation areas, 2005

Area (x 1,000 acres) 141
Number of visitors (x 1,000) 29,038
Revenues ($1,000) $34,865
    percent of operating expenditures 50.8%

National forest system land, 2007

Acres 707,387

Demographics & Population Characteristics

Population

1980 4,591,120
1990 4,877,185
2000 5,689,262
2006 6,038,803
    Male 2,950,890
    Female 3,087,913
Living in group quarters, 2006 152,407
    percent of total 2.5%
2007 (estimate) 6,156,719
    persons per square mile of land 149.4
2008 (projected) .6,124,341
2010 (projected) .6,230,852
2020 (projected) .6,780,670
2030 (projected) .7,380,634

Population of Core-Based Statistical Areas (formerly Metropolitan Areas), x 1,000

	CBSA	Non-CBSA
1990	4,350	527
2000	5,080	610
2006	5,412	627

Change in population, 2000-2007

Number 467,457
    percent 8.2%
Natural increase (births minus deaths) 168,757
Net internal migration 217,129
Net international migration 60,929

Persons by age, 2006

Under 5 years 398,252
5 to 17 years 1,044,341
18 years and over .4,596,210
65 years and over 769,222
85 years and over 97,712
    Median age 37.1

Persons by age, 2010 (projected)

Under 5 years 412,075
18 and over 4,751,937
65 and over 829,023
    Median age 37.9

Race, 2006

One Race
    White 4,855,937
    Black or African American 1,019,528
    Asian 79,665
    American Indian/Alaska Native. 18,733
    Hawaiian Native/Pacific Islander. 3,078
Two or more races 61,862

Persons of Hispanic origin, 2006

Total Hispanic or Latino 187,747
    Mexican. 126,694
    Puerto Rican 12,923
    Cuban 3,155

Persons of Asian origin, 2006

Total Asian 76,208
   Asian Indian......................17,070
   Chinese 16,270
   Filipino 5,911
   Japanese 3,655
   Korean...........................9,462
   Vietnamese.......................7,854

Marital status, 2006

Population 15 years & over 4,846,989
   Never married 1,293,537
   Married......................... 2,607,959
   Separated 116,088
   Widowed......................... 336,451
   Divorced 609,042

Language spoken at home, 2006

Population 5 years and older........ 5,639,797
   English only 5,330,469
   Spanish 171,646
   French 13,389
   German.......................... 15,994
   Chinese 13,448

Households & families, 2006

Households........................2,375,123
   with persons under 18 years 807,349
   with persons over 65 years.......... 543,746
   persons per household 2.48
Families..........................1,597,016
   persons per family.......................3.03
Married couples.................... 1,178,105
Female householder,
   no husband present..................311,624
One-person households 659,600

Nativity, 2006

Number of residents born in state 3,781,851
   percent of population 62.6%

Immigration & naturalization, 2006

Legal permanent residents admitted..... 10,042
Persons naturalized 3,334
Non-immigrant admissions 127,584

Vital Statistics and Health

Marriages

2004 67,104
2005 65,426
2006 64,028

Divorces

2004 28,858
2005 27,823
2006 25,886

Health risks, 2006

Percent of adults who are:
   Smokers.........................22.6%
   Overweight (BMI > 25)..............65.3%
   Obese (BMI > 30).....................28.8%

Births

2005 81,747
   Birthrate (per 1,000)...................13.7
   White.............................61,409
   Black 18,484
   Hispanic 7,000
   Asian/Pacific Islander 1,697
   Amer. Indian/Alaska Native ... 157
   Low birth weight (2,500g or less)....... 9.5%
   Cesarian births 31.1%
   Preterm births 14.7%
   To unmarried mothers............... 40.2%
   Twin births (per 1,000) 31.1
   Triplets or higher order (per 100,000)....153.2
2006 (preliminary)................... 84,345
   rate per 1,000 ....14.0

Deaths

2004
All causes 55,829
   rate per 100,000 .... 954.0
Heart disease 15,038
   rate per 100,000 ....259.1
Malignant neoplasms 12,586
   rate per 100,000 .... 208.6
Cerebrovascular disease................ 3,680
   rate per 100,000 ....64.7
Chronic lower respiratory disease 2,987
   rate per 100,000 ....50.9
Diabetes..............................1,882
   rate per 100,000 ....31.6
2005 (preliminary)....................57,270
   rate per 100,000 ....959.9
2006 (provisional) 56,687

Infant deaths

2004 687
   rate per 1,000 ....8.6
2005 (provisional) 737
   rate per 1,000 ....9.0

Exercise routines, 2005

None.................................. 33.1%
Moderate or greater................... 36.1%
Vigorous 17.4%

Abortions, 2004

Total performed in state................ 16,400
   rate per 1,000 women age 15-44........... 13
   % obtained by out-of-state residents 21.1%

Physicians, 2005

Total................................. 15,683
   rate per 100,000 persons 263

Community hospitals, 2005

Number of hospitals 130
Beds (x 1,000)............................20.6
Patients admitted (x 1,000) 829
Average daily census (x 1,000) 13.1
Average cost per day $1,234
Outpatient visits (x 1 mil) 11.7

Disability status of population, 2006
5 to 15 years 7.0%
16 to 64 years 16.4%
65 years and over 46.0%

Education

Educational attainment, 2006
Population over 25 years 4,037,826
  Less than 9th grade. 7.6%
  High school graduate or more 80.9%
  College graduate or more. 21.7%
  Graduate or professional degree. 7.5%

Public school enrollment, 2005-06
Total 953,928
  Pre-kindergarten through grade 8. . . . 662,219
  Grades 9 through 12 277,352

Graduating public high school seniors, 2004-05
Diplomas (incl. GED and others) 51,165

SAT scores, 2007
Average critical reading score 574
Average writing score 568
Average math score 569
Percent of graduates taking test 13%

Public school teachers, 2006-07 (estimate)
Total (x 1,000) 61.8
  Elementary 43.3
  Secondary 18.5
Average salary $43,816
  Elementary $43,238
  Secondary $44,679

State receipts & expenditures for public schools, 2006-07 (estimate)
Revenue receipts ($ mil) $7,422
Expenditures
Total ($ mil) $7,329
  Per capita $1,142
  Per pupil $7,773

NAEP proficiency scores, 2007

	Reading		Math	
	Basic	Proficient	Basic	Proficient
Grade 4	60.6%	26.9%	76.1%	28.7%
Grade 8	71.3%	25.6%	63.9%	23.1%

Higher education enrollment, fall 2005
Total 82,676
  Full-time men 29,954
  Full-time women 39,693
  Part-time men 4,929
  Part-time women 8,100

Minority enrollment in institutions of higher education, 2005
Black, non-Hispanic 55,288
Hispanic 5,142
Asian/Pacific Islander 5,277
American Indian/Alaska Native. 1,192

Institutions of higher education, 2005-06
Total 98
  Public. 22
  Private 76

Earned degrees conferred, 2004-05
Associate's. 9,707
Bachelor's 26,032
Master's 8,530
First-professional. 1,402
Doctor's 891

Public Libraries, 2006
Number of libraries. 186
Number of outlets 294
Annual visits per capita 3.2
Circulation per capita. 4.1

State & local financial support for higher education, FY 2006
Full-time equivalent enrollment (x 1,000) 170.4
Appropriations per FTE. $6,275

Social Insurance & Welfare Programs

Social Security benefits & beneficiaries, 2005
Beneficiaries (x 1,000) 1,098
  Retired & dependents. 708
  Survivors. 159
  Disabled & dependents. 231
Annual benefit payments ($ mil) $11,406
  Retired & dependents. $7,109
  Survivors. $2,010
  Disabled & dependents. $2,288
Average monthly benefit
  Retired & dependents. $978
  Disabled & dependents. $904
  Widowed. $923

Medicare, July 2005
Enrollment (x 1,000) 922
Payments ($ mil) $6,028

Medicaid, 2004
Beneficiaries (x 1,000). 1,730
Payments ($ mil) $6,945

State Children's Health Insurance Program, 2006
Enrollment (x 1,000) 0.0
Expenditures ($ mil) $0.0

Persons without health insurance, 2006
Number (x 1,000). 809
  percent. 13.7%
Number of children (x 1,000) 94
  percent of children 6.4%

Health care expenditures, 2004
Total expenditures. $32,161
  per capita $5,464

4   Tennessee

Federal and state public aid

State unemployment insurance, 2006
Recipients, first payments (x 1,000) 143
Total payments ($ mil) $408
Average weekly benefit $216
Temporary Assistance for Needy Families, 2006
Recipients (x 1,000) 2,115.4
Families (x 1,000) 803.6
Supplemental Security Income, 2005
Recipients (x 1,000) 161.1
Payments ($ mil) $752.1
Food Stamp Program, 2006
Avg monthly participants (x 1,000) 870.4
Total benefits ($ mil) $976.0

Housing & Construction

Housing units
Total 2005 (estimate) 2,637,092
Total 2006 (estimate) 2,681,150
Seasonal or recreational use, 2006 53,185
Owner-occupied, 2006 1,660,152
   Median home value $123,100
   Homeowner vacancy rate 1.8%
Renter-occupied, 2006 714,971
   Median rent $613
   Rental vacancy rate 10.5%
Home ownership rate, 2005 . . . . 72.4%
Home ownership rate, 2006 . . . . 71.3%

New privately-owned housing units
Number authorized, 2006 (x 1,000) 46.0
   Value ($ mil) $6,781.7
Started 2005 (x 1,000, estimate) 34.2
Started 2006 (x 1,000, estimate) 34.3

Existing home sales
2005 (x 1,000) 170.9
2006 (x 1,000) 173.6

Government & Elections

State officials 2008
Governor . . . . Phil Bredesen
   Democratic, term expires 1/11
Lieutenant Governor . . . . Ron Ramsey
Secretary of State . . . . Riley Darnell
Attorney General . . . . Robert Cooper Jr
Chief Justice . . . . Mickey Barker

Governorship
Minimum age 30
Length of term . . . . 4 years
Consecutive terms permitted 2
Who succeeds . . . . Speaker of Senate

Local governments by type, 2002
Total 930
   County 92
   Municipal 349
   Township 0
   School District 14
   Special District 475

State legislature
Name . . . . General Assembly
Upper chamber . . . . Senate
   Number of members 33
   Length of term . . . . 4 years
   Party in majority, 2008 . . . . Republican
Lower chamber . . . . House of Representatives
   Number of members 99
   Length of term . . . . 2 years
   Party in majority, 2008 . . . . Democratic

Federal representation, 2008 (110th Congress)
Senator . . . . Lamar Alexander
   Party . . . . Republican
   Year term expires 2009
Senator . . . . Bob Corker
   Party . . . . Republican
   Year term expires 2013
Representatives, total 9
   Democrats 5
   Republicans 4

Voters in November 2006 election (estimate)
Total 2,003,441
   Male 927,249
   Female 1,076,192
   White 1,723,048
   Black 268,473
   Hispanic . . . . NA
   Asian 2,975

Presidential election, 2004
Total Popular Vote 2,437,319
   Kerry 1,036,477
   Bush 1,384,375
Total Electoral Votes 11

Votes cast for US Senators
2004
Total vote (x 1,000) . . . . NA
Leading party . . . . NA
Percent for leading party . . . . NA
2006
Total vote (x 1,000) 1,834
Leading party . . . . Republican
Percent for leading party 50.7%

Votes cast for US Representatives
2004
Total vote (x 1,000) 2,219
   Democratic 1,032
   Republican 1,161
Leading party . . . . Republican
Percent for leading party 52.3%
2006
Total vote (x 1,000) 1,715
   Democratic 861
   Republican 800
Leading party . . . . Democratic
Percent for leading party 50.2%

Tennessee 5

State government employment, 2006
Full-time equivalent employees 83,117
Payroll ($ mil) $269.4

Local government employment, 2006
Full-time equivalent employees 240,556
Payroll ($ mil) $731.5

Women holding public office, 2008
US Congress 1
Statewide elected office. 0
State legislature 22

Black public officials, 2002
Total. 195
  US and state legislatures 18
  City/county/regional offices 118
  Judicial/law enforcement. 28
  Education/school boards 31

Hispanic public officials, 2006
Total. 2
  State executives & legislators 1
  City/county/regional offices 1
  Judicial/law enforcement. 0
  Education/school boards 0

Governmental Finance

State government revenues, 2006
Total revenue (x $1,000). $26,315,890
  per capita $4,331.90
General revenue (x $1,000) $23,644,213
  Intergovernmental 8,202,128
  Taxes 10,650,350
    general sales. 6,451,838
    individual income tax 192,764
    corporate income tax 928,349
  Current charges. 1,793,514
  Miscellaneous 2,998,221

State government expenditure, 2006
Total expenditure (x $1,000) $23,967,779
  per capita $3,945.37
General expenditure (x $1,000) $22,412,778
  per capita, total. $3,689.40
    Education. 1,208.08
    Public welfare 1,335.62
    Health 187.69
    Hospitals. 68.54
    Highways 306.58
    Police protection. 24.66
    Corrections 112.06
    Natural resources 40.32
    Parks & recreation 22.89
    Governmental administration 114.94
    Interest on general debt 31.97

State debt & cash, 2006 ($ per capita)
Debt $629.03
Cash/security holdings. $5,631.55

Federal government grants to state & local government, 2005 (x $1,000)
Total. $9,985,336
by Federal agency
  Defense 37,458
  Education 678,739
  Energy. 27,564
  Environmental Protection Agency 44,316
  Health & Human Services. 6,814,522
  Homeland Security. 37,723
  Housing & Urban Development. 515,507
  Justice 102,005
  Labor 124,103
  Transportation 734,789
  Veterans Affairs. 24,635

Crime & Law Enforcement

Crime, 2006 (rates per 100,000 residents)
Property crimes 249,297
  Burglary 62,859
  Larceny 163,845
  Motor vehicle theft 22,593
  Property crime rate. 4,128.3
Violent crimes. 45,907
  Murder 409
  Forcible rape. 2,142
  Robbery. 11,129
  Aggravated assault 32,227
  Violent crime rate 760.2
Hate crimes. 241

Fraud and identity theft, 2006
Fraud complaints. .6,871
  rate per 100,000 residents 113.8
Identity theft complaints 3,700
  rate per 100,000 residents 61.3

Law enforcement agencies, 2006
Total agencies. 450
Total employees 24,121
  Officers 14,984
  Civilians 9,137

Prisoners, probation, and parole, 2006
Total prisoners. 25,745
  percent change, 12/31/05 to 12/31/06 . . . -2.4%
  in private facilities 19.9%
  in local jails 25.1%
Sentenced to more than one year 25,745
  rate per 100,000 residents 423
Adults on probation 52,558
Adults on parole. .9,702

Prisoner demographics, June 30, 2005 (rate per 100,000 residents)
Male. 1,339
Female 151
White. 487
Black. 2,006
Hispanic 561

Arrests, 2006
Total................................. 285,475
  Persons under 18 years of age 35,228

Persons under sentence of death, 1/1/07
Total.................................. 107
  White................................ 59
  Black 43
  Hispanic 1

State's highest court
Name ....Supreme Court
Number of members....................... 5
Length of term...................... 8 years
Intermediate appeals court? ....yes

Labor & Income

Civilian labor force, 2006 (x 1,000)
Total.................................3,028
  Men 1,640
  Women 1,388
  Persons 16-19 years.................... 157
  White............................. 2,483
  Black 460
  Hispanic 127

Civilian labor force as a percent of civilian non-institutional population, 2006
Total.................................64.4%
  Men 72.5
  Women 56.9
  Persons 16-19 years...................46.0
  White.............................. 64.3
  Black 63.5
  Hispanic 82.5

Employment, 2006 (x 1,000)
Total................................. 2,872
  Men 1,557
  Women 1,315
  Persons 16-19 years................... 137
  White............................. 2,377
  Black 415
  Hispanic 123

Unemployment rate, 2006
Total.................................5.2%
  Men 5.1
  Women 5.3
  Persons 16-19 years...................12.7
  White..............................4.3
  Black 10.0
  Hispanic 3.5

Full-time/part-time labor force, 2003 (x 1,000)
Full-time labor force, employed 2,312
Part-time labor force, employed............ 429
Unemployed, looking for
  Full-time work........................ 142
  Part-time work........................ 27
Mean duration of unemployment (weeks)......18.6
  Median 9.0

Labor unions, 2006
Membership (x 1,000)................... 153
  percent of employed 6.0%

Experienced civilian labor force by private industry, 2006
Total.................................2,325,551
  Natural resources & mining 10,195
  Construction 130,251
  Manufacturing..................... 399,213
  Trade, transportation & utilities 603,477
  Information 49,085
  Finance 142,411
  Professional & business 320,065
  Education & health 328,328
  Leisure & hospitality............... 270,190
  Other............................ 70,464

Experienced civilian labor force by occupation, May 2006
Management........................ 153,090
Business & financial 81,520
Legal...............................11,930
Sales............................. 263,490
Office & admin. support............. 461,040
Computers & math 38,100
Architecture & engineering.............35,010
Arts & entertainment 27,300
Education 141,680
Social services 29,420
Health care practitioner & technical.... 155,570
Health care support 65,620
Maintenance & repair.................119,330
Construction 114,000
Transportation & moving 263,560
Production 322,630
Farming, fishing & forestry.............4,120

Hours and earnings of production workers on manufacturing payrolls, 2006
Average weekly hours 39.4
Average hourly earnings $14.04
Average weekly earnings $553.18

Income and poverty, 2006
Median household income............. $40,315
Personal income, per capita (current $)... $32,304
  in constant (2000) dollars $28,199
Persons below poverty level............. 16.2%

Average annual pay
2006 .... $37,564
  increase from 2005 .... 4.7%

Federal individual income tax returns, 2005
Returns filed.......................2,657,790
Adjusted gross income ($1,000) $123,251,823
Total tax liability ($1,000) $15,663,355

Charitable contributions, 2004
Number of contributions 563.7
Total amount ($ mil).................$3,027.3

Economy, Business, Industry & Agriculture

Fortune 500 companies, 2007 9
Bankruptcy cases filed, FY 2007 37,779

Patents and trademarks issued, 2007
Patents 807
Trademarks 1,049

Business firm ownership, 2002
Women-owned 117,935
　Sales ($ mil) $17,641
Black-owned 26,811
　Sales ($ mil) $1,755
Hispanic-owned 4,301
　Sales ($ mil) $1,004
Asian-owned 7,241
　Sales ($ mil) $2,183
Amer. Indian/Alaska Native-owned 3,567
　Sales ($ mil) $619
Hawaiian/Pacific Islander-owned 94
　Sales ($ mil) $21

Gross domestic product, 2006 ($ mil)
Total gross domestic product $238,029
　Agriculture, forestry, fishing and
　　hunting 1,392
　Mining 503
　Utilities 994
　Construction 10,465
　Manufacturing, durable goods 26,205
　Manufacturing, non-durable goods 16,178
　Wholesale trade 16,246
　Retail trade 19,852
　Transportation & warehousing 11,854
　Information 7,520
　Finance & insurance 12,938
　Real estate, rental & leasing 24,796
　Professional and technical services 12,285
　Educational services 2,410
　Health care and social assistance 20,836
　Accommodation/food services 7,480
　Other services, except government 6,084
　Government 25,131

Establishments, payroll, employees & receipts, by major industry group, 2005
Total 133,098
　Annual payroll ($1,000) $80,959,818
　Paid employees 2,378,754
Forestry, fishing & agriculture 281
　Annual payroll ($1,000) $38,712
　Paid employees 1,345
Mining 217
　Annual payroll ($1,000) $120,558
　Paid employees .2,768
　Receipts, 2002 ($1,000) $684,682

Utilities 163
　Annual payroll ($1,000) $156,536
　Paid employees .3,183
　Receipts, 2002 ($1,000) . . . . .NA
Construction 11,418
　Annual payroll ($1,000) $4,298,881
　Paid employees 112,611
　Receipts, 2002 ($1,000) $19,761,128
Manufacturing 6,671
　Annual payroll ($1,000) $15,564,711
　Paid employees 396,245
　Receipts, 2002 ($1,000) $109,293,454
Wholesale trade 7,336
　Annual payroll ($1,000) $5,574,316
　Paid employees 116,259
　Receipts, 2002 ($1,000) $97,792,030
Retail trade 23,798
　Annual payroll ($1,000) $6,874,676
　Paid employees 320,100
　Receipts, 2002 ($1,000) $60,136,403
Transportation & warehousing 4,259
　Annual payroll ($1,000) $4,315,420
　Paid employees 121,632
　Receipts, 2002 ($1,000) $11,650,494
Information 2,574
　Annual payroll ($1,000) $2,356,578
　Paid employees 55,151
　Receipts, 2002 ($1,000) . . . . .NA
Finance & insurance 9,740
　Annual payroll ($1,000) $6,237,489
　Paid employees 116,540
　Receipts, 2002 ($1,000) . . . . .NA
Professional, scientific & technical 11,082
　Annual payroll ($1,000) $5,320,454
　Paid employees 110,585
　Receipts, 2002 ($1,000) $11,022,883
Education 1,086
　Annual payroll ($1,000) $1,204,322
　Paid employees 44,848
　Receipts, 2002 ($1,000) $407,836
Health care & social assistance 13,696
　Annual payroll ($1,000) $12,325,142
　Paid employees 332,418
　Receipts, 2002 ($1,000) $24,475,539
Arts and entertainment 2,257
　Annual payroll ($1,000) $951,157
　Paid employees 29,339
　Receipts, 2002 ($1,000) $2,117,808
Real estate 5,588
　Annual payroll ($1,000) $1,274,377
　Paid employees 37,642
　Receipts, 2002 ($1,000) $4,635,964
Accommodation & food service 10,892
　Annual payroll ($1,000) $2,724,314
　Paid employees 219,970
　Receipts, 2002 ($1,000) $8,024,900

Exports, 2006
Value of exported goods ($ mil) $22,020
   Manufactured $16,943
   Non-manufactured. $1,981

Foreign direct investment in US affiliates, 2004
Property, plants & equipment ($ mil) . . . $19,890
Employment (x 1,000). 126.9

Agriculture, 2006
Number of farms 82,000
Farm acreage (x 1,000) 11,400
   Acres per farm. 139
Farm marketings and income ($ mil)
Total. $2,564.9
   Crops. $1,373.3
   Livestock. $1,191.6
Net farm income $721.8

Principal commodities, in order by marketing receipts, 2005
Cattle and calves, Broilers, Cotton, Greenhouse/
nursery, Soybeans

Federal economic activity in state
Expenditures, 2005 ($ mil)
   Total. $48,288
      Per capita $8,107.72
   Defense $4,298
   Non-defense. $43,989
Defense department, 2006 ($ mil)
   Payroll. $1,520
   Contract awards $2,866
   Grants $56
Homeland security grants ($1,000)
   2006. . . . .$13,762
   2007. . . . . $20,045

FDIC-insured financial institutions, 2005
Number 201
Assets ($ billion) $88.6
Deposits ($ billion) $61.8

Fishing, 2006
Catch (x 1,000 lbs). . . . . NA
Value ($1,000). . . . . NA

Mining, 2006 ($ mil)
Total non-fuel mineral production $807
Percent of U.S. 1.25%

Communication, Energy & Transportation

Communication
Households with computers, 2003. . . . . 56.7%
Households with internet access, 2003 . . . . 48.9%
High-speed internet providers 58
Total high-speed internet lines. 1,573,992
   Residential 969,096
   Business. 604,896
Wireless phone customers, 12/2006 5,126,510

FCC-licensed stations (as of January 1, 2008)
TV stations 40
FM radio stations. 222
AM radio stations 187

Energy
Energy consumption, 2004
   Total (trillion Btu). 2,298
   Per capita (million Btu) 390.4
By source of production (trillion Btu)
   Coal 648
   Natural gas 239
   Petroleum. 800
   Nuclear electric power 298
   Hydroelectric power. 104
By end-use sector (trillion Btu)
   Residential 512
   Commercial 378
   Industrial 776
   Transportation 632
Electric energy, 2005
   Primary source of electricity. . . . . Coal
   Net generation (billion kWh) 97.1
      percent from renewable sources. 10.2%
   Net summer capability (million kW) 20.7
   CO_2 emitted from generation 59.9
Natural gas utilities, 2005
   Customers (x 1,000) 1,176
   Sales (trillion Btu). 222
   Revenues ($ mil) $1,923
Nuclear plants, 2007 3
Total CO_2 emitted (million metric tons). 120.1
Energy spending, 2004 ($ mil) $17,666
   per capita $3,001
   Price per million Btu $12.16

Transportation, 2006
Public road & street mileage 91,416
   Urban. 21,639
   Rural. 69,777
   Interstate. 1,104
Vehicle miles of travel (millions) 70,596
   per capita 11,620.9
Total motor vehicle registrations. 5,091,328
   Automobiles. 2,878,136
   Trucks 2,193,213
   Motorcycles 134,123
Licensed drivers. .4,387,883
   19 years & under 258,702
Deaths from motor vehicle accidents 1,287
Gasoline consumed (x 1,000 gallons) 3,128,807
   per capita 515.0

Commuting Statistics, 2006
Average commute time (min) 23.5
   Drove to work alone 83.3%
   Carpooled. 10.2%
   Public transit 0.7%
   Walk to work 1.4%
   Work from home. 3.2%

State Summary

Capital city . . . . Austin
Governor . . . . Rick Perry

PO Box 12428
Austin, TX 78711
512-463-2000

Admitted as a state 1845
Area (square miles) 268,581
Population, 2007 (estimate). 23,904,380
Largest city . . . . Houston
    Population, 2006 2,144,491
Personal income per capita, 2006
    (in current dollars) $34,257
Gross domestic product, 2006 ($ mil) . . $1,065,891

Leading industries by payroll, 2005

Manufacturing, Health care/Social assistance,
    Professional/Scientific/Technical

Leading agricultural commodities by receipts, 2005

Cattle and calves, Cotton, Greenhouse/nursery,
    Broilers, Dairy products

Geography & Environment

Total area (square miles). 268,581
    land 261,797
    water 6,784
Federally-owned land, 2004 (acres) 3,130,345
    percent. 1.9%
Highest point . . . . Gaudalupe Peak
    elevation (feet) 8,749
Lowest point . . . . Gulf of Mexico
    elevation (feet) . . . . sea level
General coastline (miles) 367
Tidal shoreline (miles) 3,359
Cropland, 2003 (x 1,000 acres) 25,562
Forest land, 2003 (x 1,000 acres). 10,613
Capital city . . . . Austin
    Population 2000 656,562
    Population 2006 709,893
Largest city . . . . Houston
    Population 2000 1,953,631
    Population 2006 2,144,491

Number of cities with over 100,000 population

1990 17
2000 24
2006 27

State park and recreation areas, 2005

Area (x 1,000 acres). 589
Number of visitors (x 1,000) 10,189
Revenues ($1,000) $33,955
    percent of operating expenditures. 60.5%

National forest system land, 2007

Acres 755,365

Demographics & Population Characteristics

Population

1980 14,229,191
1990 16,986,510
2000 20,851,792
2006 23,507,783
    Male. 11,714,068
    Female 11,793,715
Living in group quarters, 2006. 594,214
    percent of total. 2.5%
2007 (estimate). 23,904,380
    persons per square mile of land 91.3
2008 (projected). 23,898,665
2010 (projected). 24,648,888
2020 (projected). 28,634,896
2030 (projected). 33,317,744

Population of Core-Based Statistical Areas (formerly Metropolitan Areas), x 1,000

	CBSA	Non-CBSA
1990	15,723	1,264
2000	19,465	1,386
2006	22,090	1,418

Change in population, 2000-2007

Number 3,052,581
    percent 14.6%
Natural increase (births minus deaths) . . 1,635,015
Net internal migration 582,078
Net international migration 842,595

Persons by age, 2006

Under 5 years 1,925,197
5 to 17 years 4,568,768
18 years and over 17,013,818
65 years and over 2,334,459
85 years and over 302,646
    Median age 33.1

Persons by age, 2010 (projected)

Under 5 years 2,077,328
18 and over 17,863,480
65 and over 2,587,383
    Median age 33.4

Race, 2006

One Race
    White. 19,452,577
    Black or African American 2,804,949
    Asian 788,356
    American Indian/Alaska Native. 163,455
    Hawaiian Native/Pacific Islander. 26,903
Two or more races. 271,543

Persons of Hispanic origin, 2006

Total Hispanic or Latino 8,385,118
    Mexican. 7,024,667
    Puerto Rican 96,034
    Cuban 35,792

Persons of Asian origin, 2006

Total Asian 787,208
  Asian Indian. 194,908
  Chinese 136,377
  Filipino 95,436
  Japanese 18,581
  Korean. 60,078
  Vietnamese. 184,096

Marital status, 2006

Population 15 years & over 18,066,247
  Never married 5,332,034
  Married. 9,790,299
  Separated 526,317
  Widowed. 1,014,640
  Divorced 1,929,274

Language spoken at home, 2006

Population 5 years and older. 21,585,556
  English only 14,289,136
  Spanish 6,278,980
  French 59,435
  German 80,770
  Chinese 114,855

Households & families, 2006

Households. 8,109,388
  with persons under 18 years 3,239,101
  with persons over 65 years. 1,598,468
  persons per household 2.83
Families. 5,686,517
  persons per family. 3.41
Married couples. 4,173,567
Female householder,
  no husband present. 1,113,815
One-person households 2,015,666

Nativity, 2006

Number of residents born in state . . . 14,320,902
  percent of population. 60.9%

Immigration & naturalization, 2006

Legal permanent residents admitted. 89,037
Persons naturalized 37,835
Non-immigrant admissions 2,450,389

Vital Statistics and Health

Marriages

2004 178,512
2005 176,768
2006 174,989

Divorces

2004 81,324
2005 75,980
2006 78,072

Health risks, 2006

Percent of adults who are:
  Smokers. 17.9%
  Overweight (BMI > 25). 62.4%
  Obese (BMI > 30). 26.1%

Births

2005 385,915
  Birthrate (per 1,000). 16.9
  White. 327,298
  Black 44,076
  Hispanic 191,445
  Asian/Pacific Islander 13,645
  Amer. Indian/Alaska Native 896
  Low birth weight (2,500g or less). 8.3%
  Cesarian births 32.6%
  Preterm births 13.6%
  To unmarried mothers. 37.6%
  Twin births (per 1,000) 28.1
  Triplets or higher order (per 100,000). . . .143.4
2006 (preliminary). 399,612
  rate per 1,000 . . . . .17.0

Deaths

2004
All causes 152,870
  rate per 100,000 . . . . .835.6
Heart disease 40,196
  rate per 100,000. . . . . .227.0
Malignant neoplasms 33,937
  rate per 100,000. . . . . .182.2
Cerebrovascular disease. 9,853
  rate per 100,000. . . . . .56.9
Chronic lower respiratory disease 7,402
  rate per 100,000. . . . . .41.9
Diabetes. 5,435
  rate per 100,000. . . . . .29.7
2005 (preliminary). 156,474
  rate per 100,000. . . . . 828.8
2006 (provisional) 152,461

Infant deaths

2004 2,407
  rate per 1,000 . . . . .6.3
2005 (provisional) 2,480
  rate per 1,000 . . . . .6.4

Exercise routines, 2005

None. 27.4%
Moderate or greater. 46.7%
Vigorous 25.3%

Abortions, 2004

Total performed in state. 74,801
  rate per 1,000 women age 15-44. 15
  % obtained by out-of-state residents 3.3%

Physicians, 2005

Total. 48,776
  rate per 100,000 persons 213

Community hospitals, 2005

Number of hospitals 415
Beds (x 1,000). 58.2
Patients admitted (x 1,000) 2,509
Average daily census (x 1,000) 36.0
Average cost per day $1,636
Outpatient visits (x 1 mil) 32.3

Disability status of population, 2006

5 to 15 years 6.7%
16 to 64 years 12.1%
65 years and over 45.5%

Education

Educational attainment, 2006

Population over 25 years 14,551,694
    Less than 9th grade. 10.5%
    High school graduate or more 78.6%
    College graduate or more. 24.7%
    Graduate or professional degree. 8.0%

Public school enrollment, 2005-06

Total 4,525,394
    Pre-kindergarten through grade 8. . .3,268,339
    Grades 9 through 12 1,257,055

Graduating public high school seniors, 2004-05

Diplomas (incl. GED and others) 239,717

SAT scores, 2007

Average critical reading score 492
Average writing score 482
Average math score 507
Percent of graduates taking test 52%

Public school teachers, 2006-07 (estimate)

Total (x 1,000) 311.7
    Elementary 159.9
    Secondary 151.8
Average salary $44,897
    Elementary $44,462
    Secondary $45,356

State receipts & expenditures for public schools, 2006-07 (estimate)

Revenue receipts ($ mil) $44,267
Expenditures
Total ($ mil) $45,157
    Per capita $1,567
    Per pupil $8,573

NAEP proficiency scores, 2007

	Reading		Math	
	Basic	Proficient	Basic	Proficient
Grade 4	65.8%	29.6%	87.4%	40.2%
Grade 8	73.0%	27.5%	77.6%	34.7%

Higher education enrollment, fall 2005

Total 159,372
    Full-time men 53,730
    Full-time women 65,978
    Part-time men 18,075
    Part-time women 21,589

Minority enrollment in institutions of higher education, 2005

Black, non-Hispanic 153,416
Hispanic 324,803
Asian/Pacific Islander 62,688
American Indian/Alaska Native 6,401

Institutions of higher education, 2005-06

Total 213
    Public 109
    Private 104

Earned degrees conferred, 2004-05

Associate's 41,778
Bachelor's 88,757
Master's 32,391
First-professional. .5,398
Doctor's 2,974

Public Libraries, 2006

Number of libraries. 553
Number of outlets 863
Annual visits per capita 3.3
Circulation per capita 4.8

State & local financial support for higher education, FY 2006

Full-time equivalent enrollment (x 1,000) 820.8
Appropriations per FTE $6,276

Social Insurance & Welfare Programs

Social Security benefits & beneficiaries, 2005

Beneficiaries (x 1,000) 2,955
    Retired & dependents. 1,990
    Survivors. 475
    Disabled & dependents. 490
Annual benefit payments ($ mil) $30,684
    Retired & dependents. $19,643
    Survivors. $6,178
    Disabled & dependents. $4,864
Average monthly benefit
    Retired & dependents. $975
    Disabled & dependents. $924
    Widowed. $940

Medicare, July 2005

Enrollment (x 1,000) 2,545
Payments ($ mil) $20,020

Medicaid, 2004

Beneficiaries (x 1,000). 3,604
Payments ($ mil) $13,214

State Children's Health Insurance Program, 2006

Enrollment (x 1,000). 585.5
Expenditures ($ mil) $371.8

Persons without health insurance, 2006

Number (x 1,000) 5,704
    percent. 24.5%
Number of children (x 1,000) 1,392
    percent of children 21.2%

Health care expenditures, 2004

Total expenditures. $103,600
    per capita $4,601

Federal and state public aid

State unemployment insurance, 2006
Recipients, first payments (x 1,000) 297
Total payments ($ mil) $1,070
Average weekly benefit $271
Temporary Assistance for Needy Families, 2006
Recipients (x 1,000) 1,836.2
Families (x 1,000) 811.4
Supplemental Security Income, 2005
Recipients (x 1,000) 501.8
Payments ($ mil) $2,190.6
Food Stamp Program, 2006
Avg monthly participants (x 1,000) 2,622.5
Total benefits ($ mil) $2,939.3

Housing & Construction

Housing units
Total 2005 (estimate) 9,025,865
Total 2006 (estimate) 9,224,361
Seasonal or recreational use, 2006 193,708
Owner-occupied, 2006 5,291,045
 Median home value $114,000
 Homeowner vacancy rate 2.2%
Renter-occupied, 2006 2,818,343
 Median rent $711
 Rental vacancy rate 13.5%
Home ownership rate, 2005 . . . . 65.9%
Home ownership rate, 2006 . . . . 66.0%

New privately-owned housing units
Number authorized, 2006 (x 1,000) 216.6
Value ($ mil) $29,206.1
Started 2005 (x 1,000, estimate) 154.9
Started 2006 (x 1,000, estimate) 149.1

Existing home sales
2005 (x 1,000) 532.5
2006 (x 1,000) 578.6

Government & Elections

State officials 2008
Governor . . . . Rick Perry
    Republican, term expires 1/11
Lieutenant Governor . . . . David Dewhurst
Secretary of State . . . . Roger Williams
Attorney General . . . . Greg Abbott
Chief Justice . . . . Wallace Jefferson

Governorship
Minimum age 30
Length of term . . . . 4 years
Consecutive terms permitted . . . . . not specified
Who succeeds . . . . Lieutenant Governor

Local governments by type, 2002
Total 4,784
 County 254
 Municipal 1,196
 Township 0
 School District 1,089
 Special District 2,245

State legislature
Name . . . . Legislature
Upper chamber . . . . Senate
 Number of members 31
 Length of term . . . . 4 years
 Party in majority, 2008 . . . . Republican
Lower chamber . . . . House of Representatives
 Number of members 150
 Length of term . . . . 2 years
 Party in majority, 2008 . . . . Republican

Federal representation, 2008 (110th Congress)
Senator . . . . John Cornyn
 Party . . . . Republican
 Year term expires 2009
Senator . . . . Kay Bailey Hutchinson
 Party . . . . Republican
 Year term expires 2013
Representatives, total 32
 Democrats 13
 Republicans 19

Voters in November 2006 election (estimate)
Total 5,525,824
 Male 2,568,765
 Female 2,957,059
 White 4,711,085
 Black 654,982
 Hispanic 503,503
 Asian 76,928

Presidential election, 2004
Total Popular Vote 7,410,765
 Kerry 2,832,704
 Bush 4,526,917
Total Electoral Votes 34

Votes cast for US Senators
2004
Total vote (x 1,000) . . . . NA
Leading party . . . . NA
Percent for leading party . . . . NA
2006
Total vote (x 1,000) 4,315
Leading party . . . . Republican
Percent for leading party 61.7%

Votes cast for US Representatives
2004
Total vote (x 1,000) 6,959
 Democratic 2,714
 Republican 4,013
Leading party . . . . Republican
Percent for leading party 57.7%
2006
Total vote (x 1,000) 4,141
 Democratic 1,831
 Republican 2,094
Leading party . . . . Republican
Percent for leading party 50.9%

State government employment, 2006
Full-time equivalent employees 281,722
Payroll ($ mil) $1,008.2

Local government employment, 2006
Full-time equivalent employees 1,033,284
Payroll ($ mil) $3,184.4

Women holding public office, 2008
US Congress 4
Statewide elected office. 2
State legislature 35

Black public officials, 2002
Total. 466
US and state legislatures 19
City/county/regional offices 306
Judicial/law enforcement. 47
Education/school boards 94

Hispanic public officials, 2006
Total. 2,109
State executives & legislators 38
City/county/regional offices 851
Judicial/law enforcement. 413
Education/school boards 807

Governmental Finance

State government revenues, 2006
Total revenue (x $1,000) $103,964,436
per capita $4,441.48
General revenue (x $1,000) $83,471,066
Intergovernmental 28,708,710
Taxes 36,591,749
general sales 18,275,210
individual income tax 0
corporate income tax 0
Current charges. 8,614,238
Miscellaneous 9,556,369

State government expenditure, 2006
Total expenditure (x $1,000) $85,513,928
per capita $3,653.25
General expenditure (x $1,000) $75,895,975
per capita, total. *$3,242.36*
Education 1,344.37
Public welfare 888.04
Health 43.77
Hospitals. 106.27
Highways 335.41
Police protection. 24.34
Corrections 130.03
Natural resources 36.17
Parks & recreation 5.01
Governmental administration 61.99
Interest on general debt 43.53

State debt & cash, 2006 ($ per capita)
Debt $1,046.73
Cash/security holdings. $10,303.13

Federal government grants to state & local government, 2005 (x $1,000)
Total. $28,912,208
by Federal agency
Defense 131,561
Education 3,221,991
Energy 79,637
Environmental Protection Agency . . . 257,803
Health & Human Services. 15,901,213
Homeland Security 527,260
Housing & Urban Development 1,733,050
Justice 425,793
Labor 590,326
Transportation 2,989,307
Veterans Affairs. 32,452

Crime & Law Enforcement

Crime, 2006 (rates per 100,000 residents)
Property crimes 959,460
Burglary 215,647
Larceny 648,384
Motor vehicle theft 95,429
Property crime rate. 4,081.5
Violent crimes. 121,378
Murder 1,384
Forcible rape. .8,372
Robbery. 37,254
Aggravated assault 74,368
Violent crime rate 516.3
Hate crimes. 292

Fraud and identity theft, 2006
Fraud complaints. 25,425
rate per 100,000 residents 108.2
Identity theft complaints 26,006
rate per 100,000 residents 110.6

Law enforcement agencies, 2006
Total agencies 981
Total employees 81,462
Officers 49,470
Civilians 31,992

Prisoners, probation, and parole, 2006
Total prisoners 172,116
percent change, 12/31/05 to 12/31/06 . . . . 1.8%
in private facilities 10.8%
in local jails 8.8%
Sentenced to more than one year 162,193
rate per 100,000 residents 683
Adults on probation 431,967
Adults on parole. 100,053

Prisoner demographics, June 30, 2005 (rate per 100,000 residents)
Male 1,772
Female 186
White 667
Black. 3,162
Hispanic 830

Arrests, 2006
Total.................................1,078,961
  Persons under 18 years of age........ 169,460

Persons under sentence of death, 1/1/07
Total................................. 393
  White............................... 121
  Black 161
  Hispanic 107

State's highest court
Name ....Supreme Court
Number of members....................... 9
Length of term....................... 6 years
Intermediate appeals court? ....yes

Labor & Income

Civilian labor force, 2006 (x 1,000)
Total.................................11,465
  Men 6,390
  Women 5,075
  Persons 16-19 years.................... 552
  White..............................9,509
  Black 1,286
  Hispanic 3,909

Civilian labor force as a percent of civilian non-institutional population, 2006
Total.................................66.8%
  Men 76.4
  Women 57.7
  Persons 16-19 years....................40.6
  White...............................66.7
  Black 65.6
  Hispanic 66.9

Employment, 2006 (x 1,000)
Total.................................10,913
  Men 6,103
  Women 4,810
  Persons 16-19 years.................... 460
  White..............................9,116
  Black 1,149
  Hispanic 3,728

Unemployment rate, 2006
Total.................................4.8%
  Men 4.5
  Women 5.2
  Persons 16-19 years....................16.7
  White...............................4.1
  Black 10.7
  Hispanic 4.6

Full-time/part-time labor force, 2003 (x 1,000)
Full-time labor force, employed.......... 8,602
Part-time labor force, employed..........1,570
Unemployed, looking for
  Full-time work.......................... 624
  Part-time work.......................... 113
Mean duration of unemployment (weeks)...... 17.1
  Median 8.9

Labor unions, 2006
Membership (x 1,000)................... 476
  percent of employed 4.9%

Experienced civilian labor force by private industry, 2006
Total.............................8,241,727
  Natural resources & mining 247,356
  Construction 605,600
  Manufacturing..................... 926,610
  Trade, transportation & utilities 2,034,037
  Information 222,814
  Finance 619,559
  Professional & business 1,229,932
  Education & health 1,116,081
  Leisure & hospitality.............. 942,155
  Other 278,929

Experienced civilian labor force by occupation, May 2006
Management........................ 444,540
Business & financial 393,790
Legal...............................69,970
Sales...............................1,052,990
Office & admin. support............. 1,740,210
Computers & math 231,420
Architecture & engineering.......... 207,350
Arts & entertainment 97,710
Education 647,030
Social services 88,020
Health care practitioner & technical.... 463,810
Health care support 231,520
Maintenance & repair................ 428,020
Construction 513,910
Transportation & moving 697,490
Production 716,600
Farming, fishing & forestry..............17,650

Hours and earnings of production workers on manufacturing payrolls, 2006
Average weekly hours.....................40.9
Average hourly earnings $14.01
Average weekly earnings $573.01

Income and poverty, 2006
Median household income............. $44,922
Personal income, per capita (current $)... $34,257
  in constant (2000) dollars $29,904
Persons below poverty level.............. 16.9%

Average annual pay
2006 .... $42,458
  increase from 2005 .... 5.7%

Federal individual income tax returns, 2005
Returns filed........................ 9,727,703
Adjusted gross income ($1,000) ...$507,165,219
Total tax liability ($1,000) $71,420,283

Charitable contributions, 2004
Number of contributions.............. 1,991.6
Total amount ($ mil)................. $9,927.6

Economy, Business, Industry & Agriculture

Fortune 500 companies, 2007 56
Bankruptcy cases filed, FY 2007 42,487

Patents and trademarks issued, 2007
Patents 6,316
Trademarks 4,410

Business firm ownership, 2002
Women-owned 468,705
  Sales ($ mil) $65,817
Black-owned 88,768
  Sales ($ mil) $6,419
Hispanic-owned. 319,340
  Sales ($ mil) $42,214
Asian-owned 77,834
  Sales ($ mil) $20,728
Amer. Indian/Alaska Native-owned 16,863
  Sales ($ mil) $3,321
Hawaiian/Pacific Islander-owned 1,391
  Sales ($ mil) $78

Gross domestic product, 2006 ($ mil)
Total gross domestic product $1,065,891
  Agriculture, forestry, fishing and
    hunting 8,339
  Mining. 100,653
  Utilities 33,135
  Construction 57,804
  Manufacturing, durable goods. 72,498
  Manufacturing, non-durable goods 67,188
  Wholesale trade. 70,755
  Retail trade. 67,262
  Transportation & warehousing 34,728
  Information 42,490
  Finance & insurance. 58,714
  Real estate, rental & leasing 101,262
  Professional and technical services 68,038
  Educational services 5,689
  Health care and social assistance 61,484
  Accommodation/food services. 25,691
  Other services, except government 21,971
  Government 112,861

Establishments, payroll, employees & receipts, by major industry group, 2005

Total 497,758
  Annual payroll ($1,000). $315,809,126
  Paid employees 8,305,102
Forestry, fishing & agriculture 1,188
  Annual payroll ($1,000). $231,834
  Paid employees 8,020
Mining 6,343
  Annual payroll ($1,000). $9,071,718
  Paid employees 126,966
  Receipts, 2002 ($1,000) $50,406,285

Utilities 2,207
  Annual payroll ($1,000). $2,889,362
  Paid employees 41,610
  Receipts, 2002 ($1,000) . . . . .NA
Construction 39,632
  Annual payroll ($1,000). $19,869,823
  Paid employees 501,694
  Receipts, 2002 ($1,000) $94,067,369
Manufacturing 20,552
  Annual payroll ($1,000). $38,224,668
  Paid employees 816,221
  Receipts, 2002 ($1,000) $310,815,965
Wholesale trade 31,133
  Annual payroll ($1,000). $23,894,136
  Paid employees 450,206
  Receipts, 2002 ($1,000) $397,405,111
Retail trade 76,335
  Annual payroll ($1,000). $24,317,534
  Paid employees 1,080,932
  Receipts, 2002 ($1,000) $228,694,755
Transportation & warehousing 15,245
  Annual payroll ($1,000). $13,537,995
  Paid employees 336,526
  Receipts, 2002 ($1,000) $32,254,393
Information 9,486
  Annual payroll ($1,000). $14,311,499
  Paid employees 251,496
  Receipts, 2002 ($1,000) . . . . .NA
Finance & insurance 35,277
  Annual payroll ($1,000). $24,080,494
  Paid employees 441,384
  Receipts, 2002 ($1,000) . . . . .NA
Professional, scientific & technical 55,618
  Annual payroll ($1,000). $31,442,127
  Paid employees 519,075
  Receipts, 2002 ($1,000) $62,549,237
Education 4,878
  Annual payroll ($1,000). $3,678,489
  Paid employees 129,348
  Receipts, 2002 ($1,000) $1,944,319
Health care & social assistance 51,460
  Annual payroll ($1,000). $38,168,221
  Paid employees 1,097,308
  Receipts, 2002 ($1,000) $81,493,532
Arts and entertainment 6,117
  Annual payroll ($1,000). $2,518,194
  Paid employees 105,477
  Receipts, 2002 ($1,000) $7,480,834
Real estate 24,868
  Annual payroll ($1,000). $5,995,928
  Paid employees 160,838
  Receipts, 2002 ($1,000) $24,304,610
Accommodation & food service 39,989
  Annual payroll ($1,000). $10,304,662
  Paid employees 800,903
  Receipts, 2002 ($1,000) $29,914,774

8   Texas

Exports, 2006
Value of exported goods ($ mil) $150,888
   Manufactured $123,094
   Non-manufactured................. $6,877

Foreign direct investment in US affiliates, 2004
Property, plants & equipment ($ mil) ... $83,739
Employment (x 1,000)................... 341.2

Agriculture, 2006
Number of farms 230,000
Farm acreage (x 1,000) 129,700
   Acres per farm 564
Farm marketings and income ($ mil)
Total............................$16,026.8
   Crops............................$5,703.0
   Livestock.......................$10,323.7
Net farm income $4,866.3

Principal commodities, in order by marketing receipts, 2005
Cattle and calves, Cotton, Greenhouse/nursery, Broilers, Dairy products

Federal economic activity in state
Expenditures, 2005 ($ mil)
   Total........................... $148,683
     Per capita $6,484.63
   Defense $30,782
   Non-defense $117,901
Defense department, 2006 ($ mil)
   Payroll...........................$11,908
   Contract awards $27,102
   Grants $168
Homeland security grants ($1,000)
   2006............................ $89,880
   2007............................$121,629

FDIC-insured financial institutions, 2005
Number.............................. 650
Assets ($ billion) $255.9
Deposits ($ billion) $193.4

Fishing, 2006
Catch (x 1,000 lbs)................... 116,860
Value ($1,000)....................... $196,856

Mining, 2006 ($ mil)
Total non-fuel mineral production $2,910
Percent of U.S. 4.52%

Communication, Energy & Transportation

Communication
Households with computers, 2003........ 59.0%
Households with internet access, 2003 .... 51.8%
High-speed internet providers 138
Total high-speed internet lines........5,452,666
   Residential 4,247,541
   Business.........................1,205,125
Wireless phone customers, 12/2006 ... 17,822,230

FCC-licensed stations (as of January 1, 2008)
TV stations 135
FM radio stations........................ 623
AM radio stations 304

Energy
Energy consumption, 2004
   Total (trillion Btu)................11,971
   Per capita (million Btu)............531.6
By source of production (trillion Btu)
   Coal.............................1,626
   Natural gas......................3,941
   Petroleum.......................5,801
   Nuclear electric power 422
   Hydroelectric power............... 13
By end-use sector (trillion Btu)
   Residential 1,555
   Commercial 1,315
   Industrial 6,400
   Transportation 2,701
Electric energy, 2005
   Primary source of electricity............. Gas
   Net generation (billion kWh) 396.7
     percent from renewable sources....... 1.7%
   Net summer capability (million kW) 101.0
   CO_2 emitted from generation 258.7
Natural gas utilities, 2005
   Customers (x 1,000) 4,311
   Sales (trillion Btu)................ 1,866
   Revenues ($ mil) $12,466
Nuclear plants, 2007 4
*Total CO_2 emitted (million metric tons).....670.2
Energy spending, 2004 ($ mil) $95,122
   per capita $4,224
   Price per million Btu $11.50

Transportation, 2006
Public road & street mileage 305,270
   Urban............................ 83,683
   Rural 221,587
   Interstate..........................3,233
Vehicle miles of travel (millions) 238,256
   per capita 10,178.6
Total motor vehicle registrations......17,538,388
   Automobiles......................8,805,316
   Trucks 8,642,899
   Motorcycles 355,825
Licensed drivers 14,906,701
   19 years & under 685,314
Deaths from motor vehicle accidents 3,475
Gasoline consumed (x 1,000 gallons) ...11,841,488
   per capita 505.9

Commuting Statistics, 2006
Average commute time (min) 24.6
   Drove to work alone 78.5%
   Carpooled........................... 12.7%
   Public transit 1.7%
   Walk to work 1.9%
   Work from home 3.5%

Utah   1

State Summary

Capital city .... Salt Lake City
Governor.................... Jon Huntsman Jr
210 State Capitol
Salt Lake City, UT 84114
801-538-1000
Admitted as a state 1896
Area (square miles) 84,899
Population, 2007 (estimate)...........2,645,330
Largest city .... Salt Lake City
Population, 2006.................. 178,858
Personal income per capita, 2006
(in current dollars) $29,108
Gross domestic product, 2006 ($ mil) $97,749

Leading industries by payroll, 2005
Manufacturing, Health care/Social assistance,
Retail trade

**Leading agricultural commodities
by receipts, 2005**
Cattle and calves, Dairy products, Hogs, Hay,
Greenhouse/nursery

Geography & Environment

Total area (square miles)............... 84,899
land 82,144
water 2,755
Federally-owned land, 2004 (acres) ...30,271,905
percent...............................57.5%
Highest point .... Kings Peak
elevation (feet) 13,528
Lowest point................. Beaverdam Wash
elevation (feet) 2,000
General coastline (miles) 0
Tidal shoreline (miles) 0
Cropland, 2003 (x 1,000 acres)...........1,682
Forest land, 2003 (x 1,000 acres)...........1,876
Capital city .... Salt Lake City
Population 2000 181,743
Population 2006 178,858
Largest city .... Salt Lake City
Population 2000 181,743
Population 2006 178,858

Number of cities with over 100,000 population
1990 1
2000 3
2006 3

State park and recreation areas, 2005
Area (x 1,000 acres)..................... 150
Number of visitors (x 1,000) 4,552
Revenues ($1,000) $10,622
percent of operating expenditures...... 39.9%

National forest system land, 2007
Acres 8,200,161

Demographics & Population Characteristics

Population
1980 1,461,037
1990 1,722,850
2000 2,233,198
2006 2,550,063
Male...........................1,282,401
Female..........................1,267,662
Living in group quarters, 2006.......... 42,646
percent of total...................... 1.7%
2007 (estimate)....................2,645,330
persons per square mile of land 32.2
2008 (projected)....................2,523,394
2010 (projected)....................2,595,013
2020 (projected)....................2,990,094
2030 (projected)....................3,485,367

**Population of Core-Based Statistical Areas
(formerly Metropolitan Areas), x 1,000**

	CBSA	Non-CBSA
1990	1,618	105
2000	2,107	126
2006	2,420	130

Change in population, 2000-2007
Number.............................412,132
percent........................... 18.5%
Natural increase (births minus deaths) 272,134
Net internal migration................. 30,709
Net international migration 63,278

Persons by age, 2006
Under 5 years 247,801
5 to 17 years 543,397
18 years and over 1,758,865
65 years and over 225,539
85 years and over 29,235
Median age 28.3

Persons by age, 2010 (projected)
Under 5 years 240,868
18 and over 1,776,028
65 and over 234,798
Median age 29.5

Race, 2006
One Race
White........................ 2,383,544
Black or African American 25,838
Asian 50,230
American Indian/Alaska Native....... 33,663
Hawaiian Native/Pacific Islander.......19,277
Two or more races......................37,511

Persons of Hispanic origin, 2006
Total Hispanic or Latino 286,113
Mexican........................... 219,599
Puerto Rican 5,174
Cuban 790

Persons of Asian origin, 2006

Total Asian	49,079
Asian Indian	4,125
Chinese	13,653
Filipino	3,513
Japanese	6,074
Korean	5,727
Vietnamese	6,944

Marital status, 2006

Population 15 years & over	1,881,043
Never married	528,268
Married	1,111,133
Separated	23,667
Widowed	73,433
Divorced	168,209

Language spoken at home, 2006

Population 5 years and older	2,302,896
English only	1,973,532
Spanish	216,327
French	9,734
German	13,116
Chinese	12,569

Households & families, 2006

Households	814,028
with persons under 18 years	351,192
with persons over 65 years	150,020
persons per household	3.08
Families	614,705
persons per family	3.56
Married couples	503,636
Female householder, no husband present	77,116
One-person households	155,746

Nativity, 2006

Number of residents born in state	1,607,096
percent of population	63.0%

Immigration & naturalization, 2006

Legal permanent residents admitted	5,749
Persons naturalized	2,740
Non-immigrant admissions	104,196

Vital Statistics and Health

Marriages

2004	23,796
2005	24,109
2006	23,678

Divorces

2004	9,811
2005	9,982
2006	9,890

Health risks, 2006

Percent of adults who are:

Smokers	9.8%
Overweight (BMI > 25)	54.9%
Obese (BMI > 30)	21.9%

Births

2005	51,556
Birthrate (per 1,000)	20.9
White	48,934
Black	482
Hispanic	7,566
Asian/Pacific Islander	1,500
Amer. Indian/Alaska Native	640
Low birth weight (2,500g or less)	6.8%
Cesarian births	21.6%
Preterm births	11.4%
To unmarried mothers	17.7%
Twin births (per 1,000)	26.5
Triplets or higher order (per 100,000)	134.8
2006 (preliminary)	53,499
rate per 1,000	21.0

Deaths

2004

All causes	13,331
rate per 100,000	760.4
Heart disease	2,942
rate per 100,000	175.0
Malignant neoplasms	2,445
rate per 100,000	141.2
Cerebrovascular disease	790
rate per 100,000	47.7
Chronic lower respiratory disease	595
rate per 100,000	35.5
Diabetes	485
rate per 100,000	28.6
2005 (preliminary)	13,434
rate per 100,000	731.3
2006 (provisional)	13,772

Infant deaths

2004	264
rate per 1,000	5.2
2005 (provisional)	226
rate per 1,000	4.4

Exercise routines, 2005

None	18.5%
Moderate or greater	55.0%
Vigorous	34.3%

Abortions, 2004

Total performed in state	3,665
rate per 1,000 women age 15-44	7
% obtained by out-of-state residents	7.8%

Physicians, 2005

Total	5,221
rate per 100,000 persons	210

Community hospitals, 2005

Number of hospitals	43
Beds (x 1,000)	4.6
Patients admitted (x 1,000)	223
Average daily census (x 1,000)	2.6
Average cost per day	$1,823
Outpatient visits (x 1 mil)	4.8

Disability status of population, 2006
5 to 15 years 5.5%
16 to 64 years 10.6%
65 years and over 38.9%

Education

Educational attainment, 2006
Population over 25 years 1,437,561
Less than 9th grade.................... 3.4%
High school graduate or more 90.2%
College graduate or more.............. 28.6%
Graduate or professional degree........ 9.4%

Public school enrollment, 2005-06
Total................................ 508,430
Pre-kindergarten through grade 8.... 357,644
Grades 9 through 12................ 150,786

Graduating public high school seniors, 2004-05
Diplomas (incl. GED and others) 30,399

SAT scores, 2007
Average critical reading score............. 558
Average writing score..................... 544
Average math score 556
Percent of graduates taking test 6%

Public school teachers, 2006-07 (estimate)
Total (x 1,000) 21.8
Elementary...........................11.8
Secondary............................10.0
Average salary $40,566
Elementary........................ $40,566
Secondary......................... $40,566

State receipts & expenditures for public schools, 2006-07 (estimate)
Revenue receipts ($ mil) $3,470
Expenditures
Total ($ mil) $3,377
Per capita $1,058
Per pupil $6,060

NAEP proficiency scores, 2007
	Reading		Math	
	Basic	Proficient	Basic	Proficient
Grade 4	68.6%	33.9%	82.7%	39.4%
Grade 8	75.0%	30.1%	72.1%	32.4%

Higher education enrollment, fall 2005
Total....................................51,731
Full-time men 21,817
Full-time women.................... 22,684
Part-time men 3,431
Part-time women.....................3,799

Minority enrollment in institutions of higher education, 2005
Black, non-Hispanic.................... 2,298
Hispanic 9,680
Asian/Pacific Islander 6,049
American Indian/Alaska Native.......... 2,269

Institutions of higher education, 2005-06
Total................................... 31
Public............................ 13
Private 18

Earned degrees conferred, 2004-05
Associate's.............................9,915
Bachelor's 20,799
Master's 4,210
First-professional........................ 423
Doctor's 373

Public Libraries, 2006
Number of libraries....................... 71
Number of outlets 135
Annual visits per capita 6.9
Circulation per capita...................12.9

State & local financial support for higher education, FY 2006
Full-time equivalent enrollment (x 1,000)....104.3
Appropriations per FTE.................$5,941

Social Insurance & Welfare Programs

Social Security benefits & beneficiaries, 2005
Beneficiaries (x 1,000) 272
Retired & dependents.................. 198
Survivors............................ 36
Disabled & dependents................. 39
Annual benefit payments ($ mil) $2,913
Retired & dependents............... $2,037
Survivors......................... $495
Disabled & dependents.............. $380
Average monthly benefit
Retired & dependents............... $1,009
Disabled & dependents.............. $928
Widowed.......................... $1,033

Medicare, July 2005
Enrollment (x 1,000).................... 237
Payments ($ mil) $1,312

Medicaid, 2004
Beneficiaries (x 1,000)................... 307
Payments ($ mil) $1,356

State Children's Health Insurance Program, 2006
Enrollment (x 1,000)....................52.0
Expenditures ($ mil)....................$56.9

Persons without health insurance, 2006
Number (x 1,000)........................ 442
percent........................ 17.4%
Number of children (x 1,000) 120
percent of children 15.0%

Health care expenditures, 2004
Total expenditures......................$9,618
per capita $3,972

Federal and state public aid

State unemployment insurance, 2006
Recipients, first payments (x 1,000) 23
Total payments ($ mil) $92
Average weekly benefit $274
Temporary Assistance for Needy Families, 2006
Recipients (x 1,000) 196.4
Families (x 1,000) 81.8
Supplemental Security Income, 2005
Recipients (x 1,000) 22.6
Payments ($ mil) $109.8
Food Stamp Program, 2006
Avg monthly participants (x 1,000) 131.8
Total benefits ($ mil) $140.4

Housing & Construction

Housing units
Total 2005 (estimate) 874,068
Total 2006 (estimate) 901,283
Seasonal or recreational use, 2006 36,886
Owner-occupied, 2006 585,929
    Median home value $188,500
    Homeowner vacancy rate 2.1%
Renter-occupied, 2006 228,099
    Median rent $697
    Rental vacancy rate 5.7%
Home ownership rate, 2005 . . . . 73.9%
Home ownership rate, 2006 . . . . 73.5%

New privately-owned housing units
Number authorized, 2006 (x 1,000) 25.9
    Value ($ mil) $4,847.4
Started 2005 (x 1,000, estimate) 19.9
Started 2006 (x 1,000, estimate) 19.8

Existing home sales
2005 (x 1,000) 51.7
2006 (x 1,000) 51.7

Government & Elections

State officials 2008
Governor . . . . Jon Huntsman Jr
        Republican, term expires 1/09
Lieutenant Governor . . . . Gary Herbert
Secretary of State . . . . (no Secretary of State)
Attorney General . . . . Mike Shurtleff
Chief Justice . . . . .Christine Durham

Governorship
Minimum age 30
Length of term . . . . 4 years
Consecutive terms permitted 3
Who succeeds . . . . Lieutenant Governor

Local governments by type, 2002
Total 605
    County 29
    Municipal 236
    Township 0
    School District 40
    Special District 300

State legislature
Name . . . . Legislature
Upper chamber . . . . .Senate
    Number of members 29
    Length of term . . . . 4 years
    Party in majority, 2008 . . . . Republican
Lower chamber . . . . House of Representatives
    Number of members 75
    Length of term . . . . 2 years
    Party in majority, 2008 . . . . Republican

Federal representation, 2008 (110th Congress)
Senator . . . . .Robert Bennett
    Party . . . . Republican
    Year term expires 2011
Senator . . . . Orrin Hatch
    Party . . . . Republican
    Year term expires 2013
Representatives, total 3
    Democrats 1
    Republicans 2

Voters in November 2006 election (estimate)
Total 602,690
    Male 293,992
    Female 308,698
    White 588,180
    Black 1,625
    Hispanic 13,066
    Asian 3,025

Presidential election, 2004
Total Popular Vote 927,844
    Kerry 241,199
    Bush 663,742
Total Electoral Votes 5

Votes cast for US Senators
2004
Total vote (x 1,000) 912
Leading party . . . . Republican
Percent for leading party 68.7%
2006
Total vote (x 1,000) 571
Leading party . . . . Republican
Percent for leading party 62.4%

Votes cast for US Representatives
2004
Total vote (x 1,000) 909
    Democratic 362
    Republican 520
Leading party . . . . Republican
Percent for leading party 57.3%
2006
Total vote (x 1,000) 570
    Democratic 244
    Republican 292
Leading party . . . . Republican
Percent for leading party 51.3%

Utah 5

State government employment, 2006
Full-time equivalent employees 50,277
Payroll ($ mil) $171.5

Local government employment, 2006
Full-time equivalent employees 78,508
Payroll ($ mil) $246.0

Women holding public office, 2008
US Congress 0
Statewide elected office..................... 0
State legislature 18

Black public officials, 2002
Total....................................... 5
  US and state legislatures 1
  City/county/regional offices 3
  Judicial/law enforcement.................... 1
  Education/school boards 0

Hispanic public officials, 2006
Total....................................... 5
  State executives & legislators 2
  City/county/regional offices 3
  Judicial/law enforcement.................... 0
  Education/school boards 0

Governmental Finance

State government revenues, 2006
Total revenue (x $1,000)............$14,163,297
  per capita $5,490.64
General revenue (x $1,000) $11,786,469
  Intergovernmental 3,235,660
  Taxes 5,459,091
    general sales.....................1,890,793
    individual income tax 2,277,478
    corporate income tax 348,129
  Current charges.................. 2,200,608
  Miscellaneous 891,110

State government expenditure, 2006
Total expenditure (x $1,000).......$12,044,631
  per capita $4,669.30
General expenditure (x $1,000) $10,966,239
  per capita, total................... $4,251.25
    Education.......................1,868.24
    Public welfare 893.57
    Health 128.99
    Hospitals........................ 260.49
    Highways 315.03
    Police protection................... 54.22
    Corrections 116.73
    Natural resources 67.42
    Parks & recreation 15.38
    Governmental administration...... 292.03
    Interest on general debt.............92.71

State debt & cash, 2006 ($ per capita)
Debt $2,299.44
Cash/security holdings..............$9,606.67

Federal government grants to state & local government, 2005 (x $1,000)
Total...............................$3,038,268
by Federal agency
  Defense 28,501
  Education 296,118
  Energy 25,388
  Environmental Protection Agency 36,723
  Health & Human Services. 1,640,721
  Homeland Security...................27,715
  Housing & Urban Development...... 146,293
  Justice 43,047
  Labor 69,148
  Transportation 289,912
  Veterans Affairs 3,206

Crime & Law Enforcement

Crime, 2006 (rates per 100,000 residents)
Property crimes 89,671
  Burglary 14,701
  Larceny 66,671
  Motor vehicle theft 8,299
  Property crime rate.................. 3,516.4
Violent crimes.........................5,722
  Murder 46
  Forcible rape........................ 869
  Robbery........................... 1,245
  Aggravated assault 3,562
  Violent crime rate 224.4
Hate crimes............................. 45

Fraud and identity theft, 2006
Fraud complaints....................... 4,563
  rate per 100,000 residents 178.9
Identity theft complaints 1,577
  rate per 100,000 residents 61.8

Law enforcement agencies, 2006
Total agencies......................... 129
Total employees 7,502
  Officers 4,495
  Civilians 3,007

Prisoners, probation, and parole, 2006
Total prisoners........................ 6,430
  percent change, 12/31/05 to 12/31/06 ....0.8%
  in private facilities 0%
  in local jails 20.7%
Sentenced to more than one year 6,339
  rate per 100,000 residents 246
Adults on probation 10,426
Adults on parole....................... 3,374

Prisoner demographics, June 30, 2005 (rate per 100,000 residents)
Male................................... 803
Female................................ 127
White................................. 392
Black.................................. 3,588
Hispanic 838

Arrests, 2006

Total...............................109,762
   Persons under 18 years of age..........23,519

Persons under sentence of death, 1/1/07

Total...................................... 9
   White..................................... 6
   Black..................................... 1
   Hispanic.................................. 1

State's highest court

Name........................Supreme Court
Number of members........................ 5
Length of term........................ 10 years
Intermediate appeals court?................yes

Labor & Income

Civilian labor force, 2006 (x 1,000)

Total.................................1,309
   Men..................................... 735
   Women................................... 574
   Persons 16-19 years...................... 92
   White.................................1,231
   Black................................... NA
   Hispanic................................ 148

Civilian labor force as a percent of civilian non-institutional population, 2006

Total.................................72.3%
   Men....................................82.0
   Women..................................62.8
   Persons 16-19 years....................56.9
   White..................................72.7
   Black................................... NA
   Hispanic...............................77.3

Employment, 2006 (x 1,000)

Total.................................1,271
   Men..................................... 715
   Women................................... 556
   Persons 16-19 years...................... 83
   White.................................1,197
   Black................................... NA
   Hispanic................................ 143

Unemployment rate, 2006

Total..................................2.9%
   Men.....................................2.8
   Women...................................3.0
   Persons 16-19 years.....................9.9
   White...................................2.8
   Black................................... NA
   Hispanic................................3.5

Full-time/part-time labor force, 2003 (x 1,000)

Full-time labor force, employed............ 834
Part-time labor force, employed............ 284
Unemployed, looking for
   Full-time work........................... 46
   Part-time work........................... 20
Mean duration of unemployment (weeks)......13.8
   Median..................................6.1

Labor unions, 2006

Membership (x 1,000).................... 61
   percent of employed................... 5.4%

Experienced civilian labor force by private industry, 2006

Total............................... 978,130
   Natural resources & mining.......... 14,456
   Construction.......................95,115
   Manufacturing.................... 122,215
   Trade, transportation & utilities..... 232,209
   Information........................31,306
   Finance............................71,413
   Professional & business............. 152,788
   Education & health................. 120,815
   Leisure & hospitality.............. 108,363
   Other..............................29,188

Experienced civilian labor force by occupation, May 2006

Management......................... 46,280
Business & financial................... 48,810
Legal.............................. 6,440
Sales.............................. 130,550
Office & admin. support...............210,570
Computers & math..................... 30,680
Architecture & engineering.............22,170
Arts & entertainment.................16,170
Education........................... 65,060
Social services.......................16,910
Health care practitioner & technical.....49,740
Health care support................... 25,860
Maintenance & repair................. 49,690
Construction...................... 84,850
Transportation & moving..............79,160
Production........................ 92,370
Farming, fishing & forestry............. 1,280

Hours and earnings of production workers on manufacturing payrolls, 2006

Average weekly hours.....................41.1
Average hourly earnings...............$15.25
Average weekly earnings.............. $626.78

Income and poverty, 2006

Median household income............ $51,309
Personal income, per capita (current $)... $29,108
   in constant (2000) dollars........... $25,409
Persons below poverty level.............. 10.6%

Average annual pay

2006................................. $35,130
   increase from 2005.................... 5.4%

Federal individual income tax returns, 2005

Returns filed.........................1,030,683
Adjusted gross income ($1,000).....$51,060,650
Total tax liability ($1,000)...........$5,732,106

Charitable contributions, 2004

Number of contributions.................363.1
Total amount ($ mil).................$2,323.8

Economy, Business, Industry & Agriculture

Fortune 500 companies, 2007 1
Bankruptcy cases filed, FY 2007 6,182

Patents and trademarks issued, 2007
Patents 790
Trademarks 905

Business firm ownership, 2002
Women-owned 48,475
   Sales ($ mil) $5,920
Black-owned 649
   Sales ($ mil) $188
Hispanic-owned 5,177
   Sales ($ mil) $555
Asian-owned 2,824
   Sales ($ mil) $707
Amer. Indian/Alaska Native-owned 1,148
   Sales ($ mil) $83
Hawaiian/Pacific Islander-owned 429
   Sales ($ mil) $152

Gross domestic product, 2006 ($ mil)
Total gross domestic product $97,749
   Agriculture, forestry, fishing and
      hunting 592
   Mining 3,108
   Utilities 1,310
   Construction 6,247
   Manufacturing, durable goods 7,824
   Manufacturing, non-durable goods 3,156
   Wholesale trade 4,935
   Retail trade 7,242
   Transportation & warehousing 3,282
   Information 3,661
   Finance & insurance 8,453
   Real estate, rental & leasing 10,662
   Professional and technical services 6,432
   Educational services 1,019
   Health care and social assistance 5,736
   Accommodation/food services 2,463
   Other services, except government 3,099
   Government 13,161

Establishments, payroll, employees & receipts, by major industry group, 2005
Total 65,549
   Annual payroll ($1,000) $30,970,696
   Paid employees 974,686
Forestry, fishing & agriculture 73
   Annual payroll ($1,000) . . . . NA
   Paid employees . . . . NA
Mining 373
   Annual payroll ($1,000) $476,697
   Paid employees .7,753
   Receipts, 2002 ($1,000) $2,455,982

Utilities 208
   Annual payroll ($1,000) $314,586
   Paid employees .4,725
   Receipts, 2002 ($1,000) . . . . .NA
Construction 10,006
   Annual payroll ($1,000) $2,485,740
   Paid employees 70,587
   Receipts, 2002 ($1,000) $10,792,051
Manufacturing 3,165
   Annual payroll ($1,000) $4,624,262
   Paid employees 116,003
   Receipts, 2002 ($1,000) $25,104,045
Wholesale trade 3,434
   Annual payroll ($1,000) $2,009,505
   Paid employees 45,994
   Receipts, 2002 ($1,000) $22,905,100
Retail trade 8,454
   Annual payroll ($1,000) $2,840,452
   Paid employees 130,073
   Receipts, 2002 ($1,000) $23,675,432
Transportation & warehousing 1,851
   Annual payroll ($1,000) $1,512,233
   Paid employees 42,063
   Receipts, 2002 ($1,000) $4,053,466
Information 1,349
   Annual payroll ($1,000) $1,452,188
   Paid employees 31,089
   Receipts, 2002 ($1,000) . . . . .NA
Finance & insurance 4,819
   Annual payroll ($1,000) $2,181,880
   Paid employees 48,763
   Receipts, 2002 ($1,000) . . . . .NA
Professional, scientific & technical 7,460
   Annual payroll ($1,000) $2,761,145
   Paid employees 64,467
   Receipts, 2002 ($1,000) $4,878,861
Education 737
   Annual payroll ($1,000) $657,061
   Paid employees 29,845
   Receipts, 2002 ($1,000) $264,917
Health care & social assistance 5,920
   Annual payroll ($1,000) $3,475,642
   Paid employees 108,171
   Receipts, 2002 ($1,000) $7,237,756
Arts and entertainment 802
   Annual payroll ($1,000) $259,806
   Paid employees 15,433
   Receipts, 2002 ($1,000) $1,910,635
Real estate 4,105
   Annual payroll ($1,000) $500,593
   Paid employees 17,266
   Receipts, 2002 ($1,000) $1,820,526
Accommodation & food service 4,360
   Annual payroll ($1,000) $1,016,166
   Paid employees 87,672
   Receipts, 2002 ($1,000) $2,984,632

Exports, 2006
Value of exported goods ($ mil) $6,798
　Manufactured $5,871
　Non-manufactured................... $764

Foreign direct investment in US affiliates, 2004
Property, plants & equipment ($ mil) $11,402
Employment (x 1,000)..................30.9

Agriculture, 2006
Number of farms 15,100
Farm acreage (x 1,000) 11,600
　Acres per farm........................ 768
Farm marketings and income ($ mil)
Total................................$1,243.7
　Crops............................$312.8
　Livestock.......................... $930.8
Net farm income $263.6

Principal commodities, in order by marketing receipts, 2005
　Cattle and calves, Dairy products, Hogs, Hay, Greenhouse/nursery

Federal economic activity in state
Expenditures, 2005 ($ mil)
　Total............................. $14,823
　　Per capita $5,952.33
　Defense $3,559
　Non-defense...................... $11,264
Defense department, 2006 ($ mil)
　Payroll..........................$1,739
　Contract awards $2,304
　Grants $22
Homeland security grants ($1,000)
　2006.............................. $8,271
　2007.............................. $6,989

FDIC-insured financial institutions, 2005
Number................................. 69
Assets ($ billion) $292.4
Deposits ($ billion) $168.5

Fishing, 2006
Catch (x 1,000 lbs).................... NA
Value ($1,000).......................... NA

Mining, 2006 ($ mil)
Total non-fuel mineral production $3,990
Percent of U.S. 6.20%

Communication, Energy & Transportation

Communication
Households with computers, 2003........ 74.1%
Households with internet access, 2003 ....62.6%
High-speed internet providers 40
Total high-speed internet lines......... 638,618
　Residential 393,338
　Business......................... 245,280
Wireless phone customers, 12/2006 1,774,755

FCC-licensed stations (as of January 1, 2008)
TV stations 17
FM radio stations......................... 73
AM radio stations 44

Energy
Energy consumption, 2004
　Total (trillion Btu)..................... 740
　Per capita (million Btu) 305.7
By source of production (trillion Btu)
　Coal 400
　Natural gas...................... 165
　Petroleum....................... 279
　Nuclear electric power 0
　Hydroelectric power....................... 5
By end-use sector (trillion Btu)
　Residential 150
　Commercial 144
　Industrial 212
　Transportation 233
Electric energy, 2005
　Primary source of electricity............ Coal
　Net generation (billion kWh) 38.2
　　percent from renewable sources....... 2.6%
　Net summer capability (million kW) 6.5
　CO_2 emitted from generation 35.9
Natural gas utilities, 2005
　Customers (x 1,000) 799
　Sales (trillion Btu)...................... 121
　Revenues ($ mil) $847
Nuclear plants, 2007 0
Total CO_2 emitted (million metric tons)......62.4
Energy spending, 2004 ($ mil) $5,673
　per capita $2,343
　Price per million Btu $11.39

Transportation, 2006
Public road & street mileage 43,769
　Urban............................10,610
　Rural 33,159
　Interstate........................ 936
Vehicle miles of travel (millions) 25,964
　per capita 10,065.4
Total motor vehicle registrations...... 2,236,088
　Automobiles.....................1,079,455
　Trucks 1,155,325
　Motorcycles 50,895
Licensed drivers 1,619,085
　19 years & under 122,857
Deaths from motor vehicle accidents 287
Gasoline consumed (x 1,000 gallons) 1,061,532
　per capita 411.5

Commuting Statistics, 2006
Average commute time (min) 20.8
　Drove to work alone 75.2%
　Carpooled......................... 13.1%
　Public transit 2.6%
　Walk to work 2.8%
　Work from home..................... 4.6%

State Summary

Capital city . . . . Montpelier
Governor . . . . Jim Douglas
109 State St
Pavilion Office Building
Montpelier, VT 05609
802-828-3333
Admitted as a state 1791
Area (square miles) 9,614
Population, 2007 (estimate) 621,254
Largest city . . . . Burlington
Population, 2006 38,358
Personal income per capita, 2006
(in current dollars) $34,264
Gross domestic product, 2006 ($ mil) $24,213

Leading industries by payroll, 2005

Manufacturing, Health care/Social assistance,
Retail trade

**Leading agricultural commodities
by receipts, 2005**

Dairy products, Cattle and calves, Greenhouse/
nursery, Hay, Maple products

Geography & Environment

Total area (square miles) 9,614
land 9,250
water 365
Federally-owned land, 2004 (acres) 443,249
percent 7.5%
Highest point .Mt. Mansfield
elevation (feet) 4,393
Lowest point . . . . Lake Champlain
elevation (feet) 95
General coastline (miles) 0
Tidal shoreline (miles) 0
Cropland, 2003 (x 1,000 acres) 587
Forest land, 2003 (x 1,000 acres) 4,129
Capital city . . . . Montpelier
Population 2000 .8,035
Population 2006 .7,954
Largest city . . . . Burlington
Population 2000 38,889
Population 2006 38,358

Number of cities with over 100,000 population

1990 0
2000 0
2006 0

State park and recreation areas, 2005

Area (x 1,000 acres) 69
Number of visitors (x 1,000) 690
Revenues ($1,000) $6,638
percent of operating expenditures 98.0%

National forest system land, 2007

Acres 398,529

Demographics & Population Characteristics

Population

1980 511,456
1990 562,758
2000 608,827
2006 623,908
Male 307,023
Female 316,885
Living in group quarters, 2006 20,760
percent of total 3.3%
2007 (estimate) 621,254
persons per square mile of land 67.2
2008 (projected) 643,905
2010 (projected) 652,512
2020 (projected) 690,686
2030 (projected) 711,867

**Population of Core-Based Statistical Areas
(formerly Metropolitan Areas), x 1,000**

	CBSA	Non-CBSA
1990	417	146
2000	449	159
2006	460	164

Change in population, 2000-2007

Number 12,427
percent 2.0%
Natural increase (births minus deaths) 10,413
Net internal migration . . . .-379
Net international migration 5,046

Persons by age, 2006

Under 5 years 32,779
5 to 17 years 100,610
18 years and over 490,519
65 years and over 82,966
85 years and over 11,714
Median age 40.4

Persons by age, 2010 (projected)

Under 5 years 34,303
18 and over 520,140
65 and over 93,442
Median age 40.6

Race, 2006

One Race

White 603,345
Black or African American 4,329
Asian 6,847
American Indian/Alaska Native 2,386
Hawaiian Native/Pacific Islander 172
Two or more races 6,829

Persons of Hispanic origin, 2006

Total Hispanic or Latino 6,644
Mexican 1,802
Puerto Rican 2,013
Cuban 336

2   Vermont

Persons of Asian origin, 2006

Total Asian 5,693
- Asian Indian. 1,263
- Chinese 1,456
- Filipino 555
- Japanese 276
- Korean. 573
- Vietnamese. 950

Marital status, 2006

Population 15 years & over 517,561
- Never married 151,292
- Married. 274,387
- Separated 8,279
- Widowed. 29,846
- Divorced 62,036

Language spoken at home, 2006

Population 5 years and older. 590,894
- English only 559,412
- Spanish 5,950
- French 10,707
- German 3,252
- Chinese 774

Households & families, 2006

Households. 253,808
- with persons under 18 years 79,330
- with persons over 65 years. 57,803
- persons per household 2.38
Families. 162,721
- persons per family. 2.90
Married couples. 127,054
Female householder,
- no husband present. 25,636
One-person households 69,822

Nativity, 2006

Number of residents born in state 328,764
- percent of population 52.7%

Immigration & naturalization, 2006

Legal permanent residents admitted. 895
Persons naturalized 569
Non-immigrant admissions 46,098

Vital Statistics and Health

Marriages

2004 5,835
2005 5,525
2006 5,385

Divorces

2004 2,442
2005 2,215
2006 2,167

Health risks, 2006

Percent of adults who are:
- Smokers. 18.0%
- Overweight (BMI > 25). 56.0%
- Obese (BMI > 30). 21.2%

Births

2005 6,295
- Birthrate (per 1,000). 10.1
- White 6,099
- Black 77
- Hispanic 72
- Asian/Pacific Islander 106
- Amer. Indian/Alaska Native 13
- Low birth weight (2,500g or less). 6.2%
- Cesarian births 25.9%
- Preterm births 9.0%
- To unmarried mothers. 32.3%
- Twin births (per 1,000) 31.9
- Triplets or higher order (per 100,000). . . .107.8
2006 (preliminary). 6,509
- rate per 1,000 . . . . .10.4

Deaths

2004
All causes 4,995
- rate per 100,000. . . . . .731.0
Heart disease 1,289
- rate per 100,000. . . . . .186.6
Malignant neoplasms 1,212
- rate per 100,000. . . . . .176.3
Cerebrovascular disease. 302
- rate per 100,000. . . . . .43.5
Chronic lower respiratory disease 296
- rate per 100,000. . . . . .44.1
Diabetes. 150
- rate per 100,000. . . . . .22.3
2005 (preliminary). 5,066
- rate per 100,000. . . . . .728.4
2006 (provisional) 5,009

Infant deaths

2004 30
- rate per 1,000 . . . . .4.6
2005 (provisional) 39
- rate per 1,000 . . . . .6.1

Exercise routines, 2005

None. 19.2%
Moderate or greater. 57.7%
Vigorous 33.1%

Abortions, 2004

Total performed in state. 1,725
- rate per 1,000 women age 15-44. 14
- % obtained by out-of-state residents 13.4%

Physicians, 2005

Total. 2,269
- rate per 100,000 persons 365

Community hospitals, 2005

Number of hospitals 12
Beds (x 1,000). 0.9
Patients admitted (x 1,000) 51
Average daily census (x 1,000) 0.6
Average cost per day $1,166
Outpatient visits (x 1 mil) 2.3

Disability status of population, 2006
5 to 15 years 8.1%
16 to 64 years 14.0%
65 years and over 39.9%

Education

Educational attainment, 2006
Population over 25 years 426,930
    Less than 9th grade..................... 3.5%
    High school graduate or more 89.8%
    College graduate or more.............. 32.4%
    Graduate or professional degree....... 12.8%

Public school enrollment, 2005-06
Total................................. 96,638
    Pre-kindergarten through grade 8..... 64,662
    Grades 9 through 12 31,856

Graduating public high school seniors, 2004-05
Diplomas (incl. GED and others) 7,179

SAT scores, 2007
Average critical reading score.............. 516
Average writing score 508
Average math score 518
Percent of graduates taking test 67%

Public school teachers, 2006-07 (estimate)
Total (x 1,000) 9.0
    Elementary...........................4.6
    Secondary............................4.4
Average salary $48,370
    Elementary........................ $48,370
    Secondary......................... $48,370

State receipts & expenditures for public schools, 2006-07 (estimate)
Revenue receipts ($ mil) $1,397
Expenditures
Total ($ mil) $1,381
    Per capita $1,986
    Per pupil $15,940

NAEP proficiency scores, 2007

	Reading		Math	
	Basic	Proficient	Basic	Proficient
Grade 4	74.4%	40.9%	89.0%	49.0%
Grade 8	84.4%	42.1%	81.1%	41.4%

Higher education enrollment, fall 2005
Total................................. 15,825
    Full-time men 6,943
    Full-time women..................... 6,409
    Part-time men 971
    Part-time women.....................1,502

Minority enrollment in institutions of higher education, 2005
Black, non-Hispanic 725
Hispanic 827
Asian/Pacific Islander 857
American Indian/Alaska Native............ 254

Institutions of higher education, 2005-06
Total................................. 25
    Public............................. 6
    Private............................ 19

Earned degrees conferred, 2004-05
Associate's...............................1,271
Bachelor's............................. 4,892
Master's...............................1,684
First-professional........................ 259
Doctor's................................ 62

Public Libraries, 2006
Number of libraries....................... 184
Number of outlets 195
Annual visits per capita 5.7
Circulation per capita.....................7.3

State & local financial support for higher education, FY 2006
Full-time equivalent enrollment (x 1,000).....18.9
Appropriations per FTE............... $3,030

Social Insurance & Welfare Programs

Social Security benefits & beneficiaries, 2005
Beneficiaries (x 1,000) 112
    Retired & dependents.................. 78
    Survivors........................... 14
    Disabled & dependents................ 20
Annual benefit payments ($ mil) $1,184
    Retired & dependents................ $802
    Survivors.......................... $184
    Disabled & dependents............... $198
Average monthly benefit
    Retired & dependents................. $995
    Disabled & dependents............... $889
    Widowed........................... $964

Medicare, July 2005
Enrollment (x 1,000)..................... 96
Payments ($ mil) $600

Medicaid, 2004
Beneficiaries (x 1,000).................... 732
Payments ($ mil) $3,574

State Children's Health Insurance Program, 2006
Enrollment (x 1,000).....................6.3
Expenditures ($ mil).....................$4.7

Persons without health insurance, 2006
Number (x 1,000)........................ 63
    percent.......................... 10.2%
Number of children (x 1,000) 11
    percent of children 8.3%

Health care expenditures, 2004
Total expenditures......................$3,768
    per capita $6,069

Federal and state public aid

State unemployment insurance, 2006
Recipients, first payments (x 1,000) 22
Total payments ($ mil) $84
Average weekly benefit $275
Temporary Assistance for Needy Families, 2006
Recipients (x 1,000) 130.8
Families (x 1,000) 53.0
Supplemental Security Income, 2005
Recipients (x 1,000) 13.1
Payments ($ mil) $62.6
Food Stamp Program, 2006
Avg monthly participants (x 1,000) 47.2
Total benefits ($ mil) $50.1

Housing & Construction

Housing units
Total 2005 (estimate) 307,348
Total 2006 (estimate) 309,557
Seasonal or recreational use, 2006 44,144
Owner-occupied, 2006 182,389
  Median home value $193,000
  Homeowner vacancy rate 1.2%
Renter-occupied, 2006 71,419
  Median rent $716
  Rental vacancy rate 3.6%
Home ownership rate, 2005 . . . . 74.2%
Home ownership rate, 2006 . . . . 74.0%

New privately-owned housing units
Number authorized, 2006 (x 1,000) 2.6
  Value ($ mil) $421.9
Started 2005 (x 1,000, estimate) 2.7
Started 2006 (x 1,000, estimate) 2.6

Existing home sales
2005 (x 1,000) 15.3
2006 (x 1,000) 15.0

Government & Elections

State officials 2008
Governor . . . . Jim Douglas
          Republican, term expires 1/09
Lieutenant Governor . . . . Brian Dubie
Secretary of State . . . . Deborah Markowitz
Attorney General . . . . William Sorrell
Chief Justice . . . . Paul Reiber

Governorship
Minimum age 18
Length of term . . . . 2 years
Consecutive terms permitted . . . . . . not specified
Who succeeds . . . . Lieutenant Governor

Local governments by type, 2002
Total 733
  County 14
  Municipal 47
  Township 237
  School District 283
  Special District 152

State legislature
Name . . . . General Assembly
Upper chamber . . . . .Senate
  Number of members 30
  Length of term . . . . 2 years
  Party in majority, 2008 . . . . .Democratic
Lower chamber . . . . House of Representatives
  Number of members 150
  Length of term . . . . 2 years
  Party in majority, 2008 . . . . .Democratic

Federal representation, 2008 (110th Congress)
Senator . . . . .Patrick Leahy
  Party . . . . .Democratic
  Year term expires 2011
Senator . . . . Bernard Sanders
  Party . . . . .Independent
  Year term expires 2013
Representatives, total 1
  Democrats 1
  Republicans 0

Voters in November 2006 election (estimate)
Total 272,854
  Male 129,914
  Female 142,939
  White 266,764
  Black 657
  Hispanic . . . . NA
  Asian 450

Presidential election, 2004
Total Popular Vote 312,309
  Kerry 184,067
  Bush 121,180
Total Electoral Votes 3

Votes cast for US Senators
2004
Total vote (x 1,000) 307
Leading party .Democratic
Percent for leading party 70.6%
2006
Total vote (x 1,000) 262
Leading party .Independent
Percent for leading party 66.1%

Votes cast for US Representatives
2004
Total vote (x 1,000) 305
  Democratic 22
  Republican 74
Leading party .Independent
Percent for leading party 67.5%
2006
Total vote (x 1,000) 263
  Democratic 140
  Republican 117
Leading party .Democratic
Percent for leading party 53.2%

Vermont 5

State government employment, 2006
Full-time equivalent employees 14,615
Payroll ($ mil) $58.3

Local government employment, 2006
Full-time equivalent employees 25,527
Payroll ($ mil) $78.4

Women holding public office, 2008
US Congress............................... 0
Statewide elected office...................... 1
State legislature 68

Black public officials, 2002
Total....................................... 1
   US and state legislatures 1
   City/county/regional offices 0
   Judicial/law enforcement................. 0
   Education/school boards................. 0

Hispanic public officials, 2006
Total....................................... 0
   State executives & legislators 0
   City/county/regional offices 0
   Judicial/law enforcement................. 0
   Education/school boards................. 0

Governmental Finance

State government revenues, 2006
Total revenue (x $1,000)............ $4,880,873
   per capita $7,862.51
General revenue (x $1,000) $4,459,078
   Intergovernmental 1,288,175
   Taxes 2,406,661
     general sales.................... 326,055
     individual income tax 542,012
     corporate income tax 86,083
   Current charges.................... 438,968
   Miscellaneous 325,274

State government expenditure, 2006
Total expenditure (x $1,000)........ $4,647,719
   per capita $7,486.93
General expenditure (x $1,000) $4,378,513
   per capita, total.................... $7,053.27
     Education 3,264.01
     Public welfare 1,817.53
     Health 217.25
     Hospitals..........................8.56
     Highways 455.96
     Police protection................. 136.53
     Corrections 166.11
     Natural resources 153.04
     Parks & recreation 26.76
     Governmental administration...... 233.58
     Interest on general debt............ 234.60

State debt & cash, 2006 ($ per capita)
Debt $4,803.82
Cash/security holdings...............$9,828.00

Federal government grants to state & local government, 2005 (x $1,000)
Total...............................$1,324,142
by Federal agency
   Defense 10,979
   Education 106,796
   Energy............................ 5,440
   Environmental Protection Agency 20,674
   Health & Human Services. 795,922
   Homeland Security...................8,018
   Housing & Urban Development........79,232
   Justice 29,435
   Labor 22,630
   Transportation 143,265
   Veterans Affairs.....................2,975

Crime & Law Enforcement

Crime, 2006 (rates per 100,000 residents)
Property crimes 14,379
   Burglary 3,300
   Larceny 10,493
   Motor vehicle theft 586
   Property crime rate.................2,304.7
Violent crimes........................ 852
   Murder 12
   Forcible rape........................ 150
   Robbery........................... 110
   Aggravated assault 580
   Violent crime rate 136.6
Hate crimes.............................. 26

Fraud and identity theft, 2006
Fraud complaints......................... 718
   rate per 100,000 residents 115.1
Identity theft complaints 178
   rate per 100,000 residents 28.5

Law enforcement agencies, 2006
Total agencies............................ 69
Total employees 1,567
   Officers 1,163
   Civilians 404

Prisoners, probation, and parole, 2006
Total prisoners.........................2,215
   percent change, 12/31/05 to 12/31/06 .... 6.6%
   in private facilities 23.7%
   in local jails .... NA
Sentenced to more than one year 1,634
   rate per 100,000 residents 262
Adults on probation 7,631
Adults on parole........................ 965

Prisoner demographics, June 30, 2005 (rate per 100,000 residents)
Male.................................... 598
Female.................................. 45
White................................... 304
Black....................................3,797
Hispanic .... NA

6   Vermont

Arrests, 2006
Total...................................13,798
   Persons under 18 years of age 1,645

Persons under sentence of death, 1/1/07
Total....................................... 0
   White...................................... 0
   Black 0
   Hispanic 0

State's highest court
Name ....Supreme Court
Number of members........................ 5
Length of term........................ 6 years
Intermediate appeals court? .... no

Labor & Income

Civilian labor force, 2006 (x 1,000)
Total.................................... 365
   Men 189
   Women 176
   Persons 16-19 years..................... 21
   White................................... 352
   Black .... NA
   Hispanic .... NA

**Civilian labor force as a percent of civilian
non-institutional population, 2006**
Total...................................72.1%
   Men 76.3
   Women 68.0
   Persons 16-19 years....................57.4
   White..................................72.0
   Black .... NA
   Hispanic .... NA

Employment, 2006 (x 1,000)
Total.................................... 352
   Men 182
   Women 170
   Persons 16-19 years..................... 19
   White................................... 339
   Black .... NA
   Hispanic .... NA

Unemployment rate, 2006
Total....................................3.6%
   Men 3.9
   Women 3.3
   Persons 16-19 years....................10.1
   White...................................3.6
   Black .... NA
   Hispanic .... NA

Full-time/part-time labor force, 2003 (x 1,000)
Full-time labor force, employed 263
Part-time labor force, employed............. 72
Unemployed, looking for
   Full-time work.......................... 12
   Part-time work........................... 4
Mean duration of unemployment (weeks)......13.8
   Median 8.2

Labor unions, 2006
Membership (x 1,000)..................... 34
   percent of employed 11.0%

**Experienced civilian labor force
by private industry, 2006**
Total............................... 251,594
   Natural resources & mining 3,048
   Construction 17,334
   Manufacturing...................... 36,233
   Trade, transportation & utilities 59,331
   Information 6,056
   Finance 12,945
   Professional & business 22,243
   Education & health 52,015
   Leisure & hospitality.................33,419
   Other 8,970

**Experienced civilian labor force
by occupation, May 2006**
Management........................8,610
Business & financial 10,870
Legal...................................1,770
Sales................................ 30,760
Office & admin. support................49,870
Computers & math 6,100
Architecture & engineering................5,920
Arts & entertainment 5,030
Education 27,060
Social services 6,790
Health care practitioner & technical......16,510
Health care support 9,470
Maintenance & repair................. 12,430
Construction 16,470
Transportation & moving 16,990
Production 24,150
Farming, fishing & forestry................ 890

**Hours and earnings of production workers
on manufacturing payrolls, 2006**
Average weekly hours....................39.6
Average hourly earnings $15.79
Average weekly earnings $625.28

Income and poverty, 2006
Median household income............ $47,665
Personal income, per capita (current $)... $34,264
   in constant (2000) dollars $29,910
Persons below poverty level.............. 10.3%

Average annual pay
2006................................. $35,542
   increase from 2005 .... 3.9%

Federal individual income tax returns, 2005
Returns filed........................ 309,831
Adjusted gross income ($1,000) $14,703,594
Total tax liability ($1,000) $1,745,492

Charitable contributions, 2004
Number of contributions 74.2
Total amount ($ mil)...................$212.7

Economy, Business, Industry & Agriculture

Fortune 500 companies, 2007............... 0
Bankruptcy cases filed, FY 2007........... 849

Patents and trademarks issued, 2007
Patents................................. 512
Trademarks.............................. 240

Business firm ownership, 2002
Women-owned....................... 18,989
   Sales ($ mil) $1,454
Black-owned........................... 211
   Sales ($ mil) $21
Hispanic-owned........................ 452
   Sales ($ mil) $38
Asian-owned 434
   Sales ($ mil) $67
Amer. Indian/Alaska Native-owned 300
   Sales ($ mil) $44
Hawaiian/Pacific Islander-owned 43
   Sales ($ mil) $1

Gross domestic product, 2006 ($ mil)
Total gross domestic product $24,213
   Agriculture, forestry, fishing and
      hunting 342
   Mining............................. 114
   Utilities............................ 597
   Construction 1,295
   Manufacturing, durable goods.........2,146
   Manufacturing, non-durable goods 784
   Wholesale trade.....................1,273
   Retail trade........................2,010
   Transportation & warehousing 480
   Information 907
   Finance & insurance.................1,479
   Real estate, rental & leasing 2,919
   Professional and technical services 1,448
   Educational services................. 518
   Health care and social assistance 2,355
   Accommodation/food services.........1,037
   Other services, except government 561
   Government 3,251

Establishments, payroll, employees & receipts, by major industry group, 2005

Total............................. 22,273
   Annual payroll ($1,000).......... $8,284,548
   Paid employees 261,656
Forestry, fishing & agriculture.............. 127
   Annual payroll ($1,000)................ NA
   Paid employees .... NA
Mining.............................. 50
   Annual payroll ($1,000)................ NA
   Paid employees .... NA
   Receipts, 2002 ($1,000) $44,884

Utilities 54
   Annual payroll ($1,000)............$131,472
   Paid employees 1,885
   Receipts, 2002 ($1,000) ....NA
Construction..........................3,067
   Annual payroll ($1,000)........... $623,572
   Paid employees 15,083
   Receipts, 2002 ($1,000) $2,253,071
Manufacturing.........................1,126
   Annual payroll ($1,000)........... $1,655,015
   Paid employees 37,170
   Receipts, 2002 ($1,000) $9,660,529
Wholesale trade 875
   Annual payroll ($1,000)........... $444,784
   Paid employees 10,482
   Receipts, 2002 ($1,000) $5,094,373
Retail trade 3,905
   Annual payroll ($1,000)........... $930,372
   Paid employees 41,385
   Receipts, 2002 ($1,000) $7,623,872
Transportation & warehousing 536
   Annual payroll ($1,000)............$189,337
   Paid employees 6,255
   Receipts, 2002 ($1,000) $405,598
Information............................ 527
   Annual payroll ($1,000)........... $280,205
   Paid employees 6,737
   Receipts, 2002 ($1,000) ....NA
Finance & insurance 983
   Annual payroll ($1,000)........... $482,077
   Paid employees 9,632
   Receipts, 2002 ($1,000) ....NA
Professional, scientific & technical 2,099
   Annual payroll ($1,000)............$587,749
   Paid employees 15,821
   Receipts, 2002 ($1,000) $1,100,405
Education 335
   Annual payroll ($1,000)........... $327,266
   Paid employees 13,692
   Receipts, 2002 ($1,000) $92,808
Health care & social assistance 2,082
   Annual payroll ($1,000)........... $1,291,378
   Paid employees 39,298
   Receipts, 2002 ($1,000) $2,526,933
Arts and entertainment 497
   Annual payroll ($1,000)............$129,531
   Paid employees 8,619
   Receipts, 2002 ($1,000) $337,453
Real estate............................ 807
   Annual payroll ($1,000).............$97,136
   Paid employees 3,370
   Receipts, 2002 ($1,000) $340,163
Accommodation & food service...........1,963
   Annual payroll ($1,000)........... $403,200
   Paid employees 29,634
   Receipts, 2002 ($1,000) $1,154,048

Exports, 2006

Value of exported goods ($ mil) $3,817
  Manufactured $2,300
  Non-manufactured.................... $83

Foreign direct investment in US affiliates, 2004

Property, plants & equipment ($ mil) $1,357
Employment (x 1,000)....................10.8

Agriculture, 2006

Number of farms 6,300
Farm acreage (x 1,000) 1,240
  Acres per farm....................... 197
Farm marketings and income ($ mil)
Total................................. $500.8
  Crops............................... $85.7
  Livestock...........................$415.1
Net farm income $103.2

Principal commodities, in order by marketing receipts, 2005

Dairy products, Cattle and calves, Greenhouse/
nursery, Hay, Maple products

Federal economic activity in state

Expenditures, 2005 ($ mil)
  Total............................... $4,645
    Per capita $7,462.63
  Defense $550
  Non-defense..................... $4,095
Defense department, 2006 ($ mil)
  Payroll.............................. $168
  Contract awards $829
  Grants $21
Homeland security grants ($1,000)
  2006......................... $10,908
  2007......................... $6,677

FDIC-insured financial institutions, 2005

Number 19
Assets ($ billion) $8.6
Deposits ($ billion) $7.1

Fishing, 2006

Catch (x 1,000 lbs)....................... NA
Value ($1,000)......................... NA

Mining, 2006 ($ mil)

Total non-fuel mineral production $101
Percent of U.S. 0.16%

Communication, Energy & Transportation

Communication

Households with computers, 2003........ 65.5%
Households with internet access, 2003 .... 58.1%
High-speed internet providers 27
Total high-speed internet lines........ 170,245
  Residential 135,596
  Business.......................... 34,649
Wireless phone customers, 12/2006 358,052

FCC-licensed stations (as of January 1, 2008)

TV stations 7
FM radio stations.......................... 58
AM radio stations 19

Energy

Energy consumption, 2004
  Total (trillion Btu)................... 169
  Per capita (million Btu) 272.7
By source of production (trillion Btu)
  Coal................................. 0
  Natural gas........................... 9
  Petroleum........................... 95
  Nuclear electric power 40
  Hydroelectric power.................. 12
By end-use sector (trillion Btu)
  Residential 51
  Commercial 33
  Industrial 32
  Transportation 54
Electric energy, 2005
  Primary source of electricity......... Nuclear
  Net generation (billion kWh) 5.7
    percent from renewable sources...... 28.6%
  Net summer capability (million kW) 1.0
  CO_2 emitted from generation 0.0
Natural gas utilities, 2005
  Customers (x 1,000) 38
  Sales (trillion Btu)..................... 9
  Revenues ($ mil) $80
Nuclear plants, 2007 1
Total CO_2 emitted (million metric tons).......6.5
Energy spending, 2004 ($ mil) $1,968
  per capita $3,170
  Price per million Btu $15.83

Transportation, 2006

Public road & street mileage 14,406
  Urban............................1,421
  Rural 12,985
  Interstate.......................... 320
Vehicle miles of travel (millions) 7,832
  per capita 12,616.4
Total motor vehicle registrations........ 587,668
  Automobiles....................... 309,972
  Trucks 275,951
  Motorcycles 32,584
Licensed drivers 532,041
  19 years & under 23,962
Deaths from motor vehicle accidents 87
Gasoline consumed (x 1,000 gallons) 348,236
  per capita 561.0

Commuting Statistics, 2006

Average commute time (min) 21.2
  Drove to work alone 75.1%
  Carpooled.......................... 11.2%
  Public transit 0.8%
  Walk to work 6.1%
  Work from home..................... 5.4%

State Summary

Capital city . . . . Richmond
Governor . . . . Tim Kaine

State Capitol
Third Floor
Richmond, VA 23219
804-786-2211

Admitted as a state 1788
Area (square miles) 42,774
Population, 2007 (estimate). 7,712,091
Largest city . . . . Virginia Beach
    Population, 2006 435,619
Personal income per capita, 2006
    (in current dollars) $39,173
Gross domestic product, 2006 ($ mil) . . . $369,260

Leading industries by payroll, 2005
    Professional/Scientific/Technical, Health care/
        Social assistance, Manufacturing

Leading agricultural commodities
by receipts, 2005
    Broilers, Cattle and calves, Dairy products, Tur-
        keys, Greenhouse/nursery

Geography & Environment

Total area (square miles) 42,774
    land 39,594
    water 3,180
Federally-owned land, 2004 (acres) 2,534,178
    percent 9.9%
Highest point . . . . Mt. Rogers
    elevation (feet) 5,729
Lowest point . . . . Atlantic Ocean
    elevation (feet) . . . . sea level
General coastline (miles) 112
Tidal shoreline (miles) 3,315
Cropland, 2003 (x 1,000 acres) 2,862
Forest land, 2003 (x 1,000 acres). 13,182
Capital city . . . . Richmond
    Population 2000 197,790
    Population 2006 192,913
Largest city . . . . Virginia Beach
    Population 2000 425,257
    Population 2006 435,619

Number of cities with over 100,000 population
1990 8
2000 8
2006 9

State park and recreation areas, 2005
Area (x 1,000 acres) 66
Number of visitors (x 1,000) 7,319
Revenues ($1,000) $10,643
    percent of operating expenditures 43.3%

National forest system land, 2007
Acres 1,664,306

Demographics & Population Characteristics

Population
1980 5,346,818
1990 6,187,358
2000 7,079,030
2006 7,642,884
    Male 3,756,771
    Female 3,886,113
Living in group quarters, 2006 235,342
    percent of total 3.1%
2007 (estimate) 7,712,091
    persons per square mile of land 194.8
2008 (projected) 7,827,657
2010 (projected) 8,010,245
2020 (projected) 8,917,395
2030 (projected) 9,825,019

Population of Core-Based Statistical Areas
(formerly Metropolitan Areas), x 1,000

	CBSA	Non-CBSA
1990	5,434	755
2000	6,269	810
2006	6,814	829

Change in population, 2000-2007
Number 633,061
    percent 8.9%
Natural increase (births minus deaths) 324,115
Net internal migration 155,205
Net international migration 159,627

Persons by age, 2006
Under 5 years 508,965
5 to 17 years 1,297,882
18 years and over 5,836,037
65 years and over 887,768
85 years and over 112,129
    Median age 36.9

Persons by age, 2010 (projected)
Under 5 years 535,955
18 and over 6,130,061
65 and over 994,359
    Median age 37.2

Race, 2006
One Race
    White 5,605,240
    Black or African American 1,519,812
    Asian 363,094
    American Indian/Alaska Native. 26,020
    Hawaiian Native/Pacific Islander. 5,624
Two or more races. 123,094

Persons of Hispanic origin, 2006
Total Hispanic or Latino 470,871
    Mexican 118,264
    Puerto Rican 51,211
    Cuban 12,702

Persons of Asian origin, 2006

Total Asian 365,515
   Asian Indian. 76,167
   Chinese 58,722
   Filipino 64,677
   Japanese 8,965
   Korean. 63,767
   Vietnamese. 48,729

Marital status, 2006

Population 15 years & over 6,153,763
   Never married 1,837,362
   Married. 3,341,125
   Separated 175,351
   Widowed. 378,532
   Divorced 596,744

Language spoken at home, 2006

Population 5 years and older. 7,139,393
   English only 6,201,784
   Spanish 412,416
   French 40,008
   German. 33,000
   Chinese 47,179

Households & families, 2006

Households. 2,905,071
   with persons under 18 years 993,568
   with persons over 65 years. 625,955
   persons per household 2.55
Families. 1,939,891
   persons per family. 3.12
Married couples. 1,466,223
Female householder,
   no husband present. 354,079
One-person households 806,999

Nativity, 2006

Number of residents born in state 3,879,738
   percent of population. 50.8%

Immigration & naturalization, 2006

Legal permanent residents admitted. 38,488
Persons naturalized 20,401
Non-immigrant admissions 377,462

Vital Statistics and Health

Marriages

2004 61,990
2005 62,023
2006 60,760

Divorces

2004 29,411
2005 30,052
2006 31,087

Health risks, 2006

Percent of adults who are:
   Smokers. 19.3%
   Overweight (BMI > 25). 61.8%
   Obese (BMI > 30). 25.1%

Births

2005 104,555
   Birthrate (per 1,000). 13.8
   White. 74,323
   Black 22,911
   Hispanic 13,058
   Asian/Pacific Islander 7,159
   Amer. Indian/Alaska Native. 162
   Low birth weight (2,500g or less). 8.2%
   Cesarian births 31.4%
   Preterm births 12.3%
   To unmarried mothers. 32.2%
   Twin births (per 1,000) 33.6
   Triplets or higher order (per 100,000). . . .154.6
2006 (preliminary). 107,817
   rate per 1,000 . . . . .14.1

Deaths

2004

All causes 56,550
   rate per 100,000. . . . . .809.2
Heart disease 14,284
   rate per 100,000. . . . . 206.5
Malignant neoplasms 13,385
   rate per 100,000. . . . . .187.6
Cerebrovascular disease. 3,788
   rate per 100,000. . . . . .55.5
Chronic lower respiratory disease 2,730
   rate per 100,000. . . . . .39.9
Diabetes. 1,602
   rate per 100,000. . . . . .22.7
2005 (preliminary). 57,857
   rate per 100,000. . . . . .801.5
2006 (provisional) 57,571

Infant deaths

2004 776
   rate per 1,000 . . . . .7.5
2005 (provisional) 760
   rate per 1,000 . . . . .7.2

Exercise routines, 2005

None. 21.3%
Moderate or greater. 50.8%
Vigorous 30.4%

Abortions, 2004

Total performed in state. 26,117
   rate per 1,000 women age 15-44. 16
   % obtained by out-of-state residents 5.1%

Physicians, 2005

Total. 20,461
   rate per 100,000 persons 270

Community hospitals, 2005

Number of hospitals 87
Beds (x 1,000). 17.5
Patients admitted (x 1,000) 780
Average daily census (x 1,000) 12.3
Average cost per day $1,394
Outpatient visits (x 1 mil) 13.2

Disability status of population, 2006
5 to 15 years 6.1%
16 to 64 years 11.0%
65 years and over 39.5%

Education

Educational attainment, 2006
Population over 25 years 5,068,993
    Less than 9th grade. 5.6%
    High school graduate or more 85.4%
    College graduate or more. 32.7%
    Graduate or professional degree. 13.2%

Public school enrollment, 2005-06
Total. 1,214,472
    Pre-kindergarten through grade 8. ... 841,435
    Grades 9 through 12. 373,037

Graduating public high school seniors, 2004-05
Diplomas (incl. GED and others) 76,860

SAT scores, 2007
Average critical reading score. 511
Average writing score. 498
Average math score. 511
Percent of graduates taking test 73%

Public school teachers, 2006-07 (estimate)
Total (x 1,000) 93.6
    Elementary. 55.5
    Secondary. 38.0
Average salary $44,727
    Elementary. $44,727
    Secondary. $44,727

State receipts & expenditures for public schools, 2006-07 (estimate)
Revenue receipts ($ mil) $13,445
Expenditures
Total ($ mil) $15,333
    Per capita $1,574
    Per pupil $10,599

NAEP proficiency scores, 2007

	Reading		Math	
	Basic	Proficient	Basic	Proficient
Grade 4	74.4%	37.6%	87.3%	41.9%
Grade 8	78.7%	33.7%	77.0%	37.5%

Higher education enrollment, fall 2005
Total. 89,971
    Full-time men 29,658
    Full-time women. 42,887
    Part-time men 6,789
    Part-time women. 10,637

Minority enrollment in institutions of higher education, 2005
Black, non-Hispanic 85,096
Hispanic 16,615
Asian/Pacific Islander 24,429
American Indian/Alaska Native. 2,153

Institutions of higher education, 2005-06
Total. 107
    Public. 39
    Private. 68

Earned degrees conferred, 2004-05
Associate's. 14,924
Bachelor's 36,970
Master's. 12,736
First-professional. 2,496
Doctor's. 1,504

Public Libraries, 2006
Number of libraries. 91
Number of outlets 373
Annual visits per capita 4.6
Circulation per capita. 8.5

State & local financial support for higher education, FY 2006
Full-time equivalent enrollment (x 1,000). ... 265.6
Appropriations per FTE. $5,223

Social Insurance & Welfare Programs

Social Security benefits & beneficiaries, 2005
Beneficiaries (x 1,000) 1,139
    Retired & dependents. 772
    Survivors. 155
    Disabled & dependents. 212
Annual benefit payments ($ mil) $12,115
    Retired & dependents. $7,883
    Survivors. $2,045
    Disabled & dependents. $2,187
Average monthly benefit
    Retired & dependents. $989
    Disabled & dependents. $945
    Widowed. $930

Medicare, July 2005
Enrollment (x 1,000) 993
Payments ($ mil) $6,171

Medicaid, 2004
Beneficiaries (x 1,000). 149
Payments ($ mil) $744

State Children's Health Insurance Program, 2006
Enrollment (x 1,000). 137.2
Expenditures ($ mil). $145.9

Persons without health insurance, 2006
Number (x 1,000). 1,006
    percent. 13.3%
Number of children (x 1,000) 185
    percent of children 10.1%

Health care expenditures, 2004
Total expenditures. $36,032
    per capita $4,822

4   Virginia

Federal and state public aid
State unemployment insurance, 2006
Recipients, first payments (x 1,000) 107
Total payments ($ mil) $347
Average weekly benefit $256
Temporary Assistance for Needy Families, 2006
Recipients (x 1,000) 447.1
Families (x 1,000) 176.2
Supplemental Security Income, 2005
Recipients (x 1,000) 137.3
Payments ($ mil) $632.2
Food Stamp Program, 2006
Avg monthly participants (x 1,000) 506.7
Total benefits ($ mil) $525.7

Housing & Construction

Housing units
Total 2005 (estimate) 3,175,095
Total 2006 (estimate) 3,230,803
Seasonal or recreational use, 2006 73,931
Owner-occupied, 2006 2,030,284
    Median home value $244,200
    Homeowner vacancy rate 1.8%
Renter-occupied, 2006 874,787
    Median rent $846
    Rental vacancy rate 8.3%
Home ownership rate, 2005 . . . . 71.2%
Home ownership rate, 2006 . . . . 71.1%

New privately-owned housing units
Number authorized, 2006 (x 1,000) 47.7
    Value ($ mil) $7,706.8
Started 2005 (x 1,000, estimate) 51.8
Started 2006 (x 1,000, estimate) 50.6

Existing home sales
2005 (x 1,000) 182.5
2006 (x 1,000) 140.1

Government & Elections

State officials 2008
Governor . . . . .Tim Kaine
    Democratic, term expires 1/10
Lieutenant Governor . . . . Bill Bolling
Secretary of State . . . . Katherine Hanley
Attorney General . . . . Bob McDonnell
Chief Justice . . . . Leroy Rountree Hassell

Governorship
Minimum age 30
Length of term . . . . 4 years
Consecutive terms permitted . . . . none
Who succeeds . . . . Lieutenant Governor

Local governments by type, 2002
Total 521
    County 95
    Municipal 229
    Township 0
    School District 1
    Special District 196

State legislature
Name . . . . General Assembly
Upper chamber . . . . .Senate
    Number of members 40
    Length of term . . . . 4 years
    Party in majority, 2008 . . . . .Democratic
Lower chamber . . . . House of Delegates
    Number of members 100
    Length of term . . . . 2 years
    Party in majority, 2008 . . . . Republican

Federal representation, 2008 (110th Congress)
Senator . . . . .John Warner
    Party . . . . Republican
    Year term expires 2009
Senator . . . . .Jim Webb
    Party . . . . .Democratic
    Year term expires 2013
Representatives, total 11
    Democrats 3
    Republicans 8

Voters in November 2006 election (estimate)
Total 2,431,144
    Male 1,143,965
    Female 1,287,179
    White 2,017,169
    Black 355,052
    Hispanic 14,165
    Asian 35,261

Presidential election, 2004
Total Popular Vote 3,198,367
    Kerry 1,454,742
    Bush 1,716,959
Total Electoral Votes 13

Votes cast for US Senators
2004
Total vote (x 1,000) . . . . NA
Leading party . . . . NA
Percent for leading party . . . . NA
2006
Total vote (x 1,000) .2,370
Leading party .Democratic
Percent for leading party 49.6%

Votes cast for US Representatives
2004
Total vote (x 1,000) 3,004
    Democratic 1,023
    Republican 1,817
Leading party . . . . Republican
Percent for leading party 60.5%
2006
Total vote (x 1,000) 2,297
    Democratic 947
    Republican 1,223
Leading party . . . . Republican
Percent for leading party 53.2%

State government employment, 2006
Full-time equivalent employees 122,634
Payroll ($ mil) $453.0

Local government employment, 2006
Full-time equivalent employees 307,987
Payroll ($ mil) $1,062.1

Women holding public office, 2008
US Congress 1
Statewide elected office..................... 0
State legislature 23

Black public officials, 2002
Total.................................... 248
   US and state legislatures 16
   City/county/regional offices 132
   Judicial/law enforcement................. 16
   Education/school boards................. 84

Hispanic public officials, 2006
Total....................................... 1
   State executives & legislators 0
   City/county/regional offices 1
   Judicial/law enforcement.................. 0
   Education/school boards.................. 0

Governmental Finance

State government revenues, 2006
Total revenue (x $1,000).......... $40,272,795
   per capita $5,271.14
General revenue (x $1,000) $32,619,477
   Intergovernmental 6,673,248
   Taxes 17,192,007
     general sales.....................3,263,647
     individual income tax 9,073,077
     corporate income tax 863,320
   Current charges...................5,440,997
   Miscellaneous 3,313,225

State government expenditure, 2006
Total expenditure (x $1,000) $34,776,228
   per capita $4,551.71
General expenditure (x $1,000) $31,831,209
   per capita, total................... *$4,166.25*
     Education 1,622.73
     Public welfare 871.10
     Health 104.00
     Hospitals.........................315.00
     Highways 347.02
     Police protection...................83.53
     Corrections 179.96
     Natural resources..................27.46
     Parks & recreation 16.13
     Governmental administration.......138.31
     Interest on general debt..............97.72

State debt & cash, 2006 ($ per capita)
Debt $2,305.04
Cash/security holdings............... $9,616.80

Federal government grants to state & local government, 2005 (x $1,000)
Total.......................... $7,745,362
by Federal agency
   Defense 73,940
   Education 799,341
   Energy............................. 60,569
   Environmental Protection Agency 97,253
   Health & Human Services.......... 3,788,133
   Homeland Security................. 80,694
   Housing & Urban Development...... 652,898
   Justice 171,669
   Labor 265,859
   Transportation 847,605
   Veterans Affairs.....................21,065

Crime & Law Enforcement

Crime, 2006 (rates per 100,000 residents)
Property crimes 189,406
   Burglary 31,913
   Larceny 142,679
   Motor vehicle theft 14,814
   Property crime rate................2,478.2
Violent crimes........................ 21,568
   Murder 399
   Forcible rape......................1,792
   Robbery...........................7,749
   Aggravated assault 11,628
   Violent crime rate 282.2
Hate crimes.......................... 389

Fraud and identity theft, 2006
Fraud complaints.................... 12,039
   rate per 100,000 residents 157.5
Identity theft complaints 5,137
   rate per 100,000 residents 67.2

Law enforcement agencies, 2006
Total agencies........................ 280
Total employees 22,872
   Officers 17,672
   Civilians 5,200

Prisoners, probation, and parole, 2006
Total prisoners...................... 36,688
   percent change, 12/31/05 to 12/31/06 .... 3.8%
   in private facilities 4.2%
   in local jails 16.3%
Sentenced to more than one year 36,688
   rate per 100,000 residents 477
Adults on probation 48,144
Adults on parole....................... 3,978

Prisoner demographics, June 30, 2005 (rate per 100,000 residents)
Male.................................. 1,393
Female 144
White................................. 396
Black................................. 2,331
Hispanic 487

Arrests, 2006

Total 276,305
    Persons under 18 years of age 34,797

Persons under sentence of death, 1/1/07

Total 20
    White 8
    Black 12
    Hispanic 0

State's highest court

Name . . . . Supreme Court
Number of members 7
Length of term . . . . 12 years
Intermediate appeals court? . . . . yes

Labor & Income

Civilian labor force, 2006 (x 1,000)

Total 3,971
    Men 2,076
    Women 1,895
    Persons 16-19 years 194
    White 2,973
    Black 761
    Hispanic 275

Civilian labor force as a percent of civilian non-institutional population, 2006

Total 68.4%
    Men 75.2
    Women 62.3
    Persons 16-19 years 45.2
    White 68.0
    Black 69.9
    Hispanic 75.1

Employment, 2006 (x 1,000)

Total 3,848
    Men 2,020
    Women 1,828
    Persons 16-19 years 171
    White 2,898
    Black 717
    Hispanic 267

Unemployment rate, 2006

Total 3.1%
    Men 2.7
    Women 3.5
    Persons 16-19 years 11.7
    White 2.5
    Black 5.7
    Hispanic 2.7

Full-time/part-time labor force, 2003 (x 1,000)

Full-time labor force, employed 3,055
Part-time labor force, employed 565
Unemployed, looking for
    Full-time work 127
    Part-time work 26
Mean duration of unemployment (weeks) 17.2
    Median 9.6

Labor unions, 2006

Membership (x 1,000) 139
    percent of employed 4.0%

Experienced civilian labor force by private industry, 2006

Total 2,976,895
    Natural resources & mining 22,092
    Construction 249,270
    Manufacturing 288,264
    Trade, transportation & utilities 657,061
    Information 91,782
    Finance 192,470
    Professional & business 629,471
    Education & health 377,108
    Leisure & hospitality 338,612
    Other 125,422

Experienced civilian labor force by occupation, May 2006

Management 118,720
Business & financial 202,700
Legal 31,200
Sales 415,380
Office & admin. support 591,390
Computers & math 176,240
Architecture & engineering 80,070
Arts & entertainment 48,250
Education 216,950
Social services 42,660
Health care practitioner & technical 159,520
Health care support 70,630
Maintenance & repair 156,630
Construction 216,400
Transportation & moving 245,660
Production 210,810
Farming, fishing & forestry 5,880

Hours and earnings of production workers on manufacturing payrolls, 2006

Average weekly hours 41.3
Average hourly earnings $16.75
Average weekly earnings $691.78

Income and poverty, 2006

Median household income $56,277
Personal income, per capita (current $) . . . $39,173
    in constant (2000) dollars $34,196
Persons below poverty level 9.6%

Average annual pay

2006 . . . . $44,051
    increase from 2005 . . . . 4.2%

Federal individual income tax returns, 2005

Returns filed 3,540,757
Adjusted gross income ($1,000) $214,671,763
Total tax liability ($1,000) $29,027,603

Charitable contributions, 2004

Number of contributions 1,239.9
Total amount ($ mil) $4,809.4

Economy, Business, Industry & Agriculture

Fortune 500 companies, 2007 17
Bankruptcy cases filed, FY 2007 17,893

Patents and trademarks issued, 2007
Patents 1,192
Trademarks 1,905

Business firm ownership, 2002
Women-owned 157,030
   Sales ($ mil) $22,123
Black-owned 41,165
   Sales ($ mil) $3,719
Hispanic-owned 18,987
   Sales ($ mil) $3,452
Asian-owned 30,457
   Sales ($ mil) $7,709
Amer. Indian/Alaska Native-owned 2,692
   Sales ($ mil) $444
Hawaiian/Pacific Islander-owned 423
   Sales ($ mil) $142

Gross domestic product, 2006 ($ mil)
Total gross domestic product $369,260
   Agriculture, forestry, fishing and
      hunting 1,522
   Mining 1,783
   Utilities 6,835
   Construction 19,568
   Manufacturing, durable goods 15,590
   Manufacturing, non-durable goods 18,573
   Wholesale trade 16,182
   Retail trade 22,354
   Transportation & warehousing 8,508
   Information 18,749
   Finance & insurance 22,834
   Real estate, rental & leasing 49,674
   Professional and technical services 43,327
   Educational services 2,771
   Health care and social assistance 19,809
   Accommodation/food services 8,655
   Other services, except government 9,088
   Government 63,083

Establishments, payroll, employees & receipts, by major industry group, 2005
Total 193,067
   Annual payroll ($1,000) $121,801,479
   Paid employees 3,060,127
Forestry, fishing & agriculture 735
   Annual payroll ($1,000) $139,548
   Paid employees 3,783
Mining 356
   Annual payroll ($1,000) $564,203
   Paid employees 10,088
   Receipts, 2002 ($1,000) $2,277,885

Utilities 309
   Annual payroll ($1,000) $1,211,784
   Paid employees 15,625
   Receipts, 2002 ($1,000) . . . . NA
Construction 24,527
   Annual payroll ($1,000) $9,166,257
   Paid employees 229,405
   Receipts, 2002 ($1,000) $33,667,129
Manufacturing 5,798
   Annual payroll ($1,000) $11,987,037
   Paid employees 290,052
   Receipts, 2002 ($1,000) $83,952,547
Wholesale trade 7,790
   Annual payroll ($1,000) $5,583,345
   Paid employees 110,990
   Receipts, 2002 ($1,000) $69,267,796
Retail trade 29,335
   Annual payroll ($1,000) $9,551,693
   Paid employees 424,451
   Receipts, 2002 ($1,000) $80,509,062
Transportation & warehousing 5,348
   Annual payroll ($1,000) $3,688,915
   Paid employees 104,237
   Receipts, 2002 ($1,000) $7,137,609
Information 4,099
   Annual payroll ($1,000) $7,107,890
   Paid employees 105,410
   Receipts, 2002 ($1,000) . . . . NA
Finance & insurance 11,482
   Annual payroll ($1,000) $10,660,107
   Paid employees 163,718
   Receipts, 2002 ($1,000) . . . . NA
Professional, scientific & technical 25,836
   Annual payroll ($1,000) $24,259,680
   Paid employees 355,406
   Receipts, 2002 ($1,000) $40,683,149
Education 2,280
   Annual payroll ($1,000) $1,532,308
   Paid employees 57,642
   Receipts, 2002 ($1,000) $989,795
Health care & social assistance 16,286
   Annual payroll ($1,000) $13,095,304
   Paid employees 346,082
   Receipts, 2002 ($1,000) $28,199,263
Arts and entertainment 2,650
   Annual payroll ($1,000) $996,562
   Paid employees 47,078
   Receipts, 2002 ($1,000) $2,781,488
Real estate 8,955
   Annual payroll ($1,000) $2,351,599
   Paid employees 60,741
   Receipts, 2002 ($1,000) $8,038,543
Accommodation & food service 14,670
   Annual payroll ($1,000) $3,927,633
   Paid employees 284,857
   Receipts, 2002 ($1,000) $10,929,429

8   Virginia

Exports, 2006
Value of exported goods ($ mil) $14,104
    Manufactured $11,122
    Non-manufactured $2,005

Foreign direct investment in US affiliates, 2004
Property, plants & equipment ($ mil) . . . $16,422
Employment (x 1,000). 133.7

Agriculture, 2006
Number of farms 46,800
Farm acreage (x 1,000) 8,500
    Acres per farm 182
Farm marketings and income ($ mil)
Total. $2,688.7
    Crops $834.1
    Livestock. $1,854.6
Net farm income $678.0

Principal commodities, in order by marketing receipts, 2005
Broilers, Cattle and calves, Dairy products, Turkeys, Greenhouse/nursery

Federal economic activity in state
Expenditures, 2005 ($ mil)
    Total. $95,097
        Per capita $12,571.83
    Defense $40,799
    Non-defense $54,298
Defense department, 2006 ($ mil)
    Payroll. $16,693
    Contract awards $29,246
    Grants $85
Homeland security grants ($1,000)
    2006. . . . . $16,888
    2007 . . . . $33,278

FDIC-insured financial institutions, 2005
Number 126
Assets ($ billion) $247.3
Deposits ($ billion) $159.1

Fishing, 2006
Catch (x 1,000 lbs). 426,217
Value ($1,000). $110,024

Mining, 2006 ($ mil)
Total non-fuel mineral production $1,230
Percent of U.S. 1.91%

Communication, Energy & Transportation

Communication
Households with computers, 2003 . . . . .66.8%
Households with internet access, 2003 . . . .60.3%
High-speed internet providers 66
Total high-speed internet lines 2,183,019
    Residential 1,451,016
    Business. 732,003
Wireless phone customers, 12/2006 5,607,350

FCC-licensed stations (as of January 1, 2008)
TV stations 36
FM radio stations. 208
AM radio stations 145

Energy
Energy consumption, 2004
    Total (trillion Btu). 2,558
    Per capita (million Btu) 342.4
By source of production (trillion Btu)
    Coal 453
    Natural gas 285
    Petroleum 1,039
    Nuclear electric power 295
    Hydroelectric power 16
By end-use sector (trillion Btu)
    Residential 617
    Commercial 578
    Industrial 591
    Transportation 772
Electric energy, 2005
    Primary source of electricity. . . . . Coal
    Net generation (billion kWh) 78.9
        percent from renewable sources. 5.0%
    Net summer capability (million kW) 22.6
    CO_2 emitted from generation 47.7
Natural gas utilities, 2005
    Customers (x 1,000) 1,158
    Sales (trillion Btu) 232
    Revenues ($ mil) $1,855
Nuclear plants, 2007 4
Total CO_2 emitted (million metric tons). 122.6
Energy spending, 2004 ($ mil) $21,298
    per capita $2,850
    Price per million Btu $12.64

Transportation, 2006
Public road & street mileage 72,331
    Urban. 21,700
    Rural. 50,631
    Interstate. 1,117
Vehicle miles of travel (millions) 81,095
    per capita 10,614.2
Total motor vehicle registrations. 6,635,976
    Automobiles. .4,031,355
    Trucks 2,586,357
    Motorcycles 81,171
Licensed drivers .5,210,685
    19 years & under 219,680
Deaths from motor vehicle accidents 963
Gasoline consumed (x 1,000 gallons) 4,011,244
    per capita 525.0

Commuting Statistics, 2006
Average commute time (min) 26.9
    Drove to work alone 77.0%
    Carpooled. 11.4%
    Public transit 4.1%
    Walk to work 2.3%
    Work from home 3.9%

State Summary

Capital city . . . . .Olympia
Governor. . . . . Christine Gregoire

Office of the Governor
PO Box 40002
Olympia, WA 98504
360-902-4111

Admitted as a state 1889
Area (square miles) 71,300
Population, 2007 (estimate). 6,468,424
Largest city . . . . Seattle
    Population, 2006. 582,454
Personal income per capita, 2006
    (in current dollars) $37,423
Gross domestic product, 2006 ($ mil) . . . $293,531

Leading industries by payroll, 2005

Manufacturing, Health care/Social assistance,
Professional/Scientific/Technical

**Leading agricultural commodities
by receipts, 2005**

Apples, Dairy products, Cattle and calves,
Wheat, Potatoes

Geography & Environment

Total area (square miles). 71,300
    land 66,544
    water 4,756
Federally-owned land, 2004 (acres) . . .12,949,662
    percent. 30.3%
Highest point . . . . Mt. Rainier
    elevation (feet) 14,411
Lowest point . . . . Pacific Ocean
    elevation (feet) . . . . sea level
General coastline (miles) 157
Tidal shoreline (miles) 3,026
Cropland, 2003 (x 1,000 acres) 6,494
Forest land, 2003 (x 1,000 acres). 12,707
Capital city . . . . .Olympia
    Population 2000 .42,514
    Population 2006 44,645
Largest city . . . . Seattle
    Population 2000 563,374
    Population 2006 582,454

Number of cities with over 100,000 population

1990 3
2000 5
2006 5

State park and recreation areas, 2005

Area (x 1,000 acres) 106
Number of visitors (x 1,000) 40,026
Revenues ($1,000) $17,627
    percent of operating expenditures. 31.2%

National forest system land, 2007

Acres 9,282,376

Demographics & Population Characteristics

Population

1980 4,132,156
1990 4,866,692
2000 5,894,140
2006 6,395,798
    Male. 3,189,630
    Female 3,206,168
Living in group quarters, 2006 140,607
    percent of total. 2.2%
2007 (estimate) 6,468,424
    persons per square mile of land 97.2
2008 (projected). 6,399,035
2010 (projected) .6,541,963
2020 (projected) .7,432,136
2030 (projected). 8,624,801

**Population of Core-Based Statistical Areas
(formerly Metropolitan Areas), x 1,000**

	CBSA	Non-CBSA
1990	4,689	178
2000	5,678	216
2006	6,168	227

Change in population, 2000-2007

Number 574,284
    percent. 9.7%
Natural increase (births minus deaths) 267,052
Net internal migration 155,491
Net international migration 164,951

Persons by age, 2006

Under 5 years 408,158
5 to 17 years 1,118,109
18 years and over 4,869,531
65 years and over 738,369
85 years and over .107,032
    Median age 36.7

Persons by age, 2010 (projected)

Under 5 years 426,590
18 and over 5,053,540
65 and over 795,528
    Median age 37.3

Race, 2006

One Race

    White. 5,420,961
    Black or African American 227,926
    Asian 422,039
    American Indian/Alaska Native. 104,405
    Hawaiian Native/Pacific Islander. 29,703
Two or more races. 190,764

Persons of Hispanic origin, 2006

Total Hispanic or Latino 580,027
    Mexican. 464,652
    Puerto Rican 19,957
    Cuban 6,746

Persons of Asian origin, 2006

Total Asian 423,976
- Asian Indian.......................... 44,271
- Chinese 81,636
- Filipino 80,896
- Japanese 38,628
- Korean.............................57,320
- Vietnamese.......................... 68,308

Marital status, 2006

Population 15 years & over 5,142,602
- Never married 1,511,538
- Married....................... 2,728,691
- Separated 86,369
- Widowed........................... 270,178
- Divorced 632,195

Language spoken at home, 2006

Population 5 years and older........ 5,988,982
- English only...................... 4,994,813
- Spanish 431,021
- French 21,683
- German........................... 39,134
- Chinese 63,390

Households & families, 2006

Households........................2,471,912
- with persons under 18 years 819,840
- with persons over 65 years...........511,029
- persons per household 2.53
Families..........................1,595,147
- persons per family....................3.11
Married couples.....................1,235,060
Female householder,
- no husband present................ 250,416
One-person households 698,549

Nativity, 2006

Number of residents born in state 3,019,592
- percent of population................ 47.2%

Immigration & naturalization, 2006

Legal permanent residents admitted..... 23,805
Persons naturalized 12,762
Non-immigrant admissions 578,192

Vital Statistics and Health

Marriages

2004 40,169
2005 40,802
2006 40,967

Divorces

2004 26,674
2005 27,022
2006 24,014

Health risks, 2006

Percent of adults who are:
- Smokers............................ 17.1%
- Overweight (BMI > 25)................60.7%
- Obese (BMI > 30)....................24.2%

Births

2005 82,703
- Birthrate (per 1,000)...................13.2
- White..............................67,917
- Black 4,230
- Hispanic 15,013
- Asian/Pacific Islander 8,473
- Amer. Indian/Alaska Native........... 2,083
- Low birth weight (2,500g or less)....... 6.1%
- Cesarian births 27.8%
- Preterm births 10.6%
- To unmarried mothers................30.9%
- Twin births (per 1,000) 29.4
- Triplets or higher order (per 100,000).....92.7
2006 (preliminary)..................... 86,848
- rate per 1,000 ....13.6

Deaths

2004
All causes 44,770
- rate per 100,000..................... 738.3
Heart disease 10,644
- rate per 100,000.....................174.7
Malignant neoplasms 10,989
- rate per 100,000.....................183.6
Cerebrovascular disease............... 3,243
- rate per 100,000.....................53.5
Chronic lower respiratory disease 2,549
- rate per 100,000.....................43.3
Diabetes............................. 1,508
- rate per 100,000.....................25.0
2005 (preliminary)..................... 46,212
- rate per 100,000.....................738.2
2006 (provisional) 44,844

Infant deaths

2004 451
- rate per 1,000 ....5.5
2005 (provisional) 414
- rate per 1,000 ....5.0

Exercise routines, 2005

None............................... 17.4%
Moderate or greater...................54.7%
Vigorous 30.6%

Abortions, 2004

Total performed in state................ 24,664
- rate per 1,000 women age 15-44........... 19
- % obtained by out-of-state residents 5.0%

Physicians, 2005

Total................................16,707
- rate per 100,000 persons 266

Community hospitals, 2005

Number of hospitals 86
Beds (x 1,000)........................11.0
Patients admitted (x 1,000) 543
Average daily census (x 1,000) 6.8
Average cost per day $2,143
Outpatient visits (x 1 mil) 10.0

Disability status of population, 2006
5 to 15 years 6.5%
16 to 64 years 13.6%
65 years and over 41.9%

Education

Educational attainment, 2006
Population over 25 years 4,253,582
   Less than 9th grade..................... 4.1%
   High school graduate or more 89.0%
   College graduate or more............. 30.5%
   Graduate or professional degree....... 10.7%

Public school enrollment, 2005-06
Total................................... 1,031,985
   Pre-kindergarten through grade 8.... 699,482
   Grades 9 through 12 332,503

Graduating public high school seniors, 2004-05
Diplomas (incl. GED and others) 61,213

SAT scores, 2007
Average critical reading score............. 526
Average writing score 510
Average math score 531
Percent of graduates taking test 53%

Public school teachers, 2006-07 (estimate)
Total (x 1,000) 54.0
   Elementary............................ 29.5
   Secondary............................ 24.4
Average salary $47,882
   Elementary......................... $47,926
   Secondary.......................... $47,828

State receipts & expenditures for public schools, 2006-07 (estimate)
Revenue receipts ($ mil) $10,395
Expenditures
Total ($ mil) $12,825
   Per capita $1,404
   Per pupil $9,334

NAEP proficiency scores, 2007

	Reading		Math	
	Basic	Proficient	Basic	Proficient
Grade 4	70.3%	36.3%	84.3%	43.8%
Grade 8	76.7%	34.1%	74.9%	35.9%

Higher education enrollment, fall 2005
Total.................................... 51,726
   Full-time men 17,651
   Full-time women.................... 23,792
   Part-time men 4,293
   Part-time women.................... 5,990

Minority enrollment in institutions of higher education, 2005
Black, non-Hispanic 15,461
Hispanic 19,530
Asian/Pacific Islander 33,269
American Indian/Alaska Native.......... 6,236

Institutions of higher education, 2005-06
Total.................................... 80
   Public.................................. 43
   Private 37

Earned degrees conferred, 2004-05
Associate's.......................... 22,338
Bachelor's 28,265
Master's 8,773
First-professional...................... 1,357
Doctor's............................... 793

Public Libraries, 2006
Number of libraries...................... 65
Number of outlets 354
Annual visits per capita 7.0
Circulation per capita................... 11.1

State & local financial support for higher education, FY 2006
Full-time equivalent enrollment (x 1,000).... 213.1
Appropriations per FTE............... $6,437

Social Insurance & Welfare Programs

Social Security benefits & beneficiaries, 2005
Beneficiaries (x 1,000) 937
   Retired & dependents................... 674
   Survivors........................... 113
   Disabled & dependents................ 150
Annual benefit payments ($ mil) $10,474
   Retired & dependents................. $7,218
   Survivors........................... $1,646
   Disabled & dependents............... $1,611
Average monthly benefit
   Retired & dependents................. $1,042
   Disabled & dependents............... $952
   Widowed........................... $1,032

Medicare, July 2005
Enrollment (x 1,000)..................... 821
Payments ($ mil) $4,334

Medicaid, 2004
Beneficiaries (x 1,000)................... 1,109
Payments ($ mil) $4,930

State Children's Health Insurance Program, 2006
Enrollment (x 1,000).................... 15.0
Expenditures ($ mil)................... $40.3

Persons without health insurance, 2006
Number (x 1,000)....................... 746
   percent............................ 11.8%
Number of children (x 1,000) 105
   percent of children 6.9%

Health care expenditures, 2004
Total expenditures.................... $31,600
   per capita $5,092

Federal and state public aid

State unemployment insurance, 2006
Recipients, first payments (x 1,000) 171
Total payments ($ mil) $710
Average weekly benefit $322
Temporary Assistance for Needy Families, 2006
Recipients (x 1,000) .1,504.6
Families (x 1,000) 637.5
Supplemental Security Income, 2005
Recipients (x 1,000) 115.6
Payments ($ mil) $616.1
Food Stamp Program, 2006
Avg monthly participants (x 1,000) 535.8
Total benefits ($ mil) $594.6

Housing & Construction

Housing units

Total 2005 (estimate) 2,651,323
Total 2006 (estimate) 2,699,333
Seasonal or recreational use, 2006 67,992
Owner-occupied, 2006 1,620,052
    Median home value $267,600
    Homeowner vacancy rate 1.3%
Renter-occupied, 2006 851,860
    Median rent $779
    Rental vacancy rate 6.3%
Home ownership rate, 2005 . . . . 67.6%
Home ownership rate, 2006 . . . . 66.7%

New privately-owned housing units

Number authorized, 2006 (x 1,000) 50.0
    Value ($ mil) $8,539.8
Started 2005 (x 1,000, estimate) 38.3
Started 2006 (x 1,000, estimate) 38.2

Existing home sales

2005 (x 1,000) 167.8
2006 (x 1,000) 154.2

Government & Elections

State officials 2008

Governor . . . . Christine Gregoire
    Democratic, term expires 1/09
Lieutenant Governor . . . . Brad Owen
Secretary of State . . . . .Sam Reed
Attorney General . . . . .Rob McKenna
Chief Justice . . . . Gerry Alexander

Governorship

Minimum age 18
Length of term . . . . 4 years
Consecutive terms permitted . . . . . . not specified
Who succeeds . . . . Lieutenant Governor

Local governments by type, 2002

Total 1,787
    County 39
    Municipal 279
    Township 0
    School District 296
    Special District 1,173

State legislature

Name . . . . Legislature
Upper chamber . . . . .Senate
    Number of members 49
    Length of term . . . . 4 years
    Party in majority, 2008 . . . . .Democratic
Lower chamber . . . . House of Representatives
    Number of members 98
    Length of term . . . . 2 years
    Party in majority, 2008 . . . . .Democratic

Federal representation, 2008 (110th Congress)

Senator . . . . Patty Murray
    Party . . . . .Democratic
    Year term expires 2011
Senator . . . . Maria Cantwell
    Party . . . . .Democratic
    Year term expires 2013
Representatives, total 9
    Democrats 6
    Republicans 3

Voters in November 2006 election (estimate)

Total 2,346,002
    Male 1,103,061
    Female 1,242,940
    White 2,131,809
    Black 25,125
    Hispanic 36,988
    Asian 74,760

Presidential election, 2004

Total Popular Vote 2,859,084
    Kerry 1,510,201
    Bush 1,304,894
Total Electoral Votes 11

Votes cast for US Senators

2004
Total vote (x 1,000) 2,819
Leading party .Democratic
Percent for leading party 55.0%
2006
Total vote (x 1,000) 2,084
Leading party .Democratic
Percent for leading party 56.9%

Votes cast for US Representatives

2004
Total vote (x 1,000) 2,730
    Democratic 1,609
    Republican 1,095
Leading party .Democratic
Percent for leading party 58.9%
2006
Total vote (x 1,000) 2,054
    Democratic 1,244
    Republican 798
Leading party .Democratic
Percent for leading party 60.6%

State government employment, 2006
Full-time equivalent employees 116,943
Payroll ($ mil) $468.6

Local government employment, 2006
Full-time equivalent employees 216,253
Payroll ($ mil) $936.6

Women holding public office, 2008
US Congress 3
Statewide elected office...................... 2
State legislature 48

Black public officials, 2002
Total..................................... 24
 US and state legislatures 2
 City/county/regional offices 9
 Judicial/law enforcement................. 11
 Education/school boards.................. 2

Hispanic public officials, 2006
Total..................................... 13
 State executives & legislators 3
 City/county/regional offices 4
 Judicial/law enforcement................. 0
 Education/school boards.................. 6

Governmental Finance

State government revenues, 2006
Total revenue (x $1,000)...........$40,832,013
 per capita........................$6,405.11
General revenue (x $1,000) $29,284,277
 Intergovernmental 7,729,139
 Taxes 16,410,977
  general sales................... 10,048,349
  individual income tax 0
  corporate income tax 0
 Current charges...................3,280,139
 Miscellaneous 1,864,022

State government expenditure, 2006
Total expenditure (x $1,000) $33,914,746
 per capita $5,320.04
General expenditure (x $1,000) $29,056,032
 per capita, total.................. $4,557.87
  Education 1,902.55
  Public welfare 1,047.85
  Health 227.95
  Hospitals.........................239.83
  Highways 362.45
  Police protection....................43.85
  Corrections 149.59
  Natural resources 103.71
  Parks & recreation 17.03
  Governmental administration........99.20
  Interest on general debt............131.14

State debt & cash, 2006 ($ per capita)
Debt $2,875.21
Cash/security holdings..............$13,174.72

Federal government grants to state & local government, 2005 (x $1,000)
Total.............................$9,046,698
by Federal agency
 Defense 59,745
 Education 695,425
 Energy............................ 50,840
 Environmental Protection Agency ... 103,394
 Health & Human Services. 5,356,936
 Homeland Security...................41,241
 Housing & Urban Development...... 639,958
 Justice 130,674
 Labor 241,040
 Transportation 851,290
 Veterans Affairs.................. 12,777

Crime & Law Enforcement

Crime, 2006 (rates per 100,000 residents)
Property crimes 286,533
 Burglary 58,307
 Larceny 182,327
 Motor vehicle theft 45,899
 Property crime rate.................4,480.0
Violent crimes....................... 22,120
 Murder 190
 Forcible rape.......................2,746
 Robbery............................ 6,405
 Aggravated assault 12,779
 Violent crime rate 345.9
Hate crimes............................ 215

Fraud and identity theft, 2006
Fraud complaints....................10,451
 rate per 100,000 residents 163.4
Identity theft complaints 5,336
 rate per 100,000 residents 83.4

Law enforcement agencies, 2006
Total agencies....................... 246
Total employees 14,420
 Officers 10,260
 Civilians 4,160

Prisoners, probation, and parole, 2006
Total prisoners.......................17,561
 percent change, 12/31/05 to 12/31/06 .... 1.0%
 in private facilities 5.4%
 in local jails 2.4%
Sentenced to more than one year 17,483
 rate per 100,000 residents 271
Adults on probation 108,076
Adults on parole.....................12,611

Prisoner demographics, June 30, 2005 (rate per 100,000 residents)
Male.................................. 831
Female 101
White................................. 393
Black................................. 2,522
Hispanic 527

Arrests, 2006
Total 246,388
    Persons under 18 years of age 34,902

Persons under sentence of death, 1/1/07
Total 9
    White 5
    Black 4
    Hispanic 0

State's highest court
Name . . . . .Supreme Court
Number of members 9
Length of term . . . . 6 years
Intermediate appeals court? . . . . .yes

Labor & Income

Civilian labor force, 2006 (x 1,000)
Total 3,335
    Men 1,792
    Women 1,543
    Persons 16-19 years 170
    White 2,802
    Black 110
    Hispanic 216

Civilian labor force as a percent of civilian non-institutional population, 2006
Total 67.4%
    Men 73.9
    Women 61.1
    Persons 16-19 years 47.6
    White 66.8
    Black 67.1
    Hispanic 72.0

Employment, 2006 (x 1,000)
Total 3,168
    Men 1,701
    Women 1,467
    Persons 16-19 years 140
    White 2,664
    Black 102
    Hispanic 201

Unemployment rate, 2006
Total 5.0%
    Men 5.1
    Women 4.9
    Persons 16-19 years 18.0
    White 4.9
    Black 7.8
    Hispanic 7.2

Full-time/part-time labor force, 2003 (x 1,000)
Full-time labor force, employed 2,293
Part-time labor force, employed 610
Unemployed, looking for
    Full-time work 196
    Part-time work 41
Mean duration of unemployment (weeks) 19.6
    Median 10.3

Labor unions, 2006
Membership (x 1,000) 549
    percent of employed 19.8%

Experienced civilian labor force by private industry, 2006
Total 2,345,531
    Natural resources & mining 87,358
    Construction 182,170
    Manufacturing .281,481
    Trade, transportation & utilities 526,402
    Information 97,725
    Finance 153,026
    Professional & business 320,487
    Education & health 317,865
    Leisure & hospitality 267,242
    Other 111,775

Experienced civilian labor force by occupation, May 2006
Management 80,480
Business & financial 125,980
Legal 20,240
Sales 299,550
Office & admin. support 457,550
Computers & math 93,500
Architecture & engineering 73,300
Arts & entertainment 39,350
Education 158,760
Social services 44,740
Health care practitioner & technical 128,730
Health care support 67,720
Maintenance & repair 113,700
Construction 151,670
Transportation & moving 206,540
Production 168,350
Farming, fishing & forestry 15,780

Hours and earnings of production workers on manufacturing payrolls, 2006
Average weekly hours 40.6
Average hourly earnings $19.90
Average weekly earnings $807.94

Income and poverty, 2006
Median household income $52,583
Personal income, per capita (current $) . . . $37,423
    in constant (2000) dollars $32,668
Persons below poverty level 11.8%

Average annual pay
2006 . . . . $42,897
    increase from 2005 . . . . 5.3%

Federal individual income tax returns, 2005
Returns filed 2,931,911
Adjusted gross income ($1,000) . . . $168,672,520
Total tax liability ($1,000) $22,605,158

Charitable contributions, 2004
Number of contributions 886.7
Total amount ($ mil) $3,435.4

Economy, Business, Industry & Agriculture

Fortune 500 companies, 2007. 10
Bankruptcy cases filed, FY 2007. 14,632

Patents and trademarks issued, 2007
Patents. 3,822
Trademarks. 2,095

Business firm ownership, 2002
Women-owned. .137,394
  Sales ($ mil) $17,368
Black-owned. 6,982
  Sales ($ mil) $1,053
Hispanic-owned. 10,261
  Sales ($ mil) $1,538
Asian-owned 26,890
  Sales ($ mil) $7,128
Amer. Indian/Alaska Native-owned 5,734
  Sales ($ mil) $938
Hawaiian/Pacific Islander-owned 728
  Sales ($ mil) $231

Gross domestic product, 2006 ($ mil)
Total gross domestic product $293,531
  Agriculture, forestry, fishing and
    hunting 5,355
  Mining. 332
  Utilities 2,798
  Construction 14,713
  Manufacturing, durable goods. 23,519
  Manufacturing, non-durable goods 9,401
  Wholesale trade. 18,246
  Retail trade. 21,392
  Transportation & warehousing 7,936
  Information 23,252
  Finance & insurance. 16,573
  Real estate, rental & leasing 42,033
  Professional and technical services 17,677
  Educational services. 1,599
  Health care and social assistance. 19,305
  Accommodation/food services. 7,747
  Other services, except government 6,565
  Government 39,465

Establishments, payroll, employees & receipts, by major industry group, 2005

Total. 175,658
  Annual payroll ($1,000). $94,928,122
  Paid employees 2,316,296
Forestry, fishing & agriculture. 1,580
  Annual payroll ($1,000). $530,207
  Paid employees 13,651
Mining. 183
  Annual payroll ($1,000). $156,374
  Paid employees 2,983
  Receipts, 2002 ($1,000) $499,595

Utilities 305
  Annual payroll ($1,000). $374,928
  Paid employees 5,637
  Receipts, 2002 ($1,000) . . . . .NA
Construction. 23,998
  Annual payroll ($1,000). $7,492,851
  Paid employees 164,391
  Receipts, 2002 ($1,000) $27,916,123
Manufacturing. 7,404
  Annual payroll ($1,000). $12,547,603
  Paid employees 256,563
  Receipts, 2002 ($1,000) $79,313,884
Wholesale trade 9,494
  Annual payroll ($1,000). $6,384,947
  Paid employees 128,315
  Receipts, 2002 ($1,000) $84,634,499
Retail trade 22,791
  Annual payroll ($1,000). $8,064,049
  Paid employees 321,048
  Receipts, 2002 ($1,000) $65,262,333
Transportation & warehousing 4,767
  Annual payroll ($1,000). $3,513,449
  Paid employees 84,341
  Receipts, 2002 ($1,000) $7,592,392
Information. 3,226
  Annual payroll ($1,000). $8,656,108
  Paid employees 105,314
  Receipts, 2002 ($1,000) . . . . .NA
Finance & insurance 10,422
  Annual payroll ($1,000). $6,460,604
  Paid employees 108,834
  Receipts, 2002 ($1,000) . . . . .NA
Professional, scientific & technical 18,399
  Annual payroll ($1,000). $9,140,640
  Paid employees 147,540
  Receipts, 2002 ($1,000) $16,730,409
Education 2,062
  Annual payroll ($1,000). $1,019,014
  Paid employees 44,690
  Receipts, 2002 ($1,000) $747,424
Health care & social assistance 17,528
  Annual payroll ($1,000). $12,130,929
  Paid employees 317,975
  Receipts, 2002 ($1,000) $24,707,761
Arts and entertainment 2,706
  Annual payroll ($1,000). $1,496,363
  Paid employees 57,737
  Receipts, 2002 ($1,000) $3,226,042
Real estate 10,031
  Annual payroll ($1,000). $1,734,609
  Paid employees 50,588
  Receipts, 2002 ($1,000) $7,660,742
Accommodation & food service. 14,963
  Annual payroll ($1,000). $3,182,478
  Paid employees 214,805
  Receipts, 2002 ($1,000) $8,642,681

8   Washington

Exports, 2006
Value of exported goods ($ mil) $53,075
   Manufactured $44,538
   Non-manufactured. $6,530

Foreign direct investment in US affiliates, 2004
Property, plants & equipment ($ mil) $17,477
Employment (x 1,000). 83.4

Agriculture, 2006
Number of farms 34,000
Farm acreage (x 1,000) 15,100
   Acres per farm. 444
Farm marketings and income ($ mil)
Total. $6,139.0
   Crops. $4,524.4
   Livestock. $1,614.5
Net farm income $958.3

Principal commodities, in order by marketing receipts, 2005
   Apples, Dairy products, Cattle and calves,
      Wheat, Potatoes

Federal economic activity in state
Expenditures, 2005 ($ mil)
Total. $46,338
   Per capita $7,364.77
   Defense $9,099
   Non-defense. $37,239
Defense department, 2006 ($ mil)
   Payroll. $5,652
   Contract awards $4,766
   Grants $60
Homeland security grants ($1,000)
   2006. . . . . $32,222
   2007. . . . . $28,926

FDIC-insured financial institutions, 2005
Number. 99
Assets ($ billion) $65.5
Deposits ($ billion) $48.3

Fishing, 2006
Catch (x 1,000 lbs). 538,791
Value ($1,000). $193,109

Mining, 2006 ($ mil)
Total non-fuel mineral production $720
Percent of U.S. 1.12%

Communication, Energy & Transportation

Communication
Households with computers, 2003. . . . . 71.4%
Households with internet access, 2003 . . . . 62.3%
High-speed internet providers 63
Total high-speed internet lines. 2,015,564
   Residential 1,360,776
   Business. 654,788
Wireless phone customers, 12/2006 4,799,143

FCC-licensed stations (as of January 1, 2008)
TV stations 35
FM radio stations. 173
AM radio stations 109

Energy
Energy consumption, 2004
   Total (trillion Btu). 2,005
   Per capita (million Btu) 323.1
By source of production (trillion Btu)
   Coal 113
   Natural gas 269
   Petroleum. 842
   Nuclear electric power 94
   Hydroelectric power. 717
By end-use sector (trillion Btu)
   Residential 469
   Commercial 371
   Industrial 559
   Transportation 605
Electric energy, 2005
   Primary source of electricity. . . . Hydroelectric
   Net generation (billion kWh) 102.0
      percent from renewable sources. 72.8%
   Net summer capability (million kW) 27.8
   CO_2 emitted from generation 14.9
Natural gas utilities, 2005
   Customers (x 1,000) 1,062
   Sales (trillion Btu). 196
   Revenues ($ mil) $1,451
Nuclear plants, 2007 1
Total CO_2 emitted (million metric tons). 78.7
Energy spending, 2004 ($ mil) $15,561
   per capita $2,508
   Price per million Btu $12.32

Transportation, 2006
Public road & street mileage 83,256
   Urban. 22,469
   Rural 60,787
   Interstate. 764
Vehicle miles of travel (millions) 56,517
   per capita 8,865.5
Total motor vehicle registrations. 5,689,497
   Automobiles. .3,087,818
   Trucks 2,590,014
   Motorcycles 194,109
Licensed drivers .4,790,864
   19 years & under 176,286
Deaths from motor vehicle accidents 630
Gasoline consumed (x 1,000 gallons) 2,730,776
   per capita 428.4

Commuting Statistics, 2006
Average commute time (min) 25.2
   Drove to work alone 72.8%
   Carpooled. 11.8%
   Public transit 5.2%
   Walk to work 3.3%
   Work from home. 5.1%

State Summary

Capital city . . . . Charleston
Governor . . . . Joe Manchin III
1900 Kanawha St
Charleston, WV 25305
304-558-2000
Admitted as a state 1863
Area (square miles) 24,230
Population, 2007 (estimate) 1,812,035
Largest city . . . . Charleston
    Population, 2006 50,846
Personal income per capita, 2006
    (in current dollars) $27,897
Gross domestic product, 2006 ($ mil) $55,658

Leading industries by payroll, 2005

Health care/Social assistance, Manufacturing,
Retail trade

**Leading agricultural commodities
by receipts, 2005**

Broilers, Cattle and calves, Turkeys, Chicken
eggs, Dairy products

Geography & Environment

Total area (square miles) 24,230
    land 24,078
    water 152
Federally-owned land, 2004 (acres) 1,146,211
    percent 7.4%
Highest point . . . . Spruce Knob
    elevation (feet) 4,861
Lowest point . . . . Potomac River
    elevation (feet) 240
General coastline (miles) 0
Tidal shoreline (miles) 0
Cropland, 2003 (x 1,000 acres) 821
Forest land, 2003 (x 1,000 acres) 10,556
Capital city . . . . Charleston
    Population 2000 .53,421
    Population 2006 50,846
Largest city . . . . Charleston
    Population 2000 .53,421
    Population 2006 50,846

Number of cities with over 100,000 population

1990 0
2000 0
2006 0

State park and recreation areas, 2005

Area (x 1,000 acres) 177
Number of visitors (x 1,000) 7,406
Revenues ($1,000) $19,602
    percent of operating expenditures 58.4%

National forest system land, 2007

Acres 1,043,028

Demographics & Population Characteristics

Population

1980 1,949,644
1990 1,793,477
2000 1,808,350
2006 1,818,470
    Male 890,588
    Female 927,882
Living in group quarters, 2006 45,532
    percent of total 2.5%
2007 (estimate) 1,812,035
    persons per square mile of land 75.3
2008 (projected) 1,827,226
2010 (projected) 1,829,141
2020 (projected) 1,801,112
2030 (projected) 1,719,959

**Population of Core-Based Statistical Areas
(formerly Metropolitan Areas), x 1,000**

	CBSA	Non-CBSA
1990	1,315	478
2000	1,348	461
2006	1,366	453

Change in population, 2000-2007

Number 3,685
    percent 0.2%
Natural increase (births minus deaths) . . . .-941
Net internal migration 7,802
Net international migration 4,246

Persons by age, 2006

Under 5 years 104,964
5 to 17 years 284,107
18 years and over 1,429,399
65 years and over 278,692
85 years and over 36,073
    Median age 40.2

Persons by age, 2010 (projected)

Under 5 years 101,135
18 and over 1,446,830
65 and over 292,402
    Median age 41.4

Race, 2006

One Race

White 1,725,687
    Black or African American 60,196
    Asian 11,778
    American Indian/Alaska Native 4,045
    Hawaiian Native/Pacific Islander 531
Two or more races 16,233

Persons of Hispanic origin, 2006

Total Hispanic or Latino 14,383
    Mexican 5,756
    Puerto Rican 1,816
    Cuban 412

Persons of Asian origin, 2006

Total Asian 10,479
  Asian Indian........................3,362
  Chinese 655
  Filipino 2,218
  Japanese 1,413
  Korean................................ 674
  Vietnamese...........................1,210

Marital status, 2006

Population 15 years & over 1,499,797
  Never married 369,318
  Married............................ 838,050
  Separated 21,287
  Widowed........................... 119,259
  Divorced 173,170

Language spoken at home, 2006

Population 5 years and older......... 1,714,041
  English only 1,675,050
  Spanish 18,207
  French 3,152
  German............................ 2,126
  Chinese 1,111

Households & families, 2006

Households........................ 743,064
  with persons under 18 years 225,948
  with persons over 65 years........... 202,011
  persons per household 2.39
Families............................ 502,381
  persons per family.....................2.89
Married couples....................... 390,066
Female householder,
  no husband present.................. 80,983
One-person households 204,778

Nativity, 2006

Number of residents born in state 1,312,058
  percent of population 72.2%

Immigration & naturalization, 2006

Legal permanent residents admitted........ 764
Persons naturalized 390
Non-immigrant admissions 14,003

Vital Statistics and Health

Marriages

2004 13,621
2005 13,418
2006 13,129

Divorces

2004 9,148
2005 9,223
2006 8,541

Health risks, 2006

Percent of adults who are:
  Smokers............................ 25.7%
  Overweight (BMI > 25)............... 67.0%
  Obese (BMI > 30)..................... 31.0%

Births

2005 20,836
  Birthrate (per 1,000)................11.5
  White.............................19,935
  Black 707
  Hispanic 174
  Asian/Pacific Islander 178
  Amer. Indian/Alaska Native 16
  Low birth weight (2,500g or less)........ 9.6%
  Cesarian births 34.2%
  Preterm births 14.4%
  To unmarried mothers................36.5%
  Twin births (per 1,000) 27.2
  Triplets or higher order (per 100,000)....105.3
2006 (preliminary).................... 20,928
  rate per 1,000 ....11.5

Deaths

2004

All causes 20,793
  rate per 100,000.................... 966.0
Heart disease 5,674
  rate per 100,000....................260.9
Malignant neoplasms 4,694
  rate per 100,000....................211.7
Cerebrovascular disease................1,178
  rate per 100,000.....................54.1
Chronic lower respiratory disease 1,225
  rate per 100,000.....................55.3
Diabetes............................. 840
  rate per 100,000.....................38.1
2005 (preliminary).................... 20,780
  rate per 100,000.................... 960.4
2006 (provisional) 20,573

Infant deaths

2004 158
  rate per 1,000 ....7.6
2005 (provisional) 169
  rate per 1,000 ....8.2

Exercise routines, 2005

None................................ 28.5%
Moderate or greater...................... 39.4%
Vigorous 17.6%

Abortions, 2004

Total performed in state................... NA
  rate per 1,000 women age 15-44.......... NA
  % obtained by out-of-state residents ...... NA

Physicians, 2005

Total.................................4,190
  rate per 100,000 persons 231

Community hospitals, 2005

Number of hospitals 57
Beds (x 1,000)..........................7.2
Patients admitted (x 1,000) 292
Average daily census (x 1,000) 4.5
Average cost per day $1,113
Outpatient visits (x 1 mil) 6.1

Disability status of population, 2006

5 to 15 years	8.6%
16 to 64 years	20.7%
65 years and over	48.1%

Education

Educational attainment, 2006

Population over 25 years	1,262,933
Less than 9th grade	7.1%
High school graduate or more	81.0%
College graduate or more	16.5%
Graduate or professional degree	6.6%

Public school enrollment, 2005-06

Total	280,866
Pre-kindergarten through grade 8	196,988
Grades 9 through 12	83,677

Graduating public high school seniors, 2004-05

Diplomas (incl. GED and others)	17,137

SAT scores, 2007

Average critical reading score	516
Average writing score	505
Average math score	507
Percent of graduates taking test	20%

Public school teachers, 2006-07 (estimate)

Total (x 1,000)	19.9
Elementary	14.2
Secondary	5.7
Average salary	$40,531
Elementary	$40,350
Secondary	$40,988

State receipts & expenditures for public schools, 2006-07 (estimate)

Revenue receipts ($ mil)	$3,042
Expenditures	
Total ($ mil)	$3,288
Per capita	$1,558
Per pupil	$10,236

NAEP proficiency scores, 2007

	Reading		Math	
	Basic	Proficient	Basic	Proficient
Grade 4	62.6%	27.8%	81.2%	32.6%
Grade 8	68.4%	22.9%	61.2%	18.5%

Higher education enrollment, fall 2005

Total	14,399
Full-time men	4,679
Full-time women	7,453
Part-time men	770
Part-time women	1,497

Minority enrollment in institutions of higher education, 2005

Black, non-Hispanic	5,220
Hispanic	1,108
Asian/Pacific Islander	1,151
American Indian/Alaska Native	371

Institutions of higher education, 2005-06

Total	44
Public	23
Private	21

Earned degrees conferred, 2004-05

Associate's	3,738
Bachelor's	9,574
Master's	2,735
First-professional	449
Doctor's	213

Public Libraries, 2006

Number of libraries	97
Number of outlets	180
Annual visits per capita	3.3
Circulation per capita	4.3

State & local financial support for higher education, FY 2006

Full-time equivalent enrollment (x 1,000)	71.7
Appropriations per FTE	$4,181

Social Insurance & Welfare Programs

Social Security benefits & beneficiaries, 2005

Beneficiaries (x 1,000)	413
Retired & dependents	239
Survivors	70
Disabled & dependents	104
Annual benefit payments ($ mil)	$4,417
Retired & dependents	$2,377
Survivors	$932
Disabled & dependents	$1,108
Average monthly benefit	
Retired & dependents	$988
Disabled & dependents	$981
Widowed	$927

Medicare, July 2005

Enrollment (x 1,000)	355
Payments ($ mil)	$2,262

Medicaid, 2004

Beneficiaries (x 1,000)	896
Payments ($ mil)	$4,314

State Children's Health Insurance Program, 2006

Enrollment (x 1,000)	39.9
Expenditures ($ mil)	$41.6

Persons without health insurance, 2006

Number (x 1,000)	245
percent	13.5%
Number of children (x 1,000)	34
percent of children	8.6%

Health care expenditures, 2004

Total expenditures	$10,783
per capita	$5,954

Federal and state public aid

State unemployment insurance, 2006
Recipients, first payments (x 1,000) 40
Total payments ($ mil) $132
Average weekly benefit $231
Temporary Assistance for Needy Families, 2006
Recipients (x 1,000) 284.9
Families (x 1,000) 127.2
Supplemental Security Income, 2005
Recipients (x 1,000) 76.7
Payments ($ mil) $375.9
Food Stamp Program, 2006
Avg monthly participants (x 1,000) 267.6
Total benefits ($ mil) $266.4

Housing & Construction

Housing units

Total 2005 (estimate) 872,147
Total 2006 (estimate) 877,784
Seasonal or recreational use, 2006 41,805
Owner-occupied, 2006 554,791
  Median home value $89,700
  Homeowner vacancy rate 2.0%
Renter-occupied, 2006 188,273
  Median rent $499
  Rental vacancy rate 10.8%
Home ownership rate, 2005 . . . . 81.3%
Home ownership rate, 2006 . . . . 78.4%

New privately-owned housing units

Number authorized, 2006 (x 1,000) 5.6
  Value ($ mil) $944.4
Started 2005 (x 1,000, estimate) 5.4
Started 2006 (x 1,000, estimate) 5.4

Existing home sales

2005 (x 1,000) 38.6
2006 (x 1,000) 32.6

Government & Elections

State officials 2008

Governor . . . . Joe Manchin III
      Democratic, term expires 1/09
Lieutenant Governor . . . . Earl Ray Tomblin
Secretary of State . . . . Betty Ireland
Attorney General . . . . Darrell McGraw Jr
Chief Justice . . . . Robin Jean Davis

Governorship

Minimum age 30
Length of term . . . . 4 years
Consecutive terms permitted 2
Who succeeds . . . . President of Senate

Local governments by type, 2002

Total 686
  County 55
  Municipal 234
  Township 0
  School District 55
  Special District 342

State legislature

Name . . . . Legislature
Upper chamber . . . . Senate
  Number of members 34
  Length of term . . . . 4 years
  Party in majority, 2008 . . . . Democratic
Lower chamber . . . . House of Delegates
  Number of members 100
  Length of term . . . . 2 years
  Party in majority, 2008 . . . . Democratic

Federal representation, 2008 (110th Congress)

Senator . . . . John Rockefeller IV
  Party . . . . Democratic
  Year term expires 2009
Senator . . . . Robert Byrd
  Party . . . . Democratic
  Year term expires 2013
Representatives, total 3
  Democrats 2
  Republicans 1

Voters in November 2006 election (estimate)

Total 512,776
  Male 245,029
  Female 267,747
  White 493,819
  Black 11,402
  Hispanic . . . . NA
  Asian 1,085

Presidential election, 2004

Total Popular Vote 755,887
  Kerry 326,541
  Bush 423,778
Total Electoral Votes 5

Votes cast for US Senators

2004
Total vote (x 1,000) . . . . NA
Leading party . . . . NA
Percent for leading party . . . . NA
2006
Total vote (x 1,000) 207
Leading party . . . . Democratic
Percent for leading party 77.0%

Votes cast for US Representatives

2004
Total vote (x 1,000) 722
  Democratic 415
  Republican 303
Leading party . . . . Democratic
Percent for leading party 57.6%
2006
Total vote (x 1,000) 455
  Democratic 264
  Republican 191
Leading party . . . . Democratic
Percent for leading party 58.0%

State government employment, 2006
Full-time equivalent employees 37,004
Payroll ($ mil) $113.4

Local government employment, 2006
Full-time equivalent employees 60,387
Payroll ($ mil) $167.6

Women holding public office, 2008
US Congress 1
Statewide elected office. 1
State legislature 19

Black public officials, 2002
Total. 19
   US and state legislatures 2
   City/county/regional offices 13
   Judicial/law enforcement. 3
   Education/school boards 1

Hispanic public officials, 2006
Total. 0
   State executives & legislators 0
   City/county/regional offices 0
   Judicial/law enforcement. 0
   Education/school boards 0

Governmental Finance

State government revenues, 2006
Total revenue (x $1,000). $11,435,205
   per capita $6,322.34
General revenue (x $1,000) $10,262,364
   Intergovernmental 3,224,309
   Taxes 4,558,219
      general sales. 1,125,766
      individual income tax 1,297,720
      corporate income tax 533,027
   Current charges. 1,100,687
   Miscellaneous 1,379,149

State government expenditure, 2006
Total expenditure (x $1,000) $9,791,417
   per capita $5,413.51
General expenditure (x $1,000) $9,199,607
   per capita, total. $5,086.31
      Education 1,889.88
      Public welfare 1,316.28
      Health 166.28
      Hospitals. 44.91
      Highways 565.15
      Police protection. 30.02
      Corrections 118.71
      Natural resources 88.18
      Parks & recreation 28.88
      Governmental administration 305.76
      Interest on general debt. 124.23

State debt & cash, 2006 ($ per capita)
Debt $2,989.10
Cash/security holdings. $6,136.06

Federal government grants to state & local government, 2005 (x $1,000)
Total. $3,808,971
by Federal agency
   Defense 17,876
   Education 272,646
   Energy. 10,653
   Environmental Protection Agency 82,613
   Health & Human Services. 2,191,826
   Homeland Security. 54,764
   Housing & Urban Development. 173,549
   Justice 55,052
   Labor 59,814
   Transportation 617,930
   Veterans Affairs. 1,459

Crime & Law Enforcement

Crime, 2006 (rates per 100,000 residents)
Property crimes 47,672
   Burglary 11,531
   Larceny 32,220
   Motor vehicle theft 3,921
   Property crime rate. 2,621.5
Violent crimes. 5,087
   Murder 75
   Forcible rape. 389
   Robbery. 853
   Aggravated assault 3,770
   Violent crime rate 279.7
Hate crimes. 37

Fraud and identity theft, 2006
Fraud complaints. 2,058
   rate per 100,000 residents 113.2
Identity theft complaints 715
   rate per 100,000 residents 39.3

Law enforcement agencies, 2006
Total agencies. 339
Total employees 4,208
   Officers 3,333
   Civilians 875

Prisoners, probation, and parole, 2006
Total prisoners. 5,733
   percent change, 12/31/05 to 12/31/06 . . . . 7.9%
   in private facilities 0%
   in local jails 23.8%
Sentenced to more than one year 5,719
   rate per 100,000 residents 314
Adults on probation 7,668
Adults on parole. 1,523

Prisoner demographics, June 30, 2005 (rate per 100,000 residents)
Male 817
Female 84
White. 392
Black. 2,188
Hispanic 211

Arrests, 2006
Total................................. 26,566
   Persons under 18 years of age 1,438

Persons under sentence of death, 1/1/07
Total...................................... 0
   White................................. 0
   Black................................. 0
   Hispanic.............................. 0

State's highest court
Name ....Supreme Court of Appeals
Number of members...................... 5
Length of term...................... 12 years
Intermediate appeals court? .... no

Labor & Income

Civilian labor force, 2006 (x 1,000)
Total.................................... 815
   Men 433
   Women 382
   Persons 16-19 years.................... 34
   White................................ 782
   Black 23
   Hispanic .... NA

Civilian labor force as a percent of civilian non-institutional population, 2006
Total..................................55.9%
   Men 61.2
   Women 50.8
   Persons 16-19 years...................35.0
   White................................55.8
   Black 56.9
   Hispanic .... NA

Employment, 2006 (x 1,000)
Total.................................... 773
   Men 411
   Women 362
   Persons 16-19 years.................... 28
   White................................ 742
   Black 21
   Hispanic .... NA

Unemployment rate, 2006
Total.................................... 5.1%
   Men 5.1
   Women 5.2
   Persons 16-19 years.................. 17.1
   White................................ 5.1
   Black 6.7
   Hispanic .... NA

Full-time/part-time labor force, 2003 (x 1,000)
Full-time labor force, employed 622
Part-time labor force, employed........... 117
Unemployed, looking for
   Full-time work......................... 42
   Part-time work......................... 6
*Mean duration of unemployment (weeks)......*20.7
   Median 11.6

Labor unions, 2006
Membership (x 1,000).................... 101
   percent of employed 14.2%

Experienced civilian labor force by private industry, 2006
Total................................. 567,898
   Natural resources & mining 28,995
   Construction 39,598
   Manufacturing......................61,007
   Trade, transportation & utilities 138,992
   Information 11,513
   Finance 28,725
   Professional & business 59,633
   Education & health 106,329
   Leisure & hospitality............... 70,805
   Other 21,767

Experienced civilian labor force by occupation, May 2006
Management.......................... 26,400
Business & financial 20,470
Legal................................ 5,690
Sales................................77,790
Office & admin. support...............117,080
Computers & math 7,330
Architecture & engineering............9,330
Arts & entertainment 5,530
Education 41,040
Social services 12,220
Health care practitioner & technical..... 46,120
Health care support 23,870
Maintenance & repair.................37,290
Construction 51,010
Transportation & moving 61,510
Production 45,460
Farming, fishing & forestry..............1,710

Hours and earnings of production workers on manufacturing payrolls, 2006
Average weekly hours 41.3
Average hourly earnings $17.89
Average weekly earnings $738.86

Income and poverty, 2006
Median household income............ $35,059
Personal income, per capita (current $)... $27,897
   in constant (2000) dollars $24,352
Persons below poverty level............. 17.3%

Average annual pay
2006................................. $32,728
   increase from 2005 .... 4.4%

Federal individual income tax returns, 2005
Returns filed......................... 753,593
Adjusted gross income ($1,000) $30,318,090
Total tax liability ($1,000) $3,287,192

Charitable contributions, 2004
Number of contributions 105.1
Total amount ($ mil)................. $386.5

Economy, Business, Industry & Agriculture

Fortune 500 companies, 2007 0

Bankruptcy cases filed, FY 2007 4,230

Patents and trademarks issued, 2007

Patents 118

Trademarks 115

Business firm ownership, 2002

Women-owned 31,301

   Sales ($ mil) $3,252

Black-owned 1,472

   Sales ($ mil) $92

Hispanic-owned 648

   Sales ($ mil) $187

Asian-owned 1,234

   Sales ($ mil) $435

Amer. Indian/Alaska Native-owned 405

   Sales ($ mil) $35

Hawaiian/Pacific Islander-owned 10

   Sales ($ mil) . . . . NA

Gross domestic product, 2006 ($ mil)

Total gross domestic product $55,658

   Agriculture, forestry, fishing and

      hunting 277

   Mining 3,834

   Utilities 2,847

   Construction 2,532

   Manufacturing, durable goods 3,393

   Manufacturing, non-durable goods 2,741

   Wholesale trade 2,864

   Retail trade 4,407

   Transportation & warehousing 1,874

   Information 1,405

   Finance & insurance 2,168

   Real estate, rental & leasing 5,243

   Professional and technical services 2,228

   Educational services 263

   Health care and social assistance 5,317

   Accommodation/food services 1,500

   Other services, except government 1,280

   Government 9,462

Establishments, payroll, employees & receipts, by major industry group, 2005

Total 40,735

   Annual payroll ($1,000) $16,323,457

   Paid employees 565,499

Forestry, fishing & agriculture 348

   Annual payroll ($1,000) $22,575

   Paid employees 1,253

Mining 631

   Annual payroll ($1,000) $1,329,536

   Paid employees 23,040

   Receipts, 2002 ($1,000) $5,429,555

Utilities 238

   Annual payroll ($1,000) $400,765

   Paid employees 6,251

   Receipts, 2002 ($1,000) . . . . NA

Construction 4,625

   Annual payroll ($1,000) $1,045,632

   Paid employees 29,842

   Receipts, 2002 ($1,000) $3,393,385

Manufacturing 1,406

   Annual payroll ($1,000) $2,574,491

   Paid employees 62,972

   Receipts, 2002 ($1,000) $18,911,332

Wholesale trade 1,641

   Annual payroll ($1,000) $785,543

   Paid employees 21,134

   Receipts, 2002 ($1,000) $10,924,279

Retail trade 7,243

   Annual payroll ($1,000) $1,658,688

   Paid employees 92,369

   Receipts, 2002 ($1,000) $16,747,900

Transportation & warehousing 1,433

   Annual payroll ($1,000) $562,945

   Paid employees 15,944

   Receipts, 2002 ($1,000) $1,927,398

Information 718

   Annual payroll ($1,000) $416,302

   Paid employees 12,673

   Receipts, 2002 ($1,000) . . . . NA

Finance & insurance 2,100

   Annual payroll ($1,000) $699,133

   Paid employees 20,338

   Receipts, 2002 ($1,000) . . . . NA

Professional, scientific & technical 3,035

   Annual payroll ($1,000) $844,354

   Paid employees 23,323

   Receipts, 2002 ($1,000) $1,860,522

Education 260

   Annual payroll ($1,000) $129,775

   Paid employees 7,598

   Receipts, 2002 ($1,000) $60,628

Health care & social assistance 4,743

   Annual payroll ($1,000) $3,499,116

   Paid employees 112,764

   Receipts, 2002 ($1,000) $7,631,590

Arts and entertainment 688

   Annual payroll ($1,000) $180,831

   Paid employees 10,558

   Receipts, 2002 ($1,000) $934,176

Real estate 1,548

   Annual payroll ($1,000) $176,376

   Paid employees 6,975

   Receipts, 2002 ($1,000) $844,390

Accommodation & food service 3,501

   Annual payroll ($1,000) $652,685

   Paid employees 58,510

   Receipts, 2002 ($1,000) $1,974,851

Exports, 2006
Value of exported goods ($ mil) $3,225
   Manufactured $2,575
   Non-manufactured $610

Foreign direct investment in US affiliates, 2004
Property, plants & equipment ($ mil) $5,716
Employment (x 1,000)....................19.0

Agriculture, 2006
Number of farms 21,200
Farm acreage (x 1,000) 3,600
   Acres per farm 170
Farm marketings and income ($ mil)
Total............................... $449.6
   Crops..............................$79.7
   Livestock...........................$369.8
Net farm income $49.7

Principal commodities, in order by marketing receipts, 2005
Broilers, Cattle and calves, Turkeys, Chicken eggs, Dairy products

Federal economic activity in state
Expenditures, 2005 ($ mil)
   Total............................ $16,087
      Per capita $8,868.07
   Defense $784
   Non-defense....................... $15,304
Defense department, 2006 ($ mil)
   Payroll............................. $384
   Contract awards $392
   Grants $25
Homeland security grants ($1,000)
   2006........................... $13,294
   2007............................ $6,712

FDIC-insured financial institutions, 2005
Number 70
Assets ($ billion) $21.3
Deposits ($ billion) $16.8

Fishing, 2006
Catch (x 1,000 lbs)...................... NA
Value ($1,000)......................... NA

Mining, 2006 ($ mil)
Total non-fuel mineral production $211
Percent of U.S. 0.33%

Communication, Energy & Transportation

Communication
Households with computers, 2003........ 55.0%
Households with internet access, 2003 .... 47.6%
High-speed internet providers 24
Total high-speed internet lines......... 268,746
   Residential 248,611
   Business...........................20,135
Wireless phone customers, 12/2006 1,040,224

FCC-licensed stations (as of January 1, 2008)
TV stations 18
FM radio stations........................ 118
AM radio stations 68

Energy
Energy consumption, 2004
   Total (trillion Btu)..................... 821
   Per capita (million Btu) 453.5
By source of production (trillion Btu)
   Coal 937
   Natural gas 143
   Petroleum............................ 280
   Nuclear electric power 0
   Hydroelectric power..................... 13
By end-use sector (trillion Btu)
   Residential 165
   Commercial 113
   Industrial 361
   Transportation 182
Electric energy, 2005
   Primary source of electricity........... Coal
   Net generation (billion kWh) 93.6
      percent from renewable sources....... 1.7%
   Net summer capability (million kW) ...16.5
   CO_2 emitted from generation 84.8
Natural gas utilities, 2005
   Customers (x 1,000) 411
   Sales (trillion Btu).................... 91
   Revenues ($ mil) $625
Nuclear plants, 2007 0
Total CO_2 emitted (million metric tons).....114.4
Energy spending, 2004 ($ mil) $5,845
   per capita $3,228
   Price per million Btu $10.66

Transportation, 2006
Public road & street mileage 37,054
   Urban..............................4,514
   Rural 32,540
   Interstate.......................... 555
Vehicle miles of travel (millions) 20,885
   per capita 11,547.0
Total motor vehicle registrations.......1,441,099
   Automobiles...................... 734,599
   Trucks 703,706
   Motorcycles 40,741
Licensed drivers 1,335,303
   19 years & under 60,611
Deaths from motor vehicle accidents 410
Gasoline consumed (x 1,000 gallons) 841,146
   per capita 465.1

Commuting Statistics, 2006
Average commute time (min) 25.6
   Drove to work alone 80.0%
   Carpooled.......................... 12.1%
   Public transit 1.0%
   Walk to work 3.1%
   Work from home...................... 2.4%

State Summary

Capital city . . . . Madison
Governor . . . . Jim Doyle
115 East State Capitol
Madison, WI 53707
608-266-1212
Admitted as a state 1848
Area (square miles) 65,498
Population, 2007 (estimate). 5,601,640
Largest city . . . . Milwaukee
Population, 2006 573,358
Personal income per capita, 2006
(in current dollars) $34,701
Gross domestic product, 2006 ($ mil) . . . $227,230

Leading industries by payroll, 2005
Manufacturing, Health care/Social assistance,
Finance & Insurance

**Leading agricultural commodities
by receipts, 2005**
Dairy products, Cattle and calves, Corn, Soybeans, Greenhouse/nursery

Geography & Environment

Total area (square miles). 65,498
land 54,310
water 11,188
Federally-owned land, 2004 (acres) 1,971,902
percent. 5.6%
Highest point . . . . Timms Hil
elevation (feet) 1,951
Lowest point . . . . Lake Michigan
elevation (feet) 581
General coastline (miles) 0
Tidal shoreline (miles) 0
Cropland, 2003 (x 1,000 acres) 10,304
Forest land, 2003 (x 1,000 acres). 14,528
Capital city . . . . Madison
Population 2000 208,054
Population 2006 223,389
Largest city . . . . Milwaukee
Population 2000 596,974
Population 2006 573,358

Number of cities with over 100,000 population
1990 2
2000 3
2006 3

State park and recreation areas, 2005
Area (x 1,000 acres). 135
Number of visitors (x 1,000) 14,964
Revenues ($1,000) $15,773
percent of operating expenditures. 74.5%

National forest system land, 2007
Acres 1,530,686

Demographics & Population Characteristics

Population
1980 4,705,767
1990 4,891,769
2000 5,363,715
2006 5,556,506
Male. 2,760,942
Female. 2,795,564
Living in group quarters, 2006 159,885
percent of total. 2.9%
2007 (estimate). 5,601,640
persons per square mile of land 103.1
2008 (projected). 5,659,640
2010 (projected) 5,727,426
2020 (projected). 6,004,954
2030 (projected). 6,150,764

**Population of Core-Based Statistical Areas
(formerly Metropolitan Areas), x 1,000**

	CBSA	Non-CBSA
1990	4,205	687
2000	4,604	759
2006	4,777	779

Change in population, 2000-2007
Number 237,925
percent. 4.4%
Natural increase (births minus deaths) 175,359
Net internal migration . . . . -5,618
Net international migration 58,366

Persons by age, 2006
Under 5 years 348,764
5 to 17 years 963,766
18 years and over 4,243,976
65 years and over 724,034
85 years and over 111,159
Median age 37.7

Persons by age, 2010 (projected)
Under 5 years 367,567
18 and over 4,408,282
65 and over 771,993
Median age 38.1

Race, 2006
One Race
White. 4,999,679
Black or African American 332,296
Asian 111,057
American Indian/Alaska Native. 51,937
Hawaiian Native/Pacific Islander. 2,128
Two or more races. 59,409

Persons of Hispanic origin, 2006
Total Hispanic or Latino 256,304
Mexican. 178,638
Puerto Rican 43,500
Cuban 1,902

Persons of Asian origin, 2006

Total Asian 110,778
  Asian Indian.........................17,949
  Chinese 15,449
  Filipino 7,296
  Japanese 3,212
  Korean...............................6,677
  Vietnamese..........................4,953

Marital status, 2006

Population 15 years & over 4,483,075
  Never married 1,340,227
  Married........................ 2,435,425
  Separated 55,011
  Widowed........................ 268,374
  Divorced 439,049

Language spoken at home, 2006

Population 5 years and older......... 5,204,804
  English only 4,781,643
  Spanish 217,550
  French 13,372
  German 46,834
  Chinese 10,348

Households & families, 2006

Households......................2,230,060
  with persons under 18 years 721,421
  with persons over 65 years........... 493,675
  persons per household 2.42
Families........................1,456,314
  persons per family......................2.98
Married couples...................... 1,147,656
Female householder,
  no husband present..................216,124
One-person households 628,248

Nativity, 2006

Number of residents born in state 4,007,850
  percent of population................. 72.1%

Immigration & naturalization, 2006

Legal permanent residents admitted...... 8,341
Persons naturalized 3,247
Non-immigrant admissions 119,990

Vital Statistics and Health

Marriages

2004 34,056
2005 33,876
2006 32,562

Divorces

2004 16,802
2005 16,297
2006 15,966

Health risks, 2006

Percent of adults who are:
  Smokers............................20.8%
  Overweight (BMI > 25)............... 63.4%
  Obese (BMI > 30)....................26.6%

Births

2005 70,984
  Birthrate (per 1,000)....................12.8
  White............................. 60,461
  Black 6,794
  Hispanic 6,252
  Asian/Pacific Islander 2,612
  Amer. Indian/Alaska Native...........1,117
  Low birth weight (2,500g or less)....... 7.0%
  Cesarian births 23.7%
  Preterm births 11.4%
  To unmarried mothers.............. 32.5%
  Twin births (per 1,000) 30.8
  Triplets or higher order (per 100,000)....160.1
2006 (preliminary)..................... 72,335
  rate per 1,000 ....13.0

Deaths

2004
All causes 45,600
  rate per 100,000.......................749.8
Heart disease 11,909
  rate per 100,000.......................191.8
Malignant neoplasms 10,861
  rate per 100,000.......................184.4
Cerebrovascular disease..................3,071
  rate per 100,000.......................48.8
Chronic lower respiratory disease 2,312
  rate per 100,000.......................38.7
Diabetes.............................1,310
  rate per 100,000.......................21.7
2005 (preliminary)..................... 46,709
  rate per 100,000.......................752.2
2006 (provisional) 46,188

Infant deaths

2004 420
  rate per 1,000 ....6.0
2005 (provisional) 468
  rate per 1,000 ....6.6

Exercise routines, 2005

None................................. 18.7%
Moderate or greater.................... 56.6%
Vigorous 32.8%

Abortions, 2004

Total performed in state..................9,943
  rate per 1,000 women age 15-44............ 9
  % obtained by out-of-state residents 2.3%

Physicians, 2005

Total................................14,093
  rate per 100,000 persons 255

Community hospitals, 2005

Number of hospitals 124
Beds (x 1,000)............................14.5
Patients admitted (x 1,000) 612
Average daily census (x 1,000) 9.0
Average cost per day $1,458
Outpatient visits (x 1 mil) 12.7

Disability status of population, 2006
5 to 15 years 6.8%
16 to 64 years 10.7%
65 years and over 35.7%

Education

Educational attainment, 2006
Population over 25 years 3,682,631
   Less than 9th grade. 4.1%
   High school graduate or more 88.4%
   College graduate or more. 25.1%
   Graduate or professional degree. 8.4%

Public school enrollment, 2005-06
Total. 875,174
   Pre-kindergarten through grade 8. . . . 583,998
   Grades 9 through 12 291,176

Graduating public high school seniors, 2004-05
Diplomas (incl. GED and others) 64,160

SAT scores, 2007
Average critical reading score. 587
Average writing score 575
Average math score 598
Percent of graduates taking test 6%

Public school teachers, 2006-07 (estimate)
Total (x 1,000) 59.3
   Elementary 40.6
   Secondary 18.7
Average salary $47,901
   Elementary $47,988
   Secondary $47,712

State receipts & expenditures for public schools, 2006-07 (estimate)
Revenue receipts ($ mil) $10,130
Expenditures
Total ($ mil) $11,833
   Per capita $1,646
   Per pupil $11,019

NAEP proficiency scores, 2007

	Reading		Math	
	Basic	Proficient	Basic	Proficient
Grade 4	70.4%	35.6%	85.3%	46.9%
Grade 8	75.9%	33.2%	75.9%	37.0%

Higher education enrollment, fall 2005
Total. 66,330
   Full-time men 18,922
   Full-time women 27,827
   Part-time men 6,530
   Part-time women. 13,051

Minority enrollment in institutions of higher education, 2005
Black, non-Hispanic 17,185
Hispanic 9,605
Asian/Pacific Islander 9,691
American Indian/Alaska Native. 3,728

Institutions of higher education, 2005-06
Total. 68
   Public. 31
   Private 37

Earned degrees conferred, 2004-05
Associate's. 11,705
Bachelor's 31,144
Master's 8,716
First-professional. 1,127
Doctor's. 946

Public Libraries, 2006
Number of libraries. 381
Number of outlets 466
Annual visits per capita 6.0
Circulation per capita. 10.3

State & local financial support for higher education, FY 2006
Full-time equivalent enrollment (x 1,000) 212.2
Appropriations per FTE. $6,226

Social Insurance & Welfare Programs

Social Security benefits & beneficiaries, 2005
Beneficiaries (x 1,000) 952
   Retired & dependents. 694
   Survivors. 120
   Disabled & dependents. 138
Annual benefit payments ($ mil) $10,551
   Retired & dependents. $7,395
   Survivors. $1,733
   Disabled & dependents. $1,423
Average monthly benefit
   Retired & dependents. $1,028
   Disabled & dependents. $939
   Widowed. $1,020

Medicare, July 2005
Enrollment (x 1,000). 826
Payments ($ mil) $4,744

Medicaid, 2004
Beneficiaries (x 1,000). 377
Payments ($ mil) $2,020

State Children's Health Insurance Program, 2006
Enrollment (x 1,000). 56.6
Expenditures ($ mil) $33.4

Persons without health insurance, 2006
Number (x 1,000). 481
   percent. 8.8%
Number of children (x 1,000) 63
   percent of children 4.9%

Health care expenditures, 2004
Total expenditures. $31,177
   per capita $5,670

4   Wisconsin

Federal and state public aid

State unemployment insurance, 2006
Recipients, first payments (x 1,000) 259
Total payments ($ mil) $786
Average weekly benefit $259
Temporary Assistance for Needy Families, 2006
Recipients (x 1,000) 462.4
Families (x 1,000) 212.5
Supplemental Security Income, 2005
Recipients (x 1,000) .92.2
Payments ($ mil) $437.4
Food Stamp Program, 2006
Avg monthly participants (x 1,000) 367.9
Total benefits ($ mil) $346.6

Housing & Construction

Housing units
Total 2005 (estimate) 2,502,536
Total 2006 (estimate) 2,534,075
Seasonal or recreational use, 2006 152,256
Owner-occupied, 2006 1,571,129
    Median home value $163,500
    Homeowner vacancy rate 1.2%
Renter-occupied, 2006 658,931
    Median rent $658
    Rental vacancy rate 8.2%
Home ownership rate, 2005 . . . . 71.1%
Home ownership rate, 2006 . . . . 70.2%

New privately-owned housing units
Number authorized, 2006 (x 1,000) 27.3
    Value ($ mil) $4,424.4
Started 2005 (x 1,000, estimate) 36.7
Started 2006 (x 1,000, estimate) 35.8

Existing home sales
2005 (x 1,000) 122.8
2006 (x 1,000) 117.3

Government & Elections

State officials 2008
Governor . . . . Jim Doyle
    Democratic, term expires 1/11
Lieutenant Governor . . . . Barbara Lawton
Secretary of State . . . . Douglas La Follette
Attorney General . . . . J.B. Van Hollen
Chief Justice . . . . Shirley Abrahamson

Governorship
Minimum age 18
Length of term . . . . 4 years
Consecutive terms permitted . . . . . . not specified
Who succeeds . . . . Lieutenant Governor

Local governments by type, 2002
Total 3,048
    County 72
    Municipal 585
    Township 1,265
    School District 442
    Special District 684

State legislature
Name . . . . Legislature
Upper chamber . . . . .Senate
    Number of members 33
    Length of term . . . . 4 years
    Party in majority, 2008 . . . . .Democratic
Lower chamber .Assembly
    Number of members 99
    Length of term . . . . 2 years
    Party in majority, 2008 . . . . Republican

Federal representation, 2008 (110th Congress)
Senator . . . . .Russell Feingold
    Party . . . . .Democratic
    Year term expires 2011
Senator . . . . Herbert Kohl
    Party . . . . .Democratic
    Year term expires 2013
Representatives, total 8
    Democrats 5
    Republicans 3

Voters in November 2006 election (estimate)
Total 2,352,105
    Male 1,101,890
    Female 1,250,214
    White 2,201,274
    Black 89,424
    Hispanic 19,516
    Asian 9,382

Presidential election, 2004
Total Popular Vote 2,997,007
    Kerry 1,489,504
    Bush 1,478,120
Total Electoral Votes 10

Votes cast for US Senators
2004
Total vote (x 1,000) 2,950
Leading party .Democratic
Percent for leading party 55.4%
2006
Total vote (x 1,000) .2,138
Leading party .Democratic
Percent for leading party 67.3%

Votes cast for US Representatives
2004
Total vote (x 1,000) 2,822
    Democratic 1,369
    Republican 1,381
Leading party . . . . Republican
Percent for leading party 48.9%
2006
Total vote (x 1,000) 2,063
    Democratic 1,003
    Republican 1,040
Leading party . . . . Republican
Percent for leading party 50.4%

State government employment, 2006
Full-time equivalent employees 68,143
Payroll ($ mil) $283.7

Local government employment, 2006
Full-time equivalent employees 219,930
Payroll ($ mil) $813.1

Women holding public office, 2008
US Congress 2
Statewide elected office. 3
State legislature 30

Black public officials, 2002
Total. 33
   US and state legislatures 8
   City/county/regional offices 15
   Judicial/law enforcement. 5
   Education/school boards 5

Hispanic public officials, 2006
Total. 13
   State executives & legislators 1
   City/county/regional offices 5
   Judicial/law enforcement. 4
   Education/school boards 3

Governmental Finance

State government revenues, 2006
Total revenue (x $1,000) $33,410,533
   per capita $5,995.44
General revenue (x $1,000) $25,707,505
   Intergovernmental 6,632,773
   Taxes 13,795,044
      general sales. 4,127,972
      individual income tax 5,906,515
      corporate income tax 808,200
   Current charges. 3,022,706
   Miscellaneous .2,256,982

State government expenditure, 2006
Total expenditure (x $1,000) $30,125,092
   per capita $5,405.87
General expenditure (x $1,000) $26,277,439
   per capita, total. $4,715.42
      Education 1,754.82
      Public welfare 1,095.78
      Health 133.85
      Hospitals. 164.70
      Highways 334.14
      Police protection. 21.13
      Corrections 170.12
      Natural resources 105.60
      Parks & recreation 6.55
      Governmental administration 113.87
      Interest on general debt 172.70

State debt & cash, 2006 ($ per capita)
Debt $3,564.94
Cash/security holdings. $15,877.40

Federal government grants to state & local government, 2005 (x $1,000)
Total. $7,538,150
by Federal agency
   Defense 39,029
   Education 610,854
   Energy. 71,947
   Environmental Protection Agency 57,456
   Health & Human Services. 4,579,319
   Homeland Security. 31,716
   Housing & Urban Development. 475,502
   Justice 89,246
   Labor 179,275
   Transportation .695,710
   Veterans Affairs. 37,337

Crime & Law Enforcement

Crime, 2006 (rates per 100,000 residents)
Property crimes 156,571
   Burglary 26,994
   Larceny 115,546
   Motor vehicle theft 14,031
   Property crime rate. 2,817.8
Violent crimes. 15,783
   Murder 164
   Forcible rape. 1,131
   Robbery. 5,567
   Aggravated assault 8,921
   Violent crime rate 284.0
Hate crimes. 103

Fraud and identity theft, 2006
Fraud complaints. 6,724
   rate per 100,000 residents 121.0
Identity theft complaints 2,536
   rate per 100,000 residents 45.6

Law enforcement agencies, 2006
Total agencies. 370
Total employees 18,111
   Officers 13,038
   Civilians 5,073

Prisoners, probation, and parole, 2006
Total prisoners. 23,431
   percent change, 12/31/05 to 12/31/06 . . . . 3.2%
   in private facilities 0.1%
   in local jails 2.9%
Sentenced to more than one year 21,881
   rate per 100,000 residents 393
Adults on probation 55,806
Adults on parole. 16,206

Prisoner demographics, June 30, 2005 (rate per 100,000 residents)
Male. 1,209
Female. 107
White. 415
Black. 4,416
Hispanic . . . . NA

6   Wisconsin

Arrests, 2006
Total.................................414,975
   Persons under 18 years of age 103,275

Persons under sentence of death, 1/1/07
Total.......................................0
   White......................................0
   Black 0
   Hispanic 0

State's highest court
Name ....Supreme Court
Number of members.........................7
Length of term.......................10 years
Intermediate appeals court? ....yes

Labor & Income

Civilian labor force, 2006 (x 1,000)
Total.................................3,079
   Men 1,615
   Women 1,464
   Persons 16-19 years..................... 195
   White................................ 2,830
   Black 145
   Hispanic 113

Civilian labor force as a percent of civilian non-institutional population, 2006
Total.................................70.7%
   Men 75.8
   Women 65.8
   Persons 16-19 years..................60.2
   White................................70.9
   Black 69.3
   Hispanic 72.1

Employment, 2006 (x 1,000)
Total.................................2,931
   Men 1,531
   Women 1,400
   Persons 16-19 years..................... 167
   White................................2,707
   Black 127
   Hispanic 104

Unemployment rate, 2006
Total..................................4.8%
   Men 5.2
   Women 4.3
   Persons 16-19 years..................14.3
   White.................................4.3
   Black 11.9
   Hispanic 7.8

Full-time/part-time labor force, 2003 (x 1,000)
Full-time labor force, employed 2,297
Part-time labor force, employed........... 607
Unemployed, looking for
   Full-time work......................... 140
   Part-time work.......................... 33
Mean duration of unemployment (weeks)......17.5
   Median 9.8

Labor unions, 2006
Membership (x 1,000)................... 386
   percent of employed 14.9%

Experienced civilian labor force by private industry, 2006
Total..............................2,389,062
   Natural resources & mining 22,043
   Construction 127,348
   Manufacturing...................... 505,599
   Trade, transportation & utilities 541,211
   Information 49,302
   Finance 157,548
   Professional & business 270,595
   Education & health 359,597
   Leisure & hospitality............... 259,380
   Other 84,651

Experienced civilian labor force by occupation, May 2006
Management......................... 95,960
Business & financial 114,390
Legal.............................. 12,530
Sales.............................. 270,760
Office & admin. support...............443,110
Computers & math 48,250
Architecture & engineering............. 50,400
Arts & entertainment 32,510
Education 153,160
Social services 30,020
Health care practitioner & technical.... 136,670
Health care support 80,480
Maintenance & repair................ 105,980
Construction 116,370
Transportation & moving 225,040
Production 346,980
Farming, fishing & forestry..............4,970

Hours and earnings of production workers on manufacturing payrolls, 2006
Average weekly hours 40.7
Average hourly earnings $16.54
Average weekly earnings $673.18

Income and poverty, 2006
Median household income............. $48,772
Personal income, per capita (current $)... $34,701
   in constant (2000) dollars $30,292
Persons below poverty level.............. 11.0%

Average annual pay
2006 .... $36,821
   increase from 2005 .... 3.8%

Federal individual income tax returns, 2005
Returns filed........................ 2,656,046
Adjusted gross income ($1,000) $132,137,153
Total tax liability ($1,000) $15,795,477

Charitable contributions, 2004
Number of contributions 861.0
Total amount ($ mil).................$2,397.3

Economy, Business, Industry & Agriculture

Fortune 500 companies, 2007. 9
Bankruptcy cases filed, FY 2007. 14,952

Patents and trademarks issued, 2007

Patents. 1,973
Trademarks. 1,673

Business firm ownership, 2002

Women-owned. .104,170
   Sales ($ mil) $17,582
Black-owned. 6,685
   Sales ($ mil) $633
Hispanic-owned. 3,750
   Sales ($ mil) $975
Asian-owned 4,957
   Sales ($ mil) $1,499
Amer. Indian/Alaska Native-owned 2,530
   Sales ($ mil) $512
Hawaiian/Pacific Islander-owned 104
   Sales ($ mil) $4

Gross domestic product, 2006 ($ mil)

Total gross domestic product $227,230
   Agriculture, forestry, fishing and
      hunting 2,929
   Mining. 322
   Utilities. 3,829
   Construction 10,270
   Manufacturing, durable goods. 28,059
   Manufacturing, non-durable goods 19,148
   Wholesale trade. 13,365
   Retail trade. 14,278
   Transportation & warehousing 7,183
   Information 6,601
   Finance & insurance. 16,935
   Real estate, rental & leasing 27,783
   Professional and technical services. 9,564
   Educational services. 1,850
   Health care and social assistance. 18,637
   Accommodation/food services. 4,955
   Other services, except government 4,968
   Government 24,726

Establishments, payroll, employees & receipts, by major industry group, 2005

Total. 145,159
   Annual payroll ($1,000). $85,781,279
   Paid employees 2,449,114
Forestry, fishing & agriculture. 550
   Annual payroll ($1,000). $113,504
   Paid employees .3,169
Mining. 159
   Annual payroll ($1,000). $238,052
   Paid employees .3,555
   Receipts, 2002 ($1,000) $518,984

Utilities 286
   Annual payroll ($1,000). $1,043,257
   Paid employees 14,874
   Receipts, 2002 ($1,000) . . . . .NA
Construction. 17,364
   Annual payroll ($1,000). $5,668,227
   Paid employees 119,663
   Receipts, 2002 ($1,000) $23,477,496
Manufacturing. 9,754
   Annual payroll ($1,000). $21,148,313
   Paid employees 493,661
   Receipts, 2002 ($1,000) $124,664,004
Wholesale trade 7,272
   Annual payroll ($1,000). $5,991,081
   Paid employees 124,033
   Receipts, 2002 ($1,000) $68,510,712
Retail trade 21,219
   Annual payroll ($1,000). $6,626,134
   Paid employees 317,423
   Receipts, 2002 ($1,000) $59,978,700
Transportation & warehousing 5,493
   Annual payroll ($1,000). $3,281,664
   Paid employees 95,390
   Receipts, 2002 ($1,000) $8,266,478
Information. 2,284
   Annual payroll ($1,000). $2,558,853
   Paid employees 55,957
   Receipts, 2002 ($1,000) . . . . .NA
Finance & insurance 9,152
   Annual payroll ($1,000). $7,125,232
   Paid employees 135,409
   Receipts, 2002 ($1,000) . . . . .NA
Professional, scientific & technical 11,492
   Annual payroll ($1,000). $4,752,212
   Paid employees 96,891
   Receipts, 2002 ($1,000) $8,961,379
Education 1,403
   Annual payroll ($1,000). $1,188,516
   Paid employees 48,148
   Receipts, 2002 ($1,000) $431,985
Health care & social assistance 14,008
   Annual payroll ($1,000). $12,542,232
   Paid employees 348,275
   Receipts, 2002 ($1,000) $24,053,322
Arts and entertainment 2,620
   Annual payroll ($1,000). $852,241
   Paid employees 39,109
   Receipts, 2002 ($1,000) $2,145,020
Real estate. 5,050
   Annual payroll ($1,000). $809,492
   Paid employees 27,250
   Receipts, 2002 ($1,000) $3,421,466
Accommodation & food service. 13,972
   Annual payroll ($1,000). $2,382,706
   Paid employees 220,168
   Receipts, 2002 ($1,000) $6,885,765

Exports, 2006
Value of exported goods ($ mil) $17,169
   Manufactured $15,103
   Non-manufactured $1,263

Foreign direct investment in US affiliates, 2004
Property, plants & equipment ($ mil) . . . $15,949
Employment (x 1,000) 86.9

Agriculture, 2006
Number of farms 76,000
Farm acreage (x 1,000) 15,300
   Acres per farm 201
Farm marketings and income ($ mil)
Total $6,791.3
   Crops $2,135.3
   Livestock $4,656.0
Net farm income $1,091.4

Principal commodities, in order by marketing receipts, 2005
Dairy products, Cattle and calves, Corn, Soybeans, Greenhouse/nursery

Federal economic activity in state
Expenditures, 2005 ($ mil)
Total $33,749
   Per capita $6,105.47
   Defense $3,191
   Non-defense $30,558
Defense department, 2006 ($ mil)
   Payroll $681
   Contract awards $2,165
   Grants $56
Homeland security grants ($1,000)
   2006 . . . . $24,431
   2007 . . . . $17,796

FDIC-insured financial institutions, 2005
Number 302
Assets ($ billion) $141.6
Deposits ($ billion) $103.6

Fishing, 2006
Catch (x 1,000 lbs) 4,449
Value ($1,000) $3,145

Mining, 2006 ($ mil)
Total non-fuel mineral production $591
Percent of U.S. 0.92%

Communication, Energy & Transportation

Communication
Households with computers, 2003 . . . . 63.8%
Households with internet access, 2003 . . . . 57.4%
High-speed internet providers 79
Total high-speed internet lines 1,247,350
   Residential 1,012,294
   Business 235,056
Wireless phone customers, 12/2006 3,509,528

FCC-licensed stations (as of January 1, 2008)
TV stations 43
FM radio stations 221
AM radio stations 112

Energy
Energy consumption, 2004
   Total (trillion Btu) 1,848
   Per capita (million Btu) 336.0
By source of production (trillion Btu)
   Coal 499
   Natural gas 385
   Petroleum 631
   Nuclear electric power 124
   Hydroelectric power 20
By end-use sector (trillion Btu)
   Residential 419
   Commercial 315
   Industrial 676
   Transportation 438
Electric energy, 2005
   Primary source of electricity . . . . Coal
   Net generation (billion kWh) 61.8
     percent from renewable sources 4.9%
   Net summer capability (million kW) 16.2
   CO_2 emitted from generation 54.0
Natural gas utilities, 2005
   Customers (x 1,000) 1,756
   Sales (trillion Btu) 358
   Revenues ($ mil) $2,639
Nuclear plants, 2007 3
Total CO_2 emitted (million metric tons) 104.8
Energy spending, 2004 ($ mil) $16,069
   per capita $2,922
   Price per million Btu $12.69

Transportation, 2006
Public road & street mileage 114,485
   Urban 21,998
   Rural 92,487
   Interstate 743
Vehicle miles of travel (millions) 59,398
   per capita 10,658.8
Total motor vehicle registrations 4,971,461
   Automobiles 2,639,984
   Trucks 2,317,130
   Motorcycles 271,145
Licensed drivers 4,049,450
   19 years & under 221,157
Deaths from motor vehicle accidents 724
Gasoline consumed (x 1,000 gallons) 2,527,993
   per capita 453.6

Commuting Statistics, 2006
Average commute time (min) 20.8
   Drove to work alone 79.9%
   Carpooled 9.2%
   Public transit 1.9%
   Walk to work 3.5%
   Work from home 3.9%

State Summary

Capital city . . . . Cheyenne
Governor . . . . David Freudenthal
State Capitol Building
Room 124
Cheyenne, WY 82002
307-777-7434
Admitted as a state 1890
Area (square miles) 97,814
Population, 2007 (estimate). 522,830
Largest city . . . . Cheyenne
Population, 2006 55,314
Personal income per capita, 2006
(in current dollars) $40,676
Gross domestic product, 2006 ($ mil) $29,561

Leading industries by payroll, 2005
Mining, Health care/Social assistance, Retail
trade

Leading agricultural commodities by receipts, 2005
Cattle and calves, Hay, Sugar beets, Hogs, Sheep
and lambs

Geography & Environment

Total area (square miles). 97,814
land 97,100
water 713
Federally-owned land, 2004 (acres) . . .26,391,487
percent. 42.3%
Highest point . . . . Gannett Peak
elevation (feet) 13,804
Lowest point . . . . .Belle Fourche River
elevation (feet) 3,009
General coastline (miles) 0
Tidal shoreline (miles) 0
Cropland, 2003 (x 1,000 acres) 2,161
Forest land, 2003 (x 1,000 acres). 949
Capital city . . . . Cheyenne
Population 2000 53,011
Population 2006 55,314
Largest city . . . . Cheyenne
Population 2000 53,011
Population 2006 55,314

Number of cities with over 100,000 population
1990 0
2000 0
2006 0

State park and recreation areas, 2005
Area (x 1,000 acres) 121
Number of visitors (x 1,000) 2,114
Revenues ($1,000) $1,343
percent of operating expenditures 8.0%

National forest system land, 2007
Acres 9,241,187

Demographics & Population Characteristics

Population
1980 469,557
1990 453,588
2000 493,782
2006 515,004
Male. 261,002
Female 254,002
Living in group quarters, 2006. 14,146
percent of total. 2.7%
2007 (estimate). 522,830
persons per square mile of land 5.4
2008 (projected). 515,408
2010 (projected) 519,886
2020 (projected) 530,948
2030 (projected). 522,979

Population of Core-Based Statistical Areas (formerly Metropolitan Areas), x 1,000

	CBSA	Non-CBSA
1990	320	133
2000	352	142
2006	368	147

Change in population, 2000-2007
Number 29,048
percent. 5.9%
Natural increase (births minus deaths) 19,423
Net internal migration 9,601
Net international migration 2,060

Persons by age, 2006
Under 5 years 33,553
5 to 17 years 88,241
18 years and over .393,210
65 years and over 62,750
85 years and over 8,367
Median age 37.1

Persons by age, 2010 (projected)
Under 5 years 32,671
18 and over 403,613
65 and over 72,658
Median age 39.5

Race, 2006
One Race
White. 486,480
Black or African American 4,867
Asian 3,605
American Indian/Alaska Native. 12,668
Hawaiian Native/Pacific Islander. 385
Two or more races. 6,999

Persons of Hispanic origin, 2006
Total Hispanic or Latino 35,732
Mexican. 26,247
Puerto Rican 500
Cuban . . . . NA

Persons of Asian origin, 2006

Total Asian	4,656
Asian Indian	1,097
Chinese	1,768
Filipino	631
Japanese	262
Korean	325
Vietnamese	265

Marital status, 2006

Population 15 years & over	416,436
Never married	103,069
Married	235,541
Separated	5,339
Widowed	22,797
Divorced	55,029

Language spoken at home, 2006

Population 5 years and older	480,876
English only	448,994
Spanish	19,830
French	2,624
German	1,566
Chinese	1,045

Households & families, 2006

Households	207,302
with persons under 18 years	65,571
with persons over 65 years	43,317
persons per household	2.42
Families	136,835
persons per family	2.94
Married couples	110,284
Female householder,	
no husband present	17,301
One-person households	56,583

Nativity, 2006

Number of residents born in state	219,327
percent of population	42.6%

Immigration & naturalization, 2006

Legal permanent residents admitted	376
Persons naturalized	169
Non-immigrant admissions	16,972

Vital Statistics and Health

Marriages

2004	4,740
2005	4,797
2006	5,027

Divorces

2004	2,656
2005	2,674
2006	2,749

Health risks, 2006

Percent of adults who are:

Smokers	21.6%
Overweight (BMI > 25)	61.4%
Obese (BMI > 30)	23.3%

Births

2005	7,239
Birthrate (per 1,000)	14.2
White	6,770
Black	63
Hispanic	828
Asian/Pacific Islander	70
Amer. Indian/Alaska Native	336
Low birth weight (2,500g or less)	8.6%
Cesarian births	24.6%
Preterm births	13.1%
To unmarried mothers	32.8%
Twin births (per 1,000)	27.3
Triplets or higher order (per 100,000)	144.6
2006 (preliminary)	7,670
rate per 1,000	14.9

Deaths

2004

All causes	3,955
rate per 100,000	789.7
Heart disease	950
rate per 100,000	191.0
Malignant neoplasms	875
rate per 100,000	170.8
Cerebrovascular disease	214
rate per 100,000	43.9
Chronic lower respiratory disease	308
rate per 100,000	62.6
Diabetes	110
rate per 100,000	22.1
2005 (preliminary)	4,100
rate per 100,000	801.4
2006 (provisional)	4,281

Infant deaths

2004	60
rate per 1,000	8.8
2005 (provisional)	42
rate per 1,000	5.8

Exercise routines, 2005

None	22.0%
Moderate or greater	56.2%
Vigorous	33.1%

Abortions, 2004

Total performed in state	12
rate per 1,000 women age 15-44	NA
% obtained by out-of-state residents	16.7%

Physicians, 2005

Total	949
rate per 100,000 persons	187

Community hospitals, 2005

Number of hospitals	24
Beds (x 1,000)	2.1
Patients admitted (x 1,000)	51
Average daily census (x 1,000)	1.2
Average cost per day	$805
Outpatient visits (x 1 mil)	1.0

Disability status of population, 2006
5 to 15 years 7.3%
16 to 64 years 13.0%
65 years and over 40.9%

Education

Educational attainment, 2006
Population over 25 years 339,398
   Less than 9th grade. 3.0%
   High school graduate or more 90.2%
   College graduate or more. 22.7%
   Graduate or professional degree. 7.4%

Public school enrollment, 2005-06
Total. 84,409
   Pre-kindergarten through grade 8. 57,195
   Grades 9 through 12. 27,214

Graduating public high school seniors, 2004-05
Diplomas (incl. GED and others) 5,653

SAT scores, 2007
Average critical reading score 565
Average writing score 544
Average math score 571
Percent of graduates taking test 8%

Public school teachers, 2006-07 (estimate)
Total (x 1,000) 6.5
   Elementary. 3.3
   Secondary. 3.2
Average salary $50,692
   Elementary. $50,428
   Secondary. $50,967

State receipts & expenditures for public schools, 2006-07 (estimate)
Revenue receipts ($ mil) $1,481
Expenditures
Total ($ mil) $1,395
   Per capita $2,190
   Per pupil $14,235

NAEP proficiency scores, 2007
	Reading		Math	
	Basic	Proficient	Basic	Proficient
Grade 4	73.5%	36.4%	88.5%	44.3%
Grade 8	79.7%	33.2%	79.8%	36.0%

Higher education enrollment, fall 2005
Total. 2,723
   Full-time men 2,608
   Full-time women. 115
   Part-time men 0
   Part-time women. 0

Minority enrollment in institutions of higher education, 2005
Black, non-Hispanic 336
Hispanic 1,612
Asian/Pacific Islander 322
American Indian/Alaska Native. 611

Institutions of higher education, 2005-06
Total. 10
   Public. 8
   Private 2

Earned degrees conferred, 2004-05
Associate's. 2,799
Bachelor's 1,695
Master's 455
First-professional. 125
Doctor's 52

Public Libraries, 2006
Number of libraries. 23
Number of outlets 76
Annual visits per capita 6.2
Circulation per capita. 9.1

State & local financial support for higher education, FY 2006
Full-time equivalent enrollment (x 1,000) 22.5
Appropriations per FTE. $13,425

Social Insurance & Welfare Programs

Social Security benefits & beneficiaries, 2005
Beneficiaries (x 1,000) 84
   Retired & dependents. 61
   Survivors. 11
   Disabled & dependents. 13
Annual benefit payments ($ mil) $908
   Retired & dependents. $629
   Survivors. $149
   Disabled & dependents. $130
Average monthly benefit
   Retired & dependents. $999
   Disabled & dependents. $936
   Widowed. $1,009

Medicare, July 2005
Enrollment (x 1,000) 71
Payments ($ mil) $429

Medicaid, 2004
Beneficiaries (x 1,000). 68
Payments ($ mil) $363

State Children's Health Insurance Program, 2006
Enrollment (x 1,000). .7.7
Expenditures ($ mil). $9.4

Persons without health insurance, 2006
Number (x 1,000). 75
   percent. 14.5%
Number of children (x 1,000) 10
   percent of children 8.1%

Health care expenditures, 2004
Total expenditures. $2,662
   per capita $5,265

Federal and state public aid

State unemployment insurance, 2006
Recipients, first payments (x 1,000) 10
Total payments ($ mil) $30
Average weekly benefit $253
Temporary Assistance for Needy Families, 2006
Recipients (x 1,000) 6.1
Families (x 1,000) 3.4
Supplemental Security Income, 2005
Recipients (x 1,000) 5.8
Payments ($ mil) $26.5
Food Stamp Program, 2006
Avg monthly participants (x 1,000) 24.2
Total benefits ($ mil) $26.3

Housing & Construction

Housing units
Total 2005 (estimate) 235,657
Total 2006 (estimate) 239,178
Seasonal or recreational use, 2006 14,167
Owner-occupied, 2006 144,117
   Median home value $148,900
   Homeowner vacancy rate 1.4%
Renter-occupied, 2006 63,185
   Median rent $601
   Rental vacancy rate 4.6%
Home ownership rate, 2005 .... 72.8%
Home ownership rate, 2006 .... 73.7%

New privately-owned housing units
Number authorized, 2006 (x 1,000) 3.5
   Value ($ mil) $638.8
Started 2005 (x 1,000, estimate) 2.2
Started 2006 (x 1,000, estimate) 2.3

Existing home sales
2005 (x 1,000) 14.3
2006 (x 1,000) 13.6

Government & Elections

State officials 2008
Governor .... David Freudenthal
   Democratic, term expires 1/11
Lieutenant Governor. . (no Lieutenant Governor)
Secretary of State .... Max Maxfield
Attorney General .... Bruce Salzburg
Chief Justice .... Barton Voigt

Governorship
Minimum age 30
Length of term .... 4 years
Consecutive terms permitted 2
Who succeeds .... Secretary of State

Local governments by type, 2002
Total 722
   County 23
   Municipal 98
   Township 0
   School District 55
   Special District 546

State legislature
Name .... Legislature
Upper chamber ....Senate
   Number of members 30
   Length of term .... 4 years
   Party in majority, 2008 .... Republican
Lower chamber .... House of Representatives
   Number of members 60
   Length of term .... 2 years
   Party in majority, 2008 .... Republican

Federal representation, 2008 (110th Congress)
Senator ....Michael Enzi
   Party .... Republican
   Year term expires 2009
Senator ....John Barrasso
   Party .... Republican
   Year term expires 2013
Representatives, total 1
   Democrats 0
   Republicans 1

Voters in November 2006 election (estimate)
Total 199,387
   Male 93,951
   Female 105,436
   White 195,111
   Black 644
   Hispanic 4,684
   Asian 544

Presidential election, 2004
Total Popular Vote 243,428
   Kerry 70,776
   Bush 167,629
Total Electoral Votes 3

Votes cast for US Senators
2004
Total vote (x 1,000) .... NA
Leading party .... NA
Percent for leading party .... NA
2006
Total vote (x 1,000) 196
Leading party .... Republican
Percent for leading party 68.9%

Votes cast for US Representatives
2004
Total vote (x 1,000) 239
   Democratic 100
   Republican 132
Leading party .... Republican
Percent for leading party 55.2%
2006
Total vote (x 1,000) 196
   Democratic 92
   Republican 93
Leading party .... Republican
Percent for leading party 47.6%

State government employment, 2006
Full-time equivalent employees 12,814
Payroll ($ mil) $43.1

Local government employment, 2006
Full-time equivalent employees 32,988
Payroll ($ mil) $103.0

Women holding public office, 2008
US Congress 1
Statewide elected office. 1
State legislature 21

Black public officials, 2002
Total. 1
   US and state legislatures 0
   City/county/regional offices 1
   Judicial/law enforcement. 0
   Education/school boards 0

Hispanic public officials, 2006
Total. 4
   State executives & legislators 1
   City/county/regional offices 3
   Judicial/law enforcement. 0
   Education/school boards 0

Governmental Finance

State government revenues, 2006
Total revenue (x $1,000) $5,616,758
   per capita $10,954.03
General revenue (x $1,000) $4,897,206
   Intergovernmental 2,009,304
   Taxes 2,122,239
     general sales. 624,924
     individual income tax 0
     corporate income tax 0
   Current charges. 148,640
   Miscellaneous 617,023

State government expenditure, 2006
Total expenditure (x $1,000) $4,011,496
   per capita $7,823.39
General expenditure (x $1,000) $3,563,917
   per capita, total. *$6,950.50*
     Education 2,084.39
     Public welfare 1,124.31
     Health 351.77
     Hospitals. 3.71
     Highways 828.97
     Police protection. 74.48
     Corrections .247.14
     Natural resources 420.21
     Parks & recreation 68.60
     Governmental administration 274.62
     Interest on general debt. 86.48

State debt & cash, 2006 ($ per capita)
Debt $1,916.61
Cash/security holdings. $29,777.62

Federal government grants to state & local government, 2005 (x $1,000)
Total. $1,898,954
by Federal agency
   Defense 13,439
   Education 121,919
   Energy 7,743
   Environmental Protection Agency 22,733
   Health & Human Services. 373,094
   Homeland Security. 2,943
   Housing & Urban Development. 37,077
   Justice 21,749
   Labor 19,235
   Transportation 220,533
   Veterans Affairs. 1,321

Crime & Law Enforcement

Crime, 2006 (rates per 100,000 residents)
Property crimes 15,350
   Burglary 2,320
   Larceny 12,254
   Motor vehicle theft 776
   Property crime rate. 2,980.6
Violent crimes. 1,234
   Murder 9
   Forcible rape. 140
   Robbery. 72
   Aggravated assault 1,013
   Violent crime rate 239.6
Hate crimes. 7

Fraud and identity theft, 2006
Fraud complaints. 657
   rate per 100,000 residents 127.6
Identity theft complaints 218
   rate per 100,000 residents 42.3

Law enforcement agencies, 2006
Total agencies. 65
Total employees 1,862
   Officers 1,313
   Civilians 549

Prisoners, probation, and parole, 2006
Total prisoners. 2,114
   percent change, 12/31/05 to 12/31/06 . . . . 3.3%
   in private facilities 37.0%
   in local jails 1.0%
Sentenced to more than one year 2,114
   rate per 100,000 residents 408
Adults on probation .5,225
Adults on parole. 674

Prisoner demographics, June 30, 2005 (rate per 100,000 residents)
Male 1,189
Female 184
White . . . . NA
Black. . . . . NA
Hispanic . . . . NA

Arrests, 2006

Total 38,780
   Persons under 18 years of age 6,682

Persons under sentence of death, 1/1/07

Total 2
   White 2
   Black 0
   Hispanic 0

State's highest court

Name . . . . .Supreme Court
Number of members 5
Length of term . . . . 8 years
Intermediate appeals court? . . . . no

Labor & Income

Civilian labor force, 2006 (x 1,000)

Total 287
   Men 158
   Women 130
   Persons 16-19 years. 17
   White. 275
   Black . . . . NA
   Hispanic 17

Civilian labor force as a percent of civilian non-institutional population, 2006

Total 71.0%
   Men 78.3
   Women 63.8
   Persons 16-19 years. 53.8
   White. 71.1
   Black . . . . NA
   Hispanic 69.5

Employment, 2006 (x 1,000)

Total 278
   Men 152
   Women 126
   Persons 16-19 years. 15
   White. 267
   Black . . . . NA
   Hispanic 16

Unemployment rate, 2006

Total 3.4%
   Men 3.5
   Women 3.2
   Persons 16-19 years. 12.0
   White. 3.1
   Black . . . . NA
   Hispanic 8.2

Full-time/part-time labor force, 2003 (x 1,000)

Full-time labor force, employed 215
Part-time labor force, employed. 52
Unemployed, looking for
   Full-time work. 10
   Part-time work. 2
Mean duration of unemployment (weeks). 13.3
   Median 6.5

Labor unions, 2006

Membership (x 1,000) 19
   percent of employed 8.3%

Experienced civilian labor force by private industry, 2006

Total $207,465
   Natural resources & mining 28,815
   Construction 23,942
   Manufacturing. 10,146
   Trade, transportation & utilities 49,852
   Information 4,173
   Finance 11,117
   Professional & business 17,048
   Education & health 21,561
   Leisure & hospitality. 32,611
   Other 8,200

Experienced civilian labor force by occupation, May 2006

Management. 12,710
Business & financial 6,740
Legal. 1,430
Sales 22,540
Office & admin. support. 36,690
Computers & math 2,070
Architecture & engineering. 4,280
Arts & entertainment 2,500
Education 17,090
Social services 3,870
Health care practitioner & technical 10,860
Health care support 6,350
Maintenance & repair. 15,640
Construction 30,180
Transportation & moving 25,020
Production . . . . NA
Farming, fishing & forestry. 430

Hours and earnings of production workers on manufacturing payrolls, 2006

Average weekly hours 41.2
Average hourly earnings $17.44
Average weekly earnings $718.53

Income and poverty, 2006

Median household income. $47,423
Personal income, per capita (current $). . . $40,676
   in constant (2000) dollars $35,508
Persons below poverty level. 9.4%

Average annual pay

2006 . . . . $36,662
   increase from 2005 . . . . 10.3%

Federal individual income tax returns, 2005

Returns filed 248,212
Adjusted gross income ($1,000) $14,299,375
Total tax liability ($1,000) $2,051,817

Charitable contributions, 2004

Number of contributions 41.4
Total amount ($ mil). $322.2

Economy, Business, Industry & Agriculture

Fortune 500 companies, 2007................ 0
Bankruptcy cases filed, FY 2007............ 784

Patents and trademarks issued, 2007
Patents.................................... 57
Trademarks............................... 145

Business firm ownership, 2002
Women-owned........................ 12,945
  Sales ($ mil) $1,130
Black-owned............................. 149
  Sales ($ mil) $10
Hispanic-owned.........................1,320
  Sales ($ mil) $221
Asian-owned 401
  Sales ($ mil) $84
Amer. Indian/Alaska Native-owned 597
  Sales ($ mil) $60
Hawaiian/Pacific Islander-owned 23
  Sales ($ mil) $1

Gross domestic product, 2006 ($ mil)
Total gross domestic product $29,561
  Agriculture, forestry, fishing and
    hunting 441
  Mining................................9,033
  Utilities..............................1,321
  Construction 1,763
  Manufacturing, durable goods........... 376
  Manufacturing, non-durable goods 618
  Wholesale trade......................1,090
  Retail trade..........................1,629
  Transportation & warehousing 1,668
  Information 426
  Finance & insurance................... 678
  Real estate, rental & leasing 2,479
  Professional and technical services 856
  Educational services.................... 64
  Health care and social assistance.......1,193
  Accommodation/food services........... 953
  Other services, except government 507
  Government 3,817

Establishments, payroll, employees & receipts, by major industry group, 2005

Total................................19,736
  Annual payroll ($1,000)..........$6,202,411
  Paid employees 191,934
Forestry, fishing & agriculture.............. 89
  Annual payroll ($1,000)................ NA
  Paid employees .... NA
Mining................................ 812
  Annual payroll ($1,000)...........$1,182,693
  Paid employees 19,443
  Receipts, 2002 ($1,000) $7,803,920

Utilities 117
  Annual payroll ($1,000)........... $150,897
  Paid employees 2,391
  Receipts, 2002 ($1,000) ....NA
Construction........................... 2,790
  Annual payroll ($1,000)........... $598,206
  Paid employees 16,372
  Receipts, 2002 ($1,000) $2,149,476
Manufacturing......................... 543
  Annual payroll ($1,000)........... $463,053
  Paid employees 10,465
  Receipts, 2002 ($1,000) $4,061,516
Wholesale trade........................ 770
  Annual payroll ($1,000)........... $288,683
  Paid employees 6,710
  Receipts, 2002 ($1,000) $3,331,043
Retail trade............................2,975
  Annual payroll ($1,000)........... $655,186
  Paid employees 30,186
  Receipts, 2002 ($1,000) $5,783,756
Transportation & warehousing............. 858
  Annual payroll ($1,000)........... $309,655
  Paid employees 8,057
  Receipts, 2002 ($1,000) $746,816
Information............................. 337
  Annual payroll ($1,000)........... $130,556
  Paid employees 4,038
  Receipts, 2002 ($1,000) ....NA
Finance & insurance 919
  Annual payroll ($1,000)........... $264,363
  Paid employees 7,108
  Receipts, 2002 ($1,000) ....NA
Professional, scientific & technical........1,745
  Annual payroll ($1,000)........... $300,600
  Paid employees 7,951
  Receipts, 2002 ($1,000) $654,070
Education 137
  Annual payroll ($1,000)........... $36,658
  Paid employees 1,730
  Receipts, 2002 ($1,000) $66,940
Health care & social assistance 1,627
  Annual payroll ($1,000)........... $908,285
  Paid employees 28,269
  Receipts, 2002 ($1,000) $1,621,193
Arts and entertainment 441
  Annual payroll ($1,000)........... NA
  Paid employees .... NA
  Receipts, 2002 ($1,000) $163,052
Real estate............................. 979
  Annual payroll ($1,000)........... $104,965
  Paid employees 3,340
  Receipts, 2002 ($1,000) $398,649
Accommodation & food service............1,749
  Annual payroll ($1,000)........... $345,459
  Paid employees 25,765
  Receipts, 2002 ($1,000) $984,684

Exports, 2006

Value of exported goods ($ mil) $830
   Manufactured $714
   Non-manufactured.................... $102

Foreign direct investment in US affiliates, 2004

Property, plants & equipment ($ mil) ... $12,444
Employment (x 1,000)......................8.5

Agriculture, 2006

Number of farms 9,100
Farm acreage (x 1,000) 34,400
   Acres per farm 3,780
Farm marketings and income ($ mil)
Total................................ $1,021.1
   Crops..............................$161.6
   Livestock........................... $859.5
Net farm income $65.2

Principal commodities, in order by marketing receipts, 2005

Cattle and calves, Hay, Sugar beets, Hogs, Sheep and lambs

Federal economic activity in state

Expenditures, 2005 ($ mil)
   Total.............................. $4,782
      Per capita $9,399.02
   Defense $486
   Non-defense...................... $4,297
Defense department, 2006 ($ mil)
   Payroll..............................$306
   Contract awards $161
   Grants $12
Homeland security grants ($1,000)
   2006.............................$7,674
   2007.............................$6,674

FDIC-insured financial institutions, 2005

Number 45
Assets ($ billion) $7.1
Deposits ($ billion) $6.1

Fishing, 2006

Catch (x 1,000 lbs) .... NA
Value ($1,000)........................ NA

Mining, 2006 ($ mil)

Total non-fuel mineral production $1,250
Percent of U.S. 1.94%

Communication, Energy & Transportation

Communication

Households with computers, 2003........ 65.4%
Households with internet access, 2003 .... 57.7%
High-speed internet providers 28
Total high-speed internet lines........ 156,940
   Residential 89,719
   Business...........................67,221
Wireless phone customers, 12/2006 387,164

FCC-licensed stations (as of January 1, 2008)

TV stations 17
FM radio stations........................... 92
AM radio stations 33

Energy

Energy consumption, 2004
   Total (trillion Btu).................... 454
   Per capita (million Btu) 898.9
By source of production (trillion Btu)
   Coal 501
   Natural gas......................... 112
   Petroleum......................... 159
   Nuclear electric power 0
   Hydroelectric power.................. 6
By end-use sector (trillion Btu)
   Residential 41
   Commercial 53
   Industrial 245
   Transportation 115
Electric energy, 2005
   Primary source of electricity............ Coal
   Net generation (billion kWh) 45.6
      percent from renewable sources....... 3.3%
   Net summer capability (million kW) 6.7
   CO_2 emitted from generation 45.4
Natural gas utilities, 2005
   Customers (x 1,000) 157
   Sales (trillion Btu)..................... 66
   Revenues ($ mil) $122
Nuclear plants, 2007 0
Total CO_2 emitted (million metric tons).....62.9
Energy spending, 2004 ($ mil) $2,906
   per capita $5,749
   Price per million Btu $10.29

Transportation, 2006

Public road & street mileage 27,834
   Urban...............................2,618
   Rural...............................25,216
   Interstate 913
Vehicle miles of travel (millions) 9,415
   per capita 18,361.5
Total motor vehicle registrations........ 645,192
   Automobiles....................... 228,057
   Trucks 414,047
   Motorcycles 35,788
Licensed drivers 390,538
   19 years & under 24,355
Deaths from motor vehicle accidents 195
Gasoline consumed (x 1,000 gallons) 360,516
   per capita 703.1

Commuting Statistics, 2006

Average commute time (min) 17.9
   Drove to work alone 76.0%
   Carpooled..........................12.5%
   Public transit 1.3%
   Walk to work 3.1%
   Work from home..................... 5.2%

National Summary

Capital city . . . . Washington, DC
President . . . . George W. Bush

The White House
1600 Pennsylvania Ave NW
Washington DC, US 20500
202-456-1414

Founded. 1776
Area (square miles) 3,794,083
Population, 2007 (estimate). 301,621,157
Largest city . . . . New York City
   Population, 2006 8,214,426
Personal income per capita, 2006
   (in current dollars) $36,276
Gross domestic product, 2006 ($ mil). . .$13,149,033

Leading industries by payroll, 2005

Manufacturing, Health care/Social assistance,
   Professional/Scientific/Technical

**Leading agricultural commodities
by receipts, 2005**

Cattle and calves, Dairy products, Corn, Broilers,
   Soybeans

Geography & Environment

Total area (square miles). 3,794,083
   land 3,537,439
   water 256,645
Federally-owned land, 2004 (acres). . . 653,299,090
   percent. 28.8%
Highest point . . . . Mt. McKinley
   elevation (feet) 20,320
Lowest point. . . . . .Death Valley
   elevation (feet) . . . . -282
General coastline (miles) 12,383
Tidal shoreline (miles) 88,633
Cropland, 2003 (x 1,000 acres) 367,900
Forest land, 2003 (x 1,000 acres). 405,600
Capital city . . . . Washington, DC
   Population 2000 572,059
   Population 2006 581,530
Largest city . . . . New York City
   Population 2000 8,008,278
   Population 2006 8,214,426

Number of cities with over 100,000 population
1990 190
2000 239
2006 258

State park and recreation areas, 2005
Area (x 1,000 acres). 13,713
Number of visitors (x 1,000) 725,361
Revenues ($1,000) $847,117
   percent of operating expenditures. 39.2%

National forest system land, 2007
Acres 192,794,673

Demographics & Population Characteristics

Population
1980 226,546,000
1990 248,709,873
2000 281,424,602
2006 299,398,484
   Male. 147,512,152
   Female 151,886,332
Living in group quarters, 2006 8,065,644
   percent of total. 2.7%
2007 (estimate) 301,621,157
   persons per square mile of land 85.3
2008 (projected). 303,597,646
2010 (projected) 308,935,581
2020 (projected). 335,804,546
2030 (projected) 363,584,435

**Population of Core-Based Statistical Areas
(formerly Metropolitan Areas), x 1,000**

	CBSA	Non-CBSA
1990	230,779	17,939
2000	262,114	19,310
2006	279,848	19,551

Change in population, 2000-2007
Number 20,196,555
   percent. 7.2%
Natural increase (births minus deaths) . . 12,212,284
Net internal migration 0
Net international migration 7,984,271

Persons by age, 2006
Under 5 years 20,417,636
5 to 17 years 53,317,926
18 years and over 225,662,922
65 years and over 37,260,352
85 years and over 5,296,817
   Median age 36.4

Persons by age, 2010 (projected)
Under 5 years 21,426,163
18 and over 234,504,070
65 and over 40,243,713
   Median age 37.0

Race, 2006
One Race
   White. 239,746,254
   Black or African American 38,342,549
   Asian 13,159,343
   American Indian/Alaska Native. 2,902,851
   Hawaiian Native/Pacific Islander. 528,818
Two or more races. 4,718,669

Persons of Hispanic origin, 2006
Total Hispanic or Latino 44,252,278
   Mexican. 28,339,354
   Puerto Rican 3,987,947
   Cuban 1,520,276

Persons of Asian origin, 2006

Total Asian 13,100,095
   Asian Indian. 2,482,141
   Chinese 3,090,453
   Filipino 2,328,097
   Japanese 829,767
   Korean. 1,335,075
   Vietnamese. .1,475,798

Marital status, 2006

Population 15 years & over 238,585,682
   Never married 72,787,209
   Married. 125,571,348
   Separated 5,404,992
   Widowed. 15,182,891
   Divorced 25,044,234

Language spoken at home, 2006

Population 5 years and older. 279,012,712
   English only 224,154,288
   Spanish 34,044,945
   French 1,997,618
   German 1,391,413
   Chinese 2,492,871

Households & families, 2006

Households. 111,617,402
   with persons under 18 years 38,628,743
   with persons over 65 years. 25,867,508
   persons per household 2.61
Families. 74,564,066
   persons per family. 3.20
Married couples. 55,521,868
Female householder,
   no husband present. 13,920,783
One-person households 30,496,588

Nativity, 2006

Persons born in state of residence . . . 176,467,918
   percent of population 58.9%

Immigration & naturalization, 2006

Legal permanent residents admitted . . .1,266,264
Persons naturalized 702,589
Non-immigrant admissions 33,667,328

Vital Statistics and Health

Marriages

2004 . . . . NA
2005 2,249,000
2006 2,160,000

Divorces

2004 . . . . NA
2005 . . . . NA
2006 . . . . NA

Health risks, 2006

Percent of adults who are:
   Smokers. 20.1%
   Overweight (BMI > 25). 61.6%
   Obese (BMI > 30). 25.1%

Births

2005 4,138,349
   Birthrate (per 1,000). 14.0
   White. 3,229,294
   Black 633,134
   Hispanic 985,505
   Asian/Pacific Islander 231,108
   Amer. Indian/Alaska Native 44,813
   Low birth weight (2,500g or less). 8.2%
   Cesarian births 30.3%
   Preterm births 12.7%
   To unmarried mothers. 36.9%
   Twin births (per 1,000) 31.9
   Triplets or higher order (per 100,000). . . .175.3
2006 (preliminary). 4,265,996
   rate per 1,000 . . . . .14.2

Deaths

2004
All causes 2,397,615
   rate per 100,000. . . . . 800.8
Heart disease 652,486
   rate per 100,000. . . . . .217.0
Malignant neoplasms 553,888
   rate per 100,000. . . . . .185.8
Cerebrovascular disease. 150,074
   rate per 100,000. . . . . .50.0
Chronic lower respiratory disease 121,987
   rate per 100,000. . . . . .41.1
Diabetes. 73,138
   rate per 100,000. . . . . .24.5
2005 (preliminary). 2,447,903
   rate per 100,000. . . . . 798.8
2006 (provisional) 2,416,000

Infant deaths

2004 27,936
   rate per 1,000 . . . . .6.8
2005 (provisional) 28,000
   rate per 1,000 . . . . .6.8

Exercise routines, 2005

None. 23.9%
Moderate or greater. 48.7%
Vigorous 27.4%

Abortions, 2004

Total performed in nation 839,226
   rate per 1,000 women age 15-44. 16
   percent obtained in different state. 8.2%

Physicians, 2005

Total. 790,128
   rate per 100,000 persons 266

Community hospitals, 2005

Number of hospitals .4,936
Beds (x 1,000). 802.3
Patients admitted (x 1,000) 35,239
Average daily census (x 1,000) 540.3
Average cost per day $1,522
Outpatient visits (x 1 mil) 584.4

Disability status of population, 2006
5 to 15 years 6.3%
16 to 64 years 12.3%
65 years and over 41.0%

Education

Educational attainment, 2006
Population over 25 years 195,932,824
Less than 9th grade. 6.5%
High school graduate or more 84.1%
College graduate or more. 27.0%
Graduate or professional degree. 9.9%

Public school enrollment, 2005-06
Total. 49,113,474
Pre-kindergarten through grade 8. . 33,998,903
Grades 9 through 12 14,788,672

Graduating public high school seniors, 2004-05
Diplomas (incl. GED and others) 2,853,262

SAT scores, 2007
Average critical reading score 502
Average writing score 494
Average math score 515
Percent of graduates taking test 48%

Public school teachers, 2006-07 (estimate)
Total (x 1,000) 3,174.4
Elementary 1,856.6
Secondary 1,317.8
Average salary $50,816
Elementary $50,684
Secondary $51,081

Total state receipts & expenditures for public schools, 2006-07 (estimate)
Revenue receipts ($ mil) $530,340
Expenditures
Total ($ mil) $552,375
Per capita $1,561
Per pupil $10,212

NAEP proficiency scores, 2007
	Reading		Math	
	Basic	Proficient	Basic	Proficient
Grade 4	67.0%	33.0%	82.0%	39.0%
Grade 8	74.0%	31.0%	71.0%	32.0%

Higher education enrollment, fall 2005
Total. 4,465,641
Full-time men .1,452,903
Full-time women 1,935,347
Part-time men 413,799
Part-time women 663,592

Minority enrollment in institutions of higher education, 2005
Black, non-Hispanic 2,214,561
Hispanic 1,881,975
Asian/Pacific Islander 1,134,382
American Indian/Alaska Native. 176,303

Institutions of higher education, 2005-06
Total. 4,276
Public. 1,693
Private 2,583

Earned degrees conferred, 2004-05
Associate's. 696,660
Bachelor's 1,439,264
Master's 574,618
First-professional. 87,289
Doctor's 52,631

Public Libraries, 2006
Number of libraries. 9,198
Number of outlets 17,368
Annual visits per capita 4.7
Circulation per capita. 7.2

State & local financial support for higher education, FY 2006
Full-time equivalent enrollment (x 1,000) . . 10,189.8
Appropriations per FTE. $6,325

Social Insurance & Welfare Programs

Social Security benefits & beneficiaries, 2005
Beneficiaries (x 1,000) 47,255
Retired & dependents. 32,727
Survivors. 6,431
Disabled & dependents. 8,097
Annual benefit payments ($ mil) $512,221
Retired & dependents. $340,499
Survivors. $88,098
Disabled & dependents. $83,623
Average monthly benefit
Retired & dependents. . . . . NA
Disabled & dependents. . . . . NA
Widowed. . . . . NA

Medicare, July 2005
Enrollment (x 1,000) 41,536
Payments ($ mil) $272,442

Medicaid, 2004
Beneficiaries (x 1,000). 55,078
Payments ($ mil) $257,722

State Children's Health Insurance Program, 2006
Enrollment (x 1,000) 6,624.2
Expenditures ($ mil) $7,034.3

Persons without health insurance, 2006
Number (x 1,000) 46,995
percent. 15.8%
Number of children (x 1,000) 8,661
percent of children 11.7%

Health care expenditures, 2004
Total expenditures. $1,551,255
per capita $5,283

Federal and state public aid

State unemployment insurance, 2006
Recipients, first payments (x 1,000) 7,349
Total payments ($ mil) $29,807
Average weekly benefit $277
Temporary Assistance for Needy Families, 2006
Recipients (x 1,000) 49,999.9
Families (x 1,000) 21,376.9
Supplemental Security Income, 2005
Recipients (x 1,000) 7,113.9
Payments ($ mil) $37,235.8
Food Stamp Program, 2006
Avg monthly participants (x 1,000) 26,671.8
Total benefits ($ mil) $30,187.3

Housing & Construction

Housing units

Total 2005 (estimate) 124,528,801
Total 2006 (estimate) 126,316,181
Seasonal or recreational use, 2006 4,213,520
Owner-occupied, 2006 75,086,485
   Median home value $185,200
   Homeowner vacancy rate 2.4%
Renter-occupied, 2006 36,530,917
   Median rent $763
   Rental vacancy rate 9.7%
Home ownership rate, 2005 . . . . .68.9%
Home ownership rate, 2006 . . . . .68.8%

New privately-owned housing units

Number authorized, 2006 (x 1,000) 1,838.9
   Value ($ mil) $291,314.5
Started 2005 (x 1,000, estimate) 1,658.0
Started 2006 (x 1,000, estimate) 1,614.0

Existing home sales

2005 (x 1,000) 7,076
2006 (x 1,000) 6,478

Government & Elections

Federal officials 2008

President . . . . George W. Bush
   Republican, term expires 1/09
Vice President . . . . Richard Cheney
Secretary of State . . . . Condoleezza Rice
Attorney General . . . . Michael B. Mukasey
Chief Justice . . . . John G. Roberts

Presidency

Minimum age 35
Length of term . . . . 4 years
Consecutive terms permitted 2
Who succeeds . . . . Vice President

Local governments by type, 2002

Total 87,525
   County 3,034
   Municipal 19,429
   Township 16,504
   School District 13,506
   Special District 35,052

Federal legislature

Name . . . . US Congress
Upper chamber . . . . US Senate
   Number of members 100
   Length of term . . . . 6 years
   Party in majority, 2008 . . . . Democratic
Lower chamber . . . . .US House of Representatives
   Number of members 435
   Length of term . . . . 2 years
   Party in majority, 2008 . . . . Democratic

Federal representation, 2008 (110th Congress)

Senators, total 100
   Democrats 51
   Republicans 49
Representatives, total . . . . 435 (3 vacant)
   Democrats 232
   Republicans 200

Voters in November 2006 election (estimate)

Total 96,118,886
   Male 45,117,695
   Female 51,001,191
   White 82,387,076
   Black 9,936,941
   Hispanic 3,006,370
   Asian 2,144,606

Presidential election, 2004

Total Popular Vote 122,295,345
   Kerry 59,028,444
   Bush 62,040,610
Total Electoral Votes 538

Votes cast for US Senators

2004
Total vote (x 1,000) 86,968
Leading party . . . . NA
Percent for leading party . . . . NA
2006
Total vote (x 1,000) 60,839
Leading party . . . . Democratic
Percent for leading party 53.2%

Votes cast for US Representatives

2004
Total vote (x 1,000) 113,192
   Democratic 52,745
   Republican 55,713
Leading party . . . . Republican
Percent for leading party 49.2%
2006
Total vote (x 1,000) 80,976
   Democratic 42,082
   Republican 35,675
Leading party . . . . Democratic
Percent for leading party 52.0%

Federal government employees, 2006
Total.................................2,700,0124
Payroll ($ mil) $160,498

State government employment, 2006
Full-time equivalent employees 4,250,554
Payroll ($ mil) $16,769.4

Local government employment, 2006
Full-time equivalent employees 11,885,145
Payroll ($ mil) $43,971.7

Women holding public office, 2008
US Congress 86
Statewide elected office...................... 74
State legislature 1,744

Black public officials, 2002
Total...................................9,430
   US and state legislatures 636
   City/county/regional offices 5,753
   Judicial/law enforcement...............1,081
   Education/school boards..............1,960

Hispanic public officials, 2006
Total..................................4,932
   State executives & legislators 244
   City/county/regional offices 2,151
   Judicial/law enforcement................ 693
   Education/school boards..............1,835

Governmental Finance

Federal government finance, 2007 (estimate)
Total Receipts ($bil)...................$2,540.1
   Individual income taxes.............. 1,168.8
   Corporate income texes 342.1
   Social Insurance and retirement receipts....873.4
   Excise taxes...........................57.1
Total Outlays ($bil) $2,784.3
   Agriculture............................88.8
   Defense - military 548.9
   Defense - civil programs 47.6
   Education 68.0
   Energy................................22.0
   Health & Human Services..............671.3
   Homeland Security.....................50.4
   Housing and Urban Development 42.8
   Justice 23.0
   Labor 47.4
   Transportation 63.8
   Treasury 490.5
   Social Security Administration:
     on-budget.........................55.7
     off-budget........................567.2
Deficit ($bil) $244.2

Federal Budget debt, 2007 (estimate)
Gross debt ($bil) $9,007.8
   Held by the public.....................5,083.3
   Federal government accounts.........3,924.5
   Gross national debt, per capita........$29,865

Federal government grants to state & local governments, 2005 (x $1,000)
Total...........................$469,579,029
by Federal agency
   Defense 3,161,336
   Education 38,053,238
   Energy...........................2,271,238
   Environmental Protection Agency ...3,972,392
   Health & Human Services. 276,352,384
   Homeland Security..............10,454,170
   Housing & Urban Development....33,786,246
   Justice 6,074,154
   Labor 7,852,666
   Transportation 41,146,849
   Veterans Affairs.................... 730,868

Crime & Law Enforcement

Crime, 2006 (rates per 100,000 residents)
Property crimes 9,983,568
   Burglary 2,183,746
   Larceny 6,607,013
   Motor vehicle theft 1,192,809
   Property crime rate...................3,334.5
Violent crimes........................ 1,417,745
   Murder 17,034
   Forcible rape...................... 92,455
   Robbery.......................... 447,403
   Aggravated assault 860,853
   Violent crime rate 473.5
Hate crimes.........................9,080

Fraud and identity theft, 2006
Fraud complaints.................... 374,907
   rate per 100,000 residents 125.2
Identity theft complaints 239,313
   rate per 100,000 residents 79.9

Law enforcement agencies, 2006
Total agencies.........................14,336
Total employees 987,125
   Officers 683,396
   Civilians 303,729

Prisoners, probation, and parole, 2006
Total prisoners......................1,570,861
   percent change, 12/31/05 to 12/31/06 ....2.8%
   in private facilities 7.2%
   in local jails 5.0%
Sentenced to more than one year 1,502,179
   rate per 100,000 residents 501
Adults on probation 4,237,023
Adults on parole.................... 798,202

Prisoner demographics, June 30, 2005 (rate per 100,000 residents)
Male..................................1,249
Female 121
White................................. 412
Black................................. 2,289
Hispanic 742

Arrests, 2006

Total.............................10,472,432
  Persons under 18 years of age.......1,626,523

Persons under sentence of death, 1/1/07

Total................................. 3,350
  White..............................1,517
  Black 1,397
  Hispanic 359

Nation's highest court

Name ....Supreme Court
Number of members....................... 9
Length of term..........................life
Intermediate appeals court? ....yes

Labor & Income

Civilian labor force, 2006 (x 1,000)

Total............................... 151,428
  Men 81,255
  Women 70,173
  Persons 16-19 years..................7,281
  White........................... 123,834
  Black 17,314
  Hispanic 20,694

Civilian labor force as a percent of civilian non-institutional population, 2006

Total...................................66.2%
  Men 73.5
  Women 59.4
  Persons 16-19 years..................43.7
  White..............................66.5
  Black 64.1
  Hispanic 68.7

Employment, 2006 (x 1,000)

Total............................... 144,427
  Men 77,502
  Women 66,925
  Persons 16-19 years..................6,162
  White...........................118,833
  Black 15,765
  Hispanic 19,613

Unemployment rate, 2006

Total.................................. 4.6%
  Men 4.6
  Women 4.6
  Persons 16-19 years..................15.4
  White..............................4.0
  Black 8.9
  Hispanic 5.2

Full-time/part-time labor force, 2003 (x 1,000)

Full-time labor force, employed .... NA
Part-time labor force, employed............ NA
Unemployed, looking for
  Full-time work......................... NA
  Part-time work........................ NA
Mean duration of unemployment (weeks)...... NA
  Median .... NA

Labor unions, 2006

Membership (x 1,000)................. 15,359
  percent of employed 12.0%

Experienced civilian labor force by private industry, 2006

Total...........................112,718,858
  Natural resources & mining 1,776,777
  Construction 7,602,148
  Manufacturing...................14,110,663
  Trade, transportation & utilities .. 26,006,269
  Information 3,040,577
  Finance 8,162,063
  Professional & business 17,469,679
  Education & health...............16,916,228
  Leisure & hospitality.............13,024,615
  Other 4,364,889

Experienced civilian labor force by occupation, May 2006

Management......................5,892,900
Business & financial 5,826,140
Legal............................. 976,740
Sales...........................14,114,860
Office & admin. support............ 23,077,190
Computers & math 3,076,200
Architecture & engineering..........2,430,250
Arts & entertainment 1,727,380
Education 8,206,440
Social services 1,749,210
Health care practitioner & technical ..6,713,780
Health care support 3,483,270
Maintenance & repair...............5,352,420
Construction 6,680,710
Transportation & moving 9,647,730
Production 10,268,510
Farming, fishing & forestry............ 450,040

Hours and earnings of production workers on manufacturing payrolls, 2006

Average weekly hours.....................41.1
Average hourly earnings $16.80
Average weekly earnings $690.83

Income and poverty, 2006

Median household income............. $48,451
Personal income, per capita (current $)... $36,276
  in constant (2000) dollars............$31,667
Persons below poverty level.............. 13.3%

Average annual pay

2006................................. $42,535
  increase from 2005 .... 4.6%

Federal individual income tax returns, 2005

Returns filed......................135,257,620
Adjusted gross income ($1,000)....$7,364,640,131
Total tax liability ($1,000) $989,191,350

Charitable contributions, 2004

Number of contributions..............40,426.9
Total amount ($ mil)...............$162,198.7

Economy, Business, Industry & Agriculture

Fortune 500 companies, 2007.............. 500
Bankruptcy cases filed, FY 2007........ 801,269

Patents and trademarks issued, 2007
Patents...........................94,618
Trademarks......................... 122,266

Business firm ownership, 2002
Women-owned.....................6,489,259
   Sales ($ mil) $939,538
Black-owned........................1,197,567
   Sales ($ mil) $88,642
Hispanic-owned....................1,573,464
   Sales ($ mil) $221,927
Asian-owned 1,103,587
   Sales ($ mil) $326,663
Amer. Indian/Alaska Native-owned 206,125
   Sales ($ mil) $26,396
Hawaiian/Pacific Islander-owned 28,948
   Sales ($ mil) $4,280

Gross domestic product, 2006 ($ mil)
Total gross domestic product $13,149,033
   Agriculture, forestry, fishing and
      hunting 122,352
   Mining............................ 256,049
   Utilities........................... 262,604
   Construction 647,882
   Manufacturing, durable goods....... 915,677
   Manufacturing, non-durable goods .. 685,475
   Wholesale trade.................... 788,674
   Retail trade....................... 863,155
   Transportation & warehousing 363,678
   Information....................... 579,232
   Finance & insurance............... 1,027,477
   Real estate, rental & leasing 1,731,115
   Professional and technical services 929,614
   Educational services............... 123,296
   Health care and social assistance.....911,681
   Accommodation/food services.......349,915
   Other services, except government ... 295,704
   Government 1,538,624

Establishments, payroll, employees & receipts, by major industry group, 2005

Total............................ 7,499,702
   Annual payroll ($1,000).......$4,482,722,481
   Paid employees 116,317,003
Forestry, fishing & agriculture.......... 24,102
   Annual payroll ($1,000)...........$5,095,741
   Paid employees 168,744
Mining............................ 24,696
   Annual payroll ($1,000).........$30,823,272
   Paid employees 497,272
   Receipts, 2002 ($1,000) $182,911,093

Utilities 17,326
   Annual payroll ($1,000)........ $46,292,766
   Paid employees 633,106
   Receipts, 2002 ($1,000) $398,907,044
Construction.........................787,672
   Annual payroll ($1,000)....... $292,519,343
   Paid employees 6,781,327
   Receipts, 2002 ($1,000) ... $1,196,555,587
Manufacturing..................... 333,460
   Annual payroll ($1,000)....... $600,696,305
   Paid employees 13,667,337
   Receipts, 2002 ($1,000) $3,916,136,712
Wholesale trade 429,823
   Annual payroll ($1,000)....... $308,918,023
   Paid employees 5,968,929
   Receipts, 2002 ($1,000) $4,634,755,112
Retail trade 1,123,207
   Annual payroll ($1,000).......$348,047,012
   Paid employees 15,338,672
   Receipts, 2002 ($1,000) $3,056,421,997
Transportation & warehousing 211,150
   Annual payroll ($1,000).,.......$154,375,938
   Paid employees 4,168,016
   Receipts, 2002 ($1,000) $382,152,040
Information........................ 141,290
   Annual payroll ($1,000)........$203,129,725
   Paid employees 3,402,599
   Receipts, 2002 ($1,000) $891,845,956
Finance & insurance 476,806
   Annual payroll ($1,000)....... $446,739,512
   Paid employees 6,431,837
   Receipts, 2002 ($1,000) ... $2,803,854,868
Professional, scientific & technical 826,101
   Annual payroll ($1,000) $456,455,965
   Paid employees 7,689,366
   Receipts, 2002 ($1,000) $886,801,038
Education 80,486
   Annual payroll ($1,000) $82,522,976
   Paid employees 2,879,374
   Receipts, 2002 ($1,000) $30,690,707
Health care & social assistance 746,600
   Annual payroll ($1,000)........ $589,654,273
   Paid employees 16,025,147
   Receipts, 2002 ($1,000) $1,207,299,734
Arts and entertainment 121,777
   Annual payroll ($1,000).........$52,935,670
   Paid employees 1,936,484
   Receipts, 2002 ($1,000) $141,904,109
Real estate 370,651
   Annual payroll ($1,000)......... $81,790,239
   Paid employees 2,144,077
   Receipts, 2002 ($1,000) $335,587,706
Accommodation & food service......... 603,435
   Annual payroll ($1,000).........$156,041,233
   Paid employees 11,025,909
   Receipts, 2002 ($1,000) $449,498,718

8   US Summary

Exports, 2006
Value of exported goods ($ mil) $1,037,320
    Manufactured $821,708
    Non-manufactured $107,955

Foreign direct investment in US affiliates, 2004
Property, plants & equipment ($ mil). . .$1,060,181
Employment (x 1,000). 5,116.4

Agriculture, 2006
Number of farms .2,089,790
Farm acreage (x 1,000) 932,430
    Acres per farm 446.18
Farm marketings and income ($ mil)
Total. $239,271.9
    Crops $119,951.5
    Livestock $119,320.4
Net farm income $59,005.5

Principal commodities, in order by marketing receipts, 2005
Cattle and calves, Dairy products, Corn, Broilers, Soybeans

Federal economic activity in states
Expenditures, 2005 ($ mil)
    Total. $2,284,760
        Per capita $7,567.85
    Defense $374,203
    Non-defense $1,910,558
Defense department, 2006 ($ mil)
    Payroll $146,858
    Contract awards $257,457
    Grants $3,934
Homeland security grants ($1,000)
    2006 . . . .$1,747,300
    2007 . . . .$1,666,460

FDIC-insured financial institutions, 2005
Number 8,680
Assets ($ billion) $11,860.3
Deposits ($ billion) $7,825.2

Fishing, 2006
Catch (x 1,000 lbs) 9,489,031
Value ($1,000). $3,993,370

Mining, 2006 ($ mil)
Total non-fuel mineral production $64,400
Percent of U.S. 100%

Communication, Energy & Transportation

Communication
Households with computers, 2003 . . . . 61.8%
Households with internet access, 2003 . . . . 54.6%
High-speed internet providers 1,397
Total high-speed internet lines 82,547,651
    Residential 58,243,921
    Business. 24,303,730
Wireless phone customers, 12/2006 . . . 229,619,397

FCC-licensed stations (as of January 1, 2008)
TV stations 1,716
FM radio stations. 9,143
AM radio stations 4,740

Energy
Energy consumption, 2004
    Total (trillion Btu). 100,279
    Per capita (million Btu) 341.5
By source of production (trillion Btu)
    Coal 22,466
    Natural gas 22,902
    Petroleum 40,593
    Nuclear electric power 8,222
    Hydroelectric power 2,690
By end-use sector (trillion Btu)
    Residential 21,243
    Commercial 17,721
    Industrial 33,415
    Transportation 27,900
Electric energy, 2005
    Primary source of electricity. . . . . Coal
    Net generation (billion kWh) 4,055.4
        percent from renewable sources. 8.8%
    Net summer capability (million kW) 978.0
    CO_2 emitted from generation 2,513.6
Natural gas utilities, 2005
    Customers (x 1,000) 68,785
    Sales (trillion Btu). 15,077
    Revenues ($ mil) $96,909
Nuclear plants, 2007 105
Total CO_2 emitted (million metric tons). . .5,800.5
Energy spending, 2004 ($ mil) $869,319
    per capita $2,961
    Price per million Btu $12.91

Transportation, 2006
Public road & street mileage 4,016,741
    Urban. 1,029,366
    Rural 2,987,375
    Interstate. 46,630
Vehicle miles of travel (millions) 3,014,116
    per capita 10,088.9
Total motor vehicle registrations 244,165,686
    Automobiles .135,399,945
    Trucks 107,943,782
    Motorcycles 6,686,147
Licensed drivers 202,810,438
    19 years & under 9,727,516
Deaths from motor vehicle accidents 42,642
Gasoline consumed (x 1,000 gallons). . . 140,320,089
    per capita 469.7

Commuting Statistics, 2006
Average commute time (min) 25.0
    Drove to work alone 76.0%
    Carpooled. 10.7%
    Public transit 4.8%
    Walk to work 2.9%
    Work from home 3.9%

Comparative Tables

Note: Rankings that are tied are listed alphabetically, with the exception of the United States, which is always listed as the final item in a group of ties.

Comparative Tables

1. Total Area (square miles)

*	UNITED STATES	3,794,083
1.	Alaska	663,267
2.	Texas	268,581
3.	California	163,696
4.	Montana	147,042
5.	New Mexico	121,590
6.	Arizona	113,998
7.	Nevada	110,561
8.	Colorado	104,094
9.	Oregon	98,381
10.	Wyoming	97,814
11.	Michigan	96,716
12.	Minnesota	86,939
13.	Utah	84,899
14.	Idaho	83,570
15.	Kansas	82,277
16.	Nebraska	77,354
17.	South Dakota	77,117
18.	Washington	71,300
19.	North Dakota	70,700
20.	Oklahoma	69,898
21.	Missouri	69,704
22.	Florida	65,755
23.	Wisconsin	65,498
24.	Georgia	59,425
25.	Illinois	57,914
26.	Iowa	56,272
27.	New York	54,556
28.	North Carolina	53,819
29.	Arkansas	53,179
30.	Alabama	52,419
31.	Louisiana	51,840
32.	Mississippi	48,430
33.	Pennsylvania	46,055
34.	Ohio	44,825
35.	Virginia	42,774
36.	Tennessee	42,143
37.	Kentucky	40,409
38.	Indiana	36,418
39.	Maine	35,385
40.	South Carolina	32,020
41.	West Virginia	24,230
42.	Maryland	12,407
43.	Hawaii	10,931
44.	Massachusetts	10,555
45.	Vermont	9,614
46.	New Hampshire	9,350
47.	New Jersey	8,721
48.	Connecticut	5,543
49.	Delaware	2,489
50.	Rhode Island	1,545
51.	District of Columbia	68

2. Federally-Owned Land, 2004

1.	Nevada	84.5%
2.	Alaska	69.1
3.	Utah	57.5
4.	Oregon	53.1
5.	Idaho	50.2
6.	Arizona	48.1
7.	California	45.3
8.	Wyoming	42.3
9.	New Mexico	41.8
10.	Colorado	36.6
11.	Washington	30.3
12.	Montana	29.9
*	UNITED STATES	28.8
13.	District of Columbia	24.7
14.	Hawaii	19.4
15.	New Hampshire	13.5
16.	North Carolina	11.8
17.	Michigan	10.0
18.	Virginia	9.9
19.	Florida	8.2
20.	Vermont	7.5
21.	West Virginia	7.4
22.	Mississippi	7.3
23.	Arkansas	7.2
24.	South Dakota	6.2
25.	Minnesota	5.6
26.	Wisconsin	5.6
27.	Kentucky	5.4
28.	Louisiana	5.1
29.	Missouri	5.0
30.	Georgia	3.8
31.	Oklahoma	3.6
32.	Tennessee	3.2
33.	New Jersey	3.1
34.	South Carolina	2.9
35.	Maryland	2.8
36.	North Dakota	2.7
37.	Pennsylvania	2.5
38.	Delaware	2.0
39.	Indiana	2.0
40.	Massachusetts	1.9
41.	Texas	1.9
42.	Illinois	1.8
43.	Ohio	1.7
44.	Alabama	1.6
45.	Nebraska	1.4
46.	Kansas	1.2
47.	Maine	1.1
48.	Iowa	0.8
49.	New York	0.8
50.	Connecticut	0.4
51.	Rhode Island	0.4

Comparative Tables

3. Population, 2000		4. Population, 2007 (estimate)	
* UNITED STATES	281,424,602	* UNITED STATES	301,621,157
1. California	33,871,653	1. California	36,553,215
2. Texas	20,851,792	2. Texas	23,904,380
3. New York	18,976,821	3. New York	19,297,729
4. Florida	15,982,824	4. Florida	18,251,243
5. Illinois	12,419,647	5. Illinois	12,852,548
6. Pennsylvania	12,281,054	6. Pennsylvania	12,432,792
7. Ohio	11,353,145	7. Ohio	11,466,917
8. Michigan	9,938,480	8. Michigan	10,071,822
9. New Jersey	8,414,347	9. Georgia	9,544,750
10. Georgia	8,186,816	10. North Carolina	9,061,032
11. North Carolina	8,046,491	11. New Jersey	8,685,920
12. Virginia	7,079,030	12. Virginia	7,712,091
13. Massachusetts	6,349,105	13. Washington	6,468,424
14. Indiana	6,080,517	14. Massachusetts	6,449,755
15. Washington	5,894,140	15. Indiana	6,345,289
16. Tennessee	5,689,262	16. Arizona	6,338,755
17. Missouri	5,596,683	17. Tennessee	6,156,719
18. Wisconsin	5,363,715	18. Missouri	5,878,415
19. Maryland	5,296,506	19. Maryland	5,618,344
20. Arizona	5,130,632	20. Wisconsin	5,601,640
21. Minnesota	4,919,492	21. Minnesota	5,197,621
22. Louisiana	4,468,958	22. Colorado	4,861,515
23. Alabama	4,447,351	23. Alabama	4,627,851
24. Colorado	4,302,015	24. South Carolina	4,407,709
25. Kentucky	4,042,285	25. Louisiana	4,293,204
26. South Carolina	4,011,816	26. Kentucky	4,241,474
27. Oklahoma	3,450,652	27. Oregon	3,747,455
28. Oregon	3,421,436	28. Oklahoma	3,617,316
29. Connecticut	3,405,602	29. Connecticut	3,502,309
30. Iowa	2,926,382	30. Iowa	2,988,046
31. Mississippi	2,844,656	31. Mississippi	2,918,785
32. Kansas	2,688,824	32. Arkansas	2,834,797
33. Arkansas	2,673,398	33. Kansas	2,775,997
34. Utah	2,233,198	34. Utah	2,645,330
35. Nevada	1,998,257	35. Nevada	2,565,382
36. New Mexico	1,819,046	36. New Mexico	1,969,915
37. West Virginia	1,808,350	37. West Virginia	1,812,035
38. Nebraska	1,711,265	38. Nebraska	1,774,571
39. Idaho	1,293,956	39. Idaho	1,499,402
40. Maine	1,274,923	40. Maine	1,317,207
41. New Hampshire	1,235,786	41. New Hampshire	1,315,828
42. Hawaii	1,211,537	42. Hawaii	1,283,388
43. Rhode Island	1,048,319	43. Rhode Island	1,057,832
44. Montana	902,195	44. Montana	957,861
45. Delaware	783,600	45. Delaware	864,764
46. South Dakota	754,840	46. South Dakota	796,214
47. North Dakota	642,204	47. Alaska	683,478
48. Alaska	626,931	48. North Dakota	639,715
49. Vermont	608,827	49. Vermont	621,254
50. District of Columbia	572,059	50. District of Columbia	588,292
51. Wyoming	493,782	51. Wyoming	522,830

Comparative Tables

5. Population, 2008 (projected)	
* UNITED STATES	303,597,646
1. California	37,262,310
2. Texas	23,898,665
3. New York	19,383,109
4. Florida	18,533,980
5. Illinois	12,835,851
6. Pennsylvania	12,525,118
7. Ohio	11,541,279
8. Michigan	10,345,033
9. Georgia	9,325,827
10. North Carolina	9,086,527
11. New Jersey	8,915,495
12. Virginia	7,827,657
13. Massachusetts	6,601,235
14. Washington	6,399,035
15. Indiana	6,337,404
16. Arizona	6,320,874
17. Tennessee	6,124,341
18. Missouri	5,860,326
19. Maryland	5,783,344
20. Wisconsin	5,659,640
21. Minnesota	5,321,587
22. Colorado	4,746,528
23. Louisiana	4,583,733
24. Alabama	4,568,983
25. South Carolina	4,365,055
26. Kentucky	4,226,659
27. Oregon	3,709,778
28. Oklahoma	3,563,865
29. Connecticut	3,550,416
30. Iowa	2,997,608
31. Mississippi	2,950,652
32. Arkansas	2,836,580
33. Kansas	2,784,728
34. Nevada	2,551,889
35. Utah	2,523,394
36. New Mexico	1,951,229
37. West Virginia	1,827,226
38. Nebraska	1,759,829
39. Idaho	1,472,584
40. New Hampshire	1,357,216
41. Maine	1,342,286
42. Hawaii	1,317,607
43. Rhode Island	1,105,525
44. Montana	954,653
45. Delaware	865,705
46. South Dakota	780,947
47. Alaska	680,082
48. Vermont	643,905
49. North Dakota	636,452
50. District of Columbia	538,487
51. Wyoming	515,408

6. Population, 2030 (projected)	
* UNITED STATES	363,584,435
1. California	46,444,861
2. Texas	33,317,744
3. Florida	28,685,769
4. New York	19,477,429
5. Illinois	13,432,892
6. Pennsylvania	12,768,184
7. North Carolina	12,227,739
8. Georgia	12,017,838
9. Ohio	11,550,528
10. Arizona	10,712,397
11. Michigan	10,694,172
12. Virginia	9,825,019
13. New Jersey	9,802,440
14. Washington	8,624,801
15. Tennessee	7,380,634
16. Maryland	7,022,251
17. Massachusetts	7,012,009
18. Indiana	6,810,108
19. Missouri	6,430,173
20. Minnesota	6,306,130
21. Wisconsin	6,150,764
22. Colorado	5,792,357
23. South Carolina	5,148,569
24. Alabama	4,874,243
25. Oregon	4,833,918
26. Louisiana	4,802,633
27. Kentucky	4,554,998
28. Nevada	4,282,102
29. Oklahoma	3,913,251
30. Connecticut	3,688,630
31. Utah	3,485,367
32. Arkansas	3,240,208
33. Mississippi	3,092,410
34. Iowa	2,955,172
35. Kansas	2,940,084
36. New Mexico	2,099,708
37. Idaho	1,969,624
38. Nebraska	1,820,247
39. West Virginia	1,719,959
40. New Hampshire	1,646,471
41. Hawaii	1,466,046
42. Maine	1,411,097
43. Rhode Island	1,152,941
44. Montana	1,044,898
45. Delaware	1,012,658
46. Alaska	867,674
47. South Dakota	800,462
48. Vermont	711,867
49. North Dakota	606,566
50. Wyoming	522,979
51. District of Columbia	433,414

Comparative Tables

7. Persons per Square Mile, 2007 (estimate)	
1. District of Columbia	9,644.1
2. New Jersey	1,171.1
3. Rhode Island	1,012.3
4. Massachusetts	822.7
5. Connecticut	722.9
6. Maryland	574.8
7. Delaware	442.6
8. New York	408.7
9. Florida	338.4
10. Ohio	280.0
11. Pennsylvania	277.4
12. California	234.4
13. Illinois	231.2
14. Hawaii	199.8
15. Virginia	194.8
16. North Carolina	186.0
17. Michigan	177.3
18. Indiana	176.9
19. Georgia	164.8
20. Tennessee	149.4
21. New Hampshire	146.7
22. South Carolina	146.4
23. Kentucky	106.8
24. Wisconsin	103.1
25. Louisiana	98.6
26. Washington	97.2
27. Texas	91.3
28. Alabama	91.2
29. Missouri	85.3
* UNITED STATES	85.3
30. West Virginia	75.3
31. Vermont	67.2
32. Minnesota	65.3
33. Mississippi	62.2
34. Arizona	55.8
35. Arkansas	54.4
36. Iowa	53.5
37. Oklahoma	52.7
38. Colorado	46.9
39. Maine	42.7
40. Oregon	39.0
41. Kansas	33.9
42. Utah	32.2
43. Nevada	23.4
44. Nebraska	23.1
45. Idaho	18.1
46. New Mexico	16.2
47. South Dakota	10.5
48. North Dakota	9.3
49. Montana	6.6
50. Wyoming	5.4
51. Alaska	1.2

8. Change in Population, 2000-2007 (estimate)	
1. Nevada	28.4%
2. Arizona	23.5
3. Utah	18.5
4. Georgia	16.6
5. Idaho	15.9
6. Texas	14.6
7. Florida	14.2
8. Colorado	13.0
9. North Carolina	12.6
10. Delaware	10.4
11. South Carolina	9.9
12. Washington	9.7
13. Oregon	9.5
14. Alaska	9.0
15. Virginia	8.9
16. New Mexico	8.3
17. Tennessee	8.2
18. California	7.9
* UNITED STATES	7.2
19. New Hampshire	6.5
20. Montana	6.2
21. Maryland	6.1
22. Arkansas	6.0
23. Hawaii	5.9
24. Wyoming	5.9
25. Minnesota	5.7
26. South Dakota	5.5
27. Missouri	5.0
28. Kentucky	4.9
29. Oklahoma	4.8
30. Indiana	4.4
31. Wisconsin	4.4
32. Alabama	4.1
33. Nebraska	3.7
34. Illinois	3.5
35. Maine	3.3
36. Kansas	3.2
37. New Jersey	3.2
38. Connecticut	2.8
39. District of Columbia	2.8
40. Mississippi	2.6
41. Iowa	2.1
42. Vermont	2.0
43. New York	1.7
44. Massachusetts	1.6
45. Michigan	1.3
46. Pennsylvania	1.2
47. Ohio	1.0
48. Rhode Island	0.9
49. West Virginia	0.2
50. North Dakota	-0.4
51. Louisiana	-3.9

Comparative Tables

9. Cities with over 100,000 Population, 2006	
* UNITED STATES	258
1. California	62
2. Texas	27
3. Florida	17
4. Arizona	9
5. Colorado	9
6. Virginia	9
7. Illinois	8
8. Michigan	7
9. North Carolina	7
10. Ohio	6
11. Connecticut	5
12. Georgia	5
13. Kansas	5
14. Massachusetts	5
15. New York	5
16. Tennessee	5
17. Washington	5
18. Alabama	4
19. Indiana	4
20. Louisiana	4
21. Missouri	4
22. Nevada	4
23. New Jersey	4
24. Pennsylvania	4
25. Oklahoma	3
26. Oregon	3
27. Utah	3
28. Wisconsin	3
29. Iowa	2
30. Kentucky	2
31. Minnesota	2
32. Nebraska	2
33. South Carolina	2
34. Alaska	1
35. Arkansas	1
36. District of Columbia	1
37. Hawaii	1
38. Idaho	1
39. Maryland	1
40. Mississippi	1
41. Montana	1
42. New Hampshire	1
43. New Mexico	1
44. Rhode Island	1
45. South Dakota	1
46. Delaware	0
47. Maine	0
48. North Dakota	0
49. Vermont	0
50. West Virginia	0
51. Wyoming	0

10. Population Living in Group Quarters, 2006	
1. District of Columbia	6.1%
2. North Dakota	4.3
3. Rhode Island	4.0
4. South Dakota	3.8
5. Pennsylvania	3.7
6. Iowa	3.5
7. Alaska	3.4
8. Massachusetts	3.4
9. South Carolina	3.3
10. Vermont	3.3
11. Connecticut	3.2
12. Mississippi	3.2
13. New York	3.1
14. North Carolina	3.1
15. Oklahoma	3.1
16. Virginia	3.1
17. Kansas	3.0
18. Delaware	2.9
19. Georgia	2.9
20. Hawaii	2.9
21. Louisiana	2.9
22. Missouri	2.9
23. Nebraska	2.9
24. Wisconsin	2.9
25. Arkansas	2.8
26. Indiana	2.8
27. Maine	2.8
28. New Hampshire	2.8
29. Kentucky	2.7
30. Minnesota	2.7
31. Montana	2.7
32. Ohio	2.7
33. Wyoming	2.7
* UNITED STATES	2.7
34. Alabama	2.5
35. Illinois	2.5
36. Maryland	2.5
37. Michigan	2.5
38. Tennessee	2.5
39. Texas	2.5
40. West Virginia	2.5
41. California	2.4
42. Florida	2.3
43. Idaho	2.3
44. New Jersey	2.3
45. Colorado	2.2
46. Oregon	2.2
47. Washington	2.2
48. New Mexico	2.1
49. Arizona	1.8
50. Utah	1.7
51. Nevada	1.3

Comparative Tables

11. Core-Based Statistical Area Population, 2006 (x 1,000)	
* UNITED STATES	279,848
1. California	36,195
2. Texas	22,090
3. New York	18,873
4. Florida	17,692
5. Illinois	12,218
6. Pennsylvania	12,056
7. Ohio	10,966
8. Michigan	9,302
9. New Jersey	8,725
10. Georgia	8,534
11. North Carolina	8,135
12. Virginia	6,814
13. Massachusetts	6,411
14. Washington	6,168
15. Arizona	5,964
16. Indiana	5,946
17. Maryland	5,533
18. Tennessee	5,412
19. Missouri	5,043
20. Wisconsin	4,777
21. Minnesota	4,510
22. Colorado	4,356
23. Alabama	4,109
24. South Carolina	4,046
25. Louisiana	3,979
26. Oregon	3,559
27. Connecticut	3,505
28. Kentucky	3,184
29. Oklahoma	3,018
30. Nevada	2,447
31. Utah	2,420
32. Kansas	2,349
33. Mississippi	2,263
34. Arkansas	2,224
35. Iowa	2,167
36. New Mexico	1,876
37. Nebraska	1,415
38. West Virginia	1,366
39. Hawaii	1,285
40. Idaho	1,267
41. New Hampshire	1,267
42. Rhode Island	1,068
43. Maine	931
44. Delaware	853
45. Montana	615
46. District of Columbia	582
47. South Dakota	560
48. Alaska	503
49. Vermont	460
50. North Dakota	442
51. Wyoming	368

12. Non-CBSA population, 2006 (x 1,000)	
* UNITED STATES	19,551
1. Texas	1,418
2. Kentucky	1,022
3. Georgia	830
4. Virginia	829
5. Iowa	816
6. Missouri	800
7. Michigan	794
8. Wisconsin	779
9. North Carolina	722
10. Minnesota	657
11. Mississippi	647
12. Tennessee	627
13. Illinois	614
14. Arkansas	587
15. Oklahoma	561
16. Ohio	512
17. Alabama	490
18. West Virginia	453
19. New York	433
20. Kansas	415
21. Florida	398
22. Colorado	397
23. Maine	391
24. Pennsylvania	385
25. Indiana	367
26. Nebraska	354
27. Montana	330
28. Louisiana	309
29. South Carolina	275
30. California	262
31. Washington	227
32. South Dakota	222
33. Arizona	203
34. Idaho	200
35. North Dakota	194
36. Alaska	167
37. Vermont	164
38. Wyoming	147
39. Oregon	142
40. Utah	130
41. Maryland	82
42. New Mexico	78
43. Nevada	49
44. New Hampshire	47
45. Massachusetts	26
46. Connecticut	0
47. Delaware	0
48. District of Columbia	0
49. Hawaii	0
50. New Jersey	0
51. Rhode Island	0

Comparative Tables

13. Median Age, 2006

1.	Maine	41.1
2.	Vermont	40.4
3.	West Virginia	40.2
4.	Florida	39.6
5.	Pennsylvania	39.5
6.	New Hampshire	39.4
7.	Montana	39.2
8.	Connecticut	39.0
9.	Massachusetts	38.2
10.	New Jersey	38.2
11.	Rhode Island	38.2
12.	Iowa	37.8
13.	Wisconsin	37.7
14.	Ohio	37.6
15.	Delaware	37.5
16.	Oregon	37.5
17.	Hawaii	37.3
18.	New York	37.3
19.	Kentucky	37.2
20.	Maryland	37.2
21.	Michigan	37.2
22.	North Dakota	37.2
23.	Alabama	37.1
24.	Missouri	37.1
25.	South Carolina	37.1
26.	Tennessee	37.1
27.	Wyoming	37.1
28.	South Dakota	36.9
29.	Virginia	36.9
30.	Arkansas	36.8
31.	Minnesota	36.8
32.	Washington	36.7
33.	North Carolina	36.6
*	UNITED STATES	36.4
34.	Indiana	36.3
35.	Kansas	36.0
36.	Nebraska	36.0
37.	Oklahoma	36.0
38.	Illinois	35.7
39.	Louisiana	35.7
40.	Nevada	35.5
41.	Colorado	35.4
42.	Mississippi	35.3
43.	New Mexico	35.3
44.	District of Columbia	35.0
45.	Arizona	34.6
46.	Georgia	34.6
47.	California	34.4
48.	Idaho	34.2
49.	Alaska	33.4
50.	Texas	33.1
51.	Utah	28.3

14. Households, 2006

*	UNITED STATES	111,617,402
1.	California	12,151,227
2.	Texas	8,109,388
3.	Florida	7,106,042
4.	New York	7,088,376
5.	Pennsylvania	4,845,603
6.	Illinois	4,724,252
7.	Ohio	4,499,506
8.	Michigan	3,869,117
9.	North Carolina	3,454,068
10.	Georgia	3,376,763
11.	New Jersey	3,135,490
12.	Virginia	2,905,071
13.	Washington	2,471,912
14.	Massachusetts	2,446,485
15.	Indiana	2,435,274
16.	Tennessee	2,375,123
17.	Missouri	2,305,027
18.	Wisconsin	2,230,060
19.	Arizona	2,224,992
20.	Maryland	2,089,031
21.	Minnesota	2,042,297
22.	Colorado	1,846,988
23.	Alabama	1,796,058
24.	South Carolina	1,656,978
25.	Kentucky	1,651,911
26.	Louisiana	1,564,978
27.	Oregon	1,449,662
28.	Oklahoma	1,385,300
29.	Connecticut	1,325,443
30.	Iowa	1,208,765
31.	Arkansas	1,103,428
32.	Kansas	1,088,288
33.	Mississippi	1,075,521
34.	Nevada	936,828
35.	Utah	814,028
36.	West Virginia	743,064
37.	New Mexico	726,033
38.	Nebraska	700,888
39.	Idaho	548,555
40.	Maine	548,247
41.	New Hampshire	504,503
42.	Hawaii	432,632
43.	Rhode Island	405,627
44.	Montana	372,190
45.	Delaware	320,110
46.	South Dakota	312,477
47.	North Dakota	272,352
48.	Vermont	253,808
49.	District of Columbia	250,456
50.	Alaska	229,878
51.	Wyoming	207,302

Comparative Tables

15. Legal Permanent Residents Admitted, 2006

*	UNITED STATES	1,266,264
1.	California	264,677
2.	New York	180,165
3.	Florida	155,996
4.	Texas	89,037
5.	New Jersey	65,934
6.	Illinois	52,459
7.	Virginia	38,488
8.	Massachusetts	35,560
9.	Georgia	32,202
10.	Maryland	30,204
11.	Pennsylvania	25,958
12.	Washington	23,805
13.	Arizona	21,530
14.	Michigan	20,911
15.	North Carolina	18,989
16.	Connecticut	18,700
17.	Minnesota	18,254
18.	Ohio	16,592
19.	Nevada	14,714
20.	Colorado	12,714
21.	Tennessee	10,042
22.	Oregon	9,192
23.	Wisconsin	8,341
24.	Indiana	8,125
25.	Hawaii	7,501
26.	Missouri	6,857
27.	Utah	5,749
28.	Kentucky	5,506
29.	South Carolina	5,292
30.	Rhode Island	4,778
31.	Oklahoma	4,591
32.	Kansas	4,280
33.	Alabama	4,278
34.	Iowa	4,086
35.	New Mexico	3,805
36.	Nebraska	3,795
37.	District of Columbia	3,775
38.	New Hampshire	2,990
39.	Arkansas	2,926
40.	Louisiana	2,693
41.	Idaho	2,377
42.	Delaware	2,265
43.	Maine	1,719
44.	Alaska	1,554
45.	Mississippi	1,480
46.	South Dakota	1,013
47.	Vermont	895
48.	West Virginia	764
49.	North Dakota	649
50.	Montana	505
51.	Wyoming	376

16. Naturalizations, 2006

*	UNITED STATES	702,589
1.	California	152,836
2.	New York	103,870
3.	Florida	90,846
4.	New Jersey	39,801
5.	Texas	37,835
6.	Illinois	30,156
7.	Massachusetts	22,932
8.	Virginia	20,401
9.	Georgia	19,785
10.	Pennsylvania	15,846
11.	Maryland	14,465
12.	Washington	12,762
13.	North Carolina	12,592
14.	Michigan	11,675
15.	Arizona	9,707
16.	Minnesota	9,137
17.	Ohio	8,796
18.	Nevada	8,202
19.	Connecticut	7,231
20.	Colorado	5,526
21.	Hawaii	5,276
22.	Oregon	4,332
23.	Indiana	3,885
24.	Missouri	3,711
25.	Tennessee	3,334
26.	Wisconsin	3,247
27.	South Carolina	2,940
28.	Utah	2,740
29.	Kansas	2,509
30.	New Hampshire	2,483
31.	Rhode Island	2,266
32.	Oklahoma	2,246
33.	Kentucky	2,049
34.	Alabama	1,946
35.	Nebraska	1,797
36.	New Mexico	1,538
37.	Louisiana	1,336
38.	Delaware	1,187
39.	Arkansas	1,133
40.	District of Columbia	1,089
41.	Idaho	980
42.	Alaska	831
43.	Iowa	805
44.	Maine	802
45.	Vermont	569
46.	Mississippi	495
47.	West Virginia	390
48.	South Dakota	342
49.	North Dakota	329
50.	Montana	225
51.	Wyoming	169

Comparative Tables

17. Persons Born in State of Residence, 2006

1.	Louisiana	79.8%
2.	Michigan	75.7
3.	Pennsylvania	75.6
4.	Ohio	75.1
5.	Mississippi	72.7
6.	Iowa	72.3
7.	West Virginia	72.2
8.	Wisconsin	72.1
9.	Kentucky	71.8
10.	North Dakota	71.1
11.	Alabama	70.9
12.	Minnesota	69.1
13.	Indiana	68.6
14.	Illinois	66.9
15.	Missouri	66.3
16.	Nebraska	65.5
17.	South Dakota	65.2
18.	Maine	65.0
19.	New York	64.5
20.	Massachusetts	64.1
21.	Utah	63.0
22.	Tennessee	62.6
23.	Oklahoma	61.7
24.	Arkansas	61.3
25.	Texas	60.9
26.	South Carolina	60.8
27.	North Carolina	59.7
28.	Rhode Island	59.2
29.	Kansas	59.1
*	UNITED STATES	58.9
30.	Connecticut	55.7
31.	Georgia	55.5
32.	Hawaii	55.2
33.	Montana	53.5
34.	Vermont	52.7
35.	California	52.4
36.	New Jersey	52.4
37.	New Mexico	50.9
38.	Virginia	50.8
39.	Maryland	47.8
40.	Washington	47.2
41.	Delaware	47.0
42.	Idaho	45.1
43.	Oregon	45.0
44.	Wyoming	42.6
45.	Colorado	42.1
46.	New Hampshire	41.8
47.	District of Columbia	40.1
48.	Alaska	38.9
49.	Arizona	35.7
50.	Florida	33.6
51.	Nevada	23.1

18. Adults who Smoke, 2006

1.	Kentucky	28.5%
2.	West Virginia	25.7
3.	Mississippi	25.1
4.	Oklahoma	25.1
5.	Indiana	24.1
6.	Alaska	24.0
7.	Arkansas	23.7
8.	Louisiana	23.4
9.	Alabama	23.2
10.	Missouri	23.2
11.	Tennessee	22.6
12.	Michigan	22.4
13.	Ohio	22.4
14.	South Carolina	22.3
15.	Nevada	22.2
16.	North Carolina	22.1
17.	Delaware	21.7
18.	Wyoming	21.6
19.	Pennsylvania	21.5
20.	Iowa	21.4
21.	Florida	21.0
22.	Maine	20.9
23.	Wisconsin	20.8
24.	Illinois	20.5
25.	South Dakota	20.3
26.	New Mexico	20.1
*	UNITED STATES	20.1
27.	Kansas	20.0
28.	Georgia	19.9
29.	North Dakota	19.5
30.	Virginia	19.3
31.	Rhode Island	19.2
32.	Montana	18.9
33.	Nebraska	18.7
34.	New Hampshire	18.7
35.	Oregon	18.5
36.	Minnesota	18.3
37.	Arizona	18.2
38.	New York	18.2
39.	New Jersey	18.0
40.	Vermont	18.0
41.	Colorado	17.9
42.	District of Columbia	17.9
43.	Texas	17.9
44.	Massachusetts	17.8
45.	Maryland	17.7
46.	Hawaii	17.5
47.	Washington	17.1
48.	Connecticut	17.0
49.	Idaho	16.8
50.	California	14.9
51.	Utah	9.8

Comparative Tables

19. Death Rate, 2005 (per 100,000 population, age-adjusted)		20. Infant Death Rate, 2004 (per 1,000 births)	
1. Mississippi	1,026.9	1. District of Columbia	12.0
2. Louisiana	1,020.6	2. Louisiana	10.5
3. Alabama	997.9	3. Mississippi	9.8
4. Oklahoma	980.8	4. South Carolina	9.3
5. District of Columbia	971.4	5. North Carolina	8.8
6. West Virginia	960.4	6. Wyoming	8.8
7. Tennessee	959.9	7. Alabama	8.7
8. Kentucky	958.4	8. Delaware	8.6
9. Arkansas	930.2	9. Tennessee	8.6
10. Georgia	905.8	10. Georgia	8.5
11. South Carolina	899.1	11. Maryland	8.4
12. Nevada	892.3	12. Arkansas	8.3
13. North Carolina	876.0	13. South Dakota	8.2
14. Missouri	869.4	14. Indiana	8.0
15. Indiana	858.7	15. Oklahoma	8.0
16. Ohio	856.8	16. Ohio	7.7
17. Delaware	830.5	17. Michigan	7.6
18. Texas	828.8	18. West Virginia	7.6
19. Pennsylvania	814.8	19. Illinois	7.5
20. Maine	813.2	20. Missouri	7.5
21. Michigan	812.3	21. Virginia	7.5
22. Kansas	806.8	22. Pennsylvania	7.3
23. Virginia	801.5	23. Kansas	7.2
24. Wyoming	801.4	24. Florida	7.1
* UNITED STATES	798.8	25. Kentucky	6.8
25. Montana	798.4	* UNITED STATES	6.8
26. Illinois	798.2	26. Alaska	6.7
27. Maryland	796.4	27. Arizona	6.7
28. New Mexico	795.0	28. Nebraska	6.6
29. Oregon	773.7	29. Nevada	6.4
30. Arizona	771.8	30. Colorado	6.3
31. Idaho	766.4	31. New Mexico	6.3
32. South Dakota	757.0	32. Texas	6.3
33. Wisconsin	752.2	33. Idaho	6.2
34. Alaska	750.8	34. New York	6.1
35. Nebraska	749.5	35. Wisconsin	6.0
36. Florida	749.4	36. Hawaii	5.7
37. Rhode Island	747.3	37. Maine	5.7
38. New Jersey	745.9	38. New Jersey	5.7
39. Colorado	742.8	39. New Hampshire	5.6
40. Iowa	742.0	40. North Dakota	5.6
41. Washington	738.2	41. Connecticut	5.5
42. New Hampshire	732.3	42. Oregon	5.5
43. Utah	731.3	43. Washington	5.5
44. Vermont	728.4	44. Rhode Island	5.3
45. Massachusetts	721.9	45. California	5.2
46. New York	718.0	46. Utah	5.2
47. California	713.1	47. Iowa	5.1
48. North Dakota	699.1	48. Massachusetts	4.8
49. Connecticut	696.0	49. Minnesota	4.7
50. Minnesota	683.9	50. Vermont	4.6
51. Hawaii	609.1	51. Montana	4.5

430

Comparative Tables

21. Twin Birth Rate, 2005 (per 1,000 births)

1.	Massachusetts	44.5
2.	New Jersey	41.8
3.	Connecticut	41.5
4.	Rhode Island	38.9
5.	New Hampshire	37.2
6.	Maryland	37.1
7.	New York	36.0
8.	Illinois	35.9
9.	Delaware	35.6
10.	District of Columbia	34.5
11.	Michigan	34.2
12.	Pennsylvania	33.7
13.	Virginia	33.6
14.	Minnesota	33.5
15.	Ohio	33.4
16.	Iowa	33.2
17.	Maine	32.8
18.	North Dakota	32.6
19.	Missouri	32.5
20.	Alabama	32.2
21.	Nebraska	32.1
22.	Indiana	31.9
23.	Mississippi	31.9
24.	North Carolina	31.9
25.	Vermont	31.9
*	UNITED STATES	31.9
26.	Colorado	31.7
27.	South Carolina	31.5
28.	Louisiana	31.3
29.	Georgia	31.2
30.	Tennessee	31.1
31.	Wisconsin	30.8
32.	Kentucky	30.6
33.	Kansas	30.3
34.	Florida	29.9
35.	Oregon	29.8
36.	Idaho	29.5
37.	Arkansas	29.4
38.	Washington	29.4
39.	California	29.0
40.	Nevada	29.0
41.	South Dakota	28.9
42.	Texas	28.1
43.	Hawaii	28.0
44.	Montana	27.6
45.	Oklahoma	27.4
46.	Wyoming	27.3
47.	West Virginia	27.2
48.	Alaska	26.9
49.	Arizona	26.5
50.	Utah	26.5
51.	New Mexico	24.2

22. Triplet Birth Rate, 2005 (per 100,000 births)

1.	Massachusetts	290.4
2.	New Jersey	288.7
3.	Nebraska	269.2
4.	Connecticut	245.5
5.	North Dakota	240.3
6.	Ohio	238.2
7.	Kentucky	234.8
8.	Illinois	234.6
9.	Indiana	234.3
10.	New York	229.9
11.	Michigan	229.0
12.	New Hampshire	214.4
13.	Minnesota	208.9
14.	Alabama	198.3
15.	Maryland	193.7
16.	Pennsylvania	192.9
17.	Delaware	180.5
18.	Rhode Island	178.4
19.	Idaho	178.1
*	UNITED STATES	175.3
20.	Missouri	170.1
21.	Arizona	164.9
22.	Wisconsin	160.1
23.	Kansas	158.8
24.	Louisiana	154.7
25.	Virginia	154.6
26.	Iowa	154.4
27.	Colorado	153.8
28.	Tennessee	153.2
29.	North Carolina	150.0
30.	California	149.6
31.	Georgia	149.6
32.	Nevada	147.0
33.	Wyoming	144.6
34.	Texas	143.4
35.	Florida	142.7
36.	South Carolina	141.8
37.	Maine	138.4
38.	Utah	134.8
39.	Mississippi	130.9
40.	Vermont	107.8
41.	West Virginia	105.3
42.	Oregon	104.0
43.	Arkansas	100.4
44.	Montana	95.6
45.	Oklahoma	92.8
46.	Washington	92.7
47.	South Dakota	91.6
48.	Hawaii	88.4
49.	Alaska	68.0
50.	New Mexico	65.9
51.	District of Columbia	NA

Comparative Tables

23. Overweight Persons, 2006

1.	West Virginia	67.0%
2.	Mississippi	66.7
3.	Kentucky	66.4
4.	South Carolina	65.4
5.	Tennessee	65.3
6.	Alabama	65.0
7.	Michigan	64.8
8.	Oklahoma	64.8
9.	North Dakota	64.5
10.	Alaska	64.2
11.	South Dakota	64.1
12.	Nebraska	63.9
13.	Ohio	63.9
14.	Arkansas	63.8
15.	Delaware	63.8
16.	Nevada	63.6
17.	Wisconsin	63.4
18.	Louisiana	63.0
19.	Iowa	62.9
20.	Missouri	62.9
21.	Indiana	62.8
22.	North Carolina	62.8
23.	Minnesota	62.7
24.	Texas	62.4
25.	Kansas	62.3
26.	Virginia	61.8
27.	Georgia	61.7
28.	Illinois	61.7
*	UNITED STATES	61.6
29.	Wyoming	61.4
30.	Pennsylvania	61.3
31.	Rhode Island	61.0
32.	Maryland	60.7
33.	New Hampshire	60.7
34.	Oregon	60.7
35.	Washington	60.7
36.	New Jersey	59.9
37.	New Mexico	59.8
38.	Idaho	59.7
39.	Maine	59.7
40.	Arizona	59.6
41.	Florida	59.6
42.	Montana	59.3
43.	California	58.8
44.	Connecticut	58.8
45.	New York	58.3
46.	Hawaii	56.1
47.	Vermont	56.0
48.	Massachusetts	55.5
49.	Colorado	54.9
50.	Utah	54.9
51.	District of Columbia	54.6

24. Obese Persons, 2006

1.	Mississippi	31.4%
2.	West Virginia	31.0
3.	Alabama	30.5
4.	South Carolina	29.4
5.	Michigan	28.8
6.	Oklahoma	28.8
7.	Tennessee	28.8
8.	Ohio	28.4
9.	Kentucky	28.0
10.	Indiana	27.8
11.	Missouri	27.2
12.	Georgia	27.1
13.	Louisiana	27.1
14.	Arkansas	26.9
15.	Nebraska	26.9
16.	North Carolina	26.6
17.	Wisconsin	26.6
18.	Alaska	26.2
19.	Texas	26.1
20.	Delaware	26.0
21.	Kansas	25.9
22.	Iowa	25.7
23.	North Dakota	25.4
24.	South Dakota	25.4
25.	Illinois	25.1
26.	Virginia	25.1
*	UNITED STATES	25.1
27.	Nevada	25.0
28.	Maryland	24.9
29.	Oregon	24.8
30.	Minnesota	24.7
31.	Washington	24.2
32.	Idaho	24.1
33.	Pennsylvania	24.0
34.	California	23.3
35.	Wyoming	23.3
36.	Florida	23.1
37.	Maine	23.1
38.	Arizona	22.9
39.	New Mexico	22.9
40.	New York	22.9
41.	New Jersey	22.6
42.	District of Columbia	22.5
43.	New Hampshire	22.4
44.	Utah	21.9
45.	Rhode Island	21.4
46.	Montana	21.2
47.	Vermont	21.2
48.	Connecticut	20.6
49.	Hawaii	20.6
50.	Massachusetts	20.3
51.	Colorado	18.2

Comparative Tables

25. People who Get No Regular Exercise, 2005

1.	Louisiana	33.4%
2.	Tennessee	33.1
3.	Mississippi	32.4
4.	Kentucky	31.5
5.	Arkansas	30.6
6.	Oklahoma	30.6
7.	Alabama	29.7
8.	New Jersey	29.2
9.	West Virginia	28.5
10.	Texas	27.4
11.	Georgia	27.2
12.	New York	27.1
13.	Florida	26.9
14.	Indiana	26.9
15.	Nevada	26.8
16.	South Carolina	26.3
17.	Rhode Island	25.9
18.	Pennsylvania	25.8
19.	Illinois	25.6
20.	North Carolina	25.6
21.	Ohio	25.6
22.	Missouri	25.4
23.	Iowa	24.7
24.	Kansas	24.4
25.	California	23.9
*	UNITED STATES	23.9
26.	Nebraska	23.8
27.	Delaware	23.3
28.	Massachusetts	23.3
29.	New Mexico	23.3
30.	North Dakota	23.1
31.	Maryland	22.9
32.	Arizona	22.6
33.	District of Columbia	22.5
34.	Michigan	22.5
35.	South Dakota	22.5
36.	Montana	22.4
37.	Maine	22.3
38.	Wyoming	22.0
39.	Idaho	21.6
40.	New Hampshire	21.6
41.	Alaska	21.4
42.	Virginia	21.3
43.	Connecticut	21.2
44.	Hawaii	19.5
45.	Vermont	19.2
46.	Wisconsin	18.7
47.	Oregon	18.6
48.	Utah	18.5
49.	Washington	17.4
50.	Colorado	17.3
51.	Minnesota	16.2

26. People who Regularly Get at Least Moderate Exercise, 2005

1.	Alaska	59.2%
2.	Vermont	57.7
3.	Wisconsin	56.6
4.	Montana	56.5
5.	Oregon	56.4
6.	Wyoming	56.2
7.	New Hampshire	56.0
8.	Utah	55.0
9.	Washington	54.7
10.	Colorado	54.4
11.	Maine	54.1
12.	Idaho	54.0
13.	Arizona	53.4
14.	California	53.4
15.	District of Columbia	53.1
16.	Massachusetts	52.6
17.	Hawaii	52.2
18.	Connecticut	51.2
19.	Rhode Island	51.1
20.	Minnesota	51.0
21.	New Mexico	51.0
22.	Virginia	50.8
23.	Nevada	50.7
24.	Michigan	49.5
25.	Ohio	49.2
26.	Maryland	49.1
27.	Kansas	48.7
28.	Pennsylvania	48.7
*	UNITED STATES	48.7
29.	North Dakota	48.4
30.	New York	48.1
31.	Indiana	47.7
32.	South Dakota	47.6
33.	Nebraska	47.3
34.	Illinois	47.1
35.	Texas	46.7
36.	Arkansas	46.4
37.	Missouri	46.4
38.	Iowa	46.2
39.	New Jersey	45.9
40.	Florida	45.3
41.	South Carolina	45.3
42.	Delaware	45.2
43.	Alabama	42.8
44.	Oklahoma	42.3
45.	North Carolina	42.1
46.	Georgia	42.0
47.	Mississippi	40.0
48.	West Virginia	39.4
49.	Louisiana	38.3
50.	Tennessee	36.1
51.	Kentucky	34.7

Comparative Tables

27. People who Regularly Get Vigorous Exercise, 2005

1.	California	36.2%
2.	Alaska	35.9
3.	Utah	34.3
4.	Montana	33.1
5.	Vermont	33.1
6.	Wyoming	33.1
7.	New Hampshire	32.9
8.	Wisconsin	32.8
9.	Colorado	32.6
10.	Nevada	32.6
11.	District of Columbia	31.5
12.	Idaho	31.1
13.	Connecticut	31.0
14.	Maine	30.8
15.	Oregon	30.7
16.	Washington	30.6
17.	Virginia	30.4
18.	Hawaii	30.2
19.	Rhode Island	29.9
20.	Massachusetts	29.7
21.	Maryland	29.6
22.	New Mexico	29.0
23.	Arizona	28.9
24.	Minnesota	28.3
25.	Michigan	28.1
26.	North Dakota	27.5
27.	Pennsylvania	27.4
*	UNITED STATES	27.4
28.	New York	27.3
29.	Ohio	27.2
30.	Indiana	27.1
31.	Illinois	25.7
32.	New Jersey	25.5
33.	Missouri	25.3
34.	Texas	25.3
35.	Kansas	25.0
36.	Delaware	24.9
37.	Arkansas	24.8
38.	Nebraska	24.7
39.	Florida	24.6
40.	South Carolina	24.6
41.	Georgia	23.7
42.	South Dakota	23.5
43.	Iowa	22.9
44.	Oklahoma	22.5
45.	North Carolina	22.2
46.	Mississippi	20.9
47.	Louisiana	20.7
48.	Alabama	20.3
49.	West Virginia	17.6
50.	Tennessee	17.4
51.	Kentucky	16.8

28. Abortions Performed, 2004

*	UNITED STATES	839,226
1.	New York	126,002
2.	Florida	91,710
3.	Texas	74,801
4.	Illinois	43,537
5.	Pennsylvania	36,030
6.	Ohio	34,242
7.	North Carolina	33,954
8.	New Jersey	32,642
9.	Georgia	32,513
10.	Michigan	26,269
11.	Virginia	26,117
12.	Washington	24,664
13.	Massachusetts	24,366
14.	Tennessee	16,400
15.	Minnesota	13,791
16.	Arizona	12,690
17.	Connecticut	12,189
18.	Oregon	11,443
19.	Colorado	11,415
20.	Alabama	11,370
21.	Kansas	11,357
22.	Louisiana	11,224
23.	Indiana	10,514
24.	Maryland	10,096
25.	Wisconsin	9,943
26.	Nevada	9,856
27.	Missouri	8,072
28.	Oklahoma	6,712
29.	South Carolina	6,565
30.	New Mexico	6,070
31.	Iowa	6,022
32.	Rhode Island	5,587
33.	Arkansas	4,644
34.	Delaware	4,588
35.	Utah	3,665
36.	Nebraska	3,584
37.	Kentucky	3,557
38.	Mississippi	3,500
39.	Hawaii	3,467
40.	Maine	2,593
41.	District of Columbia	2,401
42.	Montana	2,256
43.	Alaska	1,937
44.	Vermont	1,725
45.	North Dakota	1,357
46.	Idaho	963
47.	South Dakota	814
48.	Wyoming	12
49.	California	NA
50.	New Hampshire	NA
51.	West Virginia	NA

434

Comparative Tables

29. High School Graduates or higher, 2006

1.	Minnesota	90.7%
2.	Utah	90.2
3.	Wyoming	90.2
4.	Montana	90.1
5.	New Hampshire	89.9
6.	Vermont	89.8
7.	Alaska	89.7
8.	Nebraska	89.5
9.	Hawaii	89.0
10.	Washington	89.0
11.	Iowa	88.9
12.	Maine	88.7
13.	Kansas	88.5
14.	Wisconsin	88.4
15.	South Dakota	88.3
16.	North Dakota	88.1
17.	Colorado	88.0
18.	Connecticut	88.0
19.	Massachusetts	87.9
20.	Oregon	87.6
21.	Idaho	87.3
22.	Michigan	87.2
23.	Maryland	87.1
24.	Ohio	86.2
25.	Pennsylvania	86.2
26.	New Jersey	86.1
27.	Delaware	85.5
28.	Virginia	85.4
29.	Indiana	85.2
30.	Illinois	85.0
31.	Missouri	84.8
32.	Florida	84.5
33.	District of Columbia	84.3
34.	Oklahoma	84.3
35.	New York	84.1
*	UNITED STATES	84.1
36.	Nevada	83.9
37.	Arizona	83.8
38.	Rhode Island	82.4
39.	Georgia	82.2
40.	North Carolina	82.0
41.	New Mexico	81.5
42.	South Carolina	81.3
43.	West Virginia	81.0
44.	Tennessee	80.9
45.	Arkansas	80.5
46.	Alabama	80.1
47.	California	80.1
48.	Kentucky	79.6
49.	Louisiana	79.4
50.	Texas	78.6
51.	Mississippi	77.9

30. Bachelor's Degree or higher, 2006

1.	District of Columbia	45.9%
2.	Massachusetts	37.0
3.	Maryland	35.1
4.	Colorado	34.3
5.	Connecticut	33.7
6.	New Jersey	33.4
7.	Virginia	32.7
8.	Vermont	32.4
9.	New Hampshire	31.9
10.	New York	31.2
11.	Washington	30.5
12.	Minnesota	30.4
13.	Hawaii	29.7
14.	Rhode Island	29.6
15.	California	29.0
16.	Illinois	28.9
17.	Kansas	28.6
18.	Utah	28.6
19.	Oregon	27.5
20.	Montana	27.4
21.	Delaware	27.0
*	UNITED STATES	27.0
22.	Alaska	26.9
23.	Nebraska	26.9
24.	Georgia	26.6
25.	Maine	25.8
26.	North Dakota	25.6
27.	Arizona	25.5
28.	Pennsylvania	25.4
29.	Florida	25.3
30.	New Mexico	25.3
31.	Wisconsin	25.1
32.	North Carolina	24.8
33.	South Dakota	24.8
34.	Texas	24.7
35.	Michigan	24.5
36.	Missouri	24.3
37.	Iowa	24.0
38.	Idaho	23.3
39.	Ohio	23.0
40.	South Carolina	22.7
41.	Wyoming	22.7
42.	Oklahoma	22.1
43.	Indiana	21.7
44.	Tennessee	21.7
45.	Alabama	21.1
46.	Nevada	20.8
47.	Louisiana	20.3
48.	Kentucky	20.0
49.	Mississippi	18.8
50.	Arkansas	18.2
51.	West Virginia	16.5

Comparative Tables

31. NAEP – 4th Graders Scoring Basic or Better in Math, 2007		32. NAEP – 4th Graders Scoring Proficient or Better in Math, 2007	
1. Massachusetts	93.2%	1. Massachusetts	57.6%
2. New Hampshire	91.3	2. New Hampshire	51.8
3. North Dakota	90.8	3. New Jersey	51.8
4. New Jersey	89.6	4. Kansas	51.1
5. Kansas	89.4	5. Minnesota	50.6
6. Vermont	89.0	6. Vermont	49.0
7. Indiana	88.9	7. Pennsylvania	47.0
8. Wyoming	88.5	8. Wisconsin	46.9
9. Montana	87.7	9. Indiana	46.3
10. Minnesota	87.5	10. Ohio	45.9
11. Ohio	87.5	11. North Dakota	45.7
12. Texas	87.4	12. Connecticut	44.7
13. Virginia	87.3	13. Montana	44.4
14. Delaware	86.9	14. Wyoming	44.3
15. Iowa	86.6	15. Washington	43.8
16. Florida	86.2	16. New York	43.3
17. South Dakota	86.1	17. Iowa	43.0
18. Maine	85.5	18. Virginia	41.9
19. Wisconsin	85.3	19. Maine	41.8
20. New York	85.1	20. Colorado	41.2
21. Pennsylvania	85.1	21. North Carolina	41.0
22. North Carolina	84.9	22. South Dakota	40.6
23. Idaho	84.5	23. Florida	40.3
24. Washington	84.3	24. Texas	40.2
25. Connecticut	83.9	25. Idaho	40.1
26. Utah	82.7	26. Maryland	40.1
27. Oklahoma	82.4	27. Delaware	40.0
28. Missouri	82.0	28. Utah	39.4
* UNITED STATES	82.0	* UNITED STATES	39.0
29. Colorado	81.8	29. Missouri	38.4
30. West Virginia	81.2	30. Alaska	37.9
31. Arkansas	80.7	31. Nebraska	37.9
32. Nebraska	80.1	32. Michigan	37.1
33. Maryland	80.0	33. Arkansas	36.7
34. Michigan	79.9	34. Illinois	36.3
35. South Carolina	79.7	35. South Carolina	35.9
36. Rhode Island	79.6	36. Oregon	35.0
37. Kentucky	79.3	37. Rhode Island	34.0
38. Alaska	78.8	38. Hawaii	33.3
39. Georgia	78.6	39. Oklahoma	32.6
40. Illinois	78.6	40. West Virginia	32.6
41. Oregon	78.6	41. Georgia	31.6
42. Hawaii	76.9	42. Kentucky	30.8
43. Tennessee	76.1	43. Arizona	30.6
44. Arizona	73.7	44. Nevada	30.1
45. Nevada	73.7	45. California	29.7
46. Louisiana	72.9	46. Tennessee	28.7
47. New Mexico	70.3	47. Alabama	25.8
48. Alabama	70.2	48. New Mexico	24.5
49. Mississippi	69.9	49. Louisiana	24.4
50. California	69.6	50. Mississippi	21.3
51. District of Columbia	49.3	51. District of Columbia	13.5

436

Comparative Tables

33. NAEP – 4th Graders Scoring Basic or Better in Reading, 2007

1.	Massachusetts	81.1%
2.	New Jersey	77.2
3.	New Hampshire	76.0
4.	North Dakota	75.3
5.	Montana	75.0
6.	Vermont	74.4
7.	Virginia	74.4
8.	Iowa	73.7
9.	Wyoming	73.5
10.	Ohio	73.3
11.	Maine	73.1
12.	Minnesota	72.8
13.	Connecticut	72.6
14.	Delaware	72.6
15.	Pennsylvania	72.6
16.	Kansas	71.8
17.	South Dakota	70.9
18.	Nebraska	70.8
19.	Florida	70.4
20.	Wisconsin	70.4
21.	Idaho	70.3
22.	Washington	70.3
23.	Colorado	70.0
24.	New York	69.3
25.	Maryland	68.9
26.	Utah	68.6
27.	Kentucky	68.4
28.	Indiana	68.2
29.	Missouri	67.1
*	UNITED STATES	67.0
30.	Michigan	66.2
31.	Texas	65.8
32.	Georgia	65.6
33.	Rhode Island	65.4
34.	Illinois	65.0
35.	Oklahoma	65.0
36.	North Carolina	63.9
37.	Arkansas	63.5
38.	West Virginia	62.6
39.	Oregon	61.9
40.	Alaska	61.7
41.	Alabama	61.6
42.	Tennessee	60.6
43.	Hawaii	59.0
44.	South Carolina	58.9
45.	New Mexico	57.6
46.	Nevada	57.1
47.	Arizona	55.9
48.	California	53.2
49.	Louisiana	51.9
50.	Mississippi	51.5
51.	District of Columbia	38.7

34. NAEP – 4th Graders Scoring Proficient or Better in Reading, 2007

1.	Massachusetts	49.2%
2.	New Jersey	43.1
3.	Connecticut	41.2
4.	New Hampshire	41.1
5.	Vermont	40.9
6.	Pennsylvania	40.2
7.	Montana	38.5
8.	Virginia	37.6
9.	Minnesota	36.9
10.	Wyoming	36.4
11.	Ohio	36.3
12.	Washington	36.3
13.	Colorado	36.2
14.	Iowa	36.1
15.	Kansas	36.1
16.	New York	36.0
17.	Maryland	35.9
18.	Maine	35.8
19.	Wisconsin	35.6
20.	North Dakota	35.3
21.	Idaho	35.1
22.	Nebraska	34.6
23.	Florida	34.0
24.	Utah	33.9
25.	Delaware	33.8
26.	South Dakota	33.7
27.	Kentucky	33.5
28.	Indiana	33.0
*	UNITED STATES	33.0
29.	Michigan	32.4
30.	Illinois	32.2
31.	Missouri	31.8
32.	Rhode Island	30.8
33.	Texas	29.6
34.	North Carolina	29.1
35.	Alabama	28.9
36.	Alaska	28.7
37.	Arkansas	28.6
38.	Georgia	28.3
39.	Oregon	28.3
40.	West Virginia	27.8
41.	Tennessee	26.9
42.	Oklahoma	26.8
43.	South Carolina	25.8
44.	Hawaii	25.7
45.	Nevada	24.4
46.	Arizona	24.2
47.	New Mexico	24.0
48.	California	22.9
49.	Louisiana	20.4
50.	Mississippi	18.7
51.	District of Columbia	13.8

Comparative Tables

35. NAEP – 8th Graders Scoring Basic or Better in Math, 2007

1.	North Dakota	85.5%
2.	Massachusetts	85.0
3.	Kansas	81.4
4.	South Dakota	81.2
5.	Vermont	81.1
6.	Minnesota	81.0
7.	Wyoming	79.8
8.	Montana	79.1
9.	Maine	78.3
10.	New Hampshire	77.6
11.	Texas	77.6
12.	New Jersey	77.5
13.	Iowa	77.2
14.	Virginia	77.0
15.	Pennsylvania	76.9
16.	Ohio	76.4
17.	Wisconsin	75.9
18.	Indiana	75.7
19.	Colorado	75.1
20.	Washington	74.9
21.	Idaho	74.7
22.	Delaware	74.3
23.	Nebraska	74.3
24.	Maryland	73.6
25.	Alaska	73.0
26.	Oregon	73.0
27.	North Carolina	72.9
28.	Connecticut	72.8
29.	Missouri	72.2
30.	Utah	72.1
*	UNITED STATES	71.0
31.	South Carolina	70.9
32.	Illinois	70.3
33.	New York	70.3
34.	Kentucky	69.0
35.	Florida	68.1
36.	Arizona	66.5
37.	Michigan	66.4
38.	Oklahoma	66.1
39.	Rhode Island	65.5
40.	Arkansas	64.7
41.	Georgia	64.2
42.	Louisiana	63.9
43.	Tennessee	63.9
44.	West Virginia	61.2
45.	Nevada	60.2
46.	California	59.1
47.	Hawaii	59.1
48.	New Mexico	56.6
49.	Alabama	55.3
50.	Mississippi	53.8
51.	District of Columbia	34.1

36. NAEP – 8th Graders Scoring Proficient or Better in Math, 2007

1.	Massachusetts	50.7%
2.	Minnesota	43.1
3.	Vermont	41.4
4.	North Dakota	41.0
5.	New Jersey	40.4
6.	Kansas	40.2
7.	South Dakota	39.1
8.	Pennsylvania	38.3
9.	New Hampshire	37.9
10.	Montana	37.6
11.	Virginia	37.5
12.	Colorado	37.4
13.	Wisconsin	37.0
14.	Maryland	36.5
15.	Wyoming	36.0
16.	Washington	35.9
17.	Ohio	35.4
18.	Iowa	35.2
19.	Indiana	35.1
20.	Oregon	34.8
21.	Connecticut	34.7
22.	Texas	34.7
23.	Nebraska	34.6
24.	North Carolina	34.5
25.	Idaho	34.1
26.	Maine	34.1
27.	Utah	32.4
28.	Alaska	32.2
*	UNITED STATES	32.0
29.	South Carolina	31.9
30.	Delaware	31.3
31.	Illinois	30.8
32.	New York	30.2
33.	Missouri	29.9
34.	Michigan	28.9
35.	Rhode Island	27.7
36.	Florida	27.4
37.	Kentucky	27.3
38.	Arizona	26.3
39.	Georgia	24.7
40.	Arkansas	24.4
41.	California	23.9
42.	Tennessee	23.1
43.	Nevada	23.0
44.	Oklahoma	21.3
45.	Hawaii	21.2
46.	Louisiana	19.0
47.	West Virginia	18.5
48.	Alabama	18.2
49.	New Mexico	17.4
50.	Mississippi	13.6
51.	District of Columbia	8.0

Comparative Tables

37. NAEP – 8th Graders Scoring Basic or Better in Reading, 2007

1.	Montana	84.5%
2.	Vermont	84.4
3.	Massachusetts	83.9
4.	North Dakota	83.6
5.	South Dakota	83.5
6.	Maine	82.8
7.	New Hampshire	81.9
8.	New Jersey	81.1
9.	Kansas	80.6
10.	Minnesota	80.2
11.	Iowa	79.8
12.	Wyoming	79.7
13.	Ohio	79.4
14.	Nebraska	78.8
15.	Colorado	78.7
16.	Virginia	78.7
17.	Pennsylvania	78.6
18.	Idaho	78.5
19.	Delaware	77.2
20.	Oregon	77.2
21.	Connecticut	76.7
22.	Washington	76.7
23.	Indiana	76.1
24.	Wisconsin	75.9
25.	Maryland	75.6
26.	New York	75.1
27.	Utah	75.0
28.	Illinois	74.9
29.	Missouri	74.9
*	UNITED STATES	74.0
30.	Kentucky	73.3
31.	Texas	73.0
32.	Michigan	72.1
33.	Oklahoma	72.1
34.	Florida	71.5
35.	Tennessee	71.3
36.	North Carolina	71.0
37.	Alaska	70.8
38.	Georgia	70.1
39.	Arkansas	69.6
40.	Rhode Island	69.3
41.	South Carolina	68.7
42.	West Virginia	68.4
43.	Arizona	64.9
44.	Louisiana	64.2
45.	Nevada	63.1
46.	Hawaii	62.5
47.	New Mexico	62.5
48.	Alabama	62.3
49.	California	62.3
50.	Mississippi	60.3
51.	District of Columbia	47.9

38. NAEP – 8th Graders Scoring Proficient or Better in Reading, 2007

1.	Massachusetts	43.0%
2.	Vermont	42.1
3.	New Jersey	39.0
4.	Montana	38.9
5.	New Hampshire	37.2
6.	Connecticut	37.1
7.	Maine	36.9
8.	South Dakota	36.8
9.	Minnesota	36.6
10.	Pennsylvania	36.4
11.	Ohio	35.9
12.	Iowa	35.7
13.	Kansas	35.2
14.	Nebraska	35.0
15.	Colorado	34.6
16.	Washington	34.1
17.	Oregon	34.0
18.	Virginia	33.7
19.	Maryland	33.2
20.	Wisconsin	33.2
21.	Wyoming	33.2
22.	New York	32.2
23.	North Dakota	32.2
24.	Idaho	31.6
25.	Indiana	31.1
26.	Missouri	31.0
*	UNITED STATES	31.0
27.	Delaware	30.5
28.	Utah	30.1
29.	Illinois	29.8
30.	Michigan	28.2
31.	Florida	28.0
32.	North Carolina	28.0
33.	Kentucky	27.7
34.	Texas	27.5
35.	Rhode Island	27.2
36.	Alaska	27.1
37.	Oklahoma	26.1
38.	Georgia	25.6
39.	Tennessee	25.6
40.	Arkansas	25.4
41.	South Carolina	24.6
42.	Arizona	24.3
43.	West Virginia	22.9
44.	California	21.5
45.	Nevada	21.5
46.	Alabama	21.2
47.	Hawaii	20.3
48.	Louisiana	19.4
49.	Mississippi	17.4
50.	New Mexico	17.3
51.	District of Columbia	12.1

Comparative Tables

39. SAT Participation, 2007

1.	Maine	100%
2.	New York	89
3.	Massachusetts	85
4.	Connecticut	84
5.	New Hampshire	83
6.	New Jersey	82
7.	District of Columbia	78
8.	Pennsylvania	75
9.	Virginia	73
10.	Delaware	72
11.	North Carolina	71
12.	Maryland	70
13.	Georgia	69
14.	Rhode Island	68
15.	Vermont	67
16.	Florida	65
17.	Indiana	62
18.	South Carolina	62
19.	Hawaii	61
20.	Oregon	54
21.	Washington	53
22.	Texas	52
23.	California	49
24.	Alaska	48
*	UNITED STATES	48
25.	Nevada	41
26.	Arizona	32
27.	Montana	28
28.	Ohio	27
29.	Colorado	24
30.	West Virginia	20
31.	Idaho	19
32.	Tennessee	13
33.	New Mexico	12
34.	Kentucky	10
35.	Alabama	9
36.	Michigan	9
37.	Minnesota	9
38.	Illinois	8
39.	Kansas	8
40.	Wyoming	8
41.	Louisiana	7
42.	Missouri	6
43.	Nebraska	6
44.	Oklahoma	6
45.	Utah	6
46.	Wisconsin	6
47.	Arkansas	5
48.	Iowa	4
49.	Mississippi	4
50.	North Dakota	4
51.	South Dakota	3

40. Average Public School Teacher Salary, 2006-07

1.	California	$63,640
2.	Connecticut	60,822
3.	New Jersey	59,920
4.	District of Columbia	59,000
5.	Massachusetts	58,624
6.	New York	58,537
7.	Illinois	58,246
8.	Maryland	56,927
9.	Rhode Island	55,956
10.	Pennsylvania	54,970
11.	Michigan	54,895
12.	Delaware	54,680
13.	Alaska	54,658
14.	Ohio	51,937
15.	Hawaii	51,922
16.	Oregon	50,911
*	UNITED STATES	50,816
17.	Wyoming	50,692
18.	Georgia	49,905
19.	Minnesota	49,634
20.	Vermont	48,370
21.	Wisconsin	47,901
22.	Washington	47,882
23.	Indiana	47,831
24.	New Hampshire	46,527
25.	North Carolina	46,410
26.	Arizona	45,941
27.	Colorado	45,833
28.	Nevada	45,342
29.	Florida	45,308
30.	Texas	44,897
31.	Virginia	44,727
32.	Arkansas	44,245
33.	South Carolina	44,133
34.	Tennessee	43,816
35.	Kentucky	43,646
36.	Alabama	43,389
37.	Kansas	43,334
38.	Iowa	43,130
39.	Louisiana	42,816
40.	Idaho	42,798
41.	New Mexico	42,780
42.	Oklahoma	42,379
43.	Nebraska	42,044
44.	Missouri	41,839
45.	Maine	41,596
46.	Montana	41,225
47.	Utah	40,566
48.	West Virginia	40,531
49.	Mississippi	40,182
50.	North Dakota	38,822
51.	South Dakota	35,378

Comparative Tables

41. Expenditures for Public Schools, per capita, 2006-07

1.	New Jersey	$2,336
2.	Wyoming	2,190
3.	Connecticut	2,129
4.	New York	2,067
5.	Alaska	2,060
6.	Massachusetts	1,999
7.	Vermont	1,986
8.	Delaware	1,800
9.	Maine	1,787
10.	Michigan	1,754
11.	Rhode Island	1,748
12.	Illinois	1,717
13.	Ohio	1,717
14.	New Hampshire	1,690
15.	District of Columbia	1,685
16.	Pennsylvania	1,655
17.	Wisconsin	1,646
18.	Minnesota	1,627
19.	Virginia	1,574
20.	Texas	1,567
21.	Maryland	1,561
*	UNITED STATES	1,561
22.	West Virginia	1,558
23.	Georgia	1,531
24.	Indiana	1,530
25.	California	1,523
26.	New Mexico	1,519
27.	Kansas	1,500
28.	Colorado	1,486
29.	South Carolina	1,480
30.	Hawaii	1,466
31.	Arkansas	1,441
32.	Washington	1,404
33.	Oregon	1,367
34.	Louisiana	1,365
35.	Nebraska	1,349
36.	Montana	1,327
37.	Iowa	1,319
38.	Idaho	1,309
39.	Kentucky	1,300
40.	North Carolina	1,267
41.	South Dakota	1,267
42.	Oklahoma	1,265
43.	Missouri	1,256
44.	Florida	1,251
45.	North Dakota	1,237
46.	Alabama	1,234
47.	Nevada	1,190
48.	Mississippi	1,166
49.	Tennessee	1,142
50.	Utah	1,058
51.	Arizona	955

(calculated using 7/1/2006 population est.)

42. Expenditures for Public Schools, per pupil, 2006-07

1.	District of Columbia	$18,260
2.	Vermont	15,940
3.	New York	15,263
4.	New Jersey	14,824
5.	Wyoming	14,235
6.	Massachusetts	14,125
7.	Delaware	13,380
8.	Connecticut	13,370
9.	Maine	13,025
10.	Pennsylvania	12,121
11.	Rhode Island	12,095
12.	Ohio	11,947
13.	Alaska	11,900
14.	New Hampshire	11,879
15.	Hawaii	11,529
16.	Illinois	11,489
17.	Michigan	11,149
18.	Wisconsin	11,019
19.	Maryland	10,824
20.	Minnesota	10,809
21.	Virginia	10,599
22.	Arkansas	10,398
23.	Oregon	10,251
24.	West Virginia	10,236
*	UNITED STATES	10,212
25.	Kansas	10,119
26.	Montana	10,119
27.	New Mexico	10,106
28.	Indiana	10,044
29.	South Carolina	9,891
30.	Colorado	9,592
31.	Georgia	9,502
32.	Louisiana	9,355
33.	Washington	9,334
34.	Kentucky	9,214
35.	California	9,156
36.	North Dakota	9,036
37.	Nebraska	9,028
38.	Florida	8,928
39.	Missouri	8,857
40.	South Dakota	8,741
41.	Iowa	8,684
42.	Texas	8,573
43.	North Carolina	8,544
44.	Alabama	7,908
45.	Tennessee	7,773
46.	Idaho	7,649
47.	Oklahoma	7,593
48.	Mississippi	7,189
49.	Nevada	7,060
50.	Utah	6,060
51.	Arizona	5,896

Comparative Tables

43. Public School Revenue, 2006-07 (x $1 million)

*	UNITED STATES	$530,340
1.	California	67,460
2.	Texas	44,267
3.	New York	43,033
4.	Florida	27,556
5.	Pennsylvania	23,871
6.	Illinois	21,566
7.	Ohio	21,510
8.	New Jersey	21,167
9.	Michigan	19,580
10.	Georgia	16,777
11.	Massachusetts	14,585
12.	Virginia	13,445
13.	North Carolina	11,281
14.	Indiana	10,948
15.	Maryland	10,523
16.	Washington	10,395
17.	Wisconsin	10,130
18.	Minnesota	9,429
19.	Missouri	9,242
20.	Arizona	8,431
21.	Connecticut	8,331
22.	Colorado	7,428
23.	Tennessee	7,422
24.	Louisiana	7,115
25.	South Carolina	6,870
26.	Alabama	6,139
27.	Kentucky	6,061
28.	Oregon	5,742
29.	Oklahoma	5,054
30.	Kansas	4,923
31.	Iowa	4,814
32.	Arkansas	4,308
33.	Mississippi	3,933
34.	Utah	3,470
35.	New Mexico	3,277
36.	Nevada	3,104
37.	West Virginia	3,042
38.	Hawaii	2,801
39.	Nebraska	2,620
40.	Maine	2,425
41.	New Hampshire	2,401
42.	Idaho	1,963
43.	Delaware	1,676
44.	Rhode Island	1,636
45.	Wyoming	1,481
46.	Vermont	1,397
47.	Montana	1,372
48.	Alaska	1,346
49.	South Dakota	1,144
50.	North Dakota	967
51.	District of Columbia	882

44. State Appropriations for Higher Education, 2006 (per FTE enrollment)

1.	Wyoming	$13,425
2.	Alaska	12,097
3.	Hawaii	10,893
4.	Connecticut	9,503
5.	New Mexico	9,299
6.	Nevada	8,919
7.	Massachusetts	8,372
8.	New Jersey	8,145
9.	Georgia	7,824
10.	New York	7,784
11.	North Carolina	7,522
12.	Idaho	7,303
13.	Nebraska	6,999
14.	Kentucky	6,753
15.	Illinois	6,689
16.	Delaware	6,632
17.	California	6,586
18.	Washington	6,437
19.	Maryland	6,427
20.	Rhode Island	6,413
*	UNITED STATES	6,325
21.	Arizona	6,316
22.	Texas	6,276
23.	Tennessee	6,275
24.	Wisconsin	6,226
25.	Maine	6,096
26.	Utah	5,941
27.	Minnesota	5,907
28.	Arkansas	5,899
29.	Missouri	5,846
30.	South Carolina	5,822
31.	Iowa	5,809
32.	Michigan	5,799
33.	Kansas	5,792
34.	Pennsylvania	5,660
35.	Florida	5,641
36.	Oklahoma	5,638
37.	Alabama	5,617
38.	Louisiana	5,583
39.	Indiana	5,390
40.	Virginia	5,223
41.	Mississippi	5,053
42.	Ohio	4,690
43.	North Dakota	4,683
44.	South Dakota	4,499
45.	Oregon	4,466
46.	Montana	4,409
47.	West Virginia	4,181
48.	Colorado	3,364
49.	New Hampshire	3,193
50.	Vermont	3,030
51.	District of Columbia	NA

Comparative Tables

45. Library Visits per capita, 2006

1.	Ohio	7.2
2.	Washington	7.0
3.	Indiana	6.9
4.	Utah	6.9
5.	Nebraska	6.5
6.	Connecticut	6.4
7.	Kansas	6.4
8.	Colorado	6.2
9.	Oregon	6.2
10.	South Dakota	6.2
11.	Wyoming	6.2
12.	Idaho	6.0
13.	Wisconsin	6.0
14.	Massachusetts	5.9
15.	Rhode Island	5.9
16.	Illinois	5.8
17.	Iowa	5.8
18.	Maine	5.7
19.	New York	5.7
20.	Vermont	5.7
21.	New Jersey	5.4
22.	Alaska	5.2
23.	Minnesota	5.2
24.	Delaware	5.0
25.	Maryland	5.0
26.	Missouri	5.0
27.	New Hampshire	4.9
28.	Michigan	4.8
29.	North Dakota	4.8
*	UNITED STATES	4.7
30.	New Mexico	4.6
31.	Oklahoma	4.6
32.	Virginia	4.6
33.	Hawaii	4.4
34.	California	4.1
35.	Florida	4.1
36.	Montana	4.1
37.	Nevada	4.1
38.	Arizona	4.0
39.	Kentucky	4.0
40.	North Carolina	4.0
41.	Georgia	3.7
42.	Pennsylvania	3.6
43.	South Carolina	3.6
44.	District of Columbia	3.4
45.	Texas	3.3
46.	West Virginia	3.3
47.	Alabama	3.2
48.	Arkansas	3.2
49.	Tennessee	3.2
50.	Louisiana	3.1
51.	Mississippi	2.9

46. Library Circulation per capita, 2006

1.	Ohio	15.0
2.	Oregon	14.9
3.	Utah	12.9
4.	Indiana	12.2
5.	Washington	11.1
6.	Colorado	11.0
7.	Kansas	10.9
8.	Wisconsin	10.3
9.	Nebraska	10.1
10.	Minnesota	9.9
11.	Iowa	9.4
12.	Maryland	9.4
13.	South Dakota	9.1
14.	Wyoming	9.1
15.	Connecticut	9.0
16.	Missouri	8.9
17.	Illinois	8.6
18.	Virginia	8.5
19.	Idaho	8.3
20.	Massachusetts	7.8
21.	New Hampshire	7.7
22.	Maine	7.5
23.	New York	7.5
24.	North Dakota	7.4
25.	Arizona	7.3
26.	Vermont	7.3
*	UNITED STATES	7.2
27.	Delaware	6.9
28.	Oklahoma	6.9
29.	Rhode Island	6.8
30.	Michigan	6.6
31.	New Mexico	6.5
32.	New Jersey	6.4
33.	Montana	6.2
34.	Nevada	6.2
35.	Alaska	6.1
36.	Kentucky	6.0
37.	Florida	5.5
38.	North Carolina	5.5
39.	California	5.4
40.	Pennsylvania	5.3
41.	Hawaii	5.1
42.	South Carolina	5.0
43.	Georgia	4.8
44.	Texas	4.8
45.	Arkansas	4.4
46.	West Virginia	4.3
47.	Alabama	4.1
48.	Tennessee	4.1
49.	Louisiana	3.9
50.	Mississippi	3.2
51.	District of Columbia	2.1

Comparative Tables

47. People without Health Insurance, 2006

1.	Texas	24.5%
2.	New Mexico	22.9
3.	Louisiana	21.9
4.	Florida	21.2
5.	Arizona	20.9
6.	Mississippi	20.7
7.	Nevada	19.6
8.	Arkansas	18.9
9.	Oklahoma	18.9
10.	California	18.8
11.	North Carolina	17.9
12.	Oregon	17.9
13.	Georgia	17.7
14.	Utah	17.4
15.	Colorado	17.2
16.	Montana	17.2
17.	Alaska	16.5
18.	South Carolina	15.9
*	UNITED STATES	15.8
19.	Kentucky	15.6
20.	New Jersey	15.5
21.	Idaho	15.4
22.	Alabama	15.2
23.	Wyoming	14.5
24.	Illinois	14.0
25.	New York	14.0
26.	Maryland	13.8
27.	Tennessee	13.7
28.	West Virginia	13.5
29.	Missouri	13.3
30.	Virginia	13.3
31.	Kansas	12.3
32.	Nebraska	12.3
33.	Delaware	12.2
34.	North Dakota	12.2
35.	Indiana	11.8
36.	South Dakota	11.8
37.	Washington	11.8
38.	District of Columbia	11.6
39.	New Hampshire	11.5
40.	Iowa	10.5
41.	Michigan	10.5
42.	Massachusetts	10.4
43.	Vermont	10.2
44.	Ohio	10.1
45.	Pennsylvania	10.0
46.	Connecticut	9.4
47.	Maine	9.3
48.	Minnesota	9.2
49.	Hawaii	8.8
50.	Wisconsin	8.8
51.	Rhode Island	8.6

48. Children without Health Insurance, 2006

1.	Texas	21.2%
2.	Florida	18.9
3.	Mississippi	18.9
4.	Nevada	18.8
5.	New Mexico	17.9
6.	Arizona	17.0
7.	Louisiana	15.9
8.	Utah	15.0
9.	Colorado	14.6
10.	Montana	14.6
11.	North Carolina	14.0
12.	New Jersey	13.3
13.	Oregon	13.1
14.	Idaho	12.9
15.	California	12.8
16.	Georgia	12.8
17.	Oklahoma	12.5
18.	Delaware	11.7
*	UNITED STATES	11.7
19.	South Carolina	10.7
20.	Alaska	10.5
21.	North Dakota	10.4
22.	Nebraska	10.1
23.	Virginia	10.1
24.	Maryland	9.9
25.	Kentucky	9.7
26.	Illinois	9.5
27.	Arkansas	9.3
28.	South Dakota	9.3
29.	Missouri	9.1
30.	District of Columbia	8.7
31.	West Virginia	8.6
32.	New York	8.4
33.	Minnesota	8.3
34.	Vermont	8.3
35.	Wyoming	8.1
36.	Indiana	7.8
37.	Alabama	7.4
38.	Kansas	7.3
39.	New Hampshire	7.3
40.	Pennsylvania	7.3
41.	Massachusetts	7.0
42.	Washington	6.9
43.	Hawaii	6.4
44.	Tennessee	6.4
45.	Maine	6.3
46.	Iowa	6.2
47.	Connecticut	6.0
48.	Ohio	5.6
49.	Wisconsin	4.9
50.	Michigan	4.7
51.	Rhode Island	4.2

Comparative Tables

49. Health Care Expenditures, per capita, 2004	
1. District of Columbia	$8,295
2. Massachusetts	6,683
3. Maine	6,540
4. New York	6,535
5. Alaska	6,450
6. Connecticut	6,344
7. Delaware	6,306
8. Rhode Island	6,193
9. Vermont	6,069
10. West Virginia	5,954
11. Pennsylvania	5,933
12. North Dakota	5,808
13. New Jersey	5,807
14. Minnesota	5,795
15. Ohio	5,725
16. Wisconsin	5,670
17. Nebraska	5,599
18. Maryland	5,590
19. Florida	5,483
20. Kentucky	5,473
21. Tennessee	5,464
22. Missouri	5,444
23. New Hampshire	5,432
24. Kansas	5,382
25. Iowa	5,380
26. South Dakota	5,327
27. Indiana	5,295
28. Illinois	5,293
* UNITED STATES	5,283
29. Wyoming	5,265
30. North Carolina	5,191
31. Alabama	5,135
32. South Carolina	5,114
33. Washington	5,092
34. Montana	5,080
35. Mississippi	5,059
36. Michigan	5,058
37. Louisiana	5,040
38. Hawaii	4,941
39. Oklahoma	4,917
40. Oregon	4,880
41. Arkansas	4,863
42. Virginia	4,822
43. Colorado	4,717
44. California	4,638
45. Texas	4,601
46. Georgia	4,600
47. Nevada	4,569
48. New Mexico	4,471
49. Idaho	4,444
50. Arizona	4,103
51. Utah	3,972

50. Social Security Beneficiaries, 2005 (x 1,000)	
* UNITED STATES	47,255
1. California	4,460
2. Florida	3,424
3. New York	3,064
4. Texas	2,955
5. Pennsylvania	2,425
6. Ohio	1,965
7. Illinois	1,898
8. Michigan	1,743
9. North Carolina	1,511
10. New Jersey	1,379
11. Georgia	1,231
12. Virginia	1,139
13. Tennessee	1,098
14. Massachusetts	1,072
15. Missouri	1,064
16. Indiana	1,055
17. Wisconsin	952
18. Washington	937
19. Arizona	919
20. Alabama	904
21. Kentucky	799
22. Minnesota	786
23. South Carolina	774
24. Maryland	772
25. Louisiana	716
26. Oklahoma	635
27. Oregon	625
28. Colorado	588
29. Connecticut	585
30. Arkansas	558
31. Mississippi	552
32. Iowa	548
33. Kansas	451
34. West Virginia	413
35. Nevada	348
36. New Mexico	311
37. Nebraska	294
38. Utah	272
39. Maine	269
40. Idaho	228
41. New Hampshire	226
42. Hawaii	203
43. Rhode Island	192
44. Montana	169
45. Delaware	152
46. South Dakota	142
47. North Dakota	115
48. Vermont	112
49. Wyoming	84
50. District of Columbia	71
51. Alaska	65

Comparative Tables

51. Medicare Enrollment, July 2005 (x 1,000)		52. Medicaid Beneficiaries, 2004 (x 1,000)	
* UNITED STATES	41,536	* UNITED STATES	55,078
1. California	4,201	1. California	10,015
2. Florida	3,046	2. North Dakota	4,712
3. New York	2,776	3. Texas	3,604
4. Texas	2,545	4. Florida	2,952
5. Pennsylvania	2,132	5. Indiana	2,032
6. Ohio	1,754	6. Georgia	1,929
7. Illinois	1,691	7. Ohio	1,896
8. Michigan	1,483	8. Pennsylvania	1,835
9. North Carolina	1,277	9. Michigan	1,799
10. New Jersey	1,227	10. Tennessee	1,730
11. Georgia	1,039	11. Nebraska	1,513
12. Virginia	993	12. Mississippi	1,140
13. Massachusetts	971	13. Washington	1,109
14. Tennessee	922	14. Louisiana	1,108
15. Missouri	912	15. Maine	1,074
16. Indiana	905	16. Arkansas	1,070
17. Wisconsin	826	17. New Mexico	960
18. Washington	821	18. Iowa	946
19. Arizona	794	19. West Virginia	896
20. Alabama	755	20. Kentucky	861
21. Minnesota	698	21. South Carolina	857
22. Maryland	695	22. Alaska	808
23. Kentucky	678	23. Maryland	750
24. South Carolina	651	24. Vermont	732
25. Louisiana	610	25. Missouri	726
26. Oklahoma	541	26. Arizona	708
27. Oregon	540	27. Minnesota	698
28. Connecticut	525	28. Oklahoma	654
29. Colorado	522	29. Oregon	559
30. Iowa	490	30. Colorado	503
31. Arkansas	472	31. Connecticut	501
32. Mississippi	454	32. New York	474
33. Kansas	402	33. Idaho	383
34. West Virginia	355	34. Wisconsin	377
35. Nevada	297	35. Kansas	365
36. New Mexico	267	36. Utah	307
37. Nebraska	261	37. Massachusetts	294
38. Utah	237	38. New Hampshire	244
39. Maine	235	39. North Carolina	237
40. Idaho	192	40. Hawaii	218
41. New Hampshire	192	41. Rhode Island	208
42. Hawaii	182	42. Illinois	206
43. Rhode Island	172	43. Delaware	158
44. Montana	148	44. District of Columbia	157
45. Delaware	128	45. Virginia	149
46. South Dakota	125	46. South Dakota	128
47. North Dakota	104	47. New Jersey	119
48. Vermont	96	48. Alabama	118
49. District of Columbia	73	49. Montana	113
50. Wyoming	71	50. Nevada	78
51. Alaska	52	51. Wyoming	68

446

Comparative Tables

53. Median Home Value, 2006

1.	California	$535,700
2.	Hawaii	529,700
3.	District of Columbia	437,700
4.	Massachusetts	370,400
5.	New Jersey	366,600
6.	Maryland	334,700
7.	Nevada	315,200
8.	New York	303,400
9.	Connecticut	298,900
10.	Rhode Island	295,700
11.	Washington	267,600
12.	New Hampshire	253,200
13.	Virginia	244,200
14.	Oregon	236,600
15.	Arizona	236,500
16.	Colorado	232,900
17.	Florida	230,600
18.	Delaware	227,100
19.	Alaska	213,200
20.	Minnesota	208,200
21.	Illinois	200,200
22.	Vermont	193,000
23.	Utah	188,500
*	UNITED STATES	185,200
24.	Maine	170,500
25.	Idaho	163,900
26.	Wisconsin	163,500
27.	Georgia	156,800
28.	Montana	155,500
29.	Michigan	153,300
30.	Wyoming	148,900
31.	Pennsylvania	145,200
32.	New Mexico	141,200
33.	North Carolina	137,200
34.	Ohio	135,200
35.	Missouri	131,900
36.	Tennessee	123,100
37.	South Carolina	122,400
38.	Indiana	120,700
39.	Nebraska	119,200
40.	Louisiana	114,700
41.	Kansas	114,400
42.	Texas	114,000
43.	Iowa	112,600
44.	South Dakota	112,600
45.	Kentucky	111,000
46.	Alabama	107,000
47.	North Dakota	99,700
48.	Oklahoma	94,500
49.	Arkansas	93,900
50.	West Virginia	89,700
51.	Mississippi	88,600

54. Median Rent, 2006

1.	Hawaii	$1,116
2.	California	1,029
3.	New Jersey	974
4.	Maryland	953
5.	Massachusetts	933
6.	Nevada	917
7.	District of Columbia	914
8.	Connecticut	886
9.	Alaska	883
10.	New York	875
11.	Florida	872
12.	New Hampshire	861
13.	Virginia	846
14.	Rhode Island	840
15.	Delaware	830
16.	Colorado	780
17.	Washington	779
*	UNITED STATES	763
18.	Arizona	762
19.	Illinois	761
20.	Georgia	738
21.	Vermont	716
22.	Oregon	714
23.	Texas	711
24.	Minnesota	701
25.	Utah	697
26.	Michigan	675
27.	Pennsylvania	664
28.	Wisconsin	658
29.	North Carolina	656
30.	South Carolina	640
31.	Indiana	638
32.	Maine	636
33.	Ohio	627
34.	Idaho	623
35.	Louisiana	618
36.	New Mexico	617
37.	Tennessee	613
38.	Kansas	609
39.	Missouri	607
40.	Wyoming	601
41.	Nebraska	593
42.	Iowa	584
43.	Mississippi	584
44.	Oklahoma	580
45.	Alabama	573
46.	Montana	571
47.	Arkansas	566
48.	Kentucky	548
49.	South Dakota	522
50.	West Virginia	499
51.	North Dakota	497

Comparative Tables

55. Home Ownership Rate, 2006

1.	West Virginia	78.4%
2.	Michigan	77.4
3.	Delaware	76.8
4.	Mississippi	76.2
5.	Minnesota	75.6
6.	Maine	75.3
7.	Idaho	75.1
8.	Alabama	74.2
9.	Indiana	74.2
10.	New Hampshire	74.2
11.	South Carolina	74.2
12.	Iowa	74.0
13.	Vermont	74.0
14.	Wyoming	73.7
15.	Utah	73.5
16.	Pennsylvania	73.2
17.	Maryland	72.6
18.	Florida	72.4
19.	Ohio	72.1
20.	New Mexico	72.0
21.	Missouri	71.9
22.	Kentucky	71.7
23.	Arizona	71.6
24.	Oklahoma	71.6
25.	Louisiana	71.3
26.	Tennessee	71.3
27.	Connecticut	71.1
28.	Virginia	71.1
29.	Arkansas	70.8
30.	South Dakota	70.6
31.	Illinois	70.4
32.	North Carolina	70.2
33.	Wisconsin	70.2
34.	Colorado	70.1
35.	Kansas	70.0
36.	Montana	69.5
37.	New Jersey	69.0
*	UNITED STATES	68.8
38.	Georgia	68.5
39.	North Dakota	68.3
40.	Oregon	68.1
41.	Nebraska	67.6
42.	Alaska	67.2
43.	Washington	66.7
44.	Texas	66.0
45.	Nevada	65.7
46.	Massachusetts	65.2
47.	Rhode Island	64.6
48.	California	60.2
49.	Hawaii	59.9
50.	New York	55.7
51.	District of Columbia	45.9

56. Federal Grants to State and Local Governments, 2005 (x 1,000)

*	UNITED STATES	$469,579,029
1.	California	55,334,202
2.	New York	45,631,397
3.	Texas	28,912,208
4.	Florida	22,552,241
5.	Pennsylvania	19,868,667
6.	Ohio	17,151,707
7.	Illinois	16,634,795
8.	Massachusetts	13,748,662
9.	Michigan	13,313,206
10.	North Carolina	12,958,870
11.	Louisiana	11,388,684
12.	Georgia	11,165,966
13.	New Jersey	11,124,122
14.	Tennessee	9,985,336
15.	Washington	9,046,698
16.	Missouri	8,930,488
17.	Maryland	8,643,028
18.	Arizona	8,603,017
19.	Indiana	8,064,847
20.	Virginia	7,745,362
21.	Wisconsin	7,538,150
22.	Minnesota	7,483,670
23.	Alabama	7,346,245
24.	Kentucky	6,633,970
25.	Mississippi	6,567,356
26.	South Carolina	6,323,699
27.	Oklahoma	5,501,741
28.	Oregon	5,466,310
29.	Connecticut	5,438,708
30.	Colorado	5,433,177
31.	Arkansas	4,681,690
32.	New Mexico	4,564,332
33.	District of Columbia	4,325,307
34.	Iowa	4,035,419
35.	West Virginia	3,808,971
36.	Kansas	3,617,795
37.	Alaska	3,131,207
38.	Utah	3,038,268
39.	Nevada	2,925,545
40.	Maine	2,773,126
41.	Nebraska	2,595,784
42.	Rhode Island	2,325,111
43.	Hawaii	2,167,856
44.	Montana	2,139,765
45.	Idaho	2,092,900
46.	Wyoming	1,898,954
47.	New Hampshire	1,795,266
48.	South Dakota	1,741,877
49.	North Dakota	1,666,287
50.	Vermont	1,324,142
51.	Delaware	1,265,225

Comparative Tables

57. State Government Revenues, per capita, 2006

1.	District of Columbia	$16,023.98
2.	Alaska	16,008.29
3.	Wyoming	10,954.03
4.	New York	8,609.17
5.	Delaware	8,021.12
6.	Vermont	7,862.51
7.	Hawaii	7,708.65
8.	New Mexico	7,585.67
9.	California	7,276.29
10.	Rhode Island	7,224.88
11.	Massachusetts	7,071.25
12.	Oregon	6,974.32
13.	North Dakota	6,854.96
14.	Minnesota	6,746.03
15.	New Jersey	6,647.80
16.	Ohio	6,577.87
17.	Maine	6,563.84
18.	Connecticut	6,549.82
19.	Louisiana	6,523.16
20.	Montana	6,474.97
21.	Washington	6,405.11
22.	West Virginia	6,322.34
23.	Michigan	6,145.82
24.	Mississippi	6,120.35
25.	Wisconsin	5,995.44
*	UNITED STATES	5,934.67
26.	Pennsylvania	5,896.58
27.	Arkansas	5,846.99
28.	Iowa	5,654.57
29.	Kentucky	5,599.43
30.	Maryland	5,534.89
31.	Utah	5,490.64
32.	Oklahoma	5,483.65
33.	South Carolina	5,477.92
34.	Idaho	5,318.49
35.	South Dakota	5,295.18
36.	Virginia	5,271.14
37.	Indiana	5,212.82
38.	Nebraska	5,161.31
39.	Alabama	5,156.79
40.	North Carolina	5,127.04
41.	Nevada	4,951.60
42.	Kansas	4,940.57
43.	Missouri	4,926.70
44.	Colorado	4,923.53
45.	Illinois	4,909.50
46.	New Hampshire	4,858.25
47.	Florida	4,641.15
48.	Arizona	4,514.44
49.	Texas	4,441.48
50.	Tennessee	4,331.90
51.	Georgia	4,024.18

58. State Government Expenditures, per capita, 2006

1.	District of Columbia	$15,633.73
2.	Alaska	12,693.32
3.	Wyoming	7,823.39
4.	Delaware	7,645.80
5.	Vermont	7,486.93
6.	New York	7,408.64
7.	Hawaii	6,971.26
8.	New Mexico	6,898.53
9.	Rhode Island	6,551.99
10.	New Jersey	6,239.65
11.	California	6,215.68
12.	Massachusetts	6,198.00
13.	Minnesota	6,011.84
14.	Maine	5,973.55
15.	Connecticut	5,914.21
16.	Louisiana	5,708.00
17.	North Dakota	5,699.73
18.	Ohio	5,663.95
19.	Mississippi	5,620.03
20.	Montana	5,486.47
21.	Oregon	5,437.60
22.	West Virginia	5,413.51
23.	South Carolina	5,411.12
24.	Wisconsin	5,405.87
25.	Washington	5,320.04
26.	Michigan	5,254.97
27.	Pennsylvania	5,234.05
28.	Kentucky	5,230.74
*	UNITED STATES	5,193.48
29.	Maryland	5,170.63
30.	Arkansas	5,115.62
31.	Iowa	5,026.62
32.	Alabama	4,849.60
33.	Oklahoma	4,718.99
34.	Utah	4,669.30
35.	North Carolina	4,634.78
36.	New Hampshire	4,564.61
37.	Kansas	4,555.27
38.	Virginia	4,551.71
39.	South Dakota	4,394.95
40.	Nebraska	4,366.98
41.	Illinois	4,364.67
42.	Idaho	4,339.76
43.	Indiana	4,277.37
44.	Colorado	4,227.84
45.	Florida	4,216.65
46.	Arizona	4,173.33
47.	Missouri	4,172.21
48.	Nevada	4,149.24
49.	Tennessee	3,945.37
50.	Georgia	3,740.58
51.	Texas	3,653.25

Comparative Tables

59. Violent Crime Rate, 2006
(per 100,000 residents)

1.	District of Columbia	1,508.4
2.	South Carolina	765.5
3.	Tennessee	760.2
4.	Nevada	741.6
5.	Florida	712.0
6.	Louisiana	697.8
7.	Alaska	688.0
8.	Delaware	681.6
9.	Maryland	678.6
10.	New Mexico	643.2
11.	Michigan	562.4
12.	Arkansas	551.6
13.	Missouri	545.6
14.	Illinois	541.6
15.	California	532.5
16.	Texas	516.3
17.	Arizona	501.4
18.	Oklahoma	497.4
19.	North Carolina	475.6
*	UNITED STATES	473.5
20.	Georgia	471.0
21.	Massachusetts	447.0
22.	Pennsylvania	439.4
23.	New York	434.9
24.	Alabama	425.2
25.	Kansas	425.0
26.	Colorado	391.6
27.	New Jersey	351.6
28.	Ohio	350.3
29.	Washington	345.9
30.	Indiana	314.8
31.	Minnesota	312.0
32.	Mississippi	298.6
33.	Wisconsin	284.0
34.	Iowa	283.5
35.	Virginia	282.2
36.	Nebraska	281.8
37.	Hawaii	281.2
38.	Connecticut	280.8
39.	Oregon	280.3
40.	West Virginia	279.7
41.	Kentucky	263.0
42.	Montana	253.7
43.	Idaho	247.2
44.	Wyoming	239.6
45.	Rhode Island	227.5
46.	Utah	224.4
47.	South Dakota	171.4
48.	New Hampshire	138.7
49.	Vermont	136.6
50.	North Dakota	127.9
51.	Maine	115.5

60. Property Crime Rate, 2006
(per 100,000 residents)

1.	District of Columbia	4,653.8
2.	Arizona	4,627.9
3.	Washington	4,480.0
4.	South Carolina	4,242.3
5.	Hawaii	4,230.4
6.	Tennessee	4,128.3
7.	North Carolina	4,120.8
8.	Nevada	4,088.8
9.	Texas	4,081.5
10.	Louisiana	3,993.7
11.	Florida	3,986.1
12.	Arkansas	3,967.5
13.	New Mexico	3,937.2
14.	Alabama	3,936.1
15.	Georgia	3,889.2
16.	Missouri	3,826.5
17.	Kansas	3,750.2
18.	Ohio	3,678.6
19.	Oregon	3,672.1
20.	Oklahoma	3,604.2
21.	Utah	3,516.4
22.	Indiana	3,502.4
23.	Maryland	3,480.9
24.	Colorado	3,451.3
25.	Delaware	3,417.9
26.	Nebraska	3,340.7
*	UNITED STATES	3,334.5
27.	Michigan	3,212.8
28.	Mississippi	3,208.8
29.	California	3,170.9
30.	Minnesota	3,079.5
31.	Illinois	3,019.6
32.	Wyoming	2,980.6
33.	Wisconsin	2,817.8
34.	Iowa	2,802.7
35.	Montana	2,687.5
36.	West Virginia	2,621.5
37.	Rhode Island	2,586.9
38.	Kentucky	2,544.5
39.	Maine	2,518.7
40.	Connecticut	2,504.1
41.	Virginia	2,478.2
42.	Pennsylvania	2,443.5
43.	Idaho	2,418.8
44.	Massachusetts	2,391.0
45.	Vermont	2,304.7
46.	New Jersey	2,291.9
47.	New York	2,052.7
48.	North Dakota	2,000.3
49.	New Hampshire	1,874.1
50.	South Dakota	1,619.6
51.	Alaska	688.0

450

Comparative Tables

61. Identity Theft rate, 2006 (complaints per 100,000 residents)		62. Fraud Rate, 2006 (complaints per 100,000 residents)	
1. Arizona	147.8	1. District of Columbia	195.9
2. District of Columbia	131.5	2. Utah	178.9
3. Nevada	120.0	3. Nevada	169.2
4. California	113.5	4. Washington	163.4
5. Texas	110.6	5. Colorado	161.1
6. Florida	98.3	6. Alaska	161.0
7. Colorado	92.5	7. Virginia	157.5
8. Georgia	86.3	8. Hawaii	157.1
9. New York	85.2	9. Maryland	154.1
10. Washington	83.4	10. Oregon	150.9
11. Maryland	82.9	11. Arizona	149.6
12. New Mexico	82.9	12. New Hampshire	149.4
* UNITED STATES	79.9	13. Florida	143.2
13. Illinois	78.6	14. Idaho	137.2
14. Oregon	76.1	15. Montana	136.5
15. New Jersey	73.3	16. Maine	135.5
16. Michigan	67.2	17. California	134.6
17. Virginia	67.2	18. Connecticut	134.0
18. Delaware	66.7	19. Delaware	131.1
19. Connecticut	65.8	20. Pennsylvania	130.6
20. North Carolina	64.9	21. New Jersey	129.3
21. Pennsylvania	64.9	22. Wyoming	127.6
22. Missouri	64.2	23. Georgia	127.5
23. Massachusetts	63.7	24. Missouri	125.5
24. Oklahoma	63.0	* UNITED STATES	125.2
25. Indiana	62.2	25. Indiana	124.5
26. Utah	61.8	26. Ohio	124.1
27. Tennessee	61.3	27. New Mexico	123.1
28. Alabama	60.3	28. Wisconsin	121.0
29. Ohio	59.9	29. North Carolina	116.3
30. Kansas	58.8	30. Michigan	115.5
31. Rhode Island	57.6	31. Vermont	115.1
32. Alaska	57.3	32. Massachusetts	113.9
33. South Carolina	55.7	33. Tennessee	113.8
34. Minnesota	55.6	34. Minnesota	113.4
35. Arkansas	54.7	35. West Virginia	113.2
36. Louisiana	52.6	36. South Carolina	112.0
37. Mississippi	51.3	37. Nebraska	111.3
38. Nebraska	49.1	38. Kansas	111.0
39. Idaho	49.0	39. New York	109.4
40. Hawaii	47.8	40. Illinois	108.4
41. New Hampshire	46.1	41. Texas	108.2
42. Montana	45.9	42. Rhode Island	108.0
43. Wisconsin	45.6	43. Kentucky	106.4
44. Wyoming	42.3	44. Oklahoma	103.7
45. Kentucky	42.0	45. Alabama	102.4
46. Maine	39.7	46. Louisiana	92.8
47. West Virginia	39.3	47. Iowa	89.4
48. Iowa	34.9	48. Arkansas	86.4
49. South Dakota	30.2	49. North Dakota	85.6
50. North Dakota	29.7	50. Mississippi	79.6
51. Vermont	28.5	51. South Dakota	79.0

Comparative Tables

63. Incarceration Rate, 2006 (per 100,000 residents)

1.	Louisiana	846
2.	Texas	683
3.	Oklahoma	664
4.	Mississippi	658
5.	Alabama	595
6.	Georgia	558
7.	South Carolina	525
8.	Missouri	514
9.	Michigan	511
10.	Arizona	509
11.	Florida	509
12.	Nevada	503
*	UNITED STATES	501
13.	Delaware	488
14.	Arkansas	485
15.	Idaho	480
16.	Virginia	477
17.	California	475
18.	Colorado	469
19.	Alaska	462
20.	Kentucky	462
21.	Ohio	428
22.	South Dakota	426
23.	Tennessee	423
24.	Indiana	411
25.	Wyoming	408
26.	Maryland	396
27.	Wisconsin	393
28.	Connecticut	392
29.	Montana	374
30.	Oregon	367
31.	North Carolina	360
32.	Pennsylvania	353
33.	Illinois	350
34.	Hawaii	338
35.	New York	326
36.	New Mexico	323
37.	Kansas	318
38.	West Virginia	314
39.	New Jersey	313
40.	Iowa	296
41.	Washington	271
42.	Vermont	262
43.	Utah	246
44.	Massachusetts	243
45.	Nebraska	237
46.	North Dakota	214
47.	New Hampshire	207
48.	Rhode Island	202
49.	Minnesota	176
50.	Maine	151
51.	District of Columbia	NA

64. Incarceration Rate, White, June 2005 (per 100,000 residents)

1.	Oklahoma	740
2.	Idaho	675
3.	Texas	667
4.	Nevada	627
5.	Georgia	623
6.	Arizona	590
7.	Florida	588
8.	Kentucky	561
9.	Alabama	542
10.	Colorado	525
11.	Louisiana	523
12.	Mississippi	503
13.	Oregon	502
14.	Alaska	500
15.	Missouri	487
16.	Tennessee	487
17.	Arkansas	478
18.	South Dakota	470
19.	Indiana	463
20.	California	460
21.	Hawaii	453
22.	Kansas	443
23.	Montana	433
24.	South Carolina	415
25.	Wisconsin	415
26.	Michigan	412
*	UNITED STATES	412
27.	Delaware	396
28.	Virginia	396
29.	Washington	393
30.	Utah	392
31.	West Virginia	392
32.	Ohio	344
33.	North Carolina	320
34.	Iowa	309
35.	Pennsylvania	305
36.	Vermont	304
37.	Nebraska	290
38.	New Hampshire	289
39.	Maryland	288
40.	North Dakota	267
41.	Maine	262
42.	Illinois	223
43.	Minnesota	212
44.	Connecticut	211
45.	Massachusetts	201
46.	Rhode Island	191
47.	New Jersey	190
48.	New York	174
49.	District of Columbia	56
50.	New Mexico	NA
51.	Wyoming	NA

Comparative Tables

65. Incarceration Rate, Black, June 2005 (per 100,000 residents)	
1. South Dakota	4,710
2. Wisconsin	4,416
3. Iowa	4,200
4. Vermont	3,797
5. Utah	3,588
6. Montana	3,569
7. Colorado	3,491
8. Arizona	3,294
9. Oklahoma	3,252
10. Texas	3,162
11. Kansas	3,096
12. California	2,992
13. Oregon	2,930
14. Nevada	2,916
15. Idaho	2,869
16. Kentucky	2,793
17. Pennsylvania	2,792
18. North Dakota	2,683
19. New Hampshire	2,666
20. Florida	2,615
21. Missouri	2,556
22. Connecticut	2,532
23. Indiana	2,526
24. Washington	2,522
25. Delaware	2,517
26. Louisiana	2,452
27. Nebraska	2,418
28. New Jersey	2,352
29. Virginia	2,331
* UNITED STATES	2,289
30. Michigan	2,262
31. Ohio	2,196
32. West Virginia	2,188
33. Alaska	2,163
34. Georgia	2,068
35. Illinois	2,020
36. Tennessee	2,006
37. Maine	1,992
38. Minnesota	1,937
39. Alabama	1,916
40. South Carolina	1,856
41. Arkansas	1,846
42. Rhode Island	1,838
43. Mississippi	1,742
44. North Carolina	1,727
45. Massachusetts	1,635
46. New York	1,627
47. Maryland	1,579
48. District of Columbia	1,065
49. Hawaii	851
50. New Mexico	NA
51. Wyoming	NA

66. Incarceration Rate, Hispanic, June 2005 (per 100,000 residents)	
1. Pennsylvania	1,714
2. Idaho	1,654
3. Connecticut	1,401
4. Massachusetts	1,229
5. Arizona	1,075
6. New Hampshire	1,063
7. Colorado	1,042
8. North Dakota	848
9. Montana	846
10. Utah	838
11. Oklahoma	832
12. Texas	830
13. California	782
14. New York	778
15. Iowa	764
16. Kentucky	757
* UNITED STATES	742
17. Nebraska	739
18. Delaware	683
19. Rhode Island	631
20. New Jersey	630
21. Nevada	621
22. Ohio	613
23. Mississippi	611
24. Missouri	587
25. Indiana	579
26. Georgia	576
27. Oregon	573
28. Tennessee	561
29. Washington	527
30. Virginia	487
31. South Carolina	476
32. Illinois	415
33. Michigan	397
34. Florida	382
35. Alaska	380
36. Arkansas	288
37. District of Columbia	267
38. Louisiana	244
39. West Virginia	211
40. Hawaii	185
41. Alabama	NA
42. Kansas	NA
43. Maine	NA
44. Maryland	NA
45. Minnesota	NA
46. New Mexico	NA
47. North Carolina	NA
48. South Dakota	NA
49. Vermont	NA
50. Wisconsin	NA
51. Wyoming	NA

Comparative Tables

67. Incarceration Rate, Men, June 2005 (per 100,000 residents)		68. Incarceration Rate, Women, June 2005 (per 100,000 residents)	
1. Louisiana	2,134	1. Oklahoma	209
2. Georgia	1,877	2. Louisiana	195
3. Mississippi	1,790	3. Texas	186
4. Texas	1,772	4. Idaho	185
5. Alabama	1,665	5. Georgia	184
6. Oklahoma	1,645	6. Wyoming	184
7. South Carolina	1,558	7. Kentucky	173
8. Delaware	1,547	8. Nevada	173
9. Florida	1,541	9. Arizona	171
10. Arizona	1,443	10. Mississippi	168
11. New Mexico	1,421	11. Colorado	166
12. Virginia	1,393	12. New Mexico	163
13. Idaho	1,379	13. Alabama	161
14. Tennessee	1,339	14. South Dakota	157
15. Missouri	1,323	15. Florida	155
16. Nevada	1,319	16. Tennessee	151
17. Kentucky	1,287	17. District of Columbia	145
18. Colorado	1,279	18. Virginia	144
19. Michigan	1,262	19. Alaska	141
* UNITED STATES	1,249	20. South Carolina	137
20. California	1,246	21. Arkansas	136
21. Alaska	1,232	22. Missouri	133
22. Arkansas	1,231	23. Montana	129
23. Maryland	1,219	24. Delaware	128
24. Wisconsin	1,209	25. Utah	127
25. District of Columbia	1,202	26. Indiana	126
26. Wyoming	1,189	* UNITED STATES	121
27. Indiana	1,165	27. California	119
28. Pennsylvania	1,155	28. Kansas	117
29. North Carolina	1,154	29. Hawaii	109
30. South Dakota	1,092	30. Wisconsin	107
31. Kansas	1,054	31. North Carolina	104
32. Ohio	1,040	32. Ohio	103
33. Connecticut	1,030	33. Oregon	101
34. New Jersey	1,019	34. Washington	101
35. Oregon	965	35. Nebraska	93
36. Illinois	951	36. Pennsylvania	92
37. New York	935	37. Maryland	88
38. Montana	926	38. North Dakota	87
39. Washington	831	39. Connecticut	85
40. West Virginia	817	40. Michigan	85
41. Utah	803	41. West Virginia	84
42. Hawaii	787	42. Iowa	83
43. Nebraska	756	43. Illinois	79
44. Iowa	751	44. New Jersey	70
45. Massachusetts	687	45. New York	57
46. North Dakota	632	46. New Hampshire	56
47. Rhode Island	607	47. Minnesota	52
48. Vermont	598	48. Massachusetts	45
49. New Hampshire	590	49. Vermont	45
50. Minnesota	553	50. Maine	44
51. Maine	513	51. Rhode Island	38

454

Comparative Tables

69. Civilian Labor Force, 2006 (x 1,000)	
* UNITED STATES	151,428
1. California	17,751
2. Texas	11,465
3. New York	9,464
4. Florida	9,054
5. Illinois	6,584
6. Pennsylvania	6,308
7. Ohio	5,975
8. Michigan	5,086
9. Georgia	4,694
10. New Jersey	4,490
11. North Carolina	4,426
12. Virginia	3,971
13. Massachusetts	3,368
14. Washington	3,335
15. Indiana	3,253
16. Wisconsin	3,079
17. Missouri	3,069
18. Tennessee	3,028
19. Maryland	3,001
20. Arizona	2,969
21. Minnesota	2,933
22. Colorado	2,610
23. Alabama	2,210
24. South Carolina	2,124
25. Kentucky	2,042
26. Louisiana	1,960
27. Oregon	1,897
28. Connecticut	1,858
29. Oklahoma	1,733
30. Iowa	1,701
31. Kansas	1,480
32. Arkansas	1,374
33. Utah	1,309
34. Mississippi	1,296
35. Nevada	1,296
36. Nebraska	982
37. New Mexico	944
38. West Virginia	815
39. Idaho	759
40. New Hampshire	741
41. Maine	715
42. Hawaii	657
43. Rhode Island	577
44. Montana	505
45. Delaware	448
46. South Dakota	434
47. North Dakota	368
48. Vermont	365
49. Alaska	349
50. District of Columbia	291
51. Wyoming	287

70. Unemployment Rate, 2006	
1. Michigan	7.0%
2. Alaska	6.9
3. South Carolina	6.5
4. Mississippi	6.4
5. District of Columbia	5.8
6. Kentucky	5.6
7. Ohio	5.4
8. Oregon	5.4
9. Arkansas	5.3
10. Rhode Island	5.2
11. Tennessee	5.2
12. Massachusetts	5.1
13. West Virginia	5.1
14. Indiana	5.0
15. Washington	5.0
16. California	4.8
17. Missouri	4.8
18. New Jersey	4.8
19. Texas	4.8
20. Wisconsin	4.8
21. North Carolina	4.7
22. Pennsylvania	4.7
23. Georgia	4.6
24. Louisiana	4.6
25. Maine	4.6
* UNITED STATES	4.6
26. Illinois	4.5
27. Kansas	4.4
28. New Mexico	4.4
29. New York	4.4
30. Connecticut	4.3
31. Arizona	4.2
32. Colorado	4.2
33. Alabama	4.1
34. Nevada	4.1
35. Minnesota	4.0
36. Maryland	3.9
37. Oklahoma	3.9
38. Iowa	3.6
39. Montana	3.6
40. Vermont	3.6
41. Delaware	3.5
42. Idaho	3.5
43. New Hampshire	3.4
44. Wyoming	3.4
45. North Dakota	3.3
46. Florida	3.2
47. Nebraska	3.1
48. South Dakota	3.1
49. Virginia	3.1
50. Utah	2.9
51. Hawaii	2.7

Comparative Tables

71. Average Hourly Earnings – Production, 2006

1.	Michigan	$21.83
2.	Washington	19.90
3.	Connecticut	19.78
4.	Ohio	19.16
5.	Indiana	18.57
6.	Maine	18.57
7.	New York	18.29
8.	Massachusetts	18.26
9.	Delaware	18.13
10.	Louisiana	17.94
11.	West Virginia	17.89
12.	Maryland	17.87
13.	Kansas	17.68
14.	Wyoming	17.44
15.	District of Columbia	17.30
16.	Minnesota	17.23
17.	Missouri	17.16
18.	Kentucky	16.92
19.	Idaho	16.89
*	UNITED STATES	16.80
20.	Virginia	16.75
21.	Colorado	16.58
22.	New Hampshire	16.56
23.	New Jersey	16.55
24.	Wisconsin	16.54
25.	Iowa	16.40
26.	Illinois	16.03
27.	California	15.95
28.	Montana	15.90
29.	Hawaii	15.89
30.	Vermont	15.79
31.	Oregon	15.57
32.	Alabama	15.56
33.	Nevada	15.47
34.	Pennsylvania	15.37
35.	Utah	15.25
36.	Nebraska	15.04
37.	South Carolina	15.03
38.	North Dakota	14.97
39.	Arizona	14.88
40.	Oklahoma	14.77
41.	Florida	14.75
42.	Georgia	14.74
43.	North Carolina	14.57
44.	Alaska	14.30
45.	New Mexico	14.06
46.	Tennessee	14.04
47.	Texas	14.01
48.	Mississippi	13.78
49.	South Dakota	13.75
50.	Rhode Island	13.42
51.	Arkansas	13.35

72. Average Weekly Earnings – Production, 2006

1.	Michigan	$921.23
2.	Connecticut	834.72
3.	Washington	807.94
4.	Ohio	793.22
5.	Indiana	774.37
6.	Louisiana	771.42
7.	Maine	768.80
8.	Kansas	760.24
9.	New York	751.72
10.	Massachusetts	743.18
11.	West Virginia	738.86
12.	Maryland	725.52
13.	Delaware	723.39
14.	Wyoming	718.53
15.	Minnesota	706.43
16.	Idaho	704.31
17.	New Jersey	696.76
18.	Kentucky	695.41
19.	Virginia	691.78
*	UNITED STATES	690.83
20.	Iowa	687.16
21.	New Hampshire	682.27
22.	Missouri	674.39
23.	Wisconsin	673.18
24.	District of Columbia	669.51
25.	Illinois	658.83
26.	Colorado	649.94
27.	California	644.38
28.	Alabama	636.40
29.	Montana	636.00
30.	Oregon	630.59
31.	Pennsylvania	627.10
32.	Utah	626.78
33.	Vermont	625.28
34.	South Carolina	616.23
35.	Nebraska	615.14
36.	Hawaii	613.35
37.	Florida	612.13
38.	Nevada	609.52
39.	Arizona	604.13
40.	Oklahoma	589.32
41.	North Dakota	583.83
42.	North Carolina	582.80
43.	Georgia	582.23
44.	Alaska	579.15
45.	South Dakota	578.88
46.	Texas	573.01
47.	Tennessee	553.18
48.	New Mexico	551.15
49.	Arkansas	547.35
50.	Mississippi	542.93
51.	Rhode Island	522.04

Comparative Tables

73. Average Annual Pay, 2006

1.	District of Columbia	$70,151
2.	New York	55,479
3.	Connecticut	54,814
4.	Massachusetts	52,435
5.	New Jersey	51,645
6.	California	48,345
7.	Delaware	46,285
8.	Maryland	46,162
9.	Illinois	45,650
10.	Virginia	44,051
11.	Colorado	43,506
12.	Washington	42,897
*	UNITED STATES	42,535
13.	Texas	42,458
14.	New Hampshire	42,447
15.	Minnesota	42,185
16.	Michigan	42,157
17.	Alaska	41,750
18.	Pennsylvania	41,349
19.	Rhode Island	40,454
20.	Georgia	40,370
21.	Nevada	40,070
22.	Arizona	40,019
23.	Ohio	38,568
24.	Florida	38,485
25.	Oregon	38,077
26.	Hawaii	37,799
27.	Tennessee	37,564
28.	North Carolina	37,439
29.	Missouri	37,143
30.	Wisconsin	36,821
31.	Wyoming	36,662
32.	Louisiana	36,604
33.	Indiana	36,553
34.	Alabama	36,204
35.	Kansas	35,696
36.	Vermont	35,542
37.	Kentucky	35,201
38.	Utah	35,130
39.	New Mexico	34,567
40.	Iowa	34,320
41.	South Carolina	34,281
42.	Oklahoma	34,022
43.	Nebraska	33,814
44.	Maine	33,794
45.	West Virginia	32,728
46.	Idaho	32,580
47.	Arkansas	32,389
48.	North Dakota	31,316
49.	Mississippi	31,194
50.	Montana	30,596
51.	South Dakota	30,291

74. Median Household Income, 2006

1.	Maryland	$65,144
2.	New Jersey	64,470
3.	Connecticut	63,422
4.	Hawaii	61,160
5.	Massachusetts	59,963
6.	New Hampshire	59,683
7.	Alaska	59,393
8.	California	56,645
9.	Virginia	56,277
10.	Minnesota	54,023
11.	Nevada	52,998
12.	Delaware	52,833
13.	Washington	52,583
14.	Colorado	52,015
15.	Illinois	52,006
16.	District of Columbia	51,847
17.	Rhode Island	51,814
18.	New York	51,384
19.	Utah	51,309
20.	Wisconsin	48,772
*	UNITED STATES	48,451
21.	Vermont	47,665
22.	Wyoming	47,423
23.	Arizona	47,265
24.	Michigan	47,182
25.	Georgia	46,832
26.	Pennsylvania	46,259
27.	Oregon	46,230
28.	Florida	45,495
29.	Kansas	45,478
30.	Nebraska	45,474
31.	Indiana	45,394
32.	Texas	44,922
33.	Ohio	44,532
34.	Iowa	44,491
35.	Maine	43,439
36.	Idaho	42,865
37.	Missouri	42,841
38.	South Dakota	42,791
39.	North Carolina	42,625
40.	North Dakota	41,919
41.	South Carolina	41,100
42.	New Mexico	40,629
43.	Montana	40,627
44.	Tennessee	40,315
45.	Kentucky	39,372
46.	Louisiana	39,337
47.	Alabama	38,783
48.	Oklahoma	38,770
49.	Arkansas	36,599
50.	West Virginia	35,059
51.	Mississippi	34,473

Comparative Tables

75. Personal Income, in Current Dollars, 2006

1.	District of Columbia	$55,755
2.	Connecticut	49,852
3.	New Jersey	46,344
4.	Massachusetts	45,877
5.	Maryland	44,077
6.	New York	42,392
7.	Wyoming	40,676
8.	New Hampshire	39,311
9.	Colorado	39,186
10.	Virginia	39,173
11.	Delaware	39,022
12.	California	38,956
13.	Minnesota	38,712
14.	Illinois	38,215
15.	Washington	37,423
16.	Rhode Island	37,388
17.	Alaska	37,271
18.	Nevada	37,089
19.	Pennsylvania	36,680
20.	Hawaii	36,299
*	UNITED STATES	36,276
21.	Florida	35,798
22.	Kansas	34,743
23.	Wisconsin	34,701
24.	Nebraska	34,397
25.	Vermont	34,264
26.	Texas	34,257
27.	South Dakota	33,929
28.	Michigan	33,847
29.	Oregon	33,666
30.	Ohio	33,338
31.	Iowa	33,236
32.	Missouri	32,705
33.	North Dakota	32,552
34.	Indiana	32,526
35.	Maine	32,348
36.	Tennessee	32,304
37.	North Carolina	32,234
38.	Oklahoma	32,210
39.	Georgia	31,891
40.	Arizona	31,458
41.	Alabama	31,295
42.	Louisiana	30,952
43.	Montana	30,688
44.	Idaho	29,952
45.	New Mexico	29,673
46.	South Carolina	29,515
47.	Kentucky	29,352
48.	Utah	29,108
49.	Arkansas	27,935
50.	West Virginia	27,897
51.	Mississippi	26,535

76. Personal Income, in Constant (2000) Dollars, 2006

1.	District of Columbia	$48,671
2.	Connecticut	43,518
3.	New Jersey	40,455
4.	Massachusetts	40,048
5.	Maryland	38,476
6.	New York	37,005
7.	Wyoming	35,508
8.	New Hampshire	34,316
9.	Colorado	34,207
10.	Virginia	34,196
11.	Delaware	34,064
12.	California	34,006
13.	Minnesota	33,793
14.	Illinois	33,359
15.	Washington	32,668
16.	Rhode Island	32,637
17.	Alaska	32,535
18.	Nevada	32,376
19.	Pennsylvania	32,019
20.	Hawaii	31,687
*	UNITED STATES	31,667
21.	Florida	31,249
22.	Kansas	30,328
23.	Wisconsin	30,292
24.	Nebraska	30,026
25.	Vermont	29,910
26.	Texas	29,904
27.	South Dakota	29,618
28.	Michigan	29,546
29.	Oregon	29,388
30.	Ohio	29,102
31.	Iowa	29,013
32.	Missouri	28,549
33.	North Dakota	28,416
34.	Indiana	28,393
35.	Maine	28,238
36.	Tennessee	28,199
37.	North Carolina	28,138
38.	Oklahoma	28,117
39.	Georgia	27,839
40.	Arizona	27,461
41.	Alabama	27,319
42.	Louisiana	27,019
43.	Montana	26,789
44.	Idaho	26,146
45.	New Mexico	25,903
46.	South Carolina	25,765
47.	Kentucky	25,622
48.	Utah	25,409
49.	Arkansas	24,385
50.	West Virginia	24,352
51.	Mississippi	23,163

Comparative Tables

77. Persons Below the Poverty Level, 2006

1.	Mississippi	21.1%
2.	District of Columbia	19.6
3.	Louisiana	19.0
4.	New Mexico	18.5
5.	Arkansas	17.3
6.	West Virginia	17.3
7.	Kentucky	17.0
8.	Oklahoma	17.0
9.	Texas	16.9
10.	Alabama	16.6
11.	Tennessee	16.2
12.	South Carolina	15.7
13.	Georgia	14.7
14.	North Carolina	14.7
15.	Arizona	14.2
16.	New York	14.2
17.	Missouri	13.6
18.	Montana	13.6
19.	South Dakota	13.6
20.	Michigan	13.5
21.	Ohio	13.3
22.	Oregon	13.3
*	UNITED STATES	13.3
23.	California	13.1
24.	Maine	12.9
25.	Indiana	12.7
26.	Florida	12.6
27.	Idaho	12.6
28.	Kansas	12.4
29.	Illinois	12.3
30.	Pennsylvania	12.1
31.	Colorado	12.0
32.	Washington	11.8
33.	Nebraska	11.5
34.	North Dakota	11.4
35.	Delaware	11.1
36.	Rhode Island	11.1
37.	Iowa	11.0
38.	Wisconsin	11.0
39.	Alaska	10.9
40.	Utah	10.6
41.	Nevada	10.3
42.	Vermont	10.3
43.	Massachusetts	9.9
44.	Minnesota	9.8
45.	Virginia	9.6
46.	Wyoming	9.4
47.	Hawaii	9.3
48.	New Jersey	8.7
49.	Connecticut	8.3
50.	New Hampshire	8.0
51.	Maryland	7.8

78. Gross Domestic Product, 2006 (x $1 million)

*	UNITED STATES	$13,149,033
1.	California	1,727,355
2.	Texas	1,065,891
3.	New York	1,021,944
4.	Florida	713,505
5.	Illinois	589,598
6.	Pennsylvania	510,293
7.	Ohio	461,302
8.	New Jersey	453,177
9.	Michigan	381,003
10.	Georgia	379,550
11.	North Carolina	374,525
12.	Virginia	369,260
13.	Massachusetts	337,570
14.	Washington	293,531
15.	Maryland	257,815
16.	Indiana	248,915
17.	Minnesota	244,546
18.	Tennessee	238,029
19.	Arizona	232,463
20.	Colorado	230,478
21.	Wisconsin	227,230
22.	Missouri	225,876
23.	Connecticut	204,134
24.	Louisiana	193,138
25.	Alabama	160,569
26.	Oregon	151,301
27.	South Carolina	149,214
28.	Kentucky	145,959
29.	Oklahoma	134,651
30.	Iowa	123,970
31.	Nevada	118,399
32.	Kansas	111,699
33.	Utah	97,749
34.	Arkansas	91,837
35.	District of Columbia	87,664
36.	Mississippi	84,225
37.	New Mexico	75,910
38.	Nebraska	75,700
39.	Delaware	60,361
40.	Hawaii	58,307
41.	New Hampshire	56,276
42.	West Virginia	55,658
43.	Idaho	49,907
44.	Maine	46,973
45.	Rhode Island	45,660
46.	Alaska	41,105
47.	South Dakota	32,330
48.	Montana	32,322
49.	Wyoming	29,561
50.	North Dakota	26,385
51.	Vermont	24,213

Comparative Tables

79. Annual Payroll for Major Industry Groups, 2006 (x $1,000)	
* UNITED STATES	$4,482,722,481
1. California	588,450,315
2. New York	370,842,630
3. Texas	315,809,126
4. Florida	239,197,889
5. Illinois	217,221,786
6. Pennsylvania	189,692,284
7. Ohio	168,350,499
8. New Jersey	166,018,238
9. Michigan	148,456,286
10. Massachusetts	140,580,627
11. Georgia	128,827,270
12. Virginia	121,801,479
13. North Carolina	115,740,410
14. Minnesota	96,992,711
15. Washington	94,928,122
16. Maryland	88,964,728
17. Indiana	88,145,224
18. Wisconsin	85,781,279
19. Missouri	82,340,359
20. Tennessee	80,959,818
21. Arizona	76,340,525
22. Connecticut	75,605,605
23. Colorado	75,525,841
24. Alabama	53,365,320
25. Louisiana	50,657,624
26. Oregon	50,019,294
27. South Carolina	49,450,267
28. Kentucky	47,983,162
29. Iowa	39,420,961
30. Nevada	39,261,902
31. Oklahoma	37,620,071
32. Kansas	36,646,065
33. Utah	30,970,696
34. Arkansas	30,185,779
35. Mississippi	25,796,066
36. District of Columbia	25,152,741
37. Nebraska	24,180,753
38. New Hampshire	21,026,773
39. New Mexico	18,171,120
40. Delaware	16,875,311
41. West Virginia	16,323,457
42. Hawaii	16,163,137
43. Maine	15,873,419
44. Rhode Island	15,756,079
45. Idaho	15,397,889
46. Alaska	9,774,285
47. Montana	8,950,520
48. South Dakota	8,860,458
49. Vermont	8,284,548
50. North Dakota	7,779,322
51. Wyoming	6,202,411

80. Paid Employees for Major Industry Groups, 2006 (x 1,000)	
* UNITED STATES	116,317,003
1. California	13,382,470
2. Texas	8,305,102
3. New York	7,417,463
4. Florida	7,107,378
5. Illinois	5,235,866
6. Pennsylvania	5,082,630
7. Ohio	4,762,618
8. Michigan	3,796,876
9. New Jersey	3,594,862
10. Georgia	3,489,046
11. North Carolina	3,409,968
12. Virginia	3,060,127
13. Massachusetts	2,996,347
14. Indiana	2,610,899
15. Wisconsin	2,449,114
16. Minnesota	2,430,853
17. Missouri	2,425,403
18. Tennessee	2,378,754
19. Washington	2,316,296
20. Maryland	2,167,999
21. Arizona	2,159,823
22. Colorado	1,936,264
23. Alabama	1,667,526
24. Louisiana	1,617,507
25. South Carolina	1,584,914
26. Connecticut	1,529,827
27. Kentucky	1,514,199
28. Oregon	1,409,576
29. Iowa	1,261,108
30. Oklahoma	1,220,285
31. Kansas	1,116,216
32. Nevada	1,089,422
33. Arkansas	1,017,424
34. Utah	974,686
35. Mississippi	926,952
36. Nebraska	773,082
37. New Mexico	595,249
38. West Virginia	565,499
39. New Hampshire	562,398
40. Idaho	519,319
41. Maine	497,387
42. Hawaii	490,682
43. Rhode Island	442,291
44. District of Columbia	439,610
45. Delaware	392,840
46. Montana	326,887
47. South Dakota	310,802
48. North Dakota	270,479
49. Vermont	261,656
50. Alaska	231,088
51. Wyoming	191,934

Comparative Tables

81. Number of Farms, 2006	
* UNITED STATES	2,089,790
1. Texas	230,000
2. Missouri	105,000
3. Iowa	88,600
4. Kentucky	84,000
5. Oklahoma	83,000
6. Tennessee	82,000
7. Minnesota	79,300
8. Ohio	76,200
9. California	76,000
10. Wisconsin	76,000
11. Illinois	72,400
12. Kansas	64,000
13. Indiana	59,000
14. Pennsylvania	58,200
15. Michigan	53,000
16. Georgia	49,000
17. North Carolina	48,000
18. Nebraska	47,600
19. Virginia	46,800
20. Arkansas	46,500
21. Alabama	43,000
22. Mississippi	42,000
23. Florida	41,000
24. Oregon	39,300
25. New York	35,000
26. Washington	34,000
27. South Dakota	31,300
28. Colorado	30,700
29. North Dakota	30,300
30. Montana	28,100
31. Louisiana	26,800
32. Idaho	25,000
33. South Carolina	24,600
34. West Virginia	21,200
35. New Mexico	17,500
36. Utah	15,100
37. Maryland	12,000
38. Arizona	10,000
39. New Jersey	9,800
40. Wyoming	9,100
41. Maine	7,100
42. Vermont	6,300
43. Massachusetts	6,100
44. Hawaii	5,500
45. Connecticut	4,200
46. New Hampshire	3,400
47. Nevada	3,000
48. Delaware	2,300
49. Rhode Island	850
50. Alaska	640
51. District of Columbia	NA

82. Net Farm Income, 2006 (x $1 million)	
* UNITED STATES	$59,005.5
1. California	5,905.7
2. Texas	4,866.3
3. North Carolina	3,702.2
4. Iowa	3,274.8
5. Minnesota	2,493.6
6. Georgia	2,387.6
7. Florida	2,340.4
8. Nebraska	2,297.0
9. Arkansas	1,950.9
10. Kentucky	1,741.5
11. Missouri	1,697.3
12. Ohio	1,614.4
13. Kansas	1,614.3
14. Alabama	1,579.8
15. Indiana	1,545.4
16. Pennsylvania	1,516.4
17. Illinois	1,511.0
18. Michigan	1,321.2
19. Mississippi	1,230.3
20. Wisconsin	1,091.4
21. Washington	958.3
22. Oklahoma	876.5
23. Oregon	875.6
24. New York	868.7
25. Arizona	773.7
26. Louisiana	765.7
27. Idaho	758.4
28. South Dakota	741.5
29. Colorado	734.0
30. South Carolina	722.2
31. Tennessee	721.8
32. Virginia	678.0
33. North Dakota	605.9
34. Maryland	594.6
35. New Mexico	423.0
36. Delaware	388.2
37. New Jersey	305.4
38. Utah	263.6
39. Montana	256.8
40. Maine	216.8
41. Connecticut	182.8
42. Massachusetts	115.4
43. Hawaii	105.5
44. Vermont	103.2
45. Nevada	84.6
46. Wyoming	65.2
47. West Virginia	49.7
48. New Hampshire	42.6
49. Rhode Island	26.0
50. Alaska	20.0
51. District of Columbia	NA

Comparative Tables

83. Farm Marketing Receipts, 2006 (x $1 million)

*	UNITED STATES	$239,271.9
1.	California	31,402.7
2.	Texas	16,026.8
3.	Iowa	15,108.3
4.	Nebraska	12,042.3
5.	Kansas	10,335.8
6.	Minnesota	9,769.5
7.	Illinois	8,635.7
8.	North Carolina	8,199.3
9.	Florida	6,974.2
10.	Wisconsin	6,791.3
11.	Arkansas	6,164.1
12.	Washington	6,139.0
13.	Georgia	6,005.1
14.	Indiana	5,973.2
15.	Missouri	5,621.3
16.	Colorado	5,614.4
17.	Ohio	5,479.7
18.	Oklahoma	5,093.6
19.	South Dakota	4,716.2
20.	Pennsylvania	4,691.7
21.	Michigan	4,487.8
22.	Idaho	4,415.6
23.	Kentucky	4,007.2
24.	Oregon	3,990.6
25.	North Dakota	3,980.7
26.	Mississippi	3,788.5
27.	Alabama	3,739.1
28.	New York	3,509.0
29.	Arizona	2,879.2
30.	Virginia	2,688.7
31.	Tennessee	2,564.9
32.	New Mexico	2,463.5
33.	Montana	2,349.2
34.	Louisiana	2,186.2
35.	South Carolina	1,890.7
36.	Maryland	1,597.7
37.	Utah	1,243.7
38.	Wyoming	1,021.1
39.	Delaware	969.1
40.	New Jersey	923.9
41.	Maine	591.7
42.	Hawaii	554.6
43.	Connecticut	523.6
44.	Vermont	500.8
45.	West Virginia	449.6
46.	Nevada	446.6
47.	Massachusetts	433.0
48.	New Hampshire	161.8
49.	Rhode Island	65.6
50.	Alaska	64.2
51.	District of Columbia	NA

84. Exports, Total Value, 2006 (x $1 million)

*	UNITED STATES	$1,037,320
1.	Texas	150,888
2.	California	127,746
3.	New York	57,369
4.	Washington	53,075
5.	Illinois	42,085
6.	Michigan	40,405
7.	Florida	38,545
8.	Ohio	37,833
9.	New Jersey	27,002
10.	Pennsylvania	26,334
11.	Massachusetts	24,047
12.	Louisiana	23,503
13.	Indiana	22,620
14.	Tennessee	22,020
15.	North Carolina	21,218
16.	Georgia	20,073
17.	Arizona	18,287
18.	Kentucky	17,232
19.	Wisconsin	17,169
20.	Minnesota	16,309
21.	Oregon	15,288
22.	Virginia	14,104
23.	Alabama	13,878
24.	South Carolina	13,615
25.	Missouri	12,776
26.	Connecticut	12,238
27.	Kansas	8,626
28.	Iowa	8,410
29.	Colorado	7,956
30.	Maryland	7,598
31.	Utah	6,798
32.	Nevada	5,493
33.	Mississippi	4,674
34.	Oklahoma	4,375
35.	Arkansas	4,265
36.	Alaska	4,044
37.	Delaware	3,890
38.	Vermont	3,817
39.	Idaho	3,721
40.	Nebraska	3,625
41.	West Virginia	3,225
42.	New Mexico	2,892
43.	New Hampshire	2,811
44.	Maine	2,627
45.	Rhode Island	1,531
46.	North Dakota	1,509
47.	South Dakota	1,185
48.	District of Columbia	1,040
49.	Montana	887
50.	Wyoming	830
51.	Hawaii	706

Comparative Tables

85. Households with Computers, 2003	
1. Utah	74.1%
2. Alaska	72.7
3. New Hampshire	71.5
4. Washington	71.4
5. Colorado	70.0
6. Connecticut	69.2
7. Idaho	69.2
8. Minnesota	67.9
9. Maine	67.8
10. Oregon	67.0
11. Virginia	66.8
12. California	66.3
13. Nebraska	66.1
14. Maryland	66.0
15. New Jersey	65.5
16. Vermont	65.5
17. Wyoming	65.4
18. Iowa	64.7
19. Arizona	64.3
20. District of Columbia	64.3
21. Massachusetts	64.1
22. Kansas	63.8
23. Wisconsin	63.8
24. Hawaii	63.3
25. Rhode Island	62.3
26. South Dakota	62.1
* UNITED STATES	61.8
27. Nevada	61.3
28. North Dakota	61.2
29. Florida	61.0
30. Missouri	60.7
31. Georgia	60.6
32. Pennsylvania	60.2
33. Illinois	60.0
34. New York	60.0
35. Michigan	59.9
36. Indiana	59.6
37. Delaware	59.5
38. Montana	59.5
39. Texas	59.0
40. Ohio	58.8
41. Kentucky	58.1
42. North Carolina	57.7
43. Tennessee	56.7
44. Oklahoma	55.4
45. West Virginia	55.0
46. South Carolina	54.9
47. Alabama	53.9
48. New Mexico	53.9
49. Louisiana	52.3
50. Arkansas	50.0
51. Mississippi	48.3

86. Households with Internet Access, 2003	
1. Alaska	67.6%
2. New Hampshire	65.2
3. Colorado	63.0
4. Connecticut	62.9
5. Utah	62.6
6. Washington	62.3
7. Minnesota	61.6
8. Oregon	61.0
9. New Jersey	60.5
10. Virginia	60.3
11. California	59.6
12. Maryland	59.2
13. Massachusetts	58.1
14. Vermont	58.1
15. Maine	57.9
16. Wyoming	57.7
17. Wisconsin	57.4
18. Iowa	57.1
19. District of Columbia	56.8
20. Idaho	56.4
21. Rhode Island	55.7
22. Florida	55.6
23. Nebraska	55.4
24. Arizona	55.2
25. Nevada	55.2
26. Hawaii	55.0
27. Pennsylvania	54.7
* UNITED STATES	54.6
28. Kansas	54.3
29. South Dakota	53.6
30. Georgia	53.5
31. New York	53.3
32. Delaware	53.2
33. North Dakota	53.2
34. Missouri	53.0
35. Ohio	52.5
36. Michigan	52.0
37. Texas	51.8
38. Illinois	51.1
39. North Carolina	51.1
40. Indiana	51.0
41. Montana	50.4
42. Kentucky	49.6
43. Tennessee	48.9
44. Oklahoma	48.4
45. West Virginia	47.6
46. Alabama	45.7
47. South Carolina	45.6
48. New Mexico	44.5
49. Louisiana	44.1
50. Arkansas	42.4
51. Mississippi	38.9

Comparative Tables

87. Wireless Phone Customers, December 2006

*	UNITED STATES	229,619,397
1.	California	29,717,334
2.	Texas	17,822,230
3.	New York	15,261,760
4.	Florida	14,761,666
5.	Illinois	9,588,517
6.	Pennsylvania	8,831,238
7.	Ohio	8,380,138
8.	Georgia	7,281,724
9.	New Jersey	7,207,018
10.	Michigan	7,093,721
11.	North Carolina	6,626,582
12.	Virginia	5,607,350
13.	Massachusetts	5,128,860
14.	Tennessee	5,126,510
15.	Washington	4,799,143
16.	Maryland	4,691,026
17.	Arizona	4,405,032
18.	Missouri	4,322,458
19.	Indiana	4,271,412
20.	Minnesota	3,701,515
21.	Colorado	3,608,209
22.	Wisconsin	3,509,528
23.	Louisiana	3,492,358
24.	Alabama	3,374,701
25.	South Carolina	3,208,504
26.	Kentucky	2,966,195
27.	Connecticut	2,705,023
28.	Oregon	2,655,905
29.	Oklahoma	2,479,877
30.	Kansas	2,046,542
31.	Arkansas	2,044,217
32.	Mississippi	2,029,916
33.	Iowa	2,009,826
34.	Nevada	1,990,215
35.	Utah	1,774,755
36.	New Mexico	1,333,210
37.	Nebraska	1,272,067
38.	West Virginia	1,040,224
39.	Hawaii	1,034,788
40.	Idaho	972,825
41.	New Hampshire	943,330
42.	District of Columbia	880,077
43.	Maine	844,537
44.	Rhode Island	797,603
45.	Delaware	682,636
46.	Montana	619,620
47.	South Dakota	547,812
48.	North Dakota	472,799
49.	Alaska	412,112
50.	Wyoming	387,164
51.	Vermont	358,052

88. FCC-Licensed TV Stations, January 1, 2008

*	UNITED STATES	1,716
1.	Texas	135
2.	California	108
3.	Florida	92
4.	New York	55
5.	Michigan	54
6.	Ohio	52
7.	North Carolina	50
8.	Georgia	47
9.	Illinois	47
10.	Pennsylvania	46
11.	Alabama	43
12.	Wisconsin	43
13.	Indiana	40
14.	Tennessee	40
15.	Kentucky	38
16.	Louisiana	38
17.	Virginia	36
18.	Missouri	35
19.	Washington	35
20.	South Carolina	34
21.	Iowa	33
22.	Oregon	33
23.	Arizona	31
24.	Colorado	31
25.	Minnesota	31
26.	Mississippi	29
27.	Arkansas	27
28.	Hawaii	27
29.	Nebraska	27
30.	North Dakota	27
31.	Oklahoma	27
32.	Montana	26
33.	New Mexico	26
34.	South Dakota	26
35.	Kansas	25
36.	Massachusetts	22
37.	Idaho	21
38.	Nevada	21
39.	West Virginia	18
40.	Alaska	17
41.	Utah	17
42.	Wyoming	17
43.	Maryland	16
44.	Maine	15
45.	New Jersey	15
46.	Connecticut	13
47.	District of Columbia	8
48.	New Hampshire	7
49.	Vermont	7
50.	Rhode Island	5
51.	Delaware	3

Comparative Tables

89. Energy Spending, per capita, 2004		90. Price of Energy, 2004 (per million Btu)	
1. Alaska	$6,339	1. Hawaii	$18.05
2. Wyoming	5,749	2. District of Columbia	16.87
3. Louisiana	5,428	3. Massachusetts	16.18
4. Texas	4,224	4. Rhode Island	15.95
5. North Dakota	4,167	5. Connecticut	15.86
6. Montana	3,435	6. Vermont	15.83
7. Iowa	3,423	7. New York	15.65
8. Maine	3,403	8. New Hampshire	15.52
9. Indiana	3,364	9. Nevada	15.43
10. Alabama	3,360	10. Arizona	15.24
11. Kentucky	3,353	11. Florida	15.21
12. Kansas	3,270	12. California	15.12
13. Mississippi	3,268	13. Maryland	14.11
14. West Virginia	3,228	14. New Jersey	14.07
15. Hawaii	3,207	15. Delaware	13.64
16. Oklahoma	3,200	16. North Carolina	13.60
17. South Carolina	3,194	17. New Mexico	13.48
18. Arkansas	3,174	18. Pennsylvania	13.05
19. Vermont	3,170	* UNITED STATES	12.91
20. New Jersey	3,119	19. Missouri	12.89
21. Nebraska	3,093	20. Ohio	12.85
22. Delaware	3,066	21. Oregon	12.85
23. Ohio	3,049	22. Maine	12.80
24. Connecticut	3,032	23. Wisconsin	12.69
25. New Hampshire	3,026	24. Virginia	12.64
26. South Dakota	3,008	25. Colorado	12.54
27. Tennessee	3,001	26. South Dakota	12.54
28. Minnesota	2,989	27. South Carolina	12.53
29. District of Columbia	2,983	28. Mississippi	12.51
* UNITED STATES	2,961	29. Illinois	12.46
30. Nevada	2,949	30. Kansas	12.44
31. Wisconsin	2,922	31. Georgia	12.42
32. Pennsylvania	2,914	32. Washington	12.32
33. Georgia	2,872	33. Michigan	12.24
34. Virginia	2,850	34. Oklahoma	12.24
35. Missouri	2,846	35. Nebraska	12.18
36. Massachusetts	2,774	36. Minnesota	12.17
37. New Mexico	2,745	37. Tennessee	12.16
38. North Carolina	2,722	38. Montana	12.12
39. Michigan	2,681	39. Arkansas	11.89
40. Illinois	2,680	40. Idaho	11.82
41. Idaho	2,679	41. Iowa	11.80
42. Colorado	2,567	42. Texas	11.50
43. Maryland	2,551	43. Utah	11.39
44. Oregon	2,544	44. Kentucky	11.30
45. California	2,518	45. Alabama	11.29
46. New York	2,514	46. Alaska	11.09
47. Washington	2,508	47. West Virginia	10.66
48. Rhode Island	2,442	48. Wyoming	10.29
49. Arizona	2,398	49. Indiana	10.19
50. Florida	2,367	50. Louisiana	10.09
51. Utah	2,343	51. North Dakota	9.18

Comparative Tables

91. Energy Consumption, per capita, 2005 (x 1 million Btu)

1.	Alaska	1,186.1
2.	Wyoming	898.9
3.	Louisiana	848.9
4.	North Dakota	632.7
5.	Texas	531.6
6.	Alabama	478.1
7.	Indiana	473.3
8.	Kentucky	472.5
9.	West Virginia	453.5
10.	Montana	434.9
11.	Oklahoma	421.8
12.	Mississippi	419.8
13.	Arkansas	413.5
14.	South Carolina	409.4
15.	Iowa	408.2
16.	Kansas	403.0
17.	Tennessee	390.4
18.	Nebraska	373.2
19.	Delaware	367.8
20.	Maine	365.5
21.	New Mexico	359.0
22.	Minnesota	358.5
23.	Idaho	358.4
24.	Georgia	351.5
25.	Ohio	351.0
26.	Virginia	342.4
27.	South Dakota	342.3
*	UNITED STATES	341.5
28.	Wisconsin	336.0
29.	District of Columbia	328.3
30.	Pennsylvania	327.2
31.	Washington	323.1
32.	Missouri	321.5
33.	North Carolina	318.3
34.	Illinois	311.5
35.	Michigan	309.1
36.	Utah	305.7
37.	Oregon	304.7
38.	New Jersey	303.2
39.	Colorado	300.9
40.	Nevada	297.4
41.	Maryland	274.9
42.	Vermont	272.7
43.	Connecticut	264.4
44.	New Hampshire	262.5
45.	Hawaii	256.9
46.	Florida	256.4
47.	Arizona	250.0
48.	Massachusetts	239.7
49.	California	233.4
50.	New York	220.5
51.	Rhode Island	209.8

92. Electricity from Renewable Sources, 2005 (% of net generation)

1.	Idaho	84.2%
2.	Washington	72.8
3.	Oregon	66.1
4.	South Dakota	49.6
5.	Maine	43.3
6.	Montana	34.5
7.	California	31.6
8.	Vermont	28.6
9.	Alaska	22.3
10.	New York	18.9
11.	New Hampshire	11.2
12.	Tennessee	10.2
13.	Alabama	10.1
14.	Arkansas	10.1
*	UNITED STATES	8.8
15.	Nevada	7.4
16.	Minnesota	6.5
17.	Arizona	6.4
18.	Iowa	6.2
19.	North Carolina	5.6
20.	Hawaii	5.5
21.	Oklahoma	5.5
22.	Georgia	5.3
23.	Virginia	5.0
24.	North Dakota	4.9
25.	Wisconsin	4.9
26.	Massachusetts	4.8
27.	South Carolina	4.6
28.	Colorado	4.5
29.	Maryland	4.4
30.	Louisiana	3.8
31.	Connecticut	3.7
32.	Kentucky	3.5
33.	Mississippi	3.4
34.	Michigan	3.3
35.	Wyoming	3.3
36.	Nebraska	3.2
37.	New Mexico	2.7
38.	Utah	2.6
39.	Florida	2.1
40.	Pennsylvania	2.1
41.	Texas	1.7
42.	West Virginia	1.7
43.	New Jersey	1.5
44.	Missouri	1.3
45.	Kansas	1.0
46.	Ohio	0.6
47.	Illinois	0.5
48.	Indiana	0.4
49.	Rhode Island	0.1
50.	Delaware	NA
51.	District of Columbia	NA

Comparative Tables

93. Average Daily Commute, 2006 (minutes each way)	
1. New York	30.9
2. Maryland	30.6
3. District of Columbia	29.2
4. New Jersey	29.1
5. Illinois	27.9
6. Georgia	27.3
7. Virginia	26.9
8. California	26.8
9. Massachusetts	26.6
10. Florida	25.9
11. West Virginia	25.6
12. Hawaii	25.5
13. Washington	25.2
14. Louisiana	25.1
15. Arizona	25.0
16. Pennsylvania	25.0
* UNITED STATES	25.0
17. New Hampshire	24.6
18. Texas	24.6
19. Nevada	24.2
20. Connecticut	24.1
21. Mississippi	24.0
22. Colorado	23.9
23. Alabama	23.6
24. Delaware	23.6
25. Tennessee	23.5
26. Michigan	23.4
27. North Carolina	23.4
28. Missouri	22.9
29. South Carolina	22.9
30. Kentucky	22.4
31. Indiana	22.3
32. Maine	22.3
33. Rhode Island	22.3
34. Ohio	22.1
35. Minnesota	22.0
36. Oregon	21.8
37. Vermont	21.2
38. New Mexico	20.9
39. Utah	20.8
40. Wisconsin	20.8
41. Arkansas	20.7
42. Idaho	20.1
43. Oklahoma	20.0
44. Kansas	18.5
45. Iowa	18.2
46. Wyoming	17.9
47. Alaska	17.7
48. Nebraska	17.7
49. Montana	17.6
50. South Dakota	15.9
51. North Dakota	15.5

94. Workers who Drove to Work Alone, 2006	
1. Alabama	83.6%
2. Tennessee	83.3
3. Ohio	83.1
4. Michigan	82.9
5. Indiana	82.4
6. Mississippi	82.2
7. Kansas	81.8
8. New Hampshire	81.7
9. Louisiana	81.6
10. Kentucky	81.5
11. Rhode Island	81.1
12. South Carolina	81.1
13. Delaware	80.8
14. Missouri	80.8
15. Oklahoma	80.4
16. Arkansas	80.2
17. West Virginia	80.0
18. Wisconsin	79.9
19. North Carolina	79.8
20. Connecticut	79.7
21. Florida	79.3
22. North Dakota	79.3
23. Nebraska	79.1
24. Iowa	78.5
25. Texas	78.5
26. Georgia	78.2
27. New Mexico	78.2
28. Minnesota	78.1
29. Maine	77.6
30. South Dakota	77.5
31. Idaho	77.2
32. Virginia	77.0
33. Nevada	76.7
34. Pennsylvania	76.4
35. Wyoming	76.0
* UNITED STATES	76.0
36. Utah	75.2
37. Colorado	75.1
38. Vermont	75.1
39. Arizona	74.6
40. Illinois	74.3
41. Massachusetts	73.7
42. California	73.0
43. Maryland	72.8
44. Washington	72.8
45. Montana	72.7
46. New Jersey	71.9
47. Oregon	71.4
48. Alaska	67.7
49. Hawaii	67.0
50. New York	54.4
51. District of Columbia	35.4

Comparative Tables

95. Workers who Carpooled, 2006

1.	Hawaii	16.0%
2.	Arizona	13.9
3.	Utah	13.1
4.	Arkansas	12.9
5.	Alaska	12.7
6.	Texas	12.7
7.	New Mexico	12.5
8.	North Carolina	12.5
9.	Wyoming	12.5
10.	California	12.4
11.	Nevada	12.3
12.	Mississippi	12.1
13.	West Virginia	12.1
14.	Montana	12.0
15.	Washington	11.8
16.	Idaho	11.7
17.	Oregon	11.7
18.	Louisiana	11.6
19.	Oklahoma	11.6
20.	Georgia	11.5
21.	Virginia	11.4
22.	Alabama	11.3
23.	Kentucky	11.3
24.	South Carolina	11.3
25.	Vermont	11.2
26.	Maine	11.0
27.	Florida	10.9
28.	Iowa	10.8
29.	Maryland	10.7
*	UNITED STATES	10.7
30.	Colorado	10.6
31.	Missouri	10.4
32.	Nebraska	10.4
33.	Tennessee	10.2
34.	Indiana	9.9
35.	Pennsylvania	9.9
36.	South Dakota	9.6
37.	Delaware	9.4
38.	Illinois	9.3
39.	Minnesota	9.3
40.	New Jersey	9.3
41.	Kansas	9.2
42.	North Dakota	9.2
43.	Wisconsin	9.2
44.	Michigan	9.1
45.	Rhode Island	8.9
46.	New Hampshire	8.6
47.	Massachusetts	8.5
48.	Connecticut	8.4
49.	Ohio	8.3
50.	New York	7.6
51.	District of Columbia	6.3

96. Workers who used Public Transit, 2006

1.	District of Columbia	39.0%
2.	New York	26.1
3.	New Jersey	10.3
4.	Maryland	8.8
5.	Massachusetts	8.6
6.	Illinois	8.4
7.	Hawaii	5.4
8.	Pennsylvania	5.2
9.	Washington	5.2
10.	California	5.0
*	UNITED STATES	4.8
11.	Oregon	4.4
12.	Connecticut	4.1
13.	Virginia	4.1
14.	Nevada	3.6
15.	Colorado	3.2
16.	Minnesota	3.0
17.	Delaware	2.8
18.	Rhode Island	2.6
19.	Utah	2.6
20.	Georgia	2.4
21.	Arizona	2.1
22.	Florida	2.0
23.	Ohio	2.0
24.	Wisconsin	1.9
25.	Texas	1.7
26.	Missouri	1.4
27.	Wyoming	1.3
28.	Michigan	1.2
29.	Alaska	1.1
30.	Louisiana	1.1
31.	Indiana	1.0
32.	Iowa	1.0
33.	Kentucky	1.0
34.	North Carolina	1.0
35.	West Virginia	1.0
36.	Montana	0.9
37.	New Mexico	0.9
38.	Idaho	0.8
39.	Vermont	0.8
40.	Maine	0.7
41.	New Hampshire	0.7
42.	Tennessee	0.7
43.	Kansas	0.6
44.	South Carolina	0.6
45.	Alabama	0.5
46.	Nebraska	0.5
47.	Oklahoma	0.5
48.	Arkansas	0.4
49.	Mississippi	0.4
50.	North Dakota	0.4
51.	South Dakota	0.4

Comparative Tables

97. Gasoline Consumption, per capita, 2006 (in gallons)

1.	Wyoming	703.1
2.	Louisiana	617.7
3.	South Carolina	590.4
4.	Mississippi	578.8
5.	Alabama	572.3
6.	Iowa	562.9
7.	Vermont	561.0
8.	North Dakota	552.7
9.	Missouri	551.8
10.	New Hampshire	547.1
11.	South Dakota	543.8
12.	Delaware	538.1
13.	Maine	535.7
14.	Georgia	533.3
15.	Kentucky	530.1
16.	Montana	526.3
17.	Virginia	525.0
18.	Oklahoma	522.4
19.	Minnesota	522.2
20.	Arkansas	515.2
21.	Tennessee	515.0
22.	Indiana	511.2
23.	Texas	505.9
24.	North Carolina	500.9
25.	New Mexico	497.5
26.	Maryland	494.6
27.	New Jersey	494.0
28.	Michigan	483.0
29.	Kansas	482.4
30.	Florida	481.4
31.	Nebraska	474.4
32.	Nevada	470.7
*	UNITED STATES	469.7
33.	Arizona	465.6
34.	West Virginia	465.1
35.	Colorado	454.1
36.	Ohio	454.0
37.	Wisconsin	453.6
38.	Idaho	449.5
39.	Connecticut	448.2
40.	Massachusetts	439.3
41.	California	437.1
42.	Alaska	433.0
43.	Washington	428.4
44.	Oregon	427.4
45.	Utah	411.5
46.	Pennsylvania	411.4
47.	Illinois	406.2
48.	Rhode Island	394.1
49.	Hawaii	377.9
50.	New York	300.0
51.	District of Columbia	225.4

98. Automobile Registrations, 2006

*	UNITED STATES	135,399,945
1.	California	19,835,554
2.	Texas	8,805,316
3.	New York	8,528,457
4.	Florida	7,425,148
5.	Ohio	6,438,988
6.	Illinois	5,947,468
7.	Pennsylvania	5,842,819
8.	Michigan	4,765,547
9.	Georgia	4,141,179
10.	Virginia	4,031,355
11.	New Jersey	3,692,966
12.	North Carolina	3,659,926
13.	Massachusetts	3,310,725
14.	Washington	3,087,818
15.	Tennessee	2,878,136
16.	Missouri	2,715,297
17.	Indiana	2,694,901
18.	Maryland	2,656,597
19.	Wisconsin	2,639,984
20.	Minnesota	2,512,491
21.	Arizona	2,189,979
22.	Connecticut	1,999,809
23.	Kentucky	1,969,142
24.	South Carolina	1,964,994
25.	Louisiana	1,950,372
26.	Alabama	1,795,596
27.	Iowa	1,744,519
28.	Oklahoma	1,606,517
29.	Oregon	1,427,597
30.	Mississippi	1,118,200
31.	Utah	1,079,455
32.	Arkansas	958,640
33.	Kansas	872,878
34.	Colorado	858,967
35.	Nebraska	832,511
36.	West Virginia	734,599
37.	New Mexico	699,312
38.	Nevada	679,828
39.	New Hampshire	585,455
40.	Maine	581,797
41.	Idaho	541,487
42.	Hawaii	538,581
43.	Rhode Island	508,389
44.	Montana	447,446
45.	Delaware	432,509
46.	South Dakota	375,760
47.	North Dakota	345,502
48.	Vermont	309,972
49.	Alaska	242,487
50.	Wyoming	228,057
51.	District of Columbia	168,916

Comparative Tables

99. Vehicle-Miles Traveled, per capita, 2006

1.	Wyoming	18,361.5
2.	Mississippi	14,314.0
3.	Oklahoma	13,609.6
4.	New Mexico	13,276.5
5.	Alabama	13,161.4
6.	Vermont	12,616.4
7.	North Dakota	12,377.2
8.	Georgia	12,152.8
9.	Montana	11,898.0
10.	Missouri	11,791.4
11.	Arkansas	11,750.0
12.	South Dakota	11,627.6
13.	Tennessee	11,620.9
14.	South Carolina	11,593.0
15.	West Virginia	11,547.0
16.	North Carolina	11,445.5
17.	Maine	11,441.1
18.	Kentucky	11,355.1
19.	Indiana	11,299.2
20.	Florida	11,282.9
21.	Delaware	11,072.5
22.	Nebraska	11,007.7
23.	Minnesota	10,964.6
24.	Kansas	10,964.1
25.	Louisiana	10,703.3
26.	Wisconsin	10,658.8
27.	Virginia	10,614.2
28.	Iowa	10,548.1
29.	Idaho	10,382.0
30.	New Hampshire	10,377.9
31.	Michigan	10,312.9
32.	Colorado	10,205.3
33.	Texas	10,178.6
34.	Arizona	10,131.6
*	UNITED STATES	10,088.9
35.	Utah	10,065.4
36.	Maryland	10,050.3
37.	Ohio	9,704.4
38.	Oregon	9,613.2
39.	Connecticut	9,080.4
40.	California	9,033.9
41.	Washington	8,865.5
42.	Nevada	8,756.1
43.	Pennsylvania	8,730.1
44.	New Jersey	8,697.2
45.	Massachusetts	8,569.0
46.	Illinois	8,364.1
47.	Hawaii	7,963.2
48.	Rhode Island	7,818.1
49.	Alaska	7,331.9
50.	New York	7,330.6
51.	District of Columbia	6,188.3

100. Motor Vehicle Deaths, 2006

*	UNITED STATES	42,642
1.	California	4,236
2.	Texas	3,475
3.	Florida	3,374
4.	Georgia	1,693
5.	North Carolina	1,559
6.	Pennsylvania	1,525
7.	New York	1,456
8.	Arizona	1,288
9.	Tennessee	1,287
10.	Illinois	1,254
11.	Ohio	1,238
12.	Alabama	1,208
13.	Missouri	1,096
14.	Michigan	1,085
15.	South Carolina	1,037
16.	Louisiana	982
17.	Virginia	963
18.	Kentucky	913
19.	Mississippi	911
20.	Indiana	899
21.	New Jersey	772
22.	Oklahoma	765
23.	Wisconsin	724
24.	Arkansas	665
25.	Maryland	651
26.	Washington	630
27.	Colorado	535
28.	Minnesota	494
29.	New Mexico	484
30.	Oregon	477
31.	Kansas	468
32.	Iowa	439
33.	Nevada	432
34.	Massachusetts	430
35.	West Virginia	410
36.	Connecticut	301
37.	Utah	287
38.	Nebraska	269
39.	Idaho	267
40.	Montana	263
41.	Wyoming	195
42.	South Dakota	191
43.	Maine	188
44.	Hawaii	161
45.	Delaware	148
46.	New Hampshire	127
47.	North Dakota	111
48.	Vermont	87
49.	Rhode Island	81
50.	Alaska	74
51.	District of Columbia	37

ORDER FORM

Title	Qty	Edition	Price	Extended Price	Standing Order	
State & Municipal Profiles Series					YES	NO
Almanac of the 50 States 2008		Hardcover	$89		☐	☐
Almanac of the 50 States 2008		Paperback	$79		☐	☐
California Cities, Towns & Counties 2008		CD	$119		☐	☐
		Paperback	$119		☐	☐
Connecticut Municipal Profiles 2008		CD	$85		☐	☐
		Paperback	$85		☐	☐
Florida Cities, Towns & Counties 2008		CD	$119		☐	☐
		Paperback	$119		☐	☐
Massachusetts Municipal Profiles 2008		CD	$109		☐	☐
		Paperback	$109		☐	☐
The New Jersey Municipal Data Book 2008		CD	$119		☐	☐
		Paperback	$119		☐	☐
North Carolina Cities, Towns & Counties 2008		CD	$119		☐	☐
		Paperback	$119		☐	☐
Essential Topics Series						
Energy, Transportation & the Environment: A Statistical Sourcebook and Guide to Government Data 2008		Paperback	$77		☐	☐
American Profiles Series						
Black Americans: A Statistical Sourcebook and Guide to Government Data 2008		Paperback	$77		☐	☐
Hispanic Americans: A Statistical Sourcebook and Guide to Government Data 2008		Paperback	$77		☐	☐
Asian Americans: A Statistical Sourcebook and Guide to Government Data 2008		Paperback	$77		☐	☐

Offer and prices valid until 12/31/08

Purchase orders accepted from libraries, government agencies, and educational institutions.
Prepayment required from all other organizations.

Order Subtotal	
(Required ONLY for shipments to California) CA Sales Tax	
Shipping & Handling	
Total	

Please complete the following shipping and billing information. If paying by credit card or PO please call **(877)544-4636** or fax your completed order form to **(877)544-4635**. To pay by check, please mail this form and your payment to the address below.

Information Publications, Inc.
2995 Woodside Rd., Suite 400-182
Woodside, CA 94062

U.S. Ground Shipping Rates	
Order Subtotal	Shipping & Handling
$0-$89	$7
$90-$119	$9
$120-$240	$14
$241-$400	$19
$401-$500	$22
>$500	Call
Call for Int'l or Express Shipping Rates	

Shipping Information (UPS/FedEx tracking number sent via email)

Organization Name		
Shipping Contact		
Address (No PO Boxes, please)		
City	State	Zip
Email Address (req'd if want tracking #)	Phone #	

Payment Information (mark choice)	☐ **Check**	☐ **Credit Card** ☐ Visa ☐ MC ☐ AMEX		☐ **Purchase Order** (attach PO to this form)
	Check #	CC#		PO #
		Exp Date		

Credit Card Billing Information   ☐ Check if same as Shipping Address

Name on Credit Card		
Billing Address of Credit Card		
City	State	Zip
Signature		

2995 Woodside Rd., Suite 400-182
Woodside, CA 94062

WWW.INFORMATIONPUBLICATIONS.COM

Toll Free Phone 877-544-INFO (4636)
Toll Free Fax 877-544-4635

• Since 1980, A Trusted Ready Reference Resource for Easy-To-Use Federal, State and Local Information •

ORDER FORM

Title	Qty	Edition	Price	Extended Price	Standing Order	
State & Municipal Profiles Series					YES	NO
Almanac of the 50 States 2008		Hardcover	$89		☐	☐
Almanac of the 50 States 2008		Paperback	$79		☐	☐
California Cities, Towns & Counties 2008		CD	$119		☐	☐
		Paperback	$119		☐	☐
Connecticut Municipal Profiles 2008		CD	$85		☐	☐
		Paperback	$85		☐	☐
Florida Cities, Towns & Counties 2008		CD	$119		☐	☐
		Paperback	$119		☐	☐
Massachusetts Municipal Profiles 2008		CD	$109		☐	☐
		Paperback	$109		☐	☐
The New Jersey Municipal Data Book 2008		CD	$119		☐	☐
		Paperback	$119		☐	☐
North Carolina Cities, Towns & Counties 2008		CD	$119		☐	☐
		Paperback	$119		☐	☐
Essential Topics Series						
Energy, Transportation & the Environment: A Statistical Sourcebook and Guide to Government Data 2008		Paperback	$77		☐	☐
American Profiles Series						
Black Americans: A Statistical Sourcebook and Guide to Government Data 2008		Paperback	$77		☐	☐
Hispanic Americans: A Statistical Sourcebook and Guide to Government Data 2008		Paperback	$77		☐	☐
Asian Americans: A Statistical Sourcebook and Guide to Government Data 2008		Paperback	$77		☐	☐

Offer and prices valid until 12/31/08

Purchase orders accepted from libraries, government agencies, and educational institutions.
Prepayment required from all other organizations.

Order Subtotal	_____
(Required ONLY for shipments to California) CA Sales Tax	_____
Shipping & Handling	_____
Total	_____

Please complete the following shipping and billing information. If paying by credit card or PO please call **(877)544-4636** or fax your completed order form to **(877)544-4635**. To pay by check, please mail this form and your payment to the address below.

Information Publications, Inc.
2995 Woodside Rd., Suite 400-182
Woodside, CA 94062

U.S. Ground Shipping Rates

Order Subtotal	Shipping & Handling
$0-$89	$7
$90-$119	$9
$120-$240	$14
$241-$400	$19
$401-$500	$22
>$500	Call

Call for Int'l or Express Shipping Rates

Shipping Information (UPS/FedEx tracking number sent via email)

Organization Name		
Shipping Contact		
Address (No PO Boxes, please)		
City	State	Zip
Email Address (req'd if want tracking #)	Phone #	

Payment Information (mark choice)	☐ **Check**	☐ **Credit Card** ☐ Visa ☐ MC ☐ AMEX	☐ **Purchase Order** (attach PO to this form)
	Check #	CC#	PO #
		Exp Date	

Credit Card Billing Information   ☐ Check if same as Shipping Address

Name on Credit Card		
Billing Address of Credit Card		
City	State	Zip
Signature		

2995 Woodside Rd., Suite 400-182
Woodside, CA 94062

WWW.INFORMATIONPUBLICATIONS.COM

Toll Free Phone 877-544-INFO (4636)
Toll Free Fax 877-544-4635

• Since 1980, A Trusted Ready Reference Resource for Easy-To-Use Federal, State and Local Information •